From **Heidi M. Neck**, one of the most influential t[...] entrepreneurship education today, **Christopher P. Neck**, an award-winning professor, and **Emma L. Murray**, business writer and entrepreneur, comes this groundbreaking new text.

PRAISE FROM YOUR COLLEAGUES

"I really like the chapter on design thinking; **IT TEACHES STUDENTS HOW TO THINK** (outside the box), to identify an idea and develop it."

—*Bill Zannini, Northern Essex Community College*

"It **SPEAKS FRANKLY ABOUT SUBJECTS** in a personal manner that most other textbooks don't address—like worry and fear."

—*Timothy Ritter, Western Kentucky University*

"I think [the coverage of learning from failure] is a welcome change! Students learn so much by hearing strategies of overcoming 'what went wrong' and how to do it right the next time. **I COMMEND THE AUTHORS** for taking this approach and am glad that they included this vital part of the entrepreneurial process."

—*Amy Gresock, University of Michigan, Flint*

"I think this book is a **STRONG, LEADING EDGE VIEW** of modern entrepreneurship. The three chapters I reviewed did a wonderful job of presenting the entrepreneurial mindset, design thinking, and failing forward."

—*Charlie Nagelschmidt, Champlain College*

"I think the greatest strength of the book is that it is **CLEAR YET INSIGHTFUL**. It felt easy to read, while providing deep and important knowledge about entrepreneurship."

—*Laurent Josien, SUNY Plattsburgh*

"Neck takes research and translates it into practical examples. This is a textbook that entrepreneurs will read. Essentially, I see this as the **NEW PERFECT ENTREPRENEURSHIP TEXT**."

—*Ryan Kauth, University of Wisconsin–Green Bay*

PLAY. CREATE. EXPERIMENT. EMPATHIZE. REFLECT.

Take students on a **transformative journey** beyond the classroom by helping them develop an **entrepreneurial mindset, skillset, and toolset** that can be applied to startups as well as organizations of all kinds.

YOU BE THE ENTREPRENEUR

Mary Kay Ash began her first startup company, Mary Kay Cosmetics, with the help of her husband, who handled the financial and legal matters for their household. However, tragedy struck when her husband suddenly died of a heart attack one month before the company was scheduled to open. Her lawyer and accountant urged her to abandon the plan because she did not have a financial background and did not have the status of a man.

Source: Mary

What Wou

RESEARCH AT WORK

Study on Luck[3]

In the early 1990s, British psychologist and researcher Richard Wiseman carried out an experiment on luck to determine what defines a lucky or unlucky person. Over several years, using advertisements in newspapers and magazines, Wiseman sought out people who felt consistently lucky or unlucky. He interviewed them and identified 400 volunteers whom he asked to participate in the following experiment.

The 400 participants were divided into two groups: those who considered themselves lucky, and those who considered themselves unlucky. Both groups were given a newspaper and asked to count how many photographs it contained.

It took approximately 2 minutes, on average, for the unlucky people to count all the photos, but it only took a few seconds for the lucky people. Why? Because the lucky

Wiseman's overall findings have revealed that "although unlucky people have almost no insight into the real causes of their good and bad luck, their thoughts and behaviors are responsible for much of their fortune" (or misfortune).

CRITICAL THINKING QUESTIONS

1. Identify a successful entrepreneur. Do you believe luck played a role in their success? Why or why not?

2. Do you consider yourself a particularly lucky or unlucky person? Or do you fall somewhere in the middle? Give some reasons to support your answer.

...nity that ...e open to it? ...re open to ...e?

ENTREPRENEURSHIP MEETS ETHICS

The Rights of Research Participants

Leanna Archer with her hair product.
Credit: MARICE COHN BAND/Newscom

Before beginning testing and experimentation, the entrepreneur must consider some ethical concerns related to market research and the rights of research participants. Most notably, people participating in experiments have the right to informed consent; the right to be treated with dignity regardless of racial or ethnic background, sexual preference, or socioeconomic status; the right to privacy and confidentiality; and the right not to be deceived or harmed as a consequence of research participation. In addition, there are legal requirements for testing of food items and personal care products that come in contact with the human body, as well as regulations on the use of animals in product testing.

As long as the researcher is able to conduct the market research ethically and laws are followed, research doesn't have to be expensive. For example, entrepreneurs may enlist a group of people to try out free samples of a product in exchange for submitting an evaluation or attending a focus group afterward. There are also many laboratories that perform testing for regulatory compliance, with various price structures to suit different budgets.

Leanna Archer started her entrepreneurial venture when she was only nine years old. Archer used her grandmother's homemade hair care products and received numerous

compliments on the softness of her hair. Motivated to investigate starting her own hair care business, Archer obtained her grandmother's recipe, which used only natural, nonchemical ingredients. Her parents provided funding, and Archer began experimenting with different ingredients. Once several prototypes had been created, Archer sent samples to neighbors to get feedback. With the success of her trials and with family helping with bookkeeping and other administrative tasks, she launched the Leanna's Hair product lines. By the time she was ready to graduate from high school, her company was bringing in a six-figure income and the story of her "teenpreneurial" success had been featured in *Forbes*, *TIME*, and *INC Magazine*, among other international publications.

CRITICAL THINKING QUESTIONS

1. How would you go about finding out what kinds of testing are required for an entrepreneurial product or service?

2. If your product or service was suitable for nonprofessional testing in people's homes or at a focus group, whom would you recruit to participate in your test? Explain how you would choose your best customer types to participate.

3. How would you ensure that the participants in your experiments are treated ethically and have their rights protected?

Sources

Al Smadi, S. (n.d.). *Ethics in market research: Concerns over rights of research participants*. Retrieved from http://wbiconpro.com/Marketing/Sami.pdf

Entrepreneur Media Inc. (2016). *Small Business Encyclopedia: Market Testing*. Retrieved from Entrepreneur: http://www.entrepreneur.com/encyclopedia/market-testing

Snepenger, D. J. (2007, April 5). *Marketing Research for Entrepreneurs and Small Business Managers*. Retrieved from Montguide: http://msucommunitydevelopment.org/pubs/mt9013.pdf

Turnali, P. (2010). *Market Research Tips for Startups*. Retrieved from Go4Funding: http://www.go4funding.com/Articles/Market-Research-Tips-For-Startups.aspx

---

◄ **You Be the Entrepreneur** puts your students in the shoes of an entrepreneur and asks them to respond to obstacles faced by real entrepreneurs.

◄ **Research at Work** ties relevant research studies to chapter concepts with the goal of translating research to best practices.

▶ **Entrepreneurship Meets Ethics** illustrates the importance of ethics in entrepreneurship and helps students to practice making ethical decisions.

▼ *Learning From Failure* **chapter** is a unique chapter that aims to help students anticipate setbacks, develop grit, and understand the value of experimentation and iteration before launching into a new venture.

MINDSHIFT

Your Failure Resume[28]

In this Mindshift exercise, your assignment is to craft a "failure resume" that includes all of your biggest fails! These can be from school, work, or even in social relationships. For every failure you list, you must then describe what you learned from each fail (and, if appropriate, what others learned). By creating a failure resume, you are forced to spend time reflecting on what you learned from those experiences. As tough as this sounds, it's also a very rewarding experience.

Want to go a step further? Share your resume with a classmate and compare. Don't focus on comparing the failures but rather focus on comparing and contrasting the learning that resulted from each failure experience.

CRITICAL THINKING QUESTIONS

1. Was it easier than you expected, or more difficult, to list your biggest failures?

2. What emotions did you experience as you wrote your "failure resume"?

3. How do you think you'll be able to take the lessons learned from your failures and use them to attain more success in the future?

◀ **Mindshift Activities** take students out of the classroom to practice DOING entrepreneurship.

▶ **Entrepreneurship in Action** showcases select entrepreneurs and their journey from startup to present day.

▼ **The Pitch Deck** delivers a template to help students create a unique and memorable way to present their business idea to investors.

INSTRUCTORS:
WE MAKE IT EASY FOR YOU TO BRING YOUR CLASSROOM TO LIFE!

The book is just the beginning! A robust suite of online resources is available with this text to help bring entrepreneurship to life for your students and make your job easier.

Entrepreneurial Exercises

Written by author **Heidi M. Neck** and based on the Babson teaching philosophy, these experiential exercises aim to help you help your students develop the discovery, thinking, reasoning, and implementation skills necessary to thrive in highly uncertain environments. These lively and stimulating experiential exercises make it easy for you to facilitate hands-on in-class learning opportunities for your students to practice DOING entrepreneurship.

SAGE Premium Video

SAGE Premium Video is assignable, tied to learning objectives, and selected exclusively for this text to bring concepts to life and appeal to different learning styles, featuring:

- **Corresponding multimedia assessment options** that automatically feed to your gradebook
- **Exclusive licensed video** from Associated Press tied to key book concepts helps students contextualize and apply chapter material
- A comprehensive, downloadable *Media Guide in the Coursepack* for students that lists **every video resource**, organized by chapter and by learning objective. The *Media Guide* also includes the multimedia assessment questions and descriptions of each video.

⑤SAGE coursepacks

Our Content Tailored to Your LMS

SAGE coursepacks makes it easy to import our quality instructor and student resource content into your school's learning management system (LMS). Intuitive and simple to use, SAGE coursepacks allows you to customize course content to meet your students' needs.

SAGE coursepacks include

- Test banks, pre-tests, and post-tests built on AACSB standards and Bloom's taxonomy
- Assignable SAGE Premium Video (available via the interactive eBook, linked through SAGE coursepacks)
- Multimedia assessment
- Additional video and multimedia resources
- Entrepreneurial exercises written by Heidi M. Neck
- PowerPoint slides
- Lecture notes
- Additional exercises and suggested projects
- Case notes
- Sample answers to questions in the text
- Sample pitch decks
- Excel® spreadsheets for the appendix on financial projections

VentureBlocks is a fun and easy-to use online simulation for developing skills in conducting informative interviews, identifying potential business opportunities, and more. Students build confidence and get instant feedback in a secure environment as they compete outside the classroom in *The Nanu Challenge*. Instructor resources are included. **Instructors, request a demo!**

SAGE PUBLISHING: OUR STORY

Founded in 1965 by 24-year-old entrepreneur Sara Miller McCune, SAGE continues its legacy of making research accessible and fostering **creativity** and **innovation**. We believe in creating fresh, cutting-edge content to help you prepare your students to thrive in the modern business world and be **tomorrow's leading entrepreneurs**.

- By partnering with **top business authors** with just the right balance of research, teaching, and industry experience, we bring you the most current and applied content.

- As a **student-friendly publisher**, we keep our prices affordable and provide multiple formats of our textbooks so your students can choose the option that works best for them.

- Being permanently **independent** means we are fiercely committed to publishing the highest-quality resources for you and your students.

SAGE was founded in 1965 by Sara Miller McCune to support the dissemination of usable knowledge by publishing innovative and high-quality research and teaching content. Today, we publish over 900 journals, including those of more than 400 learned societies, more than 800 new books per year, and a growing range of library products including archives, data, case studies, reports, and video. SAGE remains majority-owned by our founder, and after Sara's lifetime will become owned by a charitable trust that secures our continued independence.

Los Angeles | London | New Delhi | Singapore | Washington DC | Melbourne

ENTREPRENEURSHIP

THE PRACTICE AND MINDSET

DEDICATION

We dedicate this book to future entrepreneurs of all types across the globe who will create opportunities and take action to change their world and the world of others. Embrace the journey, and the learning, and take pride in knowing that you are moving society forward.

ENTREPRENEURSHIP

THE PRACTICE AND MINDSET

HEIDI M. NECK

Babson College

CHRISTOPHER P. NECK

Arizona State University

EMMA L. MURRAY

Los Angeles | London | New Delhi
Singapore | Washington DC | Melbourne

FOR INFORMATION:

SAGE Publications, Inc.
2455 Teller Road
Thousand Oaks, California 91320
E-mail: order@sagepub.com

SAGE Publications Ltd.
1 Oliver's Yard
55 City Road
London, EC1Y 1SP
United Kingdom

SAGE Publications India Pvt. Ltd.
B 1/I 1 Mohan Cooperative Industrial Area
Mathura Road, New Delhi 110 044
India

SAGE Publications Asia-Pacific Pte. Ltd.
3 Church Street
#10-04 Samsung Hub
Singapore 049483

Printed in Canada

Library of Congress Cataloging-in-Publication Data

Names: Neck, Heidi M., author. | Neck, Christopher P., author. | Murray, Emma L., author.

Title: Entrepreneurship : the practice and mindset / Heidi M. Neck, Christopher P. Neck, Emma L. Murray.

Description: Los Angeles : SAGE, [2018] | Includes bibliographical references and index.

Identifiers: LCCN 2016034255 | ISBN 978-1-4833-8352-1 (pbk. : alk. paper)

Subjects: LCSH: Entrepreneurship.

Classification: LCC HB615 .N43297 2017 | DDC 338/.04—dc23 LC record available at https://lccn.loc.gov/2016034255

Acquisitions Editor: Maggie Stanley
Development Editor: Abbie Rickard
eLearning Editor: Katie Ancheta
Editorial Assistant: Neda Dallal
Production Editor: David C. Felts
Copy Editor: Ellen Howard
Typesetter: C&M Digitals (P) Ltd.
Proofreader: Caryne Brown
Indexer: Marilyn Augst
Cover Designer: Gail Buschman
Marketing Manager: Ashlee Blunk

18 19 20 21 10 9 8 7 6

BRIEF CONTENTS

DETAILED CONTENTS

Left: ©iStockphoto.com/Gumpanat
Right: ©iStockphoto.com/RyanJLane

Left: ©iStockphoto.com/swissmediavision
Right: ©iStockphoto.com/HenkBadenhorst

Left: ©iStockphoto.com/themacx
Right: ©iStockphoto.com/stellalevi

Left: ©iStockphoto.com/AndrewRich
Right: ©iStockphoto.com/solidcolours

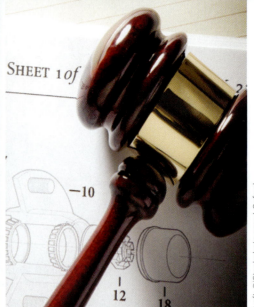

Left: ©iStockphoto.com/-Oxford-
Right: ©iStockphoto.com/andresr

PREFACE

Entrepreneurship to date has been too narrowly defined as starting a new business, with little attention given to the individuals—the entrepreneurs of all types—who have the mindset, skills, and tools to create change, improve the world, and make a difference in their lives as well as the lives of others. However, there is no single type of entrepreneur, and practicing entrepreneurship is not reserved for only those starting a new venture. The world will benefit not only from those who start new ventures but also from those who act entrepreneurially in all that they do. We are living in the entrepreneurial generation, and all students must get comfortable with creating and testing new ideas, navigating uncertain environments, and acting in order to learn rather than learning in order to act.

Entrepreneurship: The Practice & Mindset is a practice-based, realistic, and inclusive approach to entrepreneurship. It is a core textbook for college-level undergraduate and graduate students seeking methods for starting and running something new: a new business or initiative, profit or nonprofit, inside a large corporation, or within a small business. Three points guide the philosophy of this book. First, entrepreneurship education is incredibly important, but current mainstream approaches are dated. Too many still rely on writing a business plan before the customer or market is well understood. Other approaches encourage starting a business before testing assumptions and experimenting with concepts. Second, real-world experience contributes significantly to learning, but sometimes the cost of failing in the real world is too high. Finally, because of points 1 and 2, entrepreneurship within a formal education structure requires a new approach based on action and practice. Therefore, this textbook approaches teaching entrepreneurship as a method that goes beyond understanding, knowing, and talking; it requires using, applying, and acting. It is a method that requires practice.

entrepreneurship as a method that demands practice. In fact we call it "the practice of entrepreneurship" throughout the book. Today entrepreneurship is most often taught as a process which involves identifying an opportunity, understanding resource requirements, acquiring resources, planning, implementing, and harvesting. But the word "process" assumes known inputs and known outputs as in a manufacturing process. A process implies you will get to a specific destination. For example, building a car on an assembly line is a manufacturing process. You know all the parts; you know how they fit together; and you know the type of car you will have at the end. A process is quite predictable.

Entrepreneurship is not predictable and, therefore, cannot adequately be taught as a process. In fact, entrepreneurship is complex, chaotic, and lacking in any notion of linearity. The entrepreneurship practice requires creative and nimble thinking leading to a heightened level of experimentation where numerous iterations represent stages of learning rather than a series of starts and stops or even successes and failures. Finally, while a process is tested multiple times to ensure quality when used, a method is something that requires consistent practice so knowledge and expertise can be continually developed and applied to future endeavors.

Entrepreneurship: The Practice and Mindset catapults students beyond the classroom to think and act more entrepreneurially in order to create opportunities and take action in uncertain environments. Based on the world-renowned Babson program, this new text emphasizes practice and learning through action. Students learn entrepreneurship by doing entrepreneurship. By the end of the text students have the entrepreneurial mindset, skillset, and toolset that can be applied to organizations of all kinds.

OUR VISION

Our vision in writing this book was to create a practice-based text that promotes active learning and engagement with the realities of entrepreneurship, encouraging students to think like entrepreneurs rather than just learning about them. We treat

What Makes Our Book Unique

▸ A focus on the **entrepreneurial mindset** helps students develop the discovery, thinking, reasoning, and implementation skills necessary to thrive in highly uncertain environments

- An emphasis on **The Practice of Entrepreneurship**, where entrepreneurship is approached as a method that requires doing. It's not a predictive or linear process. It's messy, but clarity comes with action and practice.

- Each chapter includes a **"mindshift" activity** where students take action outside the classroom in order to practice various aspects of entrepreneurship.

- Instructors are provided with **experiential learning activities** to use inside the classroom.

- A unique chapter on **learning from failure** helps students anticipate setbacks, develop grit, and understand the value of experimentation and iteration.

- **Cutting-edge topics** such as design thinking, business model canvas, bootstrapping, and crowdfunding are covered in depth, exposing students to the latest developments in the field.

An Inclusive Approach

The media often exaggerate the meteoritic rise of so-called "overnight global sensations" such as Bill Gates (Microsoft), Steve Jobs (Apple), Mark Zuckerberg (Facebook), Elon Musk (Tesla), and Travis Kalanick (Uber). These stories have perpetuated the myth of the "tech entrepreneurial genius" and have captured the public imagination for decades. While the likes of Bill Gates and his peers are certainly inspirational, we would argue that few can personally identify with the stories surrounding them, and they do little to represent the reality of entrepreneurship.

In *Entrepreneurship*, we deconstruct the myths and stories, which we believe limits others from becoming entrepreneurs. Dominant myths include that entrepreneurship is reserved for startups; that entrepreneurs have a special set of personality traits; that entrepreneurship can't be taught; that entrepreneurs are extreme risk-takers; that entrepreneurs do not collaborate; that entrepreneurs devote large periods of time to planning; and that entrepreneurship is not a life skill.

With the support of extensive research, we show that the traditional view of the startup is not the only path for entrepreneurs; that there is no scientific evidence to suggest that entrepreneurs are any different from the rest of us in terms of personality traits or behaviors; that entrepreneurship can indeed be taught; that entrepreneurs are more calculated (rather than extreme) risk takers; that they collaborate more than they compete; act more than they plan; and perceive entrepreneurship as a life skill.

We also show that entrepreneurs do not have to come from a technology background to succeed. In *Entrepreneurship*, we include personal accounts of entrepreneurs from all types of disciplines both in the United States and around the world, including those in the fields of recruitment, science, food and beverage, tourism, engineering, finance, clothing, industrial design, pet services, tourism, fitness, costume design, sports, and promotional marketing.

These personal stories are intended to illustrate the realities of being an entrepreneur, detailing the unpredictability of entrepreneurship together with the highs and the lows; for like famous U.S. entrepreneur computer designer Adam Osborne, we believe that "the most valuable thing you can make is a mistake—you can't learn anything from being perfect."

Entrepreneurship is all around us; everyone has the ability to think and act entrepreneurially, transform opportunity into reality, and create social and economic value. But as we show, practice is key to success, and learning is inseparable from doing.

A Mindset and Action Approach

Mindset is the precursor to action. The work of researcher Darden School of Business professor Saras D. Sarasvathy has added a new dimension to the field in understanding the entrepreneurial mindset. Sarasvathy discovered patterns of thinking, a theory she calls **effectuation,** which is the idea that the future is unpredictable yet controllable. In other words, because thinking can be changed and altered, we all have the ability to think and act entrepreneurially and this thinking can be learned and taught. Moreover, entrepreneurship is not only about altering the way we think—it is about creating mindshifts to take action that yield significant change and value. And creating these mindshifts takes practice and experimentation.

We believe that it is very important to emphasize the mindset in the early development of entrepreneurship students. Often the mindset is either ignored or considered it's too difficult to teach. We introduce entrepreneurial mindset very early in the text, and then the mindset is further developed throughout the book based on the action that students take and are required to practice throughout the book.

Knowing that an entrepreneurial mindset is needed is not sufficient for a strong entrepreneurship education. Practicing the mindset and helping students develop it over time are essential components of learning the discipline of entrepreneurship today. In her previous book, *Teaching Entrepreneurship,* Heidi Neck and her co-authors Candy Brush and Patti Greene encouraged educators to build classroom environments that encouraged students to play, create, experiment, empathize, and reflect in order to build a bias toward action and become more entrepreneurial. These elements are emphasized throughout this text.

FEATURES

In each chapter, we include the following features which help students think and act like entrepreneurs.

In-Chapter Features

▶ **Entrepreneurship in Action** at the beginning of each chapter includes interviews with entrepreneurs from many different businesses and disciplines both in the United States and around the world, demonstrating how the concepts discussed in the chapter are applied in real situations. For example, in Chapter 5, the authors interview Jack McCarthy, the founder of a popular Ugly Christmas Sweater website.

▶ **Mindshift** activities in each chapter provide instructors with exercises that encourage students to think and act outside of their comfort zones. These activities can be performed inside or outside the classroom, and the accompanying critical thinking questions promote further comprehension and analysis. For example, in Chapter 2, the Three Hour Challenge prompts students to explore their goals and desires to help them identify three different business ideas based on that desire.

▶ **You Be the Entrepreneur** asks students to imagine themselves in situations based on real events from real companies to help them think critically about what they would do in the same position. Instructors can access the "What They Did" real-world responses on the instructor resources site to encourage further analysis and discussion. For example, in Chapter 13, a Shark Tank contestant must decide if he's willing to give up equity in his company to appear on the show.

▶ **Entrepreneurship Meets Ethics** provides students with examples of ethical dilemmas and challenges related to topics discussed in the chapter. These real-world scenarios and the accompanying critical-thinking questions guide students to think about how they would take action if confronted with a similar situation. For example, in Chapter 10, the authors discuss Martin Shkreli of Turing Pharmaceuticals and his decision to increase the price of a life-saving drug by 5000%.

▶ **Research at Work** highlights recent seminal entrepreneurship studies and explores their impact on and application to the marketplace. For example, in Chapter 4, Defining Social Entrepreneurship discusses how researchers have struggled to define this unique topic over the years.

▶ Short **Case Studies** tell the stories of real companies from various sectors and markets to illustrate chapter concepts and encourage further exploration of these topics. For example, Chapter 9's case study examines the prolific career of serial entrepreneur and innovator Elon Musk.

▶ **Summaries** and **Key Terms** recap important chapter information for students to aid with studying and comprehension.

▶ Topical **Appendices** offer greater depth of practice:

  • **Financial Statements and Projections for Startups** demonstrates how students can build financial projections based on sound data, using different types of financial statements.

  • **The Pitch Deck** provides an in-depth description of the pitch deck, includes sample slides, walks students through the preparation of their own pitch deck, and advises students on how to predict and prepare for the question-and-answer period that usually follows a pitch presentation.

▸ **VentureBlocks simulation** at the end of Chapter 6

- In the VentureBlocks simulation, students start from scratch, with no resources or business ideas, and must explore a new, unknown market of bearlike pets called nanus. On their journey through the simulation, students learn how to interview customers to identify business opportunities based on their needs. Most students will complete VentureBlocks in 30 to 60 minutes. The simulation includes tutorials so they know what to do and how to navigate at all times. The simulation ends when they identify business opportunities that meet the needs of nanu owners.

CONTENT AND ORGANIZATION

Part I. Introducing the Entrepreneurial Lifestyle

Chapter 1, "Entrepreneurship: A Global, Social Movement," explains the global rise and diversity of entrepreneurship and its impact; the importance of action and practice in entrepreneurship; and the myths associated with entrepreneurship.

Chapter 2, "Practicing Entrepreneurship," describes the skills most important to The Practice of Entrepreneurship, how entrepreneurship is more of a method than a process, and the concept of deliberate practice.

Chapter 3, "Developing an Entrepreneurial Mindset," outlines the effectiveness of mindset in entrepreneurship and explains how to develop the habits of self-leadership, creativity, and improvisation.

Chapter 4, "Supporting Social Entrepreneurship," defines social entrepreneurship, the different types of

social entrepreneurship, and how it can help to resolve wicked problems around the world.

Part II. Creating & Finding Opportunities

Chapter 5, "Recognizing New Opportunities," explores the pathways toward opportunity recognition, opportunity identification, and idea generation.

Chapter 6, "Using Design Thinking," describes the importance of design thinking in understanding customers and their needs, and illustrates the key parts of the design thinking process and their relevance to entrepreneurs.

Chapter 7, "Testing and Experimenting in Markets," identifies the steps of scientific experimentation and how they apply to entrepreneurs; demonstrates how to test hypotheses; and explores the power of storyboarding as a form of prototyping.

Part III. Evaluating & Acting on Opportunities

Chapter 8, "Building Business Models," examines the core areas of a business model; explores the importance of customer value propositions (CVPs); and illustrates the components of the business model canvas.

Chapter 9, "Planning for Entrepreneurs," explains TRIM (Team, Resources, Ideas, Market) and its importance to entrepreneurial planning; the different types of plans used by entrepreneurs; and provides advice for writing business plans.

Chapter 10, "Creating Revenue Models," describes the different types of revenue models used by entrepreneurs, and identifies different strategies entrepreneurs use when pricing their products and calculating prices.

Chapter 11, "Learning From Failure," explores failure and its effect on entrepreneurs; the consequences of fear of failure; how entrepreneurs can learn from failure; and the significance of "grit" and its role in building tolerance for failure.

Part IV. Resourcing New Opportunities

Chapter 12, "Bootstrapping for Resources," describes the significance of bootstrapping, and bootstrapping strategies for entrepreneurs, and also discusses crowdfunding as a form of investment for entrepreneurial ventures.

Chapter 13, "Financing for Startups," outlines the stages of equity financing, and explains the roles of angel investors and venture capital investors in financing entrepreneurs.

Chapter 14, "Developing Networks," explains the importance of networks for building social capital; describes different ways of building networks; and how networking can help build a founding team.

Chapter 15, "Navigating Legal & IP Issues," outlines the most common types of legal structures available to startups, and describes IP, IP theft, and some IP traps experienced by entrepreneurs.

Chapter 16, "Marketing & Pitching Your Idea," explores the principles of marketing and how they apply to new ventures, explains the value of social media for marketing opportunities, and describes the pitching process.

ONLINE RESOURCES

SAGE edge

SAGE edge for Instructors

A password-protected instructor resource site at **edge.sagepub.com/neckentrepreneurship** supports teaching with high-quality content to help in creating a rich learning environment for students. The SAGE edge site for this book includes the following instructor resources:

- **Test banks** built on AACSB standards, the book's learning objectives, and Bloom's Taxonomy provide a diverse range of test items with **ExamView test generation**. Each chapter includes 100 test questions to give instructors options for assessing students.

- Editable, chapter-specific **PowerPoint® slides** offer complete flexibility for creating a multimedia presentation for the course.

- **Lecture notes** for each chapter align with PowerPoint slides to serve as an essential reference, summarizing key concepts to ease preparation for lectures and class discussion.

- Carefully selected **video and multimedia content** aligned with the book's learning objectives enhances exploration of key topics to reinforce concepts and provide further insights.

- Sample **answers to questions in the text** provide an essential reference.

- **Case notes** include summaries, analyses, and sample answers to assist with discussion.

- **Entrepreneurial exercises** written by Heidi Neck and other faculty from Babson College can be used in class to reinforce learning by doing.

- Suggested **projects, experiential exercises, and activities** help students apply the concepts they learn to see how the work in various contexts, providing new perspectives.

- **Tables and figures** from the book are available for download.

- **Excel spreadsheets** accompany the appendix on financials.

- **Sample pitch decks** serve as examples to help students formulate their own pitch.

- **SAGE coursepacks** provide easy LMS integration.

SAGE edge for students

The open-access companion website helps students accomplish their coursework goals in an easy-to-use learning environment, featuring:

- **Action plans** for each chapter allow students to track their progress as they study

- **Learning objectives** with summaries reinforce the most important material

- Mobile-friendly practice **quizzes** encourage self-guided assessment and practice

- ▶ Mobile-friendly **flashcards** strengthen understanding of key concepts
- ▶ Carefully selected **video and multimedia content** enhances exploration of key topics to reinforce concepts and provide further insights.
- ▶ **Sample pitch decks** help students form their own pitch

SAGE coursepacks

SAGE coursepacks makes it easy to import our quality instructor and student resource content into your school's learning management system (LMS) with minimal effort. Intuitive and simple to use, **SAGE coursepacks** gives you the control to focus on what really matters: customizing course content to meet your students' needs. The SAGE coursepacks, created specifically for this book, are customized and curated for use in Blackboard, Canvase, Desire2Learn (D2L), and Moodle.

In addition to the content available on the SAGE edge site, the coursepacks include:

- ▶ **Pedagogically robust assessment tools** that foster review, practice, and critical thinking, and offer a better, more complete way to measure student engagement, including:
  - **Diagnostic chapter pretests and posttests** that identify opportunities for student improvement, track student progress, and ensure mastery of key learning objectives
  - **Instructions** on how to use and integrate the comprehensive assessments and resources provided

- ▶ **Assignable video tied to learning objectives, with corresponding multimedia assessment tools,** bring concepts to life that increase student engagement and appeal to different learning styles. The **video assessment questions** feed to your gradebook.
- ▶ **Integrated links to the eBook version** that make it easy to access the mobile-friendly version of the text, which can be read anywhere, anytime

Interactive eBook

Entrepreneurship is also available as an **Interactive eBook** that can be packaged with the text at no additional cost or purchased separately. The Interactive eBook offers hyperlinks to original and licensed videos, additional case studies, as well as carefully chosen videos, articles, and audio resources from the web, all from the same pages found in the printed text. Users will also have immediate access to study tools such as highlighting, bookmarking, note-taking, and more!

VentureBlocks Simulation

An engaging simulation can be packaged with the book to help students practice entrepreneurial processes. Created by Heidi Neck and Anton Yakushin, the simulation has students complete missions to practice interviewing customers, identifying new opportunities, and reflecting on what they learn. Instructors can view class analytics to help guide discussion during a debrief session, for which PowerPoint slides are available. Additionally, instructors can use available handouts to assign an in-class role-playing exercise that reinforces the concepts and further prepares students to gain insights from customers and develop a business.

ACKNOWLEDGMENTS

The authors would like to thank the following people for their support in writing this book.

Heidi Neck would like to thank Candy Brush, Patti Greene, Len Schlesinger, Dale Meyer, and the late Jeff Timmons for the inspiration behind the book—all mentors and good friends. She would also like to thank her research assistant and MBA '16, Charles Plaisimond, Anton Yakushin, her partner in VentureBlocks, and Babson College for their support in writing this book.

Chris Neck thanks Dean Amy Hillman at Arizona State (W. P. Carey School of Business) and Trevis Certo, (Department Head, Department of Management, Arizona State University) for their encouragement on his teaching and research efforts. Chris Neck thanks Duane Roen (Dean of the College of Letters and Sciences at Arizona State University) for his steadfast support and encouragement to excel in the classroom.

He'd also like to thank those behind-the-scenes individuals who assisted in the research, development, and/or editing of various parts of this book. Specifically, he thanks Elizabeth Parsons, Matthew Benedick, Gaurang Rameshchandra Bhavsar, Marisa Keegan, Amanda Rogers, Rachel Wilkerson, Nishant Mahajan, Varun Parmar, Kyle Helmle, Erich Weber, Matt Kulina, Prakrut Desai, and Alex Stanley. We would like to acknowledge and thank Jordan Jensen for writing thirteen end-of-chapter cases for the book.

We'd also like to thank Shyam Devnani, Brad George, Patti Greene, Candy Brush, Dennis Ceru, Matt Allen, Andrew Corbett, and Erik Noyes for their contributions to the experiential exercises featured on the instructor website.

We are indebted to the entrepreneurship faculty at the University of Arizona's McGuire Center for Entrepreneurship who were some of the earliest supporters of this book. Thank you Carlos J. Alsua, Randy M. Burd, K. Krasnow Waterman, Mark Peterson, Tristan Reader, and Richard Eric Yngve for your insightful feedback on the test bank. Your comments have helped us develop a better product and for that we are very grateful.

Writing a textbook is a huge undertaking that extends far beyond the author team. We would like to thank the incredibly committed team at Sage for their constant encouragement, endless patience, and thoughtful suggestions. Their passion and enthusiasm has helped to deliver a textbook of which we are extremely proud.

Maggie Stanley, our acquisitions editor, has championed this book every step of the way, and we are enormously grateful for her considerate input and constant support. Development editor Abbie Rickard has been a welcome driving force, encouraging us to explore and consider new ideas. Our talented editor Elsa Peterson helped clarify and refine the material and has significantly contributed to the quality of this textbook. Ellen Howard, our copyeditor has been meticulous in her work, for which we are very appreciative. David Felts, our production editor, oversaw the entire production process and, thanks to him, the whole project was kept on track. We'd also like to thank marketing manager Ashlee Blunk, market development manager Erica DeLuca, and marketing associate Georgia McLaughlin for their efforts promoting the book, editorial assistant Neda Dallal for handling a number of tasks during development and production, permissions assistant Tori Mirsadjadi for her work helping secure permission to use a number of items included in the text, senior eLearning editor Katie Ancheta for all of her efforts in creating and compiling the digital resources that accompany this text, and Senior Graphic Designer Gail Buschman for creating a stunning interior and cover design.

For their thoughtful and helpful comments and ideas on our manuscript, we sincerely thank the following reviewers. Our book is a better product because of their insightful suggestions.

Anuradha Basu, San Jose State University

Susan Berston, City College of San Francisco

Constant D. Beugre, Delaware State University

Martin Bressler, Southeastern Oklahoma State University

Candida Brush, Babson College

Jacqueline H. Bull, Immaculata University

Kimble Byrd, Rowan University

C.S. Richard Chan, Stony Brook University

Shih Yung Chou, The University of Texas of the Permian Basin

Diane Denslow, University of North Florida

Art Diaz, University of Texas at El Paso

Robert S. D'Intino, Rowan University

Steven Edelson, Walsh University

Kevin Ernst, Ohio Northern University

Frances Fabian, University of Memphis

David J. Gavin, Marist College

Ranjan George, Simpson University

Peter Gianiodis, Duquesne University

Amy R. Gresock, University of Michigan—Flint

Maurice Haff, University of Central Oklahoma

Sheila Hanson, University of North Dakota

Lerong He, State University of New York at Brockport

Kirk Heriot, Columbus State University

Laurent Josien, SUNY Plattsburgh

Ryan Kauth, University of Wisconsin—Green Bay

Ram Kesavan, University of Detroit Mercy

Sara Kiser, Alabama State University

Rebecca Knapp, Saddleback College

Jon Krabill, Columbus State Community College

Nancy Kucinski, Hardin-Simmons University

Thomas Lachowicz, Radford University

Denise Lefort, Arapahoe Community College

Ada Leung, Penn State Berks

Martin Luytjes, Jacksonville University

Michele K. Masterfano, Drexel University

Sue McNamara, SUNY Fredonia

Stuart Mease, Virginia Tech

Wallace W. Meyer, Jr, University of Kansas

John Edward Michaels, California University of Pennsylvania

Erik Monsen, University of Vermont

Charlie Nagelschmidt, Champlain College

David M. Nemi, Niagara County Community College

Laurel F. Ofstein, Western Michigan University

Bill Petty, Baylor University

Jonathan Phillips, Belmont University

Marlene Reed, Baylor University

Maija Renko, University of Illinois at Chicago

Rodney Ridley, Wilkes University

Timothy Ritter, Western Kentucky University

Robert W. Robertson, Independence University

Linda Wabschall Ross, Rowan University

Jacqueline Schmidt, John Carroll University

Darrell Scott, Idaho State University

Sally Sledge, Norfolk State University

Frank R. Spitznogle, Northern Arizona University

Joseph R. Stasio, Jr., Merrimack College

Sunny Li Sun, University of Missouri—Kansas City

Lauren Talia, Independence University

Keith Ward, St. Edward's University

Paula A. White, Independence University

Lei Xu, Texas Tech University

Bill Zannini, Northern Essex Community College

Thanks are also due to the individuals who developed the digital resources that accompany this book: Steven Edelson, Jordan Jensen, Eva Mika, Colette Rominger, Sally Sledge, Paula A. White, and Cecilia Williams.

ABOUT THE AUTHORS

HEIDI M. NECK, PHD

Heidi M. Neck, PhD, is a Babson College Professor and the Jeffry A. Timmons Professor of Entrepreneurial Studies. She has taught entrepreneurship at the undergraduate, MBA and executive levels. Neck is the President of the United States Association of Small Business & Entrepreneurship (USASBE), an academic organization dedicated to the advancement of entrepreneurship education. She is Faculty Director of The Babson Collaborative, a global institutional membership organization for colleges and universities seeking to increase their capability and capacity in entrepreneurship education. Additionally, Neck is Faculty Director of Babson's Symposia for Entrepreneurship Educators (SEE)—programs designed to further develop faculty from around the world in the of art and craft of teaching entrepreneurship and building entrepreneurship programs. Through her leadership she has directly trained over 2,000 educators around the world. An award-winning teacher, Neck has been recognized for teaching excellence at Babson for undergraduate, graduate, and executive education. She has also been recognized by international organizations, the Academy of Management and USASBE, for excellence in pedagogy and course design. Most recently in 2016 The Schulze Foundation awarded her "Entrepreneurship Educator of the Year" for pushing the frontier of entrepreneurship education in higher education.

Her research interests include entrepreneurship education, entrepreneurship inside organizations, and creative thinking. Neck is the lead author of *Teaching Entrepreneurship: A Practice-Based Approach* (Elgar Publishing)—a book written to help educators teach entrepreneurship in more experiential and engaging ways. Additionally, she has published 40+ book chapters, research monographs, and refereed articles in such journals as *Journal of Small Business Management*, *Entrepreneurship Theory & Practice*, and *International Journal of Entrepreneurship Education*. She is on the editorial board of the Academy of Management Learning & Education journal and is a Forbes blogger on entrepreneurship content.

Neck speaks and teaches internationally on cultivating the entrepreneurial mindset and espousing the positive force of entrepreneurship as a societal change agent. She consults and trains organizations of all sizes on building entrepreneurial capacity. She is the cofounder of VentureBlocks, an entrepreneurship education technology company and co-owner of FlowDog, a canine aquatic fitness and rehabilitation center located just outside of Boston. Heidi earned her PhD in Strategic Management and Entrepreneurship from the University of Colorado at Boulder. She holds a BS in Marketing from Louisiana State University and an MBA from the University of Colorado, Boulder.

CHRISTOPHER P. NECK, PHD

Dr. Christopher P. Neck is currently an Associate Professor of Management at Arizona State University, where he held the title "University Master Teacher." From 1994 to 2009, he was part of the Pamplin College of Business faculty at Virginia Tech. He received his PhD in Management from Arizona State University and his MBA from Louisiana State University. Neck is author of the books *Self-Leadership: The Definitive Guide to Personal Excellence* (2016, Sage); *Fit To Lead: The Proven 8-week Solution for Shaping Up Your Body, Your Mind, and Your Career* (2004, St. Martin's Press; 2012, Carpenter's Sons Publishing); *Mastering Self-Leadership: Empowering Yourself for Personal Excellence*, 6th edition (2013, Pearson); *The Wisdom of Solomon at Work* (2001, Berrett-Koehler); *For Team Members Only: Making Your Workplace Team Productive and Hassle-Free* (1997, Amacom Books); and *Medicine for the Mind: Healing Words to Help You Soar*, 4th Edition (Wiley, 2012). Neck is also the coauthor of the principles of management textbook, *Management: A Balanced Approach to the 21st Century* (Wiley 2013; 2017, 2nd Edition); the upcoming introductory to entrepreneurship textbook, *Entrepreneurship*, (Sage, 2017); and the introductory to organizational behavior textbook, *Organizational Behavior* (Sage, 2016).

Dr. Neck's research specialties include employee/executive fitness, self-leadership, leadership, group decision-making processes, and self-managing teams. He has over 100 publications in the form of books, chapters, and articles in various journals. Some of the outlets in which Neck's work has appeared include *Organizational Behavior and Human Decision Processes*, *The Journal of Organizational Behavior*, *The Academy of Management Executive*, *Journal of Applied Behavioral Science*, *The Journal of Managerial Psychology*, *Executive Excellence*, *Human Relations*, *Human Resource Development Quarterly*, *Journal of Leadership Studies*, *Educational Leadership*, and *The Commercial Law Journal*.

Due to Neck's expertise in management, he has been cited in numerous national publications, including *The Washington Post*, *The Wall Street Journal*, *The Los Angeles Times*, *The Houston Chronicle*, and the *Chicago Tribune*. Additionally, each semester Neck teaches an introductory management course to a single class of anywhere from 500 to 1,000 students.

Dr. Neck was the recipient of the 2007 Business Week Favorite Professor Award." He is featured on www.businessweek.com as one of the approximately twenty professors from across the world receiving this award.

Neck currently teaches a mega section of Management Principles to approximately 500 students at Arizona State University. Neck received the Order of Omega Outstanding Teaching Award for 2012. This award is awarded to one professor at Arizona State by the Alpha Lamda Chapter of this leadership fraternity. His class sizes at Virginia Tech filled rooms up to 2,500 students. He received numerous teaching awards during his tenure at Virginia Tech, including the 2002 Wine Award for Teaching Excellence. Also, Neck was the ten-time winner (1996, 1998, 2000, 2002, 2004, 2005, 2006, 2007, 2008, and 2009) of the "Students' Choice Teacher of The Year Award" (voted by the students for the best teacher of the year within the entire university). Also,

some of the organizations that have participated in Neck's management development training include GE/Toshiba, Busch Gardens, Clark Construction, the United States Army, Crestar, American Family Insurance, Sales and Marketing Executives International, American Airlines, American Electric Power, W. L. Gore & Associates, Dillard's Department Stores, and Prudential Life Insurance. Neck is also an avid runner. He has completed 12 marathons, including the Boston Marathon, the New York City Marathon, and the San Diego Marathon. In fact, his personal record for a single long distance run is a 40-mile run.

EMMA L. MURRAY, BA, HDIP, DBS IT

Emma L. Murray completed a Bachelor of Arts degree in English and Spanish at University College Dublin (UCD) in County Dublin, Ireland. This was followed by a Higher Diploma (Hdip) in business studies and information technology at the Michael Smurfit Graduate School of Business in County Dublin, Ireland. Following her studies, Emma spent nearly a decade in investment banking before becoming a full-time writer and author.

As a writer, Emma has worked on numerous texts, including business and economics, self-help, and psychology. Within the field of higher education, Emma worked with Dr. Christopher P. Neck and Dr. Jeffery D. Houghton on *Management* (Wiley 2013); and is the coauthor of the principles of management textbook *Management: A Balanced Approach to the 21st Century* (Wiley 2013, 2017-2nd Edition) and the coauthor of *Organizational Behavior* (Sage 2017).

She is the author of *The Unauthorized Guide to Doing Business the Alan Sugar Way* (2010, Wiley-Capstone); and the lead author of *How to Succeed as a Freelancer in Publishing* (2010, How To Books). She lives in London.

An Open Letter to All Students

Dear Student,

We suspect you are reading this now because you are on a journey—a journey in search of meaning, a desire to make a significant impact on the world, an itch to bring something new to market, a yearning not simply to find yourself but also to create yourself. Many believe that entrepreneurship can be a path to all of this. For some it can be, but it takes a lot of dedication and a lot of practice. That's what this book is all about: practicing entrepreneurship.

You are going to hear about the concept of practice throughout this entire book, and we want to take a minute to put this word in perspective. Think about a sport you're pretty good at or a musical instrument you have mastered. Even if you love the idea of playing the piano, it's very difficult to sit at the piano and start playing a piece that others really want to hear. You may be a very good soccer player today, but when you started playing, we're sure the coach didn't put you in the game immediately and say, "Go play, Kid!" Similarly, you could destroy a golf course if you didn't know the basics of hitting that little white ball. Before we play the music piece in front of others, or play in our first competitive soccer game, and before we tee up on the first hole of a prestigious golf course, we have to practice.

Rarely do we perform the entire piece of music or play the actual game, or get on the actual golf course before practicing parts of the experience. You practice scales on the piano, then you learn how to read the music, then you play simple pieces, then more complex compositions, and so on. In soccer, you work on fundamentals of kicking the ball, foot coordination, passing, heading, and tackling. A golfing instructor will make you swing different clubs for hours before you are allowed to try to hit the golf ball. Yes, just swinging. No hitting! You may also recognize in practicing these different experiences that you have to take action. We don't just read about playing the piano or soccer or golf. We have to do in order to learn. We have to take action in order to practice, and it is through practice that we can progress.

By practicing entrepreneurship, you will hone your skills and become proficient so that you can take action to reach your goals. Whether you have a concrete plan to bring something new to market, or just a passion for finding ways to make the world a better place, we hope this book will help you on your journey.

Enjoy the journey and don't forget to practice!

The Authors

PART I

INTRODUCING THE ENTREPRENEURIAL LIFESTYLE

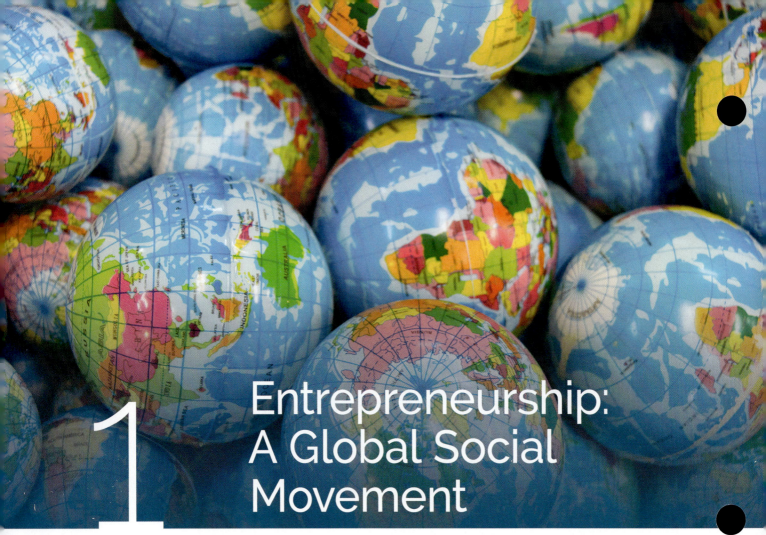

1

Entrepreneurship: A Global Social Movement

All human beings are entrepreneurs. When we were in the caves we were all self-employed . . . finding our food, feeding ourselves. That's where human history began . . . . As civilization came we suppressed it. We became labor because they stamped us, 'You are labor.' We forgot that we are entrepreneurs."[1]

—Muhammad Yunus, author and social entrepreneur

Learning Objectives

1.1 Explain the importance of action and practice in entrepreneurship.

1.2 List the seven lesser-known truths about entrepreneurship.

1.3 Explain the history of entrepreneurship in the United States.

1.4 Compare and contrast the different forms of entrepreneurship in practice today.

1.5 Illustrate the global diversity of entrepreneurship and its impact.

1.6 Propose different ways in which this book can help you practice entrepreneurship.

Chapter Outline

1.1 ENTREPRENEURSHIP REQUIRES ACTION AND PRACTICE

>> LO 1.1 **Explain the importance of action and practice in entrepreneurship.**

To fully understand the significance of these words by 2006 Nobel Peace Prize winner Muhammad Yunus, it helps to know more about Yunus's entrepreneurial achievements. As a professor of economics at the University of Chittagong in Bangladesh, Yunus founded the Grameen Bank (meaning "bank of the villages")—a bank for the poor of Bangladesh that gives very small, short-term loans to impoverished villagers who are perceived as ineligible to receive traditional bank loans to start their own businesses. Such lending programs have come to be associated with entrepreneurs in developing countries and are called **microloans**. In the 1970s, Yunus had a very simple idea that changed the landscape of entrepreneurship in Bangladesh and throughout the developing world. He placed borrowers, mostly women, into small groups, but did not permit all group members to borrow at once. While one borrower might receive a loan for $40, the other members became eligible for their own loans only when the original borrower began to pay back the loan. Such a process created motivation, accountability, and empowerment. Yunus made his first loan of $27 in 1976 to a group of women who wanted to expand their bamboo business.

As of 2007, the Grameen bank had extended credit to over seven million people, mostly in Bangladesh, who were previously at the mercy of local moneylenders who charged cripplingly high interest rates.[2] Through his revolutionary ideas, Yunus not only proved that the poor are creditworthy, but he crossed social boundaries to give the people of Bangladesh an opportunity to be entrepreneurs themselves.

The experience of Grameen Bank and its customers stands as an example of how anyone—regardless of background, ethnicity, social class, gender, sexual orientation, country, or education—can become an entrepreneur if given the opportunity

Web
Microloans

Microloan: a very small, short-term loan often associated with entrepreneurs in developing countries.

Video
Action and Practice

Nobel Peace Prize winner Muhammad Yunus founded the Grameen Bank in Bangladesh, serving the community by offering loans to underprivileged families without requiring collatoral.
Credit: Andrew Matthews/ZUMA Press/Newscom

to practice. The practice-through-action orientation is why we subtitled this book *The Practice and Mindset*. With the right mindset, or mental attitude, you are able to start practicing. We believe in all types of **entrepreneurs**—those that take action to create something new—a new idea, a new item or product, a new institution, a new market, a new set of possibilities.[3]

The *Entrepreneurship in Action* feature provides another example of how ordinary individuals with a vision can take action and use practice to reach their entrepreneurial goals.

1.2 ENTREPRENEURSHIP MAY BE DIFFERENT FROM WHAT YOU THINK

>> LO 1.2   List the seven lesser-known truths about entrepreneurship.

Our belief, as demonstrated by the previous examples, is that by taking action and putting ideas into practice, everyone "has what it takes" to be an entrepreneur. However, this is not necessarily the same message that is delivered by popular media. Let's examine some popular images of entrepreneurs. What is the truth behind these images?

Media Images of Entrepreneurs

Entrepreneurship: a discipline that seeks to understand how opportunities are discovered, created, and exploited, by whom, and with what consequences.

The media often exaggerate the meteoritic rise of so-called "overnight global sensations" such as Bill Gates (Microsoft), Steve Jobs (Apple), Mark Zuckerberg (Facebook), Elon Musk (Tesla), and Travis Kalanick (Uber). These stories have perpetuated the myth of the "male tech hero-genius" and have captured the public imagination for decades. While the likes of Bill Gates and his peers are certainly inspirational, we would argue that few can personally identify with the stories surrounding them, and they do little to represent the reality of entrepreneurship.

However, if you take a closer look at the rise of these famous entrepreneurs, you will find that their ascent to greatness has been based on a great deal of practice. In fact, Bill Gates has admitted to carrying out approximately 10,000 hours of programming practice before Microsoft was even launched.[4] The point is not the number of hours Gates spent programming, but the fact that he consistently practiced his technique over a number of years. Gates's experience also shows us that there is no such thing as an overnight success. Another example is Uber founder Travis Kalanick. Kalanick had a 10-year rocky history of startups, including threats of lawsuits, and filing for bankruptcy, before he struck gold with Uber.[5] To further debunk the myths of entrepreneurship, we have put together a parody of a stereotypical entrepreneur, loosely based on the type that we read about in the popular press.

Bob, the tech lone-wolf genius—a parody

Bob is a technical whiz. He was programming before he could talk and taking machines apart and putting them back together before he could walk. None of this is surprising, as Bob was born a genius. He came into the world with a unique set of personality traits that automatically set him on the path to success.

ENTREPRENEURSHIP IN ACTION

Niari Keverian, CEO, ZOOS Greek Iced Teas

Niari Keverian, CEO of Boston-based startup, ZOOS Greek Iced Teas.
Credit: Photo courtesy of Niari Keverian

Niari Keverian is the CEO of ZOOS, a Boston-based company founded in 2014 that sells Greek iced tea. Along with her business partner, Keverian is overseeing a healthy expansion of their low-sugar, low-calorie, all-natural indulgence. Within a year of launch, ZOOS tea was on the shelves in every Massachusetts outlet of the Wegmans grocery store chain (located in the Northeast and Mid-Atlantic United States) as well as more than 200 health food stores, spas, fitness studios, and boutique grocers.

The breadth of distribution was promising—but Keverian was cautious not to count her chickens before they hatched. "Right now we are in a very sensitive time," she said in 2015. "We have proven that we are on to something, but everything I've learned at school and through my experience says that you can't grow too fast. It's a marathon, not a sprint."

Keverian is Armenian-American, and her partner is Greek-American. Her partner long wanted to make a business out of Greek iced tea but had little experience in the food and beverage world; Keverian, however, had the perfect background with high-level corporate experience with Collective Brands, Staples and Welch's.

When Keverian met her partner, she had just graduated from her MBA a year earlier and was working as a brand manager at Welch's. "I was given advice early on in my career: build an overall business toolkit of knowledge before going out on your own. Learn from the best, then go execute. That's what I did."

Prior to Keverian's climbing on board, her partner had created a Facebook page for her dream product. With around 1,000 likes, Keverian pored through fans' info and asked pointed questions to learn more about her would-be consumer. Then, she spent an evening with glue sticks and old magazines, piecing together a collage representing that person, "what their day to day life looks like, do they work, are they in school, are they into sugar, are they concerned about health," Keverian recalls.

Keverian presented her imaginative "art piece" to a graphic designer, and "on her first try on our logo, she nailed it." In addition to the designer, Keverian had over two-year venture hired consultants in manufacturing, packaging, distribution, and law to help smooth out the edges of their fledgling business. Still, officially, it was just the two of them on the team.

Keverian believes her customers are mostly young, health-conscious professionals, college students, and older teens. Moms-to-be and new moms are another important segment. As ZOOS teas are caffeine-free and low in sugar, women who are pregnant or nursing can enjoy them.

"Though we are having some great success," Keverian reflected, "we have a very long road ahead of us. We're going to face a lot of challenges that we need to be very careful of. You only get one shot in this industry to get it right. Once you screw it up, it's very hard to get them to look at you again because it's such a saturated market."

Keverian, who describes herself as a "strong-minded personality" who "works best under pressure," reported putting in 15-hour days (weekends too), sacrificing most of her social life in the process. Her advice for her fellow entrepreneurs: "You have to be ready to dedicate your entire life to getting that business off the ground. Always know you have the control of what your future holds. No one is going to dictate that to you; it's in your court."

CRITICAL THINKING QUESTIONS

1. In what ways do you see Niari Keverian as being totally dedicated to the success of ZOOS? What does dedication mean for the entrepreneur?

2. To what extent do you agree that entrepreneurship is "a marathon, not a sprint?" Provide some examples to support your position.

3. How does an entrepreneur have control over his or her own future? How is being an entrepreneur different from working in a "regular" career when it comes to control and decision making? ●

Source: N. Keverian, personal interview, August 28, 2014.

As Bob grew into his teenage years, he dropped out of all formal education in order to start his own technology firm—from the family garage. A natural risk-taker, Bob took out a huge loan to buy the latest state-of-the-art computer equipment to enable him to bring his revolutionary computer software applications to life.

When Bob felt his business was ready to launch, he spent months laboriously putting together a business plan. When he was satisfied with the plan, he direct-dialed the CEO of one the biggest technology firms in the world, informing him of his new innovation. Blown away by the young enterprising genius, the CEO immediately agreed to buy Bob's startup company there and then. Retired at the age of 19, Bob is now a rich man living the high life in the Caribbean. When asked whom he credits for his overnight success, Bob says that he did it all by himself.

Debunking the Myths of Entrepreneurship

Video
Myths About Achieving Dreams

Of course, Bob's story is a parody of what we hear in the media, but we feel it is important to deconstruct this mythical view of an entrepreneur. Exaggerated tales like this can be intimidating, and they can form reasons why some people are afraid to embark on the entrepreneurial path. Debunking the myths is the first step to believing that each of us has the capability to be an entrepreneur.

Rather than focusing on the myths, let's take a look at some truths illustrated in Table 1.1. Separating truth from fiction can be difficult, especially when some of these truths collide with the stories we read about in the media. Let's explore these truths in more detail to further understand how entrepreneurship can be a path for many.

Truth #1: Entrepreneurship is not reserved for startups

Startup: a temporary organization in search of a scalable business model.

The term *startup* came into vogue during the 1990s dot-com bubble, when a plethora of web-based companies were born. While the term has various meanings, we subscribe to Steve Blank's definition of **startup**: a temporary organization in search of a scalable business model.[6] In the traditional of view of startups, anyone who starts a business is called an entrepreneur. The entrepreneur creates a business based on research to assess the validity of an idea or business model. The business may be partially funded by seed money from family members or investors, but usually the majority is funded by the entrepreneurs themselves.

If the business is successful, the startup does not remain a startup. It can develop into an organization in its own right, be merged with another organization, or be bought or acquired by another company. In our parody example, lone-wolf

---

TABLE 1.1

The Truths About Entrepreneurship

Truth #1	Entrepreneurship is not reserved for startups.
Truth #2	Entrepreneurs do not have a special set of personality traits.
Truth #3	Entrepreneurship can be taught (it's a method that requires practice).
Truth #4	Entrepreneurs are not extreme risk-takers.
Truth #5	Entrepreneurs collaborate more than they compete.
Truth #6	Entrepreneurs act more than they plan.
Truth #7	Entrepreneurship is a life skill.

Bob created a technology startup in his parents' garage and sold it to a hugely successful organization. This traditional view of the startup, however, is not the only path for entrepreneurs. The truth is that entrepreneurs are everywhere, from corporations to franchises, to for-profit and nonprofit organizations, to family enterprises. We will explore these different types of entrepreneurs in more detail later in the chapter.

Truth #2: Entrepreneurs do not have a special set of personality traits

In our short parody, lone-wolf Bob is a tech genius who was born with the personality traits of a brilliant entrepreneur. In reality, there is no evidence to suggest that entrepreneurs have a special set of personality characteristics that distinguishes them from the rest of us.

Early research identified four main traits that could be ascribed to entrepreneurs: a desire for achievement, an innate sense of having the ability to influence events, a tendency to take risks, and a tolerance for uncertainty. Yet there is no scientific evidence to confirm whether these traits are a result of nature or nurture or any proven patterns in the behavior of entrepreneurs versus nonentrepreneurs.[7] Academics researching traits of entrepreneurs seem to have a prevailing fascination with defining "who" the entrepreneur is, rather than what he or she does.

However, over the last couple of decades, researchers have moved away from the traits perspective in favor of how entrepreneurs think and act, and have discovered that there are patterns in how entrepreneurs think. This means that all of us have the ability to act and think entrepreneurially with practice. We can change how we think.

In particular, the work of researcher Saras Sarasvathy has added a new dimension to the field in understanding the entrepreneurial mindset. Through a study involving **serial entrepreneurs**—people who start several businesses, sometimes at the same time, or sometimes one after the other—Sarasvathy discovered patterns of thinking, a theory she calls **effectuation**, which is the idea that the future is unpredictable yet controllable.[8]

Sarasvathy believes that effectual entrepreneurs focus on creating a future rather than predicting it. This means they create new opportunities, make markets rather than find them, accept and learn from failure, and build relationships with a variety of stakeholders. Effectual entrepreneurs use their own initiative to fulfil their vision of the future.

Take Niari Keverian of ZOOS Greek Iced Teas—she created opportunities for her business by establishing a Facebook page, networking, and forming alliances with experts who could provide her with the best advice.

> *Passion is what's going to drive you, so if you don't feel 100 or 150% in, it's not going to be a success. Expect blood, sweat and tears combined. You've got to be willing to make sacrifices, work the hardest that you have ever been able to work in your entire life, network like hell, learn, talk to as many people as you can possibly talk to, in and around business industry, but also people outside, who are really smart and have had successes in their industries. Learn from them, hear what they have to say, then apply it to yourself. (personal interview, August 28, 2014)*

Keverian had the right mindset for starting a business. We strongly believe that the mindset is the precursor to action. To us, it makes sense that if entrepreneurs are in the right frame of mind; there is greater confidence, intentionality, and vision to bring

Serial Entrepreneurs (or habitual entrepreneurs): the type of entrepreneurs who start several businesses, whether simultaneously or one after the other.

Effectuation: the idea that the future is unpredictable yet controllable.

ideas from the whiteboard to the real world. We are not born with an entrepreneurial mindset, we have to work to develop it. As a result, and because it's so important, we devote a whole chapter to it (Chapter 3).

Truth #3: Entrepreneurship can be taught (it's a method that requires practice)

While lone-wolf Bob shuns formal education to follow his own entrepreneurial path, entrepreneurship can be and is being taught in colleges and universities all over the world. Many of these courses teach entrepreneurship as a linear process, which involves identifying an opportunity, understanding resource requirements, acquiring resources, planning, implementing, and harvesting (exiting a business).[9] But the word *process* assumes known inputs and known outputs, as in a manufacturing process. A process implies you will get to a specific destination. For example, building a car on an assembly line is a manufacturing process. You know all the parts, you know how they fit together, and you know the type of car you will have at the end. A process is quite predictable.

Entrepreneurship is not predictable and, therefore, cannot adequately be taught as a process. Instead, a method or practice approach advocated in this text represents a body of skills that when developed through practice over time constitute a toolkit for entrepreneurial action.[10] The entrepreneurial method requires consistent practice so that knowledge and expertise can be continuously developed and applied to future endeavors. We explore this concept in further detail in Chapter 2.

Truth #4: Entrepreneurs are not extreme risk-takers

Contrary to the stereotype that entrepreneurs like to gamble when the stakes are high, there is no evidence to suggest that entrepreneurs take more risks than anyone else. In fact, entrepreneurs with gambling tendencies are usually not successful, simply because they are leaving too much to chance.[11] Risk is very personal and relative. Things always seem more risky from the outside looking in because we really don't know what calculations were made to take the next step. In fact, most entrepreneurs are very calculated risk takers and gauge what they are willing to lose with every step taken. They practice a cycle of act–learn–build that encourages taking small actions in order to learn and build that learning into the next action (see Figure 1.1).[12] Entrepreneurship should never be a zero-sum game; never an all-or-nothing decision. It's not about ascending the summit without ropes or oxygen. It just looks that way from the outside.

FIGURE 1.1

Act – Learn – Build

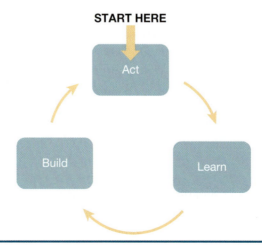

Truth #5: Entrepreneurs collaborate more than they compete

The image of lone-wolf Bob single-handedly decimating the competition in pursuit of personal gain is entirely inaccurate. Community plays an important role in entrepreneurship. Entrepreneurs draw on shared experience and desire to learn from others facing similar challenges. It can be hard to know what entrepreneurship is all about until you are actually in the throes of it, so it becomes very important to have a support group of like-minded entrepreneurs willing to help one another out with a "pay it forward" attitude—collaborating for the greater good.[13]

Not only do successful entrepreneurs collaborate with other entrepreneurs, but they also collaborate with their target customers to test new ideas, potential investors to build trust, and family and friends for support. Entrepreneurs also have a tendency to collaborate with competitors. One of the best-known examples of this is the collaboration of the late Steve Jobs of Apple and Bill Gates of Microsoft on the creation of the Apple Mac[14]—leaders of two technology giants that were seemingly at war with each other. In fact, Bill Gates had a number of Microsoft staff creating vital software for the Mac. Collaboration with customers, suppliers, and competitors can increase efficiency, spark new ideas, and generate creativity and innovation.[15]

Steve Jobs and Bill Gates collaborated on the Apple Mac despite being fierce competitors.

Credit: © User: Nafije.shabani/ Wikimedia Commons/CC-BY-SA 3.0 / https://creativecommons. org/licenses/by-sa/3.0/deed.en

Truth #6: Entrepreneurs act more than they plan

Lone wolf Bob spends an agonizing few months creating a formal business plan to present to his target technology company. But does every entrepreneur need a business plan to succeed? Not necessarily. Research revealed that fewer than half of Inc. 500 founders wrote formal business plans prior to launching their companies, and fewer than 30% had only basic plans.[16] So, how did they do it? They acted—they went out and talked to other people, connected with their customers, generated buzz about their product or service, and built a strong network. With every action, they collected real data that informed the next step. In short, they each practiced being an entrepreneur.

Today's investors want to know what the entrepreneur has done, the customers they have approached, and the interest they have generated. Facts and figures and projections are important, but they can be presented in a more visual way, through a demo or a short video clip. Ultimately, investors will want to know if the entrepreneurs have the capability to roll with the punches, take action, and accept the constructive feedback they receive from coaching.

Truth #7: Entrepreneurship is a life skill

Traditionally, entrepreneurship has been associated mostly with launching new businesses. However, these days, the meaning of entrepreneurship has transcended into something more than just the ability to begin a new venture. Many individuals and institutions perceive entrepreneurship as a life skill that helps people to deal with an uncertain future by providing them with the methods to think, act, identify opportunities, approach problems in a specific way, adapt to new conditions, and take control of personal goals and ambitions. It also provides people with a set of skills that can be applied to many other fields. Being entrepreneurial empowers us to create opportunities and reach our goals.[17]

Now that we have separated the truths from the myths, it is time to create a new narrative. Our economic future depends on entrepreneurs, and the traditional, narrow definition has stifled what it really means to be an entrepreneur. But to create a new story, we need to know how we arrived at this current narrative in the first place. The answer lies in history.

1.3 A BRIEF HISTORY OF THE EVOLUTION OF ENTREPRENEURSHIP IN THE UNITED STATES

>> **LO 1.3**   **Explain the history of entrepreneurship in the United States.**

The history of entrepreneurship in the United States can be divided into five periods or eras.[18] Let's take a brief look at each of these eras to understand how entrepreneurship has evolved over the centuries, and its contribution to the United States as an economic powerhouse and entrepreneurial nation.

Emergence of the Self-Made Man (Colonial America Before 1776)

Entrepreneur defined as: "One who undertakes a project; a manufacturer; a master builder."

—Common French usage (1600s)[19]

Founding father Benjamin Franklin, who also invented the lightning rod.

Credit: http://www.gettyimages
.com/license/51246239

Entrepreneurial ambition has always been deeply rooted in American history. Touted as the "land of opportunity," the newly discovered continent attracted immigrants, primarily from the British Isles and other northern European nations, as settlements and colonies were established. Exulting in the freedom of reinventing themselves without the burden of class or other forms of persecution, these colonists started new ventures, created new markets, and exploited opportunities in exploration, agriculture, trade, and other mercantile activities.

It was also during this era that one of history's greatest entrepreneurs emerged. Through a series of experiments with electricity, founding father Benjamin Franklin successfully invented the lighting rod, which has since become a symbol of the ingenuity of a young nation.

An Entrepreneurial Nation (First Industrial Revolution 1776–1865)

Entrepreneur defined as: "Someone who engages in exchanges for profit; someone who exercises business judgment in the face of uncertainty."

—Richard Cantillon (1755)[20]

The US Constitution could be described as a launching pad for creativity and innovation. Thanks to its democratic terms, the people had the right to own private property, access to a professional banking system, and protection for their enterprises in the form of patent laws. The industrial revolution gave rise to a significant number of inventions and innovations, which led to major business enterprises in manufacturing, agricultural, and transportation technology. Now that everyone had a fairly equal chance of being an entrepreneur, inventors became more commonplace, producing new products and services alongside the merchants and industrialists.

During this period, Charles Goodyear invented vulcanized rubber, George Crum invented the potato chip, and Daniel Hess invented the vacuum cleaner. Mary Dixon Kies, the first woman ever to be granted a US patent, invented a process for weaving straw with silk or thread that boosted the hat industry. These early innovations, together with the explosive growth in the economy, improved transportation, and increase in population, would lead on to the golden age of entrepreneurship—the second industrial revolution.

The Pinnacle of Entrepreneurship (Second Industrial Revolution 1865–1920)

> *The entrepreneur shifts economic resources out of an area of lower and into an area of higher productivity and greater yield.*
>
> —Jean-Baptiste Say (circa 1800)[21]

Video
American Entrepreneurs

During this era, entrepreneurship was at its height. A vast number of new innovations, businesses, and inventions were created to satisfy the growing consumer market and demand for technical innovation. The discovery that ore could be converted to steel changed the landscape of the continent, which became populated with skyscrapers, railroads, and heavy steel machinery. The entrepreneurs of this era were instrumental in changing the way people lived. The advent of the telephone (Alexander Graham Bell), the light bulb (Thomas Edison), and the first automatic dishwasher (Josephine Cochrane) satisfied a consumer need to be more connected with others, live in comfort, and be more efficient.

The entrepreneur or "self-made man" was very much revered in society. Novelists glorified and praised entrepreneurs in glamorous rags-to-riches stories; and countless manuals claimed to teach the secrets of entrepreneurial success. However, golden eras do not last forever, and soon the entrepreneurial landscape would become overshadowed by the industrial giants and institutions that had sprung up during the same era.

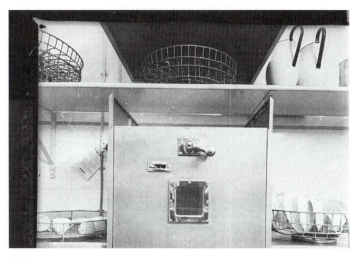

The first automatic dishwasher invented by Josephine Cochrane.
Credit: Hood Collection part I

Rise of Institutional America (Interwar and Postwar America 1920–1975)

> *Entrepreneur defined as: "[One who identifies] new combinations including the doing of new things or the doing of things that are already being done in a new way. New combinations include 1) introduction of a new good, 2) new method of production, 3) opening of a new market, 4) new source of supply, 5) new organizations."*
>
> —Schumpeter (1934)[22]

> *Entrepreneur defined as: "A decision maker whose entire role arises out of his alertness to unnoticed opportunities; therefore, entrepreneurship is the ability to perceive new opportunities. This recognition and seizing of the opportunity will tend to 'correct' the market and bring it back toward equilibrium."*
>
> —Kirzer (1973)[23]

This era signaled a shift from the traditional entrepreneur to the big corporation. Small firms founded by entrepreneurs either merged with other companies or were swallowed by larger organizations. Up until the 1930s, there was a major focus on science-based innovation, together with an increase in internal research and design; however, innovation slowed down considerably when the country plunged into the Great Depression.

The years following the Second World War saw the rise of a rapidly expanding middle class. Meeting these growing demands meant an increase in production, which superseded novel product development. By the 1950s, the big corporation had taken over the American culture, and the traditional entrepreneur was perceived as not only eccentric but a threat to the established order. Despite the institutionalization of the entrepreneur, America was still enjoying phenomenal economic prosperity, thanks to new innovations in technology, transportation, entertainment, and consumer electronics. It was during this period that the transistor radio, musical synthesizer, videotape recorder, word processor, and the microchip were invented. However, by the 1970s, corporate entrepreneurship had reached its height, and a growing interest in information technology would set the scene for impending globalization and the transition toward a knowledge-based economy.

Confined Re-Emergence (Knowledge Economy 1.0, 1975–Present)

Entrepreneur: an individual or a group who creates something new—a new idea, a new item or product, a new institution, a new market, a new set of possibilities.

> **Entrepreneur** *defined as an individual or a group who creates something new—a new idea, a new item or product, a new institution, a new market, a new set of possibilities.*[24]

As entrepreneurship regained its popularity over the last decades of the 20th century, many new definitions have sprung up, but we have chosen the one we feel fits best with the concept of entrepreneurship. In this context, the entrepreneur identifies, creates, and acts on new opportunities.[25]

The rise of information technology, advanced software development, biotech and medical research, and new materials drove transformations in the economy that created new markets and new business opportunities. Changes in patent laws made it easier for entrepreneurs to register their inventions, and the rise in venture capital funds gave them the financial capital to bring them to market. The pendulum of production and manufacturing was starting to swing in the direction of a predominantly service- and knowledge-based economy, dominated by technology-related enterprises such as Apple, Microsoft, Google, IBM, and Oracle, among others.

And thus the "tech entrepreneur" was born. Suddenly, entrepreneurship was back in fashion and courses teaching the subject started to spring up all over the world. Today, entrepreneurs are considered to be essential to the future success of any capitalistic economy. In fact, as Figure 1.2 illustrates, millennials (the generation

FIGURE 1.2

Millennials—A Highly Educated and Entrepreneurial Generation

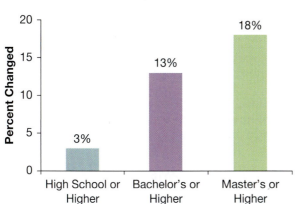

Change in the Percent of 25-to 29-Year-Olds with Selected Levels of Educational Attainment, 2007–2013

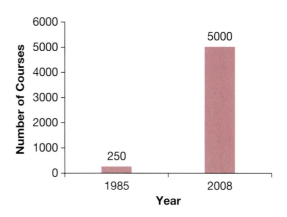

Entrepreneurship Courses Offered

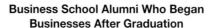
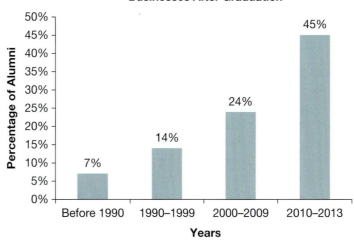

Business School Alumni Who Began Businesses After Graduation

born between 1981 and 1997) will make up 75% of the workforce by 2025. They are also considered to be the most educated generation, and the most exposed to entrepreneurship education, with high rates of entry by MBAs.

These five eras of entrepreneurial history demonstrate how the pursuits of entrepreneurs have touched every corner of our lives, affecting every aspect of the way we live—from electricity, to music, to transport, to agriculture, to manufacturing, to technology, and many more. Now it's time for a new story. It's time to bring the voices of today's entrepreneurs from all over the world to the center of the conversation. After all, it is their experiences that will open up the next page of history.

While it can be difficult to see entrepreneurial possibilities in the midst of unemployment, economic recession, war, and natural disasters, it is this sort of turbulence that often pushes us into creating new opportunities for economic progress. History

Tell Me Your Story

Every entrepreneur has a story. What beliefs and expectations do you have about entrepreneurs' stories? To what extent do you think they conform to media images of entrepreneurs? In what ways might you expect them to be different? Here is an activity to help you examine your beliefs and expectations.

Find and introduce yourself to an entrepreneur—any type of entrepreneur is fine. Ask for 20 minutes of his or her time, and simply start with the opening question: *Tell me the story of how you became an entrepreneur.*

As the story unfolds, you may want to ask other questions such as:

What worried you the most as you started the venture?

What excited you most about starting the venture?

What resources did you use to start? Where did they come from?

What moments do you remember most?

Who helped you most along the way?

How do you describe yourself to others?

What advice do you have for me as a student of entrepreneurship?

After having this 20-minute conversation, reflect on the beliefs and expectations you started with and answer the Critical Thinking Questions.

CRITICAL THINKING QUESTIONS

1. **In what ways did your chosen entrepreneur confirm your beliefs and expectations?**

2. **In what ways did the story motivate you (or not)?**

3. **What did you learn that was most unexpected?** ●

shows us that in spite of all the obstacles in their paths, all kinds of entrepreneurs have been consistently taking action to change the world. In the words of PayPal, Tesla Motors, and SpaceX entrepreneur Elon Musk: "If you go back a few hundred years, what we take for granted today would seem like magic—being able to talk to people over long distances, to transmit images, flying, accessing vast amounts of data like an oracle. These are all things that would have been considered magic a few hundred years ago."[26]

Entrepreneurs, from those like Musk, who have achieved world-acclaimed success, to our featured CEO of ZOOS Greek Iced Teas Niari Keverian, have already begun seeing and seizing opportunities to create their own contribution to history. Now it's your turn.

1.4 TYPES OF ENTREPRENEURSHIP

>> **LO 1.4**   **Compare and contrast the different forms of entrepreneurship in practice today.**

As we mentioned previously, entrepreneurship is not just reserved for startups like ZOOS Greek Iced Teas, but takes many different types and forms. The following types of entrepreneurship are most commonly in practice today.

Corporate Entrepreneurship

Corporate entrepreneurship
(or **intrapreneurship**):
a process of creating
new products, ventures,
processes, or renewal within
large organizations.

Corporate entrepreneurship (also known as **intrapreneurship**) is a process of creating new products, ventures, processes, or renewal within large organizations.[27] It is typically carried out by employees working in units separate from the organization who create and test innovations that are then assimilated back inside the broader organization.

Corporate entrepreneurs tend to explore new possibilities and seek ways in which the organization's current structure and process can enable innovation. Similar to external entrepreneurs, corporate entrepreneurs identify opportunities, build teams, and create something of value in order to enhance competitive position and organizational profitability.

Marian Croak, Senior Vice President of Domain 2.0 Architecture and Advanced Services Development at AT&T, is an excellent example of a corporate entrepreneur. In 2005, Croak was working on a voting system for the TV show *American Idol* to enable viewers to vote by text. In the same year, Hurricane Katrina struck and devastated much of the Gulf Coast. Appalled by the tragedy, Croak saw an opportunity to use the same text messaging system to enable people to make donations in disaster situations. Following the Haiti earthquake in 2010, the system was put into action and raised over $30 million in donations.[28]

Corporate entrepreneur Marian Croak raised millions in donations through her text messaging system after an earthquake struck Haiti.

Credit: Agencja Fotograficzna Caro/Alamy Stock Photo

The opportunity to be a corporate entrepreneur very much depends on the organization. AT&T was supportive of Marian Croak's ideas and encouraged her to see them though to fruition. Organizations like Google, Apple, Virgin, and Zappos are also known for encouraging an entrepreneurial spirit. However, not all organizations are as enthusiastic about employees acting entrepreneurially inside the company. Some companies fear that if they encourage their employees to be more entrepreneurial that they will leave the company and start their own.

Entrepreneurs Inside

Entrepreneurs inside consist of employees who think and act entrepreneurially within organizations. Although this sounds similar to corporate entrepreneurs (employees who work for large, established organizations), there is an important difference: entrepreneurs inside can exist and function in any type of organization, big or small, including government agencies, nonprofits, religious entities, self-organizing entities, and cooperatives.[29] These types of entrepreneurs often need to gain inside support from senior managers or other team members for their initiatives, which can be difficult if those people tend to resist new ideas, or are keen to simply "stick to the company brief" rather than pushing boundaries. Building a tribe of willing supporters is essential for getting buy-in to their ideas, and proving there is a market for them.

Entrepreneurs inside: the types of entrepreneurs who think and act entrepreneurially within organizations.

What inside entrepreneurs have in common with other entrepreneurs is the desire to create something of value, be it a new groundbreaking initiative, or a new department, product, service, or process. One of the biggest groundbreaking initiatives of 2014 was the launch of the "inglorious vegetable" by entrepreneurs working inside

Imperfect vegetables like the one shown here are sold at a discount by French supermarket Intermarche in a bid to save on food waste.

Credit: ©iStockphoto.com/ alainolympus

the French supermarket chain Intermarché as a way of reducing food waste.[30] Battling against the perception that consumers want to buy only perfect vegetables, Intermarché launched a clever campaign showing images of grotesque-looking vegetables at prices

A Jimmy John's Gourmet Sandwiches franchise location
Credit: MLADEN ANTONOV/ Staff/Getty Images

Franchise: a type of license purchased by a franchisee from an existing business, to allow them to trade under the name of that business.

Royalties: a share of the proceeds of a business from one party to another.

30% less than their more perfect counterparts. The initiative attracted over 20% more traffic to Intermarché stores and sold tons of these odd-looking vegetables, thereby successfully breaking into a previously untapped market and proving that there is a demand for "damaged goods" after all.

Buying a Franchise

A **franchise** is a type of license purchased by an entrepreneur (franchisee) from an existing business (franchisor) that allows the entrepreneur to trade under the name of that business.[31] Franchising can be a beneficial way for entrepreneurs to get a head start in launching their own businesses, as they do not have to spend the same amount of time on marketing, building the brand, developing processes, and sourcing product.

A franchise is often referred to as a turnkey operation. In other words, the franchisee turns the key to open the door and is ready for business. A franchisee not only pays the franchisor a lump sum to buy the franchise but also has to pay **royalties**, which are a share of the proceeds based on sales revenue. According to results of *Entrepreneur* magazine's 37th annual Franchise 500, announced in 2016, franchises such as Jimmy John's Gourmet Sandwiches, Anytime Fitness, Hampton by Hilton, Subway, and Supercuts, are among the most popular franchises in the United States. Today there are over 750,000 franchise establishments in the United States,[32] and the franchise cost can range from less than $50,000 to over $500,000 with approximately 50% being sold between $100,000 and $500,000.[33] Table 1.2 describes the pros and cons of owning a franchise.

Buying a Small Business

Buying a small business is another way to enter the world of entrepreneurship. In this arrangement, the entrepreneur is buying out the existing owner and taking over operations. For some entrepreneurs this is a less risky approach than starting from scratch.[34] Chris Cranston is the owner of FlowDog, a canine aquatic and rehabilitation center outside of Boston. In 2009 she bought the business, which was called Aquadog at the time, from the previous owner. Cranston changed the name but subsumed a loyal customer base, pool equipment, location, some employees, and a favorable lease. In Cranston's words, "Starting from a blank slate was too overwhelming for me. I needed something that I could build upon. That I could handle!"[35] And handle she has. FlowDog has grown an average of 20% each year since it was purchased in 2009.

Social Entrepreneurship

Since the beginning of the 21st century, social entrepreneurship has become a global movement, with thousands of initiatives being launched every year to improve social problems in areas such as water shortages, education, poverty, and global warming.

There has been considerable debate as to how to define social entrepreneurship. Some argue that all types of entrepreneurship are social, while others define it as purely an activity of the nonprofit sector. These blurred lines imply that entrepreneurs are forced to choose between making a social or an economic impact. We contend that

TABLE 1.2

Pros and Cons of Owning a Franchise

PROS	CONS
Ready-made business systems to help the franchise to become operational right away.	Franchise fee to be paid up front.
Formal training program (online modules, formal training class) after franchise agreement signed.	Royalties (percentage of sales) to be paid to franchisor every month.
Technology designed to help manage customers, and administrative tasks.	Strict franchisors' rules with no wiggle room.
Marketing/Advertising already in place to help launch your franchise.	Requirement to pay a percentage of gross sales into the franchisor's marketing fund.
Excellent support systems (in-house personnel, field reps, etc.)	Most products and supplies need to be purchased from the franchisor.
Real-estate resources to help source best location for franchise.	Sale of franchise requires approval from the franchisor.
A whole franchisee network to reach out to for help and advice.	Potential competition from other franchisees in the network.

Source: Based on material in Libava, J. (2015, February 16). The pros and cons of owning a franchise. *Entrepreneur.* Retrieved from https://www.entrepreneur.com/article/242848 Originally appeared at http://www.thefranchiseking.com/franchise-owner-ship-pros-cons

social entrepreneurs can do both. It is possible to address a social issue and make a profit—keeping a company economically stable ensures its capability to consistently meet the needs of its customers without relying on fundraising or other methods to keep it afloat.[36] We therefore define **social entrepreneurship** as the process of sourcing innovative solutions to social and environmental problems.[37]

California-based Roominate, a for-profit toy company, was founded in 2012 by Stanford engineering graduates Alice Brooks and Bettina Chen. Brooks and Chen set out to create wired building systems for girls in order to encourage innovation and help close the STEM (Science, Technology, Engineering, Mathematics) gender gap. Roominate's toy enables girls ages 6 and up to make their own unique structures using working motors and light circuits. Thanks to a successful Kickstarter campaign, plus further capital from Shark Tank regular Mark Cuban and other investors, three years after its launch Roominate had received over $1 million in funding. The founders planned to use this funding to release a new "rPower" line of kits that include the functionality to control the structures from a phone or a tablet. Roominate is an excellent example of a for-profit company created by women social entrepreneurs to encourage the next generation of women toward the traditionally male-dominated STEM fields.[38]

An example of a nonprofit social entrepreneur is former Accenture partner Lo Chay, who founded the nonprofit 1001 Fontaines Pour Demain (French for "1001 Fountains for Tomorrow") as a sustainable means of providing safe drinking water for small rural villages in Cambodia. Chay's solar-powered apparatus, which costs very little to install and operate, purifies water locally in these villages, where it is sold in large reusable jugs.[39]

Roominate and 1001 Fontaines are examples of why we believe that social entrepreneurship encompasses both for-profit and not-for-profit ventures. The point is that both the for-profit and nonprofit entrepreneurs have devised creative ways to resolve social issues, finding ways to make the world a better place. Perhaps the focus should

Social entrepreneurship: the process of sourcing innovative solutions.

Video
Social Entrepreneurship

be on what social entrepreneurs actually do rather than on the definition of what social entrepreneurship is. We believe social entrepreneurship to be so important that we have devoted a whole chapter to it (Chapter 4: Supporting Social Entrepreneurship).

YOU BE THE ENTREPRENEUR

Every entrepreneur has rough patches when getting started. In the process of creating an established company, mistakes often have to be made until the right method is found. Matthew Bellows founded Yesware, a company that sells software to make it easier for sales teams to record and analyze data. Yesware has a basic version that can be downloaded for free.

Yesware was faced with a challenge after one year in business: converting free users to paying customers. They had yet to make a profit and were struggling to sell a product designed to make sales easier for other companies—even after 10 salespeople were hired in order to try to increase sales.

What Would You Do?

Benefit corporation (or B-Corp): a form of organization certified by the nonprofit B Lab that ensures strict standards of social and environmental performance, accountability, and transparency are met.

A subcategory of social entrepreneurship is the **benefit corporation,** or **B-Corp.** This is a form of organization certified by the nonprofit B Lab that ensures that strict standards of social and environmental performance, accountability, and transparency are met.[40] The voluntary certification is designed for for-profit companies aiming to achieve social goals alongside business ones. To be certified as a B-Corp, the organization is rated on how its employees are treated, its impact on the environment, and how it benefits the community in which it operates.[41] B-Corp certification ensures that the for-profit company fulfills its social mission, and the certification protects it from lawsuits from stakeholders that may claim that the company is spending more time or resources on social issues rather than maximizing profit.

Some B-Corp members include Betterworld Books, which donates a book to someone in need every time a book is purchased; Revolution Foods, which provides affordable fresh-prepared meals to school children from low-income households; and Warby Parker, a prescription eyewear company whose "Buy a pair, give a pair" scheme involves a donation of one pair of eyeglasses for every pair it sells. The glasses are donated to nonprofit organizations all over the world to help raise awareness of the importance of eye care. Four years after its founding in 2010, Warby Parker had distributed one million pairs of glasses to people in need.[42]

Over 900 companies in 29 countries have received B-Corp certification. Not only is the certification a badge of authenticity for their social enterprises, but B-Corp members often give each other discounts in services and products; this also creates a sense of community and goodwill. In short, the certification is proof that both big and small companies are doing something to improve the quality of life in their communities.

Family Enterprising

Family enterprise: a business that is owned and managed by multiple family members, typically for more than one generation.

A **family enterprise** is a business that is owned and managed by multiple family members typically for more than one generation. What makes family enterprising part of the portfolio of entrepreneurship types is that each generation has an opportunity to bring the organization forward in new, innovative ways.[43] An entrepreneurial agenda to move the family business forward is essential to business survival, as demonstrated by the fact that the survival rate of family businesses transitioning

FIGURE 1.3

Percentage of Family-Owned Businesses

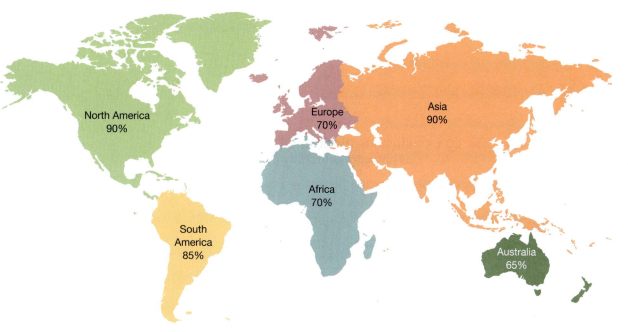

from the first to the second generation is less than 30%. However, another 50% of family businesses don't survive when they move from the second to third generation.[44] This may be because the family owners become stuck in the old ways of doing things and are unwilling to change their business structure as a result.

Video
Challenges of a Family Business

Many leading organizations that are family businesses are generally considered to be more stable, not only because of their past history and experience, but because of their ability to take a long-term view, which inspires commitment and loyalty from their employees. Yet a long-term view that becomes stagnant is detrimental and can lead the company into a downward spiral.

Family enterprises are the dominant form of business organization worldwide. It is estimated that from 80% to 90% of US businesses are family-owned or controlled by a family[45] and 65% of the US workforce is employed by a family business (see Figure 1.3).[46] Widely known businesses such as Wal-Mart in the US, supermarket chain Carrefour in France, and auto company Fiat in Italy are all long-standing family businesses that continue to go from strength to strength. To continue their cycle of growth and continuity, family members must pass on their entrepreneurial mindsets as well as their business ethos. It is this mindset that ensures the survival of the family business for many years to come.

Serial Entrepreneurs

Serial entrepreneurs, also known as **habitual entrepreneurs**, are people who start several businesses, whether simultaneously or one after another. Not satisfied with just focusing on one business, serial entrepreneurs are constantly looking out for the next big thing or exploring ways to implement their diverse range of

Serial Entrepreneurs (or **habitual entrepreneurs**): the type of entrepreneurs who start several businesses, whether simultaneously or one after the other.

ideas. Richard Branson is a good example of a serial entrepreneur: having made his fortune through Virgin, which began as a music retailer before expanding the brand to include Virgin Atlantic airlines, Branson turned his hand to railway, music, media, banking, and more. The consummate serial entrepreneur, Branson believes that "business opportunities are like buses, there's always another one coming."[47]

1.5 THE WORLD IS PARTICIPATING IN ENTREPRENEURSHIP

>> **LO 1.5** Illustrate the global diversity of entrepreneurship and its impact.

Entrepreneurs are the drivers of positive change, the ones who use energy, passion and ideas for forces of good, and the ones who will ultimately shape the world in which we live. The power of entrepreneurship is finally being recognized for its contribution to employment, societal wealth, personal wealth, innovation, economic development, and growth and innovation. Nobel Peace Prize laureate Muhammad Yunus has been given one of the highest recognitions in the world through his entrepreneurial mission to help people from deprived communities to make a life for themselves. Yet, his work has touched many communities around the world, not just the people of Bangladesh.

In the United Kingdom, the Yunus Social Business Awards recognize the endeavors of social and business entrepreneurs attending the University of Salford in Manchester to identify a social need and create a solution to address it.[48] Among the winners was student Grant Dolan, who was credited for his vending machine company, REAL Vending. The company redistributes profits from vending machines placed in schools, colleges, training centers, and local businesses, to provide grants for young people from financially disadvantaged backgrounds to help them into higher education. As part of the prize, Dolan has the opportunity to travel to Dhaka, Bangladesh, and meet with Professor Yunus, who will mentor him and help him develop his idea.

This is a good example of the legacy that existing entrepreneurs can leave behind to inspire the budding entrepreneurs of today. Yunus is not the only Nobel laureate to speak out on the importance of entrepreneurship. Dr. Dan Shechtman of Technion–Israel Institute of Technology in Haifa, Israel, who was awarded the 2011 Nobel Prize in Chemistry for the discovery of quasicrystals, believes that "entrepreneurship is the only way to maintain long-term peace." He asserts that countries that use up all their natural resources will result in tribal conflicts. Shechtman believes that education and learning are the keys to fostering the right entrepreneurial mindset.[49]

President Barack Obama also believes in the power of entrepreneurship. In a White House ceremony honoring National Small Business Week award winners in 2009, he said: "You're the job creators, responsible for half of all private sector jobs. You're innovators, producing 13 times more patents per employee than large companies. You're the starting point for the products and brands that have redefined the market. After all, Google started out as a small business; that was a research project. Hewlett-Packard began with two guys in a garage. The first Apple computers were built by hand, one at a time. McDonald's started with just one restaurant."[50]

Entrepreneurship as a Social Movement

> *The reasonable man adapts himself to the world; the unreasonable one persists in trying to adapt the world to himself. Therefore, all progress depends on the unreasonable man [and woman].*
>
> —George Bernard Shaw

The efforts of young entrepreneurs today to solve some of the world's greatest challenges are inspiring a global movement. They know that small-scale ideas can snowball into real changes. Take the global experiment, Unreasonable at Sea, which took place in 2013.[51] This was a scheme created by the founders of The Unreasonable Institute, an organization that fosters entrepreneurship by holding intensive training programs whereby entrepreneurs are matched with mentors, and the founders of Stanford's Institute of Design. These founders teamed up with the popular organization Semester at Sea, to bring a variety of entrepreneurs together for an unforgettable journey. The name "Unreasonable" is based on the George Bernard Shaw quote, above, which maintains that progress depends on perceived "unreasonable" people, as they are the ones who challenge the status quo.

The core ethos behind the Unreasonable at Sea scheme is to unite entrepreneurs to help leverage their collective technology experience to solve some of the world's most formidable challenges. Out of 1,000 applicants worldwide, the founding members of 11 tech companies were chosen to set sail with 600 students, and 20 veteran entrepreneurs and mentors (Nobel Peace Laureate Archbishop Desmond Tutu, Google executives, and the founder of Wordpress, Matt Mullenwegg, to name a few) to pitch their ideas to venture capitalists, foundations, and top government officials in 14 different countries—all in the time span of 100 days.

On the ship were a team from Botswana who had created the Solar Ear, the world's first digitally programmed rechargeable hearing aid; a company from Spain that utilizes plants to aid water purification; and a team from Mexico who invented artificial vision for the blind through a pair of glasses equipped with a camera, a mini-computer, and a transmitter that allows the wearer to see images in real time.

During the course of the voyage, the founders of the 11 tech companies brainstormed their ideas with each other and received advice from mentors, using the latest technology supplied on board to practice. It is experiments like these that help entrepreneurs practice their ideas and get them in front of a supportive audience. Through this initiative, just as in the opening chapter quote by Yunus, entrepreneurs were given the opportunity to practice.

One budding entrepreneur who took part in the 2005 Unreasonable at Sea program during college was a student called Adam Braun. Each time the ship stopped at a new country, Braun would ask the children one question, "What is the one thing you want more than anything else in the world?" One of the answers he received from a little boy begging on the street in India was "a pencil." It was this answer that would prompt Braun to leave his job at a Wall Street company a few years later to create Pencils of Promise, a nonprofit organization that builds schools in the poorest areas of the developing world. By 2014, Pencils of Promise had built over 200 schools in deprived countries and employed more than 60 people all over the world.[52]

Video
Entrepreneurship in
Developing Countries

Adam Braun, founder of nonprofit Pencils for Promise

Credit: WENN Ltd / Alamy Stock Photo

Potential entrepreneurs: individuals who believe they have the capacity and know-how to start a business without being burdened by the fear of failure.

Nascent entrepreneurs: individuals who have set up a business they will own or co-own that is less than three months old and has not yet generated wages or salaries for the owners.

New business owners: individuals who are former nascent entrepreneurs and have been actively involved in a business for over three months but less than three and a half years.

Established business owners: the people who are still active in business for over three and a half years.

Necessity-based entrepreneurs: individuals who are pushed into starting a business because of circumstance such as redundancy, threat of job loss, and unemployment.

In 2011, Braun again joined the Unreasonable at Sea voyage, but this time as a lecturer and mentor, sharing his stories with the students, and encouraging them with the words "tourists see, travelers seek"—in other words, to actively learn about the communities they visit and seek ways in which they, too, can become global citizens. Adam Braun's story is a great example of global entrepreneurship that has touched the lives of others in a meaningful way. Yet Braun is only one of millions of entrepreneurs all over the world who are in the early stages of being involved with or starting a new business.

Global Entrepreneurship

Entrepreneurship is taking off on a global scale. Let's explore some data provided by The Global Entrepreneurship Monitor (GEM)—a global research study founded by Babson College and the London Business School in 1999. Today the study is conducted by a consortium of universities around the world and measures entrepreneurial activity across 70 countries.[53]

According to the 2015/16 GEM report, the percentage of entrepreneurs in the United States has reached 13%—the highest on record. In fact, there are almost 400 million entrepreneurs worldwide—making The Practice of Entrepreneurship a global phenomenon. This means for the 10 or so iconic figures such as the late Steve Jobs, Bill Gates, and Mark Zuckerberg, there are millions of entrepreneurs globally between the ages of 18 and 64 who are in the process of starting or running a new business.

The GEM study gathers its data according to different phases of entrepreneurship (see Figure 1.4). The process begins with **potential entrepreneurs** who are individuals who believe they have the capacity and know-how to start a business without being burdened by the fear of failure. The next phase focuses on **nascent entrepreneurs**, who are individuals who have set up a business they will own or co-own that is less than three months old and has not yet generated wages or salaries for the owners. The third phase is the study of **new business owners,** who are former nascent entrepreneurs who have been actively involved in a business for over three months but less than three and a half years. The final phase explores **established business owners**—those who are still active in business for over three and a half years. Interestingly, the study found the reason that many of the established business entrepreneurs had discontinued the business after three and a half years was not necessarily because they had failed; in fact, in many cases, the entrepreneurs had instead become serial entrepreneurs or joined other companies to become inside or corporate entrepreneurs.

The GEM study also looks at opportunity-based entrepreneurs and necessity-based entrepreneurs. **Necessity-based entrepreneurs** are individuals who are pushed into starting a business because of circumstance. Layoffs, threat of job loss, and inability to find a job are some factors that drive people to start a new business. In contrast, **opportunity-based entrepreneurs** are individuals who make a decision to start their own businesses based on their ability to create or exploit an opportunity, and whose main driver for getting involved in the venture is being independent or increasing their income, rather than merely maintaining their income. Unlike necessity-based entrepreneurs, opportunity-based entrepreneurs freely make their own choice to get involved in a business.

One of the main focuses of the GEM study is the level of **Total Entrepreneurial Activity (TEA)** in different countries, which is the percentage of the population of each country between the ages of 18 and 64, who are either nascent entrepreneurs or owner-managers of a new business. For example, the early stage TEA in the United States is 13% [54] (Table 1.3). This means that 13% of the US adult population from 18 to 64 years old is involved in some type of entrepreneurial activity, such as being in the process of starting a new business or owning and managing a business less than 3 years old.

Let's take a closer look at the age ranges of entrepreneurial activity in early stages of business across the world. North America is certainly perceived as being one of the most buoyant environments for entrepreneurship, but other geographical regions such as Africa, Latin America, and the Caribbean, appear to have higher rates of entrepreneurial activity in certain age groups, while Morocco and Malaysia are the among the lowest. Europe displays the lowest TEA rates over all, with Bulgaria, Germany, and Italy, in particular, showing the lowest rates—less than 5% of the working adults begin or run new businesses. The low rates in some countries, particularly among the younger population, may be a consequence of compulsory military service or high college attendance.

Despite sub-Sarahan Africa being a less well-developed region of the world than the United States, people living in some African countries tend to see opportunities to start their own businesses, have confidence in their own skills and abilities, and have less fear of failure. These statistics prove that early-stage entrepreneurship is possible in poorer countries if the people are given the opportunity and support to grow their own businesses.

Opportunity-based entrepreneurs: individuals who make a decision to start their own businesses based on their ability to create or exploit an opportunity, and whose main driver for getting involved in the venture is being independent or increasing their income, rather than merely maintaining their income.

Total Entrepreneurial Activity (TEA): the percentage of the population of each country between the ages of 18 and 64, who are either a nascent entrepreneur or owner-manager of a new business.

Video
Frugal Innovation

FIGURE 1.4

Global Entrepreneurship Monitor Measuring Entrepreneurial Activity

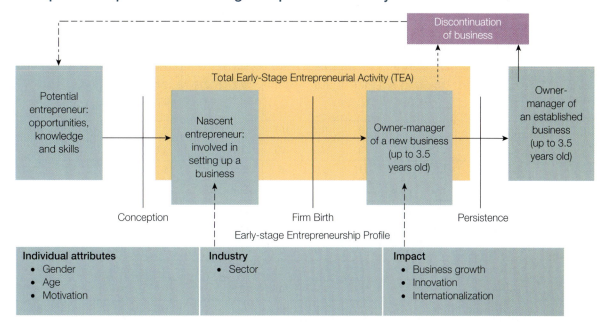

Source: http://www.gemconsortium.org/

TABLE 1.3

Entrepreneurial Activities by Geographic Region 2015

REGION	ECONOMY	NASCENT ENTREPRE-NEURSHIP RATE		NEW BUSINESS OWNERSHIP RATE		EARLY-STAGE ENTREPRE-NEURIAL ACTIVITY (TEA)		EEA		ESTABLISHED BUSINESS OWNERSHIP RATE		DISCONTIN-UATION OF BUSINESS (% ADULT POPULATION)	
		RANK /60	VALUE	RANK /60	VALUE	RANK /60	VALUE	RANK /60	VALUE	RANK /60	VALUE	RAN1K /60*	VALUE
Africa	Botswana	3	23.0	6	11.9	3	33.2	35	1.6	47	4.6	1	14.7
	Burikina Faso	4	19.7	7	11.2	5	29.8	51T	0.6	1	27.8	9	8.1
	Cameroon	6T	16.5	10	10.0	7	25.4	48T	0.7	12	12.8	5	9.0
	Egypt	46T	4.0	37T	3.4	43	7.4	38	1.3	56	2.9	14	6.6
	Morocco	58	1.3	40T	3.2	58	4.4	55T	0.4	41T	5.2	46T	2.2
	Senegal	2	24.9	2	15.0	1	38.6	29T	2.3	5	18.8	2	13.3
	South Africa	35	5.5	32T	3.8	38T	9.2	57T	0.3	53	3.4	19	4.8
	Tunisia	36	5.4	25T	4.9	33	10.1	34	1.9	44	5.0	10T	7.2
	Total		12.5		7.9		19.8		1.1		10.1		8.3
Asia & Oceania	Australia	24	7.3	20	5.8	24T	12.8	2	8.5	20	8.7	22	4.5
	China	26	6.8	17T	6.3	24T	12.8	36T	1.4	55	3.1	39T	2.7
	India	22	7.7	40T	3.2	30T	10.8	57T	0.3	38	5.5	43T	2.3
	Indonesia	31T	6.1	5	12.1	13T	17.7	60	0.2	8	17.1	27T	3.7
	Iran	21	7.9	22	5.3	23	12.9	43T	1.0	10	14.0	12T	6.7
	Israel	18	8.4	34	3.7	28	11.8	6T	6.5	51	3.9	21	4.6
	Kazakhstan	20	8.0	40T	3.2	29	11.0	46T	0.9	58	2.4	35T	3.1
	Korea	40	5.0	29	4.3	36T	9.3	27T	2.4	28T	7.0	49T	2.0
	Lebanon	12T	10.8	1	20.4	4	30.1	25T	3.3	6	18.0	4	10.6
	Malaysia	60	0.8	55	2.3	60	2.9	57T	0.3	45T	4.8	59	1.1
	Philippines	23	7.6	9	10.1	16	17.2	29T	2.3	26T	7.3	3	12.2
	Taiwan	54	2.5	27	4.8	44T	7.3	20T	4.1	16T	9.6	25T	3.8
	Thailand	43T	4.5	13	9.5	20T	13.7	48T	0.7	2	24.6	30T	3.4
	Vietnam	59	1.0	4	12.7	20T	13.7	51T	0.6	3	19.6	27T	3.7
	Total		6.0		7.4		13.1		2.3		10.4		4.6
Latin America & Caribbean	Argentina	10	11.7	17T	6.3	13T	17.7	27T	2.4	18	9.5	16	6.3
	Barbados	11	11.5	8	107	10T	21.0	41T	1.1	9	14.1	25T	3.8
	Brazil	27	6.7	3	14.9	10T	21.0	43T	1.0	4	18.9	12T	6.7
	Chile	6T	16.5	11T	9.8	6	25.9	15	5.2	21	8.2	7	8.5
	Colombia	9	15.6	16	7.5	8	22.7	29T	2.3	41T	5.2	10T	7.2
	Ecuador	1	25.9	11T	9.8	2	33.6	46T	0.9	7	17.4	8	8.3
	Guatemala	12T	10.8	15	7.6	13T	17.7	39T	1.2	22	8.1	24	4.0
	Mexico	8	16.2	24	5.0	10T	21.0	39T	1.2	30	6.9	15	6.4
	Panama	38	5.2	14	7.7	24T	12.8	54	0.5	49T	4.2	46T	2.2
	Peru	5	17.8	25T	4.9	9	22.2	48T	0.7	31	6.6	6	8.8
	Puerto Rico	28	6.6	57T	1.9	40	8.5	51T	0.6	60	1.4	60	0.9
	Uruguay	14	10.6	32T	3.8	18	14.3	19	4.2	59	2.1	20	4.7
	Total		12.9		7.5		19.9		1.8		8.5		5.7

REGION	ECONOMY	NASCENT ENTREPRENEURSHIP RATE		NEW BUSINESS OWNERSHIP RATE		EARLY-STAGE ENTREPRENEURIAL ACTIVITY (TEA)		EEA		ESTABLISHED BUSINESS OWNERSHIP RATE		DISCONTINUATION OF BUSINESS (% ADULT POPULATION)	
		RANK /60	VALUE	RANK /60	VALUE	RANK /60	VALUE	RANK /60	VALUE	RANK /60	VALUE	RAN1K /60*	VALUE
Europe	Belgium	43T	4.5	56	2.0	51	6.2	12	6.1	52	3.8	51T	1.9
	Bulgaria	57	2.0	60	1.5	59	3.5	55T	0.4	39	5.4	58	1.4
	Croatia	39	5.1	53T	2.6	42	7.7	16	4.9	57	2.8	37	2.9
	Estonia	16	8.7	28	4.7	22	13.1	10T	6.3	23T	7.7	49T	2.0
	Finland	46T	4.0	48T	2.8	50	6.6	13	5.8	14	10.2	39T	2.7
	Germany	53	2.8	57T	1.9	57	4.7	18	4.5	45T	4.8	53T	1.8
	Greece	49	3.9	48T	2.8	49	6.7	43T	1.0	11	13.1	30T	3.4
	Hungary	29T	5.3	45T	2.7	36T	7.9	5	2.1	32T	6.5	35T	2.8
	Ireland	37	6.5	52	3.0	41	9.3	33	6.6	37	5.6	38	3.1
	Italy	50T	3.2	59	1.7	56	4.9	36T	1.4	48	4.5	51T	1.9
	Latvia	17	8.6	19	6.0	19	14.1	25T	3.3	16T	9.6	30T	3.4
	Luxembourg	25	7.1	40T	3.2	32	10.2	8T	6.4	54	3.3	23	4.2
	Macedonia	52	3.0	44	3.1	52	6.1	29T	2.3	34T	5.9	43T	2.3
	Netherlands	45	4.3	45T	3.0	46T	7.2	10T	6.3	15	9.9	48	2.1
	Norway	55	2.3	39	3.3	54T	5.7	1	9.9	32T	6.5	56T	1.6
	Poland	33	5.7	36	3.5	38T	9.2	22T	4.0	34T	5.9	39T	2.7
	Portugal	34	5.6	30T	4.0	35	9.5	22T	4.0	28T	7.0	34	3.2
	Romania	31T	6.1	23	5.1	30T	10.8	17	4.6	25	7.5	33	3.3
	Slovakia	29T	6.5	37T	3.4	34	9.6	24	3.6	36	5.7	17	5.4
	Slovenia	50T	3.2	48T	2.8	53	5.9	14	5.6	49T	4.2	53T	1.8
	Spain	56	2.1	35	3.6	54T	5.7	41T	1.1	23T	7.7	56T	1.6
	Sweden	41	4.8	53T	2.6	46T	7.2	8T	6.4	41T	5.2	39T	2.7
	Switzerland	42	4.6	48T	2.8	44T	7.3	6T	6.5	13	11.3	55	1.7
	United Kingdom	46T	4.0	47	2.9	48	6.9	20T	4.1	40	5.3	43T	2.3
	Total		4.8		3.1		7.8		4.5		6.6		2.6
North America	Canada	15	9.7	21	5.5	17	14.7	3	7.1	19	8.8	18	5.0
	USA	19	8.3	30T	4.0	27	11.9	4	7.0	26T	7.3	29	3.6
	Total		9.0		4.8		13.3		7.0		8.1		4.3

*Note that discontinuation is ranked with the highest value receiving a rank of 1. Discontinuation can be regarded as either a positive or negative indicator, given that people can discontinue for both positive and negative reasons. In addition, a high discontinuation rate can mean that many people are starting businesses, with the natural result that some will discontinue.

Credit: *Global Entrepreneurship Monitor 2015–2016 Report* by D.Kelley, S.Singer and M.Herrington, p. 123, Table 3. Downloaded from http://www.gemconsortium.org/report/49480

Gender and Entrepreneurship

One of the greatest myths concerning entrepreneurship is that it is a male-only profession. As Table 1.4 shows, nothing could be farther from the truth. According to GEM studies, an estimated 200 million women are starting or running new businesses in 83 economies, and an additional 128 million are running established businesses.[55]

Most countries studied have a similar proportion of men to women early stage entrepreneurs, with the percentage of women in Vietnam, Philippines, Thailand, Malaysia, Peru, and Indonesia being equal to or exceeding their male counterparts. This shows that these countries are providing support for women-owned ventures.

TABLE 1.4

Male and Female Early-Stage Entrepreneurial Activity by Geographic Regions, 2013

REGION	FEMALE TEA RATE	MALE TEA RATE	RATIO FEMALE/MALE
Africa	25	26	0.96
Asia & Oceania (Factor- and Efficiency-Driven)	14	15	0.93
Latin America & Caribbean	15	19	0.79
Europe (Efficiency-Driven)	6	13	0.46
North America	11	16	0.69
Middle East (Innovation-Driven)	8	14	0.57
Europe (Innovation-Driven)	5	9	0.55
Asia & Oceania (Innovation-Driven)	6	11	0.54
GEM Average	11	16	0.69

Credit: *Global Entrepreneurship Monitor 2015 Special Report: Women's Entrepreneurship Report* by D.Kelley et. A., p. 17, Table 3. Downloaded from http://www.gemconsortium.org/report/49281

Why do women want to become entrepreneurs? For the same reasons as men: to support themselves and their families; to attain the fulfillment of having started something on their own and to satisfy their desire for financial independence.[56] Just like their male counterparts, women not only create jobs for themselves and others, but also work toward growing their businesses, and constantly innovating new products and services.

However, in certain countries, there are some differences in what drives women to be entrepreneurs. For example, women in less developed countries with higher rates of unemployment, poverty, and lack of choice in work are more likely to be driven by necessity, whereas women in more developed countries tend be more motivated by opportunity and innovation.

What Makes a Country Entrepreneurial?

What makes one country more entrepreneurial than another? The following are certain conditions that need to be put in place for small and medium businesses (SMEs) to flourish. Together, these conditions form The Entrepreneurship Ecosystem (Figure 1.5).

▸ Financial resources: entrepreneurs need access to appropriate financing such as grants and subsidies, loans, private equity, angel investors, venture capital funds, and so on.

▸ Support from government: entrepreneurs need support from government policies that incentivize entrepreneurship by tax incentives, lower interest rates, loans, and the like. Some countries also offer government entrepreneurship programs that provide entrepreneurs with access to tools, mentors, and educational resources.

▸ Entrepreneurship Education: certain countries provide entrepreneurship courses and training at primary and secondary levels; and at higher education such as colleges, business schools, and other institutions.

RESEARCH AT WORK

The Diana Project

The Diana Project was established in 1999 by Professors Candida Brush, Nancy Carter, Betsy Gatewood, Patricia Greene, and Myra Hart in partnership with ESBRI, Stockholm, to explore women's entrepreneurship and raise awareness of women in business.

In 1999, businesses with women on the executive team received less than 5% of venture capital in comparison with male-only companies. More than a decade later, with an estimated ten million women as majority owners of businesses across the United States, the researchers set out to find out the degree to which the gap between venture capital and women entrepreneurs has closed, if at all.

The 2014 Diana Project involved looking at 6,793 companies, seeing how many had women on the executive team, and then analyzing those companies to find out how many businesses had received venture capital between 2011 and 2013 compared with male-only teams. Compared to 1999, they found that the figure of businesses with women receiving venture capital investments had tripled—from 5% to 15%—which showed marked progress. They also found that teams involving women entrepreneurs tended to perform as well as or better than male-only companies.

Why has there been such an increase in investment in businesses involving women? Programs such as the Ernst and Young's EY Entrepreneurial Winning Women program and Springboard have helped to raise the profile of women entrepreneurs by supporting, training, and showcasing women entrepreneurs to the venture capital community through sponsored events and forums. In addition, websites such as Women 2.0, and Count Me In provide resources, business education, and support for women in business. On the investor side, the active angel investment group Golden Seeds has been set up with the sole mission of investing in companies with women on the executive team.

On the face of it, these are positive results. However, there is still a long way to go and many questions to be answered. For instance, out of 6,517 companies studied, only 2.7% (or 183 companies) had a female CEO; and there has been a decline in the number of women in the venture capital firms, which might impact the rate of investment in women entrepreneurs, given that women investors tend to seek out women entrepreneurs.

Furthermore, the study found that companies with women on their teams are more likely to receive funding in the medical technology sectors over other sectors like telecommunications; it also showed that women entrepreneurs located in certain states (North Carolina, South Carolina, Connecticut) are more likely to receive investment over those in other states. These are all facts that need to be explored further.

Overall, the evidence from The 2014 Diana Project suggests that it is not the women entrepreneurs who need to adapt, but rather the venture capital model that needs to be re-evaluated and updated in order to keep up with the changing landscape of women's entrepreneurship.

CRITICAL THINKING QUESTIONS

1. **What do you see as the value of studying women's involvement in entrepreneurship?**

2. **Even though venture capital investment has tripled for women over the past 15 years, there is still a long way to go. What do you see as the primary obstacles for women in entrepreneurship?**

3. **If you were designing a study of some other underrepresented group in entrepreneurship, how would you go about it? What would you need to know to formulate your research questions?** ●

▸ Research and Development (R&D) transfer: the extent to which scientists and research will pass on their knowledge to entrepreneurs involved in innovation. Many SMEs do not have their own R&D department so it is important that they have the opportunity to access knowledge from other resources.

▸ Commercial and Legal Infrastructure: entrepreneurs should be supported by a secure commercial and legal framework assisted by experts and advisors in property rights, accounting, law, investment banking, and technology.

▸ Entry Regulation: entrepreneurs should be able to meet the regulatory costs of starting a new business as well as undergoing administrative procedures. The extent of these costs and procedures is dependent on two factors: market

FIGURE 1.5

The Entrepreneurship Ecosystem

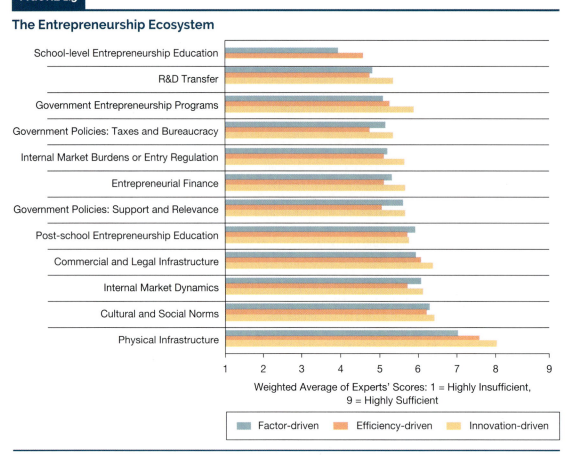

Weighted Average of Experts' Scores: 1 = Highly Insufficient, 9 = Highly Sufficient

Factor-driven   Efficiency-driven   Innovation-driven

dynamics—the annual rate of change in markets; and market openness—the degree to which new businesses have the freedom to enter new markets.

▶ Physical Infrastructure: entrepreneurs should be able to easily access or purchase at a reasonable price vital resources in the areas of communication, land, office space, and transportation.

▶ Cultural and Social Norms: entrepreneurs tend to thrive more in an environment where they feel encouraged enough to start a business, or have the confidence to choose entrepreneurship as a career path.

All these factors interact to create a very powerful force: new businesses are created, employment increases, new products hit the markets, competition is intensified, and productivity rises, all of which makes a huge contribution to social and economic development. This is why it is essential for each country all over the world to build a climate where entrepreneurship can thrive.

1.6 HOW THIS BOOK WILL HELP YOU PRACTICE ENTREPRENEURSHIP

>> LO 1.6   Propose different ways in which this book can help you practice entrepreneurship.

By now, we hope that we have proved to you that becoming an entrepreneur is a pathway for many and that the world needs more entrepreneurs of all kinds. To reinforce our message, the following are some fundamental beliefs that form the main ethos of this book.

ENTREPRENEURSHIP MEETS ETHICS

Business Practices in Developing Countries

Businesses investing in Indian companies may face a series of ethical challenges

Credit: David H. Wells/Getty Images

Marketing expert A. Coskun Samli has argued that the current top-down form of globalization is neglecting a major portion of the population. He points out that developing world markets have significant buying power due to their size and characteristics, and would be best served by entrepreneurial ventures working from the bottom up. The financial and ethical costs of doing business in developing countries, however, can be prohibitive and vary regionally.

Enterprises of all sizes, including entrepreneurs and large corporations, face significant ethical challenges in many developing countries including the world's two fastest growing markets, India and China. With India's middle class predicted to grow eightfold in the coming two decades, foreign businesses are racing to invest in the country. However, the chairman of Tata Group in India, Ratan Tata, warned investors of India's robust climate of corruption. Tata stated, "If you choose not to participate in [corruption], you leave behind a fair amount of business." Questionable ethical practices in India have been described as ranging from the "mundane to the spectacular."

Even transnational companies find the road to success in India to be treacherous. Germany's Enercon, globally the fifth-largest wind turbine manufacturer, was forced to abandon its joint venture of US$566 million due to intimidation from Indian authorities. Enercon described the firm's financial loss by their Indian subsidiary as "government-abetted theft."

Business practices that are perceived by Westerners as corrupt are commonplace in many countries. Determining how to respond to these practices is particularly difficult for entrepreneurs, as they have generally not established an infrastructure to address ethical challenges. Additionally, startups are focused on becoming profitable or maintaining the thin profits they've been able to achieve. This leaves them little time to focus on monitoring their own behavior.

CRITICAL THINKING QUESTIONS

1. **What does it mean for entrepreneurial ventures to approach global markets from the bottom up? In ethical terms, would a bottom-up approach better serve the public in developing countries?**

2. **Can a business maintain more than one set of ethical standards—one set for conducting business in the United States or Europe and another set when conducting business in a country like India or China?**

3. **In addition to people requiring bribes and kickbacks for access to infrastructure and government services, people who want to provide products and services to entrepreneurs offer bribes and kickbacks to the entrepreneur. For a struggling entrepreneur, what criteria would you use for supplier selection?** ●

Sources

Anand, A., Cherian, K., Gautam, A., Majmudar, R., & Raimawala, A. (2012, January 3). *Business vs. ethics: The India trade-off?* Retrieved from Wharton University of Pennsylvania: http://knowledge.wharton.upenn.edu/article/business-vs-ethics-the-india-tradeoff/

George, B. (2008, February 12). *Ethics must be global, not local.* Retrieved from Bloomberg: http://www.bloomberg.com/news/articles/2008-02-12/ethics-must-be-global-not-localbusinessweek-business-news-stock-market-and-financial-advice

Hanson, K. O. (2015, November 23). *The ethical challenges facing entrepreneurs.* Retrieved from The Wall Street Journal: http://www.wsj.com/articles/the-ethical-challenges-facing-entrepreneurs-1448247600

Samli, C. A. (2013). International entrepreneurship: The essence of globalization from the bottom-up. *Journal of Ethics and Entrepreneurship, 3*(1), 5–14.

Schulman, M. (March, 23 2006). *Business ethics in China.* Retrieved from Markkula Center for Applied Ethics: Santa Clara University: https://www.scu.edu/ethics/focus-areas/business-ethics/resources/business-ethics-in-china/

Video
Yunus on Entrepreneurship

1. We believe entrepreneurship can be learned and that our thinking can be altered and changed. We can develop as entrepreneurial thinkers.

2. We firmly believe in Yunus's theory that everybody has the capability to be an entrepreneur if they are given the opportunity to practice.

3. We believe entrepreneurship is a method that requires practice.

4. We believe that formal planning should be de-emphasized in favor of a continuous cycle of acting, learning, building, and acting more. There is a time for formal planning, but this book focuses on prelaunch entrepreneurship, so it's too early to talk about the business plan document.

5. We believe that each and every one of you has the power to take action to do something great that will impact the world in your own, unique way.

These guiding beliefs mean that you as the student must take action and practice entrepreneurship at every opportunity. In each chapter of this book, you will find the following features, which are designed to challenge you to do just that.

▶   *Entrepreneurship in Action:* In entrepreneurship, there is no one right answer. Role models are very important because, by learning through others, you can develop empathy for entrepreneurs around the world who may be doing the same as you someday. *Entrepreneurship in Action* includes interviews from entrepreneurs from many different businesses and disciplines both in the United States and around the world. You have already been introduced to Niari Keverian, CEO and Partner of ZOOS Greek Iced Tea in this chapter, and you will be reading more stories from a wide selection of these inspirational entrepreneurs in each of the following chapters of this book.

▶   *Mindshift*: Since entrepreneurship requires action, the *Mindshift* feature requires you to close the textbook and go and act.

▶   *You Be the Entrepreneur:* This feature asks you to imagine yourself in situations based on events that have happened in real life, so you can think critically about what you would do if you were in the same position.

▶   *Entrepreneurship Meets Ethics:* Entrepreneurs sometimes face complex ethical challenges that cause conflict. Peppered with situations faced by real-world entrepreneurs, the *Entrepreneurship Meets Ethics* feature challenges you to think about how you would take action if you were confronted with a similar ethical dilemma.

▶   *Research at Work:* This feature highlights recent seminal entrepreneurship studies and their impact and application to the real world. This will allow you to view how the latest research applies to real-life settings.

▶   *Case Study:* Finally, test your knowledge in the short case study presented at the end of each chapter. These case studies are based on real companies of all kinds including for-profit, nonprofit, technology, social, product-based, service-based, online, and others; they have been started by entrepreneurs of all types.

Video
From Learning
to Doing

Entrepreneurship is all around us—everyone has the ability to think and act entrepreneurially, to transform opportunity into reality, and create social and economic value. But remember—practice is key—learning is inseparable from doing. So, let's get started! ●

Get the edge on your studies at **edge.sagepub.com/neckentrepreneurship**

‣ Master the learning objectives using key study tools
‣ Watch, listen, and connect with online multimedia resources
‣ Access mobile-friendly quizzes and flashcards to check your understanding

SUMMARY

1.1 Explain the importance of action and practice in entrepreneurship.

Practice and action make it possible to achieve success. Many of the successful entrepreneurs behind major corporations today established their companies by acting; learning, and building what they learned into their next actions. Many entrepreneurs have learned entrepreneurship by doing entrepreneurship, but this text is design to help you practice the essentials in hope that you can avoid some of the more common pitfalls made by others.

1.2 List the seven lesser-known truths about entrepreneurship.

Contrary to popular belief, there's no research definitively confirming that character traits of successful entrepreneurs are inborn. Despite a disposition for action, entrepreneurs approach risk in a much more calculated fashion than they're given credit for, and many highly successful entrepreneurs achieve their success through collaborative actions.

1.3 Explain the history of entrepreneurship in the United States.

There are five main eras of entrepreneurship in the US: Emergence of the Self-Made Man, An Entrepreneurial Nation (1st Industrial Revolution 1776–1865), The Pinnacle of Entrepreneurship (2nd Industrial Revolution 1865–1920), Rise of Institutional America (Interwar and Postwar America 1920–1975), and Confined Re-Emergence (Knowledge Economy 1.0 1975–present).

1.4 Compare and contrast the different forms of entrepreneurship in practice today.

Corporate entrepreneurship (or intrapreneurship) is entrepreneurship within large corporations. Inside entrepreneurs are similar to corporate entrepreneurs, but they can be found in any type of organization, large or small, nonprofit or for-profit, and even among governing bodies. Franchising and buy-outs are popular ways to start relatively near the ground level. Social entrepreneurship—entrepreneurship focused on making the world a better place—is manifested in nonprofit and large, for-profit firms alike. A form of social entrepreneurship is the Benefit Corporation, or B-Corp, that has been created to designate for-profit firms that meet high standards of corporate social responsibility. Family enterprises, entrepreneurship started within the family, remain of dominant form of business development in the United States and abroad. Serial entrepreneurs are so committed to entrepreneurship that they're constantly on the move creating new businesses.

1.5 Illustrate the global diversity of entrepreneurship and its impact.

There are hundreds of millions of entrepreneurs worldwide. Known as one of the most entrepreneurial nations on the planet, the United States is eclipsed by many world regions in terms of the percentage of the population engaged in entrepreneurship. Though entrepreneurs may be born out of necessity or to exploit opportunities, they all benefit from education, financial resources, accessible knowledge, and government support providing infrastructure that will enable the fledgling businesses to achieve success.

1.6 Propose different ways in which this book can help you practice entrepreneurship.

The tools for success and methods to hone entrepreneurial skills will be available in every chapter. Thought and action exercises alike will be employed, and research and testimonials from proven academics and entrepreneurs will be provided as we move through the text. As a final test of application, case studies will follow every chapter, giving you the opportunity to employ what you've learned, a chance for entrepreneurship within a unique and real-world context.

KEY TERMS

Benefit corporation
  (or B-Corp) 20
Corporate
  entrepreneurship
  (or intrapreneurship) 16
Effectuation 9
Entrepreneur 14
Entrepreneurs inside 17
Entrepreneurship 6
Established business
  owners 24

Family enterprise 20
Franchise 18
Microloan 5
Nascent
  entrepreneurs 24
Necessity-based
  entrepreneurs 24
New business
  owners 24
Opportunity-based
  entrepreneurs 24

Potential
  entrepreneurs 24
Royalties 18
Serial Entrepreneurs
  (or habitual
  entrepreneurs) 9
Social
  entrepreneurship 19
Startup 8
Total Entrepreneurial
  Activity (TEA) 25

CASE STUDY

Dawn LaFreeda, Restaurant Franchise Owner

Dawn LaFreeda is a Denny's Restaurant franchisee from Texas. Her personal enterprise, which now includes 75 Denny's restaurants, ranks among the largest single-owner franchisee portfolios in the world, raking in close to $100 million in annual revenue.

Dawn LaFreeda's career at *Denny's* began at the bottom of the business—as a waitress and hostess. But LaFreeda had big dreams for her future. Even as a kid, she told others she would someday have her own business.

> I grew up without a lot. My mother was a single parent, and I knew anything I ever wanted I had to work for. When I was about eleven, I remember saying to my Mom one day, "I'm gonna own my own business," and my Mom looked at me and said to me, "Of course you are." I didn't know at the time exactly what form it would take, but I always knew I'd be self-employed.

In her early twenties, she went out on a limb and purchased her first *Denny's* restaurant. She credits a youthful openness to risk taking for helping her to get her start.

> When you're 23, you're not afraid to take risks. I didn't have a whole lot of money then, but I got an opportunity to buy a restaurant, and a friend of mine decided to purchase it mainly off credit cards and a few small loans.

LaFreeda faced many hurdles and difficulties as she worked to build her fledgling enterprise. One of her challenges as a younger woman was getting older bankers and businessmen to take her seriously. In her own words:

> When I was a young entrepreneur, people didn't always take me seriously. I had a hard time opening bank accounts and getting loans. I would always get a line like "Are you sure you're not just a waitress; maybe you should work at the Denny's." I actually had a banker who wouldn't open up a bank account for me, and I had to go find a bank that would actually take our money. Another time I wanted to buy a piece of real estate . . . and the banker said to me, "Young Lady, you just need to stick to the restaurant business."

LaFreeda remained resolute and persistent in the face of rejection and other difficulties. She found inspiration from her mother, who reassured her that if she failed, she could just try again a few years later. Her first Denny's franchise led to a second, and then a third, fourth, and so on, on up to the 75 restaurants in six different states she owns today.

Her tremendous successes were not without serious setbacks along the way. The 9-11 terrorist attacks created difficult burdens for LaFreeda's growing business.

It was a terrible time for us. A lot of my restaurants were by airport locations, and we know that travel drastically dropped after 9-11. The airlines also laid off thousands of workers, so it was a hard time for us. I actually had to refinance my whole company after 9–11, and it set me back a lot. But I'm grateful because I did get through it, and a lot of companies didn't.

LaFreeda's restaurants faced additional challenges during the Great Recession of 2008. She credits her success in weathering the storm to frugality and saving.

My philosophy is this: I try never to live beyond my means, and I always save for a rainy day. That philosophy has really helped me get through the times that happen that we can't predict.

How many restaurants will Dawn LaFreeda own before she retires? Only time will tell. Whatever happens, Dawn has become a nationally recognized symbol of entrepreneurial success, a legacy she will own forever.

Critical Thinking Questions

1. Dawn LaFreeda says, "When you're 23, you're not afraid to take risks." What sorts of risks do you think entrepreneurs face when they are first starting out? What risks do you think you would take when trying to get your business off the ground?

2. Think of the last time you decided to "Go for it" only to fail or be rejected? How did you respond to your *temporary* failure or rejection? After reading Dawn's story, how might you respond differently in the future?

3. Imagine you are a business owner similar to Dawn LaFreeda. What products and/or services would your business provide?

Sources
All LaFreeda quotes transcribed/paraphrased from:
Fox Business Channel. *Denny's Waitress now Owns 75 Denny's Restaurants*. Interview with Dawn LaFreeda by Fox Business Anchor Gerri Willis, August 27, 2014. Retrieved from http://video.foxbusiness.com/v/3752331760001/dennys-waitress-now-owns-75-dennys-restaurants/#sp=show-clips
For more information on Dawn LaFreeda's story, see:
Entrepreneur Magazine (online). *How a Former Denny's Waitress Amassed an Empire of Over 75 Denny's Locations*, by Jason Daley, July 11, 2014. Retrieved from http://www.entrepreneur.com/article/234985
For detailed biographical information and a Q&A with LaFreeda, see also:
Multi-Unit Franchisee Magazine (online). *Denny's Queen: Dawn LaFreeda, With 70 Units in 6 States, Is a Brand Champion*, by Debbie Salinsky. Issue III, 2014. Retrieved from http://www.franchising.com/articles/dennys_queen_dawn_lafreeda_with_70_units_in_6_states_is_a_brand_champion.html

2 Practicing Entrepreneurship

©iStockphoto.com/RyanJLane

"You may have wondered why so many things seem to be harder and take longer to accomplish than you would like—and why both things seem to be increasing. We don't have the answer in every case, but here is an explanation that probably covers the majority of situations: the way we have been taught to solve problems was designed for a different world. To deal with uncertainty today, we need a different approach."[1]

—Leonard A. Schlesinger, Charles F. Kiefer, and Paul B. Brown, authors

Learning Objectives

Chapter Outline

2.1 TWO MAIN PERSPECTIVES ON ENTREPRENEURSHIP

>> **LO 2.1** **Compare and contrast the prediction and creation approaches to entrepreneurship.**

In Chapter 1, we examined the truths behind some common images of entrepreneurs and explained why we can no longer rely on traditional conceptions of what entrepreneurship is all about. The fact that there are two main perspectives on entrepreneurship challenges us to rethink what entrepreneurship really means: It's no longer about a path of starting and growing a venture using a linear step-by-step process. Instead, it is a much messier, ongoing practice of creating opportunities, taking smart action, learning and iterating, and using a portfolio of skills to navigate an ever-changing world.

The skills and mindset presented in this book are essential to The Practice of Entrepreneurship. There is no magic formula for success, but if you develop the skills and mindset, you will learn to work smarter and faster, and be able to make decisions based on reality instead of guesses. As we will repeat many times throughout this book, entrepreneurship is a method that requires practice, and action trumps everything.

This chapter's *Entrepreneurship in Action* feature describes how Rob Hunter, founder and CEO of HigherMe, created opportunities and took action to get his venture off the ground. How can Hunter predict that his business is going to succeed? The truth is, he can't; his focus is on creating a future rather than predicting it. But, by creating what he wants and what he believes his customers need, he's in control.

The two perspectives examined in this section represent older and newer views in entrepreneurship. We like to view these perspectives as different logics—ways of thinking about entrepreneurship. The older view sees entrepreneurship as a linear process in which steps are followed and outcomes are—ideally—predictable. For this reason, it is sometimes called the **predictive logic**. In contrast to it, the newer view sees entrepreneurship—as we do—as a mindset and a method that requires practice. Recent advances in the field have termed this the **creation logic**.[2] Whereas predictive

Predictive logic: a form of thinking that sees entrepreneurship as a linear process in which steps are followed and outcomes are—ideally—predictable.

Creation logic: a form of thinking that is used when the future is unpredictable.

Rob Hunter, Founder and CEO, HigherMe http://www.higherme.com

Rob Hunter, Founder and CEO of HigherMe
Credit: Printed with permission from Rob Hunter

Kendra didn't look like much, at least not on paper. The high school student was seeking a job with a local Marble Slab Creamery ice cream shop and had sent in her resume. The chain's owner, Rob Hunter, called her for an interview anyway. He was pleasantly surprised when he met Kendra in person: "She had a wonderful personality and still has a wonderful personality," he told the technology news website Venturefizz six years later, in March 2014. "You can kind of tell or get a really good sense of work ethic and reliability a couple of minutes in." Hunter saw potential in Kendra from the beginning.

Kendra would become Hunter's most valuable employee, eventually rising to the rank of manager. She also became an inspiration for Hunter's next business venture, HigherMe, an online job-matching site that seeks to match retailers, restaurant owners and other service sector employers with stellar entry-level workers. While Hunter is long gone from the ice cream business, that time in his professional life is never far from his mind because his experience in employing Kendra inspired him to build a completely new business. "When I look back at my stores, especially the ones that failed, I think, 'What if I had had an army of Kendras?'" Smart, proactive, personable, hardworking: all those star employee qualities, hard to discern from a one-dimensional piece of paper, can be game-changers for businesses. And those are just the qualities that HigherMe, a job placement service founded in 2015, promises to unearth through its unique online system.

HigherMe invites job seekers to submit short videos answering a series of carefully selected questions. The videos, plus a ranking system, help employers decide who's worth an interview and who isn't. Hunter thinks both of these aspects help get all the critical qualities that are impossible to glean from a resume. "There's nothing more painful than that 19 and a half minutes after the first 30 seconds during which you've decided they're not going to work out," Hunter says.

Along with cofounder Evan Lodge, Hunter set his sights high. "We want to treat [workers] well, to find them jobs, to not just make money off of them, but to help them succeed in their lives. To be honest, a nice juicy exit along the way wouldn't hurt, but a big impact on the country is what we are looking for."

The startup has made some exciting inroads so far, winning more than $30,000 of funds and $50,000 of in-kind services through the MassChallenge Boston accelerator program. One advantage HigherMe enjoys is that unlike the ice cream business, overhead for this kind of tech startup is relatively low.

HigherMe is the latest phase in a life of entrepreneurship for Rob Hunter. At age 15 he built a successful enterprise selling Japanese wrestling videos and DVDs all over the world on eBay. The money was enough to send him to college and to invest in real estate, which in turn generated enough income to open a chain of ice cream stores. Some did well, some didn't. To today's aspiring entrepreneurs, he says, "Be smart with money. Have side income that can support you while pursuing your big idea. . . . Avoid personal guarantees on debts and loans. Don't underestimate the power of teamwork. . . . Try to smooth out the curve; don't get so distracted by the highs or bogged down in the lows, because there will be both."

CRITICAL THINKING QUESTIONS

1. **Does Rob Hunter's story exemplify the linear "process" approach to entrepreneurship, the nonlinear "practice" approach, or both? Explain your answer.**

2. **In what ways do you agree with the goal "to not just make money off of [job applicants], but to help them succeed in their lives"? How does this fit with your image of entrepreneurship?**

3. **To what extent do desirable qualities in an employee differ from desirable qualities in a business owner or entrepreneur? Explain your answer and give examples.** ●

Source: R. Hunter, personal interview, August 21, 2014.

thinking is used in situations of certainty, the creation logic is used when situations are more unpredictable and uncertain.[3] With a predictive approach, entrepreneurs determine the goals they need to achieve and look for the resources to enable them to reach their goals. Entrepreneurs who use the creation approach turn this thinking upside-down: they determine their goals according to whatever resources they have at hand. They use what they have rather than wait for extended periods of time to get what they need before taking action.

Prediction works best in times of certainty and when there is access to existing information and data on which to base decisions. Prediction is the dominant logic of large, established organizations, where goals are predetermined, issues are transparent, and information is reliable and accessible. Under these circumstances, it is relatively straightforward to analyze a situation, define problems and opportunities, and diagnose and find solutions. Big organizations can use sophisticated planning tools to analyze past and present data in order to predict any shifts in the business landscape. Yet this process is by no means foolproof, as demonstrated by many well-planned initiatives backed by large companies that do not end up succeeding.

Traditional entrepreneurship theory is underpinned by the prediction view: "I can control the future if I can predict it." Someone who uses prediction has a specific goal to work toward, together with a given set of means for reaching it. For example, if you are throwing a dinner party for a group of friends, you might choose a recipe or draw up a menu, buy the ingredients, and cook the meal according to a set of instructions.

In contrast, the creation logic is employed in times of uncertainty. For example, imagine that a couple of friends show up unexpectedly at your door one evening. Everybody is hungry, so you go through your kitchen cupboards to see what ingredients you can throw together to prepare a satisfactory meal. This is a simple example of the creation logic—creating something without a concrete set of instructions. However, the prediction and creation logics don't lead to opposing goals or outcomes. While the means of the goal are different, the end goal is still the same: to cook a meal for your group of friends. It's the *approach* toward action that is different.

$SAGE edge™

Master the content
**edge.sagepub.com/
neckentrepreneurship**

Video
The Creation Approach

TABLE 2.1

Prediction and Creation

PREDICTION	CREATION
Big planning	Small actions
Wait until you get what you need	Starting with what you have
Expected Return	Acceptable loss
Linear	Iterative
Optimization	Experimentation
Avoid failure at all costs	Embrace & leverage failure
Competitive	Collaborative
Knowable	Unknowable
To the extent we can predict the future, we can control it.	*To the extent we can create the future, we don't need to predict it*

Credit: Sarasvathy, S. D. 2008. *Effectuation: Elements of Entrepreneurial Expertise.* Cheltenham, UK and Northampton, MA, USA: Edward Elgar Publishing; Schlesinger, L., Kiefer, C., and Brown, P. 2012. *Just Start: Take Action, Embrace Uncertainty, Create the Future.* Cambridge, MA: Harvard Business School Press. http://www.e-elgar.com/

In reality entrepreneurs should and do employ both perspectives; but, in general, we are expert predictors because we have been honing these skills for years. We *were* expert creators when we were babies—a time when everything around us was a mystery and uncertain. The only way we learned as a baby was by trial and error. Traditional education, the need to find the correct answer, and the constant need for measurement and assessment has inhibited our creative nature. Whenever using the creation logic seems daunting, just remember that we were all born with the ability.

An early entrepreneurial venture is unlikely to have access to sophisticated predictive tools, nor is it just a smaller version of a large organization.[4] While prediction has its advantages, it is not enough in today's uncertain, complex, and chaotic business environment. Ideally, new ventures need to be able to balance both prediction and creation in order to function. Further, they need to also understand under what conditions to use which approach. Small enterprises will almost always begin with creation, but as they collect data in the real world, they will use prediction for analysis.

The majority of entrepreneurs are more likely to start out with a general idea that they feel is worth pursuing, rather than a concrete plan with a formulated strategy. The early stages of entrepreneurship emphasize creation over prediction, given the reality of what it's really like to start a business. You simply can't predict. After all, how is it possible to price a product or a service when the market does not exist? Or hire the right people for a business that hasn't yet begun to figure out who the customer is or the size of the market? Or determine the worth of a company in an industry that has only emerged very recently? It is usually possible to access some useful data; but if you are working on a truly novel idea, you must get out of the building and collect your own data. You must take action.

In many respects, prediction and creation are two sides of the same coin. Table 2.1 shows how entrepreneurs can use both creative and predictive reasoning and go back and forth between the two, depending on the circumstances. Each approach results in different types of action.[5]

Prediction and Creation in Action

To further examine the creation and prediction approaches, here is an example based on a thought experiment called "Curry in a Hurry" devised by Darden School of Business professor Saras D. Sarasvathy.[6] Say you want to start an Indian restaurant in your hometown. You could begin by assessing your market through questionnaires, surveys, and focus groups to separate those people who love Indian food versus those who don't. Then you could narrow the "love it" segment down to the customers whom you might be able to approach when your restaurant opens.

This approach would help you predict the type of diners who might become regulars at your restaurant. You could then continue your information-gathering process by visiting other Indian restaurants to gauge their business processes, and contacting vendors to gauge prices

Customers dining in a small Indian restaurant

Credit: Kumar Sriskandan/Alamy Stock Photo

and availability of goods. Having spent months acquiring all this knowledge, you could formulate a business plan, apply for bank loans and loans from investors, lease

The Creation Approach

The creation approach aligns with the work of Dr. Saras Sarasvathy and her **theory of effectuation**,[6] based on the idea that because the future is unpredictable yet controllable, entrepreneurs can "effect" the future. Sarasvathy believes it is futile for entrepreneurs to try and predict the future.

In 1997, Dr. Sarasvathy traveled to 17 states across the United States to interview 30 entrepreneurs from different types and sizes of organizations and from a variety of industries to assess their thinking patterns. The aim of her research was to understand their methods of reasoning about specific problems. Each entrepreneur was given a 17-page problem that involved making decisions to build a company from a specific product idea. By the end of the study, Sarasvathy discovered that 89% of the more experienced, serial entrepreneurs used more creative, effectual thinking more often than its contrary—predictive or causal thinking.[7]

Until Dr. Sarasvathy's study, we really didn't know how entrepreneurs think—at least previous research didn't identify such salient patterns as her work. She found that entrepreneurs, especially those entrepreneurs who have started businesses multiple times, exhibited specific thinking patterns. Thus, we are able to demonstrate that entrepreneurship can be taught because we can train ourselves to think differently—and how we think is the antecedent to how we act.

CRITICAL THINKING QUESTIONS

1. **What strengths and weaknesses do you see in the creation view of entrepreneurship? Give some examples that would apply to real life.**

2. **If you were asked to participate in Dr. Sarasvathy's study, how might she classify your ways of thinking and problem solving?**

3. **What additional research questions can you suggest that would shed light on how entrepreneurs think and solve problems?** ●

---

a building and hire staff, and start a marketing and sales campaign to attract people to your restaurant.

While this is one way to go about starting a new business, it is based on two big assumptions: (1) you have the finances and resources for research and marketing; and (2) you have the time to invest in intensive planning and research. Typically, this is the sort of path taken by novice entrepreneurs who navigate worlds that they perceive as certain; they spend huge amounts of time on planning and analysis and allow the market to take control while they take a back seat. In short, they spend lots of time and money trying to predict the future.

Given that the prediction approach to opening a new restaurant is time-consuming and expensive, what other approach could novice entrepreneurs take to carrying out the same task? If you followed the creation approach to starting your Indian restaurant, you would be going down a very different path. To learn more about the creation approach and the corresponding effectuation theory, see the *Research at Work* feature.

To implement the creation approach, first, you would take a look at what means you have to start the process. Let's assume you have only a few thousand dollars in the bank and very few other resources. You could start by doing just enough research to convince an established restauranteur to become a strategic partner, or persuade a local business owner to invest in your restaurant, or even create some dishes to bring to a local Indian restaurant and persuade them to let you set up a counter in their establishment to test a selection there.

Theory of Effectuation: the idea that the future is unpredictable yet controllable and entrepreneurs can "effect" the future.

Second, you could contact some of your friends who work in nearby businesses and bring them and their colleagues some samples of your food, which might lead to a lunch delivery service. Once the word is out and you have a high enough customer base, you might decide to start your restaurant.

Getting out in your community, meeting new people, and building relationships with customers and strategic partners can lead to all sorts of opportunities. Someone might suggest that you write an Indian cookbook and introduce you to a publishing contact; someone else might think you have just the right personality to host your own cooking show, and connect you with someone in the television industry. Others might want to learn more about Indian culture and inspire you to teach classes on the subject; or they might express an interest in travel, inspiring you to organize a food-themed tour of different regions around India. Suddenly you have a wealth of different business ideas in widely varied industries. Your original goal of starting a restaurant has evolved and multiplied into several different streams, demonstrating how it is possible to change, shape, and construct ideas in practice through action (see Figure 2.1).

But who knows what the true outcome will be? Let's say the majority of people just don't like your cooking, even though your close friends rave about it. If you are really determined to reach your initial goal, you could use their feedback to work hard at improving your recipes and try again. However, if you silently agree with your customer base, you haven't lost too much time and money in your idea—which means you have resources left over to focus on your next entrepreneurial pursuit.

Entrepreneurship under creation view is based on how entrepreneurs think. They navigate uncertain worlds to create rather than find existing opportunities; they make markets, learn from failure, and connect with a variety of stakeholders to fulfill their vision of the future.

FIGURE 2.1

The Creation Approach in Action

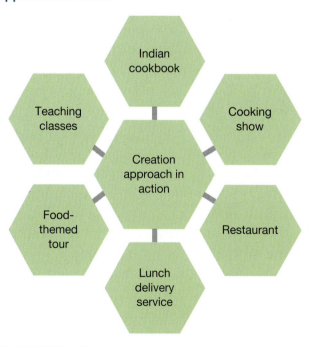

2.2 THE FIVE SKILLS MOST IMPORTANT TO THE PRACTICE OF ENTREPRENEURSHIP

>> LO 2.2   Create a portfolio of five skills essential to building a mindset for The Practice of Entrepreneurship.

By using the creation approach, entrepreneurs learn through action and manage uncertainty by focusing on developing five key skills: the skill of play, the skill of experimentation, the skill of empathy, the skill of creativity, and the skill of reflection. Throughout the book, these skills will come up time and time again through exercises that will encourage you to think and act entrepreneurially.

Skill of play: frees the imagination, opens up our minds to a wealth of opportunities and possibilities, and helps us to be more innovative as entrepreneurs.

The Skill of Play

The **skill of play** frees the imagination, opens up our minds to a wealth of opportunities and possibilities, and helps us to be more innovative as entrepreneurs.[7]

Theorists such as the famed child development psychologist, Piaget, have been extolling the benefits of play for decades, so why don't we do enough of it? Think about it. Don't you feel more interested, engaged, energized, and exhilarated when you're having fun and being playful? Why shouldn't entrepreneurship be fun? We feel that entrepreneurs benefit from creative exercises that encourage interaction with others, problem solving, idea generation, learning from trial and error, and so on.

Play can include the use of alternative reality games
Credit: ©iStockphoto.com/ EvaKatalinKondoros

In the context of entrepreneurship, play can include the use of serious games (i.e., educational games) such as alternative reality games and learning simulations that challenge you to be creative and to think like an entrepreneur.

The Skill of Experimentation

The **skill of experimentation** is best described as acting in order to learn: trying something, learning from the attempt, and building that learning into the next iteration.[8] In the context of entrepreneurship, experimentation means taking action, such as getting out of the building and collecting real-world information to test new concepts, rather than sitting at a desk searching databases for the latest research. It involves asking questions, validating assumptions, and taking nothing for granted.[9]

For example, say you have formulated a new energy drink, but you're not sure how to price it. You could spend weeks evaluating the energy drink market, researching your competitors to see how much you should charge for your own beverage. You might be able to get an idea of an average price for your drink, but it will be only a general guide. Alternatively, you could bring samples of your drink to the sidewalk, your friends, contacts, and local businesses and sell it at different prices based on what you have discovered during your research. By taking action and bringing the product directly to the customer, you acquire feedback not only on the price but also on how much they like the drink. This is experimentation—learning by doing, and taking action to create the bigger picture.

Video
The Skill of Play

Skill of experimentation: best described as acting in order to learn—trying something, learning from the attempt and building that learning into the next iteration.

The Skill of Empathy

Skill of empathy: developing the ability to understand the emotion, circumstances, intentions, thoughts, and needs of others.

The **skill of empathy** is understanding the emotion, circumstances, intentions, thoughts, and needs of others.[10] Empathy is being able to relate to how others are feeling because you have been in a similar situation yourself. For example, you know how your best friend feels when her dog dies, because the same happened to you at one stage. Similarly, a nutritionist who has struggled to lose weight knows how a patient feels when attempting to do the same thing; and a former smoker knows how it feels for someone else who is trying to quit.

Why is empathy so important for an entrepreneur? Developing empathy is essential for truly understanding the reality of being an entrepreneur as well as evaluating your own ability to become an entrepreneur. Exercises such as interviewing practicing entrepreneurs help you to develop empathy for what they have been through, and enable you to put yourself in the shoes of that person and imagine what you would do in the same situation. Furthermore, empathy allows you to connect with potential stakeholders in a more meaningful way, which could help to identify unmet needs, leading to the creation of new products and services.

The Skill of Creativity

Skill of creativity: requires a general openness to the world and relates to unleashing our creative ability to create and find opportunities and solve problems.

The **skill of creativity** requires a general openness to the world and relates to unleashing our creative ability to create and find opportunities and solve problems.[11] We believe that entrepreneurship students are more open to creativity than students from other business courses—a theory that has been supported by recent research.[12] Our aim is to harness your creative potential so you can create opportunities, rather than simply discovering or looking for them.

But how do you create opportunities? It all depends on how much you want to learn, how curious you are, and how much energy you have to implement your idea. We all have ideas; but no matter how great we think they are, we need to have the desire to see them through. We will talk a lot more about creating new ideas in Chapter 5.

Creating opportunities is also based on some of the principles outlined in the previous section: the amount of resources you have, the ability to collaborate rather than compete, the effort to build relationships, the knowledge regarding how much you can afford to lose, and the willingness to leverage the knowledge that results from possible failures along the way. Using these principles dispels all those elements that tend to stunt creativity such as fear and perceived obstacles, and helps you to take action even under extreme conditions of uncertainty and doubt to create something of value.

The Skill of Reflection

Skill of reflection: helps make sense of all of the other actions required of play, empathy, creativity and experimentation.

The **skill of reflection** helps make sense of all of the other actions required of play, empathy, creativity, and experimentation. It helps codify our learning from practicing the four other skills. You may not realize it, but taking the time out to reflect is also an action, and it can be the most important of all the five skills. Reflection makes us aware of feelings of discomfort, helps us to critically analyze our own feelings and the knowledge we possess, provides us with new perspectives, and allows us to evaluate outcomes and draw conclusions.[13]

In spite of the benefits of reflection and the substantial amount of research that supports its importance, we don't seem to practice it very much at all. When asked to

Video
Reflection

FIGURE 2.2

The Five Most Important Skills to The Practice of Entrepreneurship

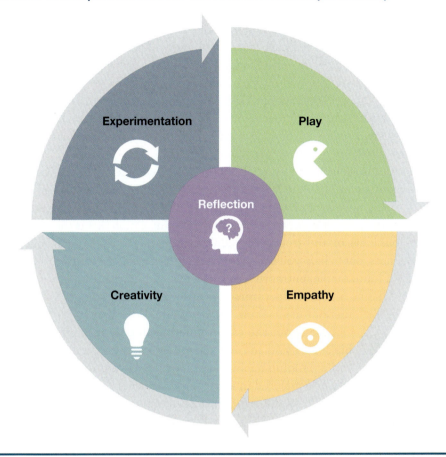

Source: Neck, H. M., Greene, P. G., & Brush, C. (2014). *Teaching entrepreneurship: A practice-based approach.* Northampton, MA: Edward Elgar.

reflect, we often don't really know how. Without intentional and focused reflection, we simply simulate writing in a diary or journal, which is interesting in practice, but it doesn't help us really learn from our actions. There are six different ways we can practice reflection:

- narrative reflection,
- emotional reflection,
- perceptive reflection,
- analytical reflection,
- evaluative reflection, and
- critical reflection.[14]

Let's further explore these different types of reflection by imagining that you have just given a presentation of your new energy drink to a small retail outlet. Following the presentation, you make time to reflect on the experience. First, through narrative reflection you could describe what happened by considering what took place, what was said, and who was involved. Second, you could use emotional reflection to focus on how you felt during the presentation and how you managed those emotions (nervousness, anxiety, etc.). Third, perceptive reflection focuses about your perceptions and reactions as well as the perceptions and reactions of others and how different viewpoints, needs, or preferences affected the experience. Fourth, you could adopt analytical reflection to analyze the situation by thinking about the skills and knowledge you gained from the experience and if anything you have learned relates to anything you have heard about before. Furthermore, you could evaluate the experience by focusing on what went well and what seemed to go badly, and if the experience was positive or negative, useful or helpful. Finally, you could practice critical reflection by considering the part you played in the presentation and the approach you took, what else you might have done, what you have learned about the experience, what questions you have, and what you need to consider as a result.

The five skills we have presented in this section (see Figure 2.2) are essential for building a mindset for The Practice of Entrepreneurship. They are designed for those who are keen to take action. This is because the skills cannot be developed without learning through doing. We want to show you that taking action first is the biggest part of getting your ideas off the ground. We don't want merely to teach you about how to create a business, but to help you live a more entrepreneurial and impactful life.

Consider, for example, entrepreneur Jim Poss. Jim is the founder of Bigbelly, Inc., which designs and manufacturers solar-powered trash compactors for commercial use.[15] From an early age, Poss had always been passionate about the environment, science, and engineering. By his senior year in high school, he knew he wanted to explore a career helping businesses go green. He attended Duke University and majored in environmental science and geology with a minor in engineering. Following university, Poss held a number of short-term jobs, working as a hydrologist, sales engineer, and production manager for different companies. It was through these experiences that he discovered his tendency to get bored easily and his dislike of being overly supervised by managers.

Bigbelly solar-powered trash compactor

Credit: Eye Ubiquitous/Newscom

Realizing that he still had a lot to learn, Poss decided to enroll in the Babson College MBA program in hopes of starting his venture prior to graduation. During his time at Babson, Poss contacted a board member he had met at the Spire Corporation, a manufacturer of solar-powered equipment, to investigate the possibility of creating solar-powered trash compactors. Although Spire wasn't interested in Poss's idea, they did offer him an internship, which resulted in Poss working 15 hours a week on top of his full-time MBA. During his time at Spire, Poss persisted in showing the feasibility of his trash compactor idea, although the company's executives still declined to pursue it.

Undeterred, Poss continued to research the trash industry and found he had more potential to make a difference than he first realized. U.S. companies were spending billions of dollars every year on trash receptacles and compaction equipment, and trash trucks were making multiple trips to high-trash volume areas like resorts, amusement parks, and beaches, resulting in a huge waste of energy and labor resources.

Confident that his idea had legs, Poss persuaded some other talented individuals to join him on his quest to make the solar-powered trash compactor a reality. His team included Jeff Satwicz and Bret Richmond, engineering students at the nearby Franklin W. Olin School of Engineering—one of whom had specialized experience in product design and welding—and Alexander Perera, a Babson Entrepreneurship Intensity Track (EIT) student with a background in renewable energy use and energy efficiency.

With $22,500 cobbled together from his own savings and some funding from Babson, Poss was able to begin the first stages of his journey. Poss found a couple of kitchen trash compactors in newspaper classified ads, which he bought for $125 each. Together with his team, they *played* around and tinkered with them to better understand how they worked. Then they *experimented* by doing some reverse engineering to test the real-world feasibility of their planned compactor. What they found encouraged them to make some cold calls in search of anyone out there who would be interested in their idea.

One of the first calls Poss made was to the ski resort town of Vail, Colorado, a place where collecting trash can be especially costly and time-consuming due to the remote locations of some of the ski lodges. In his pitch, Poss expressed how he *empathized* with this dilemma. To his surprise, Luke Cartin, who worked at the resort, jumped at the concept of a solar-powered trash compactor. Following a couple of conference calls, the resort put in an order for one Bigbelly, paying the full amount upfront. The only problem was that the product didn't exist yet.

Poss and his team knew they needed to get to work immediately. The first step they had to accomplish was to draw up engineering plans for the now-trademarked "BigBelly Solar-Powered Trash Compactor" using computer-aided design software (CAD)—an application the team had no idea how to use. Together they each committed to learning CAD so they could create the drawings they needed.

Next, they looked for quotes for building the trash compactor, but these were too high, so the team decided to build it themselves through the process of *creativity*. Poss connected with Bob Treiber, president of Boston Engineering, who charged him much less for providing his engineering team's expert assistance than what it would have cost to have the compactor fabricated. As a bonus, this work arrangement allowed Poss and the team to use Boston Engineering's company facilities.

When the first prototype was ready, Poss personally traveled to Vail to make sure it was set up correctly. The team had managed to build the first Bigbelly for $10,000, selling it to Vail for $5,500. Yet the feedback they received was worth the initial loss. The Vail crew advised Poss and the team to make a two-bin system rather than a one-bin, to put the cart inside on wheels, to put the access door on the back, and to have a wireless notification to alert the operator when the compactor was full.

Poss and the team *reflected* on this feedback and decided to incorporate it into their next production run. As a result, they presold nearly half of the compactors with a 50% down payment for each one. During this period, Poss received more funds from his parents, a business angel, and his former boss at Spire, which allowed Bigbelly to put more of the compactors into production.

Today, over 1,000 organizations in over 47 countries use Bigbelly solar-powered trash compactors as a more sustainable environmental solution to waste collection.[16] As the Bigbelly case shows, today's entrepreneurs need to identify and shape opportunities by using creative approaches to generate information that did not exist before or that is inaccessible.

Jim Poss is an example of the creation approach in action—very early on in the venture. In the next section, we will revisit the concept of entrepreneurship as a method rather than a process. The method builds on the creation approach, but it also includes the predictive approach.

2.3 ENTREPRENEURSHIP IS MORE A METHOD THAN A PROCESS

>> **LO 2.3**   Distinguish between entrepreneurship as a method and a process.

Video
Using a Method

In Chapter 1, we briefly discussed entrepreneurship as a method rather than a process. We described the *method* as a body of skills that together comprise a toolkit for entrepreneurial action; and a *process*, as the means of identifying an opportunity, understanding resource requirements, acquiring resources, planning, implementing, and harvesting.

Let's explore this concept in further detail. Table 2.2 shows the traditional approach to entrepreneurship, which is generally based on a *process* of sequential steps.

The process approach to entrepreneurship is based on planning and prediction—from firm creation right up until firm exit. It suggests that if you follow the 10 steps correctly, your new venture is more likely to succeed; and that if you use proven business models, your risk of failure is reduced. There is no doubt that the process of entrepreneurship works for larger organizations and corporations—but, as we mentioned before, entrepreneurial ventures are not just smaller versions of large corporations.[17] The 10-step process isn't enough for entrepreneurial ventures. Why? Because it relies too much on past history to predict the future, and a new venture with a new innovation does not have any history to draw from. And, simply stated, there are no steps or rules; it's just not that clean!

TABLE 2.2

The Traditional Steps of an Entrepreneurship Process

Step 1	Think of an idea
Step 2	Do market research
Step 3	Get some financial projections
Step 4	Find a partner/team
Step 5	Write a business plan
Step 6	Get financing
Step 7	Find space, build a prototype, hire people
Step 8	Bring your product/service to market
Step 9	Manage the business
Step 10	Plan an exit

Entrepreneurship is certainly not linear or predictable; it is ill-defined, unstructured, and complex. In fact, some statistics show that 8 out of 10 entrepreneurs who start businesses in the United States fail within the first 18 months[18]; others show that most failures occur in the first two years of business.[19] One reason for the extraordinary failure rate is a lack of entrepreneurial practice. Research has determined, however, that if entrepreneurs who have failed try again, they are far more likely to be successful in their second venture—even if the second venture is in a different industry. The point of these statistics is not to scare you, but to show you how unpredictable, complex, and chaotic entrepreneurship can be. The environment for entrepreneurship is fluid, dynamic, uncertain, and ambiguous. Doesn't it make sense that the way we learn needs to help us manage such "craziness"? The good news is there is a method

TABLE 2.3

Assumptions Underlying The Practice of Entrepreneurship

It applies to novices and experts regardless of experience levels.
It is inclusive, which means it includes any organization at any stage of business.
It requires continuous practice with a focus on doing, then learning.
It is designed for an unpredictable environment.

Web
Entrepreneurship as a Method

Source: Neck, H. M., & Greene, P. G. (2011). Entrepreneurship education: Known worlds and new frontiers. *Journal of Small Business Management, 49*, 55–70.

Credit: Neck, H.M.,, and Greene, P.G. 2011. Entrepreneurship education: Known worlds and new frontiers. *Journal of Small Business Management, 49*(1), 55–70. Reprinted with permission from John Wiley & Sons

to manage the chaos and craziness, and we call this method The Practice of Entrepreneurship. Table 2.3 illustrates some ideas about The Practice of Entrepreneurship.[20]

From this we can see that entrepreneurship is less an aptitude than it is a craft, and that learning and persistence are critical practices for entrepreneurial success.

Approaching entrepreneurship as a method that requires practice may be new to entrepreneurship but the concept of practice has been around for centuries. Yoga, Suzuki violin playing, and Montessori education can all be classified as methods. A method caters to the uncertainty and unpredictability of entrepreneurship. It represents a body of skills that together comprise a toolkit for entrepreneurial action.[21] It requires consistent practice so knowledge and expertise can be continuously developed and applied to future endeavors. Table 2.4 describes the differences between entrepreneurship as a method and entrepreneurship as a process.

Child learning to play the violin through the Suzuki method.

Credit: ©iStockphoto.com/ JoseGirarte

TABLE 2.4

Method Versus Process

ENTREPRENEURSHIP AS A METHOD	ENTREPRENEURSHIP AS A PROCESS
A set of practices	Known inputs and predicted outputs
Phases of learning	Steps to complete
Iterative	Linear
Creative	Predictive
Action focus	Planning focus
Investment for learning	Expected return
Collaborative	Competitive

Credit: Neck, H. M., Greene, P. G. & Brush, C. (2014). *Teaching Entrepreneurship: A Practice-Based Approach.* Northhampton, MA: Edward Elgar Publishing. http://www.e-elgar.com/

Practicing Entrepreneurship

Kathryn Minshew originally co-founded Pretty Young Professionals (PYP), a woman's networking site

Credit: © User: Techcrunch / Wikimedia Commons / CC BY 2.0 / https://creativecommons.org/licenses/by/2.0/deed.en

Entrepreneurship is understood as a social process and embedded in multiple relationships. As such, entrepreneurship is necessarily interwoven with ethical concerns including deciding how partners are selected and who has a right to be on the team. Other ethics-related concerns include how and when ownership shares should be divided.

Kathryn Minshew originally co-founded Pretty Young Professionals (PYP), a woman's networking site, which she set up with a handshake (rather than a formal contract) with four former work colleagues. She also contributed savings of $20,000. After a disagreement among the cofounders, Minshew found herself locked out of the company she helped cocreate. Realizing she would not get her $20,000 investment back, Minshew spent months trying to decide how to recover from what she perceived as an unethical betrayal. Eventually, she made a decision to move on from

the experience. She went on to cofound The Muse, an online career-development platform, and was able to leverage her prior experience to surpass PYP's 20,000 user peak with The Muse's 2 million users.

CRITICAL THINKING QUESTIONS

1. **The cofounders of PYP worked on handshakes rather than contractual agreements when they started the business. How can you know if your partners are ethical and trustworthy?**

2. **Can you think of how to get cofounders to negotiate and sign contractual agreements without implying that there is a lack of trust?**

3. **If you were Minshew, would you have sued to get your $20,000 funds back? Or, like Minshew, would you have just moved on?** ●

Sources

Fields, J. (2012, December 27). *Entrepreneurship as a practice.* Retrieved from Jonathon Fields: http://www.jonathanfields.com/entrereneurship-as-a-practice/

MacBride, E. (2014, September 30). *Kathryn Shaw: Entrepreneurship requires practice, practice, practice.* Retrieved from Stanford Business: http://www.gsb.stanford.edu/insights/kathryn-shaw-entrepreneurship-requires-practice-practice-practice

Patel, N. (2016, January 25). *7 Shortcuts for becoming a successful entrepreneur.* Retrieved from Forbes/Entrepreneurs: http://www.forbes.com/sites/neilpatel/2016/01/25/7-shortcuts-for-becoming-a-successful-entrepreneur/#2a6242b63756

Schrager, A. (2014, July 28). *Failed entrepreneurs find more success the second time.* Retrieved from Bloomberg Business: http://www.bloomberg.com/bw/articles/2014-07-28/study-failed-entrepreneurs-find-success-the-second-time-around

Wang, J. (2013, January 23). *How 5 successful entrepreneurs bounced back after failure.* Retrieved from Entrepreneur: http://www.entrepreneur.com/article/225204

Approaching entrepreneurship as a method helps give us comfort and direction, but it is not a recipe. Part of the method is learning and practicing as you go, and consciously reflecting on events as and when they take place. Part of the method is iterative. The entire method, however, is action-based and, of course, requires practice. This is why, throughout this book, we call it The Practice of Entrepreneurship.

2.4 THE PRACTICE OF ENTREPRENEURSHIP: AN INTRODUCTION

>> **LO 2.4**   **Illustrate the key components of The Practice of Entrepreneurship.**

The Practice of Entrepreneurship provides a way for entrepreneurs to embrace and confront uncertainty rather than to avoid it. It emphasizes smart action over planning. It emphasizes moving quickly from the whiteboard to the real world. It's a method that can be learned and should be repeated. There is no guarantee for success, but it does offer a few powerful assurances:

- you will act sooner, even when you don't know exactly what to do;

- for those things you can do, you will; and for those things you can't, you will try;

- you will try more times because trying early is a low-cost experiment;

- you will fail sooner—enabling better, higher quality information to be incorporated into the next iteration; and

- you'll likely begin experimenting with many new ideas simultaneously.

The practice includes the two approaches that have already been addressed: prediction and creation. Prediction requires thinking about and analyzing existing information in order to predict the future, and creation is most concerned with acting and collecting new data—real and relevant data—in order to create the future. The prediction logic is better suited when we can deduce the future from the past, while the creation logic is the only choice under conditions of extreme uncertainty.

Eight Components of The Practice of Entrepreneurship

Now that we understand the difference between the method and process of entrepreneurship, it is time to take a deeper dive into the components of the method we call The Practice of Entrepreneurship. Figure 2.3 illustrates the eight components of The Practice. Let's examine each of them in more detail.

1. **Identify your desired impact on the world**. This is a simple statement that connects to your curiosity, drive, and motivation. To be successful at creating and building a new business, a new strategy, a new product, or anything radically new requires desire—you have to have a strong feeling to achieve something larger than yourself. Rarely is entrepreneurship about the money or the profit. Granted, fast-growth companies are primarily concerned with wealth creation, but the general reasons for why people start businesses go much deeper. Some pursue what they love, others value their autonomy and ability to control their work experience, and others have a strong desire to bring something new to market.[22] The profit motive is simply not sustainable in the long run because entrepreneurship is hard work and requires satisfaction and desire that is derived from deep within.

Audio
From Curiosity to Creation

2. **Start with means at hand.**[23] Answer the following questions: Who am I? What do I know? Whom do I know? The composite answer will help you understand your current resource base—the resources you have available today that you can use for immediate action.

3. **Describe the idea today.** The idea is identified by connecting your means to your impact statement. What can you start to do today with what you have today?

4. **Calculate affordable loss.**[24] Leaving one's comfort zone is always perceived as risky, but risk is relative. What is considered high risk to one may not seem high risk to another; therefore, it can be quite difficult to calculate risk and use it as a valid decision-making criterion. Rather than calculate risk, think about taking action in terms of what you are willing to lose. What are you truly willing to give up in terms of money, reputation, time, and opportunity cost? By answering

FIGURE 2.3

The Practice of Entrepreneurship

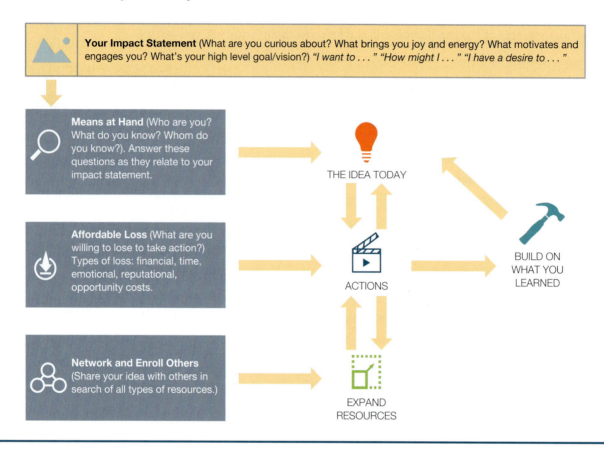

Adapted from the following sources:
Schlesinger, L., Kiefer, C., & Brown, P. (2012). *Just start: Take action, embrace uncertainty, create the future.* Cambridge, MA: Harvard Business School Press.
Sarasvathy, S. D. (2008). *Effectuation: Elements of entrepreneurial expertise.* Northampton, MA: Edward Elgar.
Neck, H. M. (2011). Cognitive ambidexterity: The underlying mental model of the entrepreneurial leader. In D. Greenberg, K. McKone-Sweet, & H. J. Wilson (Eds.), *The New entrepreneurial leader: Developing leaders who will shape social and economic opportunities* (pp. 2442). San Francisco: Berrett-Koehler.

these questions, you take control rather than allowing yourself to be controlled by risk or the fear of failure.

5. **Take small action.** Nothing drastic . . . the first action is just a small start to get you going. No excuses here. You can do it. Once you calculate your affordable loss, you control all the risk.

6. **Network and enroll others in your journey.** The Practice of Entrepreneurship is about collaboration and cocreation rather than competition. Sharing your ideas and enrolling others in your journey will increase your resource base, expand the possibilities available, and validate your idea.

7. **Build on what you learn.** Assess performance of your action. Keep in mind that assessment is not about "killing" your new idea; it's about making the idea better. There is no right or wrong answer at this stage, just better. Expect and embrace setbacks, and celebrate the learning. When Thomas Watson, the founder of IBM, was asked about the key to success he responded, "Increase the rate of failure."

8. **Reflect and be honest with yourself.** One question always arises: How do I know when I should stop or keep going? The answer is easy. Quit only if you no longer have the desire inherent in your impact statement, or if you have exceeded your affordable loss. Otherwise, the real question you have to answer now is: What are you going to do next?

As you continue with The Practice of Entrepreneurship, you'll find that your affordable loss changes (usually increases) with each action. Why? Your idea receives greater validation, you have a solid and growing knowledge base, more people have joined your team, resource stocks increase, and your overall confidence in your ability to act grows. Through the practice, you will manage to deal with extreme uncertainty, control it, and use it to help you create what others cannot.

Using the Practice to Achieve Ongoing Success

Let's observe how The Practice of Entrepreneurship works in the real world through the real-life case of the luggage design company Vera Bradley.[25] Business partners Barbara Baekgaard and Pat Miller first met in 1981. The two had a lot in common: Barbara's parents had been in the gift candle business, while Pat had worked in her grandfather's grocery store, where she gained an insight into customer relations as well as experience of running a business.

The two women soon began their first entrepreneurial venture, a wallpaper hanging business, in the 1970s. A year later, the partners were at an airport en route to a birthday celebration when they spotted something that didn't seem quite right. Many passengers were carrying Lands' End duffle bags and other run-of-the-mill bags and luggage. Baekgaard was struck by the lack of attractive bags for women and decided to investigate. It turns out there were more attractively designed bags available, but they were targeted at the high end of the market, and came with a costly price tag. Baekgaard and Miller wondered if they could produce a practical bag at a lower price for a wider market.

As soon as they returned home from the trip, they bought fabrics of many different patterns and colors and began to experiment with the design. They then hired someone to make 12 prototype bags. Now, all they needed was a brand name. After some consideration, they decided to use Baekgaard's mother's name: Vera Bradley. They sold all 12 bags at a local trunk show, and customers were asking for more. However, the trunk show customers were mostly middle-aged or older women, and Baekgaard and Miller wanted to see if their bags would appeal to a younger market.

Baekgaard had two daughters in college in different states, so she sent them each several bags to see what their friends thought of them. Both daughters provided very positive feedback from each campus. This informal market research convinced Baekgaard and Miller to take the next step. They each borrowed $250 from their husbands to make more bags.

In late 1982, the partners decided to try their luck at the Chicago Gift Show, where they sold $10,000 worth of bags. Delighted with their success, they decided to look for more financing to produce more products, but they weren't sure how to go about it. In the end, the money came from a rather unexpected source. Naturally effervescent, Baekgaard happened

Vera Bradley bags and backpacks.
Credit: RICHARD B. LEVINE/ Newscom

The 3-Hour Challenge

You may or may not have given a lot of thought to your entrepreneurial plans and goals. Either way, this activity will challenge you to clarify what plans and goals you have, and why.

You can commit to doing a lot of things for only three hours, so give this mindshift challenge a try. The three hours do not have to be spent in one continuous period. Doing it all at a stretch is probably not practical, so it is fine to spread out the time in one-hour increments, but don't go past three days.

Hour #1: Write down your impact statement. Keep in mind that this is something that drives your curiosity, motivation to engage, and enthusiasm. Your impact statement is not an idea; it's a statement that expresses your desire of the type of impact you want to make as an entrepreneur. Examples of impact statements are:

- I have a desire to help people age more gracefully.

- I have a desire to use video games to effect positive change on the world.

- I have a desire to build greater community among different populations on my college campus.

- I have a desire to design clothes that help teenagers feel more confident.

- I have a desire to create healthy snack foods.

Take a full hour to write down your impact statement. Give it deep thought and really ask yourself: What excites me? Write it as clearly, sincerely, and completely as you can.

Hour #2: Share your impact statement with your classmates or others in your life, and try to find someone who shares a similar vision. Your goal is to find just one other person with a similar vision; but if you find more, that's great too!

Hour #3: Once you find your person, schedule a one-hour meeting. Meet someplace unusual, not in the same coffee shop or restaurant where you always go. Share where your desired impact is coming from, and identify three potential business ideas that the two of you could pursue together to fulfill your desired impact. For example, if you both have a desire around healthy snack food, you may come up with an idea around healthy vending machines that hold only fresh fruit and vegetable options.

That's it . . . just craft your impact statement, find someone who shares your desire, and identify three potential business ideas. Don't judge the quality of your ideas at this point. There will be plenty of time for that.

CRITICAL THINKING QUESTIONS

1. **What assumptions and beliefs did you have before starting the 3-Hour Challenge?**

2. **In what ways did the 3-Hour Challenge confirm your existing assumptions and beliefs? In what ways did it change them?**

3. **What did you learn about yourself that was unexpected or surprising?** ●

to be enthusiastically chatting to her husband's former work colleague. He was so impressed that he cut her a check for $2,500. Events moved very quickly after that. They found a bank manager they could trust, sought advice from a retired financial executive, built relationships with fabric wholesalers, and hired people in the community to sew the bags. Armed with the mantra, "First, sell yourself, then your company, and then your product," the two partners each worked to build relationships with relevant businesses. They would simply walk into local gift shops, introduce themselves, show samples and ask if the gift shops wanted to order any of the bags. They also asked friends and family to represent the Vera Bradley brand in their different home states and to reach out, in turn, to their contacts. In every location, this involved developing relationships with local gift stores and taking orders for the bags.

As with every business, Baekgaard and Miller made their fair share of mistakes along the way. At one point, Baekgaard mistakenly ordered hundreds of 20-inch bag zippers rather than 12-inch zippers—but rather than swallowing the cost, the partners decided to simply expand their line to include a bag with a 20-inch zipper. But, of course, there were plenty of successes to make up for the mistakes. The Vera Bradley range caught the eye of the owner of the iconic New York restaurant Tavern on the Green, who asked the partners to design a collection of bags. The Tavern on the Green pattern was a big hit and gave the Vera Bradley brand even more credibility.

Since its inception in 1982, Vera Bradley has grown from a small cottage operation in Indiana to 3,500 retailers of Vera Bradley and stand-alone Vera Bradley stores all over the United States.

The brand has expanded its range from bags to backpacks, laptop backpacks, totes, purses, wallets, eyeglass and sunglass cases, cosmetic cases, wrist accessories, and jewelry cases. There are also umbrellas, napkins, placemats, rolling luggage, diaper bags, tableware, rugs, accessories, and stationery. Baby products were added to the line in 2013.[26]

The Very Bradley story is a good illustration of The Practice of Entrepreneurship in action. Both women *reflected on their desired impact on the world* to create stylish, affordable luggage for women, and they acted on this desire as soon as they returned from their trip. They began with the *means at hand* (Who am I? What do I know? Whom do I know?). They then connected their means with their *idea today* by thinking about what they could start doing right then with what they had. For example, both women had some business experience, they had both worked together in the wallpaper hanging business, they each had a passion for design, and both of them had borrowed money from their husbands to kick-start the business.

When they decided to take the plunge and expand the business, they *calculated their affordable loss* or paid only what they could afford to lose by having minimum overheads, and working with small loans from friends and the bank. They were also willing to give up their own time to make the business work. Once they calculated their affordable loss, they were able to *take small actions* to bring their bags to market by selling their prototype bags at a trunk show, simply walking into gift shops to obtain orders, and requesting feedback from friends and family. In other words, they used their personalities and their belief in their product to engage others.

Video
Practice for Continued
Success

Baekgaard and Miller also *networked and enrolled others in their journey* from the very beginning by sending Barbara's daughters a range of bags to test the student market. They also engaged a retired financial advisor, a major fabric supplier, the restaurant owner at Tavern on the Green, and a bank loan officer.

Various setbacks allowed them to *build on what they learned*; for example they leveraged perceived failures such as ordering the wrong size zippers by simply designing a new bag that would work with the larger zipper.

Both women were able to *reflect and be honest with themselves* about the challenges facing the business and spent time thinking about their next steps. The most important part of the business for them was to surround themselves by people they could trust who believed in the products as much as they did.

Baekgaard and Miller offer the following advice to entrepreneurs:[27]

‣ Concentrate on what you do best.

‣ Don't be satisfied with the status quo—innovate and practice continuous improvement.

‣ Choose the right people to work with: vendors, bankers, and employees.

‣ Networking is important; it's important when people like you and you like them.

‣ Don't be afraid to take risks.

‣ Take one day at a time.

‣ Follow your passion and have fun!

As the Vera Bradley case shows, The Practice of Entrepreneurship does work. Two women from Indiana managed to grow a successful business by using their own resources, initiative, network, and personality, with minimum financial or personal loss at the beginning. They also practiced entrepreneurship until they succeeded in getting a viable business off the ground.

The road to entrepreneurial success involves tough decisions that can continue the entrepreneur's idea to grow or make them rethink the process.

YOU BE THE ENTREPRENEUR

Mary Kay Ash began her first company, Mary Kay Cosmetics, with the help of her husband, who handled the financial and legal matters for their household. However, tragedy struck when her husband suddenly died of a heart attack one month before the company was scheduled to open. Her lawyer and accountant urged her to abandon the plan because she did not have a financial background and did not have the status of a man.

What Would You Do?

Source: Mary Kay Ash. (October 10, 2008). *Entrepreneur Magazine*.

2.5 THE CONCEPT OF DELIBERATE PRACTICE

>> **LO 2.5**   **Assess the role of deliberate practice in achieving mastery.**

In this section, we will explore the word *practice* and why we chose to call entrepreneurship a practice. We are surrounded by heroes in athletics, sports, music, business, science, and entertainment who appear to exhibit astoundingly high levels of performance. How do they do it? How do musicians play complex pieces of music from memory; and how do professional sports players perform seemingly unbelievable acts? And how do entrepreneurs move from being novices to expert serial entrepreneurs? The answer lies in a certain type of practice.

We have all heard the expression "practice makes perfect," but what does this really mean? We often associate practice with repetition and experience; for example, we picture a violinist playing a piece of music for hours every day, or a basketball player shooting hoops for prolonged periods. However, research has shown that people who spend a lot of time simply repeating the same action on a regular basis reach a plateau of capability regardless of how many hours they have put in.[28] A golf enthusiast who spends a couple of days a week playing golf will reach a certain level, but is unlikely to reach professional status solely through this form of practice. Performance does not improve purely on the basis of experience. Similarly, as studies have shown, there is no evidence to suggest that world-class chess champions or professional musicians and sports players owe their success to genes or inheritance. How, then, do people advance from novice level to top performer?

Deliberate practice: a method of carrying out carefully focused efforts to improve current performance.

Researchers have found that it all depends on how you practice. To achieve high levels of performance, high performers engage in **deliberate practice**, which involves carrying out carefully focused efforts to improve current performance.[29] Table 2.5 lists the components of deliberate practice.

While aspects of deliberate practice exist in areas such as sport, chess, and music, it is also present in such diverse areas as typing, economics, and medicine.

TABLE 2.5

Components of Deliberate Practice

- It requires high levels of focus, attention, and concentration.
- It strengthens performance by identifying weakness and improving on them.
- It must be consistent and be maintained for long periods of time.
- It must be repeated to produce lasting results.
- It requires continuous feedback on outcomes.
- It involves setting goals beforehand.
- It involves self-observation and self-reflection after practice sessions are completed.

Credit: Baron, R. A., & Henry, R. A. 2010. How entrepreneurs acquire the capacity to excel: Insights from research on expert performance. *Strategic Entrepreneurship Journal,* 4: 49–65. Reprinted with permission from John Wiley & Sons

One study explored the use of deliberate practice by identifying the study habits of medical students in learning clinical skills. Researchers found that over time, students who used deliberate practice were able to make more proficient use of their time, energy, and resources.[30] In short, they seemed to "learn how to learn."

You might not be conscious of it, but chances are you probably already use some of the elements of deliberate practice. Think of the time you first played a sport or picked up a musical instrument. You may have played the instrument for only 15 minutes a few times a week, or played football for 30 minutes twice a week; but without knowing it, during those short sessions, you were fully focused on what you were doing, intentionally repeating the activity, with a goal of improving your performance.

Deliberate practice can improve performance in many diverse areas, including soccer.
Credit: ©iStockphoto.com/ Wavebreakmedia

Video
Deliberate Practice

What does deliberate practice mean for entrepreneurs? Sustained effort, concentration, and focus have important cognitive benefits such as enhancing perception, memory, intuition, and the way in which we understand our own performance (or metacognition). Expert entrepreneurs who engage in deliberate practice are generally more skilled at perceiving situations, understanding the meaning of complex patterns, and recognizing the differences between relevant and irrelevant information.

Entrepreneurs who engage in deliberate practice are better at storing new information and retrieving it when they need to, which helps them to plan, adapt, and make decisions more quickly in changing situations. Deliberate practice also gives entrepreneurs a better sense of knowing what they know and don't know. Among the most common mistakes entrepreneurs make is getting blindsided by passion in terms of being overly optimistic and confident in their skills and abilities, and underestimating their resources—mistakes that often lead to unnecessary risk and failure.[31] While passion is an important quality to possess, it is best guided by the ability to understand your own capabilities and knowledge.

Finally, expert entrepreneurs who have consistently used deliberate practice over a number of years tend to have a higher sense of intuition, which allows them to make decisions more speedily and accurately based on prior knowledge and experience.

Years of deliberate practice may sound daunting, but you probably already have a head start! The cognitive skills that you developed through deliberate practice (e.g., by playing a musical instrument or sport, creative writing, or anything else that requires strong focus and effort) are all transferrable to entrepreneurship. You have the capability to enhance your skills—and you can demonstrate this by creating your own entrepreneurship portfolio.

Finally, we would like to end with an excerpt from a provocative article in the *Journal of Cell Science* aptly titled "The Importance of Stupidity in Scientific Research":

> *Productive stupidity means being ignorant by choice. Focusing on important questions puts us in the awkward position of being ignorant. One of the beautiful things about* science *is that it allows us to bumble along, getting it wrong time after time, and feel perfectly fine as long as we learn something each time. No doubt, this can be difficult for students who are accustomed to getting the answers right. No doubt, reasonable levels of confidence and emotional resilience help, but I think* scientific *education might do more to ease what is a very big transition: from learning what other people once discovered to making your own discoveries. The more comfortable we become with being stupid, the deeper we will wade into the unknown and the more likely we are to make big discoveries.*[32]

Now, read the above quotation again and replace "science" in sentence 3 and "scientific" in sentence 7 with the word "entrepreneurship." This is what The Practice of Entrepreneurship is all about. ●

$SAGE edge™

Get the edge on your studies at **edge.sagepub.com/neckentrepreneurship**

▸   Master the learning objectives using key study tools
▸   Watch, listen, and connect with online multimedia resources
▸   Access mobile-friendly quizzes and flashcards to check your understanding

---

SUMMARY

2.1   Compare and contrast the prediction and creation approaches to entrepreneurship.

The two main perspectives on entrepreneurship are the predictive logic, the older and more traditional view; and the creation logic, which has been developed through recent advances in the field. Prediction is the opposite of creation. Whereas prediction thinking is used in situations of certainty, the creation view is used when the future is unpredictable.

2.2   Create a portfolio of five skills essential to building a mindset for The Practice of Entrepreneurship.

The five skills of play, empathy, creativity, experimentation, and reflection support the development of different parts of our entrepreneurial selves.

2.3   Distinguish between entrepreneurship as a method and a process.

The method of entrepreneurship outlines the tools and practices necessary to take action. Entrepreneurship as a process, instead, guides would-be creators along a thorough but static path from inception to exit.

2.4 Illustrate the key components of The Practice of Entrepreneurship.

The Practice of Entrepreneurship is designed so entrepreneurs can embrace and confront uncertainty rather than avoid it. The eight components include the following: identify your desired impact on the world; start with means at hand; describe the idea today; calculate affordable loss; take small action; network and enroll others in your journey; build on what you learn; and reflect and be honest with yourself.

2.5 Assess the role of deliberate practice in achieving mastery.

Practice doesn't make perfect; rather, deliberate practice makes perfect. Starting with specific goals, deliberate practice involves consistent, targeted efforts for improvement. Feedback and self-reflection are necessary for meaningful improvement, and repetition is required to achieve lasting results.

KEY TERMS

Creation logic 37
Deliberate practice 56
Predictive logic 37
Skill of creativity 44

Skill of empathy 44
Skill of
   experimentation 43
Skill of play 43

Skill of reflection 44
Theory of
   Effectuation 41

CASE STUDY

Dr. Jordan Jensen: Writer, Speaker, and Entrepreneur

In Chapter One, we detailed the story of Dawn LaFreeda, a highly successful franchisee entrepreneur. LaFreeda is an outstanding example of an entrepreneur in the business world who has earned enormous professional success and considerable personal wealth. But are owning a company, starting a new business, and being good at sales and marketing automatic prerequisites to successful entrepreneurship?

This chapter's Case Study highlights the story of Dr. Jordan Jensen, a writer, speaker, and former high school English teacher, whose entrepreneurial spirit burns brightly, yet hasn't always aligned with stereotypical portraits and patterns of entrepreneurship.

As a teenager, Jensen came to erroneously believe that entrepreneurial success was fundamentally commensurate with success in sales and marketing. With this one-dimensional belief in mind, Jensen's entrepreneurial spirit led him to pursue several positions in sales, all of which ended in failure and disappointment. As he passed through these disillusioning experiences, he often wondered how he could ever expect to be a successful entrepreneur when he loathed sales, and got such poor results therein.

Along the pathways of his sour experiences in salesmanship, Jensen worked hard to refine and polish his ability to write and speak publicly—two activities he found incredibly fulfilling, and that he enjoyed a million times more than sales. As a high school student, he followed his entrepreneurial heart by answering an advertisement to write for a local, weekly newspaper, where hundreds of his news articles and scores of his news photographs were eventually published.

Later, after earning a bachelor's degree in English, Jensen wrote his first book and developed his first professional seminars based on his book. Still harboring the notion that entrepreneurial success was primarily contingent on his will to "pound the pavement" and "hit the phones," Jensen incorporated his business and began throwing his heart and time into willing himself to do what he hated doing: selling and marketing his seminars. His efforts included mass mailings via email and snail mail and long road trips to make personal contacts with potential clients. In doing so, he maxed out his credit cards and incurred $70,000 of personal debt, nearly leading him to declare bankruptcy. In desperation, Jensen hit a low point in his life where he had to rely on food and housing assistance from his cousins and church for a short period of time while he got back on his feet. He took a variety of low-paying, odd jobs (including several manual labor positions) in an effort to physically survive and continue to grow his business.

While he did not generate enough business for his own seminars to take off, he gained a lot of experience, and developed sufficient polish as a presenter to land a position as a professional facilitator with a seminar company. He was 28 years old and, for the first time in his life, he was finally earning consistent, professional wages.

Over time, Jensen came to realize and accept the fact that he was never destined to be a top salesman or marketing genius. By relying instead on his greatest personal assets—his capacity to teach, write, and speak, he was able to develop a strong reputation as a public speaker and professional writer.

These highly refined skills empowered Jensen to continue to nurture his entrepreneurial spirit without putting undue pressure on himself to engage in skillsets he neither enjoys nor is particularly good at. His entrepreneurial spirit prompted him to accept each opportunity that came his way—even, and especially, when it was difficult. Over time, one opportunity led to another, and each new success bred other successes.

Since becoming a professional speaker in 2005, Jensen has worked with nearly 20,000 people in almost 600 audiences in 44 US states in addition to the District of Columbia, Puerto Rico, and the U.S. Virgin Islands; five Canadian provinces, and many locations in the UK. He has also conducted training for all five branches of the US military services; as well as small, medium, and large corporations. His customer satisfaction ratings are stellar, and his superior professional reputation for consistency, dependability, and integrity have compensated for his average sales numbers. As a result, he is continually in demand as a professional speaker.

It took years to get out of debt, but gradually Jensen was able to start building a nest egg for the future. He also applied his entrepreneurial spirit to dating and romance when he was able to convince a beautiful, talented, well-educated, and highly intelligent woman—a mechanical engineer who works for a Fortune 100 Company—to marry him. This union, aside from producing a beautiful son and enormous joy and fulfillment, enabled Jensen to overcome financial challenges and continue to build his business one wise step at a time, recognizing that it would still take many years to realize his ultimate entrepreneurial vision. In the meantime, Jensen took enormous satisfaction in smaller successes that came gradually as he remained committed to the spirit of entrepreneurship.

Jensen continued to think, act, and work like an entrepreneur by taking advantage of every good opportunity to further exercise his talents and experience as a writer and speaker. One of these opportunities included the authorship of this and other case studies you are reading about in this book, an opportunity that comes with a byline and modestly handsome financial remuneration.

Unlike many successful entrepreneurs highlighted in the media, Jensen is not a salesman or tech genius. Nor is he fabulously rich like Dawn LaFreeda. But perhaps someday he will be. Either way, Jensen is grateful to have learned that entrepreneurialism can take a lot of different forms; there is not just one way to be an entrepreneur. This realization has helped him to enjoy the process of entrepreneurship instead of trying to force "square pegs into round holes" by pursuing a career that wasn't right for him.

Jensen's advice, therefore, is not to try and re-create the journeys of other entrepreneurs. Instead, he encourages everyone—no matter what your strengths and interests may be, and regardless whether you see yourself as an entrepreneur or not—to nurture the seeds of entrepreneurialism within yourself by simply working hard, planning for the future, honing your innate talents and skills, looking for and taking advantage of every good opportunity, and perhaps most importantly, listening to your heart and conscience along the pathways of your own, unique life's journey.

Jensen loves entrepreneurship and celebrates the fact that he doesn't have to be a sales champion to be a true entrepreneur. Like many entrepreneurs, Jensen is the CEO of his own company, but he understands that realizing his long-term goals will require surrounding himself with other entrepreneurially minded men and women with expertise and skill in those areas (i.e., sales and marketing) that will complement his own unique strengths. Sales and marketing expert or not, you can bet Jensen will continue to practice entrepreneurship personally and professionally throughout his life.

Critical Thinking Questions

1. What are some ways in which you have already applied an entrepreneurial spirit to personal or professional activities you have undertaken in the past (whether or not earning money was involved)?

2. What professional activities do you find most engaging and rewarding?

3. What are some preliminary steps you could start taking to apply an entrepreneurial spirit to these activities?

4. Jordan Jensen took advantage of opportunities in his life. Can you think of an opportunity in the past year or so that you chose to pass up? Was passing up this opportunity a wise decision? Why or why not?

5. What opportunities are presently available to you that taking advantage of might bolster additional entrepreneurial opportunities in the future?

Sources

Jensen, J. R. (2015). *Self-Action leadership: The key to personal & professional freedom: A comprehensive personal leadership training resource for governments, businesses, schools, homes, & individuals.* Bloomington, IN: authorHouse.

Jensen, J. R. (2013). *Self-Action leadership: An autoethnographic analysis of self-leadership through action research in support of a pedagogy of personal leadership* (Doctoral dissertation, Fielding Graduate University).

3 Developing an Entrepreneurial Mindset

I stand upon my desk to remind myself that we must constantly look at things in a different way."

—John Keating, lead character in the 1989 film *Dead Poets Society* (played by actor Robin Williams).

Learning Objectives

Chapter Outline

3.1 THE POWER OF MINDSET

>> LO 3.1 Appraise the effectiveness of mindset in entrepreneurship.

In Chapter 2, we learned about The Practice of Entrepreneurship. Part of the practice is being in the right mindset to start and grow a business. In this chapter's *Entrepreneurship in Action* feature, we describe how Robert Donat combined his knowledge from working in two diverse areas—the Army and hedge funds—to create a new hardware/software fleet tracking solution. Donat states that he owes his success to his previous work experience, and the technical and business knowledge he gained during that time.

Of course, knowledge is extremely important, but what made Donat take that knowledge and apply it so successfully to the GPS world? What motivated him to start his own business? We could say that Donat had the right mindset to start a business. He wasn't quite sure what he wanted to do, but he had an open mind, which made him curious about potential opportunities in the tracking solution industry. Thanks to experience, he had the confidence to take action by knocking on doors and gaining support for this idea. He also believed enough to persist with his idea, even in the face of high financial risk. It was Donat's mindset that kept him on the right track and ultimately led to GPS Insight's success.

Video
Mindset

Robert Donat, Founder and CEO, GPS Insight

Robert Donat, founder & CEO of GPS Insight
Credit: Used with permission from Robert Donat

Robert Donat stumbled onto his "big idea" somewhat unexpectedly. Following a stint in the Army and a long career in hedge funds, he was looking for a new job after his family relocated to Scottsdale, Arizona. A friend made an introduction, and soon Donat was applying the skills he'd learned as an artillery officer to help a local trucking business find the ideal fleet tracking product. After looking at five systems that were on the market at the time, he decided he could do it better.

Just ten years after that fortuitous 2004 decision, the hardware/software fleet tracking solution that Donat built from that one-time gig is a leader in its space. The company, GPS Insight, has placed on *Inc. Magazine's* "5,000" list of the fastest growing companies in America every year since 2009, and has been showered with awards including the TechAmerica Terman, the Deloitte Fast 500, and the Global 100. By 2014 GPS Insight was not only completely debt free, but also on track to achieve $100 million in cumulative revenue.

Yet the road hasn't been easy, and Donat still considers his venture a startup. "Every sale has to be earned from knocking on a (virtual) door or meeting at a conference, and our sales cycle ranges from 90 days (typical) to two years," he says. It took some creativity (and serious faith in the idea) to build out and pay for the infrastructure he needed. He sold a company he was part owner of, took out $150,000 in bank loans, and secured an additional $200,000 from an outside investor. The company did not become profitable until it had approached $2 million in cumulative losses. Donat explains, "We were creative about doing the most with as little as possible, and entered many obscenely expensive (18%–22%) leases

purchasing computer hardware since it was the only way to get money. We even leased three copiers at double their cost over five years in order to get a $30,000 'rebate' up front, which helped us make payroll in year three."

Yet within 18 months of becoming profitable, the company was able to pay back the money borrowed, and then some. "There was no formal business plan," Donat adds. "I just saw the potential for growth and knew that if I threw resources at the company's growth, it would pay off, given the high return on investment to customers and the recurring revenue model, which ultimately became very lucrative."

Robert Donat holds a bachelor's degree in finance, plus two master's degrees: one in finance and one in computer science. For the Army, he went through officer's school—twice. He honed his real-world business skills working for companies like the Citadel Investment Group LLC as manager of database technology. Cumulatively, he believes his robust resume and knowledge base have been key résumé success. To budding entrepreneurs, his advice is: "Wait until you have some solid skills and experience in paid positions for others before thinking you can do something on your own with a high likelihood of success. I learned a number of very costly technical *and* business lessons when working for other companies either as an employee or a contractor. Only after roughly six years of experience did I start consulting, and after four years of consulting, I was ready to start my own company. Any earlier than that and I wouldn't have had the experience, maturity, business and technical knowledge, or savings, to make this company work."

CRITICAL THINKING QUESTIONS

1. **In what ways do you see mindset, or mental attitude, playing a role in Robert Donat's success?**

2. **If you had been at the helm of GPS Insight when it was approaching $2 million in cumulative losses, would you have decided to continue in business? What information would you have needed to know in order to decide one way or the other?**

3. **Do you agree that a budding entrepreneur should wait and accumulate experience working for others before starting an entrepreneurial venture? Why or why not?** ●

Source: R. Donat, personal interview, October 5, 2014.

FIGURE 3.1

Rise and Shine

Athletes use a motivational mindset to achieve goals on the field.
Credit: "TCU Baseball 2012 - The Grind." Transcript and screenshot from a YouTube video. Red Productions, 2012. https://www.youtube.com/watch?v=MNL_DAI19_I

Master the content
**edge.sagepub.com/
neckentrepreneurship**

It's six am and your hand can't make it to the alarm clock fast enough before the voices in your head start telling you that it's too early, too cold, and too dark to get out of bed. Aching muscles lie still in rebellion pretending not to hear your brain commanding them to move. A legion of voices are shouting their permission for you to hit the snooze button and go back to dream land. But you didn't ask their opinion. The one voice you're listening to is a voice of defiance. The voice that says there's a reason you set that alarm in the first place. So sit up, put your feet on the floor and don't look back, because we've got work to do. Welcome to the grind.

For what's each day but a series of conflicts between what is the right way and the easy way. Ten thousand streams fan out like a river delta before you, each promising a path of least resistance. Thing is, you're headed upstream, and when you make that choice and decide to turn your back on what is comfortable and safe and what some would call common sense, well that's day one. From there it only gets tougher. So make sure this is something you want, because the easy way will always be there. Ready to wash you away. All you have to do is pick up your feet.

But you aren't going to, are you? With each step comes the decision to take another. You're on your way now, but this is no time to dwell on how far you've come. You're in a fight with an opponent you can't see, oh, but you can feel him on your heels can't you, feel him breathing down your neck. You know what that is, that's you, your fears, your doubts, your insecurities—all lined up like a firing squad ready to shoot you out of the sky. But don't lose heart, because while they're not easily defeated they are far

from invincible. Remember this is the grind, the battle royale between you and your mind, your body and the devil on your shoulder telling you this is a game, this is a waste of time, your opponents are stronger than you. Drown out the voices of uncertainty with the sound of your own heartbeat. Burn away your self-doubt with a fire lit beneath you. Remember what we're fighting for and never forget that momentum is a cruel mistress. She can turn on a dime with the smallest mistake. And she is ever searching for the weakness in your armor, that one tiny thing you forgot to prepare for. So as long as the devil is in the details, the question remains: is that all you got? Are you sure?

When the answer is yes and you've done all you can to prepare yourself for battle, then it's time to go forth and boldly face your enemy—the enemy within.

Only now you must take that fight in the open, into hostile territory. You're a lion in a field of lions all facing the same elusive prey, with a desperate starvation that says victory is the only thing that can keep you alive. So believe that voice that says you can, you can run a little faster, you can throw a little harder, and for you the laws of physics are merely a suggestion.

Luck is the last dying wish of those who believe winning can happen by accident; sweat is for those who know it's a choice. So decide now, because destiny waits for no man. So when your time comes and a thousand different voices are trying to tell you you're not ready for it, listen to that one lone voice of dissent that says you are ready, you are prepared, it's all up to you now.

So rise and shine.

3.2 WHAT IS MINDSET?

>> LO 3.2 **Define "mindset" and explain its importance to entrepreneurs.**

We have been using the term *mindset* since Chapter 1, so perhaps it is time we stopped to examine what it actually means. It has traditionally been defined as "the established set of attitudes held by someone."[1] The words to "Rise and Shine" in Figure 3.1 have been transcribed from an athletic and running motivation video on YouTube. It is a good description of how our mindset operates. When we wake up in the morning, we have a choice between the "easy" way and the "right" way. Depending on our mindset, we will choose one path or the other. Research has shown that our mindset needn't be "set" at all. Stanford University psychologist Carol Dweck proposes that there are two different types of mindset: a fixed mindset and a growth mindset (see Figure 3.2).[2]

In a **fixed mindset**, people perceive their talents and abilities as set traits. They believe that brains and talent alone are enough for success and go through life with the goal of looking smart all the time. They take any constructive criticism of their capabilities very personally, and tend to attribute others' success to luck (see *Research at Work*, for a study about luck) or some sort of unfair advantage. People with a fixed mindset will tell themselves they are no good at something to avoid challenge, failure, or looking dumb.

On the other hand, in a **growth mindset**, people believe that their abilities can be developed through dedication, effort, and hard work. They think brains and talent are not the key to lifelong success, but merely the starting point. People with a growth mindset are eager to enhance their qualities through lifelong learning, training, and practice. Unlike people with fixed mindsets, they see failure as an opportunity to improve their performance, and to learn from their mistakes. Despite setbacks, they tend to persevere rather than giving up.

Recent studies have found that overly praising or being praised simply for our intelligence can create a fixed mindset. For example, using a series of puzzle tests,

Fixed mindset: the assumption held by people who perceive their talents and abilities as set traits.

Growth mindset: the assumption held by people who believe that their abilities can be developed through dedication, effort, and hard work.

Video
Growth Mindset

FIGURE 3.2

What Kind of Mindset Do You Have?

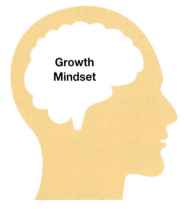

Growth Mindset

I can learn anything I want to.
When I'm frustrated, I persevere.
I want to challenge myself.
When I fail, I learn.
Tell me I try hard.
If you succeed, I'm inspired.
My effort and attitude determine everything.

Fixed Mindset

I'm either good at it, or I'm not.
When I'm frustrated, I give up.
I don't like to be challenged.
When I fail, I'm no good.
Tell me I'm smart.
If you succeed, I feel threatened.
My abilities determine everything.

Source: Created by Reid Wilson @wayfaringpath. Icon from thenounproject.com. Retrieved from http://www.coetail.com/wayfaring path/2014/12/02/growth-vs-fixed-mindset-for-elementary-students/

Study on Luck[3]

In the early 1990s, British psychologist and researcher Richard Wiseman carried out an experiment on luck to determine what defines a lucky or unlucky person. Over several years, using advertisements in newspapers and magazines, Wiseman sought out people who felt consistently lucky or unlucky. He interviewed them and identified 400 volunteers whom he asked to participate in the following experiment.

The 400 participants were divided into two groups: those who considered themselves lucky, and those who considered themselves unlucky. Both groups were given a newspaper and asked to count how many photographs in contained.

In took approximately 2 minutes, on average, for the unlucky people to count all the photos, but it only took a few seconds for the lucky people. Why? Because the lucky people had spotted a large message occupying more than half of the newspaper's second page that stated: "Stop counting. There are 43 photographs in this newspaper." The unlucky people had missed this chance opportunity because they were too focused what they thought they were *supposed* to look for.

Wiseman concluded that unlucky people tend to miss opportunities because they are too focused on something else; whereas lucky people tend to be more open to recognizing chance opportunities.

Wiseman's overall findings have revealed that "although unlucky people have almost no insight into the real causes of their good and bad luck, their thoughts and behaviors are responsible for much of their fortune" (or misfortune).

CRITICAL THINKING QUESTIONS

1. **Identify a successful entrepreneur. Do you believe luck played a role in their success? Why or why not?**

2. **Do you consider yourself a particularly lucky or unlucky person? Or do you fall somewhere in the middle? Give some reasons to support your answer.**

3. **Can you think of a chance opportunity that came your way because you were open to it? How might you make yourself more open to "lucky" opportunities in the future?**

Sources
Wiseman, R. (2003, January 9). Be lucky - it's an easy skill to learn. *The Telegraph*. Retrieved from http—//www.telegraph.co.uk/technology/3304496/Be-lucky-its-an-easy-skill-to-learn.html
Wiseman, R. (2003). *The luck factor: The four essential principles*. New York, NY: Hyperion.

Dweck discovered that 5th-grade children who were praised for their hard work and effort on the first test were far more likely to choose the more difficult puzzle next time round. In contrast, children who were praised for being smart or intelligent after the first test chose the easy test the second time around.

It seems that the children who had been praised for being smart wanted to keep their reputation for being smart and tended to avoid any challenge that would jeopardize this belief. Yet the children who had been praised for how hard they had worked on the first test and practice had more confidence in their abilities to tackle a more challenging test, and to learn from whatever mistakes they might make.[4]

Dweck observes the growth mindset in successful athletes, business people, writers, musicians; in fact, anyone who commits to a goal and puts in the hard work and practice to attain it. She believes that people with growth mindsets tend to be more successful and happier than those with fixed mindsets.

Although many of us tend to exhibit one mindset or the other, it is important to recognize that mindsets can be changed. Even if your mindset is a fixed one, it is possible to learn a growth mindset and thereby boost your chances for happiness and success. How can you do this? By becoming aware of that "voice" in your head that questions your ability to take on a new challenge, by recognizing that you have a choice in how you interpret what that voice is telling you, by responding to that voice, and by taking action.

For example, say you want to start a new business, but you're a little unsure of your accounting skills. Following are some messages you might hear from the "voice" in your head and some responses you might make based on a growth mindset.

FIXED MINDSET: *"Why do you want to start up a business? You need accounting skills. You were always terrible at math at school. Are you sure you can do it?"*[5]

GROWTH MINDSET: **"I might not be any good at accounting at first, but I think I can learn to be good at it if I commit to it and put in the time and effort."**

FIXED MINDSET: *"If you fail, people will laugh at you."*

GROWTH MINDSET: **"Give me the name of one successful person who never experienced failure at one time or another."**

FIXED MINDSET: *"Do yourself a favor; forget the idea and hang on to your dignity."*

GROWTH MINDSET: **"If I don't try, I'll fail anyway. Where's the dignity in that?"**

Next, suppose that you enroll in accounting course, but you score very low marks on your first exam. Once again, you're likely to hear messages from the "voice" in your head and respond to them as follows.

FIXED MINDSET: *"Dude! This wouldn't have happened if you were actually good at accounting in the first place. Time to throw in the towel."*

GROWTH MINDSET: **"Not so fast. Look at Richard Branson and Sean Parker—they suffered lots of setback along the way, yet they still persevered."**

Now suppose that a friend who hears about your low exam score makes a joke about your performance.

FIXED MINDSET: *"Why am I being criticized for doing badly in the accounting exam? It's not my fault. I'm just not cut out for accounting, that's all."*

GROWTH MINDSET: **"I can own this setback and learn from it. I need to do more practicing, and next time, I will do better."**

If you listen to the fixed mindset voice, the chances are you will never persevere with the accounting process. If you pay attention to the growth mindset voice instead, the likelihood is that you will pick yourself up, dust yourself off, start practicing again, and put the effort in before the next exam.

Over time, the voice you listen to most becomes your choice. The decisions you make are now in your hands. By practicing listening and responding to each of these voices, you can build your willingness to take on new challenges, learn from your mistakes, accept criticism, and take action.

As we have explored, our mindset is not dependent on luck, nor is it fixed: we each have the capability to adjust our mindset to recognize and seize opportunities, and take action even under the most unlikely or uncertain circumstances, as long as we work hard and practice. This is why the mindset is essential to entrepreneurship.

The Mindset for Entrepreneurship

Entrepreneurial mindset: the ability to quickly sense, take action, and get organized under uncertain conditions.

The growth mindset is essential to a mindset for entrepreneurship. In Chapter 2, we discussed The Practice of Entrepreneurship and how it requires a specific mindset so that entrepreneurs have the ability to alter their ways of thinking in order to see the endless possibilities in the world. While there is no one clear definition of mindset and how it relates to entrepreneurs, we believe the most accurate meaning of an **entrepreneurial mindset** is the ability to quickly sense, take action, and get organized under uncertain conditions.[6] This also includes the ability to persevere, accept and learn from failure, and get comfortable with a certain level of discomfort!

Many successful entrepreneurs appear to be very smart—but rather than being born with high intelligence, it is often the way they use their intelligence that counts. Cognitive strategies are the ways in which people solve problems such as reasoning, analyzing, experimenting, and so forth. The entrepreneurial mindset involves employing numerous cognitive strategies to identify opportunities, consider alternative options, and take action. Because working in uncertain environments "goes with the territory" in entrepreneurship, the entrepreneurial mindset requires constant thinking and rethinking, adaptability, and self-regulation—the capacity to control our emotions and impulses.

In Chapter 2 we touched on the concept of metacognition, which is the way in which we understand our own performance or the process of "thinking about thinking" (see Figure 3.3). For example, say you are reading through a complex legal document; you might notice that you don't understand some of it. You might go back and re-read it, pause

Video
An Entrepreneurial Mindset

FIGURE 3.3

Metacognition

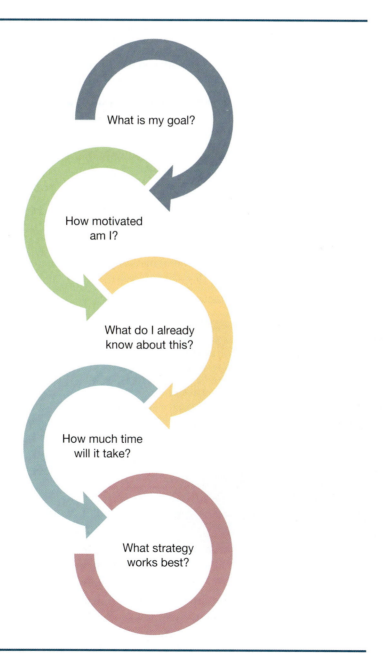

What is my goal?

How motivated am I?

What do I already know about this?

How much time will it take?

What strategy works best?

What Does Your Mindset Say About You?

Visit a place that you are unfamiliar with. It can be a park, somewhere on campus you haven't explored, a neighborhood, a new restaurant—really just about anywhere, provided you are not already familiar with the place. Bring with you a paper notepad and pen. Yes, real paper!.

For 10 minutes, just look around and write down a description of what you observe. Make sure that when you write your observations, you use adjectives to describe what you see. For example, you may see a swing set in a park, but you need to describe that swing set. The swing set may be rusty, shiny, empty, broken, vibrant, or dull. A dog you see in the park may be big, cute, dirty, ugly, friendly, or hostile.

You must record your notes in writing, and you must observe for 10 minutes.

After you've finished, sit down and look at the list of words you've written. Circle all words that have a positive connotation. Using the park example above, you would circle shiny, vibrant, cute, and friendly. Now place a square around all words that have a negative connotation. In our park example, this could be rusty, broken, dull, dirty, ugly, and hostile.

What's the point of all of this? Oftentimes what you see on the outside is a reflection of your mindset on the inside. If what you see in the world is predominantly negative, then your mindset for entrepreneurship needs to be further developed. If what you see in the world is more positive, it will be much easier for you to identify opportunities and make a difference.

CRITICAL THINKING QUESTIONS

1. **In what ways did this 10-minute observation exercise confirm your existing assumptions and beliefs about your way of looking at the world? In what ways did it change them?**

2. **Did you learn anything about yourself that was unexpected or surprising?**

3. **What do you think would happen if you repeated this exercise in a different location?**

to think it through, note the elements that don't make sense to you, and then either come back to it later or find a way to clarify the parts you don't understand. In this example, you are using your metacognitive skills to monitor your own understanding of the text, rather than simply plowing through the document without having much comprehension at all.

Entrepreneurs regularly engage in metacognitive processes to adapt to changing circumstances by thinking about alternative routes to take and choosing one or more strategies based on these options. Metacognitive awareness is part of the mindset, and it is not something that we are born with. It can be developed over time through continuous practice.

Passion and Entrepreneurship

Among many elements of the entrepreneurial mindset, one of the most talked about is the element of passion. The entrepreneurial mindset is about understanding yourself, who you are, and how you view the world. It deeply connects to your *desired impact* (described in Chapter 2), which some people equate to passion. In the past, researchers tended to use passion as a reason to explain certain behaviors displayed by entrepreneurs that were thought to be

Pierre Omidyar, founder of eBay.
Credit: Bloomberg/Bloomberg/Getty Images

unconventional, such as perceived high risk taking, intense focus and commitment, and a dogged determination to fulfill a dream.[7] Indeed, many well-known entrepreneurs such as Mark Zuckerberg (Facebook founder), Jeff Bezos (Amazon founder) and Pierre Omidyar (eBay founder) credit passion for their success.[8]

But what is passion, and is it really that important to entrepreneurial success? In the context of entrepreneurship, **passion** can be defined as an intense positive emotion, which is usually related to entrepreneurs who are engaged in meaningful ventures, or tasks and activities, and which has the effect of motivating and stimulating entrepreneurs to overcome obstacles and remain focused on their goals.[9] This type of passion is aroused by the pleasure of engaging in activities we enjoy. Studies have found that passion can also "enhance mental activity and provide meaning to everyday work,"[10] as well as fostering "creativity and recognition of new patterns that are critical in opportunity exploration and exploitation in uncertain and risky environments."[11]

Passion has also been associated with a wide range of positive effects, such as strength and courage, motivation, energy, drive, tenacity, strong initiative, resilience, love, pride, pleasure, enthusiasm, and joy—all of which can occur as part of the entrepreneurship process.

While passion is not all that is needed to be successful, research has shown that positive feelings motivate entrepreneurs to persist and engage in tasks and activities in order to maintain those pleasurable emotions.[12]

However, there can also be a dysfunctional side to passion. As we explored in Chapter 2, it is possible to become blinded by passion and so obsessed by an idea or new venture that we fail to heed the warning signs or refuse to listen to negative information or feedback. This type of negative passion can actually curb business growth and limit the ability to creatively solve problems.

Entrepreneurship as a Habit

So far, we have discussed the meaning of mindset, the different types, and the importance of passion and positive thinking for success. As we have learned, mindset is not a predisposed condition; any one of us can develop **a more entrepreneurial** mindset, but how do we do it?

A good approach is to consider developing new habits. A **habit** is a sometimes unconscious pattern of behavior that is carried out often and regularly. Good habits can be learned through a "habit loop"—a process by which our brain decides whether or not a certain behavior should be stored and repeated. If we feel rewarded for our behavior, then we are more likely to continue doing it. For example, toothpaste companies instigate a habit loop in consumers by not just advertising the hygiene benefits of brushing teeth, but also the "tingling, clean feeling" we get afterwards—the reward. People are more likely to get into a toothbrushing habit loop as a result.[13]

In the sections that follow, we present three habits that need to be cultivated for an entrepreneurial mindset: self-leadership, creativity, and improvisation. As with all good habits, they require practice.

3.3 THE SELF-LEADERSHIP HABIT[14]

>> **LO 3.3** Explain how to develop the habit of self-leadership.

In the context of entrepreneurship, **self-leadership** is a process whereby people can influence and control their own behavior, actions, and thinking to achieve the self-direction and self-motivation necessary to build their entrepreneurial business ventures. Entrepreneurship requires a deep understanding of self and an ability to

Passion: an intense positive emotion, which is usually related to entrepreneurs who are engaged in meaningful ventures, or tasks and activities, and which has the effect of motivating and stimulating entrepreneurs to overcome obstacles and remain focused on their goals.

Habit: a sometimes unconscious pattern of behavior that is carried out often and regularly.

Consumers are more likely to get into a "habit loop" of tooth-brushing when the reward (the "tingling, clean feeling") is advertised.
Credit: ©iStockphoto.com/merznatalia

Video
Self-Leadership

Self-leadership: a process whereby people can influence and control their own behavior, actions, and thinking to achieve the self-direction and self-motivation necessary to build their entrepreneurial business ventures.

FIGURE 3.4

Elements of Self-Leadership

Behavior focused strategies: methods to increase self-awareness and manage behaviors particularly when dealing with necessary but unpleasant tasks. These strategies include: self-observation, self-goal setting, self-reward, self-punishment, and self-cueing.

Self-observation: a process that raises our awareness of how, when, and why we behave the way we do in certain circumstances.

Self-goal setting: the process of setting individual goals for ourselves.

Self-reward: a process that involves compensating ourselves when we achieve our goals. These rewards can be tangible or intangible.

Self-punishment (or self-correcting feedback): a process that allows us to examine our own behaviors in a constructive way in order to reshape these behaviors.

motivate oneself to act. You cannot rely on someone else to manage you, get you up in the morning, or force you to get the work done. It can be lonely, and oftentimes no one is around to give you feedback, reprimand you, or reward you! As a result, self-leadership is required. It consists of three main strategies: behavior-focused strategies; natural reward strategies; and constructive thought pattern strategies.

Behavior-focused strategies help increase self-awareness to manage behaviors particularly when dealing with necessary but unpleasant tasks. These strategies include self-observation, self-goal setting, self-reward, self-punishment, and self-cueing (see Figure 3.4).

Self-observation raises our awareness of how, when, and why we behave the way we do in certain circumstances. For example, twice a day, you could stop and deliberately ask yourself questions about what you are accomplishing; what you are not accomplishing; what is standing in your way; and how you feel about what is happening. This is the first step toward addressing unhelpful or unproductive behaviors in order to devise ways of altering them to enhance performance.

There has been much study regarding the importance of setting goals as a means of enhancing performance. **Self-goal setting** is the process of setting individual goals for ourselves. This is especially effective when it is accompanied by **self-reward**—ways in which we compensate ourselves when we achieve our goals. These rewards can be tangible or intangible; for example, you might mentally congratulate yourself when you have achieved your goal (intangible); or you might go out for a celebratory meal or buy yourself a new pair of shoes (tangible) (see Figure 3.5). Setting rewards is a powerful way of motivating us to accomplish our goals.

Ideally, **self-punishment** or **self-correcting feedback** is a process that allows us to examine our own behaviors in a constructive way in order to reshape these behaviors. For example, if we make a mistake, we can assess why it happened and make a conscious effort not to repeat it. However, many of us have the tendency to beat ourselves up over perceived mistakes or failures; indeed, excessive self-punishment involving guilt and self-criticism can be very harmful to our performance.

Finally, we can use certain environmental cues as a way to lists or notes or constructive behaviors and reduce or eliminate destructive ones through the process of **self-cueing.** These cues might take the form of making lists, notes, or having motivational posters on your wall. They act as a reminder of your desired goals, and keep your attention on what you are trying to achieve.

Sometimes we need messages to help us to stay focused on our goals.
Credit: ©iStockphoto.com/mgkaya

Rewarding ourselves is a beneficial way to boost our spirits and keep us committed to attaining our goals. **Natural reward strategies** endeavor to make aspects of a task or activity more enjoyable by building in certain features, or by reshaping perceptions to focus on the most positive aspects of the task and the value it holds. For example, if you are working on a particularly difficult or boring task, you could build in a break to listen to some music or take a short walk outside. In addition, rather than dreading the nature of the work, you could refocus on the benefits of what you are doing and how good it will feel when it is done.

Much of our behavior is influenced by the way we think, and the habit of thinking in a certain way is derived from our assumptions and beliefs. **Constructive thought patterns** help us to form positive and productive ways of thinking that can benefit our performance. Constructive thought pattern strategies include identifying destructive beliefs and assumptions and reframing those thoughts through practicing self-talk and mental imagery.

Self-cueing: the process of prompting that acts as a reminder of desired goals, and keeps your attention on what you are trying to achieve.

As we observed earlier in this chapter, we can use positive self-talk to change our mindset and thought patterns by engaging in dialogue with that irrational voice in our heads that tells us when we can't do something. Similarly, we can engage in mental imagery to imagine ourselves performing a certain task or activity. In fact, studies show that people who visualize themselves successfully performing an activity before it actually takes place are more likely to be successful at performing the task in reality.[15]

Employees at Facebook are encouraged to take breaks and play games in the office.
Credit: Kim Kulish/Corbis News/ Getty Images

These behavioral self-leadership strategies are designed to bring about successful outcomes through positive behaviors, and suppress or eliminate those negative behaviors that lead to bad consequences. The concept of self-leadership has been related to

Natural reward strategies: types of compensation designed to make aspects of a task or activity more enjoyable by building in certain features, or by reshaping perceptions to focus on the most positive aspects of the task and the value it holds.

Constructive thought patterns: models to help us to form positive and productive ways of thinking that can benefit our performance.

many other areas such as optimism, happiness, consciousness, emotional intelligence, among others. We believe self-leadership to be an essential process for helping entrepreneurs build and grow their business ventures.

3.4 THE CREATIVITY HABIT

>> LO 3.4   Explain how to develop the habit of creativity.

Creativity is a difficult concept to define, mainly because it covers such a wide breadth of processes and people—from artists, to writers, to inventors, to entrepreneurs—all of whom could be described as creative. Yet creativity can be elusive, and sometimes we spot it only after it is presented to us. Take the classic inventions, for instance. Sometimes, we look at these inventions and wonder why on earth we hadn't thought of them ourselves. Post-it brand notes, paper clips, zippers, and Velcro—they all seem so obvious after the fact. But of course it is the simplest ideas that can change the world.

Blitab Technology's tablet computer for Braille users

Credit: Reprinted with permission from BLITAB Technology. http://www.blitab.com.

Because of its elusiveness, there is no concrete or agreed definition of creativity; however, we like to define **creativity** as the capacity to produce new ideas, insights, inventions, products, or artistic objects that are considered to be unique, useful, and of value to others.[16] For example, Slavi Slavev and Kristina Tsvetanova, cofounders of Austria-based Blitab Technology, have received multiple awards for their creativity in building the world's first tablet for the visually impaired.[17]

Again, creativity is not something we are born with, but a developed skill—creativity is creating in action. Studies have shown that people who are creative are open to experience, persistent, adaptable, original, motivated, self-reliant, and they do not fear failure.

Creativity: the capacity to produce new ideas, insights, inventions, products, or artistic objects that are considered to be unique, useful, and of value to others.

But what has creativity got to do with entrepreneurship? First, there is some evidence that entrepreneurs are more creative than others. A study published in 2008 found that students enrolled in entrepreneurship programs scored higher in personal creativity than students from other programs.[18] This tells us that while everyone has the capacity to be creative, entrepreneurs score higher on creativity simply because they are practicing the creative process more regularly.

We opened this chapter with a quote from the movie *Dead Poets Society*, which was a huge hit in the late 1980s. It is a story about a maverick English teacher named John Keating (played by Robin Williams) who challenges the strict academic structure of Welton, a traditional exclusive all-boys college preparatory school. Mr. Keating urges his students to question the status quo, adjust their mindset, change their behaviors, live life to the fullest and, famously, to seize the day (using the Latin phrase *carpe diem!*). We feel this movie is an excellent example of creativity, and especially relevant to entrepreneurs.

In one memorable scene, student Todd Anderson—a quiet, under-confident, insecure character who is full of self-doubt about his creative abilities—has not written a poem as assigned. Mr. Keating stands him at the front of the class and prods him to yell "Yawp!" like a barbarian would do, pointing to a picture on the wall of the famous poet Walt Whitman.[19]

Video
Gaining Confidence
to Be Creative

As Mr. Keating's character demonstrates in this scene, creativity is something that can be unleashed even in the most reticent person. Many of us can identify with the Todd Anderson character. It is easy for us to become blocked when we are asked to do something creative, especially when we are put on the spot. Yet, in many cases— even though we know that every single one of us has the ability to be creative—like Todd, we still find ourselves stumbling against emotional roadblocks.

Mr Keating (played by Robin Williams) encourages under-confident student Todd Anderson (played by Ethan Hawke) to be creative.
Credit: Collection Christophel / Alamy Stock Photo

The Fear Factor

James L. Adams, a Stanford University professor who specialized in creativity, identified six main emotional roadblocks preventing us from practicing creativity:

- ▶ fear,
- ▶ no appetite for chaos,
- ▶ preference for judging over generating ideas,
- ▶ dislike for incubating ideas,
- ▶ perceived lack of challenge, and
- ▶ inability to distinguish reality from fantasy.[20]

Out of these six emotional roadblocks, it is fear that has the most detrimental effect on our capacity to be creative. The danger of fear is that it can cause self-doubt, insecurity, and discomfort even before the beginning of the creative process. It can also block us from sharing our creativity with others because of the risk of failure, negative feedback, or ridicule.

Video
Challenge and Creativity

Bradley Smith, cofounder and CEO of California-based financial services company Rescue One Financial, suffered huge fear and anxiety when his business started to sink deeper and deeper into debt. Smith states, "I'd wake up at 4 in the morning with my mind racing, thinking about this and that, not being able to shut it off, wondering, when is this thing going to turn?" Less than a year later, much to Smith's relief, the business began to make money.

Similarly, Robert Donat, founder of GPS Insight, knows all about fear and admits being kept up at night by "the fear of the unknown," and what "might harm the company." Yet he manages to find ways of coping with the pressure by participating in challenging hobbies such as scuba diving, snowboarding, and learning to play the guitar. Donat has learned how to manage his fear by recognizing it, and shifting his focus to more enjoyable activities, rather than giving into it (see Entrepreneurship in Action, above at p. 64).

A Creative Mind

The importance of creativity and its necessity in navigating the uncharted waters in an uncertain world is also reflected in our biology. In human anatomy, it has long been known that the brain is divided into two hemispheres. Generally speaking, the left hemisphere controls movement, sensation, and perception on the right side of our body, and the right hemisphere does the same on the left side of our body. This is why an injury to the left side of the brain can result in impairment or paralysis on the right side of the body, and vice versa. In the 1960s, researchers proposed that each of the two hemispheres had its own distinct thinking and emotional functions. This idea was then further expanded to propose "left-brained" and "right-brained" orientations as though they were personality types (see Figure 3.5).

In his book *A Whole New Mind*, business and technology author Daniel Pink uses the right-brain/left-brain model to describe how today's society is moving from left-brain thinking to right-brain thinking.[21] Historically, Pink observes, people have tended to use left-brain thinking over right-brain thinking because most tasks and activities in the agricultural and industrial age demanded these attributes. Those were the times when jobs were more methodical and predictable. Today, many of the methodical tasks have been outsourced or have been taken over by computers. Pink holds that we now live in a "conceptual age" that requires us to use both the left and right sides of the brain to create new opportunities and possibilities—in other words, to succeed in today's world, we need a different way of thinking.

However, it is important to recognize that there has been little scientific support for the model of people being "left-brained" or "right-brained," even as the technology for brain scans had advanced. In a 2012 study, researchers at the University of Utah analyzed brain scans from more than 1,000 people between the ages of 7 and 29. They found no evidence to suggest that one side of the brain was more dominant than the other in any given individual: "[O]ur data are not consistent with a whole-brain phenotype of greater 'left-brained' or greater 'right-brained' network strength across individuals."[22]

FIGURE 3.5

Left Versus Right Brain Orientation

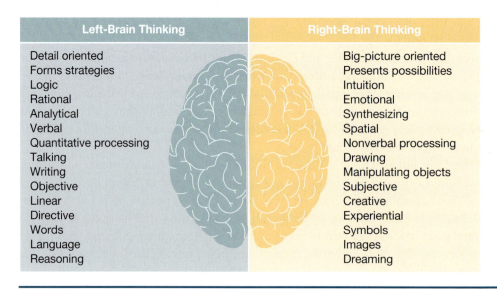

Left-Brain Thinking	Right-Brain Thinking
Detail oriented	Big-picture oriented
Forms strategies	Presents possibilities
Logic	Intuition
Rational	Emotional
Analytical	Synthesizing
Verbal	Spatial
Quantitative processing	Nonverbal processing
Talking	Drawing
Writing	Manipulating objects
Objective	Subjective
Linear	Creative
Directive	Experiential
Words	Symbols
Language	Images
Reasoning	Dreaming

Source: Neck, H. M. (2010). Idea generation. In B. Bygrave & A. Zacharakis (Eds.), *Portable MBA in entrepreneurship* (pp. 2752; Figure on p. 38). Hoboken, NJ: Wiley.

Study researcher Jared Nielsen, a graduate student in neuroscience at the university, concludes, "It may be that personality types have nothing to do with one hemisphere being more active, stronger, or more connected."[23]

Although it may be inaccurate to characterize people as "left-brained" or "right-brained," the idea of two different types of thinking can still be helpful in understanding how to foster creativity. A study carried out by psychology professor Mihaly Csikszentmihalyi between 1990 and 1995 shows an interesting relationship between personality traits and the characteristics commonly associated with left- and right-brain thinking.[24] Csikszentmihalyi and a team of researchers identified 91 people over the age of 60 whom they considered highly creative, or "exceptional," in the fields of science, art, business, and politics. They discovered that although conflicting traits are not commonly found in the same person—for example, a person is typically introverted or extroverted, not both—they were present in many of the study participants. They exhibited seemingly polarized traits like discipline and playfulness, a strong sense of reality and a vivid imagination, and pride and humility (see Table 3.1). Csikszentmihalyi referred to these highly creative individuals as having "dialectic" personalities, and concluded that for people to be creative, they need to operate at both ends of the poles.

If you compare the "polarized" traits in Table 3.1 with the left- and right-brain characteristics in Table 3.1, you will see striking similarities, suggesting that creativity involves using both sides of the brain. In this sense, Csikszentmihalyi's study is consistent with Pink's argument that we are living in a conceptual age that requires us to tap into our creative potential and think with both sides of our brain.

Although successful entrepreneurs definitely do not fit into a single profile, there is some commonality in the mindset of successful entrepreneurs. They envision success while also preparing for failure. They value autonomy in deciding and acting and, therefore, assume responsibility for problems and failures. They have a tendency to be intolerant of authority, exhibit good salesmanship skills, have high self-confidence, and believe strongly in their abilities. They also tend to be both optimistic and pragmatic. They work hard and are driven by an intense commitment to the

TABLE 3.1

Csikszentmihalyi's Polarity of Creative Individuals

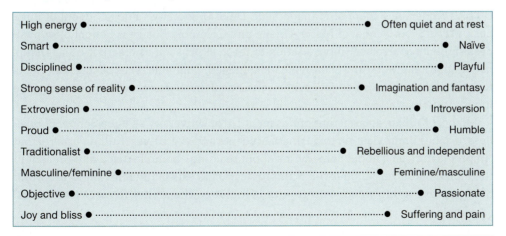

High energy	Often quiet and at rest
Smart	Naïve
Disciplined	Playful
Strong sense of reality	Imagination and fantasy
Extroversion	Introversion
Proud	Humble
Traditionalist	Rebellious and independent
Masculine/feminine	Feminine/masculine
Objective	Passionate
Joy and bliss	Suffering and pain

Credit: Adapted from in H. M. Neck, "Idea generation," In B. Bygrave & A. Zacharakis eds. *Portable MBA in Entrepreneurship* (Hoboken, NJ: John Wiley & Sons, 2010, pp. 27-52; figure on p. 40) and adapted from Mihaly Csikszentmihalyi, *Creativity: Flow and the Psychology of Discovery and Invention* (New York: Harper Collins, 1996).

success of the organization. Here again, we see evidence that an entrepreneurial mind-set requires more than one kind of thinking.

3.5 THE IMPROVISATION HABIT

>> **LO 3.5**   **Explain how to develop the habit of improvisation.**

Improvisation: the art of spontaneously creating something without preparation.

Let's explore the third of the key habits for developing an entrepreneurial mindset: improvisation. **Improvisation** is the art of spontaneously creating something without preparation. Improvisation is connected to the mindset because it helps us develop the cognitive ability to rapidly sense and act as well as change direction quickly.

For many of us, the word "improvisation" evokes images of people standing on stage in front of an audience under pressure to make them laugh or to enter-

Comedic improvisers in action.

Credit: Mark Bialek/ZUMA Press/Newscom

tain them. While it is true that world-famous comedy clubs like Second City in Chicago offer classes in improvisation to aspiring actors—including Tina Fey, Stephen Colbert, and Steve Carrell—improvisational skills can be very useful to entrepreneurs of all types.

The ability to function in an uncertain world requires a degree of improvisation. Entrepreneurs may begin with a certain idea or direction, but obstacles such as limited resources, unforeseen market conditions, or even conflicts with team members can prevent them from executing their initial plans. This means they need to find a way to quickly adapt to their circumstances, think on their feet, and create new plans to realize their vision. A recent study showed that entrepreneurs starting new ventures who displayed more signs of improvisational behavior tended to outperform those who did not have the same tendencies.[25]

Video
Entrepreneurship and Improvisation

There is a long tradition of improvisation techniques applied to the theater and to music styles such as jazz, but improvisation has also been growing in popularity in business and entrepreneurship. For example, many major business schools such as UCLA's Anderson School of Management, Duke University's Fuqua School of Business, MIT's Sloan School of Management, and Columbia Business School offer business students courses on improvisation to teach skills such as creativity, leadership, negotiation, teamwork, and communication. Indeed, Columbia takes business students to a jazz club so they can engage with professional musicians regarding how they use improvisation on stage.[26]

Robert Kulhan, an assistant professor at Duke University's Fuqua School of Business, teaches improvisation to business students and executives. Kulhan asserts that "improvisation isn't about comedy, it's about reacting—being focused and present in the moment at a very high level".[27] Improvisation is especially relevant to the world of entrepreneurship where uncertainty is high and the ability to react is essential (see Table 3.2).

For those of you who may feel a little apprehensive about the idea of engaging in spontaneous creation, it may comfort you to know that anyone can improvise. In fact, you may not realize it, but each one of us has been improvising all our lives.

TABLE 3.2

Improvisation Guidelines

- Improvisation is not just for actors or musicians.
- There's no such thing as being wrong.
- Nothing suggested is questioned or rejected (no matter how crazy it might sound!).
- Ideas are taken on board, expanded, and passed on for further input.
- Everything is important.
- It is a group activity—you will have the support of the group.
- You can trust that the group will solve a certain problem.
- It's about listening closely and accepting what you're given.
- It's about being spontaneous, imaginative, and dealing with the unexpected.

Source: Points taken from Gotts, I., & Cremer, J. (2012). *Using Improv in Business.* Retrieved from http://iangotts.files.wordpress. com/2012/02/using-improv-in-business-e2-v1.pdf

Think about it: how could any one of us be prepared for everything life has to throw at us—from our personal or business lives? Often, we are forced to react and create on the spot in response to certain events. There is simply no way we can prepare for every situation and every conversation before it takes place. We are naturally inclined to deal with the unexpected; now all we have to do is deliberately practice that ability.

However, many of us are apprehensive about sharing our ideas for fear of being shot down. One of the most useful improvisation exercises to address this fear is the "Yes, and" principle. This means listening to what others have to say, and building on it by starting with the words, "Yes, and." Consider the following conversation among three friends.

Peter: "I have a great idea for a healthy dried fruit snack for kids that contains less sugar than any other brand on the market."

Teresa: "Hasn't this been done already? The market is saturated with these kinds of products."

Sami: "I think it's an interesting idea, but I've heard that these products cost a fortune to manufacture and produce."

In this conversation, Peter has barely touched on his idea before it gets shot down by the others. Peter may not be conscious of it, but the reaction from his friends changes his mindset from positive to negative, instantly limiting his freedom to expand the idea further. Rather than offering their assistance, Sami and Teresa rely on judgment and hearsay rather than helping Peter to build on his idea.

Now let's take a look at how the "Yes, and" principle can completely change the tone and output of the conversation.

Peter: "I have a great idea for a healthy dried fruit snack for kids that contains less sugar than any other brand on the market."

Teresa: "*Yes, and* each snack could contain a card with a fun fact or maybe some kind of riddle."

Sami: "*Yes, and* if enough cards are collected, you can go online and win a small prize."

FIGURE 3.6

MRI scans from jazz improvisation

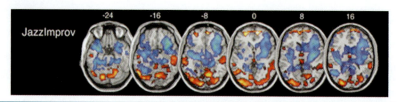

Source: Limb, Charles J. "Neural Substrates of Spontaneous Musical Performance: An fMRI Study of Jazz Improvisation." PLOS One. http://journals.plos.org/plosone/article?id=10.1371/journal.pone.0001679

By using "Yes, and," Peter and his friends have managed to expand on his original idea and inject a bit of positivity into the conversation.

Now that we know anyone can improvise, why don't more of us to do it? Self-doubt is the most common barrier to improvisation: "I don't want to pitch my idea. I hate speaking in public"; "What if I freeze up?" and even worse, "What if I make a fool of myself?" The fear underlying the self-doubt is the fear of failure, which stems from not being able to plan in advance.

Yet people who engage in improvisation are actually more tolerant of failure because it helps us to break free of traditional structured thinking, releases our need for control, opens our minds, improves our listening skills, and builds our confidence by encouraging us to think quickly under pressure. Originally actors were trained in improvisational techniques so they could overcome forgetting their lines on stage during a performance.

Improvisation has a significant effect on our brain activity. Scientists have studied the effects of improvisation on brain activity by asking six trained jazz pianists to volunteer to play a combination of learned and improvised pieces of music while lying in an MRI machine. When it came to analyzing the brain scans, the scientists found that the musicians tended to switch off the self-censoring part of the brain, which gave them the ability to freely express themselves without restriction (see Figure 3.8).[28] In other words, we have a brain that is designed to generate unpredictable ideas when the self-monitoring part is suppressed.[29]

As we have learned, developing an entrepreneurial mindset requires practice in the areas of self-leadership, creativity, and improvisation. However, all this practice is meaningless unless your mindset is geared toward action.

YOU BE THE ENTREPRENEUR

Rescue One Financial

The journey of an entrepreneur is filled with peaks and valleys. Bradley Smith, CEO of Rescue One Financial, experienced a financial dilemma. He helped clients with their debt, but secretly he shared their troubles.

Smith started his own financial services company and worked long hours counseling clients on how to get out of debt. All the while, no one knew that he was sinking deeper and deeper into debt himself. He sold the Rolex watch he had bought with his first paycheck, and had to borrow $10,000 from his father. As his debt grew, he found out his wife was pregnant with their first child. He didn't see any way to save his company.

What Would You Do?

Source: Bruder, J. (2013, September). The psychological price of entrepreneurship. *Inc. Magazine*, 110.

3.6 THE MINDSET AS THE PATHWAY TO ACTION

>> **LO 3.6** **Relate the mindset for entrepreneurship to entrepreneurial action.**

The mindset is the pathway to action. There is no entrepreneurship without action, and the mindset is antecedent to action. As we have seen in the preceding sections, the entrepreneurial mindset requires the habits of self-leadership, creativity, and improvisation. These habits create an emotional platform for entrepreneurial actions. You can have the best idea in the world, but without a mindset with a bias for action, there is nothing—no new venture, product, organization or anything else. Taking action is the only way to get results. Even the process of changing and expanding your mindset involves taking action through deliberate practice.

But taking action requires a degree of confidence, and belief in our abilities—an attribute known as self-efficacy. Let's take a look at how self-efficacy supports entrepreneurial activity.

Video
Staying Focused on Action

Self-Efficacy and Entrepreneurial Intentions

There have been an increasing number of studies on **entrepreneurial self-efficacy (ESE)**, which is the belief entrepreneurs have in their ability to begin new ventures. Self-efficacy is an essential part of the entrepreneurial mindset, and it is thought to be a good indicator of entrepreneurial intentions as well as a strong precursor to action.[30] In fact, recent research suggests that entrepreneurial self-efficacy can enable the entrepreneur to more effectively confront demands or stressors and thus improve entrepreneurial performance.[31] In other words, the research suggests that when we believe in our ability to succeed in something, we are more likely to actively take the steps to make it happen.

However, sometimes there is a fine line between self-confidence, self-efficacy, and arrogance. Arrogance leads a person to believe that he or she achieved success without help from others; further, the arrogant person may feel entitled to success and entitled to "bend the rules" to get ahead. As explored in the *Entrepreneurship Meets Ethics* feature, there is, in fact, a synergy between entrepreneurs and many other stakeholders. Healthy self-efficacy recognizes this relationship and makes use of it in constructive, mutually beneficial ways.

Sara Blakely, founder of undergarment manufacturer Spanx, believed in her vision so deeply that she committed her personal finances and all her energy to bring her product to fruition.[32] We could say that Robert Donat, the founder of GPS Insight, believed in his own ability to make things happen by building his company into the success it is today. Like many other factors of entrepreneurship, researchers have found that ESE can be heightened through training and education.

In general, people with high levels of self-efficacy tend to put in a higher level of effort, persist with an idea, and persevere with a task more than those people who possess low levels of self-efficacy, as shown by certain experiments by researchers. For example, The General Self-Efficacy Scale (GSES) (see Table 3.3) was designed by researchers to assess the degree to which we believe our actions are responsible for successful results.[33] It measures the belief we have in our ability to carry out difficult tasks, cope with adversity, persist in reaching our goals, and recover from setbacks.

Entrepreneurial self-efficacy (ESE): the belief that entrepreneurs have in their own ability to begin new ventures.

The GSES has been used all over the world since the 1990s to measure the self-efficacy levels of a whole range of ages, nationalities, and ethnicities. It is thought to be an accurate way of testing self-efficacy levels. It consists of 10 items, takes 4 minutes to complete, and is scored on a range from 10 to 40; the higher the score, the stronger the belief in your ability to take action. Take 4 minutes and complete the scale.

Keep in mind that self-efficacy can change over time. The more you practice something, such as entrepreneurship, the greater the likelihood that your self-efficacy related to entrepreneurial action will increase.

TABLE 3.3

The General Self-Efficacy Scale (GSES)

1	I can always manage to solve difficult problems if I try hard enough.
2	If someone opposes me, I can find the means and ways to get what I want.
3	It is easy for me to stick to my aims and accomplish my goals.
4	I am confident that I could deal efficiently with unexpected events.
5	Thanks to my resourcefulness, I know how to handle unforeseen situations.
6	I can solve most problems if I invest the necessary effort.
7	I can remain calm when facing difficulties because I can rely on my coping abilities.
8	When I am confronted with a problem, I can usually find several solutions.
9	If I am in trouble, I can usually think of a solution.
10	I can usually handle whatever comes my way.

Response Format
1 = Not at all true. 2 = Hardly true. 3 = Moderately true. 4 = Exactly true.

Source: Schwarzer, R. & Jerusalem, M. (1995). Generalized Self-Efficacy Scale. In J. Weinman, S. Wright, & M. Johnston (Eds.), *Measures in health psychology: A user's portfolio. Causal and control beliefs* (pp. 3537). Windsor, England: NFER-NELSON. Scale retrieved from http://userpage.fu-berlin.de/~health/engscal.htm

The Role of Mindset in Opportunity Recognition

As our mindset grows and expands through practicing self-leadership, creating, and improvising, we are more inclined to recognize and create opportunities. In fact, Richard Wiseman's study of luck, described in the *Research at Work* feature (p. 67), shows us that people who consider themselves lucky are more open to recognizing chance opportunities.

Think back to how Vera Bradley—the luggage design company featured in Chapter 2—began. Business partners Barbara Baekgaard and Pat Miller identified an opportunity to make attractive practical bags at a lower price than the competition, by simply observing the type of luggage people used at the airport. We could say that both Baekgaard and Miller were in the right mindset to recognize and pursue this opportunity. Indeed, they had already started a successful wallpaper hanging business that had given them a high degree of self-efficacy, which encouraged them to consider another venture. Through creativity and improvisation, both women succeeded in revolutionizing the luggage industry.

It is so easy to miss opportunities if we are not in the right mindset. Baekgaard and Miller just as easily could have casually exchanged remarks about the drabness of the luggage available, and then simply moved on to a new topic of conversation, forgetting all about their initial observations. Even worse, one of them might have

ENTREPRENEURSHIP MEETS ETHICS

Stakeholder Relationships and Trust

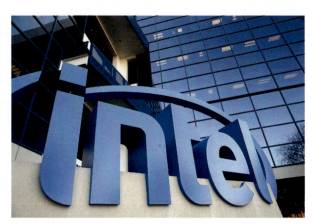

Intel practices internal and external ethical policies.
Credit: Justin Sullivan/Getty Images News/Getty Images

Although they value autonomy, entrepreneurs recognize that they also rely on many stakeholders—community networks, investors, employees, customers, and more—as keys to their success. To cultivate these relationships, successful entrepreneurs build a culture of trust by modeling ethical behavior and establishing a code of ethics.

The Silicon Valley giant Intel Corporation, maker of semiconductor chips, engages in a wide variety of ethically oriented policies, both internal and external. For example, it reaches out to the general public to stop online harassment, and is a recognized industry leader in reducing the use of "conflict minerals."[83] For its employees, Intel has an ethical code of conduct that includes, among many other provisions, a value limit on gifts that employees can accept from suppliers. The company believes that when suppliers give expensive gifts to Intel employees, it often leads the employees to feel obligated to give Intel business to those suppliers—potentially under conditions that are advantageous to the supplier and disadvantageous to Intel.

Ethical behavior can be a slippery slope, as decisions that begin in an ethically "gray area" can spiral and degenerate into unethical decisions.

CRITICAL THINKING QUESTIONS

1. **Critique the argument that entrepreneurs should establish trust with their stakeholders by modeling ethical behavior. Give some examples supporting your position.**

2. **As a CEO, would you support requiring your employees to sign a company code of ethics? If so, what would be the most important provisions of your code?**

3. **What would you do if a supplier sent a private jet to bring you to the supplier's corporate headquarters to inspect the factory?** ●

Sources

Google Inc. (n.d.). *About: Philosophy.* Retrieved from https://www.google.com/about/company/philosophy/

Intel Corporation. (n.d.). *Infographic: Online harassment is pervasive and can be vicious.* Retrieved from http://download.intel.com/newsroom/kits/diversity/pdfs/Intel-HackHarassment-Infographic-WEB.pdf

Miller, J. (2014, January 7). Intel vows to stop using "conflict minerals" in new chips. *The BBC.* Retrieved from www.bbc.co.uk

Onyemah, V., Pesquera, M. R., & Ali, A. (2013, May). What entrepreneurs get wrong. *Harvard Business Review, 91*(5), 7479.

Pannisi, E. (2012, April 18). Understanding entrepreneurship in developing countries. *Michigan State University Global Edge.* Retrieved from http://globaledge.msu.edu/blog/post/1273/understanding-entrepreneurship-in-developing-countries

Starcher, G. (1997). Ethics and entrepreneurship, an oxymoron? A transition to a free market economy in Eastern Europe. *Paris: European Baha'i Business Forum,* 112. Retrieved from http://bahai-library.com/starcher_ethics_entrepreneurship

pointed out the opportunity to design new bags, but the other could have discouraged her from persevering with the idea by saying that creating a new set of luggage would be time-consuming, expensive, and so on. Fortunately, both women were in the right mindset to identify a need for practical luggage and to support each other in their pursuit of the goal.

As we have explored, in order to develop an optimal mindset for entrepreneurship, we need to recognize its importance, and consciously take the steps to nurture it through the practice of self-leadership, creativity, and improvisation. Working on those areas helps build higher levels of self-efficacy that give us the confidence to create, pursue, and share our ideas. By building a strong mindset, we are better able to identify exciting opportunities and to take action to begin new ventures, products, or organizations. A continuously expanding and growing mindset is the key to successful entrepreneurship. ●

Video
The Skill of Self-Confidence

Get the edge on your studies at **edge.sagepub.com/neckentrepreneurship**

▸   Master the learning objectives using key study tools
▸   Watch, listen, and connect with online multimedia resources
▸   Access mobile-friendly quizzes and flashcards to check your understanding

SUMMARY

3.1   Appraise the effectiveness of mindset in entrepreneurship.

Part of The Practice of Entrepreneurship is having the right mindset (or mental attitude) to start and grow a business. Entrepreneurs who have the right mindset are more likely to persist with ideas and act on potential opportunities.

3.2   Define "mindset" and explain its importance to entrepreneurs.

An entrepreneurial mindset is the ability to quickly sense, take action, and get organized under certain conditions. Of the two mindsets proposed by Carol Dweck, the growth mindset represents a fundamental belief that failure is something to build on; and a learning mindset is essential for personal and professional growth.

3.3   Explain how to develop the habit of self-leadership.

Self-leadership is a process of self-direction that utilizes behavior strategies, reward strategies, and constructive thought patterns.

3.4   Explain how to develop the habit of creativity.

Creativity is defined as the capacity to produce new ideas, insights, or inventions that are unique and of value to others.

3.5   Explain how to develop the habit of improvisation.

Improvisation is the art of creating without preparation. Improvisation is recognized as a key skill not just for budding entrepreneurs, but for business practitioners of all types.

3.6   Relate the mindset for entrepreneurship to entrepreneurial action.

As entrepreneurship demands practice to achieve success, the right mindset is necessary for that practice to be successful. When people believe they can succeed, they're more likely to pursue the right activities to make that happen.

KEY TERMS

Behavior focused
    strategies 72
Constructive thought
    patterns 73
Creativity 74
Entrepreneurial
    mindset 68

Entrepreneurial
    self-efficacy (ESE) 81
Fixed mindset 66
Growth mindset 66
Habit 71
Improvisation 78
Natural reward
    strategies 73
Passion 71

Self-cueing 73
Self-goal setting 72
Self-leadership 71
Self-observation 72
Self-punishment
    (or self-correcting
    feedback) 72
Self-reward 72

CASE STUDY

Dr. Nathaniel J. Williams, Founder and CEO; HumanWorks Affiliates, Inc.

Dr. Nathaniel J. Williams, EdD, MHS, MPA, MBA, wears many hats: adjunct professor, author, speaker, community advocate, and *business executive*. Dr. Williams leads a $12 million per year nonprofit organization called HumanWorks Affiliates, a group of nine companies dedicated to providing management, financial, operations, and development services for nonprofit and provider agencies. Before reaching his 50th birthday, he had authored nine books; he also consults and speaks to a variety of groups throughout the world. On top of that, he is a married man and father of eight.

In 1970 little five-year old Nat Williams was orphaned upon the untimely death of his mother. After the funeral was over, five taxis waited outside to take him and his nine other brothers and sisters who were under age 18 to five separate homes in the New York City (The Bronx) foster care system.

In his own words, Nat describes his feelings and response to this difficult situation:

> I felt sorry that it happened, but rather than feeling sorry for myself, I recognized that it wasn't the end of the line for me. In time, I learned to try to find *the message*, or *the memo*, in difficult experiences I faced to see what I could learn and then internalize from those experiences.

One day, while living in a group foster home known as a cottage, Nat eagerly awaited the arrival of his brothers and sisters who were coming to visit him. Unfortunately, the van carrying his siblings broke down, and they were unable to make the trip. Saddened by this disappointment, Nat sat alone on the front steps of the foster home administration office brooding. As he sat there in his sadness, the executive director of the home, Sister Mary Patrick, came along and asked Nat what was wrong. He shared his plight with the nun, who disappeared and then returned almost magically with a bicycle to cheer Nat up. Thrilled and grateful, he rode off to show his "cottage mates" his new treasure. Then he let them take turns riding the bike. As he was observing one of his mates riding down the path on his new bike, he realized that his current mindset needed to change. He suddenly realized that if he wasn't careful, he would have a fixed mindset: *telling a sad story and then waiting for a handout*.

That wasn't the story Nat wanted told of his life, and from that point on, he began to *look at life differently*, and set his sights high. He determined that someday, he wanted to be like Sister Mary Patrick: a leader of great caring and compassion, as well as an executive director of something. He even started signing his name: *Nathaniel J. Williams, Executive Director*, a habit that spawned confusion and derision among many of his peers. In his own words:

> People were always making fun of me, and would ask, "Why the hell are you saying you're an Executive Director, and why are you signing your name that way," but it gave me a pathway. I say to people often, if it's not written, it's not going to happen, so by me just writing it down what I wanted to do, it made it very clear, so when drugs came my way, or alcohol came my way, or other things, because I knew what I wanted to do, I was able to plan my work and then work my plan. I was able to say *yes* or *no* to that based on what *I wanted* to do with my life.

Nat came to recognize over time that the true gift he had received that day was not *the bicycle*, but the lesson he learned from the experiencea lesson that would continue to inform his life's decisions and directions for the rest of his life.

> I encourage people to find the message behind the moment rather than being overwhelmed by the moment itself. I try to understand that there is something in here for me to take away from every experience—the question is: *what is it?* If I can take it away, then I can possibly turn it into a gift for other people as well.

Over time, Nat began taking more leadership initiative. At age 15, the cottage where he lived was becoming disruptive with kids from other cottages coming and going as they pleased. He decided to take action. He posted a sign that read: *All visitors must check in with the staff*. The *actual* cottage leader was infuriated to discover a 15-year-old kid had exercised such initiative without any formal authority to do so. Nat knew a need when he saw it; he wanted to be a leader, and he want to fill the needs he saw around him. Much of his time as a teen was spent taking such leadership initiative in one way or another, a harbinger of the hard work, focus, and proactivity that would mark his pathway for the next several decades.

As a teenager, he was exposed to drugs, alcohol, and other negative activities and temptations common to adolescents. As he saw a lot of people—including some of his siblings—get tangled up in the web of substance abuse and other trouble, the negative consequences of such behavior, and their incompatibility with realizing his goals, became a powerful deterrent for Williams.

After high school, Nat attended a community college in New York City for three semesters. He also began to work; one of his first jobs was in a home for mentally disabled adults. He was enthralled with the opportunity that work provided to earn money while contributing meaningfully to the lives of others. It would begin his lifelong work with the disabled, or others who needed help. Putting in 18- to 20-hour days was not uncommon as he seized on employment opportunities.

At age 28, Williams founded a company that is now a conglomerate of nine different organizations focused on human care services that help others in need. This same organization now has an operating budget of $12 million a year and employs over 200 people. Dr. Williams is also on the board of directors for three other organizations and hosts a weekly television talk show in the State of Pennsylvania.

In addition to his heavy work schedule, Dr. Williams also found time in his life for family. He got married and had two children. After a divorce from his first wife, he remarried and had five more children and adopted a sixth (his niece from Liberia), making him the father of eight.

Perhaps one of the most significant components of Dr. Williams's enormous success is that he was a minority raised in the foster care system and therefore started out in life with nothing materially or financially. His is a story that underscores the power of potential that can be found inside the body, mind, heart, and spirit of a human being. Yet, he is also quick to concede the importance of involving others along the way to help, and that a sincere relationship of complete transparency with such friends, teachers, and mentors is essential.

Instead of focusing on what he did *not* have as a young African American orphan growing up in a challenging urban environment, Nat focused on what he *did have*, what he *could do*, and what he *could learn* from his experiences. He explains that to transcend less than ideal external circumstances, it is crucial to *work with what you have* and to *believe that what you have isn't so bad*. By so doing, your focus and energy becomes directed toward framing your situation in the best possible light and then working hard to make the most of that situation.

In hindsight, he doesn't feel sorry for himself for being orphaned at five or because he had to struggle to realize his present success. Rather, he recognizes that each life experience played a distinct role in helping to mold and shape his character and and mindset.

Critical Thinking Questions

1. In your own words, how would you explain why Nathaniel J. Williams was able to rise above the difficult circumstances of his childhood?

2. In what ways does Nathaniel J. Williams's approach to life exemplify the entrepreneurial mindset avocated in this chapter? Does his approach differ in any ways?

3. Can you think of limitations you are placing on yourself that may be restricting your ability to achieve your goals? Name some specific examples.

4. How can you apply an entrepreneurial mindset to your life to help you break through these limitations in order to reach success?

Sources
This story is an abridged version of a chapter in Dr. Jordan R. Jensen's book, *Self-Action Leadership*, reprinted with permission of the author and copyright holder (Jensen).
Jensen, J. R. (2015). *Self-action leadership: The key to personal & professional freedom*. Bloomington, IN: authorHouse.
Nat Williams's personal website, http://www.nj-williams.com/
HumanWorks Affiliates, Inc. company website, http://www.humanworksaffiliates.com/

Additional Sources
1.   Robert Donat Entrepreneurship in Action interview, above at p. 000.
2.   Moore, P. (2014, June 27). Robert Donat has GPS Insight going in the right direction. *Bizjournals.com*. Retrieved from http://www.bizjournals.com/denver/print-edition/2014/06/27/robert-donat-has-gps-insight-going-in-the-right.html?page=all
3.   Suizo. G. (2012, April). Off the clock: The more personal side of fleet. *Automotive Fleet*. Retrieved from http://www.automotive-fleet.com/channel/operations/article/story/2012/04/off-the-clock-the-more-personal-side-of-fleet.aspx
4.   The Golden Bridge Awards, interview with Robert Donat: Retrieved from http://www.goldenbridgeawards.com/people/Robert-Donat.html#.VAgjl0hB4Zw

4 Supporting Social Entrepreneurship

©iStockphoto.com/HenkBadenhorst

The life purpose of the true social entrepreneur is to change the world."

—Bill Drayton, founder of Ashoka

Learning Objectives

Chapter Outline

4.1 THE ROLE OF SOCIAL ENTREPRENEURSHIP

>> **LO 4.1** Describe what role social entrepreneurship plays in society.

In Chapter 1, we introduced *social entrepreneurship* as the process of sourcing innovative solutions to social and environmental problems. What's the difference between social entrepreneurs and traditional entrepreneurs? Social entrepreneurs and business entrepreneurs share some similarities: both types found new organizations, identify opportunities, create and implement innovation solutions or services, find information and resources, form connections, and create marketing initiatives to promote offerings.[1]

However, the main difference between traditional and social entrepreneurship lies in its intended mission. Traditional entrepreneurs create ventures with a goal of making a profit, and they measure performance by the profits they generate. In contrast, social entrepreneurs create ventures to tackle social problems and bring about social change; they measure performance by advancing social and environmental goals. Some also desire profit, in the case of for-profit ventures, while others are less concerned about profit. The great number of new nonprofit and nongovernmental organizations (NGOs) being started around the globe attests to this second category. In this chapter we celebrate all types of social entrepreneurs—those who are mission-based and solving social problems—regardless of the nature of their profit motives.

As you may remember, we have described some successful social entrepreneurs who have managed to benefit society and make a profit, including Jim Poss, founder of Bigbelly Inc., a for-profit company that builds trash cans that enable garbage to be compacted using solar energy (Chapter 2). Using compaction reduces the number of pickups from traditional garbage trucks, thereby reducing carbon emissions.

Video
Social Entrepreneurship for the Community

Arthur Steingart, Founder of Symp1e

Arthur Steingart, CEO of Symp1e
Credit: Used with permission from Arthur Steingart

Still in his mid-twenties, Arthur Steingart is already an accomplished entrepreneur with a handful of small businesses under his belt, from a custom guitar shop to lucrative real estate ventures. Yet it's Symp1e, Steingart's latest company, that may just change the world—or at least, your backyard. Symp1e key innovation is Waterall, a smart, timed watering system created as an environmental solution to water-stressed areas that can save gardeners up to 40% on water usage. Its algorithm takes into account a garden's specific plant types—it knows the water needs of over 3,800 varieties—plus soil conditions and weather information in real time. With Wi-Fi and Bluetooth integration, gardeners can monitor and control their water use remotely, tracking their savings of cost and resources along the way. Waterall is the only smart watering system that considers the individual plants of a user's garden to determine ideal output.

Whether they're college students or seasoned businessmen, it hasn't been hard to convince people of the merits of Waterall. "Everyone involved has loved not just the product but the meaning," says Steingart; "how it's benefiting the community, the individual, the southwest, and the implications it could have for the world." Indeed, those implications are enormous. The United Nations predicts that by 2025, two-thirds of the world's population could be living in water-stressed areas, due to factors including climate change, population growth, and urbanization.[2] These are huge problems facing humanity and the planet, and devices like Waterall could be part of the solution.

Steingart envisions Waterall in homes across the country, helping contractors, homeowners, utility companies, and businesses make the most of a resource that is increasingly limited and precious. The idea took root over a bottle of wine at the kitchen table of J.K. and Pamela Waterman, an entrepreneurially minded couple Steingart had recently met. Steingart said, "We started talking about gardening,

because it's something we all really enjoy. . . . And we came to it! If you could save an individual 40% of their water, what would that do for the community?"
J.K Waterman, a hardware guru with over 30 years of experience, offered to build a prototype based on the trio's brainstorming. Steingart, then a freshman studying business law at Arizona State University, tapped classmates for assistance, from software development to website design to making short videos for Kickstarter. "In an environment full of ambitious, lustful people, you're really able to find anything you need," he says.

Three years later, a working prototype of Waterall is at last ready to debut, under the company name Symp1e. (Symp1e now includes Steingart as CEO, J.K. Waterman as President of Hardware Development, Pamela Waterman as Marketing Communications expert, and a fourth man, Jason Salves, as its Chief Operating Officer.) While Arthur has been its primary financier—"an expensive love, believe me," he said in 2015, Steingart is hopeful that water or construction companies might buy the Waterall in bulk, distributing it to individual homeowners for free, or at a discounted rate. "We're also talking to a major provider of infrastructure in terms of pipes for buildings, gaskets, etc. They sell everything that carries water, yet they don't have anything to control the water that goes through it, so they're very interested."

Whatever the fate of Waterall, it's clear that Steingart is determined to leave his mark as an entrepreneur. "Success for me is not just about fulfilling utilitarian needs; [success will be attained] if, 20 years from now, Arizona can avoid a water crisis because we have been able to measure water. There was a time in my life when I was making a lot of money. . . .This is not about that. It comes back to leaving behind meaning, living for others, adding something to this world."

CRITICAL THINKING QUESTIONS

1. **Should entrepreneurs exist to make money? Solve social and/or environmental problems? Or both? Explain your answer.**

2. **Explain how the Symp1e Waterall addresses concern for future generations in addition to conserving water today.**

3. **What social or environmental problem would you like to solve?** ●

Source: Personal interview, A. Steingart, May 3, 2015.

Defining Social Entrepreneurship

Social entrepreneurship is becoming a popular way of conducting business while making a social and economic impact. In the face of tough competition, it is difficult for social entrepreneurs to find the right balance between "doing good" and earning enough financially to live on, as well as growing the business. This makes social entrepreneurship difficult to define. For example, would you regard someone who sells low-cost eyeglasses to the poor and uses the profits to buy a luxury mansion a social entrepreneur?[3]

Over the years, researchers have struggled to define social entrepreneurship; some regard all social entrepreneurship as solely not-for-profit initiatives, the implication being that social entrepreneurs need to choose between making a social or an economic impact. By analyzing three successful cases of social entrepreneurship: the Grameen Bank, which gives microloans to the poor, the Aravind Eye Hospital in India, and Sekem, an initiative for sustainable development in Egypt, researchers Johanna Mair and Ignasi Marti were able to argue that these social enterprises contained both a social and economic impact. While the main focus of these cases is social value creation, creating economic value is also essential for the social enterprises to

continue with their mission of changing the lives of those at the base of the pyramid.

The researchers conclude that social entrepreneurship "differs from other forms of entrepreneurship in that it gives higher priority to social value creation—by catalyzing social change and/or catering to social needs—than to value capture."[4]

CRITICAL THINKING QUESTIONS

1. If you had to craft a definition of social entrepreneurship, how would it be? What facts would you need to know, and what issues would you take into account?

2. Describe a real business that you think embodies what social entrepreneurship should be. What is it about this business that makes it a good example?

3. Take a social entrepreneurial idea that you might pursue, and explain how it fits your definition of social entrepreneurship. Could your idea generate both social and economic value? ●

In this chapter, we have also introduced Arthur Steingart, social entrepreneur and founder of Symp1e. Symp1e's Waterall product is designed to save the amount of water we use every day and to address the serious issue of water shortages. Steingart is one of many graduates who have seized the world's most pressing problems as an opportunity to create real entrepreneurs and social value. These examples show that with the right entrepreneurial skills and a strong sense of empathy, compassion, and commitment, entrepreneurs have a real chance of preserving and protecting future generations.

In this chapter, we will discuss the different types of social entrepreneurship, discuss the global social and environmental challenges facing us today, and share some stories of social entrepreneurs who have acted on opportunities to build scalable businesses.

$SAGE edge™

Master the content
edge.sagepub.com/
neckentrepreneurship

4.2 SOCIAL ENTREPRENEURSHIP AND WICKED PROBLEMS

>> **LO 4.2** Explain how social entrepreneurship can help resolve wicked problems around the world.

In the 1960s, scholars coined the term **wicked problems**—large, complex social problems where there is no clear solution, where there is limited, confusing, or contradictory information available, and where a whole range of people with conflicting values engage in debate. More recently Jeffrey Conklin, Director of the Cognexus Institute, provided broader and more practical applications of the term (see Table 4.1).[5]

Wicked problems: large, complex social problems where there is no clear solution, where there is limited, confusing, or contradictory information available, and where a whole range of people with conflicting values engage in debate.

TABLE 4.1

Conklin's Defining Characteristics of Wicked Problems

1.	The problem is not understood until after the formulation of a solution.
2.	Wicked problems have no stopping rule.
3.	Solutions to wicked problems are not right or wrong.
4.	Every wicked problem is essentially novel and unique.
5.	Every solution to a wicked problem is a "one shot operation."
6.	Wicked problems have no given alternative solutions.

Credit: Conklin, Jeffrey (2006). *Dialogue mapping: building shared understanding of wicked problems.* Chichester, England: Wiley Publishing. Reprinted with permission from John Wiley & Sons.

Issues relating to the environment, poverty, sustainability, equality, education, child mortality, sanitation, terrorism, and health and wellness are all examples of wicked problems, whether on a global, national, or local scale (see Figure 4.1).

The dramatic increase in life expectancy—an issue affecting many countries, particularly in the Western world—is an example of a wicked problem to which there are no easy answers. An aging population is likely to result in rising health care costs, an increase in the number of people claiming pensions, and potentially higher taxes for those supporting the nonworking retirees.

Problems such as these are usually managed by policymakers who are responsible for creating ways to find solutions, but the path is fraught with obstacles. These problems

FIGURE 4.1

Global Wicked Problems

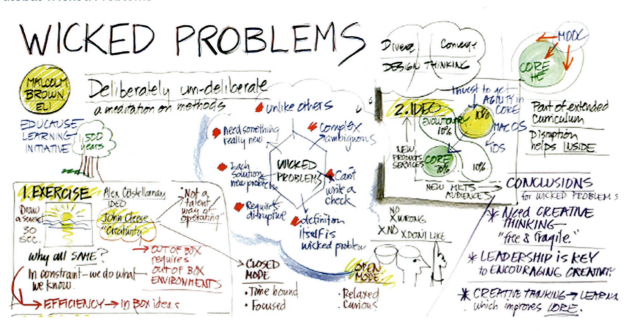

Credit: David Sibbet, CEO of The Grove. Retrieved from http://redarchive.nmc.org/news/communique-2013-future-education-summit. Reprinted with permission of David Sibbet.

are so complex that traditional linear problem-solving methods do not generally work. The nature of wicked problems poses significant challenges to social entrepreneurs, but also provides huge opportunities to make a real difference in their own countries and around the world.

For example, consider the nonprofit organization Kickstart (not to be confused with the crowdfunding website Kickstarter). Kickstart took on the challenge of solving the wicked problem of hunger in Africa. At least 75% of the children of farmers go hungry because they do not have the right irrigation tools to water their land. Kickstart provides affordable tools such as irrigation pumps to farmers that enable them to grow more food that they can sell at the local markets. The money they earn from this enterprise enables them to feed their own families and send their children to school. Kickstart successfully found a solution to a wicked problem that makes a significant difference to the livelihoods of the African poor.[6]

Whereas many of us avoid wicked problems because of their complex nature, design thinkers see wicked problems as a challenge to think differently or as an opportunity to break through constraints and develop creative solutions. Their focus lies in using their social entrepreneurs to generate the best alternative ideas.

Let's take a look at how one doctor broke through constraints to create his own solution to a complex social problem. In 1976, Dr. G. Venkataswamy set out on a mission to eradicate avoidable blindness in India, where a quarter of the world's population are afflicted with treatable cause of blindness such as cataracts. The Aravind Eye Care System began with 11 beds from his family home, which has since developed into five hospitals, a manufacturing plant, a research foundation, and a training center. Over the years, Aravind has faced Venkataswamy's challenges: the lack of access to transportation to reach the rural poor, poor people's inability to pay for the eye care, and the rising costs of ophthalmic products.

Rather than being overwhelmed by these difficult obstacles, the company met them head-on. To address the transportation issue, Aravind provides buses to bring the rural poor who need more intensive treatment to one of the hospitals in the urban areas. Those who struggle to pay for the treatment either pay nothing or are subsidized by the wealthier patients who are charged higher fees, yet still pay less than they would at other hospitals. To tackle the rising costs of eye products such as lenses, for example ($200 a pair if they are made in the West), Aravind built its own manufacturing plant in the basement of one of its hospitals, which uses less expensive technology to produce lenses for just $4 a pair.[7] As of 2013, Aravind Eye Care System had successfully treated more than 30 million patients and performed over 4 million surgeries.[8]

If Dr. G. Venkataswamy had applied conventional problem-solving techniques to this complex issue, it is unlikely his organization would have succeeded. For example, it is typical for many nonprofits to seek financial assistance from the government. Yet government support is not always available in developing countries,

Irrigation pump invented by Kickstart to address the problem of hunger in Africa
Credit: AP Photo/Tom Maliti

Video
Social Entrepreneurship and Wicked Problems

where a whole range of serious issues—disease, illiteracy, low income, and others—take up the majority of time and resources. In recognition of this, Venkataswamy provided an alternative health care system that not only supported the efforts of the government, but also supported itself. This organization began with a wicked problem, but it persisted in overcoming the constraints to seek alternative solutions for the greater good.

One particular wicked problem is getting worse every year: the global refugee crisis. By the end of 2015, almost 60 million people had been forced to flee their homes (or displaced) because of wars, conflict, and persecution—the worst figures on record.[9] This means that, globally, every 1 in 122 people is now a refugee—either displaced but still remaining in the country of conflict, or in another country seeking asylum. Children make up half of all refugees. Outbreaks of war in Africa, the Middle East, Europe, and Asia have forced many people to risk incredibly dangerous journeys across land and sea in a desperate and often fatal attempt at finding safety. While billions of dollars are spent every year on food, health, and shelter for refugees, this is still not enough to solve the problem. Rather than simply maintaining the refugee camps, new solutions must be found to address refugee displacement.

What are the options? Perhaps the first option would be to send the refugees back to their countries as soon as they are safe—but of course, in many cases, war is intractable and unending. It could take many more years before a war-torn country becomes a safe haven. A second option is for other countries to take in and resettle refugees. While 30 countries provide some sort of resettlement, only a small percentage of refugees are granted relocation status. In some cases, even when refugees are successfully relocated, they are seen as a burden to society and housed in slums or camps, eliminating the possibility of full integration.

The Nigerian investor and philanthropist Tony Elumelu may have an alternative solution: entrepreneurship. Elumelu is investing $100 million to further entrepreneurship in Africa and host countries where over 4 million refugees live in poverty.[10] This initiative could help support refugees in starting up their own businesses and boost the economic performance of the communities and countries where they live. Elumelu's solution is just one of many that are needed to tackle the wicked problem of refugee displacement, and there is plenty of opportunity for social entrepreneurs to think of more.

4.3 TYPES OF SOCIAL ENTREPRENEURSHIP

>> **LO 4.3**   **Identify the different types of social entrepreneurship.**

Video
A Social Enterprise

There are different models of social entrepreneurship. Figure 4.2 illustrates the territory of social entrepreneurship.[11] As we have described the differences between traditional and social entrepreneurship, let's take a look at (1) social purpose ventures, (2) social consequence ventures, and (3) enterprising nonprofits and their relationship to social entrepreneurship.

Social Purpose Ventures

Social purpose ventures: businesses created by social entrepreneurs to resolve a social problem and make a profit.

The aim of **social purpose ventures** is to resolve a social problem and make a profit. Organic clothing company PACT is a good example of a social venture: it designs, manufactures, and distributes premium cotton underwear without using pesticides,

FIGURE 4.2

Typology of Ventures

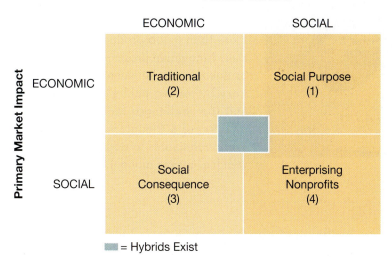

Venture Mission

	ECONOMIC	SOCIAL
ECONOMIC	Traditional (2)	Social Purpose (1)
SOCIAL	Social Consequence (3)	Enterprising Nonprofits (4)

Primary Market Impact

▨ = Hybrids Exist

Source: Neck, H. M., Brush, C., & Allen, E. (2009) The landscape of social entrepreneurship. *Business Horizons,* 52, 13–19.

fertilizers, or chemicals. As a participant in the Fair Trade movement, PACT uses family farms in India and pays a higher price on the cotton to help sustain the farms and the local communities.

Jeff Denby, founder of PACT, says, "By focusing on the people who make our products, from the farmers who grow the organic cotton to the workers who stitch the garments, PACT is fulfilling its mission to use apparel production as a means of making the world a better place."[12]

PACT has also teamed up with other ventures to add value in areas outside organic clothing. For example, in 2013, PACT partnered with the Whole Kids Foundation (a Whole Foods Market nonprofit) and crowdsourcing website Indiegogo to fund 100 urban gardens across the United States. The campaign was designed to raise awareness of healthy food, and to enable children and adults to experience how it is grown.[13]

Men's socks manufactured by Organic clothing company, PACT.

Credit: Lynne Sutherland/Alamy Stock Photo

Social Consequence Entrepreneurship

Social consequence entrepreneurship describes a for-profit venture whose primary market impact is social. A good example of a for-profit venture with a social impact is Sword & Plough, a startup founded by sisters Emily and Betsy Núñez. Sword & Plough hires army veterans to recycle surplus military materials such as parachutes, sleeping bags, and tents into fashionable bags and accessories. The company was launched in 2013, benefiting from $312,000 in funding, thanks

Social consequence entrepreneurship: a for-profit venture whose primary market impact is social.

**Emily and Betsy Núñez,
founders of Sword & Plough**

Credit: AP Photo/Bartley Young

to a powerful Kickstarter campaign. It donates 10% of its profits to veterans' organizations.

As of 2015, Sword & Plough had created almost 40 jobs for US veterans, as well as 10 nonveteran roles. It has recycled over 20,000 pounds of discarded military material, and sold more than 6,000 products globally.[14] Through their innovative products, the founders aim to bridge the gap between civilians and the military by raising public awareness of veterans and the challenges facing servicemen every day. Sword & Plough is just one of many for-profit companies in existence today that "does well [i.e., makes money] by doing good."

Video
Enterprising Nonprofits

Enterprising nonprofits:
a form of social entrepreneurship where both the venture mission and the market impact are for social purposes.

Enterprising Nonprofits

Enterprising nonprofits are a form of social entrepreneurship where both the venture mission and the market impact are for social purposes. This means that any profits made must be channeled back into the organization. Unlike with social purpose ventures, profit may not be distributed to the owners of the enterprising nonprofit. There are over 1.5 million nonprofit organizations in operation in the United States today, including charities, foundations, and others (see Table 4.2).

Compared to traditional nonprofit startups, enterprising nonprofits are more likely to survive in business after the first five years. This may have to do with revenue resources: typically, enterprising nonprofits have better access to revenue streams from universities, hospitals, and foundations. Table 4.3 illustrates the differences between traditional nonprofit entrepreneurs and enterprising nonprofits.

While there may be some differences between nonprofit entrepreneurs and traditional for-profit (also called enterprising) entrepreneurs, both types create their own ventures out of a desire to fill a gap and meet a need. Let's look at the different types of enterprising nonprofits. There are two types of enterprising nonprofits: earned-income activities, and venture philanthropy.

Earned-income activities:
the sale of products or services that are used as a source of revenue generation.

Earned-income activities, such as selling products or services, are used as a source of revenue generation. For example, the Woodland Park Zoo in Seattle, Washington, is one of several zoos that operate a "Zoo Doo" venture, selling exotic animal dung to the public as garden fertilizer. Whereas Woodland Park Zoo used to pay $60,000 to have

TABLE 4.2

Quick Facts About Nonprofit Organizations in the United States

1,571,056 tax-exempt organizations, including:	
1,097,689	public charities
105,030	private foundations
368,337	other types of nonprofit organizations, including chambers of commerce, fraternal organizations, and civic leagues.

Source: NCCS Business Master File 12/2015. Retrieved from http://nccs.urban.org/statistics/quickfacts.cfm

TABLE 4.3

Differences Between Traditional Nonprofit Entrepreneurs and Enterprising Nonprofits

	TRADITIONAL NONPROFIT ENTREPRENEURS	ENTERPRISING NONPROFIT ENTREPRENEURS
Survival rate of business for the first 5 years	50%	84%
Gender breakdown	41% women/ 59% men	60% women/ 41% men
Age of founders	Average age: 40	Average age: 53
Education level	31% have a college degree	89% have a college degree
Previous experience	55% of founders start nonprofits in industries other than those they have been working in	67% of nonprofit founders had over ten years' experience working in the private sector

Source: http://www.kauffman.org/blogs/growthology/2015/03/six-ways-non-profit-entrepreneurs-are-distinct-from-traditional-entrepreneurs

the dung removed to landfills, it now makes between $15,000 and $20,000 by selling bags of compost for $5 a bag. The money this venture generates is considered to be a bonus to the zoo's annual revenue, as well as highlighting environmentally friendly practices.[15]

In contrast to the earned-income model, **venture philanthropy funding** combines financial assistance such as grants with a high level of engagement by the funder. Venture philanthropists share their experience with nonprofit entrepreneurs to help grow and scale the company to drive social change. This might take the form of marketing and communications, executive coaching, human resources, or providing access to other contacts and potential funders. Typically, financial support is provided for three to five years with the goal of enabling the nonprofit to become financially independent by the end of this period (see Table 4.4).

New Profit Inc. is a venture philanthropy and social innovation fund led by Vanessa Kirsch, Tripp Jones, and Doug Borchard. They raise money from donors to create a large fund where money is granted to select nonprofits. New Profit has a history of growing and scaling nonprofit organizations such as Teach for America and YouthBuild USA. New Profit Inc. extended a $1 million grant investment to Food-Corps, a nonprofit organization that seeks to educate children about healthy food, what goes into food, and how to grow it themselves. FoodCorps will also receive New Profit's expertise and advice in scaling the FoodCorps model nationwide over a four-year period.[16]

Like many venture capital firms, venture philanthropists look for nonprofits whose social impact can be definitively measured and that demonstrate the potential to develop and grow. Venture philanthropy organizations include BonVenture in Germany, Impetus Trust and CAN-Breakthrough in the United Kingdom, d.o.b. Foundation in the Netherlands, Good Deed Foundation in Estonia, Invest for Children in Spain, Oltre Venture in Italy, and Social Venture Partners and Venture Philanthropy Partners in the United States.

It is possible for enterprising nonprofits to use both earned-income activities and venture philanthropy. For example, Embrace is a nonprofit set up by Stanford graduate Jane Chen in an effort to improve the survival of low-birthweight babies, particularly in developing countries where incubators are too expensive to purchase (see *Entrepreneurship Meets Ethics* in Chapter 6). The organization originated with a class project where students were tasked with designing a device to prevent neonatal hypothermia costing less than 1% of a standard incubator.

Venture philanthropy funding: a combination of financial assistance such as grants with a high level of engagement by the funder.

Video
Social Entrepreneurship for Survival

TABLE 4.4

Features of Venture Philanthropy

CHARACTERISTIC	DESCRIPTION
High Engagement	Venture philanthropists have a close, hands-on relationship with the social entrepreneurs and ventures they support, driving innovative and scalable models of social change. Some may take board places on these organizations, and all are far more intimately involved at strategic and operational levels than are traditional nonprofit funders.
Multiyear Support	Venture philanthropists provide substantial and sustained financial support to a limited number of organizations. Support typically lasts at least 3–5 years, with an objective of helping the organization to become financially self-sustaining by the end of the funding period.
Tailored Financing	As in venture capital, venture philanthropists take an investment approach to determine the most appropriate financing for each organization. Depending on their own missions and the ventures they choose to support, venture philanthropists can operate across the spectrum of investment returns.
Organizational Capacity Building	Venture philanthropists focus on building the operational capacity and long-term viability of the organizations in their portfolios, rather than funding individual projects or programs. They recognize the importance of funding core operating costs to help these organizations achieve greater social impact and operational efficiency.
Nonfinancial Support	In addition to financial support, venture philanthropists provide value-added services such as strategic planning, marketing and communications, executive coaching, human resource advice, and access to other networks and potential funders.
Performance Measurement	Venture philanthropy investment is performance-based, placing emphasis on good business planning, measurable outcomes, achievement of milestones, and high levels of financial accountability and management competence.

Source: John, Rob. *Venture Philanthropy: The Evolution of High Engagement Philanthropy in Europe.* Skoll Centre for Social Entrepreneurship Working Paper: Oxford Said Business School, 2006.

The result was the Embrace Warmer—a miniature sleeping bag that maintains the baby's body temperature without the need for electricity. It costs just $25, in stark contrast to the $20,000 cost of a typical hospital incubator. Each Embrace Warmer is durable enough to use for up to 50 premature babies. In its first four years, the product was used for more than 140,000 babies across 11 countries, and the number was expected to keep growing.

Chen states: "It is scary to go into this social impact space—or to be an entrepreneur at all. I am grateful that so many people have come together to help us with this cause. Whether it be donors, volunteers, or advisors—all these people along the way from all different walks of life pitched in to get this off the ground. I think this happened because both the founding team and I have so vehemently believed in our vision. That energy becomes contagious."[17]

Another enterprising nonprofit is the Boston-based organization Building Impact, set up in 2003 with a goal of increasing civic engagement in the wider community. Building Impact makes access to volunteering and donating easy by bringing events and opportunities right to office and residential buildings. These events can take the form of serving meals to the homeless, clothing drives, blood drives, or toy drives—all of which take place inside or right outside buildings served by Building Impact. Residents or office workers have the opportunity to work together by becoming volunteers, donors, and mentors, which further enhances civic engagement.

Building Impact connects nonprofits with almost 600 companies with more than 20,000 employees in over 50 buildings across Greater Boston. It channels 100% of its resources to other nonprofits such as Cradles to Crayons, Friends of Boston's Homeless, Goodwill Industries, and the Greater Boston Food Bank. It is funded by licensing fees paid by real estate companies as well as foundations, grants, and individual contributors. Some of the events that have recently taken place include making no-sew fleece blankets for Friends of Boston's Homeless; decorating boxes for race stops for Project Bread's Walk for Hunger; making Learning Launch Kits for the United Way; and crafting greeting cards for Ethos, an elderly and disabled service organization.[18]

Hybrid Models of Social Entrepreneurship

Through the typology of ventures illustrated in Figure 4.2, we have described several types of social entrepreneurship, but there are emerging forms of social entrepreneurship that do not fit as neatly into this four-part typology. A **hybrid model of social entrepreneurship** describes an organization with a purpose that equally emphasizes both economic and social goals.

Hybrid model of social entrepreneurship: an organization with a purpose that equally emphasizes both economic and social goals.

To further explain the hybrid model, let's take a look at two organizations with the same goal: to solve the problem of poor eyesight in developing countries. The first organization is the Centre for Vision in the Developing World, a traditional nonprofit that channels donations toward self-refraction glasses that enable the wearer to make simple adjustments at a low cost to increase vision quality. The product eliminates the need for an optometrist or prescriptions.

The second organization, VisionSpring, aims to solve the same problem but has a network of over 20,000 salespeople to sell glasses to people in their local communities who have limited access to eye care. Unlike the Centre for Vision in the Developing World, the VisionSpring model sustains itself financially through the sales of the glasses, rather than through donations.

As a result, VisionSpring is classified as a hybrid social venture model because it combines a nonprofit's concern for social issues with the for-profit goal to make money. While hybrid models can be an excellent way of exploiting the advantages of both for-profit and nonprofit models, they are less likely to receive venture capital (VC) funding or philanthropic donations because they sit in a gray zone between business and charity. As Harvard doctoral candidate Matthew Lee, who is studying hybrid organizations, explains, "It's much harder to get started and be successful if you don't fit into a well-defined form that people understand." Lee adds, "Creating a new hybrid is difficult to explain as a rational choice taking this limitation into account."[19]

However, if entrepreneurs can get it right, the hybrid model could have big social and economic payoffs. Take the for-profit coffee importer Sustainable Harvest, for instance. Sustainable Harvest is a hybrid model that earns up to $80 million in revenues, but also makes a huge social impact. The organization buys millions of pounds of Fair Trade and organic coffee from small farms in Peru, Colombia, Mexico, and Tanzania, paying them over 50% more per pound than the average rate. Sustainable Harvest also invests a large portion of its profits in training thousands of farmers in farming techniques to help grow better coffee and in infrastructure to help combat hunger in their communities.[20]

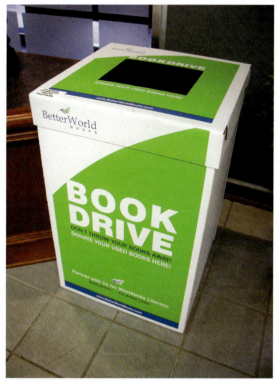

Better World Books drop box where people can drop off unwanted books.

Credit: © User: carmichaellibrary/Wikimedia Commons/CC BY 2.0/https:// creativecommons.org/licenses/ by/2.0/deed.en

Finally, Better World Books is another example of a hybrid model, which earns money by taking donations of new and unwanted books and selling them online. The venture was originally begun in 2002 by three students at the University of Notre Dame who wanted to sell their textbooks online to earn extra money. The students then decided to donate a portion of the sales from each book they sold to literacy campaigns.

Since then, Better World Books has set up relationships with almost 4,000 libraries to collect unwanted books of many different types and genres. It has also launched an initiative that provides drop boxes in certain locations, allowing people to drop off unwanted books. The collection bins even come with sensory technology that tells Better World staff when the bins are full, so they can empty them quickly.[21]

In its book-for-book program, Better World Books has learned from other organizations. One example is Toms Shoes, the subject of the *Entrepreneurship Meets Ethics* feature below. Toms Shoes is a for-profit company based in California that operates a "buy a pair of shoes, give away a pair of shoes" initiative (often shortened to Buy One Give One or BOGO). As of 2015, BetterWorld books had collected over 18 million unwanted books, and raised over $22 million in funds for literacy and libraries.[22]

4.4 CAPITAL MARKETS FOR SOCIAL ENTREPRENEURS

>> **LO 4.4**   **Explain how social entrepreneurs can use capital markets to fund their ventures.**

Just as traditional entrepreneurial ventures need capital in order to survive, so do social entrepreneurs running for-profit or nonprofit organizations, or hybrid operations. For example, social entrepreneur Jennifer McFadden (who is also Associate Director of Entrepreneurial Programs at the Yale School of Management) started her new venture, Skillcrush, with a combination of personal finance and small amounts of money from the Collaborative Fund—a company that provides financing to entrepreneurs. Skillcrush is an online course that seeks to address the gender imbalance in tech industries by teaching (primarily) women how to code in a fun, interactive way. Since its launch in 2012, Skillcrush has devised several other courses, and has acquired more than 45,000 users.[23]

For-profits can also seek investment from Social Venture Capitalists (SVC), also known as impact-investment funds. These funds look both for a return on investment and to make a specific social/environmental impact. For example, thanks to SVC, the global solar energy for-profit company d.light (see Table 4.5) has transformed lives by manufacturing and distributing affordable solar energy solutions to over 50 million people in the developing world.

TABLE 4.5

d.light Impact

• 65 million lives empowered
• $5.2 billion saved in energy-related expenses
• 17 million school-aged children reached with solar lighting
• 23 million tons of CO_2 offset
• 127 gigawatt hours generated from renewable energy source
• 34 billion productive hours created for working and studying

Source: "d.light reaches 50 millions lives empowered," http://www.dlight.com/files/2614/3172/1502/50_Million_PDF_for_Website.pdf

ENTREPRENEURSHIP MEETS ETHICS

The Unintended Consequences of Social Entrepreneurship

TOMS Shoes
Credit: Rachel Murray/Stringer/Getty Images Entertainment/Getty Images

Toms Shoes was founded by serial entrepreneur Blake Mycoskie in 2006. The for-profit operates a "Buy One Give One" (BOGO) business model—for every pair of shoes it sells, it donates a pair to people living in impoverished countries. Since it was founded, the company has given away over 35 million pairs of shoes in over 60 countries. It has won numerous awards and attracted a great deal of media attention. Such is the popularity of its business model that many other companies have followed suit; eyeglasses manufacturer Warby Parker, footwear company Roma Boots, and snack manufacturer Nouri Bar are just a few examples of companies that operate a buy-one, give-one scheme.

However, despite the efforts of these companies to do good, critics suggest that the one-for-one business model may have unintended consequences; it might actually be doing more harm than good. Andreas Widmer, director of entrepreneurship programs at Catholic University, believes that the giveaway scheme "wreaks havoc" on local businesses as it stifles local industry and potentially increases local unemployment. Why would anyone buy shoes from the local cobbler when they can get them for free? Adrien Edwards is the founder of T-shirt brand The Naked Hippie, which invests its profits in people in developing countries. Edwards believes people in developing countries should be empowered to learn how to deal with the deeper causes of poverty rather than receiving goods for free. He says the "'treating the cause' model is a step between 'giving someone a fish' and 'teaching them how to fish.'"

There is also the question whether distributing free goods fosters dependency. For example, in 2012, Bruce Wydick,

economics professor at the University of San Francisco, and two colleagues studied the effect of the Toms Shoes giveaways in El Salvador. Their research showed that children receiving free shoes were 10% more likely to say that other people should provide for the children's families, compared to children who had not received the shoes. Wydick says the level of dependency was "probably the most negative effect we found."

Mycoskie has since listened to critics and has created employment for people in Haiti by hiring local artisans to paint limited classics. He has also created partnerships with the Clinton Foundation and the Wildlife Conservation Society to produce shoes and donate the profits toward elephant conservation and sea turtle projects. Toms Shoes also supports clean water initiatives, safe births, and eye treatment through the profits it receives from some of its other products.

CRITICAL THINKING QUESTIONS

1. **To what extent do good intentions make an entrepreneurial venture ethical? Do you agree that the Buy One Give One business model may have unintended consequences? If so, how do you think the model may be altered to increase its social benefit?**

2. **Should social entrepreneurs be responsible for assessing the effects of their endeavors, or is it sufficient that they are making an effort to solve a social problem? Explain your answer.**

3. **Imagine that you are a startup social entrepreneur. How can you—or should you— make sure your business is established and run in an ethical fashion?** ●

Sources

Buchanan, L. (2016, May). What's next for Toms, the $400 million for-profit built on Karmic Capital. *Inc Magazine.* Retrieved from http://www.inc.com/magazine/201605/leigh-buchanan/toms-founder-blake-mycoskie-social-entrepreneurship.html

Costello, A. (2016, March 3). Toms Shoes is a hit at Oscars but does its shoe giveaway hit the mark? *NPR.* Retrieved from http://www.npr.org/sections/goatsandsoda/2016/03/03/468955265/toms-shoes-is-a-hit-at-oscars-but-does-its-shoe-giveaway-hit-the-mark

The one-for-one business model: Avoiding unintended consequences. (2016, February). *Wharton.* Retrieved from http://knowledge.wharton.upenn.edu/article/one-one-business-model-social-impact-avoiding-unintended-consequences/

TABLE 4.6

Examples of Impact Investment Funds

SUSTAINABLE TRADE FINANCING
A U.K.-based $65 million fund invests in sustainable trade and has provided more than $200 million in loans to 300 small and growing businesses across Latin American and Asia.
Example investment: The fund has invested in a Fair Trade and organic-certified coffee cooperative located in Ecuador. The trade finance loan allowed the cooperative to cover operating costs and invest in new processing equipment. Additional revenue gained from Fair Trade coffee sales are used to sponsor projects in reforestation, education, and community-based health clinics in the community where smallholder farmers live.

LOW-INCOME HOUSING
A private equity fund based in Brazil closed with $75 million in assets. Investments target market-rate financial returns and social benefits to rural communities in South America.
Example investment: The fund has made an investment of $4 million to a provider of affordable homes designed for low-income families in rural settings. More than 10,000 homes have been constructed in three South American countries, focusing particularly in areas affected by natural disaster.

CLEAN ENERGY ACCESS
A €150 million European private equity fund invests $2.5–12.5 million in companies that provide clean electricity to rural communities in developing countries with limited access to energy. The fund has made five investments in Asia and Africa.
Example investment: The fund made a $2.5 million equity investment in a company that provides solar energy for lighting and refrigeration in rural Indian households, schools, and hospitals that have limited access to the main electricity grid. Enabled by this investment, the company has installed more than 40,000 systems and currently offsets 25,000 tons of carbon dioxide emissions.

CLEAN DRINKING WATER
An India-based impact investing fund manager started investing in microfinance institutions more than ten years ago. The fund manager decided to raise a second fund to target businesses across a broader set of sectors, including renewable energy, agriculture, health, and education. The fund provides risk capital and support to early stage ventures with investments averaging $50,000 in size.
Example investment: The second fund invested in a company, that sets up water purification plants in rural villages. The plants are owned by the local community and operated by the installation company, which sells the purified water to the village at affordable rates. The installation company also trains local entrepreneurs to develop businesses that deliver water to neighboring villages.

Source: http://www.impactbase.org/info/examples-impact-investment-funds

Web
Using Capital Markets

In fact, the SVC market has increased over the last few years, with some estimating that it could grow to $3 trillion in the future, mainly because of the rise of more socially conscious entrepreneurs looking for impact investment opportunities.[24] Table 4.6 lists a few examples of impact-investment funds.[25]

The second type of fund is the "Community" fund, and its goal is to invest in economic development and job creation in impoverished areas.[26] Venture Philanthropy Partners (VPP), for example, is based in Washington, D.C., and focuses on helping youths and children from low-income families in the national capital region. Since its inception in 2000, VPP has recruited 26 other founding investors who together have contributed more than $30 million to VPP's investment fund.

SJF Ventures operates as a traditional VC fund but also allocates a percentage of the fund to companies seeking investment to make a positive social or environmental impact across areas such as waste reduction, heath advancement, education, and natural resource conservation. Some of these social enterprises include Community Energy, which develops solar and wind energy projects;

Pennsylvania-based company CleanScapes, which provides sustainable waste and recycling collection in Seattle; and digital health platform Validic in California, which delivers patient data into the health care system through an API (Application Programming Interface) connection, and gives nurses and doctors better insight into their daily health.[27] SJF says it "values the passion and dedication needed by entrepreneurs to convert brilliant ideas into extraordinary businesses. We help companies succeed by providing growth capital and assisting entrepreneurs, with the demanding challenges they face."[28]

In fact, a whole range of clean energy startups are emerging, offering products and services that challenge how we use power. Achates Power, Inc., is creating waves by developing an improved internal combustion engine that is designed to increase fuel efficiency, decrease the amount of greenhouse gas emissions, and cost less than a conventional engine. The startup, founded by serial entrepreneur Dr. James Lemke, was awarded $14 million by the National Advanced Mobility Consortium to support a project focused on streamlining and modernizing military vehicles.[29]

Solar-powered kiosks charge mobile phones for a low cost.
Credit: Richard Levine/Alamy Stock Photo

In the developing world, clean energy social entrepreneurs are also making a real change. For example, while millions living in rural Tanzania do not have access to electricity, most households have a mobile phone, yet struggle to find ways of charging it. This situation inspired social entrepreneurs Olivia Nava and Sachi DeCou to set up Juabar (Swahili for solar bar)—solar-powered kiosks that charge mobile phones for a low cost. Juabar also trains locals to become "Juapreneurs" to enable them to operate franchises of the business, in return for a monthly fee of less than $45. DeCou says: "I am from the US and most people there ask how we can take such a lot of money from people here. The interesting thing is that some of our entrepreneurs make up to three times what they pay us."[30]

Microfinance as a Source of Social Financing

In Chapter 1 we profiled Nobel Peace Prize winner Muhammad Yunus, who, in the 1970s, founded the Grameen Bank in Bangladesh. This bank offers microloans, or small short-term loans to the poor to enable them to set up their own businesses. Since the founding of the Grameen Bank, other microlending providers have sprung up to extend Yunus' mission of eliminating exploitation of the poor by moneylenders, and create self-employment opportunities for the disadvantaged.

For example, nonprofit organization Kiva has enhanced the microfinance concept even further by enabling anyone to loan money for as little as $25 to entrepreneurs in developing countries who lack access to traditional banking systems. The hundreds of entrepreneurs are profiled on the Kiva website, and people can choose whom they would like to fund based on this information. Kiva does not charge interest or take a cut of the loan—the entire amount goes to the entrepreneur. When the entrepreneur repays the loan, the individual can decide if he or she wants to use it to make another loan to support a different entrepreneur.

In 2014, both the Grameen bank and Kiva teamed up with Kreyol Essence in an effort to generate loans that will go toward creating 300 jobs in Haiti. Kreyol Essence, founded by Yve-Car Momperoussein, is a provider of eco-luxury beauty products with ingredients sourced from Haiti. The loans provide opportunities for Haitian farmers to grow the castor plants needed to manufacture the products, and for women to make castor oil from the seeds. Haiti is a country that has suffered high unemployment as a result of the 2010 devastating earthquake, which has left half the population without work, as well as poverty, ill-health, and poor education. In addition to stimulating economic activity by creating new employment, Momperoussein hopes to protect Haiti's land against further deforestation and soil erosion through the cultivation of the castor oil plants.[31]

Social enterprises like the Grameen Bank and Kiva have revolutionized many lives and businesses in developing countries. Nevertheless, Shivani Soroya, founder of InVenture in 2014, spotted a gap. While the informal microloans certainly helped people to start their own businesses, when it came to growing those businesses, they still had no access to formal banking institutions. Because they had no credit score, they were perceived as too risky for formal loans. Soroya's aim was to break down these barriers by providing mobile and web tools for entrepreneurs to save business data in order to build up a credit score, to prove to formal institutions that the business is growing and worth the risk of small business loans. InVenture operates in Eastern Africa, South Africa, and India—regions where over 2.5 billion people have no credit score.[32]

However, none of the social entrepreneurs profiled in this chapter carried out their mission all by themselves. They had a number of people to help them. In the next section, we will take a look at how people can help or hinder a social venture.

> ### YOU BE THE ENTREPRENEUR
>
> Not all entrepreneurs are seeking to make a personal profit on their ideas—some want to make a profit benefiting others. Hugh Evans is founder of the Global Poverty Project (GPP), an initiative that works in partnership with NGOs and business and world leaders to help people all over the world living below the poverty line, by organizing global campaigns against poverty.
>
> Evans came up with the idea to hold an annual Global Citizen Festival where people have to take action in supporting the end of poverty, such as writing to politicians, and signing petitions in order to receive free tickets. Evans wants to focus on the rights of young people and hopes to get world leaders in the discussion.
>
> **What Would You Do?**
>
> Source: Evans, H. (2014), July 30). Action will lead us to the end of extreme poverty. *Huffington Post*, p. 1.

4.5 SOCIAL ENTREPRENEURS AND THEIR STAKEHOLDERS

>> **LO 4.5** **Identify the primary attributes of stakeholders and how stakeholders can help or hinder a social entrepreneur.**

As we have learned, social entrepreneurs cannot resolve wicked problems in isolation. To gain support for their mission, social entrepreneurs need to think about how their actions affect their **stakeholders**, who are the people or groups affected by or involved with the achievements of the social enterprise's objectives.

Stakeholders may include employees, volunteers, investors, customers, suppliers, and manufacturers, leaders in nonprofit organizations, community leaders, the government,

Stakeholders: the people or groups affected by or involved with the achievements of the social enterprise's objectives.

sponsors, board members, and other entrepreneurs. By identifying your stakeholders, you will be able to better understand the impact of your enterprise's activities on others; give your stakeholders a platform to provide feedback, information, advice and direction; and allow them to raise any concerns or obstacles that may stand in the way of achieving your objectives.

Linking all these stakeholders will help you get the best out of your social enterprise. A good way to identify your key stakeholders is to draw your own stakeholder map as illustrated in Figure 4.3.

Building relationships with key stakeholders is an important way to gain support, but you must also prove to your key stakeholders how you intend to generate value for them. While "doing good deeds" is a worthy objective, your stakeholders will want to understand the value of being involved with the venture.

What stakeholders does Jim Poss, founder of Bigbelly Inc., need to think about? Jim needs to prove that he can save waste management companies money by reducing the frequency of trash collections. He must also talk to the mayor to communicate his support for "green initiatives," communicate to potential employees that Bigbelly is a place where they should be proud to work, convince the board that Bigbelly will make money, talk to the planners to address locations for the Bigbelly, and engage with the labor unions to assuage any concerns they may have regarding the potential reduction of truck drivers (see Figure 4.4).

When you create a social innovation it is unlikely that all your stakeholders will be in immediate agreement. Instead, it is your responsibility to communicate to stakeholders not only the value derived but also the potential loss or consequences of

Web
Social Entrepreneurs'
Stakeholders

FIGURE 4.3

Example of Stakeholder Map

FIGURE 4.4

Jim Poss's Stakeholders

your activities, and suggest alternative solutions. The most important question you need to ask is: What is at stake for your stakeholders, and for whom? This question will allow you to Whom risk of launching your new venture.

With the potential for so many stakeholders, how you decide which ones are the most important? Whom do you need to prioritize, and what level of attention should you give? The salience model helps social entrepreneurs select the most suitable communication approach for each group of stakeholders by classifying stakeholders based on their salience (or significance) in the social enterprise. There are three primary attributes of stakeholders to consider when you are trying to achieve your objectives: power, legitimacy, and urgency.[33]

A stakeholder in a position of power has the ability to either help or hinder your social objectives. For example, in the case of Jim Poss, the labor unions could have blocked his Bigbelly initiative on the grounds that it could lead to job loss and unemployment. Here the labor union has the power to prevent or hinder Poss from achieving his organization objectives.

The second attribute is legitimacy. Legitimate stakeholders are those whose actions are appropriate, proper, and desired in the context of the company, organization, or community.[34] For example, if you have a problem or need some advice, you may consult with the stakeholders who you feel have the most legitimacy.

The third attribute is urgency, which describes the extent to which stakeholders demand your attention. For example, in a case where there are last-minute questions that need to be answered by your investors during the due diligence process, you would need to prioritize the needs of your investors over other stakeholders until the situation has been resolved.

These three attributes are not necessarily independent of one another; in fact, a stakeholder may have both power and legitimacy, or a combination of all three.

FIGURE 4.5

Mitchell Stakeholder Typology

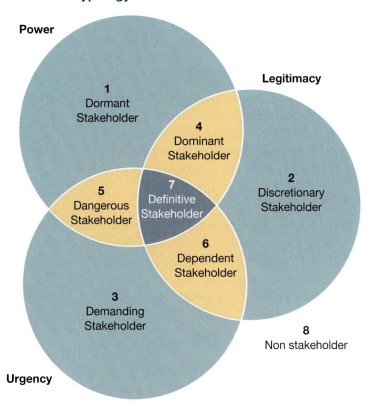

Source: Mitchell, R., Agle, B., & Wood, D. (1997). Toward a theory of stakeholder identification and salience: Defining the principle of who and what really counts. *Academy of Management Review, 22*, 853–866.

However, by identifying the different types of stakeholders, you will be better able to assess which ones are the most salient in a particular context.

Types of Stakeholders

In the 1990s, Ronald K. Mitchell and colleagues proposed a model of seven different types of stakeholders (see Figure 4.5). The model is based on the three factors of power, legitimacy, and urgency; note that each type of stakeholder occupies a position relative to these three overlapping circles. Let's examine each of these seven types using the example of nonprofit organization familiar to many young entrepreneurs—the Collegiate Entrepreneurs Organization (CEO). CEO has chapters across 200 colleges and universities in North America. Its mission is "to inform, support and inspire college students to be entrepreneurial and seek opportunity through enterprise creation."[35]

Dormant stakeholders

Dormant stakeholders are "sleepers"—they hold power but do not tend to use that power unless they are given a reason to do so. However, dormant stakeholders may become significant when they begin to utilize their power; for example, a disgruntled member may complain about CEO on social media. The key to ensuring these stakeholders are satisfied is to be transparent and keep them informed at all times. Just because they are "sleeping" doesn't mean they will never wake up.

Discretionary stakeholders

Discretionary stakeholders have no power to influence and no urgent claims, but they have legitimacy. They may come in the form of philanthropists who donate to your organization and are willing to support social causes. For example, CEO provides visitors with the opportunity to donate money on its website to support the organization.

Demanding stakeholders

Demanding stakeholders possess the urgency attribute. They have no power or legitimacy and may be the only dissenting voice in the room. For example, persons protesting outside the CEO national conference because they believe entrepreneurs create income inequality in the economy, but they do not have the power to enforce their claims. These stakeholders don't really impact CEO, and not a lot of time and energy should be devoted to them.

Dominant stakeholders

Dominant stakeholders have both power and legitimacy, which gives them strong influence in your organization. Dominant stakeholders of CEO include College Presidents or Deans of business schools where CEO chapters are located. Communicating with them regularly and responding to queries efficiently and accurately will help you maintain a good relationship with these stakeholders and keep the chapter on campus!

Dependent stakeholders

Dependent stakeholders have both urgency and legitimacy but lack the power to influence. These stakeholders are the most passionate, and their passion is likely to attract dominant stakeholders. For example, the student members of CEO are the most enthusiastic and passionate stakeholders connected to the organization, but they may not have the power necessary to effect change with the leaders of the national organization.

Dangerous stakeholders

Dangerous stakeholders possess both power and urgency but may use this power to coerce or even resort to violence. Social issues can be emotive, and power and urgency exercised against your objectives can be a significant hindrance. For example, a competing organization may emerge that could use false advertising or slander to get members from CEO to move their membership to the new organization.

Definitive stakeholders

Definitive stakeholders are the only ones who possess all three attributes of power, legitimacy, and urgency. These stakeholders have a significant role to play in your organization and must be given priority when it comes to handling their claims. In the case of CEO, the most definitive stakeholders are the foundations that fund CEO—the Kauffman and Coleman foundations.

Conclusions from the Mitchell Stakeholder Typology

Remember that stakeholders are not static—they can evolve, and through that evolution, they may either gain or lose attributes. Social entrepreneurs must continuously monitor the internal and external stakeholder environment to maintain relationships with stakeholders and ensure support for their social mission.

Stakeholders are vital to social entrepreneurship; and communities of stakeholders are emerging all over the world to share knowledge, collaborate on ideas, and build and grow social ventures. Ashoka, Social Venture Network, Investors Circle, Echoing Green,

MINDSHIFT

Practice Being "Other-Centered"

In this Mindshift, your challenge is to practice being "other-centered" for one week. Many of us live in a "me-centered" world, where events and relationships are measured by how much, and in what ways, they affect us. Being "other-centered" means stepping outside ourselves, and shifting the focus onto serving others for the good of the greater community.[36]

For example, instead of getting frustrated at an older adult taking forever to put away her change at the checkout line, give her a reassuring smile, and maybe offer to help her with her bags of groceries. Think about different ways in which you can cheer up others. Make someone else's day.

CRITICAL THINKING QUESTIONS

1. **To what extent do you feel you are already "other-centered" in your life? Give some examples of your actions and decisions in this regard.**

2. **Was it easier than you expected, or more difficult, to focus for an entire day on being other-centered? Would you want to continue this focus for a second day running?**

3. **What did you learn from this Mindshift that surprised you?** ●

Net Impact, and Social Enterprise provide a forum to connect with and learn about other stakeholders. Connecting and collaborating with others is the key to resolving wicked problems.

4.6 DIFFERENCES BETWEEN SOCIAL ENTREPRENEURSHIP AND CORPORATE SOCIAL RESPONSIBILITY

>> **LO 4.6**   **Distinguish between corporate social responsibility and social entrepreneurship.**

Corporate social responsibility (CSR) describes the efforts taken by corporations to address the company's effects on environmental and social well-being in order to promote positive change. While social entrepreneurship may sound similar to the corporate social responsibility (CSR) model, they are not the same (see Table 4.7).

The difference lies in the primary objective. In essence, CSR adds social objectives while still pursuing the main goal of making a profit. In contrast, many social entrepreneurship models, including the hybrid model, place equal emphasis on social and economic goals. An organization with a CSR strategy could reduce spending on its CSR program if it is struggling to meet revenues, whereas a social enterprise would prioritize its social goals even in the face of a reduction in profits.

Together, the biggest firms in the United States and Britain spend over $15 billion on CSR, and recent research suggests that some of these companies reap financial rewards as a result. For example, consumers may be attracted to these companies because the CSR spending may indicate high-quality products; they also may want to buy the products as an indirect way to donate to the causes the corporation supports; and they may also look on the organization favorably (the "halo" effect) because of its good deeds.[37]

On the legal side, research also suggests that if a firm is sued and prosecuted, it may tend to receive more lenient penalties if it has a record of CSR activities. For example, organizations with a focus on labor rights issues such as eliminating child labor or companies who increase CSR spending by 20% tend to be treated more leniently if they are prosecuted.[38]

A 2015 study lists corporations with the best CSR reputations including Google, Microsoft, BMW, Apple, and Sony.[39] In September 2015, Google launched a refugee

Corporate social responsibility (CSR): describes the efforts taken by corporations to address the company's effects on environmental and social well-being in order to promote positive change.

Audio
Corporate Social Responsibility

TABLE 4.7

Corporate Social Responsibility Versus Social Entrepreneurship

CORPORATE SOCIAL RESPONSIBILITY	SOCIAL ENTREPRENEURSHIP
Peripheral to mission	Core to mission
Side show	Main event
A department	The entire organization
Seeks to reduce harm	Measures social impact
Feel and look good	Do good
Stakeholder is the observer	Stakeholder is the customer
Consequence-driven	Purpose-driven
Image-motivated	Opportunity-motivated

fundraising campaign through its homepage, inviting users to donate to the migrant crisis, pledging any contribution would be matched dollar for dollar. Less than two months later, Google managed to raise $9 million for Doctors Without Borders, the International Rescue Committee, Save the Children, and the United Nations High Commissioner for Refugees (UNHCR).

While CSR has been mostly associated with large companies, it is also important to small to medium-sized companies. As Figure 4.6 shows, good CSR makes good business sense for small companies.

Smaller companies can also build a good reputation in the local community by volunteering at local libraries, hospitals and schools and by supporting local sports teams or local charities. Being connected with ethical suppliers with positive CSR is also a bonus for a small company as it builds trust with new customers.

Building trust and being socially responsible is important for all companies—big or small.

FIGURE 4.6

CSR Makes Good Business Sense

Good CSR helps to:

- engage more customers, especially if your firm is helping to support good causes
- lead to real innovations, such as environmentally safe products
- decrease costs by cutting packaging, travel, and energy expenses
- increase public image through the company's efforts to do good deeds
- bring people together by holding charity events such as sponsored walks and bake sales

Credit: R. Mitchell, B. Agle, and D. Wood. 1997. "Toward a Theory of Stakeholder Identification and Salience: Defining the Principle of Who and What Really Counts." *Academy of Management Review*, 22 (4): 853–866.

4.7 SOCIAL ENTREPRENEURSHIP AND GLOBAL INCLUSION

>> **LO 4.7**   **Assess the value of social inclusion globally within social entrepreneurship.**

Thorkil Sonne was an employee at a telecommunications firm in Denmark when his young son, Lars, was diagnosed with autism. According to research, autistic adults would always be dependent on their parents, and would have little chance of employment. In the United States alone, studies have shown that over half of Americans diagnosed with autism do not go to college or find jobs within a couple of years of graduating from high school.[40] However, at a young age Lars had begun to display a high sense of curiosity, intense focus, and close attention to detail—the very qualities companies needed in employees. Sonne quit his job and set up or "The Specialists"—a for-profit consultancy firm that hires out employees with autism. Within 12 years after its inception in 2003, *Specialisterne* had expanded from Denmark into 12 countries all over the world, including the United States of America, Canada, the United Kingdom, and Australia.[41] Sonne's mission is to create one million jobs for people with autism through social entrepreneurship.[42]

The Specialists is an example of a **work integration social enterprise (WISE)**—a social enterprise whose mission is to integrate people who have been socially excluded into work and society through productive activity.[43] Today, WISEs are becoming more or commonplace as more social entrepreneurs are realizing the social and economic potential of integrating people on the margins of society into the labor market. Typically, WISEs reach out to people who have a very low income, poor literacy, disabilities, or are homeless.

InnerCity Weightlifting (ICW) in Boston, founded by Babson graduate Jon Feinman, is another example of an organization set up to give socially excluded individuals an opportunity to turn their lives around. The main mission of ICW is to give troubled men and women, most of whom have been former gang members, or have criminal records, the chance to become personal trainers. ICW sends personal trainers over to the Microsoft New England headquarters in Cambridge, to put the Microsoft employees through their paces in an empty conference room. The ICW initiative provides a safe alternative space to the streets, where students can either become personal trainers or build networks with people who help them find roles in other areas.

Feinman's hope is to break down the barriers between social groups by encouraging them to support rather than isolate each other. Of his troubled students, he says, "There's a perception that they don't care [about trying to improve their own lives]. It's easy to write them off," he says of those enrolled in his program. "Our students do really care. What they lack is hope. How do we create that hope?"[44]

Social entrepreneurs are working all over the world to include people on the margins of society to give them new opportunities and hope. For example, in Mexico, 50% of the population released from prison ends up incarcerated again.

In an effort to fix this problem, social entrepreneur Saskia Nino de Rivera founded the nonprofit organization Reinserta un Mexicano to change the Mexican penitentiary system by working with mothers of children born in prison. Over 130 babies are born in Mexico City's women's prison every year, Reinserta un Mexicano helps the mothers raise their

Work integration social enterprise (WISE): a social enterprise whose mission is to integrate people who have been socially excluded into work and society through productive activity.

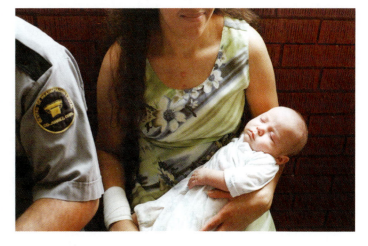

Reinserta un Mexicano helps reinsert mothers and their young children into society after being released from prison.

Credit: Joe Raedle/Hulton Archive/Getty Images

children, by providing them with rehabilitation and education, so they can rebuild their lives. The aim is to reduce the likelihood of the mothers going back to prison.[45]

Social entrepreneurs are also taking an inclusive approach to resolving problems in developing countries. As an example, by 2020, India will be one of the world's youngest populations, with an average age of 29. India is experiencing a rise in poverty and lack of access to health care and education.

Biomedical engineering graduate Dhairya Pujara founded Ycenter, an international social innovation startup that addresses problems in Africa and India, after working in a rural hospital in Mozambique for 5 months. The Ycenter aims to improve on three main shortcomings of traditional models of donations and charity.

First, these traditional models are ineffective when there is no concrete way of implementing the changes financed by the donations. For example, new medical equipment provided to hospitals in a developing country may go unused because staff members have not been trained to use it.

Second, traditional projects are not inclusive: people in these communities are not generally asked about their needs and wants, leading to lack of ownership and accountability.

Finally, Pujara believes that classroom education gets students only so far: "We need to back it up with on-the-field learning experiences, cultural awareness, and empathy."[46]

Video
Social Entrepreneurs in
Developing Countries

By empathizing and cocreating solutions with communities, using technology as a medium, Pujara believes that there is a chance these problems will eradicated forever. Pujara believes that Indian youths are the key to creating innovative and sustainable solutions to these wicked problems, if they are given a chance to practice entrepreneurship. Since the founding of Ycenter, Pujara has tackled the mortality rate of malaria in Mozambique by creating a short message service (SMS) app to enable the sick to text local community health workers, who will in turn reach out to help them. He is working with universities in the United States to send students to Africa to give them on-the-field experience and learn how to make an impact. Pujara also set up the very first TEDx conference in Mozambique.[47]

New York-based business Inspiring Capital, founded by Nell Derick Debevoise, CEO, is another social venture that brings a community of businesses and individuals together in order to devise strategies to change the world. Inspiring Capital has recently launched a program called Inspire Impact, which pairs MBA students with nonprofits and for-profit social enterprises.[48] Students benefit from experiencing firsthand how these organizations work by working on specific projects, while the organizations benefit from accessing talent that they might not otherwise have found. "By the end of the summer, they can have a 30,000 foot view of what a career in this field would be like," says Yael Silverstein, chief strategy and operations officer.

The Inspire Impact initiative ties in with the theory of Ycenter founder Pujara with its goal of getting the students out of the classroom during their study in order to learn how to apply their business skills so they can make an impact. Inspiring Capital works with a range of diverse companies including World Fund, Youth Inc., Tegu Toys, Happy Hearts Funds, Fiver Children's Foundation, and Guggenheim Partners.

Social entrepreneurs use the fundamental principles of entrepreneurship to build businesses of economic and social value. They improve the lives of whole communities by providing employment; they save the lives of premature babies; they educate people so they can make a living; they bring better eyesight to those who cannot afford treatment; they utilize our "trash" to create businesses that improve the lives of others; they employ excluded members of society and give them confidence and a sense of purpose. There is no such thing as waste or hopelessness in the mind of a social entrepreneur. Social entrepreneurs bring hope and change lives. They are making the world a better place (see Table 4.8). ●

TABLE 4.8

Resources for Social Entrepreneurs

Ashoka (www.ashoka.org)	Ashoka is a global association of social entrepreneurs. The website provides a wealth of information and resources for social entrepreneurs working in primarily nonprofit sectors. Ashoka both connects and funds social entrepreneurs in the citizen sector.
Echoing Green (www.echoinggreen.org)	Echoing Green invests in and supports social entrepreneurs launching and operating bold, high-impact social ventures.
Envirolink (www.environlink.org)	Envirolink is an online portal for environmental resources, including research, job postings, government resources, and events.
Global Social Venture Competition (www.gsvc.org)	The Global Social Venture Competition is the oldest and largest student-led business plan competition. The annual grand prize is $50,000. It receives over 500 entries from 40 countries.
Investor's Circle (www.investorscircle.net)	Investor's Circle is a group of formal and informal investors that invests patient capital in ventures that focus on building a sustainable economy.
Lewis Institute (www.babson.edu/lewis)	The Lewis Institute of Babson College strives to contribute to the solution of the world's problems through cutting-edge education, thought leadership, and entrepreneurship.
Net Impact (www.netimpact.org)	Net Impact is an international organization with graduate, undergraduate, and professional chapters. The organization brings together an extensive network of individuals who seek to positively change the world through business.
Root Cause (www.rootcause.org)	Root Cause supports social innovators and social investors through uniting and networking public, private, and nonprofit sectors. The website provides knowledge resources and how-to resources on everything from business plan writing to measuring social impact.
Schwab Foundation for Social Entrepreneurship (www.schwabfound.org)	The Schwab Foundation is a networking and support organization for leading social entrepreneurs hand-selected to join a prestigious network.
Skoll Foundation (www.skollfoundation.org)	The Skoll Foundation invests in and connects social entrepreneurs working for systemic change in areas of tolerance and human rights, health, environmental sustainability, economic and social equity, institutional responsibility, and peace and security.
Social Edge (www.socialedge.org)	Social Edge is a global online community of social entrepreneurs. Built for social entrepreneurs by social entrepreneurs where community members share resources, knowledge, and networks.
Social Enterprise Alliance (www.se-alliance.org)	The Social Enterprise Alliance brings together multiple stakeholder groups connected to social enterprise, including nonprofits, social purpose businesses, funders, investors, and consultants. The annual conference, Social Enterprise Summit, is one of the largest conferences serving social entrepreneurship today.
Social Fusion (www.socialfusion.org)	Social Fusion is an incubator for nonprofit and for-profit social ventures. The organization provides a menu of services and programs to help entrepreneurs start and build sustainable businesses.
Social Innovation Forum (www.socialinnovationforum.org)	The Social Innovation Forum connects social innovators to social impact investors in order to accelerate the creation of enduring solutions to social problems.
Social Venture Network (www.svn.org)	The mission of Social Venture Network is "to inspire a community of business and social leaders to build a just economy and sustainable planet." The organization hosts two annual conferences that bring together an extensive network of social entrepreneurs and others who support business as a way to change the world.
William James Foundation (www.williamjamesfoundation.org)	The William James Foundation offers support to mission-driven businesses through socially responsible business plan competitions, speaker series, cosponsored events, and fiscal assistance.

Get the edge on your studies at **edge.sagepub.com/neckentrepreneurship**

- ‣ Master the learning objectives using key study tools
- ‣ Watch, listen, and connect with online multimedia resources
- ‣ Access mobile-friendly quizzes and flashcards to check your understanding

SUMMARY

4.1   Describe what role social entrepreneurship plays in society.

Social entrepreneurship is the process of sourcing innovative solutions to social and environmental problems. While many companies strive simply to maximize shareholder value, social entrepreneurs are often more committed to causes centered on preserving and protecting future generations.

4.2   Explain how social entrepreneurship can help resolve wicked problems around the world.

Social entrepreneurship can help resolve wicked problems such as those related to water shortages, education, health care, poverty, energy, forced migration, and global warming by creating innovative solutions that make a real impact on the lives and livelihoods of others.

4.3   Identify the different types of social entrepreneurship.

There are three primary types of social entrepreneurship: social purpose ventures, social consequence entrepreneurship, and enterprising nonprofits.

4.4   Explain how social entrepreneurs can use capital markets to fund their ventures.

Social entrepreneurs can seek funding from Social Venture Capitalists (SVC) and community-funded venture capital to support operations. Microlending is another source of capital available for social entrepreneurs.

4.5   Identify the primary attributes of stakeholders and how stakeholders can help or hinder a social entrepreneur.

Stakeholders are all those involved in and affected by the activities of a social venture. Building relationships with key stakeholders is typically important for any entrepreneur, social or otherwise; but often social issues need additional support to gain traction with the majority of stakeholders.

4.6   Distinguish between corporate social responsibility and social entrepreneurship.

Corporate social responsibility and social entrepreneurship differ in one critical sense: the primary objective of the enterprise. Corporations seek to incorporate social initiatives into broader strategic and tactical objectives, while social entrepreneurs put those social issues front and center. To many corporations, social responsibility causes may just be another means to a successful business end.

4.7   Assess the value of social inclusion globally within social entrepreneurship.

Social inclusion is meant to directly confront some of the inequity that creates personal marginalization and its resulting social issues head-on. Many individuals will not have some of the same opportunities so common for their peers; many around the world have dedicated their careers to breaking down social issues plaguing society, encouraging inclusion with a heavy dose of hope.

KEY TERMS

Corporate social
    responsibility
    (CSR) 109
Earned-income
    activities 96
Enterprising nonprofits 96

Hybrid model of social
    entrepreneurship 99
Social consequence
    entrepreneurship 95
Social purpose
    ventures 94

Stakeholders 104
Venture philanthropy
    funding 97
Wicked problems 91
Work integration social
    enterprise (WISE) 111

Muhammad Yunus; Founder of Grameen Bank and Winner of the Nobel Peace Prize (2006)

Muhammad Yunus is a classic example of a social entrepreneur. He changed the world of moneylending by establishing the Grameen Bank—one of the first large-scale banks in the world to provide microcredit in the form of microloans to the poor. While Yunus's work is based in Bangladesh, the principles of microfinance made famous by his pioneering work have since been successfully applied in developing nations around the world. They have also been introduced to developed countries, including the United States.

Yunus was born in 1940 in what is now Bangladesh; at the time it was part of the British Raj (the areas of the Indian Subcontinent controlled by the British Empire until 1947). As a young man, Yunus was an avid Boy Scout who also demonstrated great academic potential. Later, in college, he earned two degrees in economics. After beginning a career in academia in Bangladesh, Yunus traveled to Nashville, Tennessee, in the United States to study at Vanderbilt University as a recipient of the prestigious Fulbright Scholarship. Upon receiving his PhD in economics, he opted to stay in the United States for three more years, where he taught at Middle Tennessee State University.

After returning to Bangladesh in the mid-1970s, Yunus was disheartened by the inability of the poorest members of his country to secure capital to produce wares and otherwise conduct businesses in which they were capable, willing, and eager to engage. Determined to address the problem with a real solution, he began pursuing research on concepts related to microfinance. He believed microlending would benefit the Bangladeshi underclass by providing a productive means whereby an individual could combat, and eventually escape, poverty.

In 1974, Bangladesh suffered a serious famine, which led to the deaths of thousands. Following this tragic period, Yunus saw an opportunity to begin testing his theories of microfinance. In 1976, while visiting the village of Jobra, Yunus met a woman who made a living weaving bamboo into furniture. Despite her skill and work ethic, she lacked the credit and collateral to secure capital from traditional lending sources to expand her business. Impressed with her work, and willing to take a chance on this obscure entrepreneur, Yunus took a small amount of money from his own pocket—a mere $27—and lent it to this woman *and* about 40 others in her community. When these minuscule loans were paid back on time, Yunus was encouraged to continue the practice by expanding the opportunity to other people—mostly women—in other villages.

Over time, word spread, and Yunus's work expanded. In 1983, the Grameen Bank was officially formed. Eventually, a system of group accountability was designed to encourage honest and timely repayments by lending money to individuals in groups of five, to include close associates who could hold each other accountable in making good on their debt obligations. The system proved so successful that as of 2006, the bank's 6.6 million borrowers had paid back over 98.5% of their loans! According to Yunus, this success comes in the wake of "no guarantee, no references, [and] no legal instrument. . . . It defies all the conventional wisdom . . . [yet] still it works."

As of 2006, Grameen was lending about $800 million per year in individual loans averaging only about $130. Yunus is passionate about reaching everyone who seeks a microloan for the sake of personal or professional betterment. In Yunus's own words: "Our policy is simple but different: Nobody should be left behind. We go house to house in an outreach to touch every single poor household."

Over the years, Grameen has expanded its entrepreneurial outreach to engage in other societal arenas besides microlending. These arenas include agriculture, fishing, telecommunications (specifically cellular phones), and solar power.

The success of Yunus and the Grameen Bank reached a crescendo in 2006 when the man and the bank were both awarded a Nobel Peace Prize. Yunus was the first citizen of Bangladesh to win the prestigious award. This was followed by a flurry of global recognition that included the prestigious Presidential Medal of Freedom, awarded by U.S. President Barack Obama in 2009. *Fortune* magazine named Yunus one of a dozen greatest entrepreneurs of the age, elevating him to an entrepreneurial echelon that included Steve Jobs, Bill Gates, Jeff Bezos, and Mark Zuckerberg, among others.

In Yunus's mind, a certain dollar amount is not necessary to become an entrepreneur.

> The guy who sells a hot dog on the street is as much an entrepreneur as anyone else. Getting his $50 loan to start could be as difficult as finding $50 million for someone else. All people are entrepreneurs. Some [just] never discover their talent and direction. (*Fortune Magazine* source, next page)

With unusual vision, drive, and results, Muhammad Yunus has provided opportunities for literally millions of new entrepreneurs to pursue their dreams, either on their own, or working for Grameen Bank. While you may never hear about most of these entrepreneurs, or read about them in *Fortune*, they are entrepreneurs nonetheless. Moreover, they are creating enormous amounts of positive momentum in the direction of destroying poverty throughout Bangladesh and the rest of the world.

> I strongly believe [that] . . . human beings [are not] born to remain poor. That is not the purpose of . . . life on this planet—to remain poor and struggle in poverty. I think human beings have lots [of] potential . . . to contribute, to be creative, to bring ingenuity [to] the world. (interview with Dr. Muhammad Yunus on Australian Broadcasting Corporation; see source below)

Critical Thinking Questions

1. What specific things might a social entrepreneur learn from Muhammad Yunus's amazing education and life journey that could help one find success in a future social entrepreneurship effort?

2. What social issues are being impacted by the Grameen Bank?

3. What other entrepreneurial domains might be tapped to specifically target needs and address problems we face as human beings?

Sources

Australian Broadcasting Corporation (ABC). (1997, March 25, Broadcast). *World in Focus: Interview with Prof. Muhammad Yunus.* George Negus, Interviewer. Retrieved from http://www.abc.net.au/foreign/stories/s400630.htm

Fortune Magazine Online. (2006, October 13). *From microcredit to microcapitalism: An interview with Nobel Peace Prize winner, Muhammad Yunus.* Retrieved from http://archive.fortune.com/magazines/fortune/fortune_archive/2006/10/16/8390329/index.htm

Giridharadas, A., & Bradsher, K. (2006, October 13). Microloan pioneer and his bank win Nobel Peace Prize. *New York Times.* Retrieved from http://www.nytimes.com/2006/10/13/business/14nobelcnd.html?_r=0

Harris, J. A. (2012). *Transformative entrepreneurs: How Walt Disney, Steve Jobs, Muhammad Yunus, and other innovators succeeded.* New York, NY: Palgrave Macmillan.

Yunus, M., & Jolis, A. (2008). *Banker to the poor: Micro-lending and the battle against world poverty.* New York, NY: Public Affairs.

Yunus, M., with Webber, K. (2009). *Creating a world without poverty: Social business and the future of capitalism.* New York, NY: Public Affairs.

Yunus, M., with Webber, K. (2010). *Building social business: The new kind of capitalism that serves humanity's most pressing needs.* New York, NY: Public Affairs.

PART II

CREATING AND FINDING OPPORTUNITIES

5 Generating New Ideas

Entrepreneurs have a knack for looking at the usual and seeing the unusual, at the ordinary and seeing the extraordinary. Consequently, they can spot opportunities that turn the commonplace into the unique and unexpected."[1]

—D. G. Mitton, author

5.1 THE ENTREPRENEURIAL MINDSET AND OPPORTUNITY RECOGNITION

>> **LO 5.2** Explain how the entrepreneurial mindset relates to opportunity recognition.

Through a chance occurrence, Jack McCarthy got the idea to set up a business selling ugly Christmas sweaters online. Although he was not yet out of high school, he recognized a gap in the market that needed to be filled and took action. But why was he one of the first to pursue this opportunity? Why didn't more people try to capture this niche market?

Video
Recognizing an Opportunity

In Chapter 3, we explored the concept of mindset and its importance to identifying opportunities. Applying what we have learned about mindset, we could say that McCarthy had an entrepreneurial mindset that positioned him to identify opportunities and to take to action to start his own venture. He wasn't quite sure what the outcome was going to be, but had an open mind that made him curious enough to try selling ugly Christmas sweaters again the following year. See the *Entrepreneurship in Action* feature below for McCarthy's story.

Making a success out of selling garments deemed "ugly" certainly seems unexpected, but the entrepreneurial mindset is attuned to just that—the unexpected. Entrepreneurship is all about openness to new ideas, new goals, and new ways of attaining them. Indeed, this is demonstrated time and again by countless entrepreneurs' stories, regardless of the diversity of their industries, whether for-profit or nonprofit, at startup or within an existing corporation. All the entrepreneurs featured throughout this text—from Niari Keverian, founder of ZOOS Greek Iced Teas; Jim Poss, founder of Bigbelly; to business partners Barbara Baekgaard and Pat Miller, founders of Vera Bradley—have found ways to identify new opportunities that address unmet needs in the marketplace. Let's take a closer look at what *opportunity* really means.

Jack McCarthy, Founder, UltimateUglyChristmas.com

Ultimate Ugly Christmas founder Jack McCarthy wearing an ugly christmas sweater
Credit: Used with permission from Jack McCarthy

For Jack McCarthy, success has never looked so . . . atrocious. The teenager started his business, UltimateUglyChristmas.com, as a fluke, as Jack's older sister prepared to participate in an Ugly Christmas Sweater 5K "fun run" for charity in 2008. Once the 5K was over, she decided to sell her eyesore on eBay. Jack, then a middle school student, was the model for the picture. Much to the siblings' surprise, a bidding war began. The winning bid was $50 + express shipping, a 450% profit margin on a $5 throwaway garment picked up at Goodwill.

Encouraged by his sister's success, the following Christmas seasons, Jack picked up more and more sweaters, hawking them on eBay for similar margins. Each year demand grew, profits ballooned, and he began to realize he was onto something. As a high school junior, in 2011, McCarthy started UltimateUglyChristmas.com. That year he sold a "few hundred" and even picked up some national TV news coverage. "This is when I knew it was more than a little side income," he says.

McCarthy admits that in the early years, he knew nothing about business (he went on to study the subject at Babson College in Massachusetts), and looks back on those early experiments as "market validation." "I was naïve," he said. "I started selling and went from there. After the success in 2011 is when I learned many of the things that helped to grow the business—internet marketing, search engine optimization (SEO), graphic design, accounting, etc." Indeed, McCarthy had stumbled onto a growing niche. At the time he listed the first sweater in 2008 on eBay, there were only

about 30 competing items, but since 2014, these have since grown to over 30,000.

The ugly sweater party trend got its start in Vancouver, Canada, in the early 2000s, according to *Ugly Christmas Sweater Party Book: The Definitive Guide to Getting Your Ugly On* by Brian Miller, Adam Paulson, and Kevin Wool. In 2008, ugly sweater parties earned a coveted spot on the tongue-in-cheek website StuffWhitePeopleLike.com, a reflection of their ascension into mainstream consciousness.

"I love ugly Christmas sweaters," says McCarthy. "I think they are hilarious and fun." The sweaters on his site are all vintage, sourced from thrift stores, and thus generally one-of-a-kind. "It's a treasure hunt finding inventory."

The McCarthy's are an entrepreneurial family. Jack's sister launched a social media marketing agency after college, and his father started a financial planning investment advisory firm when he was young. "I watched him grow it over the years and wanted to create something of my own like that," says Jack. His family was his main "network" in the early days: His mother helped with "operational things" (she still runs the UltimateUglyChristmas.com warehouse—the family basement) while his father helped with "accounting/legal/general business advice." Jack's sister weighed in with social media and Internet marketing ideas. SEO has been key to growing his reach.

While studying business in college, McCarthy's goal was to grow and formalize that network, seeking out the ideas and expertise of fellow entrepreneurs, VCs, and professors. Though he describes himself as thriving on pressure, competition from the "big guys" is cause for concern. "Since it's an internet business," McCarthy says, "all it takes is Amazon (or another big site) to become aggressive in this market and my site will fade into second/later pages of Google. This could really hurt my business; it has others in the industry."

CRITICAL THINKING QUESTIONS

1. **Since the idea of ugly Christmas sweaters already existed, what key factors led to Jack McCarthy's turning it into a business opportunity?**

2. **What are some advantages a teenager might have over an experienced adult when it comes to recognizing and implementing a business opportunity?**

3. **If you were in McCarthy's position as a business student who already headed a highly successful enterprise, what would your career goals be? Explain the reasons for the goals you propose.** ●

Source: J. McCarthy, personal interview, September 18, 2014.

What Is an Opportunity?

There are many definitions of opportunity, but most include references to three central characteristics: potential economic value, novelty or newness, and perceived desirability.[2] We define **opportunity** as an apparent way of generating value through unique, novel, or desirable products, services, and even processes that have not been previously exploited. For an opportunity to be viable, the idea must have the capacity to generate value.

Value can take many forms. The most common form of value is economic value: the capacity to generate profit. Two other forms of value—social value and environmental value—are less common but equally important. An opportunity has social value if it helps to address a social need. Environmental value exists if the opportunity protects or preserves the environment. The Bigbelly waste management and recycling company, for example, is a business that generates both economic and environmental value.

All forms of value, however, are predicated on the assumption that there is a market populated with enough people to buy your product or service. This does not mean that a large market is required; there are countless examples of successful businesses that run on a small scale, catering to a market that is limited in one way or another. The key is to scale the business and its costs to the size of the market—to balance supply with demand. Here again, the entrepreneurial mindset is what enables us to envision how a new product or service can generate value for a niche, an age group or interest segment, a geographic area, or a larger population.

In addition, a new idea that constitutes an opportunity, whether it is a product, service, or technology, must be new or unique or at least a variation on an existing theme that you are confident people will accept and adopt. The idea must involve something that people need, desire, and find useful or valuable. Finding these qualities in an idea is the essence of opportunity recognition.

Innovation, Invention, Improvement, or Irrelevant?

Of course, all ideas are not created equal. Part of recognizing an opportunity is the ability to evaluate ideas and identify those with the highest likelihood of success. One framework for doing this is to rate an idea on four different dimensions: the idea may be an *innovation*, an *invention*, an *improvement*, or *irrelevant*. Of these, innovations and inventions are high in novelty, while improvements and irrelevant ideas are low in novelty (see Figure 5.1).

A successful idea scores highly as an *innovation* if the product or service is novel, useful, and valuable. Today's smartphone, and the basic cellular phone of the 1980s, are both good examples of a product that meets all the requirements of a successful innovation.

Innovations and inventions are often paired together, but the difference between them lies in demand. *Inventions*, by definition, score highly for novelty; but if an invention does not reach the market or appeal to consumers, then it will be rendered useless. Inventions that succeed in finding a market move to the innovation stage.

As an example of an invention that developed into an innovation, consider the story of Bette Nesmith Graham, inventor of Liquid Paper correction fluid.[2] In the early 1950s, Graham was a single mother and an aspiring artist, working as a secretary in Dallas, Texas. Like any typist, she sometimes made typing errors and wondered if there was a way to correct them. (This, of course, was years before the word processor

Master the content
edge.sagepub.com/neckentrepreneurship

Opportunity: an apparent way of generating profit through unique, novel, or desirable products or services that have not been previously exploited.

Video
Innovation Through Collaboration

FIGURE 5.1

Idea Classification Matrix

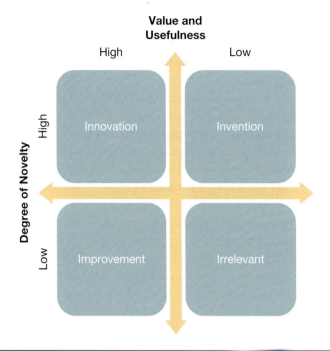

Source: H. M. Nock, "Idea generation," In B. Bygrave & A. Zacharakis eds. *Portable MBA in Entrepreneurship* (Hoboken, NJ: John Wiley & Sons, 2010, pp. 27–52).

came into use.) Her interest in art taught her that artists tend to paint over their mistakes on canvas, so she set about finding a solution to correct typing errors on paper.

Graham began by using water-based paint to correct her typing mistakes, matching it to the color of her stationery. Soon, all the other secretaries in the company where she worked were asking for some, too. Encouraged by the success of the product, Graham started the Mistake Out Company in 1956 (later renamed Liquid Paper) from her own kitchen, recruiting friends and family to fill the bottles to sell to a growing customer base. Less than 10 years later, Liquid Paper had grown into a million-dollar business. By the time Graham sold it in 1980, it was worth $47.5 million.

The Liquid Paper invention took off because it was novel, useful, and practical—but it became an innovation of high value only when it hit the market. Yet ideas do not always need to be unique or novel to appeal to customers. There are many ideas that focus on *improvement*. These improvements are based on enhancing existing products. Take folding sunglasses, serrated ice cream scoops, or reusable sticky notes, for instance. Each product has been revisited and improved on. While the products may not be high in novelty, there is still a strong market for these products, as many people will find them useful to a degree.

Bette Nesmith Graham invented Liquid Paper correction fluid in the 1950s, a product that is still widely used today.

Credit: Ingram Publishing/ Newscom

Finally, there are ideas that fall into the *irrelevant* category, scoring low on both novelty and usefulness. The beverage industry in particular has experimented with some changes over the years that have failed to meet consumer expectations. Coca-Cola changing its recipe to produce "New Coke" and Pepsi-Cola introducing colorless "Crystal Pepsi"; the Life Saver Soda drink; and Maxwell House producing coffee in a carton—all of these are arguably examples of irrelevant ideas.

However, it is difficult to fully pigeonhole ideas into neat categories. How can we really predict whether an idea is inventive, innovative, or irrelevant? Something we perceive as irrelevant and useless might appeal to someone else. For example, who would have thought ugly Christmas sweaters would be in such high demand? Or that sunglasses for dogs ("Doggles") would generate more than $3 million in sales for a small company?[3] Or that a fleece blanket with sleeves (the Snuggie) would become a viral phenomenon and generate over $500,000 in sales?[4]

"Doggles" - sunglasses for dogs
Credit: ©iStockphoto.com/damedeeso

Even the most apparently bizarre inventions can find a home. Take the Pet Rock, invented in the 1970s. The replacement of a live animal with a pet rock might seem absolutely ludicrous to some; but in less than a year, 1.5 million consumers bought their own Pet Rock, proving that even seemingly improbable ideas can be successful.[5]

Opportunities spring from ideas, but not all ideas are opportunities. While we all have the capability to generate a huge range of ideas, not every one of us knows how to turn an idea into a valuable, revenue-generating opportunity. Making an idea a reality is a process that involves time, resources, commitment, and a great deal of work, which can seem a little daunting to many of us. But if it were easy, wouldn't everyone do it?

As the idea classification matrix illustrates, most opportunities in entrepreneurship demand high value and some degree of novelty. But how do we identify the right opportunities? The first step in the opportunity identification process is generating as many ideas as we can—for it is out of thousands of ideas that opportunities are born.

5.2 OPPORTUNITIES START WITH THOUSANDS OF IDEAS

>> **LO 5.2**   Employ strategies for generating new ideas from which opportunities are born.

The way to get good ideas is to get lots of ideas and throw the bad ones away. Different strategies can be employed and not all will work for you.
                    —Linus Pauling, Nobel Laureate in Chemistry

The first step in creating and identifying opportunities is idea generation; the more ideas we generate, the greater the likelihood we will find a strong opportunity. At this stage, it's important to embrace the openness of an entrepreneurial mindset to consider ideas that might seem impractical, overly obvious, wild, or even silly. On the surface, you never know what may turn out to be a good or bad idea.

The Myth of the Isolated Inventor

Here's a quick exercise: Take a minute, close your eyes, and think of an idea. Ready? Think hard. How many ideas did you come up with? If you have come up with very few or no ideas at all, you are in good company. Ideas don't just spring fully formed into our minds, although the myth of the isolated inventor, working tirelessly from his or her workshop or laboratory, may lead us to think so.

In fact, as recent literature shows, history's greatest inventions occurred very differently from what we may have been taught. For instance, most of us learned in history class that Eli Whitney invented the cotton gin in 1793—except he didn't really. In fact, he simply improved existing cotton gins by using coarse wire teeth instead of rollers. In other words, he took an existing product and enhanced it to make it more useful. The cotton gin was actually a result of the work of a group of different people who made improvements over a number of years, which finally resulted in a popular marketable innovation.[6]

Similarly, Thomas Edison did not invent the lightbulb—in fact, electric lighting and lightbulbs already existed before he came along. Edison's discovery was a filament made of a certain species of bamboo that had a higher resistance to electricity than other filaments. Again, he took an existing product and made it more useful and valuable. Edison's biggest contribution to the light bulb was making it more marketable.[7]

Many of the most well-known inventions have evolved because of both a substantial number of people working on them simultaneously, and improvements made by groups over the years or even centuries. Many sewage-treatment plants and irrigation systems today use a rotating corkscrew type of pump known as Archimedes' screw, which dates back to the third century BC. Although its invention is attributed to the Greek scientist Archimedes, chances are he did not devise it on his own—and even if he did, it has been modified and adapted in a multitude of ways around the world. Other examples of inventions with long and varied histories include concrete (developed by the Romans around 300 BC); optical lenses (another ancient Roman discovery, made practical in thirteenth-century Europe); gunpowder (invented in the ninth century in China), and vaccination (first developed in the 1700s, but not widely implemented until more than a century later). As history shows, there is very little reason to credit just one person for the creation of a novel product or service.[8]

Regardless of who is responsible for inventions and innovations, we can safely say that each of those successful products or services began with an idea. Opportunities emerge from thousands of ideas, but how can we learn to generate the best ideas? Let's take a look at some strategies we can use for idea generation.

Seven Strategies for Idea Generation

There are countless different ways of generating ideas—from the informal (but not very effective) type illustrated above, such as "close your eyes and think of an idea!" to the more structured idea generation techniques, which we describe below.

Researchers have defined many formal methods of idea generation. Out of these, we have chosen seven main strategies that we believe are effective in the generation of new ideas for entrepreneurs. They include the following:

- ▶ analytical strategies,
- ▶ search strategies,
- ▶ imagination-based strategies,
- ▶ habit-breaking strategies,
- ▶ relationship-seeking strategies,
- ▶ development strategies, and
- ▶ interpersonal strategies.[10]

ENTREPRENEURSHIP MEETS ETHICS

Improving on Someone Else's Idea

Howard Schultz, founder and CEO of Starbucks, took the concept of Italian Gourmet coffee and built a whole new type of café culture.

Credit: Bloomberg/Bloomberg/Getty Images

Approaches to generating ideas include networking and meeting new people, keeping a journal on problems you or others have encountered and potential ways of solving them, tapping into your hobbies and interests, exploring new ways of thinking about designs and methodologies, traveling and recycling ideas from other regions, and surfing the web, among others. Engaging in these activities will often mean that you learn about ideas that have occurred to other people, whether they have acted on them or not. It can also mean that you will think of ways to implement an existing idea. Indeed, it's usually much easier to define a better implementation for an existing idea than to dream up a great idea from scratch.

Examples of companies that took the opportunity to improve on and profit from others' ideas include Starbucks and Southwest Airlines. Starbucks CEO Howard Schultz brought the concept of Italian gourmet coffees to the United States and then disseminated the model around the world. Herb Kelleher, cofounder of Southwest, created a unique culture that is equal parts playful and professional.

But is it ethical to "steal" someone else's idea and improve upon it? Seth Godin is the founder of the web service Squidoo. Godin believes that ideas can't be stolen because rather than getting smaller, ideas get bigger when they are shared. He has suggested that the role of the "stealer" is not to implement the initial idea, but instead to take responsibility for *improving* on the idea.

The answer to the question of ethics regarding ideas is not a simple "yes" or "no." Instead, there are degrees of ethical behavior involved in taking another's idea,

improving on it, and then profiting from it. While there are legal protections for what is known as intellectual property (IP; patent, trademark, and copyright[9]), even within what is legal there are practices that may be unethical. It is easy to argue that if an idea is universal and not suitable for a patent, it may be perfectly ethical for anyone to make use of it. But what about an idea that might be eligible for a patent or trademark, whose originator doesn't intend to apply for these protections? Is it ethical for someone else do to so? As another example, what are the ethics of using material eligible for copyright whose copyright hasn't yet been filed? The law states that the material belongs to the originator—but copyright cannot protect an *idea*; it protects only the tangible expression of an idea. Chapter 15 provides more information about legal issues and IP.

As you can see, there are ways in which it may be possible and legally defensible to "steal" work that does not (yet) have a patent, a trademark, or a registered copyright. Nevertheless, it is often unethical for such material to be taken, produced, and profited from by another.

CRITICAL THINKING QUESTIONS

1. **What are some reasons why governments have laws protecting IP (patent, trademark, and copyright)?**

2. **Do you agree or disagree with Seth Godin's view that ideas can't be stolen? Is it more ethical to "steal" an idea if the "stealer" improves on it? Explain your answers.**

3. **Have you ever had someone take credit for your idea or work? Did someone profit financially or receive public praise for your work? How did that make you feel? What did you do in response?** ●

Sources

Cain, A. (2015, September 18). Stealing ideas is theft. *The Sydney Morning Herald: My Small Business.* Retrieved from http://www.smh.com.au/small-business/trends/the-big-idea/stealing-ideas-is-theft-20150910-gjjpsv.html

Djurkic, J. (2014, December 16). *7 Ways to generate business ideas this year.* Retrieved from MaRS: https://www.marsdd.com/news-and-insights/seven-ways-to-generate-business-ideas/

Magley, R. (2014, May 1). *Why stealing a business idea is easier than inventing one.* Retrieved from https://www.emailanswers.com/2014/05/steal-blog-stealing-business-idea-easier-inventing/

Weinstein, B. (2004, November 19). *10 great ways to generate business ideas.* Retrieved from Entrepreneur.com: http://www.entrepreneur.com/article/74184

Although not all of the strategies may suit everyone, each can help us forge new connections, think differently, and consider new perspectives in different ways. Let's take a closer look at each.

Designing a door hinge may require use of search strategies as a stimulus.

Credit: ©iStockphoto.com/Gizmo

Analytical strategies: actions that involve taking time to think carefully about a problem by breaking it up into parts, or looking at it in a more general way in order to generate ideas about how certain products or services can be improved or made more innovative.

Search strategies: actions that involve using memory to retrieve information to make links or connections based on past experience that are relevant to the current problem using stimuli.

Imagination-based strategies: actions that involve suspending disbelief and dropping constraints in order to create unrealistic states, or fantasies.

Habit-breaking strategies: actions that involve techniques that help to break our minds out of mental fixedness in order to bring about creative insights.

Analytical strategies involve taking time to think carefully about a problem by breaking it up into parts, or looking at it in a more general way in order to generate ideas about how certain products or services can be improved or made more innovative. In some cases, you may see very little correlation between problems until you think about them analytically. For example, in one study, a group was asked to think about different ways of stacking certain items. The ideas they came up with were then considered as ways to park cars. In another study, researchers found that artists who carried out critical analysis before they started their work, as well as through the duration of the task, were more successful than those who did not use the same analysis.

Search strategies involve using memory to retrieve information to make links or connections based on past experience that are relevant to the current problem using stimuli. For example, say you were asked to design a door hinge. Here, the door hinge is a stimulus—a starting point for searching solutions to the problem. Although you may not have any prior experience of designing door hinges, you could search your memory to see if you can think of anything that you can associate with a door hinge to support the design process. For example, the search process may stimulate your memory of the opening and closing of a clam shell. By drawing on this memory, you could use your knowledge of the clam shell and apply it to the hinge design. This strategy illustrates our ability to be resourceful in generating associations between objects that at first appear to have no apparent relationship with each other.

Imagination plays an important part in idea generation. **Imagination-based strategies** involve suspending disbelief and dropping constraints in order to create unrealistic states, or fantasies. For example, the Gillette team also used imagination to come up with a new shampoo by imagining themselves as human hairs.

One of the remarkable things about generating ideas, especially ideas that come from imagination-based strategies, is that one idea can lead to another, yielding a pipeline of great ideas—that may impact the world. For example, scientists at the National Aeronautics and Space Administration (NASA) have needed to use a great deal of imagination to come up with tools, protective clothing, personal care items, foodstuffs, and other inventions that can be used in outer space. Along the way, these ideas led to other inventions that have changed many people's lives here on Earth; some of them are shown in Figure 5.2.

In order to think creatively, our mind needs to break out of its usual response patterns. **Habit-breaking strategies** are techniques that help to break our minds out of mental fixedness in order to bring about creative insights. One strategy is to think about the opposite of something you believe, in order to explore a new perspective. Another method focuses on taking the viewpoint of someone who may or may not be involved in the situation. A popular habit-breaking strategy is to take the role of a famous or admired individual and think about how he or she would perceive the situation. This is sometimes called the Napoleon technique, as in

FIGURE 5.2

Everyday Spinoffs From NASA

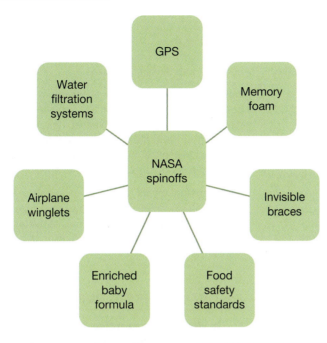

Source: Inhabitat. (2014) "INFOGRAPHIC: You Won't Believe How many World-Changing Inventions Came From NASA." Retrieved from http://inhabitat.com/infographic-you-wont-believe-how-many-world-changing-inventions-came-from-nasa/ and National Aeronautics and Space Administration (2016). *Spinoff*. https://spinoff.nasa.gov/Spinoff2016/pdf/2016_Brochure_web.pdf

"What would Napoleon do?" referring to the skills of this famous military and political leader.

Relationship-seeking strategies involve consciously making links between concepts or ideas that are not normally associated with each other. For example, you could make a list of words that are completely unrelated to the problem you are trying to solve, such as *doorknob*, then list the characteristics of each item on the list. Next, apply those characteristics to the problem with a view toward coming up with ideas to solve the problem. The purpose of this exercise is to stimulate toward the mind into making connections that would otherwise have gone unnoticed.

Development strategies are employed to enhance and modify existing ideas in order to create better alternatives and new possibilities. A common exercise in idea enhancement is to gather a group of four to six people together. Each person writes down three ideas, which are then passed around the group. Then every member spends five minutes suggesting improvements on the ideas to make them more feasible and effective.

The most dominant of the strategies within group scenarios are **interpersonal strategies**, in which group members collaborate to come up with new or improved ideas. Group brainstorming is a good example of an interpersonal strategy where members exchange thoughts and build on ideas.

The point of these seven strategies is to direct your mind toward generating enough ideas that will eventually provide pathways to new opportunities.

Relationship-seeking strategies: plans of action that involve consciously making links between concepts or ideas that are not normally associated with each other.

Development strategies: actions that involve enhancing and modifying existing ideas in order to create better alternatives and new possibilities.

Interpersonal strategies: actions that involve group members stimulating each other to come up with new or improved ideas.

In Love With Your Idea?

Find some classmates and practice this quick brainstorming exercise. It's best to have a group of five or more. The more people you have, the more powerful the exercise will be.

You'll need a few materials before you begin:

- A sheet of paper for every group member
- A pen or pencil for every group member
- A pencil that will not be used—or a picture of a pencil, if you are working with a large group
- A timer

Here are your instructions. They are quite simple: You have five minutes to brainstorm as many uses as you can for a pencil. Yes, a pencil! Go for quantity, do not judge your ideas, and keep in mind that wild ideas are just as acceptable as are mundane ideas. Start the timer and go.

After five minutes have passed, everyone should stop brainstorming uses for a pencil and count how many ideas they have generated. Identify the person with the most ideas—the winner!

Ask the winner to identify his or her first and second idea. Then ask the other group members to raise their hands if their list included at least one of these two same ideas. Usually most of the group will raise their hands.

The point of the exercise is: Don't fall in love with the first ideas that pop into your mind, because most people will come up with those same ideas.

Now ask the winner to share an idea from the very bottom of his or her list. Typically, you will find that not many people in the room have that idea on their lists. The thoughts we generate when we keep "digging," prodding ourselves to think of more and more ideas, are the ones that tend to be the most original and novel.

Brainstorming not only takes practice; it also takes energy, as it requires pushing beyond the easiest, most obvious ideas. Don't fall in love with the ideas at the top of your list. They won't be novel. Instead, keep going to get the most innovative ideas.

CRITICAL THINKING QUESTIONS

1. **In view of this exercise, can you explain the popular saying, "You always find something in the last place where you looked for it"?**

2. **Do you agree that it is always important to look for new ideas and solutions if a workable solution already exists? Give examples to support your answer.**

3. **In what ways did the exercise challenge your previous assumptions and beliefs? Did you learn anything that surprised you?** ●

5.3 TWO PATHWAYS TO OPPORTUNITY IDENTIFICATION[11]

>> **LO 5.3**   **Apply the two primary pathways to opportunity identification.**

Video
Identifying an Opportunity

Finding approach: a concept that assumes that opportunities exist independent of entrepreneurs and are waiting to be found.

When the famous explorer George Leigh Mallory was asked why he climbed Mount Everest, he answered, "Because it's there."[12] This indicates that Mallory took the opportunity to climb Everest simply because it was there for the taking.

If we apply this concept to entrepreneurship, we could argue that, like the mountain, entrepreneurial opportunities already exist—we just need to find them. This is called the **finding approach**, a concept that assumes that opportunities exist independent of entrepreneurs and are waiting to be found.[13] It is based on the concept that entrepreneurial opportunities exist as a result of the changing landscape in technology, consumer preferences, government regulations, and demographics.

In the finding approach, the role of savvy entrepreneurs is to deliberately search for these opportunities by scanning the environment, staying alert, making use of available information, and ensuring they are the first to exploit opportunities as soon as they discover them.

The finding approach views decisions as *risky*. Because opportunities already exist, it stands to reason that the information is available and the data there to be collected. Because the data exists, it can be used through a process of analysis techniques to work out the probability of the outcome, if you were to pursue the opportunity; in other words, the information is available to reasonably ascertain the level of risk. For example, using the mountain metaphor, plenty of information about Mount Everest has been collected over the years to assist mountain climbers with the knowledge they will need when considering an ascent, and it is up to a would-be climber to find this information.

Yet, what if entrepreneurial opportunities are not like mountains at all? What if entrepreneurs are the ones responsible for creating opportunities that never before existed? In other words, what if the mountains are actually created by the actions of entrepreneurs? Recall from Chapter 1 the work of Saras Sarasvathy, who proposed that entrepreneurs focus on creating a future rather than predicting it; creating new opportunities, making new markets, and producing new products and services through action. In Sarasvathy's theory of effectuation, entrepreneurs interact with their environment by observing how the markets and customers respond to their activity, and learning from the results produced by that activity.

Plenty of information is available for people who wish to climb Mount Everest.

Credit: robertharding/Alamy Stock Photo

Building approach: a concept that assumes that opportunities do not exist independent of entrepreneurs, but are instead a product of the mind.

Sarasvathy's theory is similar to the second pathway for opportunity identification we present here: the **building approach**, a concept that assumes that opportunities do not exist independent of entrepreneurs, but are instead a product of the mind.[14] In the building approach, opportunities are created, not found. They originate from the entrepreneur's prior knowledge and experience, which equip the entrepreneur to create them. To identify opportunities, this approach advocates using what you know, whom you know, and who you are. Your role as an entrepreneur is to take action and see how the market responds, recognize patterns, and learn from iteration to define the opportunity as it evolves.

Whereas decision making is perceived as risky within the finding approach, decision making is thought to be *uncertain* in the building approach. Because the opportunity doesn't exist yet, it needs to be created. The building approach acknowledges that information about how to proceed is not readily available. Unlike the finding approach, entrepreneurs do not have existing information to build a mountain because the mountains do not yet exist. In order to learn, improve, and succeed, the entrepreneur must continually take actions and adjust to changing circumstances. The entrepreneur cannot predict the probability of the outcomes, given the potential lack of information. This leaves the entrepreneur with two decisions: either to find ways to source the information and resources in order to create an opportunity or to decide against the opportunity altogether (see Table 5.1).

Consider Jack McCarthy of Ugly Christmas Sweaters. McCarthy stumbled on the market for those sweaters. He had no prior knowledge of the market for that kind of product, nor did he have any formal experience of social networks. He had no way to predict the probability of his Ugly Christmas Sweater business becoming a success or a failure since there wasn't much existing information to go on. McCarthy had two courses of action to choose from: to test the market by putting more ugly sweaters

Video
Using the Building Approach

TABLE 5.1

Finding or Building Opportunities

	FINDING OPPORTUNITIES	BUILDING OPPORTUNITIES
Origin of opportunities	Changes in technology, markets, consumer tastes, government regulations, demographics	Prior knowledge and experience
Assumptions	The opportunity exists and is waiting to be identified	Opportunities don't exist until they are created
Methods of identification	Search and scan the environment	Build networks
Role of the entrepreneur	Be alert to changes in the environment	Take action; continuous learning and iteration
Decisions	Perceived as risky	Perceived as uncertain

Source: Adapted from Sarasvathy, S. D. (2008). *Effectuation: Elements of entrepreneurial expertise.* Northampton, MA: Edward Elgar; Alvarez, S. A. & Barney, J. B. (2007). Discover and creation: Alternative theories of entrepreneurial action. *Strategic Entrepreneurship Journal, 1,* 11–26.

up for sale, or to walk away. As we know, he decided to take action and test the response of consumers by selling more sweaters online. Rather than spending time planning his next steps, or attempting to predict the end result of his actions, he put the sweaters on eBay and, without any major foresight, created his own opportunity. The overwhelming response from consumers has encouraged him to build his business by creating his own e-commerce site, sourcing more sweaters to sell, learning about entrepreneurship, building his knowledge base, and expanding his network. In this sense, we could say that he managed to bring an opportunity into existence by engaging in a repetitive process of reaction (reacting to market demands) and action (taking the necessary steps to build his business).

Both the finding and building theories attempt to explain the pathways entrepreneurs take to identify and exploit opportunities, yet they tend to differ in their effectiveness of how entrepreneurs go about forming opportunities.

5.4 OPPORTUNITIES THROUGH ACTIVE SEARCH AND ALERTNESS

>> **LO 5.4**   Demonstrate how entrepreneurs find opportunities through active search and alertness.

Active search: method used by entrepreneurs in attempting to discover existing opportunities.

As we have discussed, access to the right information is one of the key influences of opportunity identification. However, access to information is not enough—it is how this information is used that makes the real impact. In the finding approach, entrepreneurs often engage in **active search** to discover existing opportunities.[15] This implies—in accord with the finding approach—that the opportunity is already present in the environment and can be discovered through a systematic search. But where do entrepreneurs source their information? A recent study showed that entrepreneurs tend to consciously seek information through their own personal contacts and relevant publications, not from reading newspapers, magazines or other trade publications.[16] In other words—in accord with the building approach—they use whom they know and what they know to find the answers to their questions. Let's take a closer look at each of these methods of finding opportunities.

Active Search

We all possess certain information sets, or knowledge bases, established by our existing knowledge.[17] By actively searching these sets, we can access a wealth of information. For example, you could use your own knowledge base to search for people who could potentially support you in your venture, such as your inner circle of friends, family, business contacts, neighbors, and so on.

While such rational and conscious search processes are undoubtedly useful, they do not always apply to every situation, especially when discoveries can occur so randomly. For example, if we confine ourselves to the specific information sets or knowledge base we possess, we may focus only on those things that are relevant to our personal inventory of information, and run the risk of missing those random occurrences that fall outside what we think we know. This tendency to miss chance opportunities relates to the *Research at Work* feature in Chapter 3 that describes a study of "lucky" and "unlucky" people. The conclusions of this study explain why some people tend to miss opportunities: they are too focused on what they are *supposed* to be looking for, in contrast to other people who tend to have greater potential to recognize chance opportunities.

The finding approach suggests that any existing opportunity is there to be exploited, as long as we have the skills and awareness to do so. But if that were the case, why aren't there floods of people rushing in to seize every possible existing opportunity? Surely, it would be difficult to produce profit-making products and services with everybody else potentially doing the same thing. Therefore, it is not enough for entrepreneurs to identify opportunities within the confines of their existing knowledge sets. In short, active search can be very helpful in the recognition of opportunities, but we also need to be alert to nonobvious opportunities when they arise.

Web
Entrepreneurs and Luck

Alertness

To address the question of why some people spot opportunities and some don't, researchers have suggested that opportunities are everywhere waiting to be discovered. Such discovery is made by those entrepreneurs who have **alertness**, the ability to identify opportunities in their environment.[18] This means that entrepreneurs do not necessarily rationally and systematically search their environment or their particular information sets for opportunities. Rather, they become alert to opportunities that already exist through their daily activities—in some instances, even being taken by surprise by what they observe.

Alertness: the ability some people have to identify opportunities.

Think back to Bette Nesmith Graham, the inventor of Liquid Paper correction fluid mentioned earlier in this chapter. Graham was not actively searching for an opportunity to invent a specific paint to correct typing errors, but she became alert to the idea through her daily secretarial duties. She then proceeded to draw on her interest in art to create a product that would prove to be a huge market success in the future. Graham's experience adheres to this concept of alertness that suggests that we are capable of recognizing opportunities even when we are not looking for them.

The origin of the football is another interesting example of alertness.[19] Until 1860, footballs were made of animal bladders, which were blown up into a plum or pear shape, then tied and sealed. Because the bladders were constantly exploding, shoemakers were often called upon to encase the bladders in leather to protect them from bursting so easily. A young shoemaker in the town of Rugby, England, named Richard Lindon was employed in this trade, and he enlisted the help of his wife to inflate the bladders by blowing air into them. However, after his wife died from an illness attributed to contact with infected pigs' bladders, Lindon started to look for a safer option. He found a

Richard Lindon with enhanced rugby balls.

Credit: https://commons.wikimedia.org/wiki/File:Richard_Lindon_(1816-1887).jpg

way of replacing the bladders with rubber-inflated tubes, and using a pump to inflate the footballs without any contact from the mouth. He is credited with inventing the appearance of the rugby football as we know it today, as well as the invention of the air pump. The point is that although Lindon had not started out looking to revolutionize the football, he was able to recognize an opportunity when it appeared.

Some researchers believe that entrepreneurs may be more adept at spotting opportunities than nonentrepreneurs for several reasons:

▶ they have access to more information,

▶ they may be more prone to pursuing risks rather than avoiding them, and

▶ they may possess different cognitive styles from those of nonentrepreneurs.

Recall from Chapter 3 that cognitive strategies are ways in which people solve problems; similarly, cognitive styles are ways and patterns of thinking. Cognitive styles attributed to successful entrepreneurs include a higher degree of intelligence, creativity, and self-efficacy.[20] All of the above attributes are thought to influence opportunity recognition, and they may explain why some entrepreneurs are more likely to become aware of opportunities while others may remain oblivious. Keep in mind that all of these attributes can be developed with practice!

Building Opportunities: Prior Knowledge and Pattern Recognition

Video
Using Prior Knowledge

Prior knowledge: the preexisting information gained from a combination of life and work experience.

There has been a great deal of research in measuring how entrepreneurs recognize opportunities. We have explored the importance of actively searching for opportunities, alertness to recognizing opportunities when they arise, and the importance of taking action to support the formation of opportunities. But once entrepreneurs have identified opportunities, how do they go about building on them?

Researchers have identified two major factors in the building of opportunities: prior knowledge and pattern recognition.[21] As described in our earlier discussion of the finding approach, **prior knowledge** is preexisting information gained from a combination of life and work experience. Many studies indicate that entrepreneurs with preexisting knowledge of an industry or market, together with a broad network, are more likely to recognize opportunities than those who have less experience or fewer contacts.[22] Successful entrepreneurs often have prior knowledge with respect to a market, industry, or customers, which they can then apply to their own ventures.[23]

Robert Donat, founder of GPS Insight (described in Chapter 3), was able to apply the knowledge he gained from working in two diverse areas—the Army and hedge funds—to create a new hardware/software fleet-tracking solution. Donat credits his success with the invaluable knowledge he acquired during his time in those two very different roles. Similarly, Niari Keverian, founder of ZOOS Greek Iced Teas, featured in Chapter 1, was able to draw on her previous experience as an employee at Collective Brands, Staples, and Welch's to launch her business. The well-known entrepreneur

FIGURE 5.3

Nine-Dot Exercise

Puzzle: Copy the above image to paper. Draw no more
than four straight lines (without lifting the pencil) and
connect all nine dots. No back-tracking either.

Source: Raudsepp, E., & Hough, G. (1977). *Creative growth games.* New York, NY: Jove. The nine-dot exercise is referred to as "Breaking Out" and is found on page 29. The solution is on page 113.

Jack Dorsey made use of programming knowledge from his days of coding programs for taxicab dispatching to go on to become the founder of Twitter and Square.[24] These are just a few examples of how prior knowledge can be crucial in an entrepreneur's ability to build on an opportunity.

Another key factor in building and recognizing opportunities is **pattern recognition:** the process of identifying links or connections between apparently unrelated things or events. Pattern recognition takes place when people "connect the dots" in order to identify and then build on opportunities.[25] The "nine-dot exercise" (Figure 5.3) illustrates the limitations of our thinking. The challenge is to connect nine dots by drawing 4 straight lines without lifting your pen from the paper and without backtracking. If you who have difficulty completing the task, your mind may be blocked by the imaginary "box" created by the dots. To help overcome such limitations, try to think of the dots beyond any of the imaginary constraints.

Pattern recognition: the process of identifying links or connections between apparently unrelated things or events.

In a recent study, highly experienced entrepreneurs were asked to describe the process they used to identify opportunities.[26] Each entrepreneur reported using prior knowledge to make connections between seemingly unrelated events and trends. In cognitive science, pattern recognition is thought to be one of the ways in which we attempt to understand the world around us.

The types of suitcases used before compact wheeled luggage became available to consumers.

Credit: English Heritage Images/ Newscom

Some of the simplest ideas are born from making links from one event to the other. For example, compact wheeled luggage was used by airline crew for years before the same type of luggage was marketed for passengers. This idea to make the product available to airline passengers came from an airline pilot, who connected the dots between three major trends that were happening at the time, such as an increase in the number of passengers, which made airports busier and carrying traditional luggage more difficult; the overflow of bags that needed to be checked in, which opened up a need for carry-on luggage; and the inconvenience of transporting bags over large distances as a result of expanding airports. Once these trends were recognized, the product was built and marketed to a huge customer base to enormous success.[27]

Moving from the idea to identifying an opportunity may seem like a daunting prospect, but we can all train ourselves to get better at recognizing opportunities. We do so by identifying changes in technology, markets, and demographics; engaging in active searches; and keeping an open mind to recognizing trends and patterns. And always look beyond the imaginary box!

YOU BE THE ENTREPRENEUR

Entrepreneurs are creative people with the drive to pursue their ideas wherever they may lead. Where those ideas come from can be from their ingenuity or something they stumble on. Lisa Conte, founder of Napo Pharmaceuticals, identified an interesting idea, but shaping that idea into an opportunity has been a rough road.

While working as a biotechnology analyst for a venture capital firm, Conte took a vacation to Africa and climbed Mount Kilimanjaro. There she observed a fellow climber ingesting a plant to combat altitude sickness, which gave her the idea of making prescription drugs from plants. After testing many plants for their therapeutic qualities, Conte focused on crofelemer, a substance derived from a tree native to the Amazon River basin, to aid in relieving chronic diarrhea.

After many trials, there weren't enough patients who benefited from the drug to enable it to pass the regulatory hurdles needed to apply for FDA approval. In the meantime, Conte had spent all of her money—including $200 million from investors—on research and testing.

What Would You Do?

Source: Coster, H. (2010, Dec 10). One pharma entrepreneur's never ending quest. *Forbes*, 12.

5.5 FROM IDEA GENERATION TO OPPORTUNITY RECOGNITION

>> LO 5.5   **Connect idea generation to opportunity recognition.**

As we have explored, for an opportunity to be viable, the idea must be new or unique or at least a variation on an existing theme that you are confident that people will accept and adopt. It must involve something that people need, desire, find useful or valuable; and it must have the capacity to generate profit. We cannot credit divine intervention

---

FIGURE 5.4

Idea Generation, Creativity, and Opportunity Recognition[28]

Idea Generation	Creativity	Opportunity Recognition
Production of ideas for something new.	Production of ideas for something new that is also potentially *useful*.	Recognition that ideas are not only new and potentially useful, but also have the potential to generate economic value.

⟶ Increasing Relevance to Founding New Ventures ⟶

Source: Baron, R. A., & Shane, S. A. (2008). *Entrepreneurship: A process perspective* (p. 69). South-Western Educational: Mason, OH.

Credit: From BARON/SHANE. *Entrepreneurship*, 2E. © 2008 South-Western, a part of Cengage Learning, Inc. Reproduced by permission. www.cengage.com/permissions

as the source of new ideas, nor is every idea an opportunity. The best ideas are based on existing knowledge and the ability to transform the idea into a viable opportunity.

Let's take a look at the process that connects idea generation to opportunity recognition (Figure 5.4). Typically, entrepreneurs go through three processes before they are able to identify an opportunity for a new business venture: idea generation, creativity, and opportunity recognition.

The first step is generating lots of ideas for something new, potentially through the strategies we discussed earlier in the chapter. During the creativity stage, we sort out these ideas for newness and usefulness. Finally, the opportunity recognition stage allows us to sort out the remaining ideas for both newness and usefulness, and also assess them for their ability to generate economic value.

The second step is the creativity stage. As we explored in Chapter 3, we all have the ability to think creatively through practice, and to transcend the boundaries of our existing knowledge structures. While these knowledge structures are essential in making sense of the world, they tend to inhibit creative thinking, as they allow us only to interpret the familiar with what we already know. This is why it is so important to train our minds to think creatively. Let's explore the role of creativity and its relationship to opportunity identification.

Researchers have identified four approaches that we can practice to enhance our creativity with the purpose of transforming our ideas into opportunities. These approaches yield the acronym SEEC: securing, expanding, exposing, and challenging (see Table 5.2). **Securing** is the capacity not only to focus on new ideas but also to sustain them. **Expanding** is the broadening or the acquisition of new skills that enable people to generate ideas and share knowledge. **Exposing** involves the skills required to open ourselves to diverse and fluctuating circumstances and events. **Challenging** is the process of building on past failures by braving new encounters.[29]

Like many of the concepts we have described previously, opportunity recognition is a skill that can be learned and developed like any other. The *Research at Work* feature describes how the SEEC model was used to enhance students' ability to identify opportunities.

Securing: the capacity to focus on and sustain new ideas.

Expanding: the broadening or the acquisition of new skills that enable people to generate ideas and share knowledge.

Exposing: the skills required to open ourselves to diverse and fluctuating circumstances and events.

Challenging: the process of building on past failures by braving new encounters.

TABLE 5.2

SEEC Model

Securing: the capacity to focus on and sustain new ideas.	Similar to alertness, *securing* involves being consciously aware of possibilities, but also focuses on the deliberate capture of those ideas that sometimes have a habit of drifting in and out of our minds before we have a chance to focus on them. A useful way of securing those ideas is to keep a written log of opportunities that you observe during your daily activities, which is a simple but effective way to record ideas for later use.
Expanding: broadening or acquiring new skills	*Expanding* skills enables people to generate ideas and share knowledge. A useful exercise carried out in a group setting is to list recent problems you have encountered in your daily life, and design some possible solutions, which are then shared with the class for further discussion and feedback.
Exposing: opening ourselves to circumstances and events	Entrepreneurs tread a fine line between structure and turbulence, and so it is useful to build resilience by *exposing* ourselves to diverse and fluctuating circumstances and events. This exposure builds our ability to function in an unstructured and uncertain environment. Brainstorming and becoming a consumer of information about creativity are productive ways of building exposure.
Challenging: overcoming past failures by braving new encounters	We all fail at times, and the important thing is not how often we fail but how well we recover. Further, we must not let past failures stop us from *challenging* ourselves to make new efforts and try new things. Learning from failure can lead to enhanced creativity and further idea identification.

Source: Adapted from DeTienne, D. R., & Chandler, G. N. (2004). Opportunity identification and its role in the entrepreneurial classroom: A pedagogical approach and empirical test. *Academy of Management Learning and Education, 3,* 242–257. Material on pp. 246–248.

SEEC Study

Researchers applied the SEEC model to a group of students studying business-related subjects in an effort to better understand the impact of training on the ability to generate innovative ideas leading to opportunity identification. Students were asked to complete tests and questionnaires before and after the SEEC training.

During the training, the students were also asked to enter five ideas per week into an opportunity register, and were frequently encouraged to look at the world in a new way by thinking of everyday events as potential opportunities. Every time the class met, they spent time sharing ideas or investigating the origins of existing everyday products and services. Students were also given a range of SEEC exercises to help them think more creatively.

By the end of the SEEC training, researchers found not only that students had the ability to generate more ideas for business opportunities but that these ideas had the characteristic of being more innovative. The training had enabled the students to become more skilled at identifying viable opportunities.

CRITICAL THINKING QUESTIONS

1. **Describe any classes you have taken (or are currently taking) that require creative thinking or generating new ideas. What similarities do you find with the training described in this research study? What differences?**

2. **How would you measure the effectiveness of SEEC training? How would you quantify how innovative students' ideas were, or how skilled students were at opportunity recognition?**

3. **In the training, students were given "a range of SEEC exercises to help them think more creatively." Make up an exercise that would help accomplish this.** ●

Source: Page 284 of DeTienne, D. R., & G. N. Chandler, G. N. 2004. Opportunity identification and its role in the entrepreneurial classroom: A pedagogical approach and empirical test. *Academy of Management Learning and Education*, *3*(3), 242–257.

The training methods used by the SEEC researchers involve practice and action. Listing your ideas in a book, sharing ideas, and collaborating with others are all actions that can transform an opportunity into a reality. As we have explored, practicing creativity provides us with a better chance of recognizing opportunities.

Let's apply some of the concepts we have presented in this chapter to the evolution of the modern-day gourmet food truck. The mobile food business is not a new concept, but traditionally street food has been associated with fast food such as burgers, hot dogs, and ice cream; these are the menu items often sold from food trucks, kiosks, and food carts. Yet in the past few years, the nature of the mobile food business has changed as the street food industry has become increasingly upscale and popular with "foodies."

Around the time of the 2008 world economic crisis, some food truck operators *recognized a pattern* in the trends happening at the time: the slower economy meant that people were looking for less expensive meals; the nature of many jobs required employees to work longer hours with shorter lunch breaks, which increased the demand for quick and convenient food; and the trend for healthier eating habits gave rise to a growing market of people who demanded different dietary choices from burgers, hot dogs, and ice cream.[30]

David Weber, cofounder of the Rickshaw Dumpling Bar in Manhattan, used the experience he had gained from the bar to take his business mobile. What started out as a temporary way to test different locations and experiment with ways to reduce costs ended up to be such a success that it allowed Weber and his partner to expand to two storefronts, four trucks, and a much sought-after kiosk in Times Square within a short period of time. Weber believes that starting a gourmet food truck business is a viable opportunity for entrepreneurs because it requires much less capital than starting a restaurant. In addition, it allows freedom to try out recipes and experiment with cooking techniques. Because of the limited financial and regulatory commitments, it provides an opportunity to try out the brand and refine the target market.[31]

Did Weber use the *finding* or the *building* approach to identify the opportunity to launch a food truck business? The finding approach suggests that the opportunity was waiting for Weber; after all, the mobile food business has been around for decades. Surely it was just waiting for someone like him to spot the opportunity for a niche market? But, as Weber mentions, he didn't originally set out to launch a food truck business—his original intention was to use the trucks to try out different locations and different ways to reduce costs.

In this case, we could say that the *building* approach is more applicable to Weber's story. He used his *prior knowledge* and experience from running the Rickshaw Dumpling Bar restaurant to test out his market and identify locations. By taking action, he interacted directly with his environment by connecting with his customers to figure out how to meet their needs. He was then able to gain valuable *information* about the gourmet food business that had not been fully explored previously. Finally, although Weber had not originally intended to launch a food truck business, he was *alert* to the business potential as soon as he realized how popular his food trucks were becoming.

Rickshaw Dumpling Food Truck
Credit: RICHARD B. LEVINE/ Newscom

Video
A New Approach

Many other food truck operators have thought about *creative* ways in which they can be more differentiated in order to stand out in this current competitive landscape of the street food industry. For example, a whole range of gourmet food trucks representing some of the most expensive and highly rated restaurants have sprung up. They have reached a whole new demographic of consumers who may not be able to afford to eat at top restaurants, or may even feel uncomfortable dining in what can be a very formal environment. These customers now have the opportunity to sample these high-end foods at a lower cost from gourmet food trucks in an informal environment. The food is cooked fresh from the best ingredients by talented chefs who work from trucks that are branded with the restaurant's name and logo.

In another example of creativity, some gourmet food truck owners have also identified opportunities to provide high-quality, low-cost food to traditionally expensive events such as weddings, bat mitzvahs, and corporate affairs. Some food truck owners go one step further by renting out their trucks for promotions, co-branding the truck with the name of their own company, as well as the company they are working with.[32] In addition to promotional opportunities, gourmet street food has spawned cookbooks, TV shows, websites, blogs, and even a food truck computer game.

The most successful mobile food businesses are run by entrepreneurs who have used their existing knowledge gained from prior experience of running a business to generate an alternative means of providing a diverse range of food to a larger demographic. These entrepreneurs collaborate, build partnerships, and use and expand their networks to build their knowledge and gain access to the information they need to establish their business. They work long hours, are constantly thinking of creative ways to differentiate themselves from the competition, and invest huge amounts of commitment to establish a good reputation and build up a loyal customer base. The growth of the gourmet food truck business illustrates how one simple idea—selling gourmet food from a truck at lower prices—not only has succeeded in reaching a larger market, but has evolved into a whole range of diverse initiatives.

Recall that Figure 5.1, the Idea Classification Matrix, classifies business ideas as innovation, invention, improvement, irrelevant. By applying this matrix to the success of the gourmet food truck business, we could say that the business is a successful *innovation* that has a high degree of *novelty,* as it is a good example of a service that is valuable, useful, and profit generating. Although the mobile food industry has been around for a long time, this new variation on an existing theme has succeeded in creating a service that not only meets all of the requirements of a successful innovation, but has reached a whole new range of customers.

The food truck operators have taken what they know about the traditional restaurant industry, recognized the opportunity to make it into something bigger, and succeeded in starting a cultural revolution. ●

---

⑤SAGE edge™

Get the edge on your studies at **edge.sagepub.com/neckentrepreneurship**

▸   Master the learning objectives using key study tools
▸   Watch, listen, and connect with online multimedia resources
▸   Access mobile-friendly quizzes and flashcards to check your understanding

SUMMARY

5.1   Explain how the entrepreneurial mindset relates to opportunity recognition.

Having the right entrepreneurial mindset is essential to identifying opportunities and taking action to start new ventures. It gives entrepreneurs the confidence to network and find unmet needs in the marketplace, and the ability to persist with ideas and build on opportunities.

5.2   Employ strategies for generating new ideas from which opportunities are born.

Of the nearly countless ways of generating ideas, seven strategies have been outlined by researchers. Included are analytical strategies, search strategies, imagination-based strategies, habit-breaking strategies, relationship-seeking strategies, development strategies, and interpersonal strategies.

5.3   Apply the two primary pathways to opportunity identification.

The first is the finding approach, which relies on the notion that as the global societies shift and develop, undiscovered opportunities abound. Alternatively, Saras Savasvathy asserts that a building approach, which assumes that opportunities do not exist independent of entrepreneurs but are instead a product of the mind, is beneficial toward capitalizing on the opportunity.

5.4   Demonstrate how entrepreneurs find opportunities through active search and alertness.

In the finding approach, entrepreneurs often engage in active search in attempting to discover existing opportunities. While active search can be very helpful in the recognition of opportunities, entrepreneurs need to be alert to random opportunities when they arise.

5.5   Connect idea generation to opportunity recognition.

The process of moving from idea generation to opportunity recognition is primarily composed of three stages: idea generation, creativity, and opportunity recognition.

CASE STUDY

Jack Ma, Founder and Chairman, Alibaba Group

Jack Ma knows a thing or two about creating new opportunities. A self-made billionaire, Ma was ranked #33 on the *Forbes* billionaire list for 2015. He got there by orchestrating the development of Alibaba, a mega-e-commerce company that went public on the New York Stock Exchange (NYSE) with the largest initial public offering (IPO) in history, beating out erstwhile mega-IPOs including Facebook, Visa, and General Motors (GM).

Jack Ma was born as Ma Yun in Hangzhou, in China's Zhejiang Province, about 100 miles from one of the world's largest cities, Shanghai Jack's entrepreneurship efforts began at an early age. When he was only 12 years old, Ma recognized the tremendous opportunities he could create for himself if he learned English. To accomplish his goal, he would ride his bike for 40 minutes every day—regardless of the weather—to an international hotel in Hangzhou's West Lake district where he could fraternize with foreigners, offering his services as a tour guide free of charge. In return, he learned English. Just as important, he learned about the rest of the world firsthand. He quickly realized that the foreigners he spoke with had a different story to tell than did his native Chinese teachers and textbooks, which presented reality through the distorted lens of communism.

In 1979, Ma met an Australian couple and became pen pals with their two children. In 1985, the family invited Ma to visit them "Down Under," further opening up Jack's eyes to the way the rest of the world—especially the Western world—lived and worked. His efforts to seek out education and opportunities beyond the borders of his own country changed his thinking and his life.

Like virtually all entrepreneurs, Ma faced a lot of failure and disappointment in his early working years. From flunking his university admission exam to being rejected in his application to become a secretary to a *Kentucky Fried Chicken* general manager, Ma learned the hard way that success rarely happens overnight.

In 1995, Ma was able to move to the United States as an interpreter for a trade delegation. It was in Seattle that he first learned about the Internet. Jack and a friend quickly discovered that China was not yet utilizing the Internet, so they launched their own website, called *China Pages*.

With virtually zero knowledge of the Internet, or even how to properly use a keyboard, Ma invested $2,000 to start a company. He had enough early success to attract the interest of the state-owned *China Telecom*, but later parted ways when the communications giant showed little interest in Ma's vision or goals.

In 1999, Ma courageously ventured out on his own again with a single-minded vision of starting his own e-commerce corporation. With some close associates who believed in him, and $60,000, Ma and his team went to work.

> I wanted to have a global company, so I chose a global name. *Alibaba* is easy to spell, and people everywhere associate that with "Open, Sesame," the command that Ali Baba used to open doors to hidden treasures in *One Thousand and One Nights* (Fannin, 2008, online).

Alibaba began business in Ma's apartment. The company's core values included frugality, flexibility, and innovativeness. With serious irony, Ma cites three reasons for his company's initial survival: "We had no money, we had no technology, and we had no plan."

As is often the case, *Alibaba* expanded too fast initially, leading to layoffs and minuscule profits. Ma refers to these challenging times as "The dark days at Alibaba" (Fannin, 2008, online). But with determination and persistence, Ma and his associates eventually prevailed in epic fashion. Their global financial success was consummated on September 19, 2014, when *Alibaba* went public on the NYSE with the ticker symbol BABA and was valued at $231 billion (Baker, Toonkel, & Vlastelica, 2014), making Ma one of the richest people in the world.

From his childhood in Hangzhou to his mid-forties as a megacelebrity on Wall Street and around the world, Ma has been a big thinker. He has also been willing to take calculated risks to create opportunities and accomplish his vision—which has yet to be fully realized. Ma's entrepreneurial vision expands well beyond making money, as he has expressed the desire to change the world, and especially his native country of China, in positive ways.

> My vision is to build an e-commerce ecosystem that allows consumers and businesses to do all aspects of business online. We are going into search with Yahoo! and have launched online auction and payment businesses. I want to create one million jobs, change China's social and economic environment, and make it the largest Internet market in the world. . . . What is important in my life is that I can do something that can influence many people and influence China's development. When I am myself, I am relaxed and happy and have a good result. (Fannin, 2008, online)

Critical Thinking Questions

1. Describe how Ma's desire to influence and contribute to Chinese social and economic culture aided his rise as a global entrepreneur. Now identify some entrepreneurial opportunities for making a meaningful contribution to your own nation or culture.

2. Entrepreneurs tend to see the opportunity even in the most challenging circumstances. Riding his bike—rain or shine—for 40 minutes a day for years took unusual dedication and personal drive. What difficulties do you currently face—or would you be willing to face—to take advantage of entrepreneurial opportunities?

3. What is something you could learn (e.g., a foreign language), or a skill you could acquire (e.g., trade, process, function), that would empower you to create additional entrepreneurial opportunities for yourself in the future?

Sources
Note: This case study is drawn primarily from a 2007 interview of Jack Ma by Rebecca Fannin of *Inc.com* (cited below).
Baker, L. B., Toonkel, J., Vlastelica, R. (2014, September 19). Alibaba surges 38 percent on massive demand in market debut. *Reuters*. Retrieved from http://www.reuters.com/article/us-alibaba-ipo-idUSKBN0HD2CO20140919
Chen, L., Mac, R., & Solomon, B. (2014, September 22). Alibaba claims title for largest global IPO ever with extra share sales. *Forbes.com*. Retrieved from http://www.forbes.com/sites/ryanmac/2014/09/22/alibaba-claims-title-for-largest-global-ipo-ever-with-extra-share-sales/
Fannin, R. (2007; updated 2008, January 1). How I did it: Jack Ma, Alibaba.com: The unlikely rise of China's hottest Internet tycoon (transcription of interview with Ma). *Inc.com*, the Magazine (online edition). Retrieved from http://www.inc.com/magazine/20080101/how-i-did-it-jack-ma-alibaba.html
The World's Billionaire's List: #36 Jack Ma. *Forbes.com*. Retrieved from http://www.forbes.com/profile/jack-ma/

6 Using Design Thinking

Design is about making intent real. . . . When you design, something new is brought into the world with purpose."[1]

—Kevin Clark and Ron Smith, authors

6.1 WHAT IS DESIGN THINKING?

≫ LO 6.1   Define design thinking.

What pops into your mind when you hear the word "design"? You might think of design as a way of enhancing products such as clothing, furnishings, or appliances with the intent of making them more attractive to a certain target market. Traditionally, this is what design has meant: Designers take a developed product or service and make it look pretty or enhance the brand before launching it into the marketplace. Design has been generally associated with the final stages of a project; the wrapping on the gift.

However, today's business environment is driven by the need for continuous innovation and the need for strategic initiatives to support innovation. More often than ever before, businesses are faced with complex challenges that have no easy answers. There is a growing demand for companies to create ideas to meet the needs of customers, to create long-term value rather than merely enhancing existing ideas with limited value. Entrepreneurs have to do the same.

In Chapter 4, we explored the concept of opportunity and how generating valuable, useful, and economically viable ideas coupled with different approaches can improve our ability to identify meaningful opportunities. In the example of the invisible bicycle helmet, featured in *Entrepreneurship in Action* on the next page, we could say that the two Swedish students identified an opportunity to reinvent the bicycle helmet, but they also did something more: they used **design thinking,** a thinking process most commonly used by designers to solve complex problems, navigate uncertain environments, and create something that is new to the world.

In the context of design thinking, **needs** are considered to be human emotions or desires that are uncovered through the design process. Those companies that succeed in identifying and satisfying the needs of customers have a better chance of gaining that all-important competitive edge.

Video
What is Design Thinking?

Design thinking: a thinking process most commonly used by designers to solve complex problems and navigate uncertain environments.

Needs: human emotions or desires that are uncovered through the design process.

Anna Haupt and Terese Alstin, Founders, Hövding

Model wearing invisible bicycle helmet made by Hövding, showing how the "air bag" mechanism looks when deployed.

Credit: Hövding/Splash News/Newscom

Look closely at the photo on the left. Can you tell the woman is wearing an invisible bicycle helmet? If not, the helmet is fulfilling its invisible purpose. Yet, every time the wearer gets on her bike, if she falls off, or if she is struck, her head and neck will be protected. The invisible bike helmet is the brainchild of Anna Haupt and Terese Alstin, two Swedish industrial designers, who together set out to revolutionize the bicycle helmet industry. The idea took root when a new Swedish law was passed making it compulsory for children to wear bicycle helmets up until the age of 15. This sparked a debate as to whether the same law should apply to adults.

"We saw this law as a threat to adult bicyclists, because many people in Sweden and the rest of the world are really bad at using conventional helmets because they don't think they are good enough," Haupt said.[2] Haupt and Alstin, who were university students at the time, set out to find out why people didn't like wearing the conventional bicycle helmet, and they discovered some interesting insights. Through anonymous questionnaires, they found that one of the main reasons was not as much to do with safety as with vanity; many respondents said bicycle helmets made them "feel geeky", that they messed up their hair, and they were awkward to carry around.

Haupt and Alstin concluded it was not people's attitudes that needed to change, but the product itself. And so they set out to create a product that addressed both safety concerns and aesthetics by developing a helmet that doesn't mess up the hair, that looks fashionable, and that is easy to transport. Over the course of 8 years, Haupt and Alstin studied bicycle accidents—"everything from an icy road crash to getting hit by a car"—and enlisted the help of professional cyclists to help them develop the product.[3]

Take another look at the photo: the clue is in the scarf the woman is wearing. Inside the scarf is a protective nylon hood which, in the event of a collision, is inflated by a small gas canister. Built-in sensors monitor the movements of the cyclist and signal when the cyclist has either been struck or has fallen off the bike. Similar to airbag technology in cars, the hood inflates within one-tenth of a second. Furthermore, it is thought to be safer than conventional helmets. "It's actually three or four times better in terms of shock absorbance," Alstin said. "And that's the most important factor. It covers more of the head—including the entire neck—than the traditional helmets."[4]

Using the latest technology and design, Haupt and Alstin have succeeded in addressing not only the safety aspect of cycling, but the aesthetic side as well. Thanks to their innovative approach to helmets, cyclists no longer have to worry about their hair being messed up, or suffer the inconvenience of carrying a bulky helmet around. The scarf-style helmet is not just discreet, but a desirable fashion accessory, as it comes in a range of attractive colors designed to appeal to even the most discerning cyclist.

CRITICAL THINKING QUESTIONS

1. **What do you think was the main catalyst for Haupt and Alstin to design a new bicycle helmet?**

2. **How would you describe the creative process of designing something that doesn't exist?**

3. **What are some ways for an entrepreneur to go beyond convention to design a product to appeal to a particular market?** ●

Can you as an entrepreneur be trained in the art of design during this entrepreneurship course? Absolutely not. Great designers like Jonathan Ive of Apple, and home furnishings designer Jonathan Adler, have spent years in school and in practice honing their craft. Our goal here is not to introduce you to design. It's to introduce you to the benefits of *design thinking* and to describe how such an approach to problem solving is essential to The Practice of Entrepreneurship that has been introduced in this book.

While it is undoubtedly true that gifted designers Ive and Adler have the deep ability to visualize and define patterns that many of us would not be able to spot, the focus for you as an entrepreneur is not on specific studio training but on the way to solve problems to best meet the needs of the people for whom you are designing. In other words, how do you identify new solutions that meet the needs of a market? That is the essence of design thinking, and it can be taught to entrepreneurs.[5]

The concept of design thinking aligns with many of the facets of The Practice of Entrepreneurship, described in Chapter 2. Design thinking applies to everyone, regardless of experience levels; it involves getting out of the building and taking action; it requires continuous practice with a focus on doing in order to learn; and it works best in unpredictable environments. Design thinking incorporates the core elements of the practice and the essential skills of play, empathy, reflection, creation, and experimentation addressed in Chapter 2. Design thinking helps put the practice into action because it requires you to collaborate, cocreate, accept and expect setbacks, and build on what you learn.

One of the biggest obstacles to trying new things or generating new ideas is the fear of failure. What if the idea doesn't work out? What if the prototype fails to meet expectations? Design thinking does not see failure as a threat as long as it happens early and is used as a springboard for further learning—in other words, "Fail early to succeed sooner."[6] Design is a process of constructive conflict that merges into unifying solutions through the power of observation, synthesis, searching and generating alternatives, critical thinking, feedback, visual representation, creativity, problem solving, and value creation. By using design thinking, entrepreneurs will be better able to identify and act on unique venture opportunities, solve complex problems, and create value across multiple groups of customers and stakeholders.

How do we become successful design thinkers? The first step is being human.

6.2 DESIGN THINKING AS A HUMAN-CENTERED PROCESS

>> **LO 6.2** Demonstrate design thinking as a human-centered process focusing on customers and their needs.

In typical situations where new ideas are being vetted, we often jump to answer two questions: Can it be done? Will it make money? But human-centered design involves a different starting point in the creation process. Taking a design-thinking approach forces you to answer an entirely different question in the beginning. The first question is: What do people need?[7]

Leading innovation and design firm IDEO has popularized design thinking, and is featured several times in this chapter to illustrate design thinking in action. IDEO takes on all sorts of diverse design challenges—from developing new ways to optimize health care, to designing advertising campaigns, to finding different approaches to education. The CEO of IDEO, Tim Brown, credits one key phrase for sparking the

Master the content
edge.sagepub.com/ neckentrepreneurship

Video
Human-Centered Design

Tim Brown, CEO of the design firm, IDEO

Credit: Jon Shapley/Getty Images Entertainment/Getty Images

design-thinking process: "How Might We?" The "how" part presumes that the solutions to the problems already exist and they just need to be unearthed; the "might" part suggests that it is possible to put out ideas that may or may not work; and the "we" part means that the process will be a fruitful and collaborative one.[8] In short, those three words encourage the design thinker to believe that anything is possible.

Design thinkers welcome constraints and see them as opportunities to identify innovative solutions. An idea is deemed successful if it strikes a balance among three main criteria (see Figure 6.1):

▸ feasibility—what can be possibly achieved in the near future?

▸ viability—how sustainable is the idea in the long term? and

▸ desirability—who will want to use or buy the product or service?[9]

Video
Keeping Customers First

The starting point is desirability—what do you people need? It's not about building a new product and service and then searching for customers. It's about going to customers first, determining their needs, and then creating something to meet their needs.

A good example of an organization that has successfully achieved this balance is Nintendo. Rather than competing with other gaming companies which were focusing on graphics and consoles, Nintendo used new technology to create the Nintendo Wii.[10] Through innovative thinking and design, with a fresh new focus on enhancing the user experience, Nintendo broke through the competitive constraints of the gaming

FIGURE 6.1

Intersection of Desirability, Feasibility, and Viability

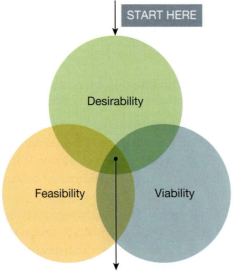

Source: Image is from Human Centered Design: An Introduction, p. 14. IDEO. http://d1r3w4d5z5a88i.cloudfront.net/assets/guide/Field%20Guide%20to%20Human-Centered%20Design_IDEOorg_English-ee47a1ed4b91f3252115b83152828d7e.pdf

Helping You Find Your Inner Adult[11]

Credit: ©iStockphoto.com/franckreporter

MassMutual Financial Group partnered with innovation and design company IDEO over the course of two years to design a service to encourage people under 40 to buy life insurance policies. What they had found was that while people under the age of 40 were happy to talk about life in terms of where they had been or where they are going, they were reluctant to delve deeper into the financial aspects of their future.

When they came together on the project, the IDEO and MassMutual teams discovered that when it comes to life insurance, age doesn't matter—people are either smart with their money or they're not. From this insight, the Society of Grownups was born. It covers a curriculum of all the "boring" financial stuff that the under 40s don't want to deal with—from investing in a 401K, saving to buy a house, and starting a family, to planning for retirement, and budgeting for the future—but within the comfort of a hip, informal environment, with a bit of wine tasting thrown in.

The Society of Grownups is now a distinct brand with its own customized section in MassMutual. It is equipped with financial advisors who are in tune with the needs of the adults whom they are advising, to help them understand their money and to design strategies to help them to get where they want to go. As MassMutual explains: "Why 'Society of Grownups'? Because we're all here to help each other become a little smarter. And a little more grown-up."

CRITICAL THINKING QUESTIONS

1. **What do you see as the value of providing life insurance services to the under-40 age group?**

2. **Do you agree that people under 40 need a "hip, informal environment" to encourage them to think seriously about the future? Why or why not?**

3. **What other strategies do you think might appeal to this demographic when it comes to life insurance and financial planning?** ●

industry to create an affordable yet profit-generating product that has become hugely popular with consumers.

Kaiser Permanente, the largest integrated health plan and health care provider in the United States, went to IDEO with a very human problem that needed to be addressed: to improve the experience of hospital patients and medical staff.[12] The IDEO team collaborated with the Kaiser team to identify opportunities for change. Early in the process, it became clear that there was something not quite right in the way nurses exchanged information regarding the status of the patients when changing work shifts. The exchanges were done at the nurses' station and could take up to 45 minutes. This delayed the incoming nurse from seeing patients, and delayed the departing nurse from leaving. Because of the informal nature of the exchange (sometimes notes hastily scribbled on scraps of paper or even on scrubs), some insights relating to patient care were habitually lost. Many patients felt there was a gap in their care with every shift change.

Following 4 weeks of shadowing the nurses, requesting their feedback, and making observations on each shift change, the IDEO team came up a with new shift change design. Rather than exchanging information at the nurses' station, information would be passed on in front of the patients, who were in turn able to provide their own input or correct any misunderstandings. The team also built some simple software that allowed the nurses to input and update patient notes throughout a shift, rather than at the end. The notes could be easily accessed by the nurse on the next shift.

The impact of these changes was significant: The nurses who had just arrived didn't have to spend the first 45 minutes being debriefed, which meant they could spend more time with their patients. The departing nurses were able leave straight after their shift. The patients were able to provide more input during the note-taking process, ensuring nothing fell through the cracks, with the added benefit of receiving more attention. By taking a human-centered approach, the IDEO team was able to see things in real time from the point of view of the people carrying out these tasks and activities; and the IDEO team created a holistic solution that could benefit everyone involved, rather than just a select few.

In an effort to improve the patient experience, this time focusing on the emergency room, an IDEO project team member feigning a foot injury went undercover to experience what it was like for people entering the emergency room.[13] A hidden camera helped the undercover agent capture the chaos of the checking-in process, the long wait times without anybody providing any information, and the bright lights and noise of the emergency room. These observations led to some significant insights: while the hospital employees were focusing on the practical elements like bed allocation, paperwork, and which patients should be seen first, they were neglecting the human element. The result: new systems, technologies, and spaces to make the whole patient emergency room experience less chaotic and stressful.

The human approach ethos is not based just on thinking about what people need, but on exploring how they behave, asking them what they think, and empathizing need how they feel. By truly understanding the emotional and cultural realities of the people for whom you are designing, you will be more able to design a better solution with real value. This is why empathy is so important to the design process.

YOU BE THE ENTREPRENEUR[14]

Entrepreneurs are designers who have to envision their final product, and then figure out how to get there. Dan Houser, founder of Rockstar Games, started the video game company with his brother. They created many famous titles such as *Grand Theft Auto*, *Red Dead Redemption*, and *Max Payne*. Many of their games involve violence, and Rockstar Games has had to deal with public criticism of the content.

Houser's company released *Grand Theft Auto* in the late 1980s but received a lot of backlash from the media. Tabloids and parent advocacy groups targeted the game for its depiction of casual violence. The series continued to be controversial, as some retail chains pulled the game from their shelves. In 2005, the Federal Trade Commission investigated several employees because hackers had found an explicit sex scene hidden in the game's source code.

What Would You Do?

6.3 DESIGN THINKING REQUIRES EMPATHY

Video
Empathy in Design Thinking

» LO 6.3   **Describe the role of empathy in the design-thinking process.**

In Chapter 2, we introduced the concept of empathy as one of the five skills essential to The Practice of Entrepreneurship. We explained the importance of being able to relate to how others are feeling in order to truly understand and connect with them, and to identify unmet needs. Empathy is essential for networking, effective leadership, and team building. Developing our empathic ability allows us to better understand not only *how* people do things but *why*; their physical and emotional needs; the way they think and feel; and what is important to them.[15] In other words, to create meaningful ideas and innovations, we need to know and care about the people who are using them.

We all have the ability to practice empathy, but how do we actually do it? The answer lies in observation, engaging people in conversation or interviewing, and watching and listening.[16] Let's take an example of a real problem challenging the design thinkers at IDEO: A woman called Shanti, living in a poor

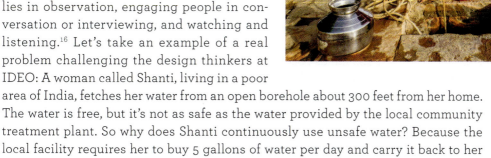

An impoverished woman in India drawing unsafe water from the ground.

Credit: ©iStockphoto.com/ BartoszHadyniak

area of India, fetches her water from an open borehole about 300 feet from her home. The water is free, but it's not as safe as the water provided by the local community treatment plant. So why does Shanti continuously use unsafe water? Because the local facility requires her to buy 5 gallons of water per day and carry it back to her home in a 5-gallon jerrycan. Not only is the weight too much for Shanti to carry, but she doesn't actually need 5 gallons of water a day.[17]

Start with developing empathy for Shanti. How would you feel if you were forced into drinking unsafe water because you could not carry the required amount you had to purchase from the local fresh-water facility? What do you think needs to be done to make Shanti's life a bit easier? Design thinkers will use their empathy for Shanti as a means of working toward constructive and experiential ways to resolve the water problem.

While rationalism and analytical techniques are important when creating products and services, as we have seen, design thinking is very much a human-centered approach and looks at the emotional as well as the functional side of problems. It allows us to express ourselves through our own feelings—to put ourselves in the shoes of someone like Shanti and think about better, safer ways of making her life a little easier. As best we can, in order for us to solve Shanti's problems, we need to be Shanti.

In another example, IDEO has been working with Ford to see how the car-making company can survive another 100 years in a world where the transportation landscape is changing. Innovations like Uber, ZipCar, and Lyft have given commuters far more transportation options and the choice to opt out of owning a car at all. With self-driving cars under development, traditional car makers need to find ways to be competitive, apart from manufacturing cars. The IDEO team was tasked with providing Ford with ideas for a unique product that would make money and differentiate it from the competition.

IDEO began by looking at the strengths and weaknesses of Chicago's "multimodal transport" system (buses, subways, water taxis, ride-hailing apps, bike shares, and walking). After experimenting with various modes of transport themselves, the design team connected with a diverse group of Chicago area commuters and followed them for weeks as they went about their daily lives. During this period, the design team asked the commuters lots of questions about why they chose one form of transport over another. They collated data from the commuters' homes and even recorded what they carried in their pockets. The team also interviewed city planners and academics to get the latest information on transportation.

Several brainstorming sessions later, the IDEO team finally came up with a concept for Ford. Studying the Chicago commuters had brought them to the conclusion that three types of commuters existed: the "Time Trumpers," who prioritize speed over comfort; the "Everyday Improvers," who try to find ways to enhance their commute; and the "Experience Seekers," who consider alternative ways of getting to their destinations, such as walking or taking a new route. The IDEO team then developed an app for each of these different personalities. For example, the app for the Time Trumpers would offer alternative routes in the face of delays; the app for the Everyday Improvers would include a text function informing them of weather conditions that might affect their commute; and the Experience Seeker app would offer different route options such as "connect with nature." IDEO is testing these apps with a view toward integrating them into Ford's new FordPass app, which offers services such as car sharing and electronic payments for parking. By taking a human-centered approach, IDEO not only has succeeded in understanding the hearts and minds of commuters, but also has created a unique product for Ford that will help the historic organization remain competitive in the future.[18]

There are many ways in which we can use empathy to relate to the people around us. In an innovative way for students to empathize with older people, researchers at the Massachusetts Institute of Technology (MIT) created the AGNES suit (Age Gain Now Empathy Suit) which is designed for the wearer to experience the physical discomfort that many elderly people have to deal with every day, such as joint stiffness, poor posture, bad eyesight and hearing, and lack of balance.[19] This is a very powerful way of encouraging people to empathize with older people to identify their needs. Given that our aging population is growing, there is ample opportunity for entrepreneurs to consider ways in which they can make the lives of the elderly more comfortable. This is yet another example of how empathy is one of the key elements of the design-thinking process used to solve complex problems and identify needs.

6.4 The Design-Thinking Process: Inspiration, Ideation, Implementation

>> **LO 6.4**   **Illustrate the key parts of the design-thinking process.**

Web
The Design
Thinking Process

Divergent thinking: a thought process that allows us to expand our view of the world to generate as many ideas as possible without being trapped by traditional problem-solving methods or predetermined constraints.

Convergent thinking: a thought process that allows us to narrow down the number of ideas generated through divergent thinking in an effort to identify which ones have the most potential.

In this section, we explore the design-thinking process and its effectiveness in designing solutions. IDEO looks on the design-thinking process as a system of overlapping phases, rather than a linear, predictive approach (described in Chapter 2), where organizations determine the goals they need to achieve and look for the resources to enable them to reach their goals. In this sense, the design-thinking process consists of three main phases: inspiration, ideation, and implementation (Figure 6.2).

The design-thinking process is based on two main types of thinking called divergence and convergence. **Divergent thinking** allows us to expand our view of the world to generate as many ideas as possible without being trapped by traditional problem-solving methods or predetermined constraints. This is a concept similar to the practice of play, which frees the imagination, opens up our minds to a wealth of opportunities and possibilities, and helps us to become more innovative. In fact, IDEO builds its whole culture around play and creating a fun environment for people to work in.[20]

The second type of thinking, **convergent thinking,** allows us to narrow down the number of ideas generated through divergent thinking in an effort to identify which ones have the most potential. These ways of thinking allow us to move from openness to understanding, from abstract to concrete, and from what is to what can be.

Let's explore the three phases of design thinking—inspiration, ideation, and implementation—in further detail.

ENTREPRENEURSHIP MEETS ETHICS

Empathy as an Ethical Challenge

Embrace baby warmer sleeping bag for babies, created by Stanford students.

Credit: © User: Rahul Panicker, Embrace Innovations/Wikimedia Commons/ CC-BY-SA 3.0/https://creativecommons.org/licenses/by-sa/3.0/deed.en

The practice of design thinking is fundamentally human-centered and requires the innovator to imagine the feelings of users as they experience a particular problem. These elements of empathy and user engagement make design thinking an inherently ethical endeavor. What could arouse more empathy than the death of an infant? Yet in developing countries, many premature and low-birthweight babies die from lack of warmth, or hypothermia. Is it ethical to turn a blind eye to these tragic deaths?

As a class project, Stanford graduate students Rahul Panicker, Jane Chen, Linus Liang, and Naganand Murty had been designing an intervention for at-risk babies that was low enough in cost to be used in developing countries. As mentioned in Chapter 4, their specific challenge was to create one that cost less than 1% as much as a state-of-the-art neonatal incubator. But when they created a prototype, collaborative field testing in Nepal with village families proved that the incubators were impractical since the families for whom the design was created lacked electricity. During their field testing, the students determined that the cold Nepal winters and limited heat sources resulted in frequent incidences of fatal hypothermia for low-birthweight babies.

Consequently, the students abandoned their electricity-powered incubator design. Instead, they began brainstorming creative solutions for a baby-warming device that didn't require electricity. The students eventually designed what looks like an infant-size sleeping bag. The bag is made of phase-change material that, after being heated, maintains its warmth for up to 6 hours, helping parents in remote villages give their vulnerable infants a chance to survive. Within 2 years of its pilot in 2011, the Embrace baby warmer had helped some 39,000 at-risk babies.

CRITICAL THINKING QUESTIONS

1. **How can you design collaboratively and inclusively when resources are highly unequal?**

2. **Design thinking requires incorporation of user feedback and possibly scrapping your original designs. Have you ever had to throw away work you've spent weeks or months on and start over? Would you perceive this as progress or failure?**

3. **Provide an example of a time when empathy, or an emotional desire to help solve a problem, prompted you to think creatively. What did you do? What were the results?** ●

Sources

Bajaj, H. (2014, March 13). *How to boost your innovation and stand out from the competition.* Retrieved from http://yourstory .com/2014/03/design-thinking-entrepreneurs/

Burnette, C. (2013, September 2). *The morals and ethics of a theory of design thinking.* Retrieved from http://www.academia.edu/4390557/The_ Morals_and_Ethics_of_A_Theory_of_Design_Thinking

Embrace global: About us. Retrieved from http://embraceglobal.org/ about-us/

The ethics of innovation: An ethical framework can bridge the worlds of startup technology and international development to strengthen cross-sector innovation in the social sector. (2014, August 5). Retrieved from Stanford Social Innovation Review: http://ssir.org/articles/entry/ the_ethics_of_innovation

Rodriguez, D., & Jaco, R. (2007, May 16). *Embracing risk to grow and innovate.* Retrieved from http://www.bloomberg.com/bw/stories/2007-05-16/ embracing-risk-to-grow-and-innovatebusinessweek-business-news-stock-market-and-financial-advice

Soule, S. A. (2013, December 30). *How design thinking can help social entrepreneurs.* Retrieved from Stanford Business Graduate School: http://www.gsb.stanford.edu/insights/sarah-soule-how-design-thinking-can-help-social-entrepreneurs

FIGURE 6.2

Three Phases of Design Thinking

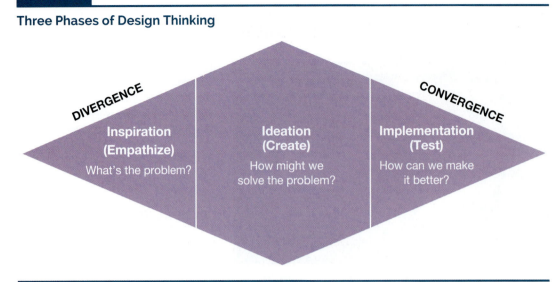

Inspiration

Inspiration: the problem or opportunity that stimulates the quest for a solution.

Inspiration is the problem or opportunity that stimulates the quest for a solution. It starts with a broad problem, or what is called a design challenge. A design challenge should not be too narrow, nor should it be too broad. You want to have the freedom to imagine, but you also want to have some boundaries in order to manage the process. Finding this sweet spot can be quite difficult and requires practice. This is where we use the question, "How Might We?"

Think about a fill-in-the-blank questionnaire as you develop your design challenge statement: How might we enhance /create /improve /redesign /expand /reimagine / grow . . . ? Here are some examples:

▸ How might we enhance the entrepreneurship education experience of students?

▸ How might we improve how the elderly live independently?

▸ How might we redesign how adults learn in virtual worlds?

▸ How might we reimagine how people get around in a town without cars?

Imagine that you see a woman in a grocery store trying to reach something on a high shelf. You might conclude, "Hey, this woman needs a ladder." If you're thinking innovatively, you may think about the type of ladder she needs. What if the woman is 80 years old? What does that ladder look like?

Now let's look at this from a broader perspective. Rather than simply saying the woman needs a ladder, what if we said, "How might we help customers reach products on a high shelf?"[21] Now the solution set is much broader—way beyond types of ladders. Ideas such as robots, mini-elevators, or moving shelves are much more innovative ideas than a simple ladder. These ideas have been inspired by observing that woman trying to reach a high shelf in the store.

Designers actively observe people in their own environment to identify their real needs. By observing the actual experiences of real people as they go through their daily lives, entrepreneurs are able to imagine themselves in the shoes of the people for whom they are designing. This gives them an opportunity to develop empathy to better identify needs and ultimately develop solutions. It is also an excellent way of seeing the world differently in order to capitalize on needs that the competition hasn't yet taken the time to recognize.

Ideation

The second phase of the design-thinking process is **ideation,** which involves generating and developing new ideas based on observations gained during the inspiration process to address latent needs. **Latent needs** are needs we have but don't know we have. For example, we didn't know we needed an iPad until we held one. The late Apple CEO Steve Jobs was very good at identifying latent needs of customers, and he possessed great observation skills; yet he was often criticized for not talking to his customers. Latent needs are more easily identified by observing rather than talking.

The ideation process is in line with the creation view described in The Practice of Entrepreneurship, as it requires a general openness to the world and involves using our creative ability to solve problems. Remember, it is up to you to come up with the big ideas; you cannot depend on the people you have been observing to generate them for you. Instead, you use your observation data as a basis for coming up with ideas. During the ideation stage, ideas are often generated in collaboration with a diverse group of people whose experience spans many different disciplines. Within IDEO, it is not uncommon for a design team to comprise a mix of architects, psychologists, artists, and engineers, most of whom have also had some kind of experience in business or marketing, or who have completed an MBA. By combining different viewpoints, the team can generate a wide variety of ideas and engage in productive debates about competing ideas.

Brainstorming is an important part of the ideation process. Brainstorming was created in the 1950s by writer and advertising executive Alex Osborne, who wrote about creativity in his text *Applied Imagination*. One of the key factors of brainstorming, in Osborne's model, was to "hold back criticism until the creative current has had every chance to flow." He considered the following four ground rules for brainstorming as pivotal to divergent thinking:

- suspending all judgment;
- being open to wild suggestions;
- generating as many ideas as possible; and
- putting ideas together and improving on them.[22]

Thus, the ideation phase uses brainstorming as a way to generate as many ideas as possible to meet the needs identified in the inspiration phase. Similarly, IDEO follows a set of rules for brainstorming (see Table 6.1); many of these are based on Osborne's four rules.

Developing a design challenge statement could involve asking how we might improve how the elderly live independently.
Credit: ©iStockphoto.com/ gpointstudio

Ideation: a creative process that involves generating and developing new ideas based on observations gained during the inspiration process to address latent needs.

Latent needs: needs we don't know we have.

TABLE 6.1

IDEO's Brainstorming Rules

1.	Avoid judging others. The whole idea of brainstorming is to make everyone comfortable enough to say whatever springs to mind. Remember, the more ideas out there, the more chance there is of building on those ideas to create the right solution.
2.	Let the creativity flow. Always encourage ideas—no matter how outlandish they may be. Seemingly "crazy" ideas can often give rise to real solutions.
3.	Be open to developing the ideas of others. However unlikely the idea may be, using positive language (use "and" rather than "but"), when investigating an idea can achieve real breakthroughs.
4.	Stay on topic. Keep your attention on the topic being discussed; otherwise you risk exploring different paths that may go far beyond the scale of the project.
5.	Follow the "one at a time" rule. There is more chance of the team developing ideas when full attention is focused on one person speaking at a time.
6.	Use visuals. Visuals such as sticky notes or rough sketches are powerful ways to get an idea across to an audience.
7.	Generate as many new ideas as possible. Try for up to 100 ideas in an 60-minute session, and then choose the ones worth developing.

Source: Adapted from http://www.designkit.org/methods/28

Implementation

Once you have used inspiration and ideation to identify some ideas that you think may have potential, it's time to enter the third phase of the design-thinking process: implementation.

Implementation: a process involving the testing of assumptions of new ideas to continuously shape them into viable opportunities.

Implementation tests assumptions of new ideas to continuously shape them into viable opportunities. During the implementation phase, ideas generated through the ideation process are transformed into concrete actions.

At the heart of the implementation process is low-cost experimentation through rapid prototyping, which creates an actual model of the product or service, which is then repeatedly tested for strengths and weaknesses until it leads from the project stage into people's lives. Prototypes need not be sophisticated or expensive.

For example, in an attempt to understand a client's requirements for a new surgical apparatus to operate on delicate nasal tissues, an IDEO designer grabbed a whiteboard marker, a film canister, and a plastic clothespin and taped them together. This crude, cheap prototype helped everyone to visualize the new surgical instrument and to clarify exactly what the client wanted.[23]

Experimentation is also relevant to the implementation stage, as it involves acting in order to learn, trying something new, learning from the attempt, and building that learning into the next iteration.

Rather than executing the ideas generated in the inspiration and ideation phases, the implementation phase focuses on early, fast, cheap testing to strengthen ideas and ensure that the design team is on the right path toward meeting the demands of the people for whom they are designing. This part is so important that we've devoted Chapter 7: Testing and Experimenting in Markets to this topic. Let's take a look at a real-life example of the three phases of design thinking in action.

The Three Phases of Design Thinking in Action

Video
Design Thinking in Action

In 2004, Shimano, a Japanese manufacturer of cycling components, noticed a flattening in growth in its components for high-end road-racing and mountain bikes in the United States. The Shimano team invited the IDEO design thinkers to collaborate on an idea for a new type of casual bike, aimed at baby boomers—people born between 1946 and 1964, who were now in their 40s and 50s.[24]

During the *inspiration* phase, the IDEO-Shimano team set out to define the problem and to identify any constraints. Working off the statistic that 90% of American adults don't ride bikes, the team set out to find out why. By talking to a range of consumers and observing them in action, the team found that while consumers admitted they had enjoyed riding bikes when they were kids, they were now put off by the cost of bikes, the number of accessories, the complex controls, and lack of knowledge about which bikes were suitable for certain surfaces. In short, these consumers yearned for the simplicity of the bikes they had ridden when they were young.

During the *ideation* phase, the team brought together what they had learned from their time with the consumers, and came up with the idea of "coasting"—a term that would promote the casual nature of a new range of bikes. These bikes would be built for pleasure and designed for simplicity; there would be no complicated controls or visible gear shifts, and they would be easy to maintain. Even the three-gear shifts on the bike would be controlled by an onboard computer that would sense the speed of the bike and adjust accordingly.

The *implementation* phase focused on the design of the new components such as the computerized gear shift, creating prototypes of the new coasting bike with these additional components to test it for strengths and weaknesses. Impressed by Shimano's innovative idea, top cycling manufacturers Trek, Raleigh, and Giant were the first to sign up to produce coasting bikes, and developed them by incorporating the cycling components put forward by Shimano.

Yet the project didn't stop there. To connect with the nostalgia many people associated with their fun, relaxed cycling childhood experiences, the team designed a brand that promoted coasting as the new, trouble-free way to enjoy life. They used slogans like "Chill. Explore. Dawdle. Lollygag. First one there's a rotten egg." The team also collaborated with local governments and cycling organizations to launch a campaign, and created a website identifying the safest places to ride bikes. Within a year of the first coasting bike's launch, seven more bike manufacturers had begun to produce coasting bikes.

A middle-aged man riding a Shimano bicycle
Credit: AP Photo/Ikea/REX

As we mentioned, the design-thinking process is not linear. It is not unusual to loop back through the three stages of inspiration, ideation, and implementation when exploring and testing new ideas. An initially successful idea, too, may need to be revisited. For example, despite initial enthusiasm for the coaster bike, sales soon flattened.[25] The concept might need a new round of inspiration, ideation, and implementation to identify key weaknesses and devise ways to remedy them. Because design thinking does not follow a strict pattern, it may at first seem like a chaotic process; however, there is structure in the chaos that serves to produce creative, meaningful results. The design challenge gives us direction, but through observation, we begin to uncover the real problems and needs. We will explore ideation and implementation in greater detail in later chapters, but here let's take a closer look at what happens during the inspiration phase.

6.5 PATHWAYS TOWARD OBSERVATION AND INSIGHTS

>> **LO 6.5**   **Demonstrate how to observe and convert observation data to insights.**

Observation: the action of closely monitoring the behavior and activities of users/potential customers in their own environment.

Video
Observation
and Insights

Insight: an interpretation of an observation or a sudden realization that provides us with a new understanding of a human behavior or attitude that results in some sort of action.

Two of the most important techniques that entrepreneurs use during the inspiration phase are observation and insight development. **Observation** is the action of closely monitoring the behavior and activities of users/potential customers in their own environment. Many of us are so very accustomed to just seeing, or simply talking to (or *at*) other people, that we don't necessarily know how to observe. Because we are so used to our own environment, we tend to lose sight of the bigger picture. It can be difficult to consciously stop and simply observe, yet observation is essential for gathering facts and developing the most interesting insights. Observing people is really where we begin to hone our empathy skill.

The other technique, insight development, is a bit more challenging to define. First, let's start with what an insight is *not*. The term is quite often misused. It is important to understand that insights and observations are not the same thing. Observations focus on the raw data that you have consciously recorded from all the things you have heard and seen, without any interpretation. An insight comes later: it is an interesting, nonobvious piece of information derived from interview or observation data that drives opportunities.

An insight is *not* just reporting what you heard in the conversations. An insight is *not* an idea. An insight *is* a statement that identifies a customer need and explains why. In other words, an **insight** is an interpretation of an observation or a sudden realization that provides us with a new understanding of a human behavior or attitude that results in some sort of action—for example, a new product or service to meet customer needs or even a new process to increase employee satisfaction.[26] Observations represent the *what* we see and insights help us better understand *why* we are seeing what we are seeing. Insights are the patterns we observe and help us identify needs of the people we are observing. Probably one of the best ways to remember what an insight is, is the following: "Why is a good insight like a refrigerator?" The answer—"Because the moment you look into it, a light comes on."[27]

In Chapter 5 we discussed pattern recognition, a process in which people identify links or connections, or "connect the dots," in order to identify and then build on opportunities between apparently unrelated events. You may remember the airline pilot who connected the dots between trends that were happening at the time, reinventing the compact wheeled luggage used by airline crews to make it suitable for passengers. Once these trends were recognized, the product was built and marketed to a huge customer base with enormous success.

Recognizing patterns generates *insights* that enable us to see everyday things in a new light. These insights can often take us by surprise. Think back to the *Entrepreneurship in Action* feature, for example. The two Swedish students, Haupt and Alstin, observed and gathered information from a whole range of adult cyclists, which helped them develop an insight about bicycle helmets: namely, on the surface, people attributed their reluctance to wear bicycle helmets to lack of safety, but the real reason lay in the aesthetics. It was this insight that led the women on a quest for a bicycle helmet that would be safe, comfortable, and aesthetically pleasing—the invisible bicycle helmet.

Insights are not ideas, but they help us generate innovative ideas…for new products or services that we didn't even know we needed. For example, how many of us have thought aloud, "Do you know what I really need? An invisible bicycle helmet!" Yet some of the greatest innovations of today have fulfilled a need that we had no idea we had, such as the Internet or the iPhone. In fact, even the most boring tasks can trigger the most illuminating of insights.

Take the relatively mundane task of mopping the floor, for instance. In an effort to find a new home cleaning product, consumer products company Procter & Gamble went to observe people cleaning floors. Although it may not sound like the most exciting assignment, the observation generated important new insights. What the researchers found is that people don't like slopping water around with a mop; nor does water really help get rid of the dirt.

From this new insight came the Swiffer brand—a range of waterless cleaning products that make surface cleaning easier and more convenient. The researchers had succeeded in looking beyond the obvious (the information that confirms our existing knowledge) to identify an unexpected pattern between the drudgery of mopping and our desire for a product that makes our lives easier. Instead of simply observing what they saw, and had seen many times over the years—the act of mopping—they had approached something very obvious from a different angle. They had asked *why*, and continued to ask why until they came up with a meaningful insight that led them to identify the primary need (the need to avoid messy and often dirty water) to create the solution to meet the need (Swiffer mop). In other words, they had spotted the gap between where the customers are today and where they want to be.[28]

Observation Techniques

Developing keen observation skills requires practice. The more we practice observation, the higher the likelihood of our developing new, meaningful insights that can lead to innovative solutions. There are nine dimensions of observation (Table 6.2) that can guide what we observe to help us to focus on the things that are not necessarily visible or obvious at first glance.

TABLE 6.2

Nine Dimensions of Observation

DIMENSION	DESCRIPTION
1. Space	The physical place or places
2. Actor	The people involved
3. Activity	A set of related acts people do
4. Object	The physical things that are present
5. Act	Single actions that people do
6. Event	A set of related activities that people carry out
7. Time	The sequencing that takes place over time
8. Goal	The things people are trying to accomplish
9. Feeling	The emotions felt and repressed

Credit: Reprinted by permission of Waveland Press, Inc. from Spradley. PARTICIPANT OBSERVATION. Long Grove, IL: Waveland Press, Inc., ©1980; reissued 2016. All rights reserved.

AEIOU framework:
acronym for *Activities, Environments, Interactions, Objects,* and *Users*—a framework commonly used to categorize observations during fieldwork.

Another technique used to guide observation efforts is the **AEIOU framework**: an acronym for *Activities, Environments, Interactions, Objects,* and *Users.*[29] This is a framework commonly used to categorize observations during fieldwork. The AEIOU framework is similar to the nine dimensions of observation, but it has a smaller number of categories that are a little easier to remember during field research. AEIOU is also the focus of the Mindshift exercise. Table 6.3 defines the five AEIOU dimensions.

TABLE 6.3

The Five AEIOU Dimensions

Activities – are goal directed sets of actions—pathways toward things that people want to accomplish. What activities and actions do people engage in when carrying out tasks?
Environments – include the entire arena where activities take place. What is the function of the individual, shared, and overall space? Taking photographs or drawing sketches of the environment is also a useful way to record environmental cues.
Interactions – take place between a person and something or someone else. What is the nature of these exchanges? Can you observe what the person enjoys the most or the least?
Objects – are the building blocks or physical items that people interact with. What are the objects and devices that people use, and how do they relate to their activities?
Users – are the people whose behaviors, needs, and preferences being observed. What are their goals, values, motivations, roles, prejudices, and relationships? Who are they?

Source: AEIOU framework. Retrieved from http://help.ethnohub.com/guide/aeiou-framework

---

In addition to the observations frameworks, there are small adjustments you can make to your own lifestyle to increase your powers of observation.[30] For example, you could deliberately change your own personal routine. Do you always take the same route to class? Or go to the same grocery stores? If so, then try to take a different route or go to a different store, and see if you can make any observations based on these changes. Imagine you are seeing things for the first time, and see if you can discover anything new. Furthermore, the act of observation doesn't have to be a solitary activity. Bringing along someone else to help spot something you didn't notice before, or offer a different point of view, can be invaluable in developing new insights.

Here's a direct challenge. Once a day, stop and observe the ordinary. Look at those everyday things that you normally take for granted, as if seeing them for the first time. Why are manhole covers round, for instance? Not only will this exercise improve your observation skills, but it will make you a better design thinker; for good design thinkers observe, but great design thinkers observe the ordinary in extraordinary ways.[31]

6.6 INTERVIEWING AS A USEFUL TECHNIQUE FOR IDENTIFYING NEEDS

>> **LO 6.6**   Demonstrate how to interview potential customers in order to better understand their needs.

Interviewing is an important part of the inspiration phase, as it is one of the most effective ways to identify and empathize with customer needs, create new ideas, and discover opportunities. It can be an alternative and/or complement to observation. It's simply another way design thinkers collect data. A skilled interviewer is open-minded, flexible, patient, observant, and a good listener. Like observation, interviewing is a skill that improves with practice.

It's very common for entrepreneurs to interview customers after they have a product or service. These are called feedback interviews. But it's also common to use interviewing much earlier in the process to also develop insights and identify needs. Doing this ensures that you are creating something that people actually need. Regardless of the type of interview you are conducting the following sections will help you develop your interviewing skills for maximum impact.

Preparing for an Interview[32]

First, think about whom you want to interview. For example, say you are looking to start your own French gourmet food truck business with a goal of selling to high-end customers, such as business executives, at exclusive business events such as conferences and office parties. As a startup, the first step is to think about whom you know. Whom do you know who works in the business world? Or, if you don't know anyone personally, who do you know who might know someone in the business world who can provide you with an introduction? Go through your list of contacts, or try networking sites like Facebook, Twitter, and LinkedIn. Research the companies and experts who might be able to offer you some guidance, and try to establish contacts there, too.

Think about what you want the end result of the interview to be. What is the aim of the interview? Do you need to test assumptions or learn about preferences and attitudes? What is it you want to gain from the interview?

Second, draft an introduction to the interview (approximately 4 or 5 sentences) that lays out your intentions and the purpose of the interview. For example, say your interviewee is an events manager at a large bank. Your goal is to find out what he thinks of your gourmet French food truck business and whether it is something that the bank staff and clients would be interested in for corporate events (see Figure 6.3).

Third, prepare your interview questions. In order to get the most information from the person you are interviewing, you need to minimize yes/no questions, such as, "Do you like food trucks?" Instead, ask open-ended questions like:

- "What do you think of the explosion of the food truck industry?"
- "What would motivate you, your clients, and your employees to buy from a food truck?"
- "Do you have any frustrations around the food from food trucks or the service provided?"

If your interviewee expresses enthusiasm at your idea, you can ask, "What do you like best about this venture concept?" If the interviewee's reaction is less than enthusiastic, you might ask, "In what ways could this venture concept be improved to have greater appeal for people like you?"

Make sure you also record some basic facts about the person (gender, occupation, age, profession, industry, affluence). There is no need to ask these questions directly, as they can be offensive. Do your best to make some reasonable guesses.

Another useful interviewing technique is "Peel the Onion," which is a way of delving into a problem one layer at a time (see Figure 6.4). Begin with the challenges the person faces, and then continue to dig deeper in order to understand the core root of the problem. Simply asking, "Why?" or saying, "Tell me more about _____" will help you gain a deeper understanding.

Observations to Insights

Now it's time to practice a little design thinking. When talking about observation as a core tenet of design thinking, it's easy to say, "I've observed all my life. I don't need to practice observing." Well, you haven't been observing your entire life . . . you've just been seeing. When we observe with purpose and intention, we often see new things. This mindshift is about getting outside of the classroom, observing, and then building insights from your observation data. The AEIOU framework is a tool to help you do this.

First, identify an area of curiosity for you. This could be fitness, video gaming, food, travel, education—any human activity you are curious about. Once you have identified an area of curiosity, find a space to observe that is related to this area. For example, if you are interested in food, you could observe waiters at a local restaurant. If you are interested in education, you could observe students in a class. If you are interested in travel, you could observe people in an airport or at a highway rest stop. What's most important is that you must observe *people*. Remember, design thinking is human-centered, and desirability comes first. By observing people, you can identify what they need.

Observe for two hours, and record your notes using a table like the one below. Using the AEIOU framework helps you organize your notes.

OBSERVATION WORKSHEET
AEIOU FRAMEWORK

Activities What are people doing?	
Environment How are people using the environment? What's the role of the environment?	
Interactions Do you see any routines? Do you observe special interactions between people? Between people and objects?	
Objects What's there and being used or not used? Describe engagement with objects? Are there any work-arounds you can identify?	
Users Who are the users you are observing? What are their roles? Are there any extreme users?	

Source: Doblin, Inc. by Rick Robinson and Stef Norvaisis Available at http://help.ethnohub.com/guide/aeiou-framework

Now think about any insights that come out of your observations. Remember, an insight is not an idea; it's a statement that drives your idea and identifies the needs of users.

CRITICAL THINKING QUESTIONS

1. **Do you agree that observing and seeing are two different skills? In what ways, if any, are they different?**

2. **In the A-E-I-O-U framework, which aspect of observation did you find the most useful? The most challenging? Explain your answers.**

3. **What insight can you identify for the space you observed in this exercise? Does your insight represent a need or a solution. Remember insights are not solutions—they lead you to solutions. Why is separating needs and solutions important?** ●

FIGURE 6.3

Sample Interview Introduction

Hello—I am Antonia, founder of the Le Gourmet food truck, which offers organic French food based on the finest ingredients, located in Boston, Mass. I was referred to you by Gavin Jones, head chef at the restaurant Beaujolais. I am interested in your views on my plans to sell my product at office conferences and other business events. I have a few questions that will take approximately 30 minutes. Everything you say will be treated as strictly confidential.

Credit: Alex's Pictures - Moscow/Alamy Stock Photo

FIGURE 6.4

Peel the Onion for Deep Understanding

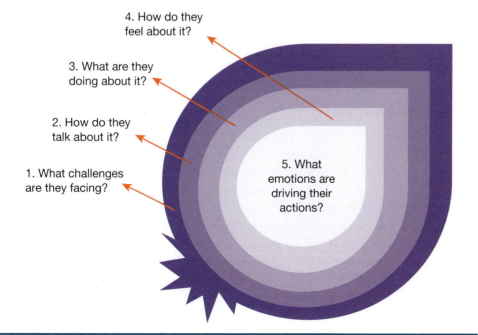

4. How do they feel about it?

3. What are they doing about it?

2. How do they talk about it?

1. What challenges are they facing?

5. What emotions are driving their actions?

Conducting the Interview

Video
Interviewing Customers

Begin by briefly stating the purpose of your interview. Take notes throughout, and if you are intending to also audio record the interview, make sure you ask permission first. Remember to use your questions as a guide only—it's best to keep the tone conversational and relaxed, but directed. The golden rule of interviewing is to actively listen to the other person. Don't become so focused on your prepared questions that you neglect to pay attention to what the other person is telling you. Furthermore, when you reflect back or paraphrase what the other person has said, this shows that you are listening. However, do not interrupt, or try and second-guess the answers. If there is a pause in the conversation, don't feel obliged to rush in and try to fill the space—your interviewee may be thinking about something or planning what to say next.

Remember, your goal here is to learn as much as possible—you're not selling to the person (although keep in mind that this person might well be a future customer of yours). The focus should be on the people you interview, getting to know them, the problems they have experienced, and how they have tried to solve them (or not); and the outcome. If you are unclear about something or have a question, don't be afraid to seek clarification. In this way, you will come away from the interview with as much concise information as possible.

One of the most common interviewing mistakes is to seek validation for your ideas. Remember, at this stage, you either have a very early idea or may not even have an idea at all. Overall, you are trying to better understand the needs of potential customers. For example, if your interviewee tells you his business associates might not be pleased about eating from a food truck at corporate events, do not rush in to tell him that he is wrong—and that food trucks are the answer to all his problems. The aim here is to listen and understand why he doesn't think food trucks would be that appealing. His answers may not be the ones you are looking for, and sometimes the truth hurts, but his feedback may lead to new insights and ideas. Figure 6.5 provides examples of "bad" interview question types to avoid and "good" interview question types that are often helpful.

As you are wrapping up the interview, it's a good idea to ask your interviewee to provide introductions to other contacts. This is a useful way to continue your research and expand your network. Finally, in addition to thanking the interviewee on the spot, it's always common courtesy to follow up with a thank-you note or email afterward. You never know when your interviewee may be in a position to tell others about you, and the more gracious you can be in your interactions, the better the chance that what he or she will say about you will be favorable.

After the Interview

As soon as the interview finishes, take some time to go through your notes, and write down any additional observations or thoughts while the interaction is fresh in your mind. Try to craft insights from your notes by looking for themes and patterns based on responses to questions, body language and tone of voice, and make note of any other questions or findings that have emerged. Develop your reflection skill; reflection is useful here, as it helps you to make sense of your own feelings, the knowledge you have gained, what questions you may have, and what you need to consider as a result. Reflecting on the interview also gives you the opportunity to come up with new perspectives, and conclusions. Also think about how you could improve the interview the next time. Practice makes perfect!

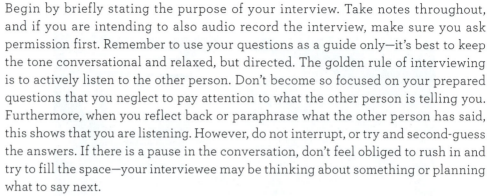

FIGURE 6.5

Bad Questions to Avoid and Good Questions to Remember

Bad Question Reminders	Good Question Reminders
Too Soon: Asking a stranger for commitment or personal information before it's appropriate in the conversation	**Ask Permission:** Getting the customer's permission to conduct a short interview
Leading: Making assumptions about your customer that may be false and bringing your own biases into the conversation	**Customer Pain:** While exercising sensitivity, encouraging the customer talking about a problem or pain that they have
Dead End: Asking questions that can be answered with a "yes" or "no" and don't give your customer a chance to tell you anything meaningful	**Existing Alternatives**: Learning what the customer has tried to do to solve his or her problem in the past
Poor Listener: Showing that you clearly didn't listen to your customer's earlier responses	**Prioritize Pain**: Clarifying that alleviating the customer's pain is one of your top priorities
Sales Pitch: Asking your customers if they're interested in a product or service instead of listening and learning about them	**Dig Deep**: Following up a question to learn more
Insulting: Offending your customer so much that they end the conversation	**Get a Story**: Asking the customer to tell you a story about his or her situation

Source: Heidi Neck & Anton Yakushin. 2015 VentureBlocks Teaching Note

The Empathy Map

One of the most useful ways to efficiently record the information from an interview is by completing an empathy map. An empathy map is a tool that helps you collate and integrate your interview data in order to discover surprising or unanticipated insights. It also enables you to uncover unmet needs, find the source of any frustrations, discover areas for improvement, explore different perspectives, and question your own assumptions and beliefs. In other words, empathy mapping gets you out of your head into someone else's.[33]

Figure 6.6 is a template that illustrates the type of content that goes into an empathy map—you can either use this one or draw your own. The map contains four main components that help you organize data from people you interview: Say, Do, Think, and Feel.[34]

Drawing from the observations you have made during your interviews, write down the following:

Say: What sort of things did the person say? What struck you as being particularly significant? Are there any interesting quotes you can use?

Do: What sorts of actions and behavior were displayed by the person? Any particular body language that you noticed?

Think: What might the person be thinking? What sort of beliefs or attitudes might be relevant?

Feel: What sort of emotions do you think the person is experiencing?

When complete, the empathy map is a useful way for you to spot contradictions and certain tensions that can spark a whole host of interesting insights. Sometimes

EMPATHY MAP

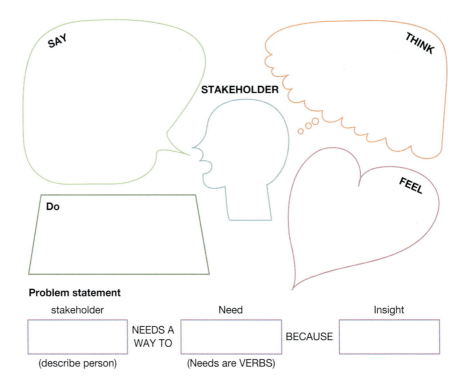

Credit: The empathy map worksheet was part of the instructional materials for the Stanford University online course Design Thinking Action Lab, taught by Leticia Britos Cavagnaro in 2013 on the NovoEd platform (https://novoed.com/designthinking/). Credit to David Grey for the original empathy map framework. More context on the use of empathy map as part of a design thinking toolkit can be found at http://dschool.stanford.edu/use-our-methods/

we have a tendency to say one thing and mean another. The Swedish students in the Entrepreneurship at Work feature spotted this disconnect when people at first claimed lack of safety as the reason for not wearing bicycle helmets when the real reason was vanity. This triggered an idea to create a helmet that addressed both safety and aesthetics.

6.7 VARIATIONS OF THE DESIGN-THINKING PROCESS

>> LO 6.7 Identify and describe other approaches to design thinking.

Earlier in the chapter we described IDEO's three phases of design thinking (inspiration, ideation, and implementation), but it is important to recognize that there are also other schools of design thought. The authors of *Designing for Growth* suggest four questions that are useful to ask during the design-thinking process—all of which have periods of divergence and convergence:

▸ What is?

▸ What if?

▸ What wows?

▸ What works?[35]

TABLE 6.4

The Stanford Design School Five Phases of Design Thinking

THE STANFORD DESIGN SCHOOL FIVE PHASES OF DESIGN THINKING
• *Empathy* is getting out and talking to your customers directly
• *Define* is defining a problem statement from that empathy work
• *Ideate* is brainstorming lots of ideas that could help you solve the problem you identified
• *Prototype* is building a crude version of the solution that you want to test with users
• *Test* is getting out and testing with users

Source: Hasso Plattner Institute of Design at Stanford. *(n.d.) An introduction to design thinking: Process guide.* Retrieved from https://dschool.stanford.edu/sandbox/groups/designresources/wiki/36873/attachments/74b3d/ModeGuideBOOTCAMP2010L. pdf?sessionID=68deabe9f22d5b79bde83798d28a09327886ea4b

Credit: *An Introduction to Design Thinking: Process Guide,* Hasso Plattner Institute of Design at Stanford.

What is encourages the entrepreneur to explore the current reality of the problem; *What if* encourages you to imagine all of the possibilities without regard to the reality of the ideas; *What wows* focuses on making decisions about what the customer really wants; and *What works* tests these solutions in the marketplace.

Another variation on the design-thinking process is from the Stanford Design School. Rather than IDEO's three phases or the four questions suggested by Designing for Growth, the Stanford Design School uses five phases: empathy, define, ideate, prototype, and test (Table 6.4).

Regardless of the variations inherent in design-thinking approaches, the themes and goals are similar. Each approach focuses on the importance of people and their needs; encourages entrepreneurs to get in front of real people in order to understand them; emphasizes the identification of needs before developing solutions; and recommends testing and experimentation, not for the purposes of killing an idea but to shape it and make it stronger.

Design thinking can be used to develop new products and services but also to build organizations, design strategy, improve processes that all bring value and deliver meaningful results. By adopting some of the methods designers use when approaching problems, entrepreneurs will be better able to find effective solutions to complex problems.

Video
From Design to
Design Thinking

So far, we have explored the different processes of design thinking, the power of design thinking in solving complex problems, and the importance of empathy, observation, and interviewing in the creation of successful design. In the next chapter, we will build on some of the concepts we have learned from design thinking to explore market testing and experimentation. ●

Get the edge on your studies at **edge.sagepub.com/neckentrepreneurship**

▸ Master the learning objectives using key study tools
▸ Watch, listen, and connect with online multimedia resources
▸ Access mobile-friendly quizzes and flashcards to check your understanding

SUMMARY

6.1   Define design thinking.

Similar to The Practice of Entrepreneurship in many ways, design thinking is ultimately a constructive and collaborative process that merges the power of observation, synthesis, searching and generating alternatives, critical thinking, feedback, visual representation, creativity, problem solving, and value creation.

6.2   Demonstrate design thinking as a human-centered process focusing on the customers and their needs.

Before business feasibility and economic sustainability are considered in the design process, entrepreneurs discover what people need. Products that achieve all three are bound to be the most successful, but the product or service must first be designed to provide a desired solution or fulfill a need for the design process to be considered human-centered.

6.3   Describe the role of empathy in the design-thinking process.

To create meaningful ideas and innovations, we need to know and care about the people who are using them. Developing our empathic ability enables us to better understand the way people do things and the reasons why; their physical and emotional needs; the way they think and feel; and what is important to them.

6.4   Illustrate the key parts of the design-thinking process.

The design-thinking process comprises three main overlapping phases: inspiration, ideation, and implementation.

6.5   Demonstrate how to observe and convert observation data to insights.

An insight in this sense is an interpretation of an event or observation that, importantly, provides new information or meaning. Observations can fall along one of nine different dimensions, and, like entrepreneurship, the ability to discern trends and patterns from each dimension is a skill that can be practiced and improved.

6.6   Demonstrate how to interview potential customers in order to better understand their needs.

Interviews should be done for two reasons: 1) to develop a better understanding of their needs during the inspiration phase of design thinking and 2) get feedback on ideas during the implementation phase. The interview must be well-prepared, the customer must be listened to and intelligent questions asked, and the interview must be evaluated when it is over.

6.7   Identify and describe other approaches to design thinking.

The authors of Designing for Growth suggest four questions that are useful to ask during the design-thinking process, all of which have periods of divergence and convergence. They are as follows: What is? What if? What Wows? What works?[36] Another variation on the design-thinking process is from the Stanford Design School, which uses five phases: empathy, define, ideate, prototype, and test. Design thinking can also be used to resolve wicked problems.

KEY TERMS

AEIOU framework 160
Convergent thinking 152
Design thinking 145
Divergent thinking 152

Ideation 155
Implementation 156
Insight 158
Inspiration 154

Latent needs 155
Needs 145
Observation 158

Anton Yakushin, Cofounder and CEO of VentureBlocks

Anton Yakushin is the cofounder of an education technology (EdTech) startup called VentureBlocks. Founded in March of 2014, VentureBlocks is a game-based online simulation that teaches student entrepreneurs how to interview customers and identify their needs (VentureBlocks is described in more detail on page 172).

A self-confessed "life-long tech nerd," Anton began coding at a young age. After high school, he sought out roles that involved building software. For several years he worked as a software engineer for a variety of employers. During this time, Anton was also working on his degree at Babson College. He signed up for an entrepreneurship course which he hoped would help him achieve his goal to be a tech entrepreneur. He was also keen to learn the business skills he felt he needed to capitalize on his vast range of tech knowledge.

After graduating from Babson in 2008, Anton had a variety of stints in consulting and startups, but returned to meet with his old entrepreneurship professor in 2014, Heidi Neck. He told Professor Neck that he wanted to make a difference in the way students were taught – specifically in the area of simulations. He says, "When I was at college, I was always surprised how limited the simulations we used were. They were limited both in terms of topics covered, and with what actions you could take while playing. More often than not, you could figure out a set of buttons to click consistently and win!"

He presented an idea to create a multiplayer online game where students would compete with each other while operating retail businesses.

Professor Neck told him that while she wouldn't use it, he should interview some other professors to verify if they were interested. Anton reflects, "After about a dozen initial conversations with professors at various business schools, I couldn't get one person to say they would use (and much less pay or have their students pay for) such a simulation."

However, the interviews had given Anton some valuable feedback which he shared with Professor Neck, who ultimately signed on as a cofounder. Upon assessing this feedback, Neck introduced Anton to the idea of game-based learning in education. The first step was to identify how game-based simulations could be enhanced for learning purposes, and who would use them. To do this, Anton needed to identify his target market, and how to address their needs.

Anton started by interviewing hundreds of people in education including students, professors, administrators, and high school students. It was during his interviews with a hundred entrepreneurship professors from different business schools that he quickly discovered a pattern. The biggest and most consistent pain point for most of the entrepreneurship professors was teaching students to identify customer needs. The reason was that each student had a different approach – some were not listening to their customers and asking the wrong questions, while others were being negatively influenced by existing biases. This made it very difficult for professors to teach customer development and need-finding, especially when this topic was typically restricted to one or two classes.

This feedback from entrepreneurship professors would eventually lead to the creation of Ventureblocks, a tool that would prepare students to effectively interview customers in order to identify their needs. In addition, Ventureblocks provides a safe and fun space for students to compete with each other. Through the simulation, students also learn how to develop empathy and build stronger customer insights. Because students receive instant feedback as they are playing, they learn quickly from their mistakes.

While Anton had not originally set out to create a simulation to sell to professors to aid student-learning in this area of entrepreneurship, the interview feedback showed that there was potential to provide a solution to this pain point and create a business. Building on this knowledge, Anton created a low-cost prototype to demonstrate for professors and to give them something tangible to play themselves.

Before writing a single line of code, Anton built the simulation as a paper prototype which underwent about 50 iterations over the course of six months. Anton said, "Since we wanted to build a software simulation, we prototyped with a paper card-based one where I took on the role of the computer, doing what the simulation would have done. We found, through iteration, how to engage groups of players, and how to embed the lessons most crucial to professors in a fun way."

In testing the prototype, Anton regularly went to the Babson College library, cafeteria, student center, and graduate school to play with undergraduate and MBA students as well as professors to get their feedback. He also contacted other colleges within driving distance to do the same, and used Craigslist to find students willing to playtest the prototype during school vacation. He took time to complete the Business Model Canvas on several occasions in order to prove that he had a product that people would buy before he went any further. After months of testing and feedback, Anton finally knew when he had a viable product to market. Though Anton did most of the coding himself using a platform called Unity, he coordinated a team of contractors to help with 3D graphics, script-writing, and user-interface design.

"We decided that our product met customer needs when (1) students confirmed that they learned what we set out teach them and (2) that the process of playing was engaging to them. We knew we achieved the first goal when a group of students told me that they were going to change their approach to identifying customer needs after playing the simulation in class. We knew we achieved our second goal when a group of professors was so engaged playing that they lost track of time and became quite competitive for top score!"

While the outlook looked positive, Anton suffered an unexpected setback in the initial stages of launching the product. During the official launch at an entrepreneurship educators' conference, the product attracted the attention of a few early adopters, but the over-riding response was quite negative. When Anton asked why, he was told that while most professors were impressed by the quality of the simulation, almost everyone was unhappy with the price for student access. Anton discovered that professors, while keen to use the product, were restricted by college budgets.

"The mistake we made with pricing was that we set it based on analyzing the competition (other simulations) and by talking to professors at a handful of private, relatively expensive colleges. We realized that we had set a price that limited the number of early adopters, and in doing so hurt our opportunity to grow and scale our user base—something critical for a brand new product in the market."

"The idea itself has been completely overhauled many times in the first 6 months through customer interviews and prototypes. We completely overhauled the software simulation after the first year because of how much we learned from our early adopters. We also pivoted with our revenue model and our channels. We changed pricing and revenue type along the way, and also changed how we reach potential customers and what we do when we reach them."

For Anton, VentureBlocks has been a labor of love, but his passion for the product is reflected in its success. To date, VentureBlocks is used by more 30 colleges and universities and even available bundled with the textbook that you are reading. "It's great that a textbook publisher actually sees the value in VentureBlocks and it will be helpful for the company to extend its reach both in the U.S. and around the world."

Critical Thinking Questions

1. The three core components of design thinking are inspiration, ideation, and implementation. Can you identify these components in the evolution of VentureBlocks?

2. The journey of Ventureblocks is populated with many tests, experiments, and prototypes. Where do you think VentureBlocks would be today if Anton had simply written a business plan and started the business? Why?

3. How might you apply design thinking to your own academic endeavors to maximize your potential for success after graduation?

Sources
Personal interview with Anton Yakushin (Nov 3rd, 2016)
Ventureblocks website: http://ventureblocks.com/

Practice interviewing customers and identifying their needs with VentureBlocks, a game-based simulation.

Simulation Goals

1. **Develop** a better understanding of approaching opportunity creation through the identification of customer needs.

2. **Practice** interviewing potential customers including:

   a. Approaching strangers and starting a conversation.

   b. Asking good open-ended questions to get useful and relevant information.

   c. Identifying bad questions that would make real-world customer interviews unsuccessful.

   d. Feeling rejection when someone does not want to engage in a conversation.

3. **Improve** listening and observation skills to identify the needs of potential customers and build strong customer insights.

4. **Cultivate** pattern recognition skills to identify potential opportunities that meet the needs of multiple customer types.

5. **Distinguish** between needs, customer insights, and solutions.

What is VentureBlocks?

In the VentureBlocks simulation, you start from scratch, with no resources or business ideas, and must explore a new, unknown market of bear-like pets called nanus. On your journey through the simulation, you learn how to identify business opportunities based on customer needs.

Most students will complete VentureBlocks in 30 to 60 minutes. The simulation includes tutorials so you know what to do and how to navigate at all times. Take your time though because this is a points-based competition. You will be able to see the top five performers at all time in your class through the real-time leaderboard!

Here's a little bit more information about the simulation.

You assume the role of a nascent entrepreneur who lives in a small town called Trepton. A few years ago, scientists in Trepton created a new pet: the nanu. These cute bear-like pets are becoming popular fast. The number of nanu owners in Trepton is growing, and a few well-known veterinarians project nanu ownership to surpass dog ownership by the year 2040. This could be disruptive! The entrepreneur (you!) believes business opportunities exist but must learn more about nanus and their owners.

The Nanu

VentureBlocks is completed when you identify business opportunities that meet the needs of nanu owners. In order to do this, you must complete missions across eight levels of play. In Levels 1–4 you develop empathy for nanu owners by talking with them. In Levels 5–7, you generate customer insights that lead to business opportunities. A simulation learning summary occurs in Level 8. Figure 1 details the missions.

VentureBlocks represents early stage entrepreneurial activity, and its foundations are rooted in design thinking that was introduced in this chapter. Figure 2 should look familiar: this is the Human-Centered Approach framework presented in the chapter. Remember, strong opportunities are found at the intersection of feasibility, viability, and desirability. Feasibility answers the question: Can it be done from a technical or organizational perspective? Viability answers the question: Can we make money doing it? Desirability answers the question: What do people need?

It is very common for entrepreneurship students to start with feasibility and viability. And these do represent two very important factors in building a sustainable business model, but sometimes we try to answer these questions too soon without giving adequate attention to what people need. As a result, VentureBlocks is designed to focus first on desirability: what nanu owners need.

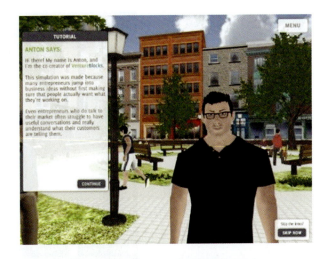

FIGURE 1

VentureBlocks Missions

Level	Mandatory Mission	Location
1	Start a conversation and get rejected	Trepton Park
2	Trash a bad question while talking to people	Trepton Park
3	Talk to a nanu owner and earn 75 XP (experience points)	Trepton Park
4	Talk to a nanu owner and earn 110 XP (experience points)	Trepton Park
5	Go home and build 3 good insights	Home
6	Choose your top insight	Home
7	Create 2 business ideas based on your chosen insight	Home

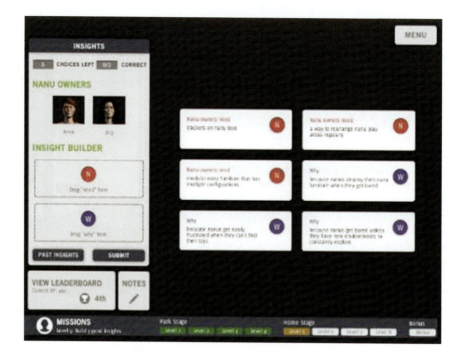

Design Thinking Framework Revisited

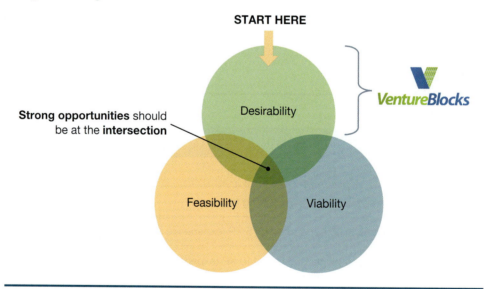

How to Use With This Text

While the concepts students will practice in this simulation are most directly connected to concepts in Chapter 6: Using Design Thinking, they will also practice concepts from Chapter 5: Recognizing New Opportunities and Chapter 11: Learning from Failure. Figure 3 demonstrates how the Chapter Learning Objectives align with the Simulation Goals.

FIGURE 3

Simulation Goals and Chapter Learning Objectives

Simulation Goals	Learning Objectives
Develop a better understanding of approaching opportunity creation through the identification of customer needs.	6.2 Demonstrate design thinking as a human-centered process focusing on customers and their needs.
Practice interviewing potential customers.	6.6 Demonstrate how to interview potential customers in order to better understand their needs.
Improve listening and observation skills to identify the needs of potential customers and build strong customer insights.	6.5 Demonstrate how to observe and convert observation data to insights.
Cultivate pattern recognition skills to identify potential opportunities that meet the needs of multiple customer types.	5.4 Demonstrate how entrepreneurs find opportunities through active search and alertness. 5.3 Apply the two primary pathways to opportunity identification.
Distinguish between needs, customer insights, and solutions.	5.5 Connect idea generation to opportunity recognition.
Apply learning from unsuccessful attempts to future attempts and develop an appreciation for the necessity of iteration.	11.5 Describe the significance of "grit" and its role in building tolerance for failure.
Reflect on both successes and failures through built-in debrief questions.	11.4 Explain the different ways entrepreneurs can learn from failure.

How to Access the Simulation

To access the VentureBlocks Simulation, visit sage.ventureblocks.com and enter your registration code. Your registration code will be available once your instructor sets up the course at sage.ventureblocks.com.

7 Testing and Experimenting in Markets

©iStockphoto.com/AndrewRich

Experiments are key to innovation because they rarely turn out as you expect, and you learn so much."

— Jeff Bezos, Amazon.com founder and CEO

7.1 WHAT ARE EXPERIMENTS?

>> LO 7.1 Define experiments and describe the steps of experimentation.

In Chapter 6, we explored the concept of design thinking and how certain thinking processes help us to navigate uncertainty to find solutions to complex problems. We also described the three phases of the design-thinking process: inspiration, ideation, and implementation—a nonlinear structure that produces creative, meaningful results.

In this chapter, we will explore in further detail the processes that take place during the *implementation* phase, specifically with regard to experimentation. The implementation phase focuses on early, fast, low-cost testing and experimentation to strengthen ideas and ensure that entrepreneurs are on the right path toward meeting the needs of their potential customers.

The implementation phase also ties in with developing the skill of *experimentation* as part of The Practice of Entrepreneurship, described in Chapter 2. This involves taking action, trying something new, and building that learning into the next iteration. Experimentation means getting out of the building and collecting real-world information to test new concepts, rather than sitting at a desk searching databases for the latest research. It involves asking questions, validating assumptions, and taking nothing for granted.

Video
Learning from
Experimentation

In the Entrepreneurs in Action feature, the founders of Parlor Skis began with a hypothesis that people want custom-built tailored skis. They then used experimentation to gauge customer feedback on their vision to build customized skis, and tested the market to ensure they had a viable product.

Over the course of four years, they asked questions and talked to as many people as they could to find out what pleased or bothered their target customer base. For instance, they discovered that their assumption that people would love that their skis were handmade was wrong—people were nervous about quality. The founders were then able to shift their focus to emphasizing the quality aspect of their skis as an effort to reassure their customers.

Mark Wallace, Pete Endres, and Jason Epstein, Cofounders, Parlor Skis

The cofounders of Parlor Skis have taken to heart that every pair of skis is unique

Credit: ©iStockphoto.com/simonkr

Parlor Skis is a custom ski business based in Boston's "Eastie" neighborhood; it was launched in 2010 in an old funeral home. While many sporting goods manufacturers claim they can give you exactly what you're looking for, Parlor goes several steps further. Every single pair of skis is one of a kind, custom designed according to a skier's height, weight, ski style and preferences; the skis are then sawed, sanded, and pieced together. The result is a completely tailored piece of equipment, right down to the graphics and colors that grace the final product.

Mark Wallace and his cofounders Pete Endres and Jason Epstein are all Williams College graduates. The three met on the racing slopes during school. After college, Wallace took to the competitive international racing circuit, while Endres and Epstein found jobs in the "real world." Still, skiing was never far from their minds.

"We realized that there was a gap out there in the market in terms of a product that was really tailored to the rider," Mark says. "Integrating people with their product is core to what we do." Endres, who was also a ski coach at Boston College, elaborates: "When you buy from a ski shop, you are trying to find the best mass-produced product for your skiing style. We custom-make the core of the ski to fit you. Our product complements skiers."

But it was the input from customers that was most important. Before Parlor Skis earned its first dollar, the three entrepreneurs took their idea through four years of process and product testing. Friends and family sales and "demo days" on the slopes gave the trio valuable feedback to tweak processes and product. "I think that we have built

this business in a low-risk way," Mark reflects, "because we test things all the time. Testing and then tweaking, then testing is a great way to de-risk the business. We have also really controlled our growth, which helps."

Parlor Skis also holds "shop nights," where the community is welcome to tour the workshop and talk to the guys face to face. "We are learning about our customers every day," Mark says. "When I look back at our first customer profiles, I realize that we were fairly wrong about who was going to buy our skis and what they cared about. For example, we thought that people were going to love that they were handmade. [It] turns out this made them nervous about quality. . . . Who knew! That's why we test."

By its fifth year in business, Parlor was pulling in small profits, yet the endeavor had already seen some setbacks. "We failed trying to get our skis into brick-and-mortar stores," recalls Mark, "[when] we thought that they would love the product. It turns out that they don't understand it and that they wanted a higher margin than we could provide." Instead, customers were able to find the company through events, or on Facebook—where Parlor Skis first launched—or via the website.

Mark urges aspiring entrepreneurs to climb the summit and take the plunge. "Get out there and do it. Fail fast and cheaply. Then keep going. Always be learning, [even though] that is a really hard thing to do. We all think we are really smart and right all the time; it's not always true. The flipside of that is people give you BAD advice so you have to know who not to listen to. Basically it comes down to judgment . . . and a bit of luck."

CRITICAL THINKING QUESTIONS

1. **Identify some ways in which the Parlor Skis founders' collective experience helped them start their own business.**

2. **In what ways do you think testing and experimentation helped the Parlor Skis entrepreneurs grow their business?**

3. **Suppose you started a business and your original assumptions about your target customer base turned out to be incorrect? How would you deal with this setback?** ●

Source: Personal interview, M. Wallace, October 16, 2014.

Parlor Skis provides a good example of how small-scale experiments also follow the tenets of affordable loss—only putting in what you can afford to lose. The founders made small experiments one at a time, refining their product based on what they learned in each experiment.

Let's take a closer look at experiments and why they are so important to an entrepreneur. We define an **experiment** as a method used to prove or disprove the validity of an idea or hypothesis. Experiments need to have a clear purpose, be achievable, and generate reliable results. Experiments guide us toward which customer opinions to listen to, what important product or service features should take priority, what might please or upset customers, and what should be worked on next.[1] They are essential when it comes to trying out new ideas, finding solutions, and providing answers to those "What if" questions.[2] It is through experimentation that we start to address feasibility and viability discussed in Chapter 6.

An experiment begins with a **hypothesis,** which is an assumption that is tested through research and experimentation. Getting out of the building and testing our hypotheses enables us to gain new insights into our target customers' wants and needs. However, testing a hypothesis is not just about gathering data—it also involves matching the results of our tests to the original hypothesis and potentially adapting our original assumptions to better understand our customer target base.[3]

In the next section, we will explore the scientific process of experimentation and its relevance to entrepreneurs.

7.2 THE SIX STEPS OF SCIENTIFIC EXPERIMENTATION

>> **LO 7.2**   **Identify and describe the six steps of scientific experimentation.**

When we hear the word *experiment,* we may think of scientists wearing white coats working with test tubes in laboratories, or the extensive clinical trials and experiments undertaken by pharmaceutical companies when testing a new drug.[4, 5] Yet the scientific method is not just limited to scientists and pharmaceutical companies; it is also extremely relevant to entrepreneurs starting new ventures. Experiments can, for example, involve observations of students studying in a library, or employees working on a group project, or consumers visiting a store. They can also involve constructing or formulating products and testing how they perform. In fact, continuous testing is an ongoing requirement for entrepreneurs.

Entrepreneurs are by definition experimenters, and that is why it is valuable to understand the process of experimentation—otherwise, the experiments could become disorganized and fruitless.

The scientific process of experimentation includes the following six steps (see Figure 7.1):

1. asking lots of questions,

2. carrying out background research,

3. developing hypotheses,

4. testing the hypotheses by running experiments,

5. analyzing the data, and

6. assessing results.[6]

FIGURE 7.1

The Scientific Method

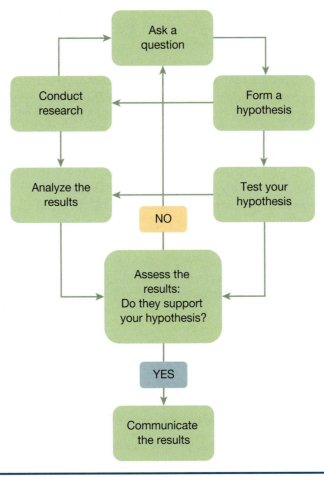

Let's apply the steps of the scientific method to the initial experimentation process undertaken by Amazon.com founder Jeff Bezos, who is also quoted at the beginning of this chapter. Bezos is an excellent example of an entrepreneur who frequently used experiments to test assumptions.[7]

While working at a Wall Street investment firm in 1994, Bezos was surfing online and came across an interesting statistic that claimed that Internet usage was growing by 2300% a year. Bezos reasoned that given the huge growth of Internet users, there could be massive potential for an online business opportunity. But what kind of business would it be?

First, he began by asking some *questions*: What kind of products would people buy online? What do people buy most from mail order versus going into a store? To find the answers to these questions, Bezos carried out some *background research*, by going through the products listed in the top 20 mail order catalogs.

From this research, Bezos was able to create a *hypothesis* that there was a market for standard products (the ones where consumers knew exactly what they were getting) that people would be happy to buy online. While it might seem obvious to us now that books fall into the category of a standard product, books weren't actually featured in the top 20 list of mail order products at all. When Bezos investigated further, he found that it simply wasn't possible to compile and publish a book catalog like the typical mail order catalogs he had researched. There were far too many books in print, and the catalog would be too expensive and weighty to produce. This explained why books were not in the top 20 standard products in catalog sales, but Bezos reasoned that selling books online still ought to be a viable idea.

Armed with the data he had gathered from his research, Bezos decided to *test his hypothesis* and run an experiment to see if there was an appetite for an online bookstore offering the widest selection of books in the world. Bezos's experiment was as low cost as it could be: rather than seeking investment or partnering with bookstores, Bezos made a deal directly with Ingram Content Group, a book wholesaler that agreed to warehouse and ship the books.

Jeff Bezos, founder of Amazon.com, experiments with new business opportunities to test assumptions.
Credit: epa european pressphoto agency b.v./Alamy Stock Photo

When Bezos *analyzed the data* generated from his initial Amazon.com book sales, he concluded from the *results* that he had created a business with tremendous potential. The success of his early experiment led to Amazon becoming the world's largest online discount retailer, selling a whole range of products—but it all started with books.

Since its inception, Amazon has reinvented itself several times: from the Kindle, the electronic reader, to renting data storage to other companies via its cloud computing services at Amazon EC2. It seems that there is no end in sight for Amazon's ability to experiment with diverse product offerings. By thinking like a scientist and applying the steps of experimentation, Bezos succeeded in learning firsthand about the value of experiments, their power to produce unexpected results, and their ability to provide an important opportunity for further learning.

While the scientific approach to experimentation is useful to entrepreneurship, keep in mind that you need to think like a scientist, not act like a scientist. Many scientific experiments take a huge amount of time, resources, and precision. As an entrepreneur, you have a goal not to build the perfect experiment but rather to use low cost, quick methods to shape ideas and to make them better through continual iteration. Entrepreneurial experimentation is about acting to learn, rather than getting bogged down in scientific rigor. By taking action and experimenting quickly and cheaply, you will have a better chance of refining your ideas into feasible and viable opportunities.

7.3 HYPOTHESES AND CUSTOMER IDENTIFICATION

>> LO 7.3 Demonstrate how to test hypotheses and identify customers.

As we have explored above, a true experiment involves a clear hypothesis. For example, Bezos's first hypothesis was to prove there is that market for standard products that people would be happy to buy online. During his quest to validate that hypothesis, he discovered that books had the most potential to be sold online. In doing so, he also created a marketplace for a host of other products.

Video
Using Hypotheses to Identify Customers

Similarly, many organizations design hypotheses to test assumptions about certain ideas before carrying out an experiment. One example comes from the sandwich retailer Subway, which is a global enterprise with more outlets around the world than any other restaurant chain. In 2008, as the United States and other countries were

Subway foot-long sandwich offered at $5 special rate.

Credit: Kristoffer Tripplaar/Alamy Stock Photo

hit with a recession, some marketers at Subway suggested a hypothesis that selling foot-long subs at the reduced price of $5 would increase sales.[8] Yet others were concerned that the promotion would distract customers from purchasing the more expensive items on the menu.

So Subway carried out an experiment: it tested the promotion in some Subway sites but not in others, and for limited time periods, such as weekends. The results showed that the $5 subs did not detract from the overall sales. However, even if the experiment had failed to support the hypothesis—if customers had stopped buying the more expensive items on the menu—it still would have raised many interesting questions: Why were customers not buying the more expensive items? What could Subway do to attract them to the other items on the menu, while offering the promotion? The Subway experiment turned out to be a useful way for the company to define customer tastes and preferences.

Limited, Low-Cost Experimentation

You don't need to be a wealthy entrepreneur or a marketer at a major sandwich chain to create a hypothesis. We all have the ability to generate a hypothesis and use low-cost experimentation to test its validity. Take a group of MBA students at Babson College, for instance. They had an early idea of creating software or some type of electronic gadget that students could use to "ping" other students when they were being distracting in the class. For example, if someone was speaking too long or spending too much time on Facebook or email, or just not staying engaged in the class, that person would be notified by their classmates through an app.

Rather than invest time and effort in developing the app or the software, the students obtained a professor's approval to conduct a quick, low-cost experiment. They used about $15 to buy fabric at a discount store, and then purchased some wine corks. With these materials they created yellow flags similar to those used by referees in American football. Each student was given a few flags at the beginning of the class and was allowed to throw them someone perceived to be distracting or unproductive in the class.

The hypothesis was that classmates "calling out" classmates would be a distraction. However, the exact opposite happened. Because the students knew they could be flagged, the flags actually served as a deterrent. In fact, the professor reflected at the end of the class that it had been one of the most engaging class discussions she had experienced in the entire semester. Not only was the experiment cheap, but it also generated an unexpected outcome, which led to many other interesting questions in need of testing to find answers.

Testing Hypotheses With Potential Customers

One of the most important parts of an experiment is customer engagement in your product or service. Involving real customers in your experiment is a great way to test hypotheses, as it provides you with immediate feedback on how your product or service is received. It is also an excellent way of making connections with people who may buy your product or service when it is fully launched.

For example, Parlor Skis spent several years integrating people into their product development process by holding "demo days" on the slopes, and "shop nights" when they opened their doors to people in the community and talked to them face-to-face. Similarly, Jeff Bezos built up a customer base by running an experiment to test Amazon.com, and was able to gauge the success of the experiment by analyzing the responses from real customers.

But how do entrepreneurs know which types of customers might be attracted to their products or services? To find out, entrepreneurs need to gain a deep understanding of the different types of customers. Typically, there are six different types of customers: end users, influencers, recommenders, economic buyers, decision makers, and saboteurs (see Figure 7.2).[9] Let's take a closer look at each of these types.

End users: the type of customers who will use your product. Their feedback will help you refine and tweak the product.

Influencers (or opinion leaders): the type of customers with a large following who have the power to influence our purchase decisions.

FIGURE 7.2

Six Types of Customers

Customer	Example
User	Teen playing a video game
Influencer	Celebrity endorsing the video game in a commercial
Recommender	Blogger writing positive reviews for the video game on a website
Economic buyer	Buyer for GameStop who decided to stock the video game in the company's stores
Decision Maker	CEO of the gaming company who decided to buy the game from the game designer
Saboteur	Parents who decided to not allow their child to purchase the game

▶ **End users:** these are the customers who will actually use your product. They will buy it (or not), touch it, operate it, use it, and tell you whether they love it or hate it. Gaining a deeper insight into the needs and motivations of end users is essential in the experimentation period, as their feedback will help you refine and tweak the product.

▶ **Influencers** (or **opinion leaders**): Sometimes the biggest influence on the success of a service or product comes from "customers" who have no involvement in it all. Celebrities, journalists, industry analysts, and bloggers with a large following have the power to influence our purchase decisions. For example, famous celebrities have tremendous influence on fashion; a dress worn to the Oscars by a movie star can launch a designer's career. Make a list of all the outside influencers you would like to target and ways in which you can reach them, for example via social media or by attending events where your target influencers will be present.

Kate Middleton, Duchess of Cambridge is an example of an "influencer."
Credit: AP Photo/Chris Jackson

▶ **Recommenders:** Popular bloggers, experts in an industry, or CEOs of major corporations carry a lot of weight when they evaluate your product and tell

Recommenders: The type of customers who have the power to make or break a sale.

Economic buyers: the type of customers who have the ability to approve purchases, such as office managers, corporate VPs, or even teens with their own allowances.

Decision makers: the type of customers (similar to economic buyers) who have even more authority to make purchasing decisions as they are positioned higher up in the hierarchy.

Saboteurs: the type of customers who can veto or slow down a purchasing decision.

the public about it. Their opinions have the power to make or break your reputation. For example, a games blogger who recommends a new game could do wonders for a new product.

▶ **Economic buyers:** These are the customers who have the ability to approve large-scale purchases, such as buyers for retail chains, corporate office managers, and corporate VPs. Economic buyers have the power to put your product on the shelves, physically or virtually. Connecting with economic buyers brings you one step closer to the type of end-user customers you want to have the opportunity to buy your service or product.

▶ **Decision makers:** These are similar to economic buyers, but they might have even authority to make purchasing decisions as they are positioned higher up in the hierarchy. The ultimate decision makers do not need to be CEOs—they could also be "mom" or "dad," who have the power to approve purchases for their family.

▶ **Saboteurs:** These types of customers can be anyone who can veto or slow down a purchasing decision—from top managers, to friends, spouses, to even children. Identify your saboteur customers and find out what's putting them off. You might learn a lot from their feedback.

Let's take a look at how Zappos founder, Nick Swinmurn, involved real customers to test his hypothesis that enough people in the market would be prepared to purchase shoes online.[10] First, Swinmurn approached local shoe stores and persuaded them to give him permission to take pictures of their shoes to put online, in exchange for buying each pair of shoes at full price should an online customer purchase them. His experiment brought him in contact with shoe retailers and enabled him to build up a relationship with them, even before putting the products online.

Zappos.com founded by Nic Swinmurn

When customers started buying the shoes from ShoeSite (whose name was soon changed to Zappos, a takeoff on the Spanish word for shoes: *zapatos*), Swinmurn took the opportunity to interact with them through customer support, handling returns, and taking payment. By having such direct interaction he was able to observe real customer behavior, which made him better able to meet customer needs and demands. In the end, Swinmurn had proved his simple hypothesis with a small-scale experiment by observing real customer behavior. Yet Zappos grew to be anything but small-scale; ten years after its 1999 inception, it was sold to Amazon for a reported $1.2 billion.[11]

We could say that the marketers at Subway, the students at Babson College, and Zappos founder Nick Swinmurn used the "test and learn" approach to experimentation.[12] Test and learn is a quick, cheap way to generate knowledge about what works and what doesn't. It allows you to put your ideas and hypotheses to the test and generates results that help you to make tactical decisions.

ENTREPRENEURSHIP MEETS ETHICS

The Rights of Research Participants

Leanna Archer with her hair product.
Credit: MARICE COHN BAND/Newscom

Before beginning testing and experimentation, the entrepreneur must consider some ethical concerns related to market research and the rights of research participants. Most notably, people participating in experiments have the right to informed consent; the right to be treated with dignity regardless of racial or ethnic background, sexual preference, or socioeconomic status; the right to privacy and confidentiality; and the right not to be deceived or harmed as a consequence of research participation. In addition, there are legal requirements for testing of food items and personal care products that come into contact with the human body, as well as regulations on the use of animals in product testing.

As long as the researcher is able to conduct the market research ethically and laws are followed, research doesn't have to be expensive. For example, entrepreneurs may enlist a group of people to try out free samples of a product in exchange for submitting an evaluation or attending a focus group afterward. There are also many laboratories that perform testing for regulatory compliance, with various price structures to suit different budgets.

Leanna Archer started her entrepreneurial venture when she was only nine years old. Archer used her grandmother's homemade hair care products and received numerous compliments on the softness of her hair. Motivated to investigate starting her own hair care business, Archer obtained her grandmother's recipe, which used only natural, nonchemical ingredients. Her parents provided funding, and Archer began experimenting with different ingredients. Once several prototypes had been created, Archer sent samples to neighbors to get feedback. With the success of her trials and with family helping with bookkeeping and other administrative tasks, she launched the Leanna's Hair product lines. By the time she was ready to graduate from high school, her company was bringing in a six-figure income and the story of her "teenpreneurial" success had been featured in *Forbes*, *TIME*, and *INC Magazine*, among other international publications.

CRITICAL THINKING QUESTIONS

1. **How would you go about finding out what kinds of testing are required for an entrepreneurial product or service?**

2. **If your product or service was suitable for nonprofessional testing in people's homes or at a focus group, whom would you recruit to participate in your test? Explain how you would choose your best customer types to participate.**

3. **How would you ensure that the participants in your experiments are treated ethically and have their rights protected?** ●

Sources

Al Smadi, S. (*n.d.*). *Ethics in market research: Concerns over rights of research participants.* Retrieved from http://wbiconpro.com/Marketing/Sami.pdf

Entrepreneur Media Inc. (2016). *Small Business Encyclopedia: Market Testing.* Retrieved from Entrepreneur: http://www. entrepreneur. com/encyclopedia/market-testing

Snepenger, D. J. (2007, April 5). *Marketing Research for Entrepreneurs and Small Business Managers.* Retrieved from Montguide: http://msucommunitydevelopment.org/pubs/mt9013.pdf

Tumati, P. (2010). *Market Research Tips for Startups.* Retrieved from Go4Funding: http://www.go4funding. com/Articles/Market-Research-Tips-For-Startups.aspx

For example, because the promotion took off in the test stores, Subway was able to roll it out to all of its stores; the students at Babson were encouraged to further test or modify their "flagging" idea after their experiment gleaned some surprising results; and the feedback Swinmurn gained from real customers and retailers through his low-cost experiment allowed him to grow his idea of an online shoe store into a hugely successful business.

One of the major benefits of testing hypotheses is the real-time data it generates. Entrepreneurs operating a startup will be far more likely to gather evidence and data from conducting simple, low-cost experiments. Experimentation can be used to produce real and current data as we will explore in the next section.

7.4 GENERATING DATA AND THE RULES OF EXPERIMENTATION

>> **LO 7.4**   **Explore different ways of generating data and describe the rules of experimentation.**

Video
Ways of Generating Data

Organizations have traditionally relied on large amounts of historical data to gauge customer tastes and preferences. Direct mail, surveys, advertising, and catalogs are just a few of the methods that larger companies use to gather data about their customers.[13]

Yet not all of these methods are reliable, especially in terms of advertising, where it is almost impossible to observe direct outcomes and acquire reliable feedback. As the 19th-century retail giant John Wanamaker once said, "Half the money I spend on advertising is wasted; the trouble is, I don't know which half."[14]

Even the greatest volume of data and complex data systems don't necessarily provide all the answers. Consider the experience of the century-old department store chain JC Penney. When Ron Johnson, known for his successes with Target and The Apple Store, became CEO in the fall of 2011, the company possessed a huge amount of data on its customers. While it wanted to modernize the Penney brand, it had no way of predicting how the public would react to big changes in the customer experience. Less than 18 months after Johnson's initiatives to get rid of clearance racks and coupons and replace them with boutiques and "fair and square" everyday pricing, JC Penney had suffered big financial losses, and Johnson was fired. Despite all the data JC Penney had on its customers, it turned out that people did not like the new changes. Furthermore, Johnson did not call for testing of his new ideas before they were implemented. The problem with data is that they serve only to provide insights into past behaviors—they cannot predict how people might react to new products and innovations.[15]

But what about when the data are lacking altogether? Often, when there is insufficient or nonexistent data, people tend to use either their intuition or their experience to make decisions. The problem with intuition is that it is often unreliable and doesn't provide the knowledge or evidence to support the feasibility of an idea.

Similarly, we can't rely wholly on experience and conventional wisdom—in fact, many innovations challenge what we thought we knew or what we thought we wanted. For example, when the nationwide pet specialties retailer Petco faced competition from big box stores, it came up with a new pricing strategy to price products sold by weight for an amount that ended in $0.25. This challenged the conventional wisdom that all prices should end in $.9 ($5.99 etc.), yet Petco's new pricing strategy led to a huge increase in sales.[16]

Fear of failure tends to discourage some organizations from experimenting at all. Experiments can be perceived as risky and sometimes requiring a trade-off between short-term loss and long-term gain, and nobody likes the idea of failing. Yet not all organizations have shied away from experimentation. Scott Cook, founder of tax software firm Intuit, says he cultivates an organizational culture of experimentation where failure is completely acceptable. Cook reasons that failure is key to creating evidence, which he believes is far more productive than using intuition.[17]

Entrepreneurial experiments are different from analytical experiments involving big data. Unlike major corporations like JC Penney, smaller organizations and especially startups usually do not have the resources to fund data systems analytics, nor may they even have existing data to rely on. In this sense, how can entrepreneurs get the data they need that doesn't exist?

Recall Parlor Skis, featured in our *Entrepreneurship in Action* feature. The business was founded on an idea of making customized snow skis. As this had never been done before, the founders had no data to rely on, and so they spent four years testing the market and experimenting with their product to get to know their customers better. This is how they identified customer needs in order to satisfy them. In short, Parlor Skis built up their own data with very little up-front investment and conducted low-cost experiments to shape their idea into a scalable and viable business model.

The point is that unlike larger organizations, entrepreneurs do not need expensive systems or large amounts of cash to generate the data they need to gauge customer needs and preferences. Small-scale experiments do not need to be risky or expensive. Entrepreneurs have more freedom to experiment, as they have a lot less to lose in the beginning than larger organizations do.

The essential thing to remember about experiments, large or small, is that all results must be taken into account, even if they fail to support the hypothesis and contradict original assumptions. Ignoring data just because they tell us what we don't want to hear is detrimental to the success of any venture.

The goal of experimentation is not to conduct the "perfect" experiment but to see it as an opportunity for further learning and better decision making. Failure is also important, for if you cannot fail, you cannot learn.[18]

Video
Experimentation and
Entrepreneurship

YOU BE THE ENTREPRENEUR[19]

Canadian entrepreneur Andrew Reid, founder of the software company Vision Critical, discovered a big problem with how many companies conduct their market research. While many companies used business intelligence to monitor what customers did and how they did it, they never wondered why customers acted the way they did. Reid took this idea and developed customer intelligence software to gain insights on customers by using cloud-based, real-time customer feedback.

Reid had attended the Vancouver Film School and had seemed headed for a career path opposite that of his father Angus Reid, who ran an extremely successful market research firm. Although Andrew knew nothing about the business world, he was determined to start a new market research company using online communities.

What Would You Do?

Though there is no one best or perfect way to conduct an entrepreneurial experiment, there are a few "rules" based on the information we have provided in this chapter so far. Table 7.1 shows some rules key to learning through experimentation.

In the next section, we will take a look at the three most commonly used experiments that are used today to help us to generate future data.

Utpal M. Dholakia, associate professor of marketing at Rice University's Jones Graduate School of Business, and Emily Durham, founder and president of Houston-based consulting firm Restaurant Connections, collaborated on an experiment to explore the effectiveness of social media on marketing. They set out to assess just how much influence businesses had on consumers when they set up dedicated online pages designed to attract "fans" by sending them messages and posting offers.

The first step to finding the results they needed was to partner with a bakery and café chain called Dessert Gallery (DG), based in Houston, Texas. Everyone on DG's mailing list was sent a survey asking for opinions of DG. Out of the 13,270 people who were sent a survey, 689 responded.

The experimenters then launched a Facebook page that was regularly updated with news, promotions, and reviews, and sent a Facebook fan request to everyone on the mailing list. Three months later, the same survey was re-sent to the original people on the mailing list. This time, 1,067 responded to the survey. Some of the respondents were Facebook fans, some were not Facebook fans, and some were not on Facebook at all.

When the experimenters analyzed the three groups, they found that the customers who had completed the survey twice and were Facebook fans happened to be DG's best, most frequent, and most loyal customers, as well as the best in spreading positive word of mouth.

While this experiment shows promise in just how effective social media can be for certain businesses, there is more work to be done. For example, another study shows that out of 50 Zagat-rated Houston restaurants, Facebook pages showed an average of only 340 fans, even though these were highly successful restaurants with thousands of customers. Still, the experiment suggests that Facebook can be a useful tool for some businesses when it is used effectively.

CRITICAL THINKING QUESTIONS

1.   **How would you describe Dholakia and Durham's hypothesis?**

2.   **Do you think the two experimenters used the most effective approach to test their hypothesis? Why or why not?**

3.   **Choose a particular kind of business that you imagine you are starting. How would you use social media to test a reaction of your target audience?** ●

TABLE 7.1

The Rules of Experimentation

1.	Focus on all stakeholders. Entrepreneurs need to focus on all the stakeholders potentially involved in the startup—these include customers, partners, suppliers, distributors, even real estate agents.
2.	Ask lots of questions. Remember, every question you have about your idea is fertile ground for an experiment.
3.	Think like a scientist, but don't act like a scientist. In other words, it's important to think through your hypothesis, what you want to test, and how you are going to test; but don't get bogged down in the rigor.
4.	Build your learning into the next iteration. Don't ignore negative information, just as you don't want to ignore positive information. A general rule of thumb is that six pieces of information saying the same thing can be a fact!
5.	Keep track of your data. You may think a piece of information is not important, but it is essential to keep track of everything.
6.	Keep your experiments low cost and quick; and use them to shape and improve ideas.
7.	Don't just talk with stakeholders—interact with them.
8.	Don't ignore data just because you don't like what they're telling you.

7.5 TYPES OF EXPERIMENTS[21]

>> **LO 7.5** **Identify three types of experiments most commonly used.**

A recent study has shown that entrepreneurs who launch new businesses and new products tend to use at least one of the following three forms of experiments (Figure 7.3): trying out new experiences; taking apart products, processes, and ideas; and testing ideas through pilots and prototypes.[22]

Trying Out New Experiences

Entrepreneurs who try new experiences such as going to different countries, working for multiple businesses, or learning new skills are more likely to generate new business ideas. For example, Apple cofounder Steve Jobs spent several months in an ashram in India, and attended calligraphy classes when he was a student at Reed College in the early 1970s. At the time, Jobs could not have predicted that his calligraphy experience would have any practical application in later life, but it very much influenced the typography on the first Apple Macintosh computer. As Jobs put it: "You can't connect the dots looking forward. You can only connect them looking backward. So you have to trust that the dots will somehow connect in your future."[23]

Similarly, entrepreneur Kristin Murdock could never have predicted that her unusual interest in collecting dried cow manure—also known as "cow pies"—would lead to a successful business. When they started to fall apart, she used a glaze to hold them together and was pleased with the otiose (moo) result. Then she had an idea to put a clock inside a cow pie and present it as a joke gift; she gave these to a few of her friends and relatives with funny messages such as "You Dung Good," or "Happy Birthday, You Old Poop." While many of Murdock's friends thought her clocks were disgusting, they

Video
Trying Out a
New Experience

FIGURE 7.3

Three Types of Experiments

Experimenting

Try out new experiences	Take apart products, processes, and ideas	Test ideas through pilots and prototypes
Examples	**Examples**	**Examples**
• Live in a different country	• Disassemble a product	• Build a prototype
• Work in multiple industries	• Visually map out a process	• Pilot a new process
• Develop a new skill	• Deconstruct an idea	• Launch a new venture on the market
Useful for generating new business ideas	Useful for generating new business ideas	Useful for generating and testing new business ideas to see what works

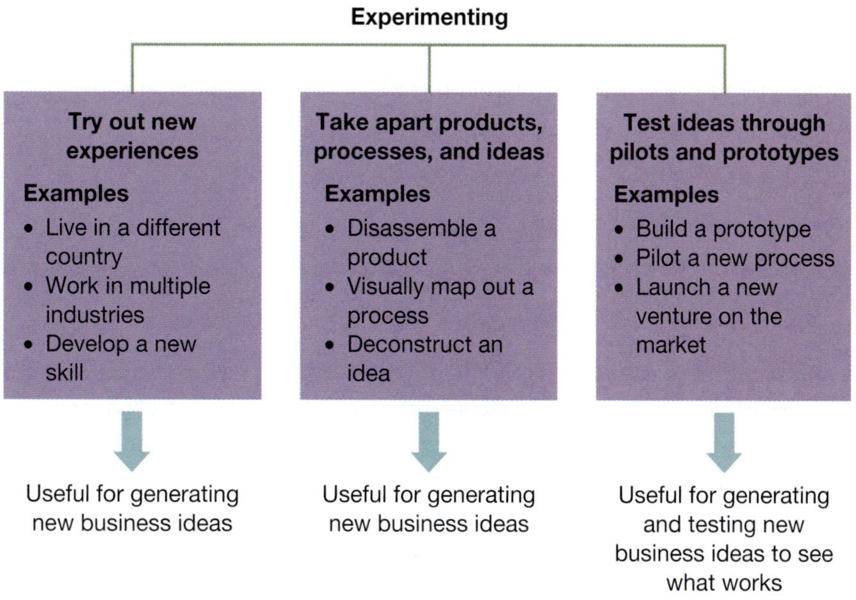

Source: Figure is from page 149/ibook of *The Innovator's DNA: Mastering the Five Skills of Disruptive Innovators* (Boston, MA: Harvard Business Review Press, 2011). P. 141 Kindle edition.

An example of a cow pie clock.

Credit: BOB EIGHMIE/KRT/ Newscom

caught the eye of the singer and television presenter Donny Osmond, who was a friend of one of Murdock's relatives. The clock was featured on the *Donny and Marie* show, and Murdock became inundated with orders for her creations. The cow-pie clocks went on to make millions of dollars, and Murdock expanded the cow-pie brand to a line of greeting cards. She jokingly refers to herself as an "entre-manure."[24]

The point is that exposing ourselves to diverse experiences broadens our mind, which improves our ability to make connections and expand our knowledge, and helps us become more innovative.

Taking Things Apart

As the story goes, at a young age Jeff Bezos attempted to take apart his own crib with a screwdriver; Google founder Larry Page was fascinated by what lay inside power tools; and Michael Dell disassembled a brand-new Apple II just to see how it worked. By taking the computer apart, Dell was able to find ways to enhance it, which eventually led to setting up his own company, Dell Inc.

Erin McKean, founder of the news discovery app Reverb and the online dictionary Wordnik.com, also applies her entrepreneurial experimentation to dressmaking and fashion creation. She observes, "Taking things apart and putting them back together again symbolizes the inquisitive, creative, disruptive entrepreneurial mindset, with an additional dose of 'I can do it better' arrogance."[25]

The point is that experimenting by exploring how things work, and deconstructing ideas, can also lead to different and better ways of doings things. Taking apart products, processes, and ideas often generates questions and triggers new ideas about how we can make our products or services work better.

Testing Ideas Through Pilots and Prototypes

The third type of experimentation, testing ideas through pilots and prototypes, is probably the most relevant to the types of experiments entrepreneurs conduct today. A **pilot experiment** is a small-scale study conducted to assess the feasibility of a product or service. Pilots and prototypes are not the same thing—in fact, a prototype, at least in its crude version, is often created before the pilot testing.

Pilot experiment: a small-scale study conducted to assess the feasibility of a product or service.

As we found in Chapter 6, prototyping is an essential part of the design process. You may remember the IDEO designer's attempt to understand clients' requirements for a new surgical apparatus to operate on delicate nasal tissues. He used a whiteboard marker and a film canister taped to a plastic clothespin to make a crude but effective prototype, which led to testing ideas to see what worked before the product was developed and launched. Prototypes can come in the form of basic models, or sketches that inform others and communicate what our ideas look like, behave like, and work like before the real product or service is launched.[26]

Entrepreneurs have different ways of testing their ideas: many of them, like Zappos founder Nick Swinmurn, launch their products and services quickly to the market and then use feedback from their customers for further testing and development; others first carefully test ideas through pilots and prototypes by conducting a range of experiments. This is the approach Jennifer Fleiss and Jennifer Hyman took before launching Rent the Runway, a business renting designer dresses initially online, followed by bricks-and-mortar locations.[27]

Fleiss thought of the idea to rent designer dresses when she noticed her sister, who was an accessories buyer at Bloomingdale's, struggling to find something to wear for a wedding. It occurred to Fleiss that if her sister, who had a successful well-paid job, couldn't afford a designer dress, then there wasn't much hope for anyone else. She also thought about the problem from the designer's side. How were designers going to get young, fashionable women to build their brand when the dresses were so far out of their price range? Fleiss teamed up with her Harvard Business School friend Jennifer Hyman to find the answers to those questions and to investigate the following hypothesis: there is a market for women who want to rent designer dresses online. Now all Fleiss and Hyman had to do was to test their assumptions.

But before launching the website, Fleiss and Hyman ran three experiments to test their idea. In their first experiment, they purchased one hundred dresses from top fashion designers, and offered them up for rent on the Harvard University campus, having let the students try them on in advance. The results of this pilot were encouraging: not only did the dresses rent, but they were returned in good condition. This experiment proved that there was a market for women who wanted to rent designer dresses and who would return them in good shape.

In the second experiment, they offered the dresses for rent on the Yale campus. This time prospective buyers were allowed to see the dresses but not try them on first. Even though not as many women rented the dresses as in the first experiment, the pilot was still considered a success.

In the final experiment, Fleiss and Hyman took photos of the dresses and offered the dresses for rent to New Yorkers through PDF photos and descriptions only. This was a test to see if women would prefer to rent the dresses from a store versus online. It turned out that approximately 5% of women showed an interest in renting the dresses online, which was enough for the founders to launch Rent the Runway: an online service renting designer dresses at only one-tenth of the cost, which the *New York Times* called "a Netflix model for haute couture."[28]

Launched in 2009, Rent the Runway attracted 600,000 members and 50,000 clients in its first year. By carrying out very few thoughtful experiments, Fleiss and Hyman had managed to create a hugely successful business. Furthermore, they didn't need to go down the traditional market research route and use methods like surveys. Their experiments allowed them to get immediate hands-on feedback from the participants, as well as knowledge about their buying behavior. This gave Fleiss and Hyman the opportunity to enlist early customers in the Rent the Runway model, and eventually launch the website with an established customer base. By starting small, the two businesswomen were able to realize their vision without huge financial costs and waste down the road.

These examples demonstrate that you don't need to run a whole range of complex, expensive experiments to get the answers you are looking for. The more questions you

Rent the Runway, founded by Jennifer Fleiss and Jennifer Hyman, makes designer dresses more affordable for everyone.

Credit: Astrid Stawiarz/Getty Images Entertainment/Getty Images

ask, observations you make, and people you involve, the more powerful are your data. Keep it simple and inexpensive, but also look for patterns across your data to draw accurate conclusions.

As we have learned, Fleiss and Hyman, Swinmurn, the founders of Parlor Skis, and the IDEO designers have all used some form of prototyping to experiment and test their ideas. Let's take a look at one of the easiest and most powerful forms of prototyping: storyboarding.

7.6 THE POWER OF STORYBOARDING

>> **LO 7.6**   **Illustrate the power of storyboarding as a form of prototyping and a basis for experiments.**

Storyboarding: an easy form of prototyping that provides a high-level view of thoughts and ideas arranged in sequence in the form of drawings, sketches, or illustrations.

Video
Storyboarding
a Prototype

Storyboarding is an easy form of prototyping that provides a high-level view of thoughts and ideas arranged in sequence in the form of drawings, sketches, or illustrations (see Figure 7.4).

Walt Disney animator Webb Smith has been credited with developing the idea of storyboarding in the 1930s by pinning up sketches of scenes in order to previsualize cartoons and spot any problems or inconsistencies before the animation goes into production.[29] Since then, not only has storyboarding become standard for movies, commercials, documentaries, and advertising, but it is also becoming popular as a business and management tool for explaining projects or products to employees, clients, customers, stockholders, and others.[30]

What does storyboarding mean to the entrepreneur? A storyboard provides you with a better understanding of your own idea and how it interacts with customers. It is a way of compiling your thoughts and ideas into one visual, easy-to-understand, logical document or set of documents.[31] Often, it is helpful to draw a storyboard before interacting with customers or other stakeholders because it can bring clarity to the idea, better tell the story of the idea, and highlight the potential value it brings to customers.

FIGURE 7.4

Storyboard

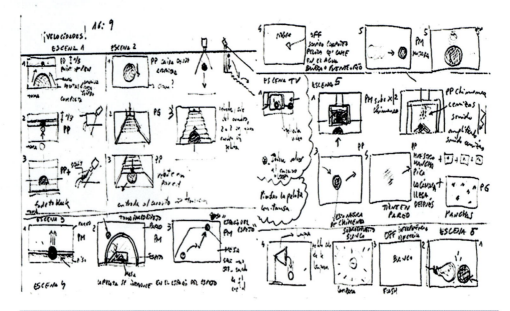

Source: Retrieved from http://www.fastcodesign.com/1672917/the-8-steps-to-creating-a-great-storyboard
Credit: ©iStockphoto.com/Rudimencial

While there are no hard and fast rules for storyboarding, there must be a clear sense of what needs to be accomplished and an effort to maintain the flow or sequence of thoughts and ideas.

Remember the old adage, "A picture is worth a thousand words." Because of the visual element, storyboards have a way of getting the main message across very quickly. It is also more likely than a lengthy, detailed, written document or speech to provoke reactions, discussion, and feedback from the people who are viewing it. As long as your storyboard flows well and is interesting and interactive, you can expect it to generate ideas and further questions.[32]

Storyboarding requires that the customer be at the center of the story. It is a way for you to draw the idea in action, which generates further questions for additional experimentation.

Basic storyboards are simple and inexpensive to create, and they do not require any artistic training or talent. They can be rough, hand-drawn sketches, or simple PowerPoint slides. If you are sketching on a piece of paper, separate your page into quadrants, and then you can start to fill in each one. Your goal is not to create a work of art but to communicate: to use visual imagery to make your entrepreneurial idea more understandable.[33]

The problem–solution–benefit framework (see Figure 7.5) provides a basic structure for storyboarding. In this structure, there are three main questions to keep in mind:

▸ What is the problem your customer is experiencing?

▸ What are you offering as a solution to the problem?

▸ How will your customer benefit from your product/service offering?

Let's apply these questions to the Rent the Runway example we described above.

The problem: Many women (even those in well-paid jobs) cannot afford designer dresses to wear to special occasions. "I want to wear a designer dress, but they are very expensive, and I would probably wear it only once."

The solution: Give women access to designer dresses by creating an online business renting designer dresses for one-tenth of the original cost. "I get access to the latest dresses, but I get to rent for the night rather than buy!"

The benefit: The rental model gives many more women the opportunity to wear designer dresses, which they could have never afforded before. It provides designers with an opportunity to build their brand because their dresses are being showcased

FIGURE 7.5

The Problem–Solution–Benefit Framework

State the Problem	Show the Solution	Show the Benefit
• What is the problem your customer is experiencing?	• What are you offering as a solution to the problem?	• How will your customer benefit from your solution?

by a larger demographic of young, fashionable women. "This service would let me feel like a movie star for my fancy party that's coming up next month."

Video
Using a Storyboard
to Solve Problems

Another version of a storyboard (Figure 7.6) uses a four-quadrant framework. The storyboard illustrates an idea for a new entrepreneurship course. The idea is for faculty members to create an Introduction to Entrepreneurship course for first-year college students with the goal of creating, developing, operating, and launching a new business.

This storyboard shows a before-and-after scenario. The upper left quadrant shows a traditional classroom setting, with a professor standing at the top of the class, lecturing students on the theory of entrepreneurship. One student is sleeping; another student is hoping a friend will text him to give him something else to do; a third student doesn't understand the theory that the professor is teaching. The *problem* is that students are not engaged during the entrepreneurship course.

The second part of the story board (the upper right quadrant) suggests a *solution* to boost student engagement by separating them into teams, and loaning each team $3,000 (funded by the college) as startup money for the new ventures.

In the third (lower left) quadrant, the students armed with the money *organize* their businesses into different function units. While they are given the freedom to create their own ideas, they are encouraged to think about how their product or services satisfies a human need. They sell their product; but they also suffer from challenges, setbacks, and great victories—as depicted in the zigzag graph illustrated with happy and unhappy faces.

The final quadrant, on the lower right, shows the *outcome*. Students pay the startup money back to the college, and the remaining profits go to charity. What are the *benefits* of this idea? The students are much more engaged because they acted in order to learn. They were given the opportunity to build something real, practice entrepreneurship, and get a taste for the real entrepreneurial experience.

This storyboard generated lots of questions that needed to be answered before the course could be rolled out. Early questions are listed in Table 7.2.

FIGURE 7.6

Storyboard of an Idea to Boost Student Engagement

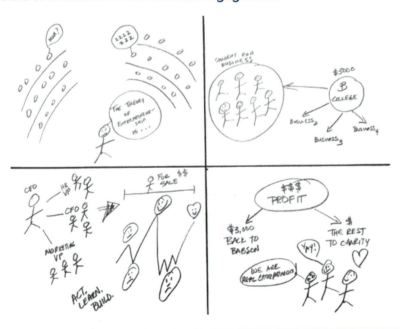

MINDSHIFT

Create a Storyboard and One Simple Experiment

By this point in the book, we are sure you have at least one idea, if not hundreds, floating around in your mind. We hope you've developed a practice of writing down your ideas. Now it's time to take one of your ideas and draw it in action using a storyboard format. The simplest format is the four-quadrant version depicted in Figure 7.6—the storyboard to boost student engagement.

Artistic talent is not required. Simply focus on visually representing the four aspects of your idea: problem, solution, organization, and outcomes/benefits. As you create your sketches, questions will probably arise related to your idea. Once you've completed the storyboard, write a list of all the questions that you have, now that you have envisioned your idea in action. It's okay if you have a long list. As a matter of fact, the longer the better.

Once you have your questions, identify the top three questions you want to answer first, and develop an action-oriented experiment to answer each question. Be specific: What's the question the experiment is designed to examine? What do think you'll find (i.e., what is your hypothesis)? Next, conduct the experiments. What did you learn? How will you build this learning into the next iteration?

CRITICAL THINKING QUESTIONS

1. **At the outset of this exercise, how did you feel about being asked to create a storyboard? Do you think people with artistic training or talent have an advantage in storyboarding? Why or why not?**

2. **Is your list of questions longer or shorter than you expected? How easy or difficult was it to translate your top three questions into experiments?**

3. **What did you learn from this exercise that surprised you?** ●

The list of questions can go on and on, but it's amazing how many questions come from simply drawing the idea in action. It is likely the list would have been much shorter if the idea was simply being discussed rather than sketched. But in this case, each question represents a need for an experiment.

Depending on the result of each experiment, the original idea may change slightly and for the better. This is the point of experimenting. Once most of the questions have been answered, then a pilot course can be built and rolled out to all students.

This class is actually being taught today at Babson College, and has been since 1996. Many experiments have been conducted over the years to better refine the course. Most recently, this course has been combined with the organizational behavior

TABLE 7.2

Early Questions Generated by Storyboarding

• Will Babson College give first-year students $3,000?
• What happens if the money is lost and cannot be repaid?
• What should the size of the business teams be?
• Do students want to participate?
• Do faculty want to teach this type of class?
• How should students be graded?
• What content is necessary to have before a business can be started?
• Should this be for first-year students, or is it better for seniors?

(OB) course, and is known as Foundations of Management and Entrepreneurship. It is taught by an entrepreneurship faculty member and an OB faculty member.

The idea is that as the venture grows (entrepreneurship), so do the individual and team (organizational behavior). As you can see from the original storyboard, the intention to combine two courses was not in the original design, but the idea has evolved and grown over the years to become even more innovative and inclusive. Local charities have also benefited from the student startups and have received over $400,000 in donations since 1999.[34]

In the next chapter, we will explore the concept of evaluating opportunities through the medium of business models. ●

$SAGE edge™

SUMMARY

7.1   Define experiments and describe the steps of experimentation.

Experiments are mechanisms for testing the validity of a hypothesis. The starting point of an experiment is the hypothesis—the assumption to be tested—but the formulation of the hypothesis itself begins with asking questions and conducting background research to identify the right questions to be explored further.

7.2   Identify and describe the six steps of scientific experimentation.

The scientific process of experimentation includes the following steps: asking lots of questions; carrying out background research; developing hypotheses; testing the hypotheses by running experiments; analyzing the data; and assessing results.

7.3   Demonstrate how to test hypotheses and identify customers.

It's critical that when testing hypotheses, entrepreneurs need not actually develop elaborate, extremely robust experiments; the goal is to think like a scientist, not to emulate one perfectly. The type of customer to be targeted must also be carefully weighed. Customers differ in terms of their levels of consumption, rate of adoption, and ability to influence. Furthermore, many factors influential to the perception of a new product or service need not stem from actual customers but could instead come from critics or celebrity endorsements.

7.4   Explore different ways of generating data and describe the rules of experimentation.

When experimenting, entrepreneurs should build on learning, including recently acquired information (positive and negative) into future experiments. Again, a scientific mentality should be adopted, but not to an extreme degree. Data should be well tracked, and many questions should be explored; but cost and experiment duration should be kept to a minimum whenever possible. Finally, all possible stakeholders should be the focus, both in terms of consideration and interaction.

7.5   Identify three types of experiments most commonly used.

The three most commonly employed types of experiments areas follows: trying new experiences; deconstructing products, processes, and ideas to better understand how and why they function; and conducting trials and pilots.

7.6   Illustrate the power of storyboarding as a form of prototyping and a basis for experiments.

Engaging, simple, and effective in communicating a point or position—storyboards exemplify the old adage that a picture is worth a thousand words. Inexpensive and easy to make, storyboards are also great tools for eliciting questions from the audience or getting them involved in the creative process.

CASE STUDY

Marissa Mayer, Yahoo Inc. CEO

In 2013, *Fortune* magazine listed Marissa Mayer in the #1 slot on their prestigious *40 Under 40* list, ahead of well-known Internet tycoons such as Mark Zuckerberg (Facebook), Ben Silberman (Pinterest), and Kevin Systrom (Instagram). In 2014, *Fortune* magazine listed Mayer as #14 on its *Most Powerful Women in Business* list, and #18 on its *Most Influential Women in the World* list. Yet, by 2015, her star quality seemed to be getting tarnished.

Hailing from the farmland of central Wisconsin, Marissa Mayer had a typical small-town American upbringing. In high school, she was active in extracurricular activities, where she demonstrated leadership abilities as captain of her school's successful debate team and pom-pom squad. She continued in her upward trajectory of success at Stanford University, where she initially studied to become a doctor but earned both a bachelor's and master's degree in computer science.

Mayer's successes coming out of college opened many doors of opportunity. Despite receiving 14 different job offers from a variety of prestigious organizations, Mayer chose to accept an offer with a computer startup company called Google, which at the time was still in its infancy. When Mayer joined Google in 1999, she was only the 20th person hired by the company, which had been incorporated just a year previously.

An entrepreneur at heart, Mayer made contributions to Google in the early days of the company that were prominent, far-reaching, and in many ways foundational to the overarching success the company has enjoyed. She started out as a programmer writing code. Over time, however, she became increasingly involved in leadership roles that allowed her to experiment with policy strategies that proved highly successful. For example, her leadership and example led to clearer communication between executives and floor-level employees, and to the development of a mentoring program that has since been replicated at numerous other tech companies.

During her decade-plus stint with Google, Mayer became known for "her work ethic, eye for detail and vision" (Marissa Mayer Biography, 2016). Her perfectionism led her to experiment and research until she had found design, market, and policy solutions that met her unusually high standards. For example, Mayer once "wanted to test out 41 shades of blue for the toolbar on Google pages to see which one appealed the most to the user." While such fastidious decision-making processes have surely caused anxiety among some of her colleagues over the years, they seem to have ultimately served her—and the companies she has worked for—very well.

Like all entrepreneurs, Mayer has always kept her eyes open for new opportunities.

> In a 2008 interview . . . she seemed to [already] be looking ahead to her next act. "I helped build Google," Mayer said, "but I don't like to rest on [my] laurels. I think the most interesting thing is what happens next (Marissa Mayer Biography, 2016).

What happened next caught the attention of Silicon Valley and the rest of Corporate America in unprecedented fashion. In July 2012, Yahoo Inc.—the search engine giant and competitor of Google—hired Mayer to be its new CEO. With the hire, Mayer became one of only 20 female CEOs in the Fortune 500. And at only 37 years of age, Mayer became *the* youngest of *all* Fortune 500 CEOs, male and female.

Yahoo hired Mayer for her entrepreneurial vision hoping she could turn around a troubled company that was facing "a lack of innovation" and "a culture problem." Innovation and culture building were two things Mayer had excelled in at Google, and she immediately went to work. Her immediate shake-up of Yahoo included a line of executive firings and several new hires to replace them.

With her new leadership team in place, Mayer began leading Yahoo in a series of substantial investments and acquisitions. However, one decision made before she came on board was the sale of over $7 billion dollars of Yahoo stock to the Chinese e-commerce giant Alibaba in order to increase Yahoo's cash reserves. With added capital for experimentation and expansion, Mayer spent her first year on the job overseeing the acquisition of over 20 smaller companies. The company's highest profile, and most expensive, move was to acquire the hugely successful microblogging company Tumblr for a price of just over a billion dollars. Ever willing to demonstrate her entrepreneurial capacity for flexibility and experimentation, Mayer pioneered a new path for Yahoo with her nod to acquire Tumblr—a move that "analysts hailed . . . as a shift in industrial strategy" (Riggins, 2014).

After only 22 months at the helm, Mayer was able to announce an 84% profit rise from the previous year. Observers commented that Yahoo's decision to place its future in the hands of a young and gifted math and science whiz from Upstate Wisconsin had been touched by King Midas. And Marissa Mayer, worth an estimated $300 million, was goldenly compensated for her leadership as well.

Given such accolades, it was a shock to many when, in the summer of 2014, Mayer was forced to announce Yahoo's lowest quarterly earnings in a decade. By the end of 2014, analysts were questioning not only Yahoo's financial viability but also Mayer's leadership.

> She may be a woman of power, but she's been heavily criticised [sic] for her lack of support in helping other women break through the glass ceiling of her industry's heavily male-dominated hierarchy. Meanwhile, her cold, calculated style has continued to chase some of Yahoo's most talented engineers into the arms of rivals like Google and Facebook. (Riggins, 2014)

No stranger to ambition and audacity, Mayer was known for following a personal working style that includes the following two principles: "a) work with the smartest people she can find, and b) go for a challenge that makes her feel like she's in over her head." As impressive as it is for a woman under the age of 40 to have taken over one of the most prominent tech companies in the world, Mayer faced the risk of being blamed for Yahoo's demise. Nevertheless, if the company were to be sold, she would take with her a severance package valued at over $150 million.

Critical Thinking Questions

1. Marissa Mayer's early successes were rooted in her proficiency as a student in math and science. Why are subjects like math, statistics, logic, and critical thinking essential to product experimentation and market hypotheses?

2. How might you apply the "Rules of Experimentation" to discovering and developing your own entrepreneurship and leadership skills?

3. Data generation is critical to market research and product experimentation. What "Data" might you begin collecting to better prepare yourself for a career in entrepreneurship (journal writing, subscribing to a professional journal or blog, asking questions of entrepreneurial role models, seeking out a mentor, etc.)?

4. Marissa Mayer's executive opportunity at Yahoo came about because of her outstanding work at Google, and skilled marketing of her own career along the way. In what ways are you currently expanding or contracting future opportunities for yourself based on your present performance as a student, employee, entrepreneur, networker, friend, and human being. Secondly, how are you marketing your own career to achieve future success?

Sources

Carlson, N. (2014, December 17). What happened when Marissa Mayer tried to be Steve Jobs. *New York Times*. Retrieved from http://www.nytimes.com/2014/12/21/magazine/what-happened-when-marissa-mayer-tried-to-be-steve-jobs.html

Forbes (Online). (*n.d.*). *The world's 100 most powerful women*. Retrieved from http://www.forbes.com/power-women/list/#tab:overall

Fortune Magazine (Online). (*n.d.*). *40 under 40 2013*. Retrieved from http://fortune.com/40-under-40/2013/

Fortune Magazine (Online). (*n.d.*). The most powerful women in business. Retrieved from http://fortune.com/most-powerful-women/ginni-rometty-1/

Goel, V. (2015, December 5). Yahoo board is quiet on any shake-up plans. *New York Times*.

Goldman, D. (2016, March 11). Marissa Mayer is in the fight of her life. *CNN*: 11:49 AM ET. "Mayer is battling for her job on multiple fronts: the public, customers, in vestors and potential buyers."

Hare, B. (2013, March 13). How Marissa Mayer writes her own rules. *CNN*. Retrieved from http://www. cnn.com/2013/03/12/tech/web/marissa-mayer-yahoo-profile/

Marissa Mayer Biography. (2016) .Retrieved from http://www.biography.com/people/marissa-mayer-20902689

The Richest (Online). (*n.d.*). *Marissa Mayer net worth*. Retrieved from http://www.therichest. com/celebnetworth/celebrity-business/ceo/marissa-mayer-net-worth/

Riggins, N. (2014, July 3). *Marissa Mayer: Queen of Silicon Valley*. World Finance: The Voice of the Market (online). Retrieved from http://www.worldfinance.com/home/featured/queen-of-silicon-valley/

PART III

EVALUATING AND ACTING ON OPPORTUNITIES

8 Building Business Models

"Today countless innovative business models are emerging. Entirely new industries are forming as the old ones crumble. Upstarts are challenging the old guard, some of whom are struggling feverishly to reinvent themselves."

—Alexander Osterwalder and Yves Pigneur, authors of *Business Model Generation: A Handbook for Visionaries, Game Changers, and Challengers*

Learning Objectives

Chapter Outline

8.1 WHAT IS A BUSINESS MODEL?

>> **LO 8.1** **Define the business model.**

In Chapter 7, we explored how entrepreneurs can test their ideas through small-scale experiments. As you may recall, an experiment begins with a hypothesis in need of testing. In this chapter, we will look at how business models support experimentation by illustrating the different components of a business model and how each component represents a hypothesis that needs to be tested, then validated or changed. Let's begin by exploring the definition of a business model.

A **business model** is a conceptual framework that describes how a company creates, delivers, and extracts value.[1] It includes a network of activities and resources to create a sustainable and scalable business that delivers value to target customers. Business models help entrepreneurs generate value and scale. They do this in several ways: by fulfilling unmet needs in an existing market, by delivering existing products and services to existing customers with unique differentiation, and by serving customers in new markets.

A business model is not the same as a business plan, although people often confuse the two. A **business plan** is a formal document that provides background and financial information about the company, outlines your goals for the business, and describes how you intend to reach them. A business plan supports the business model and explains the steps necessary to attain the business model's goals.

Entrepreneurs like Tanzeel urRehman, profiled in the *Entrepreneurship in Action* feature, have the freedom to create, test, and adapt their business models until they find a compelling value proposition that meets the needs of most customers. For example, as soon as VF realized that startups were struggling to pay fees for its services, it quickly adapted its business model to a subsidy-based one in exchange for a percentage of equity in the product or the company itself. This approach appealed more to its target customer base.

Because new businesses tend to be small in the beginning, it is much easier to be agile and make quick, efficient changes to the business model during

Video
What is a Business Model?

Business model: a conceptual framework that describes how a company creates, delivers, and extracts value.

Business plan: a formal document that provides background and financial information about the company, outlines your goals for the business, and describes how you intend to reach them.

ENTREPRENEURSHIP IN ACTION

Tanzeel urRehman, Cofounder and CEO, Virtual Force (VF)

**Tanzeel urRehman,
Cofounder and CEO, Virtual Force (VF) together with his team.**
Credit: Used with permission from Tanzeel urRehman

With a background in computer engineering, Tanzeel urRehman worked in a number of roles in technology, business development, and sales before earning an MBA at Babson College in 2013. Keen to share his vast experience, passion, and knowledge, urRehman hit on exactly the right kind business for him when he cofounded Virtual Force (VF) in late 2011.

Based in Pakistan, VF is an innovation platform that supports startups, SMEs, and large enterprises in need of tech expertise in order to get their businesses off the ground. Since being founded in late 2011, VF has grown to 50 staff members and worked with more than 30 startups on a range of diverse products in health care, home care, financing, education, sports, agriculture, beauty, and clothing, among others.

In providing this service, VF offers a solution to one of the biggest challenges to early-stage tech startups in particular: finding the right expertise to build a testable product quickly and efficiently with the least number of resources possible. By taking this approach, VF enables startups to reach the market with a testable product available for customer feedback and further iteration where necessary.

As urRehman says, "Not having the right tech cofounder and eventually not being able to build the correct product in a timely manner has been one of the most important causes of failure for many startups. We at VF identified this niche and then started working with startups, helping them build their products, taking the role of their tech cofounders."

VF also takes a streamlined approach to its business model. Initially, VF started off with a fee-based business model where the startup would pay a fee for the services provided by VF. However, the model has evolved to offer subsidized engineering and design services to startups in exchange for a percentage of equity in the product or the company itself. Through trial and error, VF quickly learned that many startups could not afford to pay the fees for this service, so a shift to an equity-based business model made more sense.

Tanzeel urRehman believes his business brings people together and satisfies two primary needs: the need for startups to find the right talent to help build and scale their products; and the need for his engineers to work on new, exciting products. He states, "Startups in the US face a huge issue of finding the right talent for their product needs. Similarly, engineers in Pakistan generally do not get to work on brilliant new ideas. For engineers, it is more fun to work on new and unique ideas that they can see scale up. We identified this gap and created a bridge between these two markets through VF. Our business connects talent from across the continents to work together and make that important 'dent' in the universe."

Success for urRehman is collaborating with great minds from all over the world to build unique, innovative products. "It is more valuable to see the sort of impact I have had. I had a chance to stay in the US and work in some organization, instead I worked to expand this business. Now in my company, brilliant minds of Pakistan get to work with brilliant minds of US and Europe. We are creating amazing products that are changing the world *and* we have created a company with a culture that is turning out to be a role model for other companies in Pakistan."

CRITICAL THINKING QUESTIONS

1. How would you describe the business model used by VF? Why do you think VF changed its business model?

2. Think about all VF stakeholders (employees, clients, customers of clients, and local communities). How is VF providing value for these stakeholders?

3. Do you think taking ownership in his client's businesses will be valuable in the long run? Explain your reasoning ●

Source: Tanzeel urRehman, personal interview, April 5, 2016.

the startup stage. Then, if successful, the business can scale as the young business model is tested and validated through early action. Equally, if the changes don't seem to work, then it is easy to spot the flaws and adjust them accordingly before large-scale investments are made. This is the logic behind the often-quoted saying from Steve Blank, a Silicon Valley entrepreneur and professor: "A startup is a temporary organization in search of a scalable business model."[2]

However, the ability to tweak and change business models is not as quick or as efficient for some larger or more established organizations, and some of them have ultimately failed because of their inability to change their business models. Consider BlackBerry, which stormed the business, government, and consumer markets with its smartphone technology in the early 2000s. Within a decade, BlackBerry failed to adapt to new competitors who were offering sleeker smartphones with additional functions such as touch interface and video/photo transmission, putting the company on the decline.[3] Similarly, Kodak failed to adapt to the digital camera revolution quickly enough, and as a result struggled for years before filing for Chapter 11 bankruptcy protection in 2012. The point is that the business model in any company (big, small, new, old) must always be poised for adjustment and changes as new information is received and markets change.

But who says business models have to be reinvented at all? Remember the Swiffer brand by Procter & Gamble that we mentioned in Chapter 6? The Swiffer brand is a range of waterless cleaning products that makes surface cleaning easier and more convenient. While Swiffer is often hailed as a big innovation, Procter & Gamble didn't need to change its business model to accommodate it—in fact, the product fit squarely with its existing business model of selling cleaning products. While Swiffer did disrupt the traditional mop makers, it didn't disrupt Procter & Gamble.

The key to a successful business model is focusing on what customers want and where they are going. In Chapter 7 we explored the rise of Amazon founder Jeff Bezos, who excelled at experimenting with new business opportunities to test assumptions behind various business models. Amazon is a great example of a company that continually invents new business models to stay relevant, moving from selling books to other products to brokering sales for other companies (small companies as well as other retailers) to selling cloud computing IT services to selling hardware (the Kindle). As Bezos says, "I really look where the customer is going and where I need to deliver value for that customer, and I don't care about legacy. I will do what it takes."[4]

8.2 THE FOUR PARTS OF A BUSINESS MODEL

>> LO 8.2 Identify the four core areas of a business model.

Let's begin with a deeper exploration of the business model by breaking it down into its four major components. The business model consists of four main interlocking parts that together create "the business." These are as follows: the *offering*, the *customers*, the *infrastructure*, and the *financial viability*.[5] Without these four parts, there is no business, no company, no opportunity. All must coexist, and none can be ignored; however, each can be a source of innovation and advantage over the competition. In other words, competitive advantage doesn't always come from the product or service you are offering. It can come from the other areas of the business as well.

Video
Parts of a Business Model

The Offering

Offering: what you are offering to a particular customer segment, the value generated for those customers, and how you will reach and communicate with them.

The first part of the business model is the **offering**, which identifies what you are offering to a particular customer segment, the value generated for those customers, and how you will reach and communicate with them. The offering includes the **customer value proposition (CVP)**, which describes exactly what products or services your business offers and sells to customers. It explains how you can help customers do something more inexpensively, easily, effectively, or quickly than before. We will explore the concept of the CVP in greater detail later in this chapter.

Customer value proposition (CVP): a statement that describes exactly what products or services your business offers and sells to customers.

Customers

Customers: people who populate the segments of a market served by the offering.

Customers include the people who populate the segments of a market that your offering is serving. Entrepreneurs typically can't serve everyone in a market, so you have to choose whom best to target. In addition, you have to determine how you will reach those segments and how you will maintain a relationship with the customer. Remember Niari Keverian, founder of ZOOS Greek Iced Teas, featured in Chapter 1? Keverian created a Facebook page to collate information about their potential customers. Eventually, this led to defining a target market that included mostly young, health-conscious professionals, college students, and older teens, as well as moms-to-be and new moms.

Infrastructure

Infrastructure: the resources (people, technology, products, suppliers, partners, facilities, cash, etc.) that an entrepreneur must have in order to deliver the CVP.

The **infrastructure** generally includes all the resources (people, technology, products, suppliers, partners, facilities, cash, etc.) that an entrepreneur must have in order to deliver the CVP. For example, when Anna Haupt and Terese Alstin wanted to make their idea for the invisible bicycle helmet become a reality, they enlisted investors, cycling experts, designers, suppliers, and retailers to support the creation, promotion, and sales of the product.

Financial Viability

Financial viability: defines the revenue and cost structures a business needs to meet its operating expenses and financial obligations.

Financial viability defines the revenue and cost structures a business needs to meet its operating expenses and financial obligations: How much will it cost to deliver the offering to our customers?

For example, when the founders of Parlor Skis, featured in Chapter 7, failed to get their skis into brick-and-mortar stores, they had to ensure that their custom-made skis were still profitable by being sold primarily online.

People often make a mistake in thinking that the business model is just about revenue and costs, but a business model is more than a financial model. It has to describe more than how you intend to make money; it needs to explain why a customer would give you money in the first place and what's in it for the customer. This is where the CVP comes in.

8.3 THE CUSTOMER VALUE PROPOSITION (CVP)

>> **LO 8.3**   **Explore the importance of the Customer Value Proposition in further detail.**

The Customer Value Proposition, or CVP, is perhaps the most important part of your business model. The key word in CVP is "customer." The focus should always be on the value generated for the customer and how this value is then captured by the business in the form of profit.[10]

Attack of the Clones[6]

Oliver Samwer, cofounder of Berlin-based Rocket Internet
Credit: REUTERS/Alamy Stock Photo

Three German brothers, Oliver, Marc, and Alexander Samwer, have managed to create a hugely successful business model by cloning the most successful Internet businesses in the United States and launching them internationally.

Staffed with finance and management specialists, Berlin-based Rocket Internet provides its team members with the financial backing they need to create duplicate versions of proven business models executed by well-known Internet companies. These copycat businesses are then launched in different countries, and often in emerging markets.

Since creating their copycat business model in 1999, Rocket Internet has created duplicate versions of eBay, GrubHub, Airbnb, eHarmony, Pinterest, and Zappos, to name just a few. In the case of Zappos, within four years of its launch, the German copy called Zalando was present in 15 countries, and was valued at around $5 billion. Alando, Rocket's German version of eBay, was actually bought by eBay for $50 million less than a year after its launch. Similarly, less than six months after Rocket introduced a Groupon clone, Citydeal, Groupon bought it for 14% of its shares.[7]

Rocket also focuses on investing in tech startups, hiring entrepreneurs to run the businesses in places where their US rivals are not so prevalent. Its geographic distribution is organized into four regions: Africa, Asia Pacific, Latin America, and the Middle East. It has a global portfolio of startups in more than 110 countries, employs 30,000 people, and earns almost $850 billion in annual revenue.[8] Yet there is a time limit on how long these tech startups are given to prove their worth—if they don't succeed within six months of starting, then they face the prospect of being shut down.

While the Samwer brothers are both revered and criticized for their cloning tactics and for profiting from the ideas of others, they believe there is a skill to applying proven tech ideas to emerging markets. "There are pioneering entrepreneurs and execution entrepreneurs, and maybe we belong more to the execution entrepreneurs," says Oliver Samwar.[9] Yet, there is nothing to prevent Rocket from copying existing tech businesses, as long as it doesn't infringe on copyrights and trademarks; equally, there is otiose nothing to stop competitors from duplicating Rocket's business model—something that has already begun.

CRITICAL THINKING QUESTIONS

1. **What do you think are the ethical implications of copycat business models?**

2. **Do you think cloning products and services is good business practice? Why or why not?**

3. **What would you do if someone else cloned your product or service?** ●

For your CVP to be truly effective, it needs three qualities:

▸ it must offer better value than the competition,

▸ it must be measurable in monetary terms (i.e., you must be able to prove that your CVP is better value than other offerings on the market), and

▸ it must be sustainable (i.e., you must have the ability to execute it for a considerable length of time).[11]

In Chapter 6 we explored the concept of design thinking and the processes entrepreneurs go through to create value, generate new options, and find the most functional solutions to problems. As we have learned, design thinking is ultimately a constructive and collaborative process that combines the skills of observation, synthesis, searching and generating alternatives, critical thinking, feedback, visual representation, creativity, problem solving, and value creation. Applying design thinking to your CVP enables you to create uniqueness and differentiation.[12] As with design thinking, the CVP means thinking about your business from the customer's viewpoint rather than from an organizational perspective. Your CVP must demonstrate that you are meeting the needs of various customer segments.

Getting the Job Done

Video
The Customer's Need

The key to a successful CVP involves a deep understanding of what the customer really wants or needs—not just how the customer does things now. It is an exciting opportunity to meet the needs of a real customer who wants to accomplish a goal, to get the job done.[13] Creating your CVP does not begin with trying to persuade customers to buy your product or service. Rather, it's about finding a goal—a job that the customer needs done—and then proposing a way to fulfill that goal.[14] It's about uncovering what your customer needs and providing solutions to meet those needs. The first question to ask, then, is this: "What job is the customer trying to get done?"

For example, the Swedish home-furnishings company IKEA understood the goal of customers who needed to furnish their rooms or apartments on a tight budget but did not want to settle for unattractive, worn, secondhand pieces. By providing do-it-yourself furniture kits at a lower cost than ready-made furniture sold in major furniture stores, IKEA solved the problem of obtaining good quality new, stylish furniture for a low price. Similarly, FedEx made the job of transporting a letter or package overnight from point A to point B effortless in comparison with the regular mailing and parcel delivery services that existed in the 1970s when FedEx (then called Federal Express) was launched.[15]

In creating their CVPs, both IKEA and FedEx first focused on the jobs that the customer needed to get done before coming up with a solution to meet this need. The CVP also involves identifying ways in which your company best fits into customers' lifestyles; it means analyzing the relationships you need to establish with customers versus the relationships your customer expects to establish with you; finally, it emphasizes how much customers are willing to pay for value, rather than trying to extract money from your customers.[16] To illustrate these points, let's look at an example of a successful CVP in action.

Tata Motors, an automotive manufacturing company in India previously known for building trucks and buses, created a CVP to provide radically low-cost cars for the people of India. Prior to the introduction in 2008 of Tata's highly affordable car, millions of citizens mostly used scooters to get around. Sometimes whole families would put themselves at risk by crowding onto a scooter, exposed to rain, wind, and traffic hazards. The problem was that many families could not afford to buy a car—even the cheapest car cost five times more than a scooter—so they had to make do with what they could afford.

A Tata car— the world's cheapest car

Tata Motors created a CVP focused on providing an affordable, safer, more comfortable mode of transport for the low price of $2,500. This price was intended to make the car price-competitive with scooters, which its target customers were currently buying due to affordability.

Yet Tata Motors' existing business model did not allow the company to create a car at the price it wanted. Creating such a radically low-cost car would require a new business model that would support such a low price point. Tata needed to find ways to cut the costs of manufacturing in order to make the car affordable for its target customers.

How did Tata do it? First, it created a product design process that removed as much cost as possible from the car. Tata looked at eliminating everything it possibly could to reduce the number of parts used in the car. The resulting car has no air conditioning, no power steering, no power windows, no fabric covering the seats, no radio, no central locking of doors; and only the driver's seat is adjustable.[17] Tata also used 60% fewer suppliers than are needed for a typical economy car, thus giving more business to fewer suppliers and reducing coordination costs.

Tata then outsourced 83% of the car's components to find the lowest possible cost. What's more, Tata worked closely with its suppliers from the start, getting them involved in designing the components rather than merely building them to Tata's specifications. For example, instead of specifying, "build a windshield wiper X inches long with a Y diameter," Tata issued a more functional goal: "wipe water from the windshield." This allowed suppliers to come up with new, innovative, and low-cost ways to meet goals. In the case of the car's wipers, the suppliers came up with the idea of having only one wiper blade rather than the standard two wipers.

Next, Tata created a different manufacturing process that reduced the cost of final assembly. It made the innovative decision to save costs by not assembling its cars. Instead, Tata ships a "kit" with all the required parts in modules to a network of local entrepreneurs who assemble the cars on demand. The modules are designed to be glued together rather than welded because gluing is less expensive and doesn't require costly welding equipment. In addition to assembling the cars, the local entrepreneurs sell and service the cars.

By reinventing its business model to meet the needs of its CVP, Tata's innovation approach to the production, design, and manufacturing of cars enabled it to open up a whole new market to meet the needs of hundreds of thousands of people who previously couldn't afford cars.[18] Tata didn't simply create a low-cost car; the company created a car that delivered the base value customers were willing to pay for a no-frills car that accomplished the customer goal. Tata Motors succeeded in resolving the problem of affordability for its customers.

Like Tata, you can find opportunities to help customers do a better job or accomplish a goal that they haven't been able to reach before, by considering the deeper categories of problems faced by customers.

Four Problems Experienced by Customers

Typically, customers face at least one of four problems that prevent them from getting a job done. These problems include lack of time, lack of money, lack of skills, and lack of access (see Figure 8.1). As an entrepreneur, if you can find a new way to solve one of these problems, you're on your way to creating a good CVP. Let's take a look at how some companies have resolved each of these problems with their own CVPs.

Video
The Customer Value Proposition

Lack of time

Think of the last time you or a loved one had a minor health issue like a sore throat or a mildly strained muscle. Chances are you didn't visit the doctor because of how much time it would take to request an appointment, how many days it would be until an appointment was available, and the length of time you'd have to spend in the doctor's office waiting room before being called in to be seen.

MinuteClinic partnered with CVS pharmacy to provide people with minor ailments with greater access to medical care.

Credit: AP Photo/Andy King

MinuteClinic, a division of CVS Health, solved this problem by identifying a wide range of minor ailments and procedures that were so common and well understood that they could be handled by nurse practitioners rather than doctors.[19] MinuteClinic then partnered with CVS pharmacy chains to set up a nurse's station inside the store. Customers can just walk in without an appointment and be treated in about 30 minutes. By solving one of the major problems experienced by patients with minor ailments, MinuteClinic's CVP is increased availability and access to medical care.

Lack of money

Delivering previously unaffordable products or services for less money can help beat the competition and open up a whole new market. As we have seen, Tata Motors was able to solve the problem of lack of money by creating an affordable car to sell to people in India, and IKEA solved the problem of obtaining new, stylish furniture on a tight budget. Similarly, in Chapter 5, we looked at the rise of gourmet food trucks representing many expensive and highly rated restaurants, which have succeeded in reaching a whole new demographic of consumers who are unable to afford to eat at top restaurants. Customers now have the opportunity to sample these high-end foods at a lower cost from gourmet food trucks in an informal environment.

Lack of skills

In many areas of life, people might like to accomplish a task but lack the specialized skills to get the job done. This common problem creates an opportunity to provide

---

FIGURE 8.1

Four Problems Experienced by Customers

a. Lack of time

b. Lack of money

c. Lack of skills

d. Lack of access

Cerdit: a: ©iStockphoto.com/diego_cervo. b: ©iStockphoto.com/-Oxford-. c: ©iStockphoto.com/svetikd. d: ©iStockphoto.com/Terraxplorer

easy-to-use solutions; ease of use is a big plus in converting complex professional-level tools into consumer products.

In the early 20th century, as fewer households had servants or custom tailors, many women wished to sew clothing for themselves and their families but lacked the skills to make a well-fitting garment based on a picture in a fashion magazine. The solution was the sewing pattern that was printed on tissue paper, sold in sizes, and accompanied with instructions that a nonexpert could follow.

A more recent example of how ease of use transformed customers' lives is the shift from computers with arcane command-line interfaces to computers with graphical user interfaces like Apple's Macintosh or Microsoft Windows. These computers meant that you no longer had to have expertise in computer programming to use a computer. To solve another common problem, lack of accounting skills, software maker Intuit enabled individuals and small business owners to do their own accounting by developing Quicken and the somewhat more robust Quickbooks. Quicken and Quickbooks are both software programs that eliminate the need for specialized accounting knowledge. They make it possible for individuals to manage their household finances, and small-business owners to do their company accounting, without having to learn how to use complicated accounting packages designed for experts.

Lack of access

Finally, people struggle with lack of access, which prevents them from getting a job done. For example, science has made DNA testing possible, but the general public did not have a way to take advantage of this testing. To address the lack of access to DNA information, the company 23andMe took advantage of the declining cost of genetic analysis to provide a personalized service available with a simple mail-in testing kit.[20] A customer submits a saliva sample to the company, and the company analyzes the person's DNA. In particular, 23andMe identifies common genetic variations that can inform if the customer is a carrier of certain diseases that can

be passed from parent to child. Additionally the DNA can give customer insights on their ancestry as well as explain different traits such as why you may or may not sneeze when exposed to bright sun!

Another example of the lack-of-access problem is solar energy. The technology for small-scale solar collectors has been available since the 1970s, but it is generally suitable only for commercial buildings and homes with a large amount of roof space—and they need to be located where they receive direct sunlight for many hours per day. Moreover, it requires a sizable investment beyond the means of low-income homeowners, let alone rental tenants. To solve this problem of access, companies like SolarCity have devised community solar programs. Community solar makes solar energy accessible by enabling an entire neighborhood to pool resources to buy a solar installation and share the energy it produces.[21]

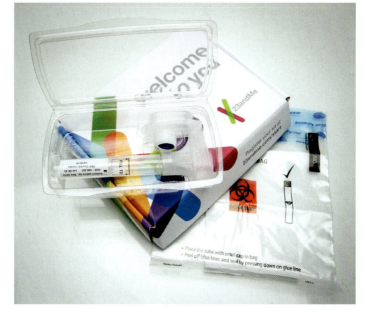

A mail-in DNA testing kit from 23and Me

Credit: David Bro/ZUMA Press/ Newscom

8.4 DIFFERENT TYPES OF CVPs AND CUSTOMER SEGMENTS

>> **LO 8.4**   **Describe the different types of Customer Value Propositions and learn how to identify your target customers.**

You may feel you have the greatest product or service idea in the world, but how do you convince others of its greatness? This is where many entrepreneurs fall short: they have the idea in mind but may not be so clear on the marketing or the execution. In fact, some entrepreneurs cannot even prove that customers want to buy their offering. This is where the CVP really fulfills its potential, as it delineates the value of your idea in meeting customer needs. In this section, we will explore different types of CVPs and learn how to identify your target customers.

Types of Value Propositions

Some CVPs are better than others. Let's explore three main types of approaches in creating value propositions: the all-benefits, points-of-difference, and resonating-focus approaches (see Figure 8.2).[22]

All-benefits: a type of value proposition that involves identifying and promoting all the benefits of a product or service to target customers, with little regard to the competition or any real insight into what the customer really wants or needs.

Points-of-difference: a type of approach that focuses on the product or service relative to the competition and how the offering is different from others on the market.

The **all-benefits** approach to CVP involves identifying and promoting all the benefits of your product or service to target customers, with little regard to the competition or any real insight into what the customer really wants or needs. This is the least impactful approach for creating a value proposition because it's overly product focused. In other words, you are promoting features and benefits that customers may not even need.

The **points-of-difference** approach produces a stronger CVP than all benefits because it focuses on your product or service relative to the competition and recognizes that your offering is unique and different from others on the market. However, although focusing on the differences may help you differentiate your business from the competition, it still doesn't provide evidence that customers will also find the differences valuable. Simply assuming that customers will find these points of difference favorable is not evidence enough to prove they will buy from you.

A CVP that stems from the **resonating-focus** approach (also called "just what the customer wants" or **product-market fit**) is the "gold standard." All-benefits and points-of-difference CVPs each provide a laundry list of the presumed benefits to the customers, and the differences between your products or services in comparison with the competition, but a resonating-focus CVP drills down to what is most important to the customer. It describes why people will buy your product and focuses on the customers and what they really need and value. Your offering shows an understanding of your customers' problems and needs and describes how you intend to meet their demands.[23]

Resonating-focus: a type of CVP that describes why people will really like your product and focuses on the customers and what they really need and value.

Product-market fit: an offering that meets the needs of customers.

Defining Your Target Customer

When it comes to defining your customer, you may be tempted to think that everyone will want to buy your product or service. In fact, trying to aim the CVP at "everyone" is a very common mistake made by young entrepreneurs. As a knowledgeable entrepreneur, you must realize that a major part of your business proposition is to figure out which customers to focus on and which ones to ignore. For example, if you're trying to sell luxury yachting experiences, you may target professionals between 30 and 65, with a high income, who live in a location close to water, and who have an interest in water sports. Remember, if you're not clear on your customer segment, your CVP will also not be clear.[24]

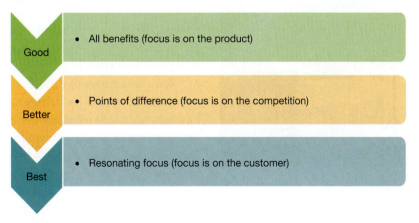

The questions to ask: Who are your customers? For whom are creating value? And why would they buy from you?[25] Table 8.1 outlines some more questions to ask when identifying your target customer.

An interesting way to answer some of these questions is by looking at unusual toys like the Frozen Smiles Ice Mold in the photo at left.[26]

Using the questions listed above, who do you think might use this product? What would be the target customer segment? How would you develop the CVP for such a product?

Frozen Smiles Ice Mold
Credit: Copyright © Lifetime Brands, Inc.

Video
The Target Customer

FIGURE 8.2

Three Types of Value Propositions

Good	• All benefits (focus is on the product)
Better	• Points of difference (focus is on the competition)
Best	• Resonating focus (focus is on the customer)

Identifying Your Target Customer

What age is your customer?
What gender is your customer?
What sort of income do they earn? For example, are they able to afford your product?
What is their location?
What nationality are they?
What sort of profession do they work in?
Is your customer a risk taker?
Does your customer buy products spontaneously?
Do they like to invest in new offerings?
Are they traditionalists or trendsetters?

Source: Retrieved from http://www.slideshare.net/leslieforman/customer-segments-value-proposition-based-on-business-model-canvas-framework-presented-to-chile-startup-school-on-october-12-2011-leslie-forman

Types of Customer Segments

Video
Product Differentiation

Many products and services are attractive to more than one customer segment. How, then, can a "gold standard" CVP be developed if the focus is supposed to center on the customer? The answer is that businesses often have different CVPs for each customer segment. This is to ensure they are meeting the needs of the customers within each segment. In this section, we will explore how businesses adjust their CVPs to cater for different types of customer segments.

As an example, consider Diet Coke and Coca-Cola Zero. The two products have very similar ingredients, but they are aimed at different target markets. Why? Market research indicated that young men shied away from Diet Coke because they associated it with women who were trying to lose weight.[27] In response, a new CVP was created, resulting in Coca-Cola Zero, which many people believe is clearly aimed at men.[28] By understanding the motivations, desires, and unmet needs of your customers, you are better able to create a product or service that they will be willing to buy.

Some examples of different customer segments targeted by different types of businesses include mass market, niche market, segmented market, diversified market, and multisided market. Let's take a closer look at each of these.

Flytopgrapher, founded by Nicole Smith, connects travelers with professional photographers in their travel destinations

Credit: ©iStockphoto.com/ Nadiamik

A **mass market** comprises a large group of customers with very similar needs and problems. You may have heard of the phrase "it's gone mass market," which means a product or a service is being purchased by an enormous proportion of customers all looking for the same thing. A few examples of mass market products include computers, soap, cars, insurance, and health care. Coke and Pepsi are products that are considered mass market because they target a wide range of large groups, from youths to families.

A **niche market** is a small market segment comprising customers with specific needs and requirements. The CVP is tailored to meet these particular needs. For example, Canadian entrepreneur Nicole Smith set up her business, Flytographer, in response to people who wanted high-quality vacation photos as keepsakes of their time abroad. Through the Flytographer website, travelers can connect with professional photographers from all over the world who meet the vacationers at their destinations to capture special moments—at affordable prices starting at $250 for a 30-minute photo session.

A **segmented market** involves breaking customer segments into groups according to their different needs and problems. For example, a bank might provide different services to its wealthier clients than they would to people with an average income, or offer different products for small versus large businesses. Segmenting customers is a good way of generating more business.

A **diversified market** offers a variety of services to serve two or more customer segments with different needs and problems, which bear no relationship to each other. Amazon is a good example of an organization that diversified from its retail business—selling books and other tangible products—to sell cloud computing services, online storage space, and on-demand server usage. In short, Amazon adapted its CVP to cater for a whole new wave of customers, such as web companies, that would buy these computing services.[29]

Multisided markets describe two or more customer segments that are linked but are independent of each other. For example, a free newspaper caters to its readership customer base by providing commuters with newsworthy content. The newspaper also needs to prove to advertisers that it has a large readership in order to get the funding to produce and distribute the free publication. The newspaper is dependent on both of these two distinct segments in order to be successful.[30]

Matching the right CVP to targeted customer segments is essential to the development of a scalable business model.

8.5 THE BUSINESS MODEL CANVAS (BMC)

>> **LO 8.5** Identify the nine components of the business model canvas.

As we have learned, there are four major parts of the business model: the offering, the customers, the infrastructure, and the financial viability. In this section, we further explore the process of how a company intends to create, deliver, and capture value for customers through a more in-depth study of the **business model canvas (BMC)**.[31] The BMC, introduced in 2008 by Swiss business theorist Alexander Osterwalder, divides the business model's four parts into nine components in order to provide a more thorough overview of the logic of the business model. When the four parts are divided into nine components, the result looks like this:

▸ The offering constitutes the (1) value proposition.
▸ Customers relate to (2) customer segments, (3) channels, and (4) customer relationships.
▸ Infrastructure includes (5) key activities, (6) key resources, and (7) key partners.
▸ Financial viability includes (8) cost structure and (9) revenue streams.

Mass market: a large group of customers with very similar needs and problems.

Niche market: a small market segment comprising customers with specific needs and requirements.

Segmented market: a marketing strategy that involves breaking customer segments into groups according to their different needs and problems.

Diversified market: a variety of services that for two customer segments with different needs and problems, and which bear no relationship to each other.

Multisided markets: platforms that serve two or more customer segments that are mutually independent of each other.

Business model canvas (BMC): a type of visual plan that depicts the business on one page by filling in nine blocks of a business model.

Web
The Business
Model Canvas

The BMC (Figure 8.3) illustrates the nine components through an idea for a new retail store that sells trendy T-shirts emblazoned with original designs by young, emerging artists.

Let's apply the T-shirt store example to some questions that each of the nine components must address.

1. **Customer Value Proposition:** As described earlier in this chapter, the CVP is designed to solve a customer problem or meet a need. With regard to your new T-shirt business, ask yourself the following: What value do we deliver? What bundle of products and services are we offering? What are we helping customers achieve by providing a new range of T-shirts?

2. **Customer Segments:** As defined above, a customer segment is a part of the customer grouping of a market. For example, gluten-free is a segment of the grouping of customers who buy food; another segment would be customers who are lactose intolerant. In Chapter 1 we saw that the caffeine-free ZOOS Greek Iced Tea would appeal to pregnant and new moms. The customer segmentation questions for the T-shirt business are these: Who are your most important customers? What segment of the market would be most likely to buy your T-shirts?

3. **Channels:** The value proposition is delivered through communication, distribution, and sales channels. The core question here: What are all the ways in which you can reach your customer? For example, you could reach your customers online, through a brick-and-mortar store, and/or through word of mouth.

4. **Customer Relationships:** Relationships can be developed on a one-to-one basis in a brick-and-mortar T-shirt store and/or through a purely automated process of selling the T-shirts online. Customer relationships go beyond just buying and selling; they depend on engendering positive feelings about your business, building a sense of customer identity ("I am a so-and-so T-shirt customer"), and motivating customers to want to bring their friends into the relationship. The key here is one of the most important questions an entrepreneur can answer: How do you establish and maintain relationships with your customers?

5. **Key Activities:** What are the most important activities that the company participates in to get the job done? When running a T-shirt business, you will need to consider such activities as stock management, sales management, and T-shirt design selection.

6. **Key Resources:** Resources are what you need to develop the business, create products and services, and deliver on your CVP. Resources take many forms and include people, technology, information, and physical and financial resources. How much and which resources will you need if your company has 1,000 customers or 1,000,000? What resources do you need to accomplish the key activities? If you're opening up a store, then you need to figure out the location and size; you also need people who are going to sell your T-shirts; space to store inventory; and a range of artists who will provide the designs for your T-shirts. You will also need to calculate how much money you will need to set up, as well as accumulate the skills, knowledge, and information you need to start your own business.

7. **Key Partners:** Entrepreneurs are not able to do everything by themselves, so partnering with suppliers, associates, and distributors is a logical option, not only for strategic purposes but also for efficiency needs. For example, you could partner with a designer who could advise you on the artwork of the T-shirts as well as provide you with a network into other designers. You could ask the

questions around outsourcing: Could some activities be outsourced? Do you have a network of suppliers/buyers you could tap into or negotiate with?

8. **Revenue Streams:** Revenue is generated if a successful value proposition is delivered. Here you need to ask: How much are my customers willing to pay? How many customers do I need? How much cash can be generated through T-shirt sales in the store or T-shirt sales online? How much does each stream contribute to the total? (We will explore revenue models in further detail in Chapter 10).

9. **Cost Structure:** The cost structure represents all expenses required to execute and run the business model. What are the most important costs inherent in the business model? Which resources are the most expensive to get? Which activities are the most expensive? Store rental, employee salaries, the cost of purchasing T-shirt materials and designs, and the cost of sales and marketing are all factors to consider when formulating a cost structure.

FIGURE 8.3

The Business Model Canvas

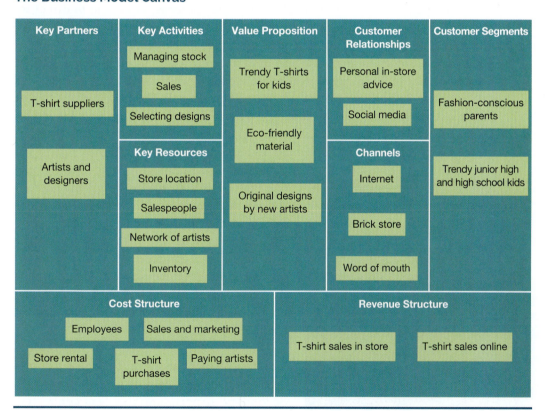

Credit: BMC is from the book *Business Model Generation* by Osterwalder and Pigneur, 2010. http://www.businessmodelgeneration.com/canvas/bmc

Remember a business model is about creating, capturing, and delivering value. The Business Model Canvas is a great tool to help you think about this. The right side of the BMC is about creating value and the left side is about delivering that value as efficiently as possible. Additionally, the business model canvas encourages you to find answers to the most important questions and think about them in a structured way, using the canvas to unlock your creativity. The process is iterative—you'll probably be moving back and forth between the boxes as you test ideas in relation to each other. Not only that, some of your ideas will need to be tested through experimentation before you have a solid answer.

Video
The Business Model Canvas

The most important thing in staying competitive is to keep refining and revisiting your business model, because as we saw at the beginning of this chapter with the examples of BlackBerry and Kodak, the implications of leaving your model to stagnate can lead to business failure.

Thinking through all nine components of your business model helps you understand how the various parts work together: the value you'll create for customers, the processes you must have to deliver value, the resources you need, and the way you'll make money. Overall, the goal is to lay out your assumptions so that you can test them. Be ready to change, because your ideas will likely evolve before you get the formula right.

The BMC in Action

Let's choose two of the components of the BMC—key activities and resources—to illustrate how they work together to alter the customer value proposition in order to deliver on the CVP to the customer segments. In the airline industry, Southwest Airlines pioneered an innovative approach to low-cost air travel by paying careful attention to aligning its activities and resources to satisfy its target customer base. For example, Southwest changed the sales process, switching to direct-to-consumer sales while the rest of the airline industry was still using travel agents. This change enabled Southwest to eliminate travel agent fees.

Secondly, Southwest wanted to minimize time on the ground and eliminate delays because a plane on the ground doesn't earn money. This led to a number of decisions that changed Southwest's processes and resource needs. For example, Southwest eliminated extras like onboard food and entertainment to reduce resource needs. Having no food meant less labor, less supplies costs, and less delay in the ground processes such as cleaning and restocking the aircraft.

Southwest Airlines has created its own CVP to improve customer service and increase efficiencies

Credit: ©iStockphoto.com/ SkyCaptain86

In addition, Southwest decided to fly only one type of aircraft, Boeing 737s. This reduced the costs of maintenance processes as well as the amount of resources devoted to spare parts. Moreover, having one type of plane simplified the often complex process of assigning pilots and flight attendants to flights. Because Southwest flies only one type of aircraft, any aircrew is qualified to work on any plane, which again reduces delays and costs.

Finally, Southwest chose to fly into secondary airports, not the big hubs. These airports offered lower gate fees and operating costs. Secondary airports are also less congested, which meant that Southwest airplanes waste less time in taxiing to and from gates, less time waiting for takeoff clearance, and less time in holding patterns. All of these processes and decisions had a big impact on Southwest's resource requirements. The average Southwest plane takes five or more flights per day.[32] Southwest also has fewer employees per aircraft and higher seat-miles-per-employee than other major airlines.

Create Your Own BMC

Download a free copy of the Business Model Canvas from **http://www.businessmodelgeneration.com/canvas/bmc**.

Yes, we want you to fill out the canvas with one of the many business ideas you probably have at this stage of the book. But most students don't know where to start. Do you start with the value proposition, key resources, or customer segments first?

To answer this question, fold the canvas in half so there is a crease down the middle of the canvas. Now open the page to its original position. The area of the canvas to the right of the crease is all about *creating* value. The area of the canvas to the left of the crease is all about *delivering* that value in an efficient way.

In order to build an innovative and sustainable business model, always focus on the right (value creation) side of the canvas first. The left (value delivery) side of the canvas is operational and process-oriented. Don't spend too much time on the left until you have established something truly valuable for customers.

Again, every completed box is just a guess. Once your canvas is completed, your job is to begin testing. Start with testing the value proposition with the customer segment you've identified—the product-market fit. Are you offering something people want?

Now you are ready to complete your first canvas. Take an idea, and complete a canvas using the example in Figure 8.3 as a guide.

CRITICAL THINKING QUESTIONS

1. **Why do you think this tool is called the Business Model Canvas?**

2. **In what ways does the division between value creation and value delivery help clarify the process of refining the business model?**

3. **In completing a BMC for your idea, which boxes were more difficult to fill out? Why? What are you going to do now with your completed BMC?** ●

The common thread running through examples like Southwest Airlines and Tata Motors isn't that a particular set of processes are best. Each company has created its own particular processes and resource models to suit its CVP and industry. Both Southwest and Tata have not only succeeded in creating their own tailored CVP but also have given some serious thought to how much money they will need to action their processes. Without sound financial models built into their respective business models, the companies never would have succeeded. One of the biggest considerations in building your own business model is money—it matters.

Peer-to-Peer Business Models

Although there are many complex descriptions of a business model, the core definition is a conceptual framework that describes how a company creates, delivers, and extracts value. In the peer-to-peer model, businesses sell the same products and services that traditional businesses sell. Their products and services are not necessarily better, they are just distributed in a different way. For example, Uber and traditional taxis services both transport customers from one point to another by providing a car with a driver; Airbnb and traditional hotel booking services both enable travelers to book lodging. However, there are differences in their business models: Uber and Airbnb eliminate much of the traditional structure by enabling the end user to make a direct transaction with the service provider—at a low cost. In other words, the peer-to-peer business model breaks down the distinction between traditional companies and customers, and consumers versus providers, by empowering customers to become part-time business people by offering the use of their own homes, cars, or other goods in return for cash. Equally, users are able to take advantage of arguably more affordable, flexible services than a traditional provider could offer. Essentially, the peer-to-peer businesses simply play matchmaker by matching their affordable services to individuals who require those services.

The most recognized peer-to-peer businesses are Airbnb, eBay, Uber, Lyft, and Etsy; but there are over 9,000 peer-to-peer businesses in nearly every industry, including office space rentals, philanthropy (such as businesses that donate money to entrepreneurs in developed and developing countries), travel, money-lending, education, food, recreation, and clothing.

Peer-to peer businesses are based on transparency, which generates trust; and without that trust, the business will likely fail. Additionally, if a customer experiences a problem, there must be some assurance that the problem will be resolved before the customer will be willing to use the service again. With the ubiquity of the Internet, companies can't prevent dissatisfied customers' voices from being universally heard.

While transparency and accountability are no doubt essential to the peer-to-peer business model, peer-to-peer businesses have not been without controversy. Uber has landed in regulatory hot water on several occasions, sparking protests and bans in several countries. Airbnb also has its critics; public advocate Letitia James charges that the "illegal hotel operators it enables are contributing to the affordable housing crisis." Peer-to-peer businesses also face the risk of being disrupted themselves thanks to the rise of blockchain (or chained blocks of data), a transparent public ledger or shared database which allows transactions to be made without the need for middlemen or intermediaries. This new technology has the power to disrupt some of the most successful peer-to-peer businesses by making transactions faster, cheaper, more efficient, and more secure than third party intermediaries.

While peer-to-peer businesses continue to grow, there is a chance that the peer-to-peer model could not only outgrow and replace the traditional business model, but might end up being replaced altogether by the latest disruptor, blockchain.

CRITICAL THINKING QUESTIONS

1. **Do you think the peer-to-peer business model is better than the traditional business model? Why or why not?**

2. **What do you think the impact will be if traditional businesses fail to adapt to peer-to-peer business models?**

3. **How would negative press or reviews influence your decision to use peer-to-peer services?**

4. **Do you think peer-to-peer businesses should regard blockchain as a threat or an opportunity? Why or why not?** ●

Sources

Bryant, B. J. (n.d.). *List of business models*. Retrieved from Chron: Small Business: http://smallbusiness.chron.com/list-business-models-338.html

CurencyFair. (2014, March 26). The peer-to-peer marketplace revolution: 50+ Companies that are changing the world. Retrieved from https://www.currencyfair.com/blog/peer-to-peer-marketplace-revolution-50-companies-changing-world/

French, L. (2015, April 13). Sharing economy shakes up traditional business models. *The New Economy.* Retrieved from http://www.theneweconomy.com/business/the-sharing-economy-shakes-up-traditional-business-models

Ryan, V. (n.d.). Most successful business models. Retrieved from eHow: http://www.ehow.com/list_7227436_successful-business-models.html

Schnackenberg, A. K., & Tomlinson, E. C. (2014, March 12). Organizational transparency: A new perspective on managing trust in organization stakeholder relationships. *Journal of Management.* doi:10.1177/0149206314525202

Tomasicchio, A. (2016, February 24). The Next Step: How Blockchain Could Disrupt Uber, Airbnb, and iTunes. Retrieved September 16, 2016, from https://cointelegraph.com/news/Blockchain-disrupt-uber-airbnb-itunes The titans of the sharing economy meet their match. (n.d.) Retrieved September 16, 2016 from http://www.nesta.org.uk/2016-predictions/titans-sharing-economy-meet-match

Get the edge on your studies at **edge.sagepub.com/neckentrepreneurship**

▶ Master the learning objectives using key study tools
▶ Watch, listen, and connect with online multimedia resources
▶ Access mobile-friendly quizzes and flashcards to check your understanding

SUMMARY

8.1 Define the business model.

The business model is the framework for creating and delivering consumer value, while extracting value for the entrepreneur as well.

8.2 Identify the four core areas of a business model.

Broken into four parts, each business model includes an offering, customers, infrastructure, and financial viability.

8.3 Explore the importance of the CVP in further detailExplore the importance of the Customer Value Proposition in further detail.

The CVP outlines exactly how the firm will generate value, how it will generate it in excess of its competition, and how it will continue to do so in the future. As the true measure of any business is creating value, the true measure of a business model is its customer value proposition.

8.4 Describe the different types of Customer Value Propositions and learn how to identify your target customers.

Businesses tend to have different CVPs for each customer segment. This is to ensure they are meeting the needs of the customers within each segment. Examples of different customer segments targeted by different types of businesses include mass market, niche market, segmented market, diversified market, and multisided markets. Types of CVPs include all-benefits, points of difference, and resonating focus.

8.5 Identify the nine components of the business model canvas.

The four core elements of a business model can be expanded to nine business model components. Separating core elements into their respective components makes them easier to define and integrate with one another. The offering constitutes the (1) value proposition. Customers relate to (2) customer segments, (3) channels, and (4) customer relationships. Infrastructure includes (5) key activities, (6) key resources, and (7) key partners. Financial viability includes (8) cost structure and (9) revenue streams.

KEY TERMS

All-benefits 212
Business model 203
Business model
  canvas (BMC) 215
Business plan 203
Customer value
  proposition (CVP) 206

Customers 206
Diversified market 215
Financial viability 206
Infrastructure 206
Mass market 215
Multisided markets 215
Niche market 215

Offering 206
Points-of-difference 212
Product-market fit 213
Resonating-focus 213
Segmented market 215

CASE STUDY

Meredith Perry, Founder & CEO of uBeam

Meredith Perry achieved recognition as an inventor when she was in her mid-twenties and had been out of college for only a few years. As a student studying astrobiology at the University of Pennsylvania, Perry grew weary of having to use a power cord to charge her laptop and smartphone. With her problem-solving-oriented work ethic, she began investigating whether there might be a better way. In her own words:

> In the beginning . . . I just wanted to solve a problem. And that was: I don't want to plug in my laptop anymore. I want to be able to move around a room and use all my devices without plugging them in.

Despite being told by scientists and engineers that her ambition was impossible, Perry knew that *anything* was possible, as long as she obeyed the laws of physics. The result? She successfully invented "a transmitter that emits ultrasonic waves that make tiny crystals in a receiver vibrate, [thus] generating electrical power." Put another way, uBeam uses "transducers . . . [to] convert . . . electrical energy into ultrasound waves and then back into electrical energy." The power that is generated can theoretically charge any device (small or large) that is attached to the receiver, thus eliminating the need for any chargers or wires. In her own words, the process involves "thinking about sound as a form of energy, which people don't often think about."

Thanks to Perry's remarkable invention, all of us could someday be cordlessly powering everything in our lives, including power appliances and electric cars, "introducing the prospect of a truly wireless world." In 2016, Perry was named to Forbes' prestigious *30 Under 30* list for her remarkable accomplishments and progress in making her dream become a reality. Billionaire entrepreneur Mark Cuban has called Perry's concept "a zillion-dollar idea"—if uBeam can get it to work and then profitably market and sell it.

Herein lies the issue for Perry as a long-term entrepreneur. There is no doubt the power Perry is striving to harness and the technology she is trying to create would revolutionize the way we operate our technological devices, both personally and professionally. The challenge uBeam faces is successfully getting Perry's invention to the marketplace. uBeam is currently in the process of constructing a working prototype; it predicts that a sellable product could be available to the public within the next few years. Until then, voices critical of uBeam's product viability are quite loud. Their concerns are that Perry's idea breaks the laws of physics and that it could also prove unsafe, but Perry claims that both charges are unfounded.

Entrepreneurs are often known for inventing new devices or creating new products or services that have not existed before. Such undertakings can prove extremely challenging. Perry, who has invented something new points out the inherent difficulties in designing and building a product without a technological precedent. In her own words:

> To create something really new is extremely difficult, because there's no protocol. I can't Google it online and find [answers to many of our questions]. . . . Sometimes you have to create your own materials, your own design, your own manufacturing process. You have to create your own shipping materials that can cover the parts that you built. And we were building all of these tiny little devices by hand. . . . So that's the level of minutiae you have to get involved with in order to actually execute on something that hasn't been done before.

The concept behind Perry's genius and uBeam's business model is something that could truly change the world. On the other hand, it could also end in a bust. In order to find out what is truly possible, a lot of capital is required to conduct the research, development, construction and testing necessary to support uBeam's business model. Perry has shown herself capable of raising large sums of money.

Perry first grabbed the tech world's attention as a fundraiser when she attracted Yahoo's CEO Marissa Mayer (see Chapter 7 Case Study) to become one of her first major investors. Mayer provided Perry with a $1.7 million dollar startup investment "after a simple cold email and a 12-minute in-person pitch."

uBeam's business model is based on stretching the limitations of wireless technology and getting practical results in the process. Is a CEO as young and inexperienced as Perry up to the challenge? Venture Capitalist Mark Suster believes she is. Convinced Perry has the right plans, skills, and business acumen to create a successful business model, Suster's VC firm, Upfront Ventures, recently invested $10 million in uBeam. Physicist Danny Rogers claimed that such a sizable investment in a yet-unproven product is foolish. Despite the voices of such critics, uBeam has since increased its overall funding to $24 million.

To help uBeam build the scientific and technical side of its business, Perry has attracted the attention and recruited the help of MIT grad Marc Berte, as well as some in his MIT network. Berte has previous experience with Raytheon, Sparta Consulting, and the Aerospace Corporation.

While it is still early on in the game, if money is any indicator, Perry is laying the foundation for a company that could be an authentic game-changer in Silicon Valley and beyond in coming years. This idea is ambitious and extends beyond just cell phones and laptop computers. In the words of Suster (2014), "The practical use for uBeam technology is limitless." Time will tell if she can create a scalable business model to match the investments of her current advocates, but one thing is for sure, Meredith Perry is not afraid to take risks and blaze new trails in the tech world.

Critical Thinking Questions

1. What do you think Meredith Perry's business model will look like, assuming uBeam is successful in building a working prototype of a wireless charger? Complete a business model canvas for uBeam and draw conclusions regarding the future of the business.

2. What specific customer value propositions (CVPs) do you think Meredith Perry and her company, uBeam, are taking into account as they plan for the future?

3. Assuming they succeed in producing a profitable wireless charger, what customer segments do you think uBeam will eventually target?

4. What additional related products and services might a company like uBeam consider inventing, building, and selling if it succeeds with its wireless chargers?

Sources

Brady, E., Derenzo, N., & Wright, C. (2014, October). Wonder women: Five female tech entrepreneurs who never got the memo that the field was dominated by men. *Hemisphere Magazine* (United Airlines), 6974.

Forbes. (2016). 30-under-30 in energy. Retrieved from http://www.forbes.com/pictures/mef45jdde/meredith-perry-23/#39332aea708d

Roberts, D. (2015, December 2). Meredith Perry responds to uBeam's critics. *Fortune.com*. Retrieved from http://fortune.com/2015/12/02/meredith-perry-ubeam-criticism-science/

Roberts, D. (2014, December 30). She's an inventor. She's 25. And she wants to make true wireless charging a reality. *Fortune.com*. Retrieved from http://fortune.com/2014/12/30/meredith-perry-ubeam/

Suster, M. (2014, October 30). The audacious plan to make electricity as easy as WiFi. BothSides Blog. Retrieved from http://www.bothsidesofthetable.com/2014/10/30/the-audacious-plan-to-make-electricity-as-easy-as-wifi/

9 Planning for Entrepreneurs

Failed plans should not be interpreted as a failed vision. Visions don't change, they are only refined. Plans rarely stay the same, and are scrapped or adjusted as needed. Be stubborn about the vision, but flexible with your plan."

—John C. Maxwell, American author

Learning Objectives

9.1   Examine "planning" from an entrepreneurial perspective.

9.2   Define TRIM and explain its importance to entrepreneurial planning.

9.3   Explain the different types of plans used by entrepreneurs.

9.4   Debate the value of writing business plans.

9.5   Implement the tips for writing business plans.

Chapter Outline

9.1   The Importance of Planning to Entrepreneurs

9.2   The TRIM Framework

9.3   Plans Take Many Forms

9.4   The Business Plan Debate

9.5   Tips for Writing Business Plans

9.1 THE IMPORTANCE OF PLANNING TO ENTREPRENEURS

>> LO 9.1   **Examine "planning" from an entrepreneurial perspective.**

Over the course of this book, we have emphasized the importance of learning by doing and acting in order to learn. Taking action in the real world, collecting data, gathering feedback, and testing business models are the most beneficial ways to develop a product or service that people actually want and build a scalable business.

As we have learned, when you are first starting out as an entrepreneur, it is important to think about whom you know, what you know, and how you're going to implement your idea. This is why it is important to have a plan that helps take the first steps on your journey to building a new venture and proving it is viable and feasible before you go any further. From an entrepreneurial perspective, **planning** is a description of the future you envision for your business, including what you plan to do and how you plan to do it.[1]

As described in the *Entrepreneurship in Action* feature, Bark 'N Leash founder Michele Pytko learned through action by researching her competitors, gathering data through social media, and carefully listening to potential customers. By using her network, business, and people skills, she had a clearer idea of her business strategy months before she launched her dog-walking business. By taking action, learning, and planning, Pytko proved to herself that Bark 'N Leash was worth pursuing.

Like Bark 'N Leash, every business needs to start with some type of plan, whether it is as informal as a sketch on the back of a napkin or as formal and structured as a written business plan. Plans help you to get out of your head and see your idea for what it really is—the good, the bad, and even the ugly! They help crystalize your thoughts, allow you to clearly articulate where you want your business to go, and can be the foundation for an overall business strategy. In short, planning pushes you to move forward.

Planning is different from a plan. Planning is a verb and therefore implies action. If planning pushes you to move forward and take action, then a plan helps you organize

Video
Planning is Important

Planning: a description of the future one envisions for a business, including what one plans to do and how one plans to do it.

Video
Making a Plan

Michele Pytko, Bark 'N Leash

Michelle Pykto, founder of Bark 'N Leash
Credit: Used with permission from Bark 'n Leash

When her role as Global Director of Performance Marketing at footwear company Sperry was eliminated in 2014 due to cutbacks, Michele Pytko decided it was time for a change. "For quite some time . . . I wasn't overly happy with my role and was at odds with being so stressed out over shoes," says Pytko. "It's not exactly like we were curing cancer; I just longed to do something different, and knew I would be most happy if it involved animals."

With the support of her wife, former colleagues, and several close friends, Pytko finally made the leap to realizing a dream: starting her own animal-centered small business. Her new venture, Bark 'N Leash, is a dog-walking, -sitting, and -training operation based in Watertown, Massachusetts. After just 18 months, the business was in the black and well ahead of the average income for other dog walkers in the area; however, she said, "I have not been overly concerned with the initial numbers. Using the 'If you build it (correctly), they will come' [model], I know the clients will follow."

Part of Bark 'N Leash's success may be attributed to Pytko's tenacity in analyzing the market, and then building her business to meet its needs. First, she thoroughly researched the competitive landscape, starting with Google and Google maps to identify similar service providers within her target towns. Then she learned everything she could about them: their services, staff, pricing, location, schedules, and more. Facebook and Instagram were especially useful in allowing her to examine the level and frequency of activity, likes and followers, and the "voices" and branding of these various small businesses. "There were very obvious things that emerged throughout this research—lack of professionalism, limited training, poor communication and

customer service, poor marketing/operational skills," Pytko recalls. Though there were a few bright spots, "60% to 70% did not offer the level of professionalism I had come to expect from my corporate career."

Next, Pytko examined who she thought would be her target customer: the discriminating pet owner, "one who treats their dog as a child." She learned through conversations with friends and friends of friends that while few dog owners were "in love" with their dog walker, most did not have time to find a new one. She also listened to her potential customers and compiled a "wish list" for a dog walker/pet sitter. "The level of communication and access to their walker wasn't what they would prefer, for instance, if they went out of town," she recalls. "Many walkers would actually NOT SHOW UP FOR THE SERVICE—who does that?" Customers seemed to be voicing a desire for professionalism, and for customization and personalized care.

Armed with a mountain of competitive and customer intelligence, Pytko was ready to launch. She hired a designer to build a professional website and poured her resources into marketing: mailings to licensed dog owners in her area; targeted Facebook and Google advertising; social media campaigns; and advertising on Pet Sitter's International, Rover, and Pet Tech sites. The Bark 'N Leash difference, communicated across every platform: professionalism and customer service. "We just communicate more openly and provide more services for them (bringing packages in, dropping a little rock salt on the stairs, dragging trash cans out of the street into the driveways)," says Pytko; "nothing overly special, just an attention to detail that is not common among dog walkers." During the on-boarding process, for example, tablets are utilized to answer a 50-point questionnaire with drop-down menus; the number and thoughtfulness of the questions helps to reassure clients that Bark 'N Leash is serious about the canines it cares for. All walkers/employees are trained in pet CPR, which, to Pytko's surprise, has become a big selling point for discerning pet owners shopping for animal care.

Not long after Bark 'N Leash was launched, a need for quality puppy training became apparent. "One puppy turned into a third of my business, and I catered an exercise/training/playgroup package that no one else offers in the area. . . . And adding puppies to the funnel, assuming you do a good job with them, means you will have a customer for life, or for as long as they are in the area." Pytko also scouted locations for commercial space to open a doggie day care/wellness facility, with sitting, training, agility courses, therapy, and aquatics for fun and rehab. Still, she kept backup plans in mind: "Worst case, I stick with the low overhead model, and build the best dog-walking/pet-sitting/puppy-training business outside of Boston, and be the company by which everyone else is measured."

Bark 'N Leash is proof that pursuing a life and career you love can be profitable. Yet, as Michele Pytko advises, do so with forethought and planning. "Do your homework and understand the competition. Understand how you will be different from other brands/services. Be clear about what you want and don't want to do or be known for. Be open to surrounding yourself with other smart people, and don't think you have all of the answers. Be open to change, and to course corrections along the way."

CRITICAL THINKING QUESTIONS

1. **What evidence of planning can you identify in Michele Pytko's launch of Bark 'N Leash?**

2. **Pytko's plan also caters for "worst case"— do you think all plans should include this element? Why or why not?**

3. **What aspects of Pytko's planning strategy would you apply to your own business? ●**

Source: M. Pykto, personal interview, February 1, 2015.

those actions in some way. Planning is essentially about answering the most important questions we have posed throughout the book. A **plan** is a written description of the future you envision for your business, including what you plan to do and how you plan to do it.

The plan, then, is the document that records the answers to questions. As this chapter will illustrate, there are many types of plans available to entrepreneurs today, including simplified plans, plans that emphasize planning with preparation, and those that flow from planning with imagination. What is most important, regardless of the type of document created, is that the questions get answered. In the next section, we take a look at the most important questions through a framework called TRIM.

9.2 THE TRIM FRAMEWORK

>> **LO 9.2** **Define TRIM and explain its importance to entrepreneurial planning.**

The **TRIM (Team, Resources, Idea, Market) framework** (Table 9.1) is a planning tool that identifies the types of people needed for the team, the resources available and needed, the details of the idea, and the potential market for the product or service.

It serves as a tool for determining the types of people you would like on your team and how you might go about attracting them to your business, the resources you have available to grow the business and the types of access you may have to other resources, the validity of your idea, and the potential market for your product or service.

The questions in the TRIM framework deal with issues that you have been tackling up to this point and will continue to deal with throughout this book. The important thing is to recognize that these are the questions that must be answered. The answers to all or a subset of these questions can be formatted into a document called "the plan"; but the plan can take many forms, and they range far in both complexity and purpose.

9.3 PLANS TAKE MANY FORMS

>> **LO 9.3** **Explain the different types of plans used by entrepreneurs.**

As we discussed, plans are an important way to develop a vision, gain clarity, answer important questions, estimate timelines, and set goals. Many entrepreneurs are initially resistant to the idea of sitting down and writing a plan, or feel that they lack the time for this task. However, this section demonstrates that there are several alternatives to

SAGE edge™

Master the content
edge.sagepub.com/ neckentrepreneurship

Plan: a written description of the future you envision for your business, including what you plan to do and how you plan to do it.

TRIM (Team, Resources, Idea, Market) framework: a planning tool that identifies the types of people needed for the team, the resources available and needed, the details of the idea, and the potential market for the product or service.

Web
TRIM

Video
Selecting a Team

TABLE 9.1

The TRIM Framework

Team (or individual founder)	Who needs to be on the team at the start?	Do you have ways of attracting new team members?
	What skills does each person bring to the table?	What are the personal and business goals of each member?
	Are there any skill gaps? Can these gaps be outsourced?	What is the role of each member, and is each role distinct?
	What type of work experience is related to the idea?	How are you dividing ownership?
	What is the network of each member?	
Resources	What do you currently have that you can use to get started?	Can you lease equipment, or is it necessary to own?
	What cash resources do you have at your disposal?	Do you need to rent space, or can you leverage your apartment, a garage, or an incubator?
	What people resources can you use beyond the founding team?	How can you use limited resources to get the business started?
	Can you tap into advisors or mentors for knowledge and other resources?	What are your startup costs?
	What assets (equipment, people, and technology) are needed to start?	What are your primary expenses?
Idea	What is the clearest and most simple description of the idea?	Is there anyone doing what you're doing? If yes, how are you doing it better? How can you learn from what they've already done? If no, how are people solving the problem currently?
	How is the idea unique or differentiated?	What is the most important benefit of your product/service? Do people really care about this benefit?
	What problem is being solved? How do you know this is a problem?	Is there intellectual property involved? Is there anything patentable?
	What needs are being met? How do you know this is a need?	What trends support the idea?
	What is the value proposition?	
Market	Who are your primary customers?	How many potential customers are there? Is this number growing?
	What do they care about?	What are they willing to pay?
	How will you reach them?	What feedback have you received from your customers?
	How will they hear and learn about your product/service?	What is the overall size of the market in dollars?
	How much does it cost to acquire a customer?	What percent of the market can you realistically acquire in year 1, 2, and 3?
	How will you keep them? How much does that cost?	

choose from to help you take action and envision a future for your business—or decide, based on solid information, whether your business idea even *has* a future.

It's not a matter of writing or not writing a business plan, but what type of plan is most appropriate for the entrepreneur at what stage. Different types of plans include back of a napkin, sketches on a page, the business model canvas, the business brief, the feasibility study, the pitch deck, and the business plan.

Back of a Napkin

The simplest of all entrepreneurial plans is sketching out the idea on the back of a napkin. While this type of plan would not pass muster in a formal presentation to investors, it can be a highly effective way of gaining clarity on the business idea and how it will work. There is something about sketching and pictures that makes an

Ethical Business Planning

Planning is a critical activity for business success. A new venture can quickly become derailed if customers, employees, and investors perceive that there are ethical issues related to the company's processes. The planning process must consider a framework for ethical behavior and the resolution of ethical issues.

Many unethical decisions are a consequence of structural and procedural inadequacies. However, even companies that have plans in place for ethical behavior can still slip up. For example, the infamous energy company Enron, whose bankruptcy made headlines in 2001, had a corporate Code of Conduct. This was hardly a fail-safe method of preventing some of its employees from disguising the billions of dollars in debt that had accumulated from failed deals. Still, the planning process should include enterprise plans that define, reward, and provide training for ethical behavior as well as define specific consequences for unethical behavior. This kind of ethical planning will go a long way toward preventing unethical behavior and the damage it can do to the company.

Most decisions are not definitively ethical or unethical, but land in "gray areas" that lie between these binaries. Misrepresenting a product or service to get the sale is an example of deliberate deception that can not only alienate customers, but even result in lawsuits from those who were deceived.

CRITICAL THINKING QUESTIONS

1. Can you think of instances when the quality of a product or service was exaggerated and you were disappointed or even angry?

2. How many times are you willing to give a company another chance once you've had a bad experience?

3. How do you think these ethical considerations should be built into the planning process? ●

Sources

BDC. (n.d.). The benefits of strategic planning for your business. BDC: Entrepreneurs First. Retrieved from https://www.bdc.ca/en/articles-tools/business-strategy-planning/define-strategy/pages/strategic-planning-your-business.aspx

Canada Business Network. (n.d.). Strategic planning. Info Entrepreneurs. Retrieved from http://www.infoentrepreneurs.org/en/guides/strategic-planning/

Duff, V. (n.d.). Examples of unethical behavior in the workplace. Houston: Small Business. Retrieved from http://smallbusiness.chron.com/examples-unethical-behavior-workplace-10092.html

Hill, B. (n.d.). Entrepreneurship and business planning. Houston Chronicle. Retrieved from http://smallbusiness.chron.com/entrepreneurship-business-planning-2532.html

Schulman, M. (2006, March 22). Incorporating ethics into the organization's strategic plan. Santa Clara University: Markkula Center for Applied Ethics. Retrieved from https://www.scu.edu/ethics/focus-areas/business-ethics/resources/incorporating-ethics-into-the-organization/

idea come alive. According to Dan Roam, author of *The Back of the Napkin*, we can visually solve problems with pictures. "We can use simplicity and immediacy of pictures to discover and clarify our own ideas, and use those same pictures to clarify our ideas for other people, helping them to discover something new for themselves along the way."[2]

Video
Visual Planning

The back-of-the-napkin technique has connotations of social settings in cafes, restaurants, and bars, where people meet to discuss their ideas and find themselves jotting down spontaneous ideas on the closest thing to hand. Indeed, many great ideas started on the back of a napkin. For example, Allison Rugen and Carlo Marchiondo jotted down a plan on the back of a cocktail napkin in a local bar for a chili distribution company, which was eventually to become Southwest Chili Supply. The company sells chilies online and distributes them to restaurants and wholesalers. Similarly, North Carolina publicist Lisa Jeffries came up with the idea for RaleighNYE.com—a one-stop guide to Raleigh's New Year's Eve parties—over drinks at a pizza restaurant with her friend Evan Roberts, who was keen to find out New Year's party recommendations.[3]

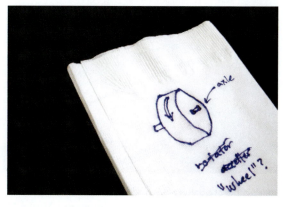

Every business starts with a plan, even if the plan is as informal as a sketch on a napkin

Credit: ©iStockphoto.com/mcmenomy

Sketches on a Page

Using sketches on a page to write your plan is a little more complicated than the back of the napkin. While it is also informal, it requires a more focused approach based on how the product works or can work in the future. Sketches on a page help you think about the idea today and also what it could become in the future. You can sketch your idea by hand on blank paper, or you can do this electronically using PowerPoint, Prezi, or other software of your choosing.

A simple technique is to create a gallery sketch. With a large piece of white paper as your "canvas," use color, arrows, and labels to indicate all of the major components of the idea. Add clarifying notes as needed. Make an effort to sketch boldly, avoiding faint lines and small pictures. If the idea is for a service, try sketching a map of the events that take place when the service is provided.

Taking the gallery sketch one step further, draw a "before and after" scenario. Scenarios are short stories that depict your business, or the product/service, in action. The "before" scenario shows what the lives of your customers are like today. The "after" scenario shows what their lives could be like after your venture is started. The "after" scenario represents what you dream the business could be and the impact it can have on customers in the near future.

Another type of sketch to try is the "Vivid Vision" exercise. Cameron Herold, a business coach and mentor, presented the concept of Vivid Vision in his book *Double Double*. Vivid Vision challenges the entrepreneur to imagine what a business could be three years into the future. Three years is a reasonable amount of time to "nail down" specific, measurable goals; Vivid Vision is not just fantasizing so far into the future that it becomes pure speculation. Three years makes you stretch just enough to think about how to get from today to your idea of success in year three.

The best way to begin the Vivid Vision exercise is to get out of your usual working environment (your class, or your office) and go to a spot that for you is relaxing and peaceful—it could be a nearby park or someplace farther away such as the ocean, mountains, or a lake. Start sketching or writing and aim to create a document no more than three pages long.

Once you have visualized the answers to these questions, then you can write a three-page description or draw a large sketch of these thoughts, detailing what your company will look and feel like in three years' time. Remember that this exercise does not involve how you are going to build the business or the steps you need to take to get there. It is simply a description of how your business might look in the future—specifically, just three years down the road.

Cameron Herold created his own Vivid Vision (see Table 9.2). Keep in mind that although Herold presented his vision in writing, the vision can also be shown as a visual such as a gallery sketch, a photo montage, or a video.

An example of a gallery sketch.

Credit: ©iStockphoto.com/
RawpixelLtd

Your own Vivid Vision should describe what the future looks like rather than detailing how you're going to get there.

TABLE 9.2

Cameron Herold's Vivid Vision

The following is an example of Vivid Vision elements from Cameron Herold. Herold believes that "Creating a vivid vision brings the future into the present, so we can have clarity on what we are building now. It is a detailed overview of what my business will look like, feel like, and act like three years out."

What I Do	Why I "do what I do" is simple and clear—I love helping CEOs turn their dreams into reality.
My Programs	My content is about my leadership and growth expertise, and is designed specifically for CEOs and entrepreneurial minds. I am frequently invited to present at conferences and keynote talks at large-scale events. I set a firm limit for the number of annual speaking events I do, which increases the demand for my services, and my fees increase each year. This allows me more time with my family.
Live Programs	While on the road speaking, I book half-day and full-day workshops for groups or companies, in the same city, to teach their employees the systems to become more entrepreneurial. I run two-day growth camps and leadership team retreats in my home cities that attract companies and employees from around the globe.
Remote Programs	I leverage webinar technology, and companies book me to do remote training for their employees. Prior webinars I've done are available online for thousands of companies around the world to use—and for their employees to learn from as well.
Coaching/ Mentoring	My clients stay with me for an average of twenty-four months. Those who leave do so only because they've learned enough to no longer need me to guide them. I am coaching twenty-four clients per month by reducing the number of lower-leverage speaking events I do. My fees increase each year for new clients.
Leadership	Clients say that I hold them accountable for doing the things they need to do in order to successfully grow their company. Clients I coach love setting goals with me because our efforts directly correlate to an increase in their company's productivity. CEOs value having me on their team as a senior leader who they normally couldn't afford. Clients consistently say I've made (or saved) them millions of dollars.
Communication	People trust me because I say what's on my mind. I am respected for that. People say I'm a breath of fresh air and that I say what other people are thinking but won't say. My inner voice helps me filter my decisions.
Customer Service	My clients are very clear about what I promise them and say that I overdeliver with every interaction. My client companies feel grateful to have me helping them, as I feel grateful to play a role in their growth. I deliver incredible value. They are thrilled they have time with me consistently.
My Mentors	I connect and learn from those who have already "figured it out." I study fiercely—what the great companies do and how they do it—so I don't have to reinvent the wheel. I'm known as a "connector" because of how many people I know and regularly call on, leveraging social networks and the CEOs I meet globally. My track record of hyper-growth with my clients and honesty in my relationships is what accelerates and grows my network.
Profitability	I continue to be extremely profitable doing exactly what I love. My revenues have grown 100 percent [in 3 years].
Balance	I choose international engagements where I'm able to add days of personal time to enjoy the country with my wife; and as our four children get older, we include them more as well.
Core Values	I live the core values that I have set for my company—and I ask people to call me on any deviation. • Do What You Love • Be Authentic • Deliver What You Promise • Balance Is Key

Source: Adapted from Herold, Cameron. 2011. *"Double Double: How to Double Your Revenue and Profit in Three Years,"* Greenleaf Book Group, Austin, Texas. ISBN 9781608320998

MINDSHIFT

The Vivid Vision Checklist

Using the Vivid Vision checklist, try to imagine your business in three years' time.

When you finish your own Vivid Vision, share it with your friends, family, and anyone else you may feel would be interested in seeing it. The act of publicly sharing your picture makes your vision more real and compels you to take action in order to achieve your goals. Besides, as Herold says, "the more people who know with clarity what my company looks and feels like, the better chance there is that people will be able to help me to make it happen."[4]

Pretend you have traveled in a time machine into the future. The date is December 31, three years from now. You are walking around your company's offices (the startup you founded three years before) with a clipboard in hand.

- What do you see?
- What do you hear?
- What are clients saying?
- What does the media write about you?
- What kind of comments are your employees making at the water cooler?
- What is the buzz about you in your community?
- What is your marketing like? Are you marketing your goods/ services globally now? Are you launching new online and TV ads? What is being said on social media?
- How is the company running day to day? Is it organized and running like a clock?

- What's in the office space? Are people sitting, standing, talking? When they move from their workspace, where do they go?
- What kind of stuff do you do every day? Are you focused on strategy, team building, customer relationships, and so on?
- What do the company's financials reveal?
- How are you funded now?
- How are your core values being realized among your employees?

CRITICAL THINKING QUESTIONS

1. **Is three years a useful and reasonable time period to look ahead and envision your business? If you think three years is too long or too short, explain why.**

2. **In the Vivid Vision checklist, which questions did you find the most useful? The most challenging? Explain your answers.**

3. **Is there anything in your plans for your business that is not covered in the Vivid Vision checklist? Anything that is not relevant to your business?** ●

Source: Herold, C. (2011). *Double double: How to double your revenue and profit in three years*. Austin, TX: Greenleaf Book Group.

Business Model Canvas

The Business Model Canvas (BMC), introduced in Chapter 8, is another type of visual plan. It is especially useful for identifying any gaps in the business idea and integrating the various components. We say it's visual because the entire business is depicted on one page by filling in the nine blocks of the business model. These blocks are:

- Key partners
- Key activities
- Value proposition
- Customer relationships
- Customer segments
- Key resources
- Channels

FIGURE 9.1

Sample Business Model Canvas

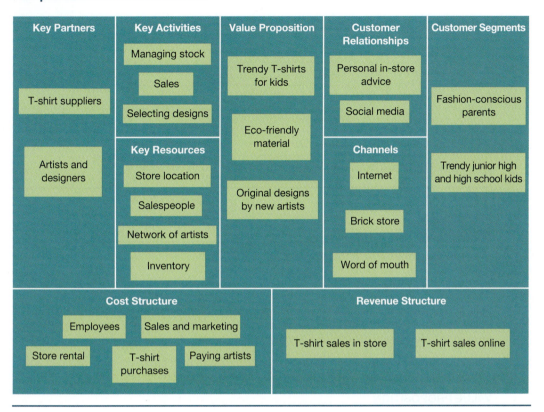

- ▸ Cost structure
- ▸ Revenue streams

The sample BMC (Figure 9.1) illustrates the nine components through an idea for a new T-shirt store that sells trendy T-shirts emblazoned with original designs by young, emerging artists.

By thinking through all nine components of your business model, you will be able to visualize how all the various parts work together: the value created for customers, the processes you must have to deliver value, the resources you need, and the way you'll make money.

The Business Brief

The business brief is less visual than the two previous types of plans, and requires a bit more detail and writing. Typically a business brief is a 2- to 3-page document outlining the company overview, value proposition, customer, and milestones (see Table 9.3). It's something you can easily send to stakeholders that will give them an at-a-glance understanding of who you are, the business, and its potential. Creating a business brief is not too time intensive, and it indicates that you're doing your homework and thinking critically about the business. Table 9.3 lists the points to include in a business brief. Figure 9.2 is a sample business brief for an online meal service called India in a Box.

TABLE 9.3

Points to Include in a Business Brief

• Description of the business idea (company overview)
• Value proposition that highlights the problem being solved or need being met
• Customer profile and market size
• Proof of market demand and future growth
• Description of the entrepreneur/team
• Actions taken to date and future actions planned
• Simple pro forma income statement (up to 3 years)

FIGURE 9.2

Sample Business Brief: India in a Box

COMPANY OVERVIEW

India in a Box is an online meal service (subscription and on-demand) delivering authentic Indian food that is healthy and can be prepared in 5 to 10 minutes. We are on a simple mission to bring a taste of India to every home in the United States.

Through the India in a Box online store, customers receive their choice of curry and can add on rice or naan. Curries are easily prepared by adding water, stirring, and heating.

VALUE PROPOSITION

Cooking a traditional Indian meal requires time, knowledge, and passion. We captured and simplified the essence of this process. By using a specialized dehydration process, we ensure that each dish has a simple ingredient list; and 95% of its nutrients are preserved in the packaging process, compared to 50% provided by our competitors. Each dish has a simple ingredient list; is 100% vegetarian and gluten-free; and contains no added preservatives, sodium, or sugar. We start with whole, fresh ingredients and slowly simmer to develop complex sauces and then naturally condense through dehydration to lock in flavor and nutrition. The shelf life of our products is nine months.

MARKET

Key trends supporting the startup and scale up of India in a Box:

- Ethnic food industry is $11 billion growing at 15% Year on Year (YOY).
- Indian cuisine is the 2nd fastest growing cuisine with a 20% YOY growth projected until 2018.
- Ongoing concerns with health and wellness: 88% of people are willing to pay more to get healthy and great quality food (Nielsen 2015 report).
- Growth of food-based services: Over $750 million invested in just the first half of 2015 in food technology companies, including meal kits & subscriptions.

CUSTOMER

Our target consumers are Indian food lovers and enthusiasts. There are over 5 million Indians and 130,000 Indian students in the US. Indians are now the largest international nationality for students represented in the US. Specifically, our customers are the following:

- **Urban Food Explorers:** Whole Foods shoppers (health conscious), time constrained, looking for convenience
- **Indian Americans:** Highly influential group who will be our brand evangelists, helps builds brand credibility
- **Millennials:** Young, yet particular about food consumption and their current and future wellness

ACTIONS TAKEN

We have product. 5 recipes have been developed by us. With the help of a professional chef and our head of nutrition, Sucheta Gehani, we created 5 delicious recipes from scratch. We partnered with Spicebox, a state-of-the-art commercial kitchen in India, to create, iterate, and finalize our recipes.

We have co-packers. We have developed strategic partnerships for co-packing our food in India. Our food is created in a commercial kitchen in Mumbai and then dehydrated by a separate manufacturer in Mumbai, India. Both of these companies meet the necessary FDA approvals and production standards required.

We have a supply chain process. Product is shipped by air freight from Mumbai, India, and warehoused by Ship Bob, which has 2 warehouses across the United States (New Jersey and Chicago).

We have sales. In May, India in a Box launched its first batch of five products, and completely sold out doing $1,200 in one day. After we launched our online platform, www.indiainabox.us, we sold $6,000 in 3 months, fulfilling orders from 8 different states.

OUR TEAM

Shyam Devnani, Founder and CEO:

Shyam is a Babson MBA 2015 alumni with an undergraduate degree in Computer Engineering. He has 3 years of experience as CEO of a startup garment textile manufacturing firm.

Sucheta Gehani, Head of Nutrition and Wellness:

Sucheta is a Registered Dietitian and brings to bear her expertise as a nutrition and health expert. Sucheta is passionate about Health and Wellness and is also a certified Yoga instructor.

Meet Kouchar, Operations Partner:

Meet is a serial food entrepreneur with companies such as SpiceBox (www.spicebox.in), Oye Kiddan, and the Bohri Kitchen in India. He is our new Operations Partner for food production in India and will help us set up our own kitchen and dehydration unit in India.

Vinayak Agarwal, Marketing Intern:

Vinayak is studying his Master's in International Marketing from Hult University. He is a foodie and a passionate photographer, who will bring to the company his Digital marketing expertise to help us execute our social media strategies.

We are also looking at bringing on board a full time Marketing/Sales person and creating a board of advisors with industry experts.

FINANCIAL PROJECTIONS

Our revenue model is selling our meal boxes online at a price of $24 for 3 curries and 3 rice or naan. Our second product line will be curated regional experience boxes, which will be priced at $35. We project to have year 1 revenue of $261,000. Our gross profit margin is 61%, and we will have a net profit of $1 Million in Year 3.

	YEAR 1	YEAR 2	YEAR 3
REVENUE	$261,000	$820,000	$2,540,000
EXPENSES	$132,000	$343,000	$980,000
GROSS PROFIT	$129,000	$477,000	$1,560,000
SG&A	$84,000	$225,000	$530,000
NET PROFIT	$45,000	$252,000	$1,030,00

FUTURE MILESTONES

We are currently looking to raise a $250K round of seed funding. This will enable us to bring the dehydration unit in house and also help expand our marketing and sales efforts to the West Coast. With the addition of the new capital, we will grow our physical and online

(Continued)

FIGURE 9.2   (Continued)

presence in highly Indian-populated locations with a demand for Indian food, such as New York, New Jersey, San Francisco, and Austin.

SPRING 2016

- Bring operations of manufacturing in-house with partner in India.
- Raise a round of seed funding.
- Bring on board an experienced marketing person to push online sales strategies.
- Target sales in Boston and Bay Area.

SUMMER 2016

- Launch curated regional subscription boxes.
- Increase product offerings to 15 with help of operations partner.
- Invest in our web platform and improve warehousing/fulfillment.

Credit: Reprinted with permission from Shyam Devnani

Feasibility Study

Feasibility study: a planning tool that allows entrepreneurs to test the possibilities of an initial idea to see if it is worth pursuing.

Video
Feasibility

A **feasibility study** is an essential planning tool that allows entrepreneurs to test the possibilities of an initial idea to see if it is worth pursuing. It serves as a solid foundation for developing a business plan when the time comes. The feasibility study focuses on the size of the market, the suppliers, distributors, and the skills of the entrepreneur. Every entrepreneur should conduct a feasibility study because it determines whether your idea is workable and profitable. It is typically created to assess the viability of a business concept.

The information you gather for your feasibility study will help you identify the essentials you need to make the business work: any problems or obstacles to your business, the customers you hope to sell to, marketing strategies, the logistics of delivering your product or service, your competition, and the resources you need to start your business and keep it running until it is established.

From the entrepreneurs' perspective, the feasibility study is a useful way to assess whether they have the time, energy, abilities, and resources to get their venture off the ground. The conclusions you draw from the study will determine whether your venture is viable or not. Ultimately, the feasibility study is a valuable exercise in answering the question: Will my venture work? This feasibility study is for your eyes only, which means you need to be as honest as possible with the conclusions you draw from the study. If there are constraints, describe them and be realistic about whether your idea is worth further investigation.

The feasibility study is a written document of no more than 10 pages. It takes all of the action components we've been talking about in the book and places the learnings from the actions into a structure that can be used for decision making, such as "I do or do not want to move forward with this venture"—or, in short, a "Go/No Go" decision.

The feasibility study addresses the most critical elements entrepreneurs need to consider during the initial conceptualization of the venture (see Table 9.4). The key to the feasibility study is speed. It is a quick way to prompt you to zero in on what you need to know. It requires you to pursue answers to your questions, and to gather real data from your interactions with potential customers, suppliers, distributors and others. The feasibility study template (see Table 9.5) also prompts you to quickly find out the rules and regulations surrounding your startup, which could save you time and money.

To produce a feasibility study, there must be action, testing, information gathering, and analysis in order to reduce uncertainty and gain greater confidence about the opportunity and your approach. For example, if you haven't talked to at least 50 potential customers, *you are not ready to decide whether the business idea is viable.* "Talking" can include contacts by phone, social networking, and other electronic "conversations;" but don't overlook the value of interviewing prospective customers face-to-face.

Though there is no one best format for a feasibility study, Table 9.5 gives a sample template that can be used to organize all the data you have collected from the idea generation and business model stage, allowing you to clearly articulate where you are and where you want to go.

Talking to people face to face is a valuable way to test the viability of your business idea

Credit: ©iStockphoto.com/vm

Using a gourmet food cart venture as an example, suppose you want to offer mayonnaise as a condiment and grated cheese as a topping for your featured menu items. If you conduct a proper feasibility study before you progress with your plan, you will find that most health departments do not allow food carts to sell dairy-based or edible-oil-based condiments. This is useful information to know before you go out and buy dozens of bottles of mayonnaise and packets of cheese.

One of the main aims of the feasibility study is to establish whether your idea is a "go" or a "no go." Is your idea feasible and worthwhile, or should you just draw a line through it and move on?

Whether your decision is a "go" or "no go," you will need to state the reasons why. For example, if it's a "go," then you will need to develop and test prototypes, carry out due diligence, find a management team, try to get some early customers, seek funding if necessary, and prepare a launch plan.

While a "no go" may feel disappointing, remember that a decision not to go ahead is also a valid and valuable result of a feasibility study. It has saved you the time, effort, and expense that you may have spent on a concept that does not have the potential to succeed in the market.

Knowing your constraints can also lead to doors opening in other areas you might not have imagined. Take Jorge Heraud and Lee Redden, the founders of Blue River Technology, for instance.[5] They had an idea to build robotic mowers for commercial spaces. Having spoken to 100 customers over a period of 10 weeks, they learned that their original target market—golf courses—did not think their solution was viable.

TABLE 9.4

Critical Elements of Feasibility Study

• Does the idea fulfill a need or solve a big problem?
• Is there both a short- and long-term market potential?
• Who are the customers, and what are they willing to pay?
• Does the opportunity provide competitive uniqueness?
• Is the business model feasible (can it be done) and viable (can it be sustainable)?

Credit: D. Kelley, B. George, D. Ceru, H. Neck. Babson's Feasibility Blueprint Assignment for MBA students, Babson College, 2013.

One of Blue River Technology's many agricultural machines.

Credit: Photo courtesy of Blue River Technology

However, during their market research, the two entrepreneurs discovered a huge demand from farmers for an automated way to kill weeds without chemicals. This gave the two entrepreneurs the "go" they were looking for. They built and tested the prototype and received $3 million in venture funding less than a year later.

The more data you gather during the feasibility study, the more evidence you will have to show investors when the time comes to develop your pitch deck or write a business plan.

The Pitch Deck

The pitch deck is a brief presentation highlighting many of the essential elements found in a feasibility study and a business plan. Some call this the launch plan. This is such an important part of the planning process that we've devoted a whole chapter to the pitch (Chapter 16), but let's briefly discuss the specifics of the deck here. (An example Pitch Deck can be found in Appendix B, p. 477.)

The pitch deck has replaced the formal business plan in most venues. A pitch deck is needed for collegiate competitions, applications to accelerators and incubators,

TABLE 9.5

Sample Feasibility Study Template

Need Identification	Describe why there is a need for your business to exist.
Venture Concept	Have a clear, concise description in 2–3 sentences.
Value Propositions	What makes you unique and why is this valuable for the customer? Prove that the customer wants what you are providing.
Market	Discuss the market size, potential market size, and target market size. Is the market large enough to meet your goals? Discuss trends and growth estimates.
Competitive Environment	Identify and compare your venture against the competition. By understanding the competition, you will have a better understanding of the dynamics of the industry in which you are competing and how you are differentiated. Are there specific laws or regulations you should be aware of?
Revenue Model	Describe your revenue model in terms of the revenue streams and the key factors that will influence those streams. You will also need to examine your cost model and determine the key drivers of your costs. Overall, you are assessing your potential profitability. Provide a simple income statement.
Startup Requirements	Identify the resources needed to start the business. What is absolutely essential before a sale can be made? What don't you have, but need?
Team	Critically assess your current team, its fit with the venture, and your ability to act (or not).
Decision	Based on the analysis laid out in the feasibility study, do you want to move forward? Why or why not?

Source: Kelley, D., Ceru, D., George, B., & Neck, H. (2014). *Feasibility Blueprint Guidelines.* Wellesley, MA: Babson College.

and for angel and venture capital funding. There are many variations on the "ideal" pitch deck on the Internet, so we encourage you to do your own research before preparing. The purpose of the pitch is to describe and get interest. In the case of using your pitch deck in front of professional investors, the goal is to get to the next meeting!

There are no strict rules for the length or style of pitch decks. Author and entrepreneur Guy Kawasaki advises keeping pitch deck slides to a minimum of 10, while Timothy Young, founder of professional online collaboration tool Socialcast and a cofounder of the personal web hosting service About.me, achieved success by using only five Powerpoint slides. With these five slides on his iPad, he presented his pitch to investors, raising over $10 million in funding for both startups.[6] Young also believes that presenting on his iPad was an advantage because it forced him and his investors to share a screen, which he believed made the process more relaxed and informal.

The Business Plan

In Chapter 8, "Building Business Models," we defined the *business plan* as a formal document that provides background and financial information about the company, outlines your goals for the business and describes how you intend to reach them. We also explained that the business plan supports the business model by outlining the steps necessary to attain the necessary goals.

As stated earlier, the business plan has been replaced by the pitch deck in most venues—but when it comes to traditional investors and bankers, they are likely to require a traditional business plan. The business plan needs to show that you are serious and that you've done your homework, given the level of detail that is necessary to complete a strong business plan. However, there is an ironic angle to this: when a business plan is created, it must be thought of as a work in progress because nothing goes according to plan. It is important to realize this ahead of time, as some entrepreneurs struggle when things don't go according to plan because so much energy has been put into creating the actual business plan.

A traditional business plan usually consists of 20 to 40 pages, plus additional pages for appendices and financial statements. It also includes the organization's mission, strategy, tactics, goals, financials, and objectives, together with a five-year forecast for income, profits, and cash flow.[7] This information is divided into three main parts.[8]

The first part is the business concept, where you discuss the industry, business structure, products and services, and how you plan to make your

About.me founder Timothy Young believes that presenting on an iPad is less formal and more relaxed as everyone shares a screen.

Credit: ©iStockphoto.com/ lovro77

business a success. The second part is the market section, where you describe potential customers, and the competitors in your market. The third part describes how you intend to design, develop, and implement the plan; and provides some detail on operations and management. Finally, the financial section includes details of income and cash flow, balance sheets, financial projections, and the like. In addition to these components, a business plan also has a cover, title page, and table of contents (Table 9.6).

It can be a complex task to start writing a business plan too early, especially for a startup when there are still so many questions to be answered. Business plans are useful for established companies with a history of data and operations because this

---

TABLE 9.6

Components of a Traditional Business Plan

BUSINESS PLAN OUTLINE

1. *Cover*

2. *Table of Contents*

3. *Executive Summary* (2–3 pages)
   - Brief introduction & description of the opportunity
   - Company overview
   - Product or service description
   - Industry overview
   - Marketplace & target market
   - Competitive advantage
   - Business model (with summary of financials)
   - Management team
   - Offering

4. *Company Overview* (1–2 pages)
   - Company description
   - History & current status (stage of development)
   - Products & service description
   - Competitive advantages
   - Entry, growth, & exit strategies

5. *Industry, Marketplace, & Competitor Analyses* (3–6 pages)
   - Industry analysis
   - Marketplace analysis
   - Competitor analysis

6. *Marketing Plan* (1–4 pages)
   - Target market strategy
   - Product/service strategy
   - Pricing strategy
   - Distribution Strategy
   - Advertising and promotion strategy
   - Sales strategy
   - Marketing and sales forecasts
   - Marketing expenses

7. *Operations Plan* (2 pages)
   - Operations strategy
   - Scope of operations
   - Ongoing operations
   - Operations expenses

8. *Development Plan* (1–2pages)
   - Development Strategy
   - Development timeline (milestones)
   - Development expenses

9. *Management* (1–2 pages)
   - Company organization
   - Management team
   - Ownership & compensation
   - Administrative expenses

10. *Critical Risks* (1–2 pages)
    - Market, customer, financial risks
    - Competitor retaliation
    - Contingency plans

11. *Offering* (up to 1 page)
    - Investment requirements
    - Offer

12. *Financial Plan* (up to 2 text pages, including financial statements)
    - Detailed financial assumptions
    - Pro forma financial statements
    - Breakeven analysis and other calculations
    - Do include statement within this section; do not place statements in the appendix.

13. *Appendices* (no maximum)
    - Customer survey and results
    - Other items to include may be menus, product specifications, team résumés, sample promotions, product pictures.

data will help the business to plan and forecast more accurately, but startups have no such history. Startups are not just smaller versions of bigger companies—a startup begins with guesswork and untested assumptions. Nevertheless, in order to get later stage funding, a business plan will likely be needed.

In the order of entrepreneurial activities, business plans come after idea generation, business model canvas, feasibility study, and pitch deck. Figure 9.3 illustrates the path from idea generation to business plan.

By following the steps of The Practice of Entrepreneurship, which we introduced in Chapter 2, you have a better chance of creating a solid, evidence-based business plan to present to potential investors when the time comes. By gathering, testing and analyzing real data, you will be more able to illustrate your passion to create, the resources you have used, the actions you have taken to get your business on the move, the risks you have taken (and the ones you are prepared not to take), the people who have been enrolled in your journey, the experiments you have carried out to test what works and what doesn't, and where you would like the business to go next. In short, you will be able to prove that your product works, a real market exists, and your financials are not based just on guesswork.

FIGURE 9.3

Path From Idea Generation to Business Plan

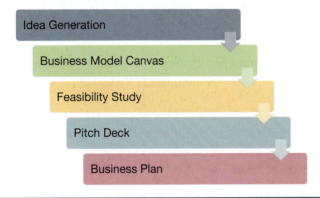

Summary of Different Types of Plans

Although we are not advocating one type of plan over another, we believe it's important that entrepreneurs understand what is available to them and for what purposes. Table 9.7 summarizes the different types of plans we have outlined for entrepreneurs.

In addition to the plans we've outlined here, there are other options used by entrepreneurs to showcase their businesses. Among them are the following:

▸ LeanLaunchLab, which allows you to test hypotheses and refine your business model;

▸ Lean Stack, a paid service that compresses the essential parts of your business down to one page to send to investors who have little time to read through a large document; and

▸ free tool Plan Cruncher that, like Lean Stack, allows you to summarize your idea in one page.

TABLE 9.7

Summary of Different Types of Plans

TYPE OF PLAN	PRIMARY AUDIENCE	PURPOSE	OUTPUT
Back of a Napkin	Friends and prospective team members	Gain clarity on the idea	A drawing on a napkin
Sketches	Team members, early employees	Visualize the future potential	More detailed drawing or informally written
Business Model Canvas	Team members, advisors	Identify gaps and critically evaluate each part of the business and how the components integrate	Completed and tested business model canvas
Business Brief	Friends and family investors, advisors, other interested stakeholders	To have something in writing to show anybody interested in the business; also good practice for describing the business in a concise way	2- to 3-page typed document that is well formatted and professional looking
Feasibility Study	Team members, maybe early investors	Assess the potential of a new concept; can act as proof that the venture has market potential	10-page typed documents that is well formatted and professional looking
Pitch Deck	Early investors, judges of venture competitions, incubators, accelerators	To get the next meeting with a potential investor; to apply to an incubator program; win a competition; get funding	10 to 20 slides, depending on length and purpose of the presentation
Business Plan	Banks, investors	Get funding	25+ page document plus appendices

How do you know what plan to create? Depending on your business, you may use a different type of plan in the beginning from other entrepreneurs. The best plan for you is the one that helps gives you the clarity and direction to take action to create your future venture. Use The Practice of Entrepreneurship to take action and get out of the building, just as our featured entrepreneurs have done: test your ideas, get market feedback, generate momentum, revise assumptions, make continuous iterations, use your social network, make contacts, and get potential customers interested in your product or service.

Most of the successful entrepreneurs featured throughout this book started out by testing their ideas in the real world to see if they really had wings and if they could make them into a business, long before they sat down to write their formal business plan and many never wrote a formal business plan at all. They also used the time to equip themselves with the basic skills required for a successful venture—financial management, production capabilities, and marketing and sales—either by learning the skills themselves or partnering with other people. When you, too, have proved your concept, and gathered the data to go with it, then you will be able to produce a solid, credible business plan.

9.4 THE BUSINESS PLAN DEBATE

>> LO 9.4   **Debate the value of writing business plans.**

Of all the types of plans presented in this chapter, the business plan is the most complex and time-consuming document to create. There is considerable debate on the value of spending the time writing a business plan. Proponents of writing a business plan say it helps you gain clarity, keeps you organized, establishes the core message, and creates alignment among team members.[10] It also helps establish legitimacy because, if nothing else, you have a business plan.

Video
Skipping the Formal Business Plan

Some entrepreneurs in the very early stages find the practice of writing a simple business plan *just for themselves* a great exercise in thinking about things they may not have thought of before. It allows you to make sure that you truly understand the components of the plan and the best way to communicate these details to your team and investors. Practicing your plan also helps you to question the validity of your ideas, the markets you intend to target, and the customers you would like to attract.

Others point out that many ideas are pursued but may not be opportunities. The process of writing a business plan helps you vet the idea and shape it into an opportunity. As a result, spending time writing a business plan could help save the entrepreneur a lot of time and money down the road. For example, it can take up to 200 hours to write a comprehensive business plan. That's about a $10,000 investment assuming you might get $50 per hour for writing a plan ($50 x 200). However, launching a poor idea and unproven concept could cost you millions.[11]

A business plan can be useful at the stage when you have partners or team members on board. It allows everyone to articulate vision and strategy, and ensures that everyone is aligned with current and future plans for the business. It is also a valuable benchmarking tool, as it forces you to be honest about your company's performance by showing not only areas where your business exceeded expectations but also those instances when your strategies didn't work out, and the lessons you learned from this.

Nevertheless, there is growing support for the advantages of *not* writing a business plan.[12] Those against writing a business plan say that the plan is old as soon as it comes off the printer, it's based on untested assumptions, financial projections are too far out to have validity, and the actual writing and compiling discourages action and gathering real data.[13] As just mentioned, it can take 200 hours to write a comprehensive business plan. Opponents of the business plan feel these hours could be spent on actual activities that can help shape the business idea, get customer input, make early sales, and so on.

The idea that the business plan—the most formal and complex of plans—is the first step for an entrepreneur is an outdated view. The business plan is more often used for bank loans and professional investment, but many other types of plans should be generated prior to the formal business plan.

Eric Ries, author of *The Lean Startup*, argues that one reason startups fail is due to "the allure of a good plan, a solid strategy, and thorough market research." Ries hints that corporate strategic planning led us to the conundrum that if [a business plan] works for the greatest corporations in the world, then it must be good for startups too! Ries notes, "Planning and forecasting are only accurate when based on a long, stable operating history and a relatively static environment. Startups have neither."[14]

In sum, although formal business plans have their place, they may not necessarily be relevant to the new entrepreneur. Entrepreneurs are explorers—they take action to find answers, rather than basing their assumptions on speculation. They are also experts in using social capital—the people and connections you need to make your business a success. No entrepreneur is an island.

So, what should come before the business plan? As we have pointed out many times, at the early stages it is essential to follow The Practice of Entrepreneurship, to take action, and get out of the building. And make sure you have mastered the basic skills required for a successful venture—financial management, production capabilities, and marketing and sales. When you have proved your concept, and gathered the data to go with it, then you will be able to produce a solid, credible business plan.

9.5 TIPS FOR WRITING BUSINESS PLANS

>> LO 9.5 Implement the tips for writing business plans.

Web
Business Plan Tips

When it comes to the stage where you feel you need a business plan, it is important to think about the purpose of the plan. Do you need the plan in order to secure funding? Or do you just want to convey to your audience your future plans for the company?

Remember, different audiences require different plans, and each plan should be tailored accordingly. For example, potential investors will be keen to know more about the financials because they will want to know details of the return on their investment, as well as a time frame for getting their money back.

The key to a successful business plan is knowledge—showing that you have done your homework through exploration, experimentation, and market research is one of the best ways to impress your audience. If your plan does not have a solid basis in fact or research, then do not waste time writing one. Following are some more tips for writing business plans.[17] Keep in mind, though, that these tips are good for all types of planning!

Remove Any of the Fluff

Decorative language can sound nice, but do not be tempted to use it in a business plan. Too much wordiness or jargon can detract from the main message. For example, opening with "In our current environment of fast food, hot dogs are still a much sought-after food enjoyed by people all over the US" is purely a waste of space. Most people will know that hot dogs are a popular fast food, and they don't need to be reminded of this.

A better introduction to your business is to describe what it is, its current location, and the target market. For example, "Harry's Gourmet Hot Dogs is a food truck located

RESEARCH AT WORK

How Valuable Are Business Plans?

The traditional school of thought teaches that a business plan is a must, but other evidence suggests otherwise. William Bygrave, a professor emeritus and entrepreneurship researcher at Babson College, studied graduates over a number of years to figure out how successful those people were who started out writing formal business plans versus those who didn't. Bygrave concluded that there was no difference in success between those with a formal business plan at the outset and those without one.

Similarly, in a study of over 200 startups, Bill Gross, founder of business incubator Idealab, found that business plans rank pretty low in the five factors for startup success, crediting timing as the most important (are customers really ready for what you have to offer them?), and business plans and funding as the least important.[15]

However, another study, carried out by entrepreneurship professor William Gartner from Clemson University using data from Panel Study of Entrepreneurial Dynamics, shows that writing a business plan can increase the likelihood of entrepreneurs' setting up their own companies.[16]

In addition, Bygrave believes that having any type of plan, formal or informal, is better than having no type of plan at all. He observes that plans are essential in helping entrepreneurs clarify ideas, recognize opportunities, build the right team, and work out financial projections. After all, 40% of Babson students who have taken the business plan writing course tend to start their own businesses after graduation, which is twice the rate of those who didn't take the class at all.

Bottom line, how valuable are business plans? Bygrave thinks it's all in the timing: "We're saying that writing a business plan ahead of time, before you open your doors for business, does not appear to help the performance of the business subsequently." The debate continues.

CRITICAL THINKING QUESTIONS

1. **What value do you think a business plan adds to an early-stage venture?**

2. **Do you think writing a business plan is a worthwhile exercise for every entrepreneur? Why or why not?**

3. **At what stage do you think you might start writing a business plan for your startup?** ●

in southwest Washington that offers 25 different hot dog varieties to satisfy the discerning tastes of local office workers, residents, and seasonal tourists." Here, instead of fillers and unnecessary detail, you have used direct language to quickly and clearly convey a description of your company without taking up too much space.

Be Realistic

Outline the challenges ahead, potential risks, lessons you have learned, and opportunities to progress. A strong idea will stand on its merit when you are realistic about it. Everything you write or present must be based in fact or well-researched assumptions.

Avoid the Exaggerated Hockey Stick

Even though it can be difficult to establish solid financial projections, be conservative in your approach to financials. While you may feel certain that your business will capture 50% of the market next year, it is better to present a more credible percentage, for example 10%. There is no use presenting figures based on guesswork or blown wildly out of proportion. If possible, back up your projections with examples to show investors that you are at least in the right ballpark.

Avoid Typos, Grammatical Mistakes, and Inconsistencies

Revise your plan thoroughly for any mistakes before you show it to investors. For example, if your plan's summary includes the requirement for $60,000 in investment, but your projection shows that you plan to have $70,000 in cash flow in the first year, you have clearly made a mistake. Careless mistakes like these will not impress investors.

Use Visuals

Visuals are a good way to break up the text, help the plan flow better, and bring your idea to life. However, be careful not to crowd the plan with too many graphs, charts, and images. Use adequate white space for optimal legibility and a clean, uncluttered look.

The right time to write a business plan is when your business is more established, you have a fully functioning team involved, and you have the data to prove your concept. If you are considering expanding the business and seeking funding, now would be a good time to write a business plan. Table 9.8 lists some useful resources for writing a business plan when the time comes. ●

TABLE 9.8

Business Plan Resources

WEBSITE ADDRESS	DESCRIPTION
https://www.sba.gov/writing-business-plan	The U.S. Small Business Administration guide to writing a business plan
http://www.entrepreneur.com/landing/224842	*Entrepreneur* magazine's "How To Write A Business Plan"
http://www.entrepreneur.com/formnet/form/561	A free template for writing a business plan from *Entrepreneur* magazine's Business Form Template Gallery
http://www.caycon.com/resources.php?s=4	A collection of business plan resources in the Entrepreneur's Library—Startup Resources from Cayenne Consulting
http://www.businessnewsdaily.com/5680-simple-business-plan-templates.html	8 Simple Business Plan Templates for Entrepreneurs from *Business News Daily*

Get the edge on your studies at **edge.sagepub.com/neckentrepreneurship**

‣   Master the learning objectives using key study tools
‣   Watch, listen, and connect with online multimedia resources
‣   Access mobile-friendly quizzes and flashcards to check your understanding

SUMMARY

9.1   Examine "planning" from an entrepreneurial perspective.

From an entrepreneurial perspective, planning helps clarify the entrepreneurial vision and helps the entrepreneur articulate where the business is going and how it can succeed. Entrepreneurs can use alternative planning methods, including simplified plans, planning with preparation, and planning with imagination.

9.2   Define TRIM and explain its importance to entrepreneurial planning.

The TRIM framework (Team, Resources, Idea, Market) lists the most important questions that must be addressed in any type of entrepreneurial planning.

9.3   Explain the different types of plans used by entrepreneurs.

Different types of plans include back of a napkin, sketches on a page, the business model canvas, the business brief, the feasibility study, the pitch deck, and the business plan.

9.4   Debate the value of writing business plans.

Experts disagree on the value of spending the time writing a business plan. Some see a business plan as complex, time-consuming, and based on untested assumptions; while others believe it is a useful way to crystallize and organize ideas. Formal business plans have their place, but they may not necessarily be relevant to the new entrepreneur.

9.5   Implement the tips for writing business plans.

Some tips for writing business plans include: using visuals; removing any fluff; avoiding typos, grammatical mistakes, and inconsistencies; avoiding the exaggerated hockey stick; and being realistic.

KEY TERMS

Feasibility study 236
Plan 227
Planning 225

TRIM (Team, Resources, Idea, Market) framework 227

CASE STUDY

Elon Musk, CEO and CTO of Tesla Motors, CEO and Chief Designer of SpaceX, Chairman of Solar City, and Cofounder of PayPal

Elon Musk is the ultimate entrepreneur. Aside from his extraordinary intellect, business acumen, and billionaire status, he is also willing to risk huge sums of money in achieving unprecedented scientific breakthroughs and technological advancements. He has been labeled as "this generation's well known biggest risk taker,"[1] due to his willingness to invest billions in projects that have no precedent for accomplishment, but are theoretically feasible. This unusual capacity for risk taking has landed Musk with a reputation as the quintessential 21st- century explorer, and entrepreneur.

Musk was born in 1971 in Pretoria, South Africa. He likely derived some of his extraordinary intellectual capacities from his father, an engineer with expertise in fields both mechanical and chemical. As a teenager, Musk emigrated to Canada, and later moved to the United States to attend the Wharton School at the University of Pennsylvania, where he earned two bachelor's degrees: one in economics and one in physics. With undergraduate degrees in hand, Musk was accepted to an applied physics doctoral program at Stanford in 1995. He moved to California to pursue his degree, but soon opted out of his academic pursuits to turn his attention to entrepreneurship. Musk became a US citizen in 2002.

Working with his brother Kimbal, Musk's first entrepreneurial venture was to build Zip2, an Internet software company. After only four years, the Musk brothers were able to sell their business to Compaq for over $300 million. His next venture was to build a new company called X.com.

Just a few years after starting up, X.com merged with Cofinity to form what we know today as PayPal. Applying his economic and technological savvy to help his colleagues build PayPal, Musk is credited with being a cofounder of this online money transfer services giant. After only three years, Musk and company had developed PayPal into a billion-dollar business that was bought by e-Bay in 2002. A visionary entrepreneur, Musk consistently puts his money where his mouth is.

After the sale of PayPal, Musk turned his attention to investigating the feasibility of new ventures that interested him even more than computers and the Internet—electric cars and space exploration. A cofounder of Tesla Motors, Musk is also the chief product architect of this new-age automobile brand, widely considered the finest electric vehicles available on the market.

Tesla is one of the most expensive and audacious investments of the 21st century. Critics questioned the feasibility of making electric cars affordable for the masses. Undaunted, Musk invested tens of millions of dollars of his own fortune and raised hundreds of millions more from sources in both the public and private sector to analyze feasibility and overcome obstacles. Analysts predicted it would take ten years to achieve profitability; yet by 2015, Tesla Motors was on its way to unprecedented success in the electric automobile industry, and was expected to compete with traditional automakers in the future.

If Musk's feasibility analyses and achievements with Tesla sound ambitious, his endeavors with SpaceX have been truly remarkable—and revolutionary—throughout the aerospace industry. Tapping liberally into the fortunes he accrued in other endeavors, Musk has invested more than a $100 million dollars of his own money into building SpaceX. A private-sector competitor to NASA itself, SpaceX became the first private space exploration company to send rockets into orbit and to the International Space Station. But Musk's goals do not stop at building rockets. As of 2015, feasibility studies were under way to accomplish feats never before achieved in human history, such as sending human beings to the planet Mars, where Musk hopes to eventually settle and colonize the "red planet." "I really want SpaceX to help make life multiplanetary" in our solar system, he says.

Elon Musk likely has several decades of productive work still ahead of him. What will the future bring? Elon himself may not fully know yet. One thing is for sure; his goals for the future are big, ambitious, and not reserved exclusively for automobile transportation and space exploration. Another of his key interests is solar energy. Musk is the largest shareholder of the company Solar City, which seeks to improve on the acquisition and delivery of solar energy around the country.

Musk is also passionate about improving land-based travel, as he finds the current options for public rapid transit uninspiring. Specifically, he supports what he calls a Hyperloop. If materialized, hyperloops would send passengers safely through land-based, pressurized tubes at supersonic speeds. For example, imagine traveling from Los Angeles to San Francisco (a 75-minute airplane flight, not counting time involved in clearing airport security) on the ground through a tube in just half an hour! It would be like taking an ultramodern train ride, except you would be traveling on land faster than you could travel in the air. It seems that the sky is the only limit to Musk's technological and entrepreneurial ambitions; and he is rapidly working on breaking barriers there as well. What will he come up with next?

Critical Thinking Questions

1. Entrepreneurship always involves varying kinds and degrees of risk. What kinds of feasibility, safety, and capital guidelines do you think should govern the decision-making processes surrounding entrepreneurial risk taking?

2. Why is it important for science and technology to play a prominent role in future entrepreneurial efforts around the world?

3. What new inventions in science and technology do you believe inventors and entrepreneurs will create and market in your lifetime?

Sources

A brief history of Tesla. (2016, June). Techcruch.com Retrieved from http://techcrunch.com/gallery/a-brief-history-of-tesla/

Elon Musk: I'll put a man on Mars in ten years: The Big Interview with Alan Murray. (2011, April 22.) *Wall Street Journal. Retrieved* from http://www.wsj.com/video/elon-musk-ill-put-a-man-on-mars-in-10-years/CCF1FC62-BB0D-4561-938C-DF0DEFAD15BA.html

Garber, M. (2013-, July 13). The real i-Pod: Elon Musk's wild idea for a "Jetson Tunnel" from S.F. to L.A. *The Atlantic*. Retrieved from http://www.theatlantic.com/technology/archive/2012/07/the-real-ipod-elon-musks-wild-idea-for-a-jetson-tunnel-from-sf-to-la/259825/

Vance, A. (2015). *Elon Musk: Tesla, SpaceX, and the quest for a fantastic future*. New York, NY: HarperCollins.

Official website for Solar City. Retrieved from www.solarcity.com

Official website for SpaceX. Retrieved from www.spacex.com

Official website for Tesla Motors. Retrieved from www.teslamotors.com

Vance, A. (2015). *Elon Musk: Tesla, SpaceX, and the quest for a fantastic future*. New York, NY: HarperCollins.

Wikipedia article on Hyperloops. (2016). Retrieved from https://en.wikipedia.org/wiki/Hyperloop

10 Creating Revenue Models

Remind people that profit is the difference between revenue and expense. This makes you look smart."

—Scott Adams, *Dilbert* cartoonist

Learning Objectives

10.1 Define a revenue model and distinguish it from the business model.

10.2 Illustrate the ten most popular revenue models being used by entrepreneurs.

10.3 Explain how companies generate revenue by profiting from "free."

10.4 Identify the drivers that affect revenue as well as cost.

10.5 Identify different strategies entrepreneurs use when pricing their product and service.

10.6 Explain different methods of calculating price.

Chapter Outline

10.1 WHAT IS A REVENUE MODEL?

>> **LO 10.1** Define a revenue model and distinguish it from the business model.

Over the course of the previous chapters, we have described numerous different enterprises founded by entrepreneurs from all sorts of industries and backgrounds, from ugly Christmas sweaters to designer dress online rentals, to invisible bicycle helmets, among many others. Diverse though the businesses may appear to be, they all have one very important thing in common: the ability to generate **revenue,** which is the income gained from sales of goods or services.

In Chapter 9, we presented several ways in which entrepreneurs use planning for different stages and purposes. However, planning and business modeling cannot be complete without an understanding of the revenue model. In other words, how will the business earn revenue, manage costs, and produce profit?

While the terms are sometimes used interchangeably, a business model and a revenue model are not the same thing. Recall from Chapter 8 that business models fulfill three main purposes: they help entrepreneurs to fulfill unmet needs in an existing market, to deliver existing products and services to existing customers with unique differentiation, and to serve entirely new customers in new markets. In other words, a business model describes how a venture will create, deliver, and capture value.

A **revenue model** is a key component of the business model and identifies how the company will earn income and generate profits. In other words, it explains how entrepreneurs will make money and capture value from delivering on the customer value proposition (CVP) that is outlined as part of their business model. As an entrepreneur, if you have a clear strategy for generating revenue from your business, this will give you a better chance of attracting investment when the time comes. Part of this strategy is asking a few simple questions, such as:

▶ How much are my customers willing to pay?

▶ How many customers do I need?

Video
Revenue Models

Revenue: the income gained from sales of goods or services.

Revenue Model: a key component of the business model and identifies how the company will earn income and make profits.

Shane Kost, Founder, Chicago Food Planet Food Tours and Food Tour Pros

Shane Kost, founder of Chicago Food Planet Tours and Food Tour Pros
Credit: Used with permission from Shane Kost

After whetting his entrepreneurial appetite with a small apparel company and a seasonal indoor/outdoor lighting outfit, Shane Kost settled on his big idea, inspired by his own passion for travel. "I thought, what are the main questions that people have when they are going to travel? 'Where are we going to stay, and where are we going to eat?'" Kost recalls. His research showed that 13 million people in the United States traveled with food as their top motivation, so after talking to many restaurateurs and food shops in his adopted hometown of Chicago, he launched Chicago Food Planet Food Tours in 2006.

The company conducts culinary tours with various themes. Costing between $35 and $58 per person (with less expensive tickets for teens and children), the tours include all food tastings and beverages in the price, as well as the expertise of a trained guide. Chicago Food Planet Food Tours has an office on North Michigan Avenue and employs 25 people—and also pays the food vendors, where groups stop for tastings.

From the beginning, these vendor relationships have been instrumental. "They were a real partner in our growth and vice-versa—as we grow, so do they," says Kost. While the locations benefit from exposure to new potential patrons, "we pay the tasting locations because it's the right thing to do, and nobody should give away their product for free." The company does receive substantial discounts based on volume, however. "The more people we bring, we tend to get better pricing (basic economics), which lowers our per-person price and keeps the relationships, which is the most important part of our business, intact. Every discount and how it is set up is slightly different, but they

average from anywhere between 5% and 50% at times," Shane explains.

As Chicago Food Planet Food Tours' reputation began to grow, so did interest from other like-minded entrepreneurs who were keen to learn Shane's recipe for success. In 2009, Shane launched a sister operation, Food Tour Pros, "to help industrious people make a successful living by providing them the tools they needed to succeed." Food Tour Pros offers two and three-day intensive courses in Chicago that teach new and aspiring business owners everything they need to get started, or to improve an existing operation.

"The average cost for starting a Food Tour Pros business is $4,994," says Shane. "This includes the fees for our courses at Food Tour Pros, but also includes other startup costs including building and launching a company website, R&D, legal fees, etc." Since 2009, Food Tour Pros has helped launch food tours in over 100 cities across the world in over 20 countries.

While the accolades and financial returns are nice, and the opportunity to help others realize their dreams is deeply rewarding, success for Kost is "about lifestyle and working toward goals that are not related to money. If the metric is 'are you profitable,' then yes we are, and for a lot of people, but is that enough? . . . I wanted to work around food, people, and travel. I wanted to travel two months out of the year at least, so I created that by building this lifestyle business." As of 2015, Kost had traveled to more than 40 countries.

Chicago Food Planet Food Tours and Food Tour Pros are all about people—the tour-goers, the tour operators, the vendors, the employees—who together provide a great experience. The joy is in the journey, not the destination.

CRITICAL THINKING QUESTIONS

1. **What do you consider to be the most important factors driving revenue in Chicago Food Planet Food Tours and Food Tour Pros?**

2. **How does the company use revenue to grow the business?**

3. **Kost believes that lifestyle and working toward goals are more important than accolades and financial returns. Do you agree with his view? Why or why not?** ●

Source: S. Kost, personal interview, December 23, 2014.

▸   How much revenue can be generated through sales?

▸   If I have more than one revenue stream, how much does each stream contribute
to the total?

As an example, consider Shane Kost, founder of Chicago Food Planet Food Tours
and Food Tour Pros. Kost has managed to set up a business that generates revenue in
two principal ways: from food tasting tours and from business courses for other entrepreneurs wishing to start food tasting tour businesses. The revenue and business climate of Chicago Food Planet Food Tours and Food Tour Pros has also provided him
with the lifestyle he has always wanted.

In the next section, we will take a look at the different types of revenue models that
are available to the startup entrepreneur.

10.2 DIFFERENT TYPES OF REVENUE MODELS

>> **LO 10.2**   **Illustrate the ten most popular revenue models
being used by entrepreneurs.[1]**

As we have discussed, different types of revenue models have different revenue streams.
Some companies operate on just one primary revenue model while others use a combination
of models. Each type determines different ways in which revenue is generated, which also
affects who your customers will be. For example, a retailer that generates revenue through
online sales tends to attract the type of customers who prefer shopping from their computers
or mobile devices rather than traveling to the local mall. Remember: the customer is not
always your end user! Let's take a look at 10 main types of revenue models.

Unit Sales Revenue Model

The **Unit Sales Revenue Model** measures the amount of revenue generated by the
number of items (units) sold by a company. Typically, retail businesses rely on the

⑤SAGE edge™

Master the content
**edge.sagepub.com/
neckentrepreneurship**

Video
Types of Revenue Models

**Unit Sales Revenue
Model:** the amount of
revenue generated by the
number of items (units) sold
by a company.

FIGURE 10.1

The Razor-and-Razor-Blade Model

a.   b.

Credit: ©iStockphoto.com/JoseAntonioRevidiegoPavon   Credit: ©iStockphoto.com/delihayat

Source: http://www.rogersfamilyco.com/index.php/story-2-0-brewer/

unit sales revenue model by selling products or service directly to consumers, whether face-to-face or online. The idea is that you earn revenue when you sell the product or service to the end user. There are two different types of unit sales: physical goods, which include clothing, food and beverages, housewares and hardware, furniture, cars, and so forth; and intangibles, which are often digital products such as music sold through iTunes, or games and apps sold to smartphones and tablets. Software support may also be unit-priced, meaning that customers pay by the minute or by the hour.

Another variation of the unit sales revenue model is called the razor-and-razor-blade model. This phrase was coined by Gillette, which generates huge revenue from offering a physical product like razors at no or low cost to encourage sales of the more expensive razor blades (see Figure 10.1). This has also become known as the printers-and-ink model, which most of us have encountered: The printer is sold at a low cost, but the ink or toner cartridges are priced much higher, generating ongoing revenue for the printer manufacturer. Single-serve coffee machines that use cartridges or "pods" may also be priced this way.

Advertising Revenue Model

Advertising Revenue Model: the amount of revenue gained through advertising products and services.

The **Advertising Revenue Model** relies on the amount of revenue gained through advertising products and services. Advertising has been around for a long time, as has this revenue model: A century ago, magazines and newspapers accepted advertisements and charged by the space or by the word, and early radio and television charged by the minute or second to broadcast ads. Today the ad revenue model has evolved from its traditional format to encompass the digital world.

Meaningful advertising revenue generated in the digital world is dependent on attracting traffic or developing a dominant niche. For example, Google AdWords is not only Google's main advertising product but also its main source of revenue. The AdWords service is a type of advertising revenue model called cost-per-click (CPC) which charges the advertiser a fee every time a user clicks on the ad. The model is intended to attract traffic to the advertiser's business while generating income for providing the AdWords service. AdWords also includes the cost-per-action (CPA) advertising model, whereby advertisers pay only when the click converts to an actual sale of a product or service. Google is an example of a business that has developed a niche by offering this form of advertising to people running businesses all over the world.

Another form of online advertising is called promoted content (also known as "sponsored" or "suggested" content), which works by having ads appear in the flow of the content that the users are reading. Often, these ads are blended in so neatly to the content that users may not even realize that they have been paid for.

Many types of businesses use digital platforms such as Twitter, Facebook, LinkedIn, and Yelp to publish paid ads to promote their services. For example, *The Economist* advertises its weekly newspaper by posting articles regularly on Facebook. Although these postings are marked as "sponsored," they generally attract more people than traditional ads because they are perceived as more credible than others. The ads also increase brand awareness by reminding people of *The Economist*'s existence, thereby encouraging more customers to purchase the publication.

Data Revenue Model

Companies use the **Data Revenue Model** when they generate revenue by selling high-quality, exclusive, valuable information to other parties. The social network PatientsLikeMe is a forum for people with certain diseases to share factual, quantified information about their condition. PatientsLikeMe generates revenue from this forum by aggregating the data and selling it to companies in the health care industry. If you predict that this would raise privacy concerns, you are correct—however, the site does not pass on the contact information of the members; it keeps their details strictly anonymous.

Similarly, while other social networks such as Google, Twitter, and Facebook have huge databases of users' personal contact information, they tend to use this data for targeted advertising only, and do not sell these databases to third parties. Despite anonymizing and de-identifying users, there is still a sense of discomfort from users who resent their data being manipulated for the sake of research or advertising.[2] Another social network, Ello, addresses these data issues by making its site ad-free and promising not to harvest or sell its users' data. Users are given a free basic account; Ello generates revenue by charging users for additional features.[3]

Data Revenue Model: a type of revenue model whereby companies generate revenue by selling high-quality, exclusive, valuable information to other parties.

Intermediation Revenue Model

The **Intermediation Revenue Model** describes the different methods by which third parties such as brokers (or "middlemen") can generate money. **Brokers** are people who organize transactions between buyers and sellers. These "middlemen" play important roles in connecting people to different services. For example, eBay acts as an auction broker as it manages the transaction between seller and buyer, and generates revenue by charging a listing fee or commission on a sale. Other common examples of intermediaries include real estate brokers who take a percentage of commission each time they match a buyer and seller; and credit card companies, which earn revenue through the sales transactions process.

In recent years, various entrepreneurial ventures have emerged to put a new creative spin on the role of the middleman in an effort to connect people with services in a more efficient and less expensive way. An example is Airbnb, which offers short-term accommodation that private homeowners rent out to visitors, usually tourists, at a fraction of the price of hotels. Airbnb has low overhead since it is purely web-based, and it makes money by taking a 3% commission from the fee earned by the homeowner, as well as a booking fee of 6% to 12% for every booking made by the visitors. Similarly, New York-based website Homethinking connects home buyers and home sellers to specific realtors by providing statistics on homes sold, such as the amount they sold for and the length of time they took to sell. The site also includes mortgage research tools, as well as ratings and reviews of Realtors from homeowners who have been through the process.[4]

Intermediation Revenue Model: the different methods by which third parties such as brokers (or "middlemen") can generate money.

Brokers: the people who organize transactions between buyers and sellers.

Licensing Revenue Model

The **Licensing Revenue Model** is a way of earning revenue by giving permission to other parties to use protected intellectual property (copyrights, patents, and trademarks) in exchange for fees. We will explore intellectual property in more detail in Chapter 15. Licensing frequently takes place in the technology

Licensing Revenue Model: a way of earning revenue by giving permission to other parties to use protected intellectual property (patents, copyrights, trademarks) in exchange for fees.

Music-streaming app Pandora which generates revenue from subscriptions, licensing, and on-screen advertising.
Credit: RICHARD B. LEVINE/ Newscom

Franchising Revenue Model: a type of revenue model whereby franchises are sold by an existing business to allow another party to trade under the name of that business.

industry where technological innovations are licensed to other users. For example, when we use our personal computers, they are under license from the developer of that software.

Licensing frequently takes place in the technology industry, where technological innovations are often sold to larger companies that have the financial and technical expertise to maximize their potential. Take apps, for instance. Many people design iPhone apps and then license them to Apple, which has the capability to market them to a wider audience. The most successful apps, such as music-streaming company Pandora, generate revenue not only from licensing but also from user subscriptions and from on-screen advertising.[5]

Franchising Revenue Model

The **Franchising Revenue Model** describes the process whereby an existing business allows another party to trade under the name of that business. In Chapter 1, we explained the concept of franchising and how it can be a beneficial way for entrepreneurs to get a head start in launching their own businesses. With a franchise, entrepreneurs do not have to spend the same amount of time on marketing, building the brand, developing processes and sourcing product. Chapter 1's *Case Study* highlights Dawn LaFreeda, a Denny's Restaurant franchisee in Texas. LaFreeda's personal enterprise, consisting of 75 Denny's restaurants, ranks among the largest single-owner franchisee portfolios in the world, earning close to $100 million in annual revenue.

While familiar franchises such as Anytime Fitness, Hampton Inns, Subway, and Supercuts regularly appear on lists of the top 500 franchises in the United States, some lesser-known (and somewhat quirky) franchises are also causing a bit of a stir. For example, there are 15 franchises in the Northwest and the Midwest dedicated to chasing away geese. Geese Police is a franchise that uses specially trained border collie dogs to chase Canada geese off the lawns at business properties, parks, and golf courses.

Robert Burck—The Naked Cowboy.
Credit: ©iStockphoto.com/ Onfokus

Or how about a franchise that involves standing in the street in just your underwear while strumming a guitar? The Naked Cowboy is franchised by the original naked cowboy, Robert Burck, who in 1997 began entertaining passers-by in New York's Times Square by simply donning a cowboy hat, underwear, and an artfully placed guitar. Burck made money from his quirky business through allowing strangers to take pictures with him in exchange for spare change, as well as officiating weddings and making appearances at events. Then he hit on the idea of franchising Naked Cowboy performance artists in other cities, who regularly entertain the public in major cities like Los Angeles and Nashville.[6]

Subscription Revenue Model

The **Subscription Revenue Model** involves charging customers to gain continuous access to a product or service. This type of model has been traditionally applied to magazines and newspapers where customers pay a subscription fee to receive each issue of the publication. Today, a growing number of startup companies also use the subscription revenue model. For example, Netflix earns revenue by providing subscribers with access to movies, Birchbox delivers monthly beauty products to subscribers, and Barkbox charges a subscription fee to deliver a monthly box of doggy treats to dog lovers. Another type of subscription model is applied to user communities such as Angie's List, where members pay for access to a network of reviews on local businesses.

Subscription Revenue Model: a type of model that involves charging customers to gain continuous access to a product or service.

Professional Revenue Model

The **Professional Revenue Model** provides professional services on a time and materials contract. For example, consultants, lawyers, and accountants often charge by the hour for their services. Websites like Get a Freelancer and Elance also use this model by allowing freelancers to charge a fixed fee for projects posted online by other companies.

Professional Revenue Model: professional services on a time and materials contract.

Utility and Usage Revenue Model

The **Utility and Usage Revenue Model** charges customers fees on the basis of how often goods or services are used. This is also known as a pay-as-you-go model. Some mobile phone carriers use this model by charging users a fee for the number of minutes used on calls, or for the volume of text messages.[7] The greater the number of minutes or volume of texts, the higher the payment. Hotels also use this model by charging customers by the night. Car rental companies also generate revenue through this model by charging per unit of time. For example, Avis and Hertz rent cars on a daily or weekly basis, while Zipcar rents cars by the hour, allowing multiple customers to use the same car at different times on the same day.[8]

Utility and Usage Revenue Model: a pay-as-you-go model that charges customers fees on the basis of how often goods or services are used.

Freemium Revenue Model

The **Freemium Revenue Model** involves mixing free (mainly web-based) basic services with premium or upgraded services. In this model, businesses create at least two versions or tiers of products or services. The company gives away the low-end version of the service for free. The free "basic" version usually comes with limits on usage and functionality. The company also creates and sells higher-end versions that offer more functionality and performance. The photo-sharing website Flickr, for example, gives everyone a free basic account that allows them to upload and share a limited numbers of images. For a small annual fee, users can pay for unlimited uploads and much bigger storage space. Similarly, the business networking site LinkedIn gives members free access to build a profile and maintain a professional network. It charges a fee for its premium service, which further benefits job seekers and recruiters with added functions such as search filtering, sending personalized messages, and tracking visits to one's profile.

Freemium Revenue Model: a type of revenue model whereby free (mainly web-based) basic services are mixed with premium or upgraded services.

Audio
Freemium

So far, we have explored the typical ways in which different businesses generate revenue through different types of revenue models. These are summarized in Table 10.1.

In the next section we take a closer look at how some companies have generated revenue by profiting from "free."

TABLE 10.1

Ten Types of Revenue Models

Unit Sales	The amount of revenue generated by the number of items (units) sold by a company.
Advertising	The amount of revenue gained through advertising products and services.
Data	The amount of revenue generated by selling high-quality, exclusive, valuable information to other parties.
Intermediation	The amount of revenue generated by third parties
Licensing	The amount of revenue generated by giving permission to other parties to use protected intellectual property (patents, copyrights, trademarks) in exchange for fees.
Franchising	The process whereby franchises are sold by an existing business to allow another party to trade under the name of that business.
Subscription	The amount of revenue generated by charging customers payment to gain continuous access to a product or service.
Professional	The amount of revenue generated by providing professional services on a time and materials contract.
Utility and Usage	The amount of revenue generated by charging customers fees on the basis of how often goods or services are used.
Freemium	The amount of revenue gained by mixing free (mainly web-based) basic services with premium or upgraded services.

10.3 GENERATING REVENUE FROM "FREE"

Web
From "Free" to Revenue

>> **LO 10.3**   **Explain how companies generate revenue by profiting from "free."**

Many of us like getting a bargain, but most of us love the idea of getting something for free. Yet as an entrepreneur running your own business, how comfortable would you feel giving away your products and services for nothing? Unlikely as it may sound, the freemium revenue model, which offers a product or service for zero cost, is becoming more popular as a means of encouraging widespread customer adoption (see Figure 10.2).[9]

Skype is an example of a freemium model that provides the functionality to make free calls, which are fully routed through the Internet. Because of its lack of infrastructure, the costs of running Skype are minimal. It earns its revenue by charging for Skypeout, a premium service that charges users low rates for calling landlines and cell phones. In 2011, Skype was acquired by Microsoft for $8.5 billion.

Free newspaper, *The Metro*. Britain's most popular newspaper.

Credit: Ton Koene/VWPics/Newscom

However, making "free" work financially is not without its risks. Obviously, if you are giving away something for nothing, you need to make sure you are still earning

Creating Revenue Models

Martin Shkreli, founder of Turing Pharmaceuticals.
Credit: AP Photo/Tom Williams

Pricing can be fraught with ethical ambiguities. Two disparate examples from the health industry can bring ethical decisions related to pricing sharply into focus.

Martin Shkreli, entrepreneur and founder of Turing Pharmaceuticals, caused huge controversy when he raised the price of one particular life-saving drug, which is used to treat parasitic infections such as toxoplasmosis and malaria. Although the manufacturing cost is about $1, Shkreli increased the price by 5,500%—from $13.50 to $750. The increased cost may be a severe hardship for people who need the drug, especially those from low-income and middle-class families, as well as taxpayers who cover pharmaceutical costs for Medicaid recipients using the drug. Martin Shkreli is estimated to have a personal net worth valued between $45 and $100 million.

Juxtapose Shkreli's approach to pricing with that of Elizabeth Holmes. After dropping out of Stanford University at age 19, Holmes founded the blood testing company Theranos and worked for 12 years to make blood test procedures widely available and inexpensive. Holmes's company makes cholesterol tests available for $2.99, less than the cost of a gourmet coffee. Theranos makes a basic test for HIV available for $15.40.

CRITICAL THINKING QUESTIONS

1. **Do you believe there should be an ethical boundary on the percent of profit a company should get? If so, who would decide on the boundary and how would it be enforced?**

2. **Should the ethical boundary on profit margins depend on the type of product or service?**

3. **Does the ethical boundary on profit margins depend on whether the company "earned" the profit?** ●

Sources

Jawaharlal, D. M. (2015, September 28). A tale of two CEOs: Elizabeth Holmes and Martin Shkreli. *HuffPost: Education.* Retrieved from http://www.huffingtonpost.com/dr-mariappan-jawaharlal/tale-of-two-ceos-elizabeth-holmes-martin-shkreli_b_8197094.html

MaRS Discovery District. (2009, December 6). *Revenue models, product pricing and commercializing new technology.* Retrieved from https://www.marsdd.com/mars-library/revenue-models-product-pricing-and-commercializing-new-technology/

substantial revenues. The key to a sustainable revenue model involving "free" is earning enough money on some part of the business to pay for the costs of supporting the free side of the business.

The free newspaper *Metro* is a great example of a free business model that gives away a free product yet still makes huge profits. The *Metro* was first circulated in Stockholm, Sweden, before being made available in dozens of cities all over the world. In Britain in particular, the *Metro* has become the nation's most profitable newspaper.[10] But how does the *Metro* team make money from giving away free newspapers?

First, its readership is aimed at wealthy commuters, on average around 37 years old (coined as "urbanites")—a demographic that attracts advertisers such as large supermarket chains and businesses that pay generously to reach this target audience. The *Metro* is also paid to feature major events such as Wimbledon Tennis and other

FIGURE 10.2

Freemium

Credit: ©iStockphoto.com/venimo

Video
Free Financial Models

annual occasions. Second, the *Metro* keeps its editorial costs low by keeping its content short, punchy, and easy to read—just engaging enough for a quick 20-minute read on the train or bus to or from work. Finally, it has developed its own distribution network by controlling news racks in train and bus stations where commuters can help themselves to the free publication.

Let's look at the two types of free financial models.

Direct Cross-Subsidies

Direct cross-subsidies: pricing a product or service above its market value to pay for the loss of giving away a product or service for free or below its market value.

Direct cross-subsidies refers to pricing a product or service above its market value to pay for the loss of giving away a product or service for free or below its market value. For example, cell phone companies lose money by giving away the phone handsets for free, but then cover the loss by charging monthly service fees.[11] Similarly, some airlines advertise amazingly low fares, but then add fees for amenities like checked bags, additional legroom, or the ability to choose one's seat. Hotels may offer a low nightly rate but then add a mandatory "resort fee"—even if the guest doesn't use any of the hotel's "resort" facilities.

Cross-subsidization attracts customers by eliminating, or reducing, the up-front cost of a product or service. It then makes up the loss with subsequent charges, which the company expects customers to be willing to pay because they are pleased with the product or service and don't want to go through the hassle of switching. The added business gained by attracting customers with the below-market price generates more revenues for the organization through the cross-subsidy fees. Table 10.2 lists several ways of implementing direct cross-subsidies.

Multiparty Markets

Multiparty business: a type of free model that involves giving one party product or service free, but charging the other party(s).

A **multiparty business** is a type of free model that involves giving a product or service to one party for free, but charging the other party or parties (see Table 10.3). The classic example of a multiparty market is the ad-supported free content model so

TABLE 10.2

Ideas for Direct Cross-Subsidies

- Give away services, sell products
- Give away products, sell services
- Give away software, sell hardware
- Give away hardware, sell software
- Give away cell phones, sell minutes of talk time
- Give away talk time, sell cell phones
- Give away the show, sell the drinks
- Give away the drinks, sell the show

common on the Internet: consumers get access to content for free while advertisers pay for access. Similarly, some online dating services allow women to enroll for free while men pay substantial charges to participate. Other examples include allowing job seekers to post résumés for free while charging employers for posting jobs, or giving children free admission while charging adults.

The challenge for the multiparty market model is to prevent costly overuse by those who get the service for free, as well as making the business valuable enough to the party that does pay.

Financially, the freemium model is often a viable option for web-based companies because of the low marginal cost of providing the service for free users: online storage and bandwidth are cheap. However, companies running freemium models need to be constantly focused on the average cost of running the service for free users, as well as the rates at which free users convert to paying users. If the costs of

TABLE 10.3

Ideas for Multiparty Markets

IDEA	EXAMPLE
Give away scientific articles, charge authors to publish them	Public Library of Science
Give away document readers, sell document writers	Adobe
Give away listings, sell premium search	Match.com
Sell listings, give away search	Craigslist New York Housing
Give away travel services, get a cut of rental car and hotel reservations	Travelocity
Give away house listings, sell mortgages	Zillow
Give away content, sell stuff	Slashdot/ThinkGeek
Give away résumé listings, charge for power search	LinkedIn

Source: Anderson, C. (2009). *Free: The future of a radical price.* New York, NY: Hyperion.

supporting free customers grows too high or the number of paying customers is too low, the freemium business model will not work. Table 10.4 gives examples of some freemium ideas.

TABLE 10.4

Freemium Ideas

IDEA	EXAMPLE
Give away basic information, sell richer information in easier-to-use form	BoxOfficeMojo
Give away federal tax software, sell state	TurboTax
Give away online games, charge a subscription to do more in a game	Club Penguin
Give away computer-to-computer calls, sell computer-to-computer calls	Skype
Give away free photo-sharing services, charge for additional storage space	Flickr

Source: Anderson, C. (2009). *Free: The future of a radical price.* New York, NY: Hyperion.

10.4 REVENUE AND COST DRIVERS[13]

>> **LO 10.4**   Identify the drivers that affect revenue as well as cost.

Now that we have explored the freemium model, let's take a look at how companies drive revenue. Revenue models influence who your customers are and how you reach them. While choosing and establishing your revenue model is an important step, it is equally important to have a deep understanding of what is driving both your revenue and your cost, in order to generate as much value (profit) as possible for your company.

YOU BE THE ENTREPRENEUR[12]

All entrepreneurs have to determine how they will earn revenue when starting their businesses. Many find their successful business ideas from experiences they've had, and then turn them into helpful tools for consumers. That's what CEO of Porch, Matt Ehrlichman, did when he founded his business that bridges the gap between customers and the right service job company for them. Ehrlichman was a confused customer who, like many, didn't know where to look for trustworthy home improvement companies.

Ehrlichman came up with his idea for Porch when he was trying to find a contractor for his own home renovations. After, its first successful year in business, Porch partnered with home improvement giant Lowes to develop a sales boosting system that links associated contractors with certain home improvement items.

Ehrlichman wanted to move the company to the next step by launching a database called "Porch Home & Neighborhood Report." This site would detail information about professionals' projects all across the country. The only hiccup was that the site would be free to users, so it would not generate revenue.

What Would You Do?

Revenue Drivers

It's tempting to believe that merely selling products or services will make you money, but more factors must be taken into consideration. Drawing from the information we have provided so far in this chapter, let's apply some key revenue drivers to the idea for a new funky coffee shop. The coffee shop provides unlimited coffee for free, but charges a per-minute flat fee for the amount of time your customers spend in the café.[14]

Video
Driving Revenue

As illustrated in Figure 10.3, the first key revenue driver is your *customers*. How many customers will come into your coffee shop? How much are they willing to pay to stay? How will you attract customers to your location?

The second key driver is *frequency*. How often will your customers come into your coffee shop? What incentives can you offer to keep them coming back?

The third driver is *selling process*. How much time will you be able to sell? What kind of upselling or cross-selling opportunities can you find? For example, you might add products such as snacks to sell alongside the unlimited free coffee to generate more revenue.

The fourth driver is *price*. If you think your price per minute should be higher than what your competitors charge, what are the factors that increase the value of your product? If you raise or lower prices, what will be the impact on your customer base?[15]

But how do you determine your revenue drivers when your business hasn't even begun yet? By getting out of the building! Actively testing your assumptions and hypotheses is the best way of figuring out the underlying factors that will drive revenue for your business.

For example, let's take a look at the first key revenue driver: your customers. You might be able to sketch a brief outline of the number of customers you think will come to your coffee shop, but how do you get a more accurate estimate? You may think that customers will be attracted to your coffee shop because it is unique and trendy, but no matter how great you think your coffee shop is, people won't come if it's in the wrong location. A coffee shop situated on the outskirts of town, with very

---

FIGURE 10.3

Four Key Revenue Drivers

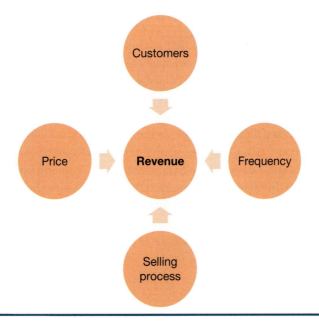

For more details about revenue drivers, see Appendix A: Financial Statements and Projections for Startups.

little around it, is not conducive to attracting foot traffic. Ideally, you want your coffee shop to be in a location with a high density of shoppers, which means city centers and shopping malls. If your target customer base is students, then you would want to be close to a university campus.

Renting a retail space in these shopping districts is expensive, so you need to be sure that enough people will be attracted to your coffee shop to walk in and pay to spend time there on a regular basis. How do you justify paying high rent before you even open for business?

One of the best ways to scout suitable locations for your coffee shop and determine the number of customers that might potentially buy from you is to go to your local shopping mall and watch customers as they go in and out of different coffee shops. Do this on different days, and at different times of day. Record the busy and slow periods. This will give you a better idea of the volume of customers you might expect to walk into your coffee shop and therefore the revenue you can expect to get. This in turn will allow you to determine whether the volume of traffic will justify the expense of the high rent you will need to pay for an advantageous location.

Cost Drivers

Understanding the factors that drive costs are just as important as your key revenue drivers.

In order to teach others how to run their own food tour businesses, Shane Kost identified the main startup costs, which include the cost of creating and launching the company website, legal fees, and research and development. His detailed and transparent costings are among the attributes that attracted customers to Food Tour Pros, enabling Kost to help launch food tours in over 100 cities across the world in over 20 countries.

When it comes to cost drivers, two different types of costs should be taken into consideration: **cost of goods sold (COGS)** and operating expenses. While both COGS and operating expenses are both types of expenses, there are some differences between them.

Cost of goods sold (COGS): the value of goods sold when a sale takes place.

Cost of goods sold (COGS)

COGS occur when a sale takes place. For example, with regard to a T-shirt store, the cost is in how much money it takes to produce each T-shirt: the material, the design, the manufacturing, the packaging, and so on. Once you know how much goes into producing your T-shirts, you can think about ways to reduce costs if you need to. For example, you might find a lower-cost manufacturer, or use less expensive material, or even negotiate with young artists to see if they can provide their designs at a lower cost. Lowering the COGS means you could potentially sell your T-shirts at a lower price to your customers.

However, there also needs to be a balance between reducing your costs and satisfying your customer. In other words, you would need to ensure that you are not devaluing your product to the extent that it would reduce your customers' willingness to buy it at all. For example, if your customers are attracted to your T-shirts because of their great quality, then it would be unwise to use cheaper material to save costs. If you can get the balance right, you can use the savings you make to invest in other areas such as marketing, or reducing debt.

Operating Expenses: the costs of running your business, including your rent, utilities, administration, marketing/advertising, employee salaries, and so on.

Operating expenses

Operating expenses are the costs of running your business, including your rent, utilities, administration, marketing/advertising, employee salaries, and so forth

FIGURE 10.4

Retail Operating Expenses

Operating Expenses	
• Rent	• Insurance
• Utilities	• Transportation
• Administration	• Taxes
• Marketing/Advertising	• Legal Fees
• Salaries	• Office Supplies
• Accounting	• Benefits

(see Figure 10.4). These kinds of expenses are more difficult to reduce. Cutting operating expenses can yield beneficial short-term gains, but it generally doesn't work in the long term—for reasons we explore next.

Imagine that you have a retail store and wish to cut operating expenses. If you move your store to a cheaper but less popular location to save on rent, you will save more money. However, over time you might lose out on revenue because the new location might not attract as many customers—or the right kind of customers—compared to the more expensive location. Similarly, you will save costs if you cut out advertising and marketing expenses; but as sales depend on marketing, in the long term, you will lose customer awareness. When people don't know about your store, or start forgetting about it, your sales will suffer.

Another way to decrease operating costs is to reduce employee salaries or reduce the number of employees altogether, which has an immediate positive effect on the bottom line. However, it also might damage customer relationships if there isn't enough skilled, knowledgeable staff to help drive sales. For example, Shane Kost of Chicago Food Planet Food Tours credits his excellent employees with creating quality, which not only makes his company a great place to work but also keeps his tour customers coming back—and referring their friends.

Striking the right balance in the areas of COGS and operating expenses can be tricky, but if you know your business inside out, it becomes more manageable over time. Covering your expenses depends on sales of your product and service, and successful sales require a carefully constructed pricing strategy.

Income Statement

When your company is finally up and running, you will need some financial tools to help you measure the revenue generated and your company's profitability. The **income statement** (or **profit and loss statement**) is a financial report that measures the financial performance of your business on a monthly or annual basis. It subtracts the COGS and expenses (administrative, marketing, research, and other operating expenses) from the total revenue to give you a net income figure, which will be either a profit or a loss. (Other useful financial reports include the balance sheet and the cash flow statement, both of which can be viewed in Appendix A: Financial Statements and Projections for Startups.

The income statement also reflects depreciation and amortization of your company's assets. Depreciation really means the cost of wear and tear of your physical assets such as machinery, equipment, and the building in which you operate.

Income statement (or profit and loss statement): a financial report that measures the financial performance of your business on a monthly or annual basis.

FIGURE 10.5

Sample Income Statement

Revenue	$200,000
(-) Cost of Goods	$100,000
Gross Profit	$100,000
(-) Sales, General & Administrative	$50,000
(-) Marketing	$5,000
(-) Research & Development	$2,000
(-) Depreciation & Amortization	$2,000
Operating Profit	$41,000
(-) Interest Expense	$1,230
(-) Taxes	$8,500
Net Income	$31,270

When you purchase an asset that has a useful life of more than one year, you will not include the entire cost of that asset on the income statement in the year that it is purchased. Instead, you are able to spread the cost of that asset over a predetermined period of time; therefore, you record only a portion of the cost each year until the asset is fully depreciated. Amortization works similarly to depreciation; the main difference is that amortization relates to intangible assets such as patents, trademarks, copyrights, and business methodologies. Amortization matches the useful life of an intangible asset with the revenue it generates. Sample income statements are illustrated in Figure 10.5.

The operating profit represents the amount left over from revenue once all costs and expenses are subtracted. The interest expense is a good indicator of the company's debt, as it represents interest due in the period on any borrowed money. Taxes are the last expense item before net income. This line item includes all federal, state and municipal taxes (if any) that are due for the period.

Net income is what is left after all costs, expenses, and taxes have been paid; it shows the company's real bottom line. Over time, you can begin to compare your company's income statements; this helps you chart trends in your company's financial performance. The trends will, in turn, help you to set future financial goals and strategies.

10.5 PRICING STRATEGIES

Video
Pricing

» LO 10.5   **Identify different strategies entrepreneurs use when pricing their product and service.**

Startup entrepreneurs often struggle with how much to charge for their products or services. If your price is too high, you might drive customers away, but if your price is too low, then you run the risk of making very little profit. So, where do you begin?[18]

Let's say you want to start an online luxury cupcake business. You plan to make the cupcakes from fresh, natural, organic ingredients, at home with some part-time help from a friend. A courier service will deliver the beautifully packaged and

From Freemium to Premium

Over the past decade, the freemium business model has become more popular among startups and iOS apps, yet despite its popularity, many startups have failed to make it work. This is largely because the dynamics of freemium pricing are poorly understood, making it more difficult for entrepreneurs to optimize a company's revenue through providing products and services for free.[16] In other words, it is not that easy to convert customers from freemium to premium.

Harvard Business Professors Vineet Kumar, Clarence Lee, and Sunil Gupta carried out a study in an effort to better understand the dynamics of freemium by focusing on customer behavior. On the basis of the study, the researchers provide several key recommendations that can aid companies making decisions about the pricing and design of freemium products. These include:

- if free products are not attracting enough new customers, then the features need to be improved;

- when lots of new users sign up for free products, but not many upgrade to premium, then the free products are too fruitful and need to be scaled back;

- when customers don't understand why they should upgrade to premium, they are less likely to convert; and

- when the rewards given to existing users for referring new users are too generous, then they may discourage multiple referrals.

The study also raised some interesting questions around conversion rates, specifically that a very high conversion rate may not be such a good thing. When a conversion rate is too high, it suggests that the free product may not be very good, and this can impede the amount of traffic, especially when it comes to free trials for new products. Furthermore, companies that introduce new features see a rise in conversion rates; for example, the video streaming service Hulu experiences a boost in conversion rates when it introduces a new show in its premium, rather than free, version. Finally, early adopters (people who sign up for the product as soon as it becomes available) are generally less price sensitive than later adopters and tend to convert much more quickly.

While the study raises some interesting questions, the results are by no means conclusive. Further research has been planned to assess the reasons why users convert from freemium to premium.[17]

CRITICAL THINKING QUESTIONS

1. **What do you see as the benefits and disadvantages to the freemium business model?**

2. **What considerations would you take into account when designing your freemium model strategy?**

3. **How would you encourage your user to convert from freemium to premium?** ●

---

personalized cupcakes up to a distance of 200 miles from your location. Your cupcake business is designed to target events such as weddings, children's parties, and corporate gatherings. If the business takes off, you aim to open a retail space in your local area and hire a couple of employees to help you run the business.

To find out how much to charge, you need to find out the going rate of cupcakes. The best place to begin is to check out your competition. Visit cupcake stores and other online cupcake companies and see how much they charge. Don't be afraid to ask people in the cupcake business direct questions about pricing and running a cupcake business; most people want to help and will be happy to give advice. Besides, making connections in this way may lead to partnerships or collaborations in the future.

In addition, talk to your friends and family to see how much they would pay, or have paid for cupcakes in the past, and ask them to share their experiences of online cupcake companies if they have used them before. You could even send out a survey to all your contacts asking them what price they would be willing to pay for a single delicious cupcake or box of premium cupcakes.

Gigi Butler built America's most successful cupcake business with 93 outlets operating in 23 states

Credit: ZUMA Press Inc/Alamy Stock Photo

The next step is to think about your customers. What can they afford to pay? For example, you may decide to charge a higher rate for catering corporate events versus providing cupcakes for children's parties.

The key to sustaining a new business is to create consistent revenue streams. Once you have acquired new customers, your goal is to hear from them again and again. For events like weddings and children's parties, this may be difficult as they are typically one-time events. However, these customers may tell their friends how pleased they were with your service, and guests at the events may be impressed with how delicious and beautifully decorated your cupcakes were. Thus, you will rely largely on referrals and word of mouth to get more business in those areas. For corporate events, on the other hand, there are ample opportunities for repeat business. You could approach a corporations and offer a contract agreeing to provide cupcakes for all their corporate events, or a certain number of events per year. This would bring you a steady stream of revenue from a regular client.

In addition, it is helpful to compare yourself to others in the field. Do you have the right credentials to run an online cupcake business? What experience do you have in the bakery business? What sort of business experience do you have to operate as an online cupcake company? If you have less experience than others, then you might want to consider charging lower prices to win new clients and gain real experience. However, if you have a background in bakery and catering, already have a solid customer base, and have business qualifications to match, then you could feasibly charge higher rates.

Once you have a better idea of your competition, your target market, and how your qualifications measure up against others, it is time to plan your pricing strategy.

Pricing Products and Services

There is no right way to determine your pricing strategy, nor is there any such thing as long-term fixed pricing. As your business evolves, your prices will adjust according to demand. The best way to set a price is to base it on the information you have already gathered.

Several factors might influence your pricing strategy. For example, the positioning and brand of your product or service will affect how much it sells for. Understanding your brand is also very important when defining your business. Start defining your brand by choosing a name, logo, and design for your website. A useful exercise is to think of three to five words to describe your business that sets it apart from other competitors; for example, if very few competitors offer home delivery, you could include this in your brand description: "Luxury cupcakes delivered at home." Once you have defined your brand, you can carry the theme through your packaging, website, marketing materials and other communications with potential customers.[19]

Using the cupcake example, think about how you are positioning your online cupcake business in the market. As you are promoting your cupcakes as a luxury product, you need to aim for a price that isn't too low. A low price on a luxury product can cause customers to doubt the quality of the item being sold.

Different Types of Pricing Strategies[20]

There are many different pricing strategies used by different companies. Let's take a look at some common pricing strategies (see Figure 10.6).

Competition-led pricing

In **competition-led pricing,** prices are guided by other businesses selling the same or very similar products and services. For example, for products that match those of your competitors, you can copy your competitors' pricing for your own product. However, matching a price is not generally enough to encourage customers to buy from you, especially if you're not an established brand. You need to find other ways to differentiate your product from your competitors', in order to attract more customers.

Competition-led pricing: a type of pricing strategy when prices are guided by other businesses selling the same or very similar products and services.

Customer-led pricing

In **customer-led pricing,** you ask customers how much they are willing to pay, and then offer it at that price. This is a technique used by some airlines signed up to the commercial website Priceline to offer passengers a chance to name their own price for flights. Passengers make bids—however, they don't ultimately control the fares; the airline accepts or rejects each bid depending on how acceptable it is and whether other customers are willing to pay more for the same flight. This "name your own price technique" is a useful way of attracting people to your company, and it still allows you a measure of control over your own pricing.

Customer-led pricing: a type of pricing strategy when you ask customers how much they are willing to pay, and then offer it at that price.

Loss leader

A **loss leader** is the practice of offering a product or service at a below-cost price in an attempt to attract more customers. This involves giving special discounts and reducing prices. Loss leaders can be an effective way of competing with an established brand offering similar products and services.

Loss leader: a pricing method whereby a business offers a product or service at a lower price in an attempt to attract more customers.

This approach is often used by retail stores. Discounted goods or "sales" attract more people to the store, and help shift merchandise. When applied by retailers, loss leader pricing strategy also tempts the customers to look at the goods that are not on sale. For example, Walmart attracts customers by selling low-price DVDs.[21] The "loss" made on the discounted goods is made up by customers purchasing the non-discounted merchandise.

However, there has be some kind of consistency to raising and lowering prices; for example, a customer who has just bought a product at full price the previous day will not be pleased if that same product is being sold at a deep discount the next day. Therefore, it is important to know how long the lower price can be sustained, and to know when to readjust pricing before the business begins to lose money.

Loss leaders like discounted goods entice customers to stores and encourage them to look at nonsale goods.
Credit: B.O'Kane/Alamy Stock Photo

FIGURE 10.6

Pricing Strategies

Source: www.learnmarketing.net

Introductory offer

Introductory offer:
a pricing method to
encourage people to try
a new product by offering
it for free or at a heavily
discounted price.

The idea of the **introductory offer** is to encourage people to try your new product by offering it for free or at a heavily discounted price for a certain number of days, or for the first 100 customers. Introductory pricing is generally used for new products or services on the market. For example, in the UK, Uber offers new customers a free ride worth £10 ($14.98), simply for signing up online with the car-sharing service.[22]

Skimming

Skimming: a form of high
pricing method, generally
used for new products or
service that face very little,
or even no competition.

Skimming is a form of high pricing, generally used for new products or services that face very little or even no competition. If your product is the first on the market, then you can sell it at a higher price and retain the maximum value upfront, until you are forced to gradually reduce your prices when competitors launch rival products. Innovative products like the iPad and Sony PlayStation 3, which were originally priced high when they were launched, are good examples of price skimming.[23]

Psychological pricing

Psychological pricing: a
pricing method intended to
encourage customers to buy
on the basis of their belief
that the product or service is
cheaper than it really is.

Customers' perceptions of price points are also important to the sale. **Psychological pricing** is intended to encourage customers to buy based on their belief that the product or service is cheaper than it really is. Flash sales, "buy one get one free," and bundled products are all methods of psychological pricing. In addition, specific prices such as those ending in $0.99 are popular with customers, as $19.99 is a more appealing figure to most than $20. Odd though it may sound, pricing your product or service one cent lower can make a difference between selling and not selling.

Fair pricing

Fair pricing: the degree to
which both businesses and
customers believe that the
pricing is reasonable.

Fair pricing is the degree to which both businesses and customers believe that the pricing is reasonable. Having done your financial homework as an entrepreneur, you might think your product or service is priced fairly—but that doesn't mean your customers will. Regardless of how much benefit to the customer or how valuable you think your offering is, there are some customers who are simply unwilling to pay the asking price for items or services that they do not perceive as being fair. This is where market testing can help to define the perception between what people perceive as a fair maximum price, versus an unfair price.

Bundled pricing

A form of psychological pricing, **bundled pricing** is packaging a set of goods or services together; they are then sold for a lower price than if they were to be sold separately (see Figure 10.7). The customers feel they are getting a bargain, and the increased sales generate more profit for the company. Common examples of bundled pricing include fast-food value meals, *prix fixe* meals at restaurants, cell phone packages, and cable TV packages.

Once you have decided on which type of pricing is the right one for your business, then it's time to start making some proper calculations.

Bundled pricing: a type of pricing strategy whereby companies package a set of goods or services together and then sell them for a lower price than if they were to be sold separately.

FIGURE 10.7

Bundled Pricing

Credit: ©iStockphoto.com/Epine_art

10.6 CALCULATING PRICES[24]

>> **LO 10.6**   **Explain different methods of calculating price.**

Number crunching is not an exact science, but there are a few ways to calculate prices that will help you decide which one is best for your business. The key to pricing is to ensure you make a profit, as well as to create value for your customers.

Is Value the Same Thing as Price?

Product	What do I pay, or what would I pay?	Actual price found online (or price range)	Price difference
Extra whitening toothpaste with mouthwash in the paste (average size tube)			
Artisan, wood-fired pizza with local ingredients (large)			
100% electric car, 4 door			
Bath soap (1 bar)			

Using the chart on this page, identify what you think you pay, or would pay, for the listed items. Then, look up the actual price on the Internet.

CRITICAL THINKING QUESTIONS

1. **What are the differences between your pricing estimates and the actual pricing? What do you believe is the source of the differences?**

2. **As a consumer, do you care more about the price of certain items than others? What influences your level of concern about price?**

3. **In this exercise, did you learn anything that surprised you?** ●

Cost-Led Pricing

Cost-led pricing: a type of pricing strategy that involves calculating all the costs involved in manufacturing or delivering the product or service, plus all other expenses, and adding an expected profit or margin by predicting your sales volume to get the approximate price.

Cost-led pricing involves calculating all the costs involved in manufacturing or delivering the product or service, plus all other expenses, and adding an expected profit or margin by predicting your sales volume to get the approximate price.

For example, say it costs you a total of $2 to make a cupcake. To cover your costs, you could add a 50% markup, which would mean selling each cupcake at $3, resulting in a profit of $1 per cupcake. However, you would need to make sure that this price was competitive—too low and it will put people off by giving an impression of poor quality; too high and you may be pricing your cupcakes out of the market. You also need to ensure that you will have enough people buying the cupcakes to generate profit for your business.

Target-Return Pricing

Target-return pricing: a pricing method whereby the price is based on the amount of investment you have put into your business.

Target-return pricing involves setting your price based on the amount of investment you have put into your business. Using the cupcake business example again, you can save significant costs by working from home, but you still have expenses from investing in machinery, ingredients, paying a part-time worker, and utility and delivery costs.

Let's assume you have invested $3,000 in startup costs for your business. Your expected sales volume is 10,000 cupcakes per year. This means you need to cover your $3,000 investment from your cupcake sales as well as generate a profit. If your cupcakes sell for $3 each, that means 10,000 cupcakes sold per year will generate $30,000 in gross profit (profit before operating expenses).

However, remember that your cupcakes cost you $2 to produce, which amounts to $20,000 in production costs, leaving you with $10,000. Take away the $3,000 you have invested in the company, and you make a profit of $7,000. This means you make 70 cents profit on each $3 cupcake.

Value-Based Pricing

Value-based pricing involves pricing your product based on how it benefits the customer. Your buyers have a major influence over your pricing strategy. Think about what your product means to your buyers. Is it going to save them money, or make them money? Let's say you have created a water softener suitable for homeowners to install. Because hard water is full of minerals that build up in the water lines, forcing appliances to work harder, your water softener guarantees the customer a significant saving in energy bills. On this basis, you could build in a higher price because you can assure your customers that they will make back that money within, say, two years of purchasing your water softener.

But what if there is no monetary benefit to your buyers? Certainly your cupcake business will not help your customers save or make money, yet there is still a value in pleasure. What is it about your cupcakes in particular that could appeal to customers? You may price your cupcakes the same as your competitors in the beginning, but what makes them different enough for customers to pay more? Value-based pricing would reflect whatever added value your customers perceive in your cupcakes.

You could also think about different ways of generating additional revenue: selling cupcake mix, decorations, and other accessories might be ways of bringing in extra money.

In addition to the factors associated with the various pricing calculations described so far, there are two more factors your pricing calculation needs to take into consideration: your livelihood and your mistakes. For example, are you taking a salary for yourself, or do you intend to live off the profit and use any additional income to re-invest in the company? Your price also has to cover the costs of any mistakes. Say your sales volume predictions are off. You might not sell 10,000 cupcakes in a year. How much leeway have you built in to your pricing to cover the costs of inaccurate estimates and other errors? Typically, you need to account for being off by a factor of two or more and still be profitable—that is, if you plan to sell 10,000 cupcakes, you need to be able to make a profit even if you end up selling only half that many, or 5,000 cupcakes. ●

Value-based pricing: a pricing method that involves pricing a product based on how it benefits the customer.

Video
Value and Pricing

Get the edge on your studies at **edge.sagepub.com/neckentrepreneurship**

▸ Master the learning objectives using key study tools
▸ Watch, listen, and connect with online multimedia resources
▸ Access mobile-friendly quizzes and flashcards to check your understanding

$SAGE edge™

SUMMARY

10.1 Define a revenue model and distinguish it from the business model.

The revenue model specifies exactly how income and earnings will be generated from the value proposition, whereas the business model is the framework established to create value for the consumer while preserving some of that value for the entrepreneur.

10.2 Illustrate the ten most popular revenue models being used by entrepreneurs.

There are many effective revenue models. Commonly employed models include unit sales revenue model, advertising revenue model, data revenue model, intermediation revenue model, licensing revenue model, franchising revenue model, subscription revenue model, professional revenue model, utility and usage revenue model, and freemium revenue model.

10.3 Explain how companies generate revenue by profiting from "free."

The freemium concept has exploded in popularity in recent times. Many companies are finding that small, experience-amplifying transactions can be profitable after introducing consumers to a limited version of their product or service for free.

10.4 Identify the drivers that affect revenue as well as cost.

Revenue drivers include the customer, purchase frequency, selling process, and price.

10.5 Identify different strategies entrepreneurs use when pricing their product and service.

Pricing is critical for a product or service. Some common pricing strategies include competition-led pricing, customer-led pricing, loss leader, introductory offer, skimming, psychological pricing, fair pricing, and bundled pricing.

10.6 Explain different methods of calculating price.

There are several methods to help you calculate the best price for your product or service, such as cost-led pricing, target-return pricing, and value-based pricing.

KEY TERMS

CASE STUDY

Oprah Winfrey, Media Magnate

Virtually everyone knows *who* Oprah Winfrey is. Her fame is a result of her wildly popular television talk show, the *Oprah Winfrey Show*, which ran for 25 years between 1986 and 2011. What some people don't know is that Winfrey was born into extreme poverty in rural Mississippi at a time in history (1954) when prejudice and segregation were still the predominating culture—if not the law of the land—in the South.

Oprah's mother was an unmarried teenager at the time of Winfrey's birth. At age six, Oprah moved to Milwaukee, Wisconsin, where things got even worse as Oprah faced sexual abuse from multiple offenders. At age 13, she ran away from home. At age 14, she became pregnant and gave birth to a son who died shortly after he was born.

In high school, Oprah moved to Nashville, Tennessee, to live with her stepdad. Life in Nashville led to a better life for Winfrey. She was popular among her peers and began successfully developing her talents as a communicator. Her prep efforts and achievements earned her a full-tuition scholarship to Tennessee State University, where she majored in communication. She also won first place in a Black beauty pageant and began her career in journalism as a part-time radio host.

Her journalism career led to television work in Chicago in the mid-1980s, where she went from worst to first in the ratings. Bolstered by her Academy Award–nominated performance in her movie debut (*The Color Purple* in 1985), she eclipsed the highly rated *Phil Donahue Show* and in 1986 got the opportunity to launch her own talk show. *The Oprah Winfrey Show* was televised uninterrupted for a quarter of a century, consistently earning stellar ratings.

During her unprecedented run of television talk show success, Winfrey conducted some of the highest-profile and most-watched interviews in television history. Her guests included world leaders, business tycoons, entertainment stars, as well as ordinary people with extraordinary talents, skills, or stories. Her promotion of relatively obscure experts and authors often catapulted those same writers and professionals into visible, successful, and lucrative careers of their own. This was particularly true of new authors, who gained massive exposure for their books through Oprah's Book Club—a series of discussions about new books that ran on her show for many years. For example, Dr. Phil—who has since become a household name—can trace his rise to stardom back to Oprah's stage.

As her name recognition grew, she became increasingly philanthropic and entrepreneurially minded. As a philanthropist, she has donated hundreds of millions of dollars to educational causes. Among her many educational gifts are hundreds of scholarships for students to attend Morehouse College, a historically African American school in Atlanta, Georgia. She contributed $12 million to the Smithsonian Institution's National Museum of African American History and Culture, whose grand opening was slated for 2016. She also founded the Oprah Winfrey Leadership Academy for Girls, an all-girls boarding school in South Africa dedicated to providing girls from disadvantaged backgrounds with the opportunity to become educated servant leaders.

A multitalented woman, Winfrey has also coauthored several best-selling books and acted in highly acclaimed television specials, miniseries, and films. As an entrepreneur, she launched her own radio station on Sirius XM radio, created her own magazine—*O, The Oprah Magazine*—and sponsors her own website, Oprah.com. She was the first African American woman to earn the rarified financial status of billionaire, a title held by fewer than 2,000 people around the globe, and by fewer than 200 women worldwide.

Oprah Winfrey's influence on contemporary society has been incalculable, and nearly unprecedented. New words and/or phrases have been coined in her honor. For example, the *Wall Street Journal* coined the term "Oprahfication" to refer to the therapeutic benefits that may arise from making a personal confession in public, as her guests would often do on her show. The "Oprah Effect" is another term created in her honor; it refers to her power to influence just about anything she endorses or draws attention to. Her life story epitomizes what it means to embrace and realize the American Dream.

Critical Thinking Questions

1. What revenue models did Oprah Winfrey utilize to make her fortune?

2. How do (or how might) Winfrey utilize a "Freemium Model" to further expand her posttalk show business empire?

3. Oprah Winfrey is an entrepreneurial outlier. Statistically speaking, very few people will ever rise to such heights of affluence and influence as she has. Nevertheless, what are some positive lessons that *every* entrepreneur can learn from the examples of such an extraordinary woman?

Sources
Davis, D. (2011). *The Oprah Winfrey Show: Reflections on an American legacy*. New York, NY: Abrams.
Kelley, K. (2011). *Oprah: A Biography*. New York, NY: Three Rivers Press.
Vergotte, M. (2013). *Oprah Winfrey: 100 Fascinating facts, stories, & inspiring quotes*. People With Impact Series. iFame Group.
Watson, G. (2014). *The inspirational life story of Oprah Winfrey: From the little speaker to the Queen of Talk*. Inspirational Life Stories by Gregory Watson Series.
Weston, R. (2012). *Oprah Winfrey: A biography of a billionaire talk show host*. African American Icons Series. Berkeley Heights, NJ: Enslow.

11 Learning From Failure

Nine out of ten businesses fail; so I came up with a foolproof plan—create ten businesses."[1]

—Robert Kiyosaki, American author and businessman

Learning Objectives

11.1 Describe failure and its effect on entrepreneurs.

11.2 Identify several reasons for failure.

11.3 Describe the consequences of fear of failure for entrepreneurs.

11.4 Explain the different ways entrepreneurs can learn from failure.

11.5 Describe the significance of "grit" and its role in building tolerance for failure.

Chapter Outline

11.1 Failure and Entrepreneurship

11.2 The Failure Spectrum

11.3 Fear of Failure

11.4 Learning From Failure

11.5 Getting Gritty: Building a Tolerance for Failure

11.1 FAILURE AND ENTREPRENEURSHIP

>> LO 11.1   Describe failure and its effect on entrepreneurs.

In Chapter 2, we explained the ill-defined, unstructured, unpredictable, chaotic, and complex nature of entrepreneurship. We also presented some daunting statistics showing that not all attempts to grow a business will be successful, especially when many of the attempts end in bankruptcy. The reality is that many startups fail; therefore, it is important to include the topic of failure when discussing entrepreneurship.

A business failure is generally conceived as the termination of a commercial organization that has missed its goals and failed to achieve investors' expectations, preventing the venture from continuing to operate and resulting in bankruptcy or liquidation. Failure can intensify the cognitive processes involved in learning, resulting in improvements in future performance and increasing the probability for future success. For this reason, many see failure as a journey and the path by which individuals travel to develop into entrepreneurs. Having learned from failure, entrepreneurs often feel more confident, prepared, and motivated to attempt another startup venture.

Despite these perceived benefits, the failure of a venture can be not only financially costly but also emotionally painful, even traumatic. It can be experienced as the end of an intimate relationship, resulting in feelings of grief and loss, leaving the entrepreneur's self-efficacy and inclination for risk-taking in tatters.

Big failures (or "epic fails") in business are the ones we hear about the most. Bankruptcy or forced sale is probably the biggest failure for a startup. Social network Friendster is a good example of an epic fail.[2] Founded by Jonathan Abrams in 2002 (the year before MySpace and two years before Facebook), Friendster is often credited with kicking off the era of social networks. Just a year after it was launched, Google offered Abrams $30 million to buy the company, but Abrams turned down the offer. Not long afterwards Abrams was pushed out as CEO by the board of directors because of his lack of experience in running a company. A few years later, Friendster collapsed due to technical glitches and failure to keep up with the competition as its users moved on to MySpace and Facebook. Friendster was eventually acquired by one of Asia's biggest internet companies, MOL Global, and went on to operate as a social gaming site.

Video
The Reality of Failure

Tom Hatten, Founder and CEO, Mountainside Fitness

Tom Hatten, founder and CEO of Mountainside Fitness

Credit: Used with permission from Tom Hatten

Tom Hatten was 22 when he first launched Mountainside Fitness in Ahwatukee, Arizona, over 25 years ago. Since then, Mountainside Fitness has grown from a single strip mall entity to the largest locally owned fitness chain in the state, with 13 fitness centers (and more in the works), over 1,000 employees, and 60,000 active members.

Yet success has not come easy. Hatten learned his first hard lesson when he was still in his mid-twenties. With a great location and concept, Mountainside had gotten off to a promising start, but a competitor had moved in, offering lower fees, which Hatten could not afford to match. "At one point we had 15 days left of money to make the last payroll," he recalls. "I had to lock myself in and figure out how to keep my current members, bring in new ones, and get back those who had left." After a great deal of thought, number-crunching and hand-wringing, "I got on the phone, called 1,000 current, former, and prospective members, and offered memberships that were $3 *higher* than my currently advertised rates." The hook was to introduce a loyalty program: The longer a member stayed on, the more his or her fees dropped, eventually shrinking to $24 per person, which was well below the competition. "Not only did we avoid going under, we were making money by the end of the year. . . . Failure wasn't there yet," says Hatten, "but it was coming fast."

Ten years later, Hatten found himself staring down disaster yet again. "We were growing faster than my reserves would allow. I had several clubs under construction, and I was going to run out of [operating] money, because I didn't have a plan in place for growth." He came away with a new resolution: never to grow without planning first, no matter the momentum, or temptation. "Growing too fast and not staying focused caused setbacks. Today plans must be in place and measurable. Those and only those dictate tomorrow—not emotions."

By 2008, business was going so well it was time to grow again—this time, with a solid plan. Between Arizona and Colorado, five Mountainside Fitness clubs were under construction, to the tune of $35 million total. That's when "my CFO called; she said that our bank had frozen or cancelled the forward commitments to pay for all the equipment. I was on my cell phone, watching them unload it from the truck." The greatest American financial crash since the Great Depression was under way, and though his credit was excellent, banks nationwide were panicking. It wasn't long before Hatten's other lines of credit were yanked out from under him.

"The actual clubs were doing quite well, but my operation simply couldn't withstand $11 million credit cut," says Hatten. He was forced to declare bankruptcy for Mountainside, and because all of his business loans were personally backed, he had to file for personal bankruptcy as well. "I thought to myself, 'If I'm going to file bankruptcy—I've got to leverage it into something good, so how do I do it? We knew values of all the buildings were shooting down. The banks were taking a huge hit too. I basically said to them, 'just because I'm going down, and everyone's going down, I don't want to lose you, but if you don't negotiate with me, that's what's going to happen [because I can't pay on these current terms.]'." With deals in place with his main banking institutions, "they held my hand as I went to everyone—the vendors, the landlords—to reset everything. With the landlords, instead of paying 18 bucks a square foot, I renegotiated to 8. Then we walked, sometimes hand-in-hand too, to *their* bank to renegotiate *their* terms." At one point in 2012, the Mountainside Fitness parent operation was valued at 0; and Hatten, too, had 0 in the bank, with $1.5 million due in attorney fees. One partner disappeared, while the other committed suicide. Tom was left with all ownership, the debt, the responsibility.

Then *he* was offered an out. "One of my massive competitors approached me—and I knew at this point, I was going to file for personal bankruptcy, though no one else knew—and they wanted me out of Arizona," Hatten recalls. "They gave me an offer that was so lucrative, neither I nor my kid would ever have to work again. I knew the value of my business at the time was 0; this was 90 days before filing for bankruptcy. But I turned them down. I had started with $2,000 and a dream. And I wasn't done. I needed to get us through it. I felt like I would be quitting, and I didn't do this to be a millionaire." He salvaged what he could of the situation (and his pride) by taking charge of what he could.

Hatten is a millionaire today, and still at the helm of Mountainside Fitness, which despite its struggles remains the largest and most successful fitness franchise in the state. Though Hatten's experiences may be somewhat extreme, they offer a lesson in what is possible when one faces adversity with humility, perseverance, and a willingness to learn and to grow. "Don't be afraid of the unknown," he says; "embrace the reality of . . . how much is possible to overcome if you're passionate about what you're doing. If you're willing to work very hard and be patient for success and never ever give up, it will happen!"

CRITICAL THINKING QUESTIONS

1. Tom Hatten turned down a lucrative offer from a competitor, even though his business had

failed and he was facing bankruptcy. Do you think he made the right choice? Why or why not?

2. What positive or constructive lessons can you derive from Hatten's story?

3. Imagine one or more failure scenarios for a business of your own. How do you think you would respond to the threat of failure? ●

Source: Personal interview, T. Hatten, July 2, 2015.

While technical glitches and failure to keep up with the competition were the main causes of Friendster's downfall, we can usually find many reasons behind the closure of a startup. Contributing factors often include lack of market need, poor marketing, and loss of focus. Figure 11.1 lists the most common reasons behind the failure of startups.

It is also useful to hear how entrepreneurs themselves articulate the underlying reasons as to why their startups failed. Table 11.1 provides examples of entrepreneurs who attribute their failures to three main causes: their psyche, inaction, and hiring issues.

However, there is an important difference between the epic fail and small failures.

No one wants or even expects catastrophic failure such as bankruptcy, but all entrepreneurs experience countless small "fails" that require a quick reaction and sometimes a change in direction, often known as the **pivot**. A small fail is an event—an obstacle to overcome to get through the other side—whereas a big fail like the collapse of a business is a process that unfolds over time; it is more personal and can be more difficult to recover from.

The most successful entrepreneurs embrace and leverage failure and pivot when they need to—a key component of The Practice of Entrepreneurship that we presented in Chapter 2 and have built on throughout this book. Recall from Chapter 2 that Barbara Baekgaard and Pat Miller, the founders of the luggage design firm Vera Bradley, did not view ordering the wrong size zippers as a failure but rather as an opportunity to design a new bag that would work with the larger zipper. This is a good example of how failures can be opportunities to build on what you learn. By following the eight components of The Practice of Entrepreneurship, you are more likely to embrace setbacks rather than allowing them to defeat you.

Small failures are considered the "valleys" in the entrepreneurial journey that include the setbacks, the missteps, the ill-planned experiments, the misplaced

Master the content **edge.sagepub.com/ neckentrepreneurship**

Video
Types of Failure

Pivot: a quick reaction and sometimes a change in direction.

Social network site Friendster collapsed due to technical glitches and failure to keep up with the competition
Credit: ©iStockphoto.com/ GAnayMutlu

FIGURE 11.1

The Top 20 Reasons Startups Fail

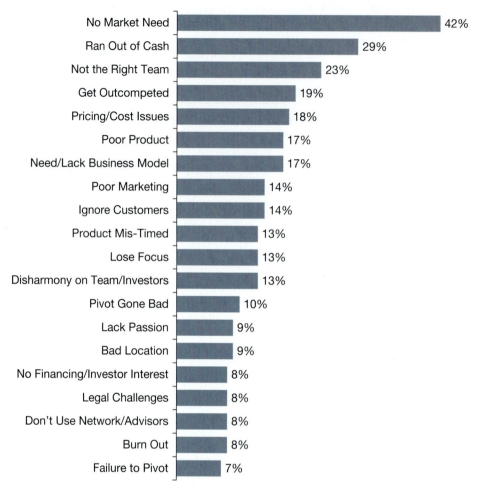

Based on an Analysis of 101 Startup Post-Mortems

Reason	%
No Market Need	42%
Ran Out of Cash	29%
Not the Right Team	23%
Get Outcompeted	19%
Pricing/Cost Issues	18%
Poor Product	17%
Need/Lack Business Model	17%
Poor Marketing	14%
Ignore Customers	14%
Product Mis-Timed	13%
Lose Focus	13%
Disharmony on Team/Investors	13%
Pivot Gone Bad	10%
Lack Passion	9%
Bad Location	9%
No Financing/Investor Interest	8%
Legal Challenges	8%
Don't Use Network/Advisors	8%
Burn Out	8%
Failure to Pivot	7%

Credit: CB Insights https://www.cbinsights.com/blog/startup-failure-reasons-top/

decisions—all manageable events that can help you build on what you learn. Small, reversible, informative failures along the way can highlight key issues and set you on a better path to success. The point is that if we can expect and embrace the learning from the small failures, then perhaps we can mitigate the risks of the big failures.

11.2 THE FAILURE SPECTRUM

>> LO 11.2   Identify several reasons for failure.

Amy C. Edmondson, a professor of leadership and management at Harvard Business School, believes that failure ranges from big to small along a failure spectrum (Figure 11.2). While many of us link the admission of failure with taking the blame, Edmondson believes that not all failures are blameworthy; her spectrum of failures runs from blameworthy to praiseworthy. Some of the reasons for failure on the

TABLE 11.1

Entrepreneurs Share Their Reasons for Failure

PSYCHE "MISTAKES"
"Fear." —Philip Rosedale, *Founder, High Fidelity, Inc. & Second Life*
"Letting opinions cloud your purpose." —Scott Lewallen, *Founder, Grindr*
"Trusting by default." —Jay Adelson, *Chairman & Founder, Opsmatic*
"Not believing in myself was the biggest mistake I made as an entrepreneur." —Sam Shank, *Cofounder/CEO, HotelTonight*
"Spending too much time worrying about competition and not enough time making what I'm building amazing." —Brenden Mulligan, *Founder/CEO, Cluster Labs*
"Thinking that entrepreneurship was the most meaningful part of my life." —Mick Hagen, *Founder, Zinch.com, Spatch, Undrip.com & Mainframe*
WAITING TOO LONG MISTAKES
"My biggest mistake as an entrepreneur was waiting too long to start." —Jason Nazar, *Founder, Docstoc.com*
"Not pivoting soon enough." —Peter Kazanjy, *Founder, TalentBin*
"Waiting to see if a problem would resolve itself." —Joshua Forman, *Cofounder, Inkling*
HIRING MISTAKES
"Hiring too fast and firing too slow." —Dan Yates, *Cofounder/CEO, OPOWER*
"Hiring bad fits." —John Battelle, *Cofounder/CEO, NewCo, Federated Media, Web 2.0 Summit, Wired*
"Getting the wrong people on the bus was the biggest mistake I made as an entrepreneur." —Hooman Radfar, *Partner, Expa & Founder, AddThis*

Source: Eleanor Rae Carman. E. R. (2015, June 25). Successful entrepreneurs reveal their biggest mistakes. *FounderDating*. Retrieved from http://founderdating.com/successful-entrepreneurs-reveal-biggest-mistakes/

spectrum are indeed blameworthy. For example, entrepreneurs who intentionally violate certain rules and regulations ("Deviance" at the top of the spectrum) are more likely to have failed businesses as well as a tarnished reputation. However, not all of the failures in the spectrum are bad—in fact, many of them are at least preventable or even praiseworthy. Someone who doesn't have the skills to do a job can receive more training; processes can be monitored and refined; and "failed" hypotheses and exploratory testing can be opportunities to expand knowledge, iterate, and set the scene for different, better approaches.[3]

Despite our misgivings about failure, it is not always bad. The failure spectrum describes situations that may be perceived as failures, yet can sometimes have positive rather than negative outcomes. The factors listed on the spectrum are discussed here.

Deviance

An entrepreneur defies legal and ethical boundaries leading to mismanagement of the venture. Napster is a good example of a company that demonstrated **deviance** from social norms, as well as its defiance of legal and, some say, ethical boundaries. Founded by Shawn Fanning and Sean Parker in the late 1990s, the music-sharing website allowed users to swap music for free, enraging musicians all over the world. When the band Metallica took Napster's founders to court, other musicians followed suit; and Napster eventually collapsed under the weight of the lawsuits, filing for bankruptcy in 2001.[4]

Deviance: a situation where an entrepreneur defies legal and ethical boundaries leading to mismanagement of the venture.

FIGURE 11.2

The Failure Spectrum

Deviance	• The entrepreneur defies legal and ethical boundaries leading to mismanagement of the venture.
Inattention	• The entrepreneur gets sidetracked from the core business—either in a new business direction or by delegating too much too soon without following up.
Lack of Ability	• The entrepreneur is overextended and lacks the skillset to get the job done.
Process Inadequacy	• The wrong (or lack of) processes are set up in the organization such that communication breaks down among employees and things begin to fall through the cracks.
Uncertainty	• The entrepreneur takes unreasonable actions due to a lack of clarity about future events.
Exploratory Experimentation	• The entrepreneur conducts market tests to get early feedback and acquire important learning and information.

Source: Adapted from Amy C. Edmondson, Strategies for Learning from Failure, *Harvard Business Review*, April 2011. https://hbr.org/2011/04/strategies-for-learning-from-failure

Inattention

An entrepreneur gets sidetracked from the core business by **inattention**—either in a new business direction or by delegating too much too soon without following up. Entrepreneur Jason DeMers became sidetracked from his main business, AudienceBloom, a social media marketing firm, by turning his attention to a new startup. As he became more involved with the new venture, his original company stopped growing, as he did not have enough resources to run two companies. The new venture failed, and DeMers went back to working on AudienceBloom full time. This incident helped DeMers realize that a "successful venture requires 100% attention, focus, and effort."[5]

Inattention: a condition whereby an entrepreneur becomes sidetracked from the core business.

Lack of ability

Lack of ability: the lack of skillset to get the job done.

With **lack of ability**, the entrepreneur is overextended and lacks the skillset to get the job done. He or she may have been good at the start but as the business grew, more skills were needed. It is very common for companies to outgrow their founders because the founders lack the skills and abilities to get the company to the next level. In some cases, the founders either can't or won't develop the necessary skills to develop the organization, and they may have to step aside as a result.[6]

For example, founding CEO Kyle Sandler of online media publication *Nibletz: The Voice of Startups Everywhere Else*, admitted that he didn't have the skills to

Video
Why a Business Can Fail

grow the company. Sandler stepped down as CEO in favor of his cofounder, Nick Tippman. Referring to the transition, Tippman said, "It's hard to step away from the role that you once had and understand that as the business grows that maybe your skill sets don't fit where they used to."[7]

Music-sharing website Napster collapsed under the weight of legal pressure

Credit: digitallife / Alamy Stock Photo

Process inadequacy

Process inadequacy or the wrong processes are set up in the organization so communication breaks down among employees and things begin to fall through the cracks. Shaun Swanson, Mark Cicoria, and Mark Johnson are the founders of Ayloo, an online and mobile shared forum to broadcast events and interests in a particular city. Johnson believes lack of communication was one of the reasons that the startup failed: "Communication was a problem. We butted heads a lot. Shaun would come up with these big ideas and I would try to be reasonable, but he thought I was shooting him down."[8]

Process Inadequacy: The wrong (or lack of) processes set up in the organization causing communication breakdown.

Uncertainty

Uncertainty or lack of clarity about future events can cause entrepreneurs to take unreasonable actions. Today Gary Swart is a venture partner at Polaris Partners, but his first business was Intellibank, which he describes as "sort of like Dropbox done wrong." Swart believes Intellibank failed because he and his team lacked focus and certainty about how to define the startup and where it was going. "We failed because we tried to go too broad. We were trying to be all things to all people. . . . We were pivoting so often for different types of customers that we completely lost the big picture."[9]

Uncertainty: the lack of clarity about future events that can cause entrepreneurs to take unreasonable actions.

Exploratory experimentation

Market tests are conducted to get early feedback and acquire important learning and information. Some of these tests may fail miserably. Jim Belosic, founder of self-service, app-building tool ShortStack, believes that **exploratory experimentation** is crucial for learning. "Most people see the word *failure* and think 'unrecoverable.' Instead, I see failures as mini test results. I tried something, it didn't work, so let's gather up what we learned and try again. I've never let my business get to a point of failure. I've set my guidelines and pivot if we start heading toward something that's failing."[10]

Exploratory experimentation: a method whereby market tests are conducted to get early feedback and acquire important learning and information.

As Figure 11.2 (p. 282) illustrates, there are different kinds of failures. Some failures are small, adjustable, informative, linked to bigger goals, and designed to highlight key issues. Others involve rigid thinking, discouragement, and may result in reputational damage.[11] Whatever the type or reason for the failure, the most important part for entrepreneurs comes from the lessons they learn.

11.3 FEAR OF FAILURE

>> **LO 11.3** Describe the consequences of fear of failure for entrepreneurs.

Despite the learning and opportunities that may arise from perceived failures, many of us view failure in a negative way and try our best to avoid it. This is because the concept of failure provokes an emotional reaction or antifailure bias that inhibits us

Learning From Failure

**Ben Huh, former CEO of Raydium, current
CEO of The Cheezburger Network**

Credit: Joe Kohen/WireImage/Getty Images

When a business is making a profit and employees are happy it's easy to be ethical. But when revenue and funding are insufficient to acquire necessary resources or meet debt obligations such as employee compensation or investor repayment, there is a higher temptation to neglect ethical responsibilities.

Ben Huh was a 22-year-old student majoring in journalism when he managed to cobble together $750,000 from investors to found Raydium, a software analytics firm, in 2000. Less than two years later the dot-com bubble burst, and Raydium's funding dried up. Huh had previously worked at startups, but he had no experience in raising capital—a shortcoming that stood out starkly as he realized he had exhausted external investor funding and was

unable to meet payroll. Huh later reflected on his sense of failure: "These investors had put a fortune on their faith in me, and you feel like you should have rewarded their faith."

With his sense of self-esteem at stake and employees and investors relying on Huh, he had to struggle with emotions and try to make a rational evaluation of several paths he could take. He could mislead employees and investors about the enterprise's financial circumstances while he attempted to increase sales or find other funding alternatives. He could close the business, lay off employees, declare bankruptcy, and liquidate the assets. He could throw his meager personal assets into the firm in an effort to postpone bankruptcy.

CRITICAL THINKING QUESTIONS

1. **How would you decide which course of action is the right one if you were Huh?**

2. **How difficult is it to remove the emotional aspect of decision making in order to make the most ethical decision?**

3. **Do you believe there are reasons that an entrepreneur might "deserve" to fail, or "need to learn a lesson the hard way" through failure? If not, why not? If so, give some examples** ●

Sources

Cope, J. (2011, November). Entrepreneurial learning from failure: An interpretative phenomenological analysis. *Journal of Business Venturing, 26,* 604623. Retrieved from http://www.dge.ubi.pt/msilva/Papers_MECE/Paper_5.pdf

Mack, S. (*n.d.*). What is the meaning of ethical responsibility? *Chron.* Retrieved from http://smallbusiness.chron.com/meaning-ethical-responsibility-56224.html

Wang, J. (2013, January 23). How 5 successful entrepreneurs bounced back after failure. *Entrepreneur.* Retrieved from https://www.entrepreneur.com/article/225204

from learning from the experience. This causes us to put the failure out of our minds rather than tackling the reasons behind it.[12]

It is not surprising that we never hear much about the emotions of failure (pain, humiliation, shame, guilt, self-blame, and anger—often associated with grief) that entrepreneurs experience when their businesses go under. Expressing these emotions is often too much to bear, as admitting our failures can be emotionally unpleasant and can damage our self-esteem.

Mikkel Svane, founder of software company Zendesk (his third startup), believes failure is a tough thing to recover from because of these unpleasant emotions.

Not being able to pay your bills is a terrible thing. Letting people go and disappointing them and their families is a terrible thing. Not delivering your promises to customers who believed in you is a terrible thing. Sure, you learn from these ordeals, but there is nothing positive about the failure that led you there.[13]

Mikkel Svane, founder of software company Zendesk
Credit: Anthony Harvey/Getty Images Entertainment/Getty Images

However, it is only by managing these emotions that entrepreneurs can begin the process of learning from failure. But this is not an easy process; sometimes we would rather blame others or external events for failures in order to maintain our self-esteem and sense of control.

For entrepreneurs, failure is especially difficult because it is hard to separate personal failure from professional failure, given how closely associated the identity of the business is tied to the identity of the entrepreneur. Featured entrepreneur, Tom Hatten, founder of Mountainside Fitness, is a good example of an entrepreneur who is so emotionally attached to his business that he is willing to persevere rather than let it go.

What Tom Hatten, Mikkel Svane, and many successful entrepreneurs have realized is that it is acceptable and human to try and fail. Feelings of doubt, uncertainty, frustration, and a yearning for help are all perfectly normal. Svane believes that it is possible to recover and learn from failure when we feel comfortable enough to make and admit our mistakes; in which case, "failing is ultimately just another step on the road to success." Yet before entrepreneurs are able to move forward or even start their businesses, they need to first overcome their fear of failure.

Video
Fear of Failure

As we have learned, fear of failure can be a major impediment to seizing opportunities and transforming entrepreneurial objectives into real action.[16] While many of us have a degree of fear of failure, some have a higher level than others. Researchers have suggested that the origins of fear of failure may lie in parent-child relations. For example, a child is likely to have a higher fear of failure if he or she is punished for failures and receives little or neutral praise for successful achievements. Studies also suggest that there is a connection between high parental expectations and a child's fear of failure, as well as other factors such as maternal irritability and paternal absence.[17]

Overall, studies show that individuals who are raised to believe that failure is unacceptable and has negative consequences, will go out of their way to avoid failure. This means that rather than seeing mistakes as opportunities to learn and improve skills, or to compete against others, they will view them as threatening and judgment-oriented experiences. Here, failure is associated with shame—a painful emotion that many of us will avoid—even if it means losing out on lucrative opportunities. Avoiding the potential to make mistakes stunts the growth and maturity of individuals with a high fear of failure, which leads only to more mistakes and failures over time.[18] Understanding that failure is an important part of growth and learning is a vital lesson for entrepreneurs who want to succeed in their personal and professional lives.

People with a strong fear of failure tend to be anxious, lack self-esteem, and demonstrate reluctance to try new things. Table 11.2 illustrates some symptoms of fear of failure.

Once you establish the extent of your fear of failure, you can begin to develop some coping strategies to deal with it.[19] First, you can reframe specific goals so they

Grief and Business Failure[14]

There is a strong emotional relationship between entrepreneurs and their businesses. Many entrepreneurs often describe their businesses as their "baby." Often the business is not about personal gain but rather a personal belief or loyalty to the product or service, together with the entrepreneurial desire to grow and demonstrate skills and abilities.

Studies carried out by Dean A. Shepherd, Professor of Management and Entrepreneurship at the Kelley School of Business, Indiana University, show that entrepreneurs who experience the loss of a business can suffer similar symptoms to grief (anger, guilt, self-blame, distress, and anxiety). This negative emotional response impedes their ability to learn from the loss. Researchers have suggested that entrepreneurs who have suffered big failures such as bankruptcy may benefit from the steps involved in a grief recovery process. The entrepreneurs would need to be aware that the feelings they are experiencing are normal, which may help to minimize feelings of shame and embarrassment. This may encourage the entrepreneurs to articulate their feelings of grief, which may help to quicken the recovery. Researchers also proposed a coping model where the griever oscillates between two grieving strategies (a dual process of grief recovery) to speed up the healing process. The first strategy involves focusing on analyzing what went wrong in order to process information about the business loss; while the second part of the process shifts the focus to the entrepreneur thinking about other aspects of his or her life in order to

distract him- or herself from the loss. When entrepreneurs alternate between these two processes, they have a better chance of learning to regulate their negative emotions. This allows them to recover enough from the loss to see the opportunities for growth and learning, and to move forward.

Dean A. Shepherd says, "We have to realize that when we pursue opportunities, the opportunity exists only because there's uncertainty, and failure is a high possibility. It's normal to have a negative emotional reaction to the loss of a project or a new business. While time does heal all wounds, we can do something to speed the process. The way you approach the failure—before and after—can impact how quickly you recover, how much you learn, and how willing you are to try again."[15]

CRITICAL THINKING QUESTIONS

1. **Would you agree that entrepreneurs have an emotional connection to their businesses? Why/Why not?**

2. **How do you think the grief recovery process can help entrepreneurs overcome the loss of their businesses?**

3. **What steps would you take to get over the loss of a failed venture?** ●

become more achievable; for example, rather than setting a goal of earning $100,000 from a new product launch, you can expand the goal to focus also on what you learn from launching a new product. That way, even if the product does not meets its monetary target, you will not feel you have failed, as you have already committed to learning something of value from the experience. This ties in with the concept of acceptable loss outlined in The Practice of Entrepreneurship.

Second, if the product failed to generate as much revenue as you would like, it is helpful to separate your personal feelings from facts. Instead of thinking, "I feel terrible because I have failed," you can ask yourself, "What did I learn from this experience?" and "What are the positive things about what happened?"

Third, many of us try to suppress the emotions associated with fear; but by deliberately allowing yourself to feel the fear, you are more likely to diminish the fear of failure. Taking deep breaths for two minutes is a useful exercise to shift negative feelings and trigger a calm response.

Finally, a good way to deal with your fear is to seek support from the role models in your life. For example, Arianna Huffington, founder of The Huffington Post, credits her mother for her positive attitude toward failure:

My mother instilled in me that failure was not something to be afraid of, that it was not the opposite of success. It was a stepping-stone to success. So I had no fear of failure. Perseverance is everything. I don't give up. Everybody has failures, but successful people keep on going. . . . She was my life mentor.[20]

TABLE 11.2

10 Signs You Might Have a Fear of Failure

1.	Failing makes you worry about what other people think about you.
2.	Failing makes you worry about your ability to pursue the future you desire.
3.	Failing makes you worry that people will lose interest in you.
4.	Failing makes you worry about how smart or capable you are.
5.	Failing makes you worry about disappointing people whose opinion you value.
6.	You tend to tell people beforehand that you don't expect to succeed in order to lower their expectations.
7.	Once you fail at something, you have trouble imagining what you could have done differently to succeed.
8.	You often get last-minute headaches, stomach aches, or other physical symptoms that prevent you from completing your preparation.
9.	You often get distracted by tasks that prevent you from completing your preparation; in hindsight, the tasks were not as urgent as they seemed at the time.
10.	You tend to procrastinate and "run out of time" to complete your preparation adequately.

Source: Adapted from Winch, G. (2013, June 18). 10 Signs that you might have fear of failure. *Psychology Today*. Retrieved from https://www.psychologytoday.com/blog/the-squeaky-wheel/201306/10-signs-you-might-have-fear-failure

Global Fear of Failure

A strong fear of failure is often rooted in one's national culture. The Global Entrepreneurship Monitor report (GEM) measures fear of failure on a global level according to country.[21] When you look at this on a map, you can also recognize regional differences (see Figure 11.3). The GEM failure rate is based on those who admit to perceiving opportunities to start a business but feel prevented from acting on those opportunities due to fear of failure. The lower the percentage shown on the map, the lower the fear.

Overall, different countries and the cultures associated with countries had different tolerances for failure, but perhaps not as much difference as you would think. For example, fear of failure is lowest in Africa, Latin America, and the Caribbean. In contrast, fear of failure is highest in Asia, Oceania, and Europe. In particular, fear of failure was lowest in Barbados and Senegal (less than 16%) and highest in Kazakhstan (76%). In the United States, while the fear of failure rate is lower than most of the Asian, Oceanian, and European countries, it is still higher than less developed countries such as Cameroon, Botswana, and Senegal.

Arianna Stassinopoulous Huffington, founder of the *Huffington Post*.

Credit: Bryan Bedder/Getty Images Entertainment/Getty Images

FIGURE 11.3

Fear of Failure Rates Around the World

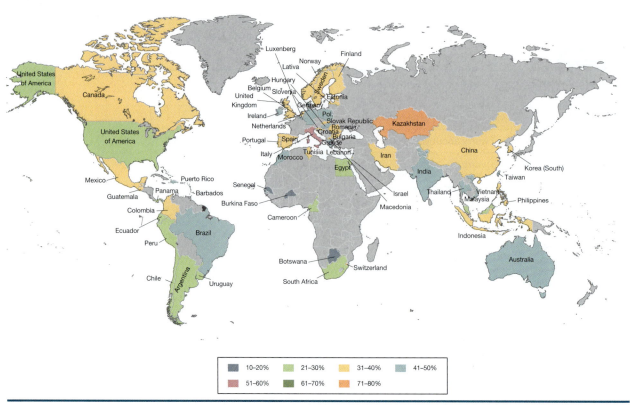

| ▮ 10–20% | ▮ 21–30% | ▮ 31–40% | ▮ 41–50% |
| ▮ 51–60% | ▮ 61–70% | ▮ 71–80% | |

Source: Global Entrepreneurship Monitor Adult Population Survey 2015

Video
Effects of Fear

How does fear of failure influence our ability to spot opportunities and act on them? To find the answer, GEM also assessed the personal perceptions about entrepreneurship experienced by people between the ages of 18 and 64 (see Figure 11.4). The study focused on three types of economies across 60 countries:

1. factor-driven economies (countries that use unskilled labor and natural resources to compete with other countries, such as India);
2. efficiency-driven economies (where economic growth is dependent on more efficient production processes, higher wages, and better product quality , such as Poland, Estonia, Chile); and
3. innovation-driven economies (countries that compete by producing innovative products and services, such as the US, the UK, South Korea, Japan, and Singapore).

The GEM study focused on how people's personal perceptions in these three economies have influenced their decision to start a business. These perceptions include the extent to which people see opportunities around them to start a business (perceived opportunities); how capable they think they are of starting a business (perceived capabilities); how many people would feel constrained by their own fear of failing (fear of failure); and the degree to which those capable of starting a business may intend to do so over the next three years (entrepreneurial intentions).

As Figure 11.4 illustrates, people in the factor-driven economies have the highest entrepreneurial self-perceptions, with over half seeing opportunities to start a business and feeling they have the capabilities to do so; both of these factors lead to high entrepreneurial intentions. In contrast, perceived opportunities are lower in

FIGURE 11.4

Self-Perceptions About Entrepreneurship

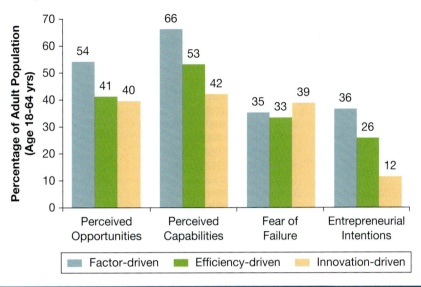

Source: GEM 2015/2016 global report, Figure 5. Retrieved from http://gemconsortium.org/report

efficiency-driven economies, and people in these economies have a lower rate of perceived capabilities and fewer intentions to start a business. The innovation-driven economies score the lowest on self-perception, particularly in the area of entrepreneurial intentions. While people in these economies may perceive opportunities and score relatively high in perceived capabilities, very few intend to take the next step into entrepreneurship. Some of the reasons for this may lie in lack of confidence, cultural differences, types of skills, the level of entrepreneurship education, and different types of businesses that exist in the economy. For example, many businesses are started in Africa for sustenance and survival, whereas many businesses in the United States are high-tech. These different businesses require different levels of skills, which may account for differences in perceived capabilities.

Yet despite the differences between the economic groups, Figure 11.5 shows similar fear of failure rates across the different types of economies. The question then becomes, what makes some people act when others don't, even if their fear of failure is almost the same? The answer lies in how we manage failure and our ability and willingness to learn from it.

YOU BE THE ENTREPRENEUR

One of the most devastating aspects of the entrepreneurship experience is failure. People learn from failure; and those in business know that from failure comes knowledge, which is sometimes worth more than success. Steve Blank, founder of Rocket Science Games and E.piphany, knows all too well about what it is like to fail. He found that some failed business ideas can lead to much better opportunities.

Steve Blank started the video gaming company Rocket Science in 1995, and everyone thought it would revolutionize the industry. But shortly after his company was founded, he made a phone call to his mother saying that he was about to lose $35 million in investor funding, which threatened to ruin his business. Blank had many choices of what to do, one of them being to quit.

What Would You Do?

Source: Porter, J. (2013, June 14). *How failure made these entrepreneurs millions. Entrepreneur.* Retrieved from https://www.entrepreneur.com/article/227011

FIGURE 11.5

Failure Fear Factor Around the World

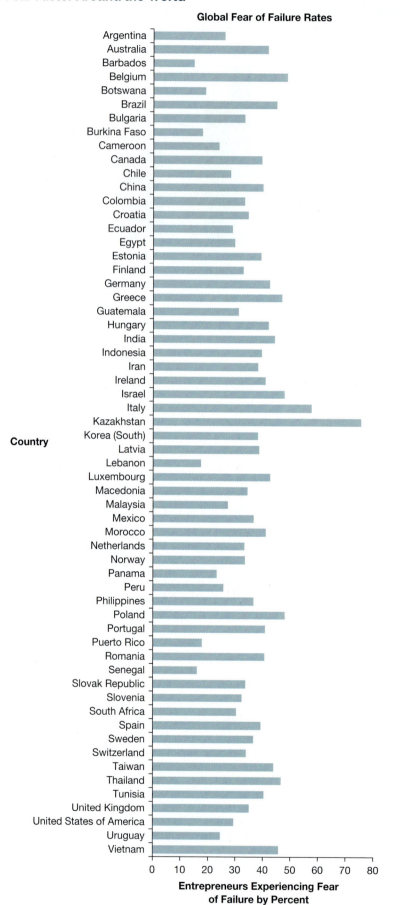

Global Fear of Failure Rates

Country (y-axis)

Argentina, Australia, Barbados, Belgium, Botswana, Brazil, Bulgaria, Burkina Faso, Cameroon, Canada, Chile, China, Colombia, Croatia, Ecuador, Egypt, Estonia, Finland, Germany, Greece, Guatemala, Hungary, India, Indonesia, Iran, Ireland, Israel, Italy, Kazakhstan, Korea (South), Latvia, Lebanon, Luxembourg, Macedonia, Malaysia, Mexico, Morocco, Netherlands, Norway, Panama, Peru, Philippines, Poland, Portugal, Puerto Rico, Romania, Senegal, Slovak Republic, Slovenia, South Africa, Spain, Sweden, Switzerland, Taiwan, Thailand, Tunisia, United Kingdom, United States of America, Uruguay, Vietnam

x-axis: 0, 10, 20, 30, 40, 50, 60, 70, 80

Entrepreneurs Experiencing Fear of Failure by Percent

Source: Global Entrepreneurship Monitor Adult Population Survey 2015

11.4 LEARNING FROM FAILURE

>> LO 11.4   Explain the different ways entrepreneurs can learn from failure.

As shown by the statistics we presented in Chapter 2, the reality of entrepreneurship is that businesses do fail, which is why it is important for aspiring entrepreneurs to learn from others who have experienced failed businesses. Learning from others can help them, not only in taking steps to preventing it from happening to them, but also to understand how to take valuable lessons from failure. As we have explored, the use of the term *failure* evokes fear that discourages entrepreneurs from trying again or attempting new approaches.

In Chapter 7 we introduced experimentation and described how each "failed" experiment is an opportunity to build our knowledge and increase evidence. Jeff Bezos, founder of Amazon.com, is a big believer in experimentation, especially when it comes to learning from failures. "I've made billions of dollars of failures at Amazon. com," he said. "Literally billions.... Companies that don't embrace failure and continue to experiment eventually get in the desperate position where the only thing they can do is make a Hail Mary bet at the end of their corporate existence."[22]

Experimentation is about trying something, seeing what happens, learning from it, and then moving forward, adapting or pivoting based on those findings. The goal of experimentation is not to conduct the "perfect" experiment; but to see it as an opportunity for further learning and better decision making, rather than a series of failed tests.

In this context, perhaps it would be better to reframe the term "failure" as "intentional iteration"—a process that involves prototyping, testing, analyzing, and refinement. This may encourage entrepreneurs to perceive failure as simply a process of experimenting and learning from the setbacks, false starts, wrong turns, and mistakes, which will in turn help them develop the skills they need to tackle potential obstacles that may lie ahead.

This process of "intentional iteration" involves making **intelligent failures**—good failures that provide valuable new knowledge that can help a startup innovate and stride ahead of its competition (see Figure 11.6). Intelligent failures take place when experimentation is deemed necessary in order to find answers in situations that have never been explored before. Designing a new, innovative product, or testing consumer reactions in an untapped market are all tasks that may result in intelligent failures. With the right kind of experimentation, entrepreneurs can produce quick failures with positive results.[23]

Video
Learning From Failure

Intelligent failures: a way of describing failures that provide valuable new knowledge that can help a startup innovate and stride ahead of its competition.

FIGURE 11.6

Intelligent Failure

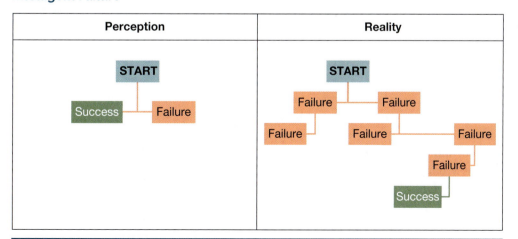

For example, global design firm IDEO (discussed in Chapter 6) benefited from intelligent failure when it introduced a new strategy-innovation service for its clients. This meant that rather than helping clients to design new products within their own product range, which was IDEO's usual approach, the new service would help clients create new lines of business that would take them in new directions.

Before publicly rolling out the new service, IDEO tested it with one of its clients, a small firm that sold mattresses. The project failed: The firm was not convinced enough by IDEO's new service to change its product strategy to create new lines. However, rather than canceling the new service, IDEO took the time to learn lessons from the failure and figure out what went wrong.

In the end, IDEO hired people with MBAs who could help clients think strategically, and it even included clients' managers in the team. The result of IDEO's intelligent failure? IDEO's strategy-innovation service now accounts for over one third of its revenues. The IDEO example shows how a company can learn important lessons from small failures in order to achieve big success.

Lessons Learned by Successful Entrepreneurs

We began this chapter with a quote from Robert Kiyosaki—"Nine of ten businesses fail; so I came up with a foolproof plan—create ten businesses." But what does this plan actually look like in real life? Kurt Theobald is the cofounder and CEO of the e-commerce firm Classy Llama—the 11th of ten failed startups over the course of five years. Despite 10 failures behind him, Theobald learned valuable lessons and persevered until he achieved success. Table 11.3 lists some of the lessons he learned along the way.

Theobald learned some valuable lessons from his 10 failed businesses that helped him to finally succeed with his eleventh new venture. Yet Theobald is only one of many entrepreneurs who have been knocked down, only to come back even stronger. Table 11.4 describes more lessons learned by successful entrepreneurs who have made mistakes.

Building a Blame-Free Environment

Many of us are guilty of playing the "blame game" when things don't go our way. Music entrepreneur Pharrell Williams struggled with accepting the failure of his 2006 album. Williams says, "I blamed everyone around me but myself"—but after further analysis, he realized that his album was "too full of ego" and lacked purpose, and so he went back to the drawing board. By understanding the reasons that led to his failed album, Williams was able to define what he really wanted: to make music to lift people up. In 2014, Williams struck gold with hugely successful hit single, "Happy."[24]

Similarly, important lessons could be learned from failures that led to the demise of many startups by building blame-free cultures that encourage people to share, accept, learn from, and recover from failure. To do this, employees in a startup would also need to feel assured that they will not receive a negative reaction when they admit mistakes. When people feel comfortable enough to report failures, there is an opportunity for the team to work together toward understanding and analyzing what went wrong, and to explore new approaches in order to prevent the same thing from happening again.

The key to building a blame-free culture is to communicate clearly what sorts of failures are acceptable and unacceptable. For example, lack of commitment, reckless

TABLE 11.3

Lessons Learned by Kurt Theobald

Beware of "shiny object syndrome"	Theobald admits he was guilty of pursuing multiple opportunities that came his way, but failed to be strategic about it, which led to many failures. He suggests that all entrepreneurs need to be strategic about pursuing opportunities, and to understand how to identify the right opportunity at the right time.
Fail fast . . . but not too fast	While failing fast is useful when it comes to warding off really big failures, Theobald also advises against giving up too soon. He admits that sometimes he was too impatient to stick out his past businesses, when he should have tried different things to get the formula right.
Find your formula	One of Theobald's businesses failed because he hadn't worked out the exact formula—the fundamental underlying method of why a business is viable. In the end, there wasn't enough revenue coming in to sustain the startup, and Theobald was forced to file for bankruptcy.
Know who you are	Theobald believes that entrepreneurs who know who they really are have a better chance at success, as they are better equipped to deal with failure. He explains, "I wrote two things in my journal: One, when I fall, I am getting up. Every single time. And two; I get up because it's who I am as an entrepreneur. Therefore to not get up is to betray who I am. And so that's what kept me going through all the failure. You can't stop. You don't really have a choice because if you choose that then you might as well sacrifice your whole life."
Find your deeper purpose	Theobald believes that entrepreneurs must have a deeper purpose to cope with failure—a deeper reason for starting and growing a business other than potential wealth, and the freedom of working for themselves. He cites Steve Jobs's return to Apple (Jobs demanded only a $1 salary) as an example of an entrepreneur with a deeper purpose who prioritized changing the world with his products, over money.
Focus on others	Being an entrepreneur is not about you, but about focusing on others—your customer, team member, supplier, stakeholders—and helping them succeed. This is not about giving up control, but rather sharing it with others. Remember the more value you give, the more you get back. By shifting your thinking to others, the people around you will be more likely to help you resolve problems and overcome obstacles.
Recognize when your approach is wrong	Many of Theobald's businesses failed because he was using the same approach every time. He quotes a mentor who advised, "Nothing's going to give if *you* keep doing the same thing you've been doing. If you keep banging your head against the concrete wall, the wall doesn't suddenly give way. Instead, you end up knocking yourself out. You need to pick a different approach."

Source: Wagner, E. (2013, October 22). 9 Lessons from a 10-time startup failure. *Forbes*. Retrieved from http://www.forbes.com/sites/ericwagner/2013/10/22/9-lessons-from-a-10-time-startup-failure/

conduct, violation of laws or standards, negligence, or wasting resources would be deemed unacceptable; whereas small fails that tend to occur through experimentation would be regarded as acceptable.

Entrepreneurs also need to be open about their own knowledge limitations, and admit the mistakes they have made in the past. This degree of openness encourages the rest of the team to be just as open and more willing to admit mistakes when they happen. Derek Sivers, founder of online music retailer CD Baby, is a big believer in protecting company culture. He admits there was a time when he blamed his employees for "turning against him" as they prioritized their benefits and entitlements over the well-being of their clients. Later, however, Sivers realized he was to blame for a toxic culture: "I realized it was all my fault. I let the culture of the company get corrupted. I ignored problems instead of nipping them in the bud."[25] Having learned from this experience, Sivers now believes that in a startup, followers must be treated as equal to leaders in order for the team to work well together.

In essence, founders must give careful thought to making demands, giving orders, overruling thoughtful decisions, shooting the messenger, and assigning blame in order to build a culture where people feel comfortable enough to share bad news and make the right choices.[26]

John Danner is an author and senior fellow at the Institute for Business Innovation in the Haas School of Business of the University of California, Berkeley. Like Sivers and

TABLE 11.4

Five Lessons Learned from Entrepreneurial Mistakes

1. Reason for failure: "We wasted $1,000,000 on a company that never launched"
Hiten Shah, Cofounder of KISSmetrics, person-based analytics firm, and analytics firm Crazy Egg.
Prior to launching KISSmetrics, Shah and his cofounder spent $1,000,000 on a web hosting company that never launched because they were too focused on building the best product in their eyes, rather than considering what customers wanted.
Lesson learned: Both cofounders have learned how to spend smart, optimize for learning and focus on customer satisfaction.
2. Reason for Failure: "We built the website first and asked our customers about it later"
Robin Chase, Cofounder of Zipcar, and founder of Buzzcar.
Like Shah Chase did not have a clear understanding of what customers wanted before he spent money on the website for GoLoco—the online ridesharing site that was built before Zipcar.
Lesson Learned: When it came to building Zipcar, Chase ensured she understood customer needs prior to launching.
3. Reason for Failure: "I built a product without understanding the market or the users"
Sandi MacPherson—Editor-in-Chief, Quibb
MacPherson made the mistake of spending 6 months on a product that she didn't really understand or would use very often herself. As a result, she ended up creating a product that nobody else wanted. Like Chase and Shah, MacPherson didn't give enough consideration to potential customers.
Lesson learned: MacPherson realized that she was not a product expert, which she believed was an important skill for a founder/CEO.
4. Reason for Failure: "I tried to do it all by myself"
Leo Laporte—Founder of the TWiT network
Laporte made the mistake of thinking he could run his startup all by himself because of his background knowledge of media, content, and technology. However, he lacked the business skills necessary for running the company, such as finance, marketing, human resources, and advertising. Laporte, like MacPherson, was overly confident in his expertise. While Laporte's company experienced rapid growth in the first few years, the company stalled because of his lack of knowledge in some vital areas.
Lesson Learned: Laporte hired a business partner to help out, which put the company back on track once more.
5. Reason for Failure: "I made the big mistake of being a 'parallel entrepreneur'"
Dharmesh Shah—Cofounder and CTO of HubSpot
When HubSpot became successful, Shah decided to become a "parallel entrepreneur" by attempting to run two different startups at the same time. As his interests were divided, his original startup team felt abandoned, and Shah didn't feel enough of an impetus to make the new startup work.
Lesson Learned: Shah realized that it was not possible to run two startups at the same time and decided to give total focus to one company only. Like Laporte, Shah had to accept that one person can do only so much.

Source: Adapted from Belle Beth Cooper, "The 13 Biggest Failures from Successful Entrepreneurs and What They've Learned from Them," *buffersocial* (September 5, 2013) https://blog.bufferapp.com/failure-entrepreneur-12-

others we have described earlier, Danner believes that failure in organizations should not be treated as a "regrettable reality," but rather as "a strategic resource—one that can help you make better decisions, create a more trusting and higher-performing culture, and accelerate your company's growth and innovation."[27]

Your Failure Résumé[28]

In this Mindshift exercise, your assignment is to craft a "failure résumé" that includes all of your biggest fails! These can be from school, work, or even in social relationships. For every failure you list, you must then describe what you learned from each fail (and, if appropriate, what others learned). By creating a failure résumé, you are forced to spend time reflecting on what you learned from those experiences. As tough as this sounds, it's also a very rewarding experience.

Want to go a step further? Share your résumé with a classmate and compare. Don't focus on comparing the failures but rather focus on comparing and contrasting the learning that resulted from each failure experience.

CRITICAL THINKING QUESTIONS

1. **Was it easier than you expected, or more difficult, to list your biggest failures?**

2. **What emotions did you experience as you wrote your "failure résumé"?**

3. **How do you think you'll be able to take the lessons learned from your failures and use them to attain more success in the future?** ●

11.5 GETTING GRITTY: BUILDING A TOLERANCE FOR FAILURE

>> **LO 11.5**   **Describe the significance of "grit" and its role in building tolerance for failure.**

Angela Lee Duckworth is a psychologist at the University of Pennsylvania who has spent more than a decade researching how character relates to achievement. Traditional wisdom leads us to believe that talent—as measured by things like IQ, SAT, and GMAT scores—is a predictor of achievement. Yet Duckworth found something different. She identified "grit" as a trait that supersedes traditional methods of measuring talent.

According to Duckworth, **grit** is the quality that enables people to work hard and sustain interest in their long-term goals. Grit is also related to resilience, not just in the face of failure, but in perseverance to stick to long-term commitments and goals.[29]

One of the first studies Duckworth carried out to show the relationship between grit and high achievement took place at the United States Military Academy at West Point—one of the most selective and rigorous military training facilities in the United States, and one with an infamously high dropout rate. Duckworth received permission to have incoming cadets complete a short "grit questionnaire," along with all the other evaluative methods employed by West Point such as The Whole Candidate Score (which includes SAT scores, class rank, etc.). Her intent was to find out what qualities would predict whether a cadet would remain at West Point through the "beast" summer program or would drop out.

Examples of the questions on Duckworth's grit questionnaire: "I have overcome setbacks to conquer an important challenge," "Setbacks don't discourage me," "I have been obsessed with a certain idea or project for a short time but later lost interest," "I have difficulty maintaining my focus on projects that take more than a few months to complete," and "I finish whatever I begin." Participants were asked to rate themselves on a five-point scale ranging from "very much like me" to "not like me at all."[30]

Web
Working With Failure

Grit: the quality that enables people to work hard and sustain interest in their long-term goals.

The findings showed that the cadets with higher levels of grit were more likely to stay until the end of the summer, and grit proved to be a better predictor than The Whole Candidate Score. Since the West Point study, Duckworth has found that grit predicts the effectiveness of sales agents, the survival of first-year teachers in tough schools, and even the identity of the finalists of U.S. National Spelling Bee contests.[31]

Duckworth's research on grit is also related to Stanford psychologist Carol Dweck's research on mindset, which we explored in Chapter 3. Dweck believes that people with a fixed mindset tend to believe that intelligence and talent is something we're born with, and they avoid failure at all costs, whereas people with growth mindset develop their abilities through dedication, effort, and hard work. They think brains and talent are not the key to lifelong success, but merely the starting point. They see failure as an opportunity to improve their performance, and to learn from their mistakes. Despite setbacks, they tend to persevere rather than giving up. Over the course of her research, Duckworth has found that children who have more of a growth mindset tend to have more grit.

Like Dweck, Duckworth also believes in the concept of deliberate practice, which is the conscious effort to practice things that we can't yet do. However, this type of practice does not involve doing the same thing over and over again; deliberate practice is a highly structured activity that must have a purpose, and be carried out with an eye on long-term achievement. Deliberate practice can be frustrating, confusing, and even boring; but the fact is that we are supposed to feel confused when we are tackling the unknown—feeling frustrated can be a sign that we are on the right track.[32] In sum, deliberate practice allows us to refine our skills, by making and accepting our mistakes in order to help us progress toward the achievement of long-term goals. This ties in with one of the key messages of this text—that entrepreneurship is a method that demands practice.

Video
Developing Grit

Building Grit

As defined in psychological studies by Duckworth and others, grit incorporates several different attributes. Let's examine each of these.

Courage

In the context of grit, people are courageous when they are not afraid to fail. They understand that failure is an important part of the learning process if they want to succeed. For example, when Jody Porowski, founder of online platform Avelist, ran out of funding, she refused to let her business die. Instead, she persevered (by selling her house) and wholly believes that "success comes from a refusal to give up."[33]

Conscientiousness

Often, when we hear of someone being conscientious, we picture a person being meticulous in carrying out painstaking tasks. However, in the context of grit, being conscientious means working tirelessly in the face of challenges and toward the achievement of long-term goals.

Perseverance

Perseverance is the commitment to long-term goals through purposeful deliberate practice. Tesla founder Elon Musk is a big believer in perseverance, but he also acknowledges that for entrepreneurs, the road to success isn't always easy. Musk states, "Entrepreneurship is like eating glass and walking on hot coals at the same time."[34]

Resilience

Resilience means the strength to recover from failure and overcome obstacles in order to persevere toward the achievement of long-term goals. Gritty people believe "everything will be all right in the end, and if it is not all right, it is not the end."[35]

Excellence

In the context of grit, striving for excellence means committing to activities that enhance skills, as well as prioritizing improvement over perfection. In other words, striving for excellence is an ongoing process, as each activity highlights new opportunities.

Removing the Stigma of Failure

Failure is still a topic that many of us would like to avoid, but that is changing. Initiatives are springing up to remove the stigma (feelings of shame and embarrassment) traditionally associated with failure.

Video
Embracing Failure

Mobile technology nonprofit MobilActive runs an annual event called FAILFaire, which provides a forum for nonprofits to "openly, honestly, and humorously discuss [their] own failures." FAILFaire gives the opportunity for the participants to share their mistakes so others may understand and learn from them, in order to make better decisions in the future.

One failure that was openly discussed involved an initiative undertaken by the World Lung Foundation as part of an antismoking campaign. The World Lung Foundation promoted an application called Pack Head using the Facebook platform. The idea was that users would be able to add evidence of smoking-related health damage to their profile pictures (rotting teeth, throat tumors, etc.) and then share the pictures with their friends to warn them of the dangers of smoking. The project failed because Pack Head users were not happy modifying their pictures to depict health problems, and their smoker friends felt they were being judged for their smoking habit.[36]

Global Giving, a nonprofit that connects donors with grassroots projects around the world, gives out the "Honest Loser Award" to staff members who have tried and failed at implementing a new initiative. The recipient of the award then shares the story of the failure, why it didn't work, and what was learned from it. The culture of the company honors honest mistakes because they are seen as an opportunity to learn and innovate, rather than a source of shame and embarrassment.

DoSomething.org, a nonprofit set up to encourage people to take action on social change initiatives, holds a Pink Boa FailFest once a quarter. The presenters wear a pink feather boa during a 10-minute presentation where they discuss the history of their failure, what went wrong, and the lessons learned. Presenters allow two minutes of Q&A from the group at the end of the talk. They also employ fun, silly metaphors in discussing the lessons learned, such as a photo of a celebrity or a song lyric that takes the sting out of the failure.[37]

Other organizations take an even more eccentric approach to removing the stigma of failure. MomsRising, an organization that runs online campaigns to build a more family-friendly America, holds a "joyful funeral" for their failed campaigns. This involves giving the initiative a formal burial, along with a eulogy during which they discuss lessons learned and generate ideas for future campaigns.

For those who are still unsure about sharing their failures in public, how about adjusting your physiology to better cope with failure? Improvisation teacher Matt Smith developed the "failure bow," which consists of raising your hands in the air, saying "I failed," grinning submissively, and moving on. Smith reports that athletes who use the failure bow find it helps them get over the fear of making a mistake. When they adjust their physiology, it helps them to change their mindset from embarrassment and shame to a more positive state that welcomes learning opportunities.[38] ●

⑤SAGE edge™

Get the edge on your studies at **edge.sagepub.com/neckentrepreneurship**

▸   Master the learning objectives using key study tools
▸   Watch, listen, and connect with online multimedia resources
▸   Access mobile-friendly quizzes and flashcards to check your understanding

SUMMARY

11.1 Describe failure and its effect on entrepreneurs.

Learning and further opportunities often come with failure. Failure does, however, come with extreme costs (financial and emotional) that need to be well managed to enable success down the road. If failure is seen as an acceptable step on the path to success, it is much more likely that failure may serve to hone the business and the entrepreneurs behind it.

11.2 Identify several reasons for failure.

Failures come in all shapes and sizes. Common types of failure include deviance, inattention, lack of ability, process inadequacy, poor business process flow, communication uncertainty, and exploratory experimentation.

11.3 Describe the consequences of fear of failure for entrepreneurs.

Fear of failure makes the entrepreneur less likely to pursue and achieve the transformative power of learning from failure.

11.4 Explain the different ways entrepreneurs can learn from failure.

Failure often goes hand-in-hand with experimentation, with each iteration bringing a product or service nearer to the state necessary for market success. Something can be learned from any failure, and it's important that the firm and its founders establish a blame-free climate in which learning can be maximized.

11.5 Describe the significance of "grit" and its role in building tolerance for failure.

Grit is that "special something" that enables people to persevere though prolonged hardship to maintain commitment and achieve long-term goals.

KEY TERMS

Deviance 281	Inattention 282	Process Inadequacy 283
Exploratory experimentation 283	Intelligent failures 291	Uncertainty 283
	Lack of ability 282	
Grit 295	Pivot 279	

CASE STUDY

Abraham Lincoln, Sixteenth U.S. President

To live is to experience failure. There appears to be no way around it. Sooner or later, everyone fails. Some failures are small and private, such as indulging in a donut while on a self-imposed diet. Other failures are larger and more public, like flunking out of school. . . . All of us experience failure many times in our lives. Some fail miserably and get over it quickly, while others let it completely take over their lives. However, failure is not a permanent state, and there are actions that can facilitate recovery.

Boss & Sims (2008)

Abraham Lincoln was the 16th president of the United States. At first, it might seem strange to have a story about him in a textbook on entrepreneurship. When you study Lincoln's life closely, however, you begin to recognize an entrepreneurial quality to Lincoln's political career that served him well. Regardless of the field or industry in which you happen to work, the ability to think and act like an entrepreneur can prove very helpful in the attainment of success—as was the case with Lincoln's rise to the top of his political world. This case study specifically addresses Lincoln's capacity to manage and leverage failure along the pathways of his ultimate ascent to the highest office in the land.

Abraham Lincoln was no stranger to failure. In fact, he is often typecast in popular culture as the man who failed at everything leading up to his stunning election as President of the United States. In truth, Lincoln did experience many heartbreaking tragedies and failures in his life. Accompanying these failures, however, was a consistent string of successes and growth that eventually paved the way for him to realize the extraordinary position he achieved in the government—and later on, in the history books.

From the loss of precious loved ones to the loss of elections; from professional failures to experiencing terrible bouts of depression, Lincoln was no stranger to defeat and adversity. But Abraham Lincoln did not become great because of his failures. Everyone fails, but not everyone goes down in history like Abraham Lincoln. The thing that defined greatness in Abraham Lincoln's life was *how* he responded to failure and defeat. By choosing not to let his failures define or break him, he was able to turn his greatest defeats into inspiring victories.

Abraham Lincoln was born and raised in obscurity in the backwoods of Kentucky and Indiana, and his family's social class positioned him better for splitting rails and planting crops than pursuing politics. His father was an uneducated man whom Lincoln never had much understanding of, nor affection for. His mother died of illness when he was only nine years old.

Although he had little opportunity for formal education, Lincoln not only learned to read and write but developed a voracious appetite for books. He was known for reading anything and everything he could get his hands on, although he had only limited time to spend reading due to the unremitting demands of farm life.

The events surrounding Lincoln's entrepreneurial spirit and rise in politics began in his early twenties when he left home to strike out on his own. Some of his early adventures included river-boating down the Mississippi to transport a load of cargo on a flatboat headed to New Orleans. When he and his colleague reached their destination, Lincoln witnessed a slave auction for the first time in his life. The callous nature with which human beings were whipped and rounded up like animals to be sold at auction disturbed him. His firsthand observations of slavery in the Deep South left a lasting impression that would influence his thinking for the rest of his life.

In 1832, Lincoln served as a volunteer in the Illinois militia during the Black Hawk War, a brief conflict involving the US territories of Illinois and Michigan and a coalition of Native Americans led by a chief called Black Hawk. Here Lincoln showed early signs of leadership capacity, being elected captain of his company. Around the same time, he and a friend from the militia purchased a small general store.

While managing the store, Lincoln became known for being unusually honest, a trait that would figure prominently in his reputation for the rest of his life. Famously, if "Honest Abe" found he had accidentally overcharged a customer, he would walk as far as necessary to return the customer's money. What is not so well known is the fact that the business soon failed, leaving Lincoln and his friend deep in debt. Not only that, but Lincoln's friend died, leaving half of the debt completely unpaid. Though Lincoln was not legally obligated to cover his friend's debt, he insisted on paying the full amount to their creditors. It took several years, but Lincoln eventually paid the debts in full.

In 1832, while the store was still a going concern and his business partner still alive, Lincoln also got his start in politics—and with it, his first dose of election failure when he lost his bid to become a member of the Illinois State Legislature. He learned from his mistakes, however, and after gaining more knowledge, experience, and polish on the stump, won election to the same body in 1834.

In 1835, Ann Rutledge, his romantic interest at the time, died of illness. This turn of events was devastating to Lincoln. It would be seven more years before Lincoln would eventually marry.

In 1836, Lincoln won re-election to the Illinois State Legislature, where he would serve for a total of 12 years. That year, he also was admitted to the bar and began practicing law, a career he would pursue for much of the rest of his life.

In the early 1840s, following his marriage to Mary Todd, Lincoln began setting his sights on the United States House of Representatives. He failed in his first attempt to win election, but succeeded in his second attempt in 1846. For partisan political reasons, he agreed to not run for a consecutive term in 1848. In 1854, Lincoln made another run at national office, this time running for the U.S. Senate representing Illinois. He lost. In 1856, he was considered as a nominee for running mate of presidential candidate John C. Frémont in the newly formed Republican Party, but he lost that bid too. In 1858, he again ran to represent Illinois in the U.S. Senate, but was again defeated.

Despite his poor election performance during the 1850s, Lincoln's political star continued to rise through a series of speeches that began attracting a nationwide audience. These speeches included the famous *House Divided* speech (June, 1858), the Cooper Union address (February, 1860), and his legendary Senate debates with Stephen Douglas (1858). Although he lost the election to Douglas, his articulate speeches and debates propelled him into the national spotlight where he became a prominent contributor to national political conversations.

Riding this wave of attention and publicity, Lincoln was able to apply all the skills he had developed over the course of three decades into his campaign for the presidency in 1860. A remarkable series of events followed, shaped in no small part by his own adroit political entrepreneurship. Abraham Lincoln, the prairie lawyer from Illinois viewed as a "dark horse" candidate, was able to win not only his party's nomination but also the general election, becoming the first Republican president.

Political tensions surrounding the issue of slavery had been running high throughout the 1850s, and Lincoln's victory sent shock waves that exacerbated hostilities. Before Lincoln was even inaugurated, the states of the Deep South had seceded from the union, initiating a conflict that burgeoned into the Civil War. Despite the enormous challenges of the war, along with his own personal tragedy when his son Willie died of an illness in 1862, Lincoln was able to again defy the odds and win re-election in 1864. In his final months in office—and on Earth—Lincoln issued the Emancipation Proclamation, brought about the passage of the 13th Amendment to the Constitution to end slavery nationwide, and led the Union to victory in the Civil War. Five days after the Confederate surrender, he was murdered by an assassin's bullet, cementing his legacy as a national martyr.

Lincoln's greatest achievement is found in the opportunity for success he opened up for others, particularly African Americans. His words from the Gettysburg Address are a continual reminder that "all men are created equal," going on to inspire generations of successful African American entrepreneurs. Seen through a long historical lens, Lincoln's courageous actions can be credited as setting the stage for Barack Obama to achieve the same office of President that Lincoln once occupied.

Critical Thinking Questions

1. What role did failure play in creating Abraham Lincoln's many successes?

2. What failures or tragedies have you experienced in your life that could potentially serve as a platform for future joys and successes?

3. Consider the opportunities Lincoln opened up for others, particularly African Americans. What is something you could do as an entrepreneur to open up new avenues for others who may not be as fortunate as you?

Sources

Abraham Lincoln Online. *Lincoln's failures?* Retrieved from http://www.abrahamlincolnonline.org/lincoln/education/failures.htm

Abraham Lincoln Online. *Pre-Presidential political timeline.* Retrieved from http://www.abrahamlincolnonline.org/lincoln/education/polbrief.htm

Blaisdel, B. (2005). *The wit and wisdom of Abraham Lincoln: A book of quotations.* Mineola, NY: Dover.

Boss, A. D., & Sims, H. P., Jr. (2008). *Everyone fails!: Using emotion regulation and self-leadership for recovery. Journal of Managerial Psychology, 23,* 135150. doi:10.1108/02683940810850781

Donald, D. H. (1995). *Lincoln.* New York, NY: Touchstone. *The Glurge of Springfield.* (2009, February 11). Snopes.com. Retrieved from http://www.snopes.com/glurge/lincoln.asp

Godwin, D. K. (2006). *The political genius of Abraham Lincoln.* New York, NY: Simon & Schuster.

Leidner, G. (1999). Lincoln's honesty. Great American History website. Retrieved from http://www.greatamericanhistory.net/honesty.htm Reprinted from an article in the Washington *Times* printed February 20, 1999.

National Park Service. (*n.d.*).Lincoln Home. *Lincoln's New Salem 1830-1837.* Retrieved from http://www.nps.gov/liho/historyculture/newsalem.htm

White, R. C. (2010). *A. Lincoln: A biography.* New York, NY: Random House.

PART IV

RESOURCING NEW OPPORTUNITIES

12 Bootstrapping for Resources

©iStockphoto.com/GoodLifeStudio

Waiting until you get funding for all your ideas can be compared with taking the chances of getting struck by lightning while you are standing at the deep end of a swimming pool on a very sunny day."[1]

—Gordon Sharp, author

12.1 WHAT IS BOOTSTRAPPING?

>> **LO 12.1** Define bootstrapping and illustrate how it applies to entrepreneurs.

One of the most common beliefs held by prospective entrepreneurs is that vast amounts of money are needed to start a business: "I can't start a business because I don't have any money—how do I get money?" Looking at entrepreneurship from the outside, it's common to believe that the key to success is to raise as much capital as possible in the beginning, but this is simply not the case. Very few entrepreneurs manage to get formal funding for their new ventures—bank loans are notoriously difficult for newly emerging businesses to access, and investments from "angels" or other investors aren't as common as people would like to believe. This is because entrepreneurs often have difficulty proving to potential investors the value of a business that hasn't gotten off the ground yet.

In fact, if you are intending to start a business without any external financing, then you are not alone—98% of startup businesses begin without any formal investment.[2] Some research has reported that 14% of the 500 fastest growing companies had begun with less than $1,000.[3] This method of starting a business is so well established that its name is borrowed from the old expression "pull yourself up by your bootstraps" (the small fingerholds used to pull on the entire boot), meaning to lift yourself by your own efforts. In entrepreneurship, **bootstrapping** is the process of building or starting a business with very little funding or capital or virtually nothing at all.[4]

Lawson and the Smeaton brothers bootstrapped their business, MorphCostumes, by working in their homes, keeping their day jobs, and each contributing $1,500 of their personal savings to get their venture off the ground. Many of the world's

Video
Bootstrapping and Entrepreneurs

Bootstrapping: the process of building or starting a business with very little funding or capital or virtually nothing at all.

Gregor Lawson, AFG Media/MorphCostumes (formerly Morphsuits)

Attire from MorphCostumes.
Credit: Simon Dack / Alamy Stock Photo

MorphCostumes, based in Edinburgh, Scotland, boasts over $15 million in revenue, 30 employees, and several lucrative licensing agreements with companies such as Disney and its Marvel division. MorphCostumes are made of skin-tight spandex that is designed in a range of different colors and patterns. They have recently taken center stage at parties and publicity stunts. In one instance, the "Power Rangers" descended on major global cities; in another, GAP Store "mannequins" suddenly came to life.

The company carries more than 300 costumes, including its "bread and butter," the morph costume, plus digitally enhanced T-shirts, masks, accessories, and ugly Christmas sweaters. MorphCostumes is backed by the Business Growth Fund (BGF), a venture capital firm that invests in small- to medium-sized British businesses.

MorphCostumes' meteoric success is all the more impressive considering it was launched in 2009 by three pretty regular guys. Gregor Lawson, along with his friends, brothers Fraser and Ali Smeaton, got the idea after attending a party where the guests were asked to dress head-to-toe in a single color. One partygoer went the extra mile, donning a stretchy one-piece costume in electric blue, which he had purchased on eBay. Though the costume was ill-fitting, Gregor was struck by the excitement and attention it attracted. "He walked through Temple Bar that night and was like a superhero celebrity, and that was when the first lightbulb moment struck," Gregor told *London Loves Business* in 2014. Gregor, who was then a product manager with Procter & Gamble, had worked with a number of brands over the years, but "I've never seen a response to a product like that," he noted.

So the trio got to work in Gregor's living room, thinking if they could perfect and sell the one-piece costume, they might make enough money to pay for an extra vacation or two. Each partner contributed almost $1,500 of his own money to get the business started. "We spent months getting the product perfect. It was critical consumers could see through, breathe through and drink through," says Gregor. Next Gregor, Ali, and Fraser built a website. With very little cash leftover, MorphCostumes (then Morphsuits) launched on Facebook.

"When we first launched, we thought we were the only idiots in the world that really liked this product," Gregor stated in the same *London Loves Business* article, "and there may be another 20,000 or so who might also like it." After many a late night, packing and shipping orders sometimes until 2 a.m., they saw over a million dollars in sales. Ten months after the launch, the trio quit their day jobs.

Though MorphCostumes was launched 100% through bootstrapping, the company's growth over the past few years is in large part thanks to a $6 million investment from the Business Growth Fund (BGF). The group took a minority stake in MorphCostumes, which allowed the team to hire more employees, build and tweak necessary infrastructure, and go after the big licensing opportunities. The investment capital freed them from the need to beg for bank loans, which would likely carry stiff terms and high interest rates.

Though MorphCostumes was already profitable by the time it sealed the deal with BGF, the money—and connections—set the stage for its next phase of growth. With little advanced skills in running a major business, the team's introduction to Ralph Kugler proved invaluable. Kugler had sat on the boards of major corporations including Unilever and InterContinental Hotels, and had turned his career to joining entrepreneurial businesses, either as a non-exec chairman or director, often investing his own funds and frequently backed by private equity.[5] "He is someone who the company would just never have met, let alone persuaded to join, without our introduction," said Duncan Macrae, an investment director in BGF's Edinburgh office, in an article about MorphCostumes in *The Telegraph U.K.* When Kugler joined the MorphCostumes as Chairman, he provided much needed expertise—and more introductions.

Today, MorphCostumes continues to roll out new product lines and gather new customers. While the company is a household name in the UK and many parts of Europe, there's still room for substantial growth in the United States. With a continued laser-like focus on innovation along with smart, hard-hitting PR (the company "pranked" the world press on April Fool's day into believing MorphCostumes had created the first-ever "invisible man" suit, for example), the MorphCostumes' star continues to rise.

CRITICAL THINKING QUESTIONS

1. **What evidence do you see of Gregor Lawson and his cofounders using assets other than cash to get their business started?**

2. **What level of accomplishment did the entrepreneurs have to achieve before they were able to secure investment capital?**

3. **What insights does this example provide to help you get your venture started with little to no cash? ●**

Source: G. Lawson, personal interview, September 27, 2014.

most successful businesses began as bootstrapped ventures, such as Coca-Cola, Apple, and Microsoft. It took only $1,000 for Michael Dell to start Dell Computers.[6] In fact, most of the entrepreneurial ventures we have described started off operating on a shoestring—from ugly Christmas sweaters sold from the basement of the family home, to bars and restaurants that started life as gourmet food trucks—demonstrating that great success can be achieved with very little money and a lot of ingenuity. Bootstrapping is all about finding creative ways to access every resource you have available to launch your venture while minimizing the amount of cash you spend.[7]

This means applying the following eight components of The Practice of Entrepreneurship as described in Chapter 2. Here is a quick reminder:

1. Identify your desired impact on the world;
2. Start with means at hand;
3. Describe the idea today;
4. Calculate affordable loss;
5. Take small action;
6. Network and enroll others in your journey;
7. Build on what you learn; and
8. Reflect and be honest with yourself.

The Practice of Entrepreneurship as reflected in the components above will enable you to think creatively about starting a business with little or no money.

Take entrepreneur Lon McGowan, for instance, who at the age of 22 started his first venture with $1,500 plus an extra $20 to secure a business license.[8] His idea? To import a low-cost digital camera called the iClick, made in Asia, and distribute it in the United States. Worried that he had only $7,500 in savings, he made his home his office to save on rent, created inexpensive business cards, and built his own website to advertise the product.

Yet he still had to figure out how to pay over $20,000 for the 500 cameras he would need to sell. So he decided to sign up for eight no-annual-fee credit cards that, combined, enabled him to draw $35,000 in credit, giving him the opportunity to jump-start his business. As a result, iClick is now a highly successful Seattle business selling low-cost digital cameras and other products.

Lon McGowan cleverly used credit cards to raise the funds he needed, but of course what he did was not without risk when you consider that interest rates on credit card debt can reach as high as 25%. Other entrepreneurs go down different

$SAGE edge™

Master the content
edge.sagepub.com/neckentrepreneurship

paths to find the money they need. For example, rather than seeking formal investment, it is more likely that entrepreneurs will turn to friends, family, and fools (sometimes called "the 3 Fs") for financial assistance. Many entrepreneurs have borrowed money from friends and family or people who are just simply won over by an idea and are willing to invest some cash in the business. While borrowing from these sources can be an easier and quicker way to get the cash you need for your business, it is better to treat the arrangement as a formal loan or investment with terms agreed by both parties. Many families have fallen out over arrangements like this due to lack of understanding, or broken promises. You do not want this to happen to you.

Bootstrapping or External Financing?

Video
Bootstrapping for
Resources

Bootstrapping is fundamentally an entrepreneurial approach to acquiring the use of resources without accessing long-term external financing sources such as raising equity from venture capitalists or borrowing from banks. Reasons for bootstrapping can include complementing current traditional financing sources, reducing reliance on them, or eliminating them entirely. Entrepreneurs may simply not have access to traditional forms of financing due to the lack of business history and credit. Additionally, entrepreneurs may voluntarily choose self-funding or funding from family and friends for all or most of the venture's financing to maintain most or complete control and autonomy over business decisions.

Although it is more difficult to acquire funding from more formal channels such as venture capital firms or angel investors, there are some real benefits to the formal route. Not only do you get the money you need, but you also gain advice and guidance from people who are far more experienced than you, as well as their contacts and connections that will, ultimately, help your business become more profitable. This was the case with MorphCostumes, featured in *Entrepreneurship in Action*, which benefited greatly from a $6 million investment from the Business Growth Fund, enabling the company to grow by hiring more employees, building necessary infrastructure, and pitching for licensing opportunities. (More details about external financing are presented in the next chapter.)

However, most entrepreneurs choose not to seek out angel investors or other external investors—at least not in the beginning. The truth is that most entrepreneurs appreciate the degree of independence and control they acquire by funding the business themselves. It keeps them focused and determined and allows them to grow the business the way they want to—on their own terms. They have the freedom to test their products and services and make decisions without having to explain themselves to outside investors. By not relying on outside investors, the business is not obliged to share ownership or give away equity. There is also no pressure to repay bank loans or any other debt. In addition, any cash flow or income from the business goes straight to the entrepreneur or back into the business rather than to the investors.[9]

The hard reality, however, is that in the beginning most new ventures are just simply not ready for investment. Outside investors are more likely to invest in a business that has been bootstrapped from the beginning, as it showcases the entrepreneur's level of commitment and resourcefulness as well as the market reaction to and demand for the product or service. Conversely, an entrepreneur who bootstraps a business with a good product-market fit, a committed team, and a decent customer base is in a much better negotiating position with investors should they express an interest in the business.

The Bootstrapped Startup

Most new ventures begin as marathon, not a race. This means that you are better off starting off at a steady pace and achieving desired milestones than trying to launch your dream business as quickly as possible. Beginning a business on a shoestring is the norm. By spending the time to build up the business piece by piece, you are more likely to generate a larger customer base as well as a steady stream of income. Once these building blocks are in place, there is a better chance of rapid growth and scalability.

As law firm president and author Jack Garson says, "You don't need to open your dream business on the first day. It's better to start with a successful hot dog stand than to get halfway through the construction of a full-service restaurant and run out of money."[10]

There are several different ways of bootstrapping your new venture. You can use cash from your savings, carefully use certain credit cards (like iClick founder Lon McGowan), fund your startup out of your salary from your existing job, or take equity out of your home if you are a homeowner. However, all these methods require careful thought—you need to consider how far you are willing to risk your own personal finances before getting yourself into debt.

Once you have a cutoff point in mind, then you will be able to gauge whether you need to move beyond bootstrapping to find more financial resources or to end the business altogether. This ties in with the concept of affordable loss discussed in Chapter 2—how much are you willing to lose to take the next step to bring your venture to life?

Whatever your chosen bootstrapping strategy (discussed next), it is certain that you will put in a huge amount of effort to get your business up and running. In the entrepreneurial context, this is called **sweat equity**: the increase in value or ownership interest created by someone as a result of hard work. For example, if you have decided to renovate houses for a living, you might save on the cost of hiring laborers by doing some of the work yourself, and adding value to the properties at the same time. Or you might build your own prototype of a product, again creating value while saving the cost of hiring a designer or manufacturer. Beyond sweat equity, let's take a look at a range of strategies entrepreneurs can use to bootstrap their businesses.

Sweat equity: the increase in value or ownership interest created as a result of hard work.

12.2 BOOTSTRAPPING STRATEGIES[11]

>> **LO 12.2** **Identify common bootstrapping strategies used by entrepreneurs.**

The key to successfully bootstrapping your business is to look for creative ways and use whatever resources you have to save money while you are getting your business off the ground. These "penny pinching strategies," illustrated in Table 12.1, will not only help minimize the costs of running your business but will also delay or alleviate the need for external funding through investments or bank loans.

Above all, remember the old saying, "cash is king." Rather than spending too much time fretting over balance sheets, forecasts, and profit and loss, focus on the amount of cash you have to keep your business operative. How long can you keep your business afloat with the cash you have? Weeks? Months? It's important to be mindful of your cash flow: cash in, cash out, and overall all cash needs.

Video
Penny Pinching

TABLE 12.1

Common Bootstrapping Strategies

- Work from home to save on renting an office; or if you need an office, use coworking spaces instead.

- Never buy new what you can borrow, lease, or get for free; for example, borrow or lease office equipment such as computers, printers, and so on.

- Take as little salary for yourself for as long as possible.

- Use your network of friends and family to get what you need at a reduced rate or for free.

- Educate yourself on basic legal and accountancy matters before paying high fees to a lawyer or accountant.

- Reimburse advisers and consultants with equity and goodwill where possible.

- Be frugal with your travel—drive rather than fly, and choose cheap accommodation.

- Hire help if you need it, but keep in mind that some employees may agree to work temporarily for an equity share in the business rather than a cash payment.

- Attend every possible networking event to make connections and get introductions to people who may be able to contribute to or enhance your business.

- Offer discounts to early customers to ensure a consistent cash flow. Not only will this help to cover overhead, but it will also help you build a loyal customer base.

- Negotiate payment terms with suppliers (if you have them), and explain how they will benefit when your business takes off.

- Outsource some tasks if you are struggling to keep up with the workload. For example, 99designs and Elance are good examples of websites that can provide you with the services you need, allowing you more time to focus on the parts of the business that generate the most income.

- Don't give up your day job until the business is being productive and making proper money.

Source: Based on information from Sharp, G., (2014). *The ultimate guide to bootstrapping: How you can build a profitable company from day one* [Kindle ed.]. Real. Cool. Media.

12.3 CROWDFUNDING VERSUS CROWDSOURCING

>> **LO 12.3**   **Explain the difference between crowdsourcing and crowdfunding.**

Crowdfunding: the process of raising funding for a new venture from a large audience (the "crowd"), typically through the Internet.

Crowdsourcing: the process of using the Internet to attract, aggregate, and manage ostensibly inexpensive or even free labor from enthusiastic customers and like-minded people.

As new entrepreneurs quickly learn, formal investment is very difficult to get, and bootstrapping can take you only so far. The emergence of **crowdfunding**—the process of raising capital for a new venture from a large audience (the "crowd"), typically through the Internet—has been a new pathway for many entrepreneurs. People who use crowdfunding to raise money are known as "crowdfunders," and people who contribute financial support to crowdfunding ventures are known as "backers."[12] Usually, crowdfunding works by drawing on small contributions from a large number of people to fund entrepreneurial ventures.[13]

Crowdfunding is often confused with crowdsourcing, but the two are not the same. Crowdfunding focuses on raising capital for new ventures, whereas **crowdsourcing** involves using the Internet to attract, aggregate, and manage ostensibly inexpensive or even free labor from enthusiastic customers and like-minded people. Thus, crowdfunding is a resource for money, and crowdsourcing is a resource for talent and labor.

Bootstrapping for Resources

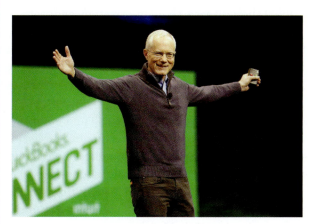

Scott Cook, founder of software company, Intuit
Credit: John Medina/Getty Images Entertainment

Entrepreneurial startups struggling to acquire resources are confronted daily with ethical decisions and temptations. Scott Cook is the founder of Intuit, the umbrella organization for such software products as TurboTax and Quicken. Cook tells of how Intuit, as a startup, was rejected in a request for a $2 million investment from venture capitalists. Product development costs quickly exhausted Cook's $151,000 bootstrapped investment, and the company had three desperate years of struggling to remain in business.

Cook noted that the shame associated with the very real potential of failure tests entrepreneurs' ethical foundations. Entrepreneurs often make decisions to "embellish" details about their product or service based on the possibility of failure—in Cook's words, "Gee, if I don't fib about this, I'm going to fail, and if I fail, I'll lose all my money, and my wife and kids, and my self-respect." Cook suggests that entrepreneurs should instead consider the possibility of success as a consequence of an unethical decision. What happens, Cook asks, if you decide to lie, and the lie is successful? Both customers and employees may know you lied. The outcome is a culture in which lying is acceptable behavior, and while it may be linked with short-term success, it also leads to an erosion of trust.

Each daily decision is a brick in the foundational culture of the company, so it is important to consider the ethics of each decision. Accumulated over time, decisions create cultures, and cultures generate stories through which employees, customers, suppliers, and investors learn about the character of the organization and the people who inhabit it. Cook emphasized that when an entrepreneur creates the right culture, employees will do the right thing.

CRITICAL THINKING QUESTIONS

1. **Do you want to work in a company with a cultural story about success achieved from lying or tricking others?**

2. **How much "embellishment" is it acceptable for entrepreneurs to convey about their product or service?**

3. **How do you determine the point at which an embellishment has to be acknowledged and the truth told—or the embellishment exaggerated even further?** ●

Sources
Cook, P. (1992, September 1). *The ethics of bootstrapping.* Retrieved from Inc.com: http://www.inc.com/magazine/19920901/4288.html
Malmström, M. (2013, December 10). Typologies of bootstrap financing behavior in small ventures. *Venture Capital: An International Journal of Entrepreneurial Finance, 16*(1), 2750. doi:10.1080/13691066.2013.863064

Like crowdfunding, crowdsourcing is a form of bootstrapping because it is a valuable method of saving money by utilizing the expertise and knowledge of the crowd to bring your ideas to life.

Throughout this text we have emphasized the importance of information as a critical and valuable resource, and finding ways to access this information is key to the success of your business. However, sometimes it can be difficult or even costly to acquire this information. Crowdsourcing is a means of obtaining information that is contributed and shared by the members of a given crowdsourcing platform. Companies have capitalized on information resources by tapping into crowdsourcing social media platforms and social networking sites. Let's take a look at three different ways in which crowdsourcing is used to gain knowledge and information.

Video
Crowdfunding Concepts

Crowdsourcing to Improve Medical Treatment

PatientsLikeMe is a social network for people who are living with a wide variety of diseases and medical conditions, ranging from various types of cancer, organ transplants, and heart ailments to infertility and mental health issues. PatientsLikeMe provides a space where members can talk about their disease, share information, and learn from others. Instead of a privacy policy, the site has an "openness policy," encouraging its members to document everything they can about their disease: test results, diagnoses, symptoms, treatments, and so forth. Then PatientsLikeMe aggregates the data, removes any way to trace it back to a specific individual, and sells it to companies in the health care industry.

What is the advantage for patients? Why would people enroll and enter highly personal data about themselves and their disease and then let PatientsLikeMe sell it? The answer is that patients want to see improvements in the products and treatments for their disease, and they know their contributions help achieve that goal.

PatientsLikeMe appeals to members because of the future benefit from improved drugs, products and treatments—if not for themselves, then at least for others who suffer from that disease in the future. PatientsLikeMe's business model gets a key resource for free: detailed patient data that patients input themselves. The company funds the platform (investment), and the company's key processes aggregate and anonymize the data and identify interested buyers (pharmaceutical companies, medical device companies, and health care providers.) It is a business model that satisfies PatientsLikeMe, its members, and its customers.

Crowdsourcing to Reduce Labor Costs

The company Local Motors used crowdsourcing to develop the design for a new sports car by asking its community of members, many of whom are designers, engineers, and car hobbyists, to submit ideas. Thanks to 3D design software, over 200 members were able to bring to life their vision for a new sports car. In the end, it was Sangho Kim's Rally Fighter design that won the crowd's favor.

Sangho Kim's Rally Fighter design.
Credit: Gene Blevins/ZUMA Press/Newscom

Once Kim's Rally Fighter car design was chosen, members competed to develop the secondary parts, such as the side vents and the light bar. While the community was designing the exterior parts, Local Motors designed or outsourced the chassis, engine, and transmission—those parts that require expertise to ensure safety, performance, and manufacturability. The time from design sketch to market was 18 months, and the total number of employees at Local Motors was 10. By using crowdsourcing, Local Motors succeeded in saving on labor costs as well as inventing creative ways to improve efficiency in the car-making process.

Crowdsourcing Through Technology

Technological advances are greatly reducing the costs of design, manufacturing, and sales. What's especially exciting for entrepreneurs with product companies is the low cost of 3D printing and other tools that enable small companies to become microfactories. For example, free software tools like Google's Sketchup enable users to create a sketch of a 3D model of their own invention; this can then be turned into a 3D physical prototype using a specialized desktop printer like the MakerBot, which costs less than $1,000.

Once you're happy with your prototype, you can have it manufactured into the real thing in China. Chinese manufacturers have become efficient enough to manufacture in small batches (as small as a batch of one) while maintaining low costs—something that was previously impossible. Now small companies and even individuals have access to manufacturing lines that had been previously reserved for large factories.

Websites like Alibaba.com list China's manufacturers, products, and capabilities.[14] You can search the site to find companies that make items similar to yours. When you've selected your top choices, you can instant-message the factory using Alibaba's real-time English-Chinese instant-messaging system. Within a decade, Alibaba has become a $1 billion business by offering these tools.

Where does crowdsourcing come in to 3D printing? Plastic is not the only material used by 3D printers—other materials like wood can be used. Wikihouse, for example, designs and builds houses through a form of 3D printing without involving a construction team.[15] Thanks to crowdsourcing, Wikihouse blueprints are submitted by the crowd that has created plans and designs of any type of house imaginable. These blueprints are freely available online for anyone who fancies building an affordable custom-built home. Aspiring homeowners can get the parts digitally printed before assembling the parts themselves, much in the manner of an IKEA furniture pack kit.

Wikihouse designs and digitally prints the parts of a house for later assembly.
Credit: View Pictures/Luke Hayes/VIEW/Newscom

12.4 CROWDFUNDING STARTUPS AND ENTREPRENEURSHIPS

>> LO 12.4 Describe the effects of crowdfunding on entrepreneurship.

Just as crowdsourcing is a useful way to acquire valuable feedback and information, crowdfunding can be an effective way of getting the funds needed to start a business or at least show proof of concept. Crowdfunding is rapidly gaining momentum and shows no signs of slowing down. Crowdfunding has helped raise billions for all types of businesses, including art, theatre, photography, charity, retail, fashion, gaming, real estate, and much more.

Crowdfunding makes all types of entrepreneurship accessible to those who want to start their own business. In a time when banks have become more nervous about lending money and investors are more cautious than ever before, crowdfunding has become a democratized method of raising money for many budding entrepreneurs.

An estimated market value of $34 billion was raised through crowdfunding campaigns in 2015, with North America and Europe dominating the industry. Many crowdfunding projects seek small amounts of money (often under $1,000) to fund one-off occasions like community or arts events, with family and friends being the

Video
Crowdfunding

main contributors. However, more and more projects are becoming a valuable source of funding for entrepreneurial ventures.[16] California-based Pebble Time, which makes smartwatches, holds the record for the largest amount of money raised on a crowdfunding platform. Since the Pebble Time launch in 2012, backers have given over $20 million through crowd-funding platform Kickstarter.[17]

What kind of people tend to back crowdfunding campaigns? According to the 2012 American Dream Composite Index,[18] crowdfunding backers tend to be between the ages of 24 and 35, are more likely to be men, and to have an income of over $100,000 per year. This is a basic demographic snapshot of people who are most likely to invest in your startup through crowdfunding. Let's explore the different types of crowdfunding sites used by entrepreneurs and participants today.

Types of Crowdfunding Sites

Launched in 2009, US-based Kickstarter is the most established crowdfunding site, as well as the largest platform for creative projects in the world. Kickstarter makes its money by charging a percentage of the funds collected from each successful project, in addition to payment processing fees.[19] It does not accept projects associated with charitable donations, loans, or general business expenses.[20] The expectation is that the money raised will be used to further develop or complete a project, and that backers will receive some reward for contributing. As of January 2016, over $2 billion had been pledged to over 100,000 projects by almost 10 million backers on Kickstarter.[21]

North American entrepreneurs can join the Kickstarter community for free and start their own campaign by pitching ideas directly to a huge worldwide audience of potential online backers. There are three basic rules:

▶ Projects must create something to share with others.

▶ Projects must be honest and clearly presented.

▶ Projects can't fund-raise for charity, offer financial incentives, or involve prohibited items.[22]

Each Kickstarter project is set up to run during a set period of time with a set fundraising goal. Project creators can build web pages that describe the projects they are looking to fund and the specific goals they would like to reach, and that broadcast their ideas through promotional videos, photos, and other information. Kickstarter also includes a facility to get feedback before the page is launched, notifies you of funds donated, allows you to track funds and the number of backers, includes a way of notifying backers of progress, and includes a mechanism to reward backers for their support. While campaigns are allowed to last from 1 to 60 days, it is worth keeping in mind that the most successful campaigns tend to last 30 days or less, with the most contributions coming in during the first and the last week.[23]

When setting a funding goal, Kickstarter crowdfunders must be aware that a project must be fully funded by the time the period of the campaign ends, or they get nothing. For example, on Kickstarter if you decide to set a funding goal of $10,000, and receive pledges of only $5,000 within your specified funding period, then you will still not receive anything. In contrast, if you surpass your funding goal early on, you will still be able to receive contributions right up until the campaign comes to an end. Yet in most cases, potential backers are less likely to fund a project once it has reached its original goal.[24]

Rewards tend to come in many different forms; for example, if you are look-ing to put on a play, you might offer potential backers free tickets on opening night, front row seats, or the chance to meet the actors backstage after the event. Similarly, in the case of a clothing line, you might give away some items of clothing for free or for a discounted price to your early backers. However, as noted in the basic rules, Kickstarter does not allow monetary rewards or equity in a company. Recent studies have shown that backers who are promised to be first to receive a certain product when it is launched, alongside the reward, tend to give larger amounts of money.[25]

Not all Kickstarter projects are successful, of course—and some have had unex-pected twists and turns. One of the most infamous Kickstarter campaigns is the Coolest Cooler, a modern take on the ice cooler, which not only keeps drinks and food cool but also features a USB charger, a battery-powered blender, Bluetooth speakers, cutting board and easy rolling tires. Oregon-based entrepreneur Ryan Grepper was initially looking for $50,000 in donations from the online community, and ended up receiving over $13 million from more than 60,000 backers. However, despite the huge amount of money raised, the Coolest Cooler suffered from a range of setbacks, includ-ing delayed production and selling the cooler on Amazon before fulfilling its promise to deliver to its backers first. These "growing pains" led some of its supporters to lose faith in the product.[26]

The Coolest Cooler, which broke Kickstarter's funding record in 2014.
Credit: NBCNewsWire/ NBCUniversal/Getty Images

There are several alternatives to Kickstarter. Another crowdfunding platform, Indiegogo, is the largest global fundraising site in the world. Anybody on earth, regardless of their geo-graphic location, can use Indiegogo. Although it has a smaller community of backers than Kickstarter, it has a larger international pres-ence. Unlike the Kickstarter model, Indiegogo accepts projects where almost anything goes. For example, a couple who found out they had very little chance of conceiving a baby requested $5,000 from backers to pay for IVF treatment. In the end, the couple received over $8,000 from generous supporters.[27]

Other crowdfunding sites that are popular with entrepreneurs include RocketHub, which focuses on science-related projects; Peerbackers, which funds creative, civic, and entrepreneurial projects; and Quirky, which helps inventors raise funds. Quirky might be considered both a crowdfunding and crowdsourcing platform as it involves collaboration with backers on the development of a product or prototype. Also worth examining are Tilt, a platform for people to pool their money and raise funds together, and Crowdrise, which focuses solely on fundraising for nonprofits.

Table 12.2 provides some additional statistics on the crowdfunding industry.

Equity Crowdfunding

For those startups that are seeking investment in return for shares or equity, there is a new form of crowdfunding on the horizon called **equity crowdfunding**—a form of crowdfunding that gives backers the opportunity to become shareholders in a company. In 2012 President Obama showed his support for this type of funding by signing the JOBS Act, which legalizes equity crowdfunding in the United States.[28]

Equity crowdfunding: a form of crowdfunding that gives investors the opportunity to become shareholders in a company.

TABLE 12.2

Key Crowdfunding Statistics

Key Global Crowdfunding Statistics 2014
• $16.2 billion raised through crowdfunding platforms worldwide
• North America is the largest market for crowdfunding, followed by Asia, and then Europe
• Crowdfunding volumes are also vastly increasing in South America, Oceania, and Africa
Most popular crowdfunding categories worldwide
• Business and Entrepreneurship is the lead category for crowdfunding, accounting for a 40% share of the funding.
• Social causes account for almost 20% of the funding share
• Films and performing arts account for just over 10% funding share.
• Real estate accounts for 5% in funding share.
• Music and Recording Arts account for just under 5% in funding share.

Source: Based on data from Erin Hobey. (March 31, 2015). "Massolution Posts Research Findings: Crowdfunding Market Grows 167% in 2014, Crowdfunding Platforms Raise $16.2 Billion" Retrieved from http://www.crowdfundinsider.com/2015/03/65302-massolution-posts-research-findings-crowdfunding-market-grows-167-in-2014-crowdfunding-platforms-raise-16-2-billion/

US sites like Crowdfunder and Circle Up provide investors with the opportunity to invest in companies in exchange for ownership or the promise of future returns.

The equity crowdfunding model is also gaining popularity all over the world. Crowdcube, a leading equity crowdfunding platform based in Britain, had attracted almost $200 million from investors as of 2014. It also offers a service that provides an independent professional fund manager to monitor the money invested, as an extra reassurance for investors.[29] Or what about OurCrowd, which exclusively focuses on global investment in Israeli startups? These are only two examples of many international equity crowdfunding sites that are changing the way people invest.

12.5 THE FOUR CONTEXTS FOR CROWDFUNDING

>> **LO 12.5**   Define the four contexts for crowdfunding.[30]

Video
Crowdfunding Contexts

As we have explored, different crowdfunding sites offer different things to both crowdfunders and backers. We have already taken a look at some entrepreneurs who have raised funds through crowdfunding, but what about the backers themselves? What sort of reasons do people have for donating, lending, or investing in a startup? To answer this question, we need to explore four different contexts or circumstances in which people fund a project through crowdfunding: patronage model, lending model, reward-based crowdfunding, and investor model (see Figure 12.1).

Patronage Model

Patronage model: a context for crowdfunding that describes the financial support given by backers without any expectation of a direct return for their donations.

The **patronage model** describes the financial support given by backers without any expectation of a direct return for their donations. A large proportion of these donations are given to the arts. For example, when sculptor Carrie Fertig failed to get funding for a giant pair of glass dove wings to hang in Chichester Cathedral in the UK, she turned

Crowdfunding: A Revolutionary Change in Funding New Ventures

Crowdfunding is such a recent phenomenon that very little research on it has been conducted. One study used data from the largest and most well-known crowdfunding site, Kickstarter.

The study utilized data from 48,526 projects representing $237 million from backers. Of these projects, 48% succeeded in raising their goal investment. Failed projects tended to receive $900 in pledges in comparison with successful projects, which raised an average of $7,825.

The projects that raised the most money were in hardware, software, games, or product design. Geography also seems to play a role in successful fundraising; for example, people proposing music projects based in Nashville are more likely to receive funds because of the cultural associations people have with Nashville. Further analysis showed that alongside social networks, the most successful Kickstarter projects included a high-quality video, and consistent communication with backers. Interestingly, the study also found that the majority of projects that were successfully funded were subject to delays; for example, of the 247 projects analyzed, only 24.9% delivered on time. Projects that are overfunded are particularly likely to be delayed because of the increase in demand and expectations.

While crowdfunding is considered to be a revolutionary change in funding new ventures because it gives more people access to startup capital than ever before, the research questions the long-term implications of crowdfunding, given the high rate of products that fail to deliver on time.

CRITICAL THINKING QUESTIONS

1. **What would you consider to be the pros and cons of crowdfunding?**

2. **How would you use crowdfunding to raise funds for your own project?**

3. **How would you ensure your product was delivered on time to meet demand and expectations?** ●

Source: Mollick, E. (2014). The dynamics of crowdfunding: An exploratory study. *Journal of Business Venturing*, 29, 116, at 1.

FIGURE 12.1

Four Types of Crowdfunding

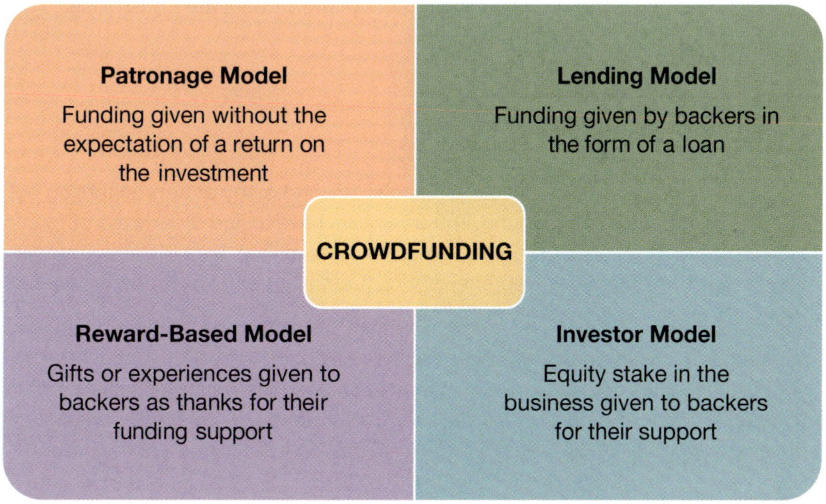

Patronage Model
Funding given without the expectation of a return on the investment

Lending Model
Funding given by backers in the form of a loan

CROWDFUNDING

Reward-Based Model
Gifts or experiences given to backers as thanks for their funding support

Investor Model
Equity stake in the business given to backers for their support

to crowdfunding website Indiegogo for help.[31] Fertig received the funds with no strings attached and was able to realize her artistic dream.

Lending Model

Lending model: a context for crowdfunding where funds are offered as loans with the expectation that the money will be repaid.

In the **lending model** funds are offered as loans with the expectation that the money will be repaid. Lending models can take different forms; for example, some backers will expect interest to be paid on the loan, while other backers might expect to be reimbursed only if and when the project starts generating revenue, or if it begins to make a profit. There can also be elements of the patronage model within the lending process; for example, in the case of microfinanced loans, where small amounts of money are loaned to impoverished people in developing countries, backers might waive any expectation of repayment as the loans are promoting the social good.

Reward-Based Crowdfunding

Reward-based crowdfunding: a context for crowdfunding which involves rewarding backers for supporting a project.

Reward-based crowdfunding involves rewarding backers for supporting a project. As in the example of Kickstarter, this is the most popular form of crowdfunding today. Rather than giving away precious equity or a large share in the profits, entrepreneurs give rewards to their backers, which can often take the form of more unique offerings such as product samples or experiences.

For example, Coolest Cooler founder Ryan Grepper rewards his backers by giving them the option to receive a discount on the Coolest Cooler product, or branded T-shirts and beverage cups. Backers who donate more than $2,000 receive a promise from Grepper himself to attend parties featuring the Coolest Cooler and to personally man the bar!

The Investor Model

Investor model: a context for crowdfunding that gives backers an equity stake in the business in return for their funding.

The **investor model** involves giving backers an equity stake in the business in return for their funding. This model takes a few different forms; for example, investors can either buy shares in the company, which means they would be given a degree of ownership or certain rights in a project; or investors can take a share of the future revenue or profits of a company without taking ownership. MorphCostumes, described in the *Entrepreneurship in Action* feature, gave away a minority stake in their business to investors in exchange for £4.2 million (nearly $6 million) in order to grow their costume enterprise.

YOU BE THE ENTREPRENEUR

Finding money to start a business can be difficult, and many entrepreneurs do not have thousands of dollars lying around. Entrepreneurs have to find other ways of funding their business, and it can be a struggle to get to that first million. Sara Blakely, Founder of Spanx, was one of those entrepreneurs who had to figure out a way to finance her idea.

Sara Blakely majored in legal communications, but failed the LSAT twice and ended up working as a "cast member" wearing a chipmunk costume at Disneyland. After that, she sold fax machines door to door. She had only $5,000 in savings when she came up with the idea for Spanx foundation garments. With no money to pay employees or pay for development, she would have a difficult time getting her business of the ground.

What Would You Do?

Source: Karol, G. (2014, Oct. 22). *How Sara Blakely built a million dollar business from scratch. Entrepreneur,* 1–2.

12.6 THE ADVANTAGES OF CROWDFUNDING[32]

≫ LO 12.6   **Explain the advantages of crowdfunding for global entrepreneurs.**

There are many benefits to crowdfunding for entrepreneurs all over the world. Not only will crowdfunding provide the money you need to get your business off the ground, but it also provides you with an idea of the level of enthusiasm and interest in your product or service before launch. This saves you money on expensive marketing as well as enabling you to gather valuable customer feedback, and to test ideas at very little cost.

Video
Advantages of Crowdfunding

Crowdfunding also enables you to build early relationships with customers who have a keen interest in your product and who will most likely purchase it when it is launched. When backers choose to fund a project, they become emotionally invested— not only in the development process but in the product itself when it comes to fruition.

For example, South African singer Verity Price set up a crowdfunding campaign to help fund her desire to record her own album. In return, backers were able to vote on which songs should be on the album, and help design the artwork. Price did raise the money she needed and was able to launch her album to a ready-made fan base as a result.[33] The point is that committed, emotionally invested customers are more likely to spread the word about your offering and help to promote it through their own social networks.

Another major advantage to crowdfunding is that there are different options to choose from. Just because you have a backer does not mean you have to give away ownership or an equity stake in your venture. In many cases, you will be able to keep hold of your equity and your independence. Most types of crowdfunding websites offer different things, and an entrepreneur is in the fortunate position of being able to choose which crowdfunding method to use.

Finally, crowdfunding is an exciting process. It is an excellent way for you to make new contacts, build your brand, attract customers, raise awareness for your products, and create a buzz before your product even hits the market.

However, do not be fooled into thinking that crowdfunding is a quick and easy process. By setting up a crowdfunding campaign, you are exposing your business idea to the world, so it is important to ensure that it's ready for that level of scrutiny. To succeed in crowdfunding, you need to plan ahead; think deeply about the type of customers you would like to attract, consider how to reach them, clearly communicate your vision, and convince your online audience that your product or service is worth investing in. You must also gather support from your friends, family, and other contacts, not only to donate or invest in it through your chosen crowdfunding model, but also to help promote your product with *their* friends, family, and other contacts.

12.7 A QUICK GUIDE TO SUCCESSFUL CROWDFUNDING[34]

≫ LO 12.7   **Describe 10 ways in which entrepreneurs can conduct a successful crowdfunding campaign.**

Crowdfunding may seem like a temptingly easy way to get your hands on the funds you need for your new venture. However, like anything worthwhile, it involves a lot of thought, commitment, and hard work. The following tips have been provided by entrepreneurs who have successfully raised funds through crowdfunding sites such as Kickstarter and Indiegogo.

Kickstarter Assessment

Kickstarter has projects in 15 different categories—from games to music to food, just to name a few. For this Mindshift exercise, go to the STATS area of Kickstarter (https://www.kickstarter.com/help/stats?ref=footer) and choose a project category that interests you most. Then, identify what you believe to be the top five reasons for successful AND unsuccessful campaigns in that category.

2. **Of the top five reasons for success, which do you think are most attainable for your entrepreneurial idea?**

3. **Of the top five reasons for failure, which do you think your entrepreneurial idea is most vulnerable to?** ●

CRITICAL THINKING QUESTIONS

1. **What conclusions can you draw about the project category you chose? In what ways is it typical or atypical of Kickstarter projects?**

1. Make Sure Your Product or Service Solves a Real Problem

Many of the entrepreneurs described in this text have become successful through their ability to solve a problem—they have managed to create something that people want to buy. If you think you have identified a product that provides a solution to a problem, then you will need to convey this message to your prospective backers. See if you can communicate your idea to your audience in no more than two sentences—if you can't, then spend time getting a clearer sense of the essence of your product.

2. Test and Refine Your Idea

There is no sense in setting up a crowdfunding campaign and presenting an idea that is half-baked. The most successful crowdfunding efforts are a result of testing, refining, and planning. For example, the first time Ryan Grepper, inventor of the Coolest Cooler, launched his product on Kickstarter, he failed to get the funding he was looking for.[35] In response, Grepper went back to the drawing board and refined the cooler to produce a much sleeker model with additional features. Eight months later, Grepper put his product on Kickstarter for a second time, only to earn over $13 million in pledges from enthusiastic backers. Grepper's success shows the merit in refining and testing your idea until it is ready for launch.

3. Be Prepared

You launch your product on a crowdfunding site, and suddenly the pledges start pouring in. Suddenly, thousands of people want your product! Exciting though this is, many entrepreneurs make the mistake of failing to plan for how they will deliver their product to such a large group of consumers. Successful entrepreneurs prepare for this possibility in advance by setting up links with their suppliers, distributors, and warehouses before launching their products on a crowdfunding site, to ensure they are able to deliver as promised.

Industry watchers have noted a number of common crowdfunding mistakes (see Table 12.3). Review those so that you are clear on what *not* to do; then read the rest of this section for more tips on what you *should* do to achieve success in crowdfunding.

TABLE 12.3

Common Crowdfunding Mistakes

• Choosing the wrong crowdfunding platform
• Setting an unrealistic funding goal
• Not having enough presence on social media
• Lack of updates or communication with your backers
• Failure to get feedback and advice from the "crowd" and other crowdfunders
• Insufficient media coverage
• Failure to deliver product or rewards post-campaign

4. Seek and Accept Advice

It is always useful to seek guidance from other entrepreneurs who have been through the crowdfunding process and have either succeeded or failed. You can ask the successful entrepreneurs for advice about how they did it, as well as requesting feedback on your idea. It is also very important to talk to entrepreneurs who have failed at crowdfunding, so you can learn about the type of things to avoid. Not all advice you get will be useful, of course, but listen with an open mind and think critically about how you can constructively apply the lessons others have shared.

5. Get your Campaign Started—Now!

Don't rely on crowdfunding sites alone to broadcast your product and attract an audience. Successful entrepreneurs have already started to build their customer base by spreading the word through social media and other outlets, before they even sign up to crowdfunding. For example, Danish entrepreneur Jonas Gyalokay, founder of wireless dongle Airtame, and his team each sent out 100 personal emails to their respective contacts explaining the importance of their idea and how meaningful it was to them. They ended the note by asking for support.

Video
Tips for Crowdfunding

You can even rally support by using local resources in your own neighborhood to raise awareness of your forthcoming campaign. For example, Allison Huynh, a mother of two and founder of gaming company MyDream, threw a Kickstarter party in her backyard. By inviting all her friends and contacts, she was able to showcase her game and whip up excitement for the launch.[36]

Even if your product isn't ready before your crowdfunding launch, you can release drawings or post a photo of the prototype on sites like Facebook or Twitter so your audience can provide feedback. People who are already familiar with your product will be more likely to pledge when it is officially launched on a crowdfunding site.

6. Money Matters

There are very few successful crowdfunding entrepreneurs who have launched a product without some kind of financing beforehand. Whether you use your own money, max out credit cards as iClick founder Lon McGowan did, or seek an investor, you will need some cash not only to manufacture your product but to cover delivery costs should your product be a hit.

When you are setting a funding goal, be aware of how much money you will actually *need* rather than how much you would *like*. Many projects fail because of crowdfunders setting unreasonable funding targets. If your goal is perceived by potential backers to be "too high," then they will not support you. By the same token, setting a target that is too low might attract backers but leave you with insufficient funds to deliver your product. It is important to do your financial homework to make sure the amount you set is realistic and conservative enough to attract backers, while also high enough to cover all your manufacturing and delivery costs.

7. Focus on the Pitch

In a crowdfunding model, the video pitch is everything (see Figure 12.2). Remember, you are launching a product to people from all over the world, most of whom you've never met and who don't know you. Your job is not to just sell them your vision but also to earn their trust. The way to do this is to be totally transparent about your idea. Why do you truly believe your product will change/improve their lives? How are you solving a problem? If you have competitors, why is your product better than theirs? One of the best ways to get your message across is to make a video (80% of Kickstarter

FIGURE 12.2

Example of a Kickstarter Campaign Site

Credit: ZUMA Press Inc / Alamy Stock Photo

projects include a video),[37] which you can even shoot on your phone if you have a tight budget. The goal is to let your potential backers see who you are.

In many cases, backers invest in a project based on their impression of the person as well as the product. If you are making a video, make sure your video is high quality and free of sound and signal problems. Also, when you are writing the description of your project, it is important that it be free of grammatical and spelling errors. As recent studies have shown, projects with spelling mistakes are 13% less likely to be successful than projects without.[38]

8. Make the Most of Crowdfunding Opportunities

Crowdfunding isn't just a money-making operation—it comes with additional perks. You get important feedback from backers, which can lead to more ideas and opportunities; and if you're successful, you also get the added benefit of press coverage, which can open lots of doors into other industries. For example, Gabriel Bestard-Ribas, founder of the Goji Smart Lock, attracted the interest of office supplies giant Staples, which contacted him during his Indiegogo campaign. The Goji Smart Lock entered into partnership with Staples, which includes the smart lock in its range of connected devices—however, the product ran into the supply shortage problem described earlier, being forced to announce delays in product delivery—a problem encountered quite often by crowdfunded projects.

9. Commit to Your Campaign

Successful crowdfunders commit to managing the campaign. If your idea proves to be popular with backers, you will need to reply to a lot of emails, and potentially send out surveys to gain valuable feedback. In the first week of launching his product on Indiegogo, Canary home security device founder Adam Sager replied to 3,000 emails. Overwhelming as this may sound, never underestimate the importance of engaging with your audience. Once you have made this connection, then you can continue the dialogue after the campaign is over, which can lead to all sorts of exciting opportunities. For example, Oculus Rift founders Palmer Luckey and Brendan Iribe originally raised over $2.4 million through Kickstarter, only to be later purchased by Facebook for $2 billion.

10. Avoid the Crowdfunding Curse!

Delays and setbacks in product delivery, and failure to deliver the promised rewards, are the biggest problems experienced by successful crowdfunders, who are often unprepared for the extent of the demand. Research has shown that over 75% of products are delivered later than expected.[39] In addition, funded projects sometimes fail altogether to deliver what they promised, which causes bad feeling among those who have been generous enough to donate.

If your product is not ready to be shipped and you know you are going to miss your initial deadline, then be honest about it. Make sure you update your backers via email and through the crowdfunding site. The worst thing you can do is to not communicate with your backers. Frustrated, impatient backers can destroy an entrepreneur's reputation and a product. They have put their faith in you by pledging to fund your idea, and they deserve to know what is happening. Don't let them down. If you are honest with them about the situation, and they are enthusiastic about your product, then many of them will cut you some slack. The lesson is to make a good-faith effort at all times to fulfill your promises.

FIGURE 12.3

Crowdfunding Checklist

Crowdfunding Tip	Stage of Completion from 1-5 with 5 = Fully Accomplished
1. Make sure your product or service solves a real problem.	
2. Test and refine your idea.	
3. Be prepared.	
4. Seek and accept advice.	
5. Get your campaign started—now!	
6. Money matters.	
7. Focus on the pitch.	
8. Make the most of crowdfunding opportunities.	
9. Commit to your campaign.	
10. Avoid the crowdfunding curse!	

Figure 12.3 summarizes the ten tips we have presented in this section in the form of a checklist where you can track your stage of completion in carrying out the advice given in each tip.

If your first crowdfunding campaign does not succeed, it doesn't mean that all is lost. Small changes can go a long way to ensuring your chances of success next time around. ●

Get the edge on your studies at **edge.sagepub.com/neckentrepreneurship**

- ‣ Master the learning objectives using key study tools
- ‣ Watch, listen, and connect with online multimedia resources
- ‣ Access mobile-friendly quizzes and flashcards to check your understanding

SUMMARY

12.1 Define bootstrapping and illustrate how it applies to entrepreneurs.

Entrepreneurs use their own sweat equity in combination with other bootstrapping strategies to make enough progress to get in a better position to attract more formal types of funding.

12.2 Identify common bootstrapping strategies used by entrepreneurs.

The list of common bootstrapping techniques is extensive. It includes ideas like using the home as the office, renting or leasing before buying, minimizing personal salary initially, developing and reaching out to contacts, offering equity reimbursement, and maintaining low operating inventories.

12.3 Explain the difference between crowdsourcing and crowdfunding.

Crowdfunding involves raising funds from a large audience, typically through the Internet. Crowdsourcing involves using the Internet to attract and manage free labor generated by enthusiasm for the product or service.

12.4 Describe the effects of crowdfunding on entrepreneurship.

The crowdfunding movement has provided a democratic means of funding that has never before existed on the scale it exists today. Equity crowdfunding has emerged as a popular crowdfunding alternative, where ownership stakes (stock) are issued in exchange for funding.

12.5 Define the four contexts for crowdfunding.

Crowdfunding largely falls into one of four types: patronage model, lending model, reward-based model, and investor model.

12.6 Explain the advantages of crowdfunding for entrepreneurs.

Crowdfunding is not just a means to generate necessary cash, but also a good direct line of contact with end users. Many crowdfunding options exist, and entrepreneurs are free to use whichever method they chose.

12.7 Describe 10 ways in which entrepreneurs can conduct a successful crowdfunding campaign.

Crowdfunding is flexible and exciting but not without its challenges; it's not free money. Entrepreneurs still need to make sure their product/service addresses a real business need, a benefit to customers that is being under-addressed or unaddressed. Successful campaigns start as early as is feasible, maintain commitments, and do not overpromise.

KEY TERMS

Bootstrapping 305
Crowdfunding 310
Crowdsourcing 310
Equity crowdfunding 315

Investor model 318
Lending model 318
Patronage
  model 316

Reward-based
  crowdfunding 318
Sweat equity 309

CASE STUDY

Goldstar

Goldstar is a successful online event ticket reseller. It was founded in 2002 by entrepreneurs Jim McCarthy, Rich Webster, and Robert Graff. Within a decade after its inception, Goldstar had grown to become "the world's largest online seller of half-price tickets to a broad range of live entertainment" (Walling, 2011) with nearly 50 employees (25 to 30 full-time) serving 1 million members (Mixergy, 2010).

Despite earning such lucrative success within their first ten years of doing business, McCarthy, Webster, and Graff got off to a rocky start—just like most entrepreneurs. Many successful entrepreneurial ventures are launched with seed funding provided by venture capitalists. Not Goldstar. It had no venture capital or other outside investors starting out. As a result, it had to bootstrap for resources to get its business off the ground.

Initially, the runners of Goldstar started out with $1,000 of their own money, $800 of which went directly to the state of California to get their business started. From there, they relied on "inside money . . . [making] the company one hundred percent founder, employee, and family owned." To remain solvent and growing in the early days of Goldstar, McCarthy, Webster, and Graff and their associates were organized, creative, frugal, and highly strategic in how they allocated company funds.

According to McCarthy, who is the company's CEO, Goldstar's business model is "based on the idea of getting people over all the barriers to going out to live entertainment more often."

Recognizing that almost everyone loves to go see live entertainment, and would love to do so more often if provided an affordable opportunity to do so, Goldstar sought to bring that opportunity within the grasp of more people, more often.

Before his Goldstar days, CEO Jim McCarthy earned an English degree. He also spent time teaching English in Japan as a young man in his early 20's. This experience broadened his perspective about the different ways people see the world. Later, he worked for Noah's Bagels (a forerunner of Einstein's Bagels) during a period of rapid growth for the company in California.

He eventually left Noah's to pursue an MBA from UCLA. It was at the Anderson School of Management at UCLA where McCarthy first met future cofounder, Richard Webster. Robert Graff also attended UCLA as an undergraduate student prior to becoming acquainted with McCarthy and Webster later on in his career.

After earning his MBA, McCarthy got a job working for GeoCities, one of the early eCommerce companies of the late 1990s. Later, McCarthy teamed up loosely with Webster and Graf for the first time when they concurrently decided to join Kiko, a new web-based business that dealt in eCommerce and eLearning. The dot.com bust of the late 1990s and early 2000s hit Kiko hard, and all three men eventually left the company.

Because of their proximity to each other (they all lived in Pasadena, California), as well as the friendships and professional synergy they had mutually developed while at Kiko, McCarthy, Webster, and Graff decided to join forces and start up a business of their own. In February 2002, Goldstar—originally Goldstar Events—was born. At the new company's inception, the three men agreed to dedicate 6 to 12 months to their new venture to see if they could get it off the ground with the fuel of their united efforts and the limited startup cash they were able to pool together.

Their new company was not an overnight success. The three entrepreneurs had to rely on unrelated, freelance side projects to pay their bills and keep Goldstar afloat that first year. Their willingness to flexibly do whatever was necessary to grow their business over time eventually paid off. This willingness is typically an essential component of any successful entrepreneurial venture. According to McCarthy:

> Everyone has bills to pay and obligations to meet. Somehow you've got to keep body and soul together in the midst of building a new venture and I think any entrepreneur that's not prepared to face the challenge of that probably isn't ready to be an entrepreneur. You've got to survive somehow both personally and professionally and if the business isn't paying you enough, you've got to figure out another way. Side projects are how we survived for a year and a half while we built the business from the ground up. It was kind of like having a full time job and a full time job.

McCarthy and his cofounders wanted to avoid going into debt to start their business. They also sought the executive freedom and autonomy that came from not involving outside monies from venture capitalists or other seed funders. According to Robert Graff, "We purposefully didn't want anyone else's money because we didn't want their advice." Hindsight being 20/20, McCarthy acknowledges now that investors seed money of $500,000 would have helped them grow much faster in their first year, but they were still able to earn success over time by patiently bootstrapping for resources and making things work on a shoestring budget.

Early on, McCarthy, Webster, and Graff relied on their own salesmanship abilities and previous experiences working with e-Commerce companies like GeoCities and Kiko. According to McCarthy, the goal of their sales pitch was to make it hard for potential customers to say no by demonstrating to potential vendors and customers how their service provided a "no-lose" opportunity. In addition to attractive sales pitches that provided legitimately beneficial services that many people wanted, the three men strove to make sign-up and other processes as easy as possible for any would-be vendor or customer.

As they began pitching their service, they relied a great deal on cold-calling venues, especially those whom the founders could identify as already provided discounts to other companies—information they were able to secure through market research. They also relied on their own personal networks, working to grow their business ONE satisfied, loyal customer at a time. Because they didn't have a big budget to advertise in the early days, they also worked hard visiting HR departments of big companies where they would promote lists of event deals and invite HR managers to share it with their employees through in-house e-mail lists.

McCarthy attributes Goldstar's initial sales success to focus and hard work, or as he puts it, "hustle." As a result, Goldstar didn't cost much to get off of the ground, sweat equity excluded, of course.

Because the three men all lived in the Los Angeles area, they initially focused their efforts on a local audience. As their business grew, they gradually began expanding to the Northern California market and beyond. By the year 2010, they had strong footholds in nearly a dozen major metropolitan markets and were selling approximately 25 million tickets a year. These sales raked in approximately $5 million in sales for Goldstar. In the process, they accrued a million and a half subscribers and were able to offer tickets to as many as 900 different live performances at any given time.

Jim McCarthy, Richard Webster, and Robert Graff—the three cofounders of Goldstar— successfully demonstrated that you don't necessarily have to possess a large pot of money to start a new business that eventually makes you a large pot of money. By courageously bootstrapping for resources, effectively applying their combined experience and education, and doggedly investing a lot of old-fashioned hard work and stick-to-itiveness, these entrepreneurs eventually became very successful. In the process, they made live performance ticket purchasing more affordable and convenient for millions of people throughout America and around the world.

Critical Thinking Questions

1. What kind of bootstrapping strategies did the *Goldstar* cofounders use to start their business?

2. What kinds of bootstrapping strategies did they not use?

3. How might the cofounders have utilized crowdfunding to further bolster their initial seed capital?

4. What risks does an entrepreneur take by bootstrapping for resources instead of securing seed capital?

5. What risks does an entrepreneur take by securing seed capital instead of bootstrapping for resources?

Sources

Mixergy. (2010, February 9). How 3 friends bootstrapped Goldstar into a $5+ mil per year discount ticket site. *Mixergy.com* Retrieved from https://mixergy.com/interviews/jim-mccarthy-goldstar/

Walling, R. (2011). *Ten highly successful bootstrapped startups. Softwarebyrob.com* Retrieved from http://www.softwarebyrob.com/2011/09/01/ten-highly-successful-bootstrapped-startups/

13 Financing for Startups

"There are two times for a young company to raise money: when there is lots of hope, or lots of results, but never in between."

—George Doriot, American Venture Capitalist

Learning Objectives

13.1 Define equity financing for entrepreneurs and outline its main stages.

13.2 Illustrate the basics of enterprise valuation.

13.3 Describe angel investors and how they finance entrepreneurs.

13.4 Explain the role of venture capitalists (VCs) and how they finance entrepreneurs.

13.5 Describe how investors carry out due diligence processes.

13.6 Explain the money versus power trade-off and the funding life cycle.

Chapter Outline

13.1 What Is Equity Financing?

13.2 The Basics of Valuation

13.3 Angel Investors

13.4 Venture Capitalists (VCs)

13.5 Due Diligence

13.6 The Entrepreneur's Dilemma

13.1 WHAT IS EQUITY FINANCING?

>> **LO 13.1** Define equity financing for entrepreneurs and outline its main stages.

In Chapter 12, we explored the different ways in which entrepreneurs can raise money for their startups through bootstrapping. We also explained how many entrepreneurs use bootstrapping in order to retain control over their business, grow it the way they want to, and keep hold of the company's equity.

While bootstrapping may be ideal in the beginning, as the company begins to grow and show potential, many entrepreneurs begin to look at the possibility of **equity financing**, which is the sale of shares of stock in exchange for cash. Most student entrepreneurs are not in a position to seek investment just yet; still, it is important to at least be familiar with the language of equity financing for the future.

One of the most difficult parts of being an entrepreneur is raising funds for start-ups. Balancing growth while preserving equity is a challenge, and entrepreneurs need to give serious thought as to whether—or at what point in time—they really need outside investment to grow. The general rule of thumb is to avoid seeking investment for as long as possible; to give your enterprise time to grow and build value so that you can secure a good deal with investors later on. However, sometimes competition will drive you to seek investment as early as you can. For example, if you have proprietary technology that has a proven market but you need additional funds to get the next version of the technology produced to reach a larger market, then equity financing is a logical next step.

Video
Defining Equity Financing

Equity financing: the sale of shares of stock in exchange for cash.

Jason Craparo, Cofounder, Contap, Inc.

Jason Craparo, cofounder of Contap, Inc.

Even in our hyperconnected world, there is disconnect—at least according to the founders of Contap, Inc., a pre-revenue startup based in Philadelphia. Kip Taylor realized that the process of swapping information was clunky. Business cards took up valuable wallet space, and although Facebook, Twitter, Instagram, Google Groups, LinkedIn were useful, each required separate searches and separate invitations.

Taylor wished for a way to share appropriate social media pages and contact information with others instantly, yet selectively. When he shared his concept with fellow Babson College MBA students Jason Crapraro and Det Ansinn, they both jumped on board.

With the Contap mobile app, users point their phones at one another's while tapping-and-holding down the Contap logo. The app allows users to share only the information they want: any combination of phone numbers, emails, websites, or any of their social media handles from Twitter, LinkedIn, Facebook, Google Groups, Instagram, and even Salesforce. The users can then view and interact with all their new contact's info from one convenient location. Contap is all about connecting with others quickly, seamlessly, and on the user's own terms, letting "you connect how you want, to who you want," according to the company website.

Explains Craparo, "There was a need in the market, technology startups were gaining tremendous momentum, and the mergers and acquisitions activity was blowing up. We thought if we could build something that was easy to use and instantly useful, that people would love it. And if people loved it, the money would follow."

Taylor, Craparo and Ansinn began the company with no formal business plan and no outside funding. They had only enough money to pay for a few rudimentary renderings, "then little by little over time, we funded the development in waves, $2,000 here, $5,000 there, etc.," Craparo explains. Taylor had been the one to start the business, pouring in $50,000 from savings and what was left over from his financial aid money. He lived modestly by sleeping on friends' couches, forgoing expensive Boston rent and the nightlife scene. When Craparo climbed aboard, he invested $20,000 from personal resources and also opened a convertible note, in which a few people on the Babson campus pieced together $15,000 at a critical point in development. Later on, with the help of that $15,000, they were able to show a finished working prototype to venture capitalists (VCs), who invested $275,000 in exchange for 15% equity of the business.

The prototype was not just useful in courting investors; it was leveraged to test their product within the target market: socially active 17- to 24-year-old college students with three or more social media accounts. A secondary market was identified along the way: young professionals who had recently graduated from college and entered the workforce. "These professionals are in an interesting position of having to create and manage a professional image but also have a social presence on the web," says Craparo. "They have many social medias, including LinkedIn. This market will really value the fact that Contap allows you to share only select social or contact information, depending on the occasion/relationship." During testing, the team wanted to reveal what these demographics liked, didn't like, and what they would do differently. The feedback proved critical to building and tweaking an app that fits users' needs and wants.

The founders' network continues to be crucial every step of the way. "We mapped out all the people we personally knew who could potentially contribute to our success," says Craparo. "Whether they had expertise in venture capital, tech, marketing, accounting, whatever, we enlisted and activated each person . . . disclosed what we were doing, and asked them very specific questions. We received great feedback and information from these informal conversations."

Craparo sees evaluating Contap's success as twofold. The first aspect of success is quantitative and customer-driven: the number of people who download and use the app. The second measure of success is financial. "This success only comes if we are successful with the first success," Jason explains. "If there are enough people on the app (over 4 million) then we could make a serious marketing play on the app, which would attract a potential acquirer of the app. That would mean success."

There are obstacles, of course. The biggest one is captured by the question that keeps Jason up at night: "Will people download this app?" Though the team members have researched their target market by testing, questioning, and refining according to feedback, Jason can't help but wonder about all the what-ifs: if the messaging is somehow "off," a server crashes, or a competitor gets a similar product to market before Contap does. "It's frustrating because we can work our tails off trying to plan for everything, but in the end, the customers will tell us if they like it by telling friends to download it too," Craparo reflects. He is all too aware that attracting further capital will be a lot more difficult without a solid user base.

If the app flops, Craparo and his cohorts are out two plus years of time, elbow grease, and tens of thousands of their own money. In his 20s, with a new wife and plans to start a family, Craparo says he realizes life could be easier with

a stable, 9-to-5 type job in, say, banking. But for now, the risk seems worth it. He feels the app could truly "add value to people's lives," and that's something he can't walk away from. "Living the life of an entrepreneur, is much more of the life I would like to live . . . whether financially successful or not."

CRITICAL THINKING QUESTIONS

1. **What are the potential risks involved in personally financing startups in the early stages?**

2. **When do you think is the right time to seek outside financing as an entrepreneur?**

3. **How would you use external financing to enhance your offering?** ●

Source: J. Craparo, personal interview, December 15, 2014.

Splitting the Ownership Pie

The idea behind equity is similar to splitting a pie. When you are the only owner of the company, you own 100% of a small pie. When someone invests in your company to enhance growth, then your pie becomes bigger. As you need to give away equity in exchange for the investment, the company is no longer fully yours. However, if the company does well, then your smaller slice of the bigger pie will be much larger than the original smaller pie.

There is no magic formula telling you how much equity to keep or give away. The founders of Contap managed to secure $275,000 from venture capitalists by giving up 15% of their business in order to help the company grow. As another example, Google gave up the majority of its ownership, so that cofounders Larry Page and Sergey Brin collectively own just 16% of Google stock. Though 16% for the founders may not sound like very much, think about it: 16% of an enormous Google-size pie is pretty lucrative.[1] At the time of this writing, Google was worth close to $530 billion, so 16% works out to almost $85 billion.

Let's take a look at the different ways in which entrepreneurs may receive equity financing.

Stages of Equity Financing

There are several stages of investment,[2] but for the purposes of this chapter we focus on the initial stages of equity financing usually provided to young companies: seed-stage financing, startup financing, and early-stage financing. **Seed-stage financing** usually consists of small or modest amounts of capital provided to entrepreneurs to prove a concept. **Startup financing** is the money provided to entrepreneurs to enable them to implement their idea by funding product research and development; and **early-stage financing** consists of larger amounts of funds provided for companies that have a team in place and a product or service tested or piloted, but as yet show little or no revenue. Contap Inc., as explained in the *Entrepreneurship in Action* feature,

Master the content
edge.sagepub.com/
neckentrepreneurship

Audio
Splitting the Pie

Seed-stage financing: a stage of financing in which small or modest amounts of capital are provided to entrepreneurs to prove a concept.

Startup financing: a stage of financing in which the money is provided to entrepreneurs to enable them to implement the idea by funding product research and development.

Early-stage financing: a stage of financing which involves larger funds provided for companies that have a team in place and a product or service tested or piloted, but has little or no revenue.

is a good example of an early-stage company that managed to acquire $250,000 in seed-stage financing before the app was fully built or target market validated.

One of the most important factors to consider when you are thinking about seeking investment is to find investors who are most suitable for your stage of the company. Timing is also a factor. There is no use trying to raise funds when the venture is down to its last dollar. For one thing, it can take at least six months to raise money; in addition, a desperate early venture may give away far too much equity than it should to investors, which can seriously dilute the position of its founders.

As the business grows and starts to take in more revenue, entrepreneurs may seek *second-stage or later-stage financing*. Even further down the road, a profitable company looking to expand and go public through an initial public offering (IPO) may seek investment through the *third or mezzanine stage of financing*. Finally, entrepreneurs may need *bridge* financing to cover the expenses associated with the IPO. These stages are displayed graphically in Figure 13.1.

Forms of Equity Financing

Depending on the stage of their venture, entrepreneurs have several equity financing options available to them. As we discussed in Chapter 12, entrepreneurs looking to raise initial funds tend to turn to friends, family, and fools (the 3 Fs). Typically, the 3 Fs either invest cash in exchange for equity in the business, provide a loan, or lend money in the form of a loan that can later be converted to equity (called convertible debt). Entrepreneurs may also use crowdfunding to raise money from their immediate network, as well as reaching out to a wider market. In general, entrepreneurs may raise from $1,000 to $100,000 through the 3 Fs.

However, entrepreneurs seeking more formal financial capital to fund a growing business may choose to seek an **angel investor.** They are investors who use their own

Angel investor: a type of investor who uses his or her own money to provide funds to young startup private businesses run by entrepreneurs who are neither friends nor family.

FIGURE 13.1

Stages of Equity Financing

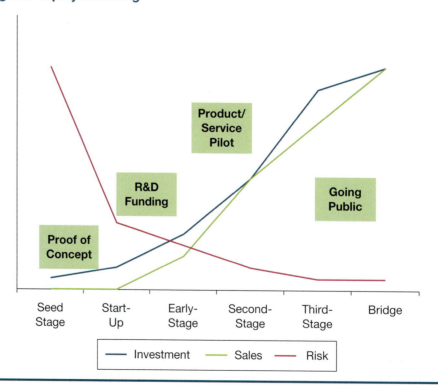

Source:https://www.marsdd.com/mars-library/angel-investors-seed-or-venture-capital-investors-that-depends-on-your-stage-of-company-development/

money to provide funds to young startup private businesses run by entrepreneurs who are neither friends nor family.[3] Entrepreneurs may choose to seek a **venture capitalist (VC)** who is a professional investor who generally invests in early-stage and emerging companies because of perceived long-term growth potential.

While angel investors and VCs tend to be looking for the same types of opportunities, there are differences between them, as illustrated in Table 13.1.

Seed-stage and startup entrepreneurs tend to seek out angel investors when they are initially trying to grow and scale the organization. While VCs also invest in startups, they are more likely to invest in companies in the early- to third-stage of business.

Venture capitalist (VC): a type of professional investor who generally invests in early-stage and emerging companies because of perceived long-term growth potential.

TABLE 13.1

The Differences Between Angels and VCs

ANGELS	VCS
Individuals worth more than $1million	Formed as fund consisting of Limited Partnerships
Invest from $25k to $100k personal funds	Invest from $500,000 upwards in VC funding
Fund seed- or early-stage companies	Fund from early-stage to third-stage companies
Carry out informal due diligence	Conduct formal due diligence
Responsible for own decisions	Decisions made with committee
Exit with returns on personal investment	Exit with returns to fund's partners

Source: Adapted from Peter Adams, "How do angel investors differ from venture capitalists?" (January 12, 2014). http://www.rockies ventureclub.org/colorado-capital-conference/how-do-angel-investors-differ-from-venture-capitalists/ retrieved on May 3, 2015.

13.2 THE BASICS OF VALUATION

>> LO 13.2 Illustrate the basics of enterprise valuation.

Before entrepreneurs begin to seek equity investment, it is essential for them to know the value of their company so that, when the time comes to raise funds, they will know how much equity to give up. This is where the basics of valuation come into play. Putting a value on a company that has very little or no financial history is not an exact science. However, when it comes to fund-raising, most investors will expect to see an approximate valuation of your business. This is needed so both the entrepreneur and investor can negotiate the equity percentage and division of ownership. But how do you value a business without any financial history?

The valuation of a seed-stage, startup, or early-stage company is based on the anticipation of future growth. How much time will it take for the business to become profitable? What potential does it have to grow? How can you prove to investors that your business is worth investing in? What is the exit strategy so investors can see how they might realize a return on their investment?

Video
Enterprise Valuation

How Can Entrepreneurs Value Their Companies?

As we have learned, there are very few overnight successes; entrepreneurs need to use the tools available to them to determine just how much their company is actually worth. Typically entrepreneurs value their companies based on the firm's potential in their chosen market. The easiest way to do this is to check out similar companies operating in the same industry to see how they are being valued.

Sites such as BizBuySell and BizQuest will help you to find out how much businesses are worth in your industry and how much they have been valued at when they have reached profitability. For example, a company that's currently valued at $10 million at profitability after 5 years could mean that it was valued at a fraction of that price at the startup stage. You can also seek advice from lawyers and accountants who can help to determine the market rates for companies like yours.

However, be careful not to get too carried away by other valuations. Just because a similar company is worth millions doesn't mean your company is worth the same. Overvaluing your startup is dangerous—not only does it put investors off, but it puts the company and the entrepreneur's reputation at risk. Entrepreneurs are wise to value their startups by thinking like an investor.

How Do Investors Value Startups?

Expert investors do deals all the time, so they will have a very good idea of what your business is worth. There are a number of reasons investors fund startups, and their decisions are not necessarily just based on the numbers. By knowing the criteria that matter to them, you can better position your company to attract investors.

First, investors will want to know your experience and your team's past successes. Second, they will want to see how many people use your product or service. Even if your business is not currently profitable, showing that you have 100,000 users, for example, proves to the investor that you have a potentially scalable business if provided with the appropriate amount of funding.

Having a distribution channel already set up is also attractive to investors. For example, the founders of MorphCostumes (see Chapter 12 *Entrepreneurship in Action*) attracted investment because they had already spent months perfecting their product, and set up a website and a Facebook page that became distribution channels to customers all over the world. Thirdly, the industry in which you are operating might just be very popular at the moment. VCs are typically interested in investing in technology, as it usually means big business. For example, Jason Craparo, founder of Contap Inc., managed to acquire $275,000 pre-revenue investment in exchange for 15% equity by showing investors a working prototype.

TV show *Shark Tank*, where budding entrepreneurs get to pitch their ideas to millionaires in the hope of receiving investment

Credit: Tyler Golden/© ABC/ Getty Images

However, it often takes quite a bit of negotiation before entrepreneurs and investors agree on what they both consider a fair valuation of the company. Take the show *Shark Tank* in the United States (also called *Dragon's Den* in the UK), where budding entrepreneurs get to pitch their ideas to angel investors in the hope of receiving investment. On any given episode, you will hear something like the following:

Entrepreneur: "We are asking for $150,000 for 10% of the company."

Shark: "Your pre-money valuation is too high at $1.35 million. I'll give you $150,000 for 30% of the company."

What does all of this mean? First, let's talk about two important definitions: pre-money valuation and post-money valuation. Pre-money valuation is the company's value before it receives outside investment while post-money valuation is the company's

TABLE 13.2

Valuation Factors That Investors Take Into Account

FACTOR	KEY QUESTIONS
Market conditions:	Is the market ready for your product/service?
Competition:	What are the competitors in your industry?
Market opportunity:	What is the opportunity for your product? What kind of customers will be attracted to it?
Value add:	How much value can investors bring to your business through their expert advice and guidance?
Market comparables:	How does your product compare with similar items in the market?

Source: Adapted from Richard Harroch, 20 things all entrepreneurs should know about angel investors." Forbes. (February 5, 2015) http://www.forbes.com/sites/allbusiness/2015/02/05/20-things-all-entrepreneurs-should-know-about-angel-investors/ retrieved on May 3, 2015.

value after it receives a round of financing. In the *Shark Tank* exchange below, what is the entrepreneur's valuation of the company before receiving funding?

The entrepreneur is asking for $150,000 for 10% of the company, which means that the post-money valuation is $1.5 million ($150,000 / .10 = $1.5M). The pre-money valuation is simply the post-money valuation less the investment. In this case, $1.35M ($1.5M–$150K = $1.35M). The Shark, however, thinks that a $1.35 million valuation is far too high, so they counter with the new offer of $150,000 for 30% of the company. With this offer, the Shark believes the pre-money valuation of the company is really only $350,000.

It is with certainty that entrepreneurs and investors will always disagree on the valuation! Table 13.2 lists some other factors and key questions that investors take into account when valuing your company.

The answers to the key questions will help investors determine an approximate value for your business before giving you an idea of how much they are willing to invest. This is why it is important to do your own homework in order to prove that your business is worth investing in. By providing an estimated valuation of your business before you meet with investors, you can display business savvy and commitment to growth.

Convertible Debt

Because valuation can be complicated when a business is new, entrepreneurs and investors often opt for **convertible debt** (also known as a *convertible bond* or *convertible note*), which is a short-term loan that can be turned into equity when future financing is issued. Convertible debt is a middle ground between debt and equity financing.

For example, say you are running a startup and you fully believe that you need to attract a significant amount of venture capital to make your business succeed. However, you are aware that VC investment doesn't happen overnight, so you still need to raise money in the immediate future to get your business off the ground. In this early stage of business, you might first ask potential lenders such as friends, family, and angel investors to invest; but you will need to think about the terms to offer them in exchange for their investment.

In the context of seed financing, these early lenders will loan you the money to help you attract venture capital. But rather than get the money back with interest when you

Convertible debt: (also known as convertible bond or a convertible note)—a short-term loan that can be turned into equity when future financing is issued.

Web
Convertible Debt

do receive investment from a VC, these lenders receive stock instead. In other words, the initial debt converts to shares of stock after an agreed certain point, which is called a conversion event—for example, entrepreneurs and investors may agree to set the conversion after a product reaches $100,000 in profit or achieves $1 million in revenue.

Benefits and advantages

One of the main advantages of issuing convertible debt is that it removes the need for valuation—in other words, you don't have to spend lots of time trying to figure out how much your company is worth to establish a stock share price. In fact, valuation becomes much easier after the first round of financing when there is a lot more data and information to work with.

Another benefit of convertible debt is that if your company succeeds, your investors may be entitled to a discount off the share price or bonus when converting the debt into equity, which can provide an incentive for your investors to commit. However, caution must be taken when setting a discount—if the discount is too low, investors may not want to commit, and if the discount is too high, the investor may take this into account when pricing the stock, which may end up coming out of your own shares.

Finally, by issuing convertible debt, you the entrepreneur, will remain the majority stockholder, with no interference from your lenders. Depending on the terms, they will have no control, no voting rights, nor any say over how you run your company.

Cautions and disadvantages

However, there are also some disadvantages to convertible debt: Early lenders may not want to take the risk of having their money tied up until the debt is converted into equity. They may also be wary of losing money if the conversion event doesn't happen (i.e., if profits don't reach $100,000 or revenue does not reach $1 million) or if the company ends up filing for bankruptcy. However, a clause can be added to address the possibility of the conversion event not occurring. For example, the initial investment could remain as debt (which the entrepreneur must repay).

For entrepreneurs, convertible debt can be a daunting prospect: Accumulating debt before the company takes off can be significantly risky. Similarly, if entrepreneurs fail to pay back the loan, they could be sued by the lenders. In addition, convertible debt requires a lawyer to draft the terms, which can be an expensive bill to pay early on in the life of a startup.

To summarize, entrepreneurs using convertible debt to gain financial support from early lenders such as friends, family, and angels, can be condensed into the following: "I need money, and you have it. But I don't know how much my company is worth, so let's see if professional investors or the passage of time will set the value for us while giving you an upside that's more in keeping with the risk."[4]

In the following sections, we will explore how angel investors and VCs can help entrepreneurs grow their businesses.

13.3 ANGEL INVESTORS

Video
Angel Investors

>> LO 13.3 **Describe angel investors and how they finance entrepreneurs.**

In the past, an "angel" in the context of investment was used to describe wealthy people who invested in Broadway theatrical productions.[5] Over the years, the term "angel" has evolved to anyone who uses personal capital to invest in an entrepreneurial venture. Angels are eligible to invest as long as they are *accredited investors*, which is anyone who earns an income over $200,000 or has a net worth of over $1 million.

Apple, Google, and Netscape are just a few well-known companies that have benefited from angel funding in the early stages.

We may tend to think of angels as motivated by a pure spirit of goodness—so it's important to remember that the primary reason why an angel (or anyone else, for that matter) chooses to invest is to earn money. However, angel investment is not just about the money. Often experienced self-made entrepreneurs themselves, angel investors can add significant value by providing advice, skills, and expertise, as well as lucrative contacts. They typically enjoy the experience of mentoring others and the personal fulfilment of nurturing a new business and watching it grow. It is generally thought that the typical amount invested by angels can range from $25,000 to $100,000.[6] Angel investors usually look for opportunities in young startups that can be expected to return 10 times their investment in five years.[7]

Angels originally were wealthy patrons who supported theatrical productions.
Credit: David M. Benett/Getty Images Entertainment

Finding an Angel Investor

Angels used to be a notoriously elusive group, but thanks to sites like AngelList, today it is much easier to find a business angel. There are still some angels who will accept only referrals, but most angels will consider unsolicited submissions of ideas. Even so, when looking for an angel, it's always best to start with whom you know. Tap your network and think about who could provide you with an introduction to an angel. For example, Steve Jobs was introduced to his business angel through another investor, and Google's Sergey Brin and Larry Page found their angel through a faculty member at Stanford University.[8] Among those who can provide you with referrals to angels are attorneys, other entrepreneurs, work colleagues, university faculty, VCs, and investment bankers. Angels receive many unsolicited ideas every day, but having a professional vouch for you is always a good start.

Table 13.3 outlines some reasons why angels and entrepreneurs can sometimes be a good match. The most successful working relationships are based on finding the right match for your business. The perfect match very much depends on the type of angel you are looking for.

Types of Angel Investors[9]

Business angels have many different objectives and styles of operating. They range from silent investors to those who want full involvement in the operations of the company, either as a consultant or as a full-time partner in the business.

To help you choose the angel who is most suited to your venture, it is useful to know the different types of business angels. There are five main types of business angels: entrepreneurial, corporate, professional, enthusiast, and micromanagement. Let's take a look at each of these.

Entrepreneurial angels

Entrepreneurial angels are entrepreneurs who have already successfully started and operated their own businesses, which they may or may not still be running. Either way, they generally have a steady flow of income that allows them to take higher investment

TABLE 13.3

Why Angels and Entrepreneurs Are Good for Each Other

• After friends and family, angel investors support up to 90% of outside equity raised by startups.
• Angels invested $24.6 Billion in startups in 2015 (estimate).
• Angels funded almost 71,000 early-stage ventures in 2015.
• Angel-invested early companies (less than 5 years old) over a 25-year period accounted for all of the net new jobs in the US.
• Economic research shows that the largest growth comes from innovative startups, the kind angels fund.
• Angels provide entrepreneurs with mentoring, monitoring and guidance.
• Angels provide entrepreneurs with connections and introductions to their widespread network.
• Angels teach entrepreneurs valuable business strategies that go beyond funding.

Source: "Angels and the Entrepreneurial Ecosystem" on the Angel Capital Association website. http://www.angelcapital association.org/about-aca/

risks. Entrepreneurial angels are the most valuable to early ventures—not only are they knowledgeable about the industries in which they invest, but because of their personal experience, they are in a great position to advise and mentor entrepreneurs.

Corporate angels

Corporate angels are individuals who are usually former business executives, often from big multinationals, looking to use their savings or current income to invest. While they primarily seek profit, many corporate angels want to play a larger part in the company, often seeking a paid position in the venture. Because of their experience managing in bigger corporations, corporate angels can often become frustrated with working in a small company with limited resources. As a result, corporate angels may be very controlling; in some cases this can result in a clash of cultures, even leading ultimately to a breakdown of the investor–entrepreneurial relationship.

Professional angels

Professional angels are doctors, lawyers, dentists, accountants, consultants, and the like, who use their savings and income to invest in entrepreneurial ventures. For the most part, they are silent investors, but some of them (the consultants, for example) may wish to be taken on by the company as paid advisers.

Enthusiast angels

Enthusiast angels are independently wealthy retired or semiretired entrepreneurs or executives who often invest their personal capital in startups as a hobby. They tend to invest in several different companies and rarely take a role in active management.

Micromanagement angels

Micromanagement angels are entrepreneurs who have achieved success through their own companies and want to be involved in the ventures they invest in. Many micromanagement angels demand directorship or a position on the board of advisors and expect regular updates on the running of the company. They will intervene in the running of the business if it does not perform to their expectations.

There are many types of angels, including the five principal types described above and summarized in Figure 13.2. The majority of them will be looking to invest in an entrepreneurial venture headed by someone who is passionate, committed, and genuine. They will also want to know your level of expertise in your chosen area of business, the extent of the market opportunity for your product or service, the estimated valuation of your business, the current state of your finances, and your expenses and projections for the future.

There are several reasons business angels will reject a pitch, some of which will be beyond your control. For example, sometimes business angels will reject a pitch for geographical reasons—in fact, most angels like to invest locally. Unless you are willing to move your company to their locale, then there's not much you can do in this instance. Another reason for rejection is that the angel does not operate in the same sector as you do—this is why researching the most appropriate angel for your business is paramount before you get in touch. Angels might also reject approaches that do not come via a trusted referral, so make sure to use your resources to find the right way to connect.

Angels will also reject entrepreneurs who do not come across as knowledgeable or passionate; they may decline to invest in a project because they believe the market is too small, the financial projections exaggerated/not believable, or there is very little need for your product or service at all. It is useful to review these reasons for

FIGURE 13.2

Types of Angels

Entrepreneurial Angels

- Experienced entrepreneurs
- Willing to take bigger risks
- Provide mentorship

Corporate Angels

- Commonly former business executives
- Looking for ROI or a paid position in the new venture
- May clash with startup culture

Professional Angels

- Professionals from other fields (doctors, lawyers, etc.)
- Commonly silent investors
- May want to become paid advisors

Enthusiast Angels

- Independently wealthy
- Retired entrepreneurs or executives
- Investing is a hobby

Micromanagement Angels

- Experienced entrepreneurs
- Looking for hands-on involvement in new ventures

rejection when you are preparing to meet with an angel investor, so that you can come prepared with excellent arguments that will convince him or her that your business is worth a shot.

Angel Groups

In recent years, angel investors have begun to form into groups in order to share their knowledge and collaborate to find startups to invest in. Table 13.4 illustrates the top 10 angel groups in the United States and the startups they have funded. These angel groups are spread all over the country and tend to specialize in specific areas. For example, Golden Seeds focuses solely on women-led startups, while Tech Coast Angels looks for technology startups in particular.

Yet the formation of angel groups has not been the only way angels have evolved over the last few years. Angel investing in entrepreneurs is also breaking barriers for women. There has been a major increase in the percentage of angel investors (from 22% to 50%), many of whom are more likely to invest in women-led companies than men.[10]

Research also suggests that women are better investors than men, as they take more time researching potential entrepreneurial ventures, and take on less risk.[11] Women-led angel funds such as Belle Capital, Golden Seeds, and the Texas Women Ventures fund are doing much to increase the visibility of women angels by showing the amount of value they can add to entrepreneurial ventures.

In stark contrast to the rise in women angels, there are very few minority business angels (defined as African American, Hispanic, Asian, or Native American), accounting for just 4.5% of the angel population. In an effort to address this imbalance, groups like TiE Angels, a South Asian funding community, have been set up for entrepreneurs seeking minority investors.[12]

Generally, if your venture is at an early stage, then business angels are the most likely source of funding. However, at a later stage, when your concept is proven and

TABLE 13.4

Most Active Angels Groups in the US 2015

Alliance of Angels
Central Texas Angel Network
Desert Angels
Houston Angel Network
Hyde Park Angels
Keiretsu Forum
Launchpad Venture Group
Maine Angels
New York Angels
Sand Hill Angels
Tech Coast Angels
Wisconsin Investment Partners

Source: Angel Resource Institute of Willamette University. (2015). The Halo Report: 2015 Annual Report. Retrieved from http://www.angelresourceinstitute.org/~/media/Files/Halo%20Report%202015%20Annual%20vFinal.pdf

you have obtained initial revenues, you may choose to seek venture capital in order to expand the company more quickly.

YOU BE THE ENTREPRENEUR

Giving up equity is not an exact science, and entrepreneurs need to think very carefully about the possible pros and cons of giving away a part of their young business. Derek Pacque, founder of Coatchex—a company that has developed an automated system for checking coats and bags at events—had to make a tough decision to give up equity for the sake of growing his business.

When Pacque had the opportunity to appear on *Shark Tank* in 2012, he had to agree to the conditions for appearing on the show—which included giving up 2% of the company's annual profits, or 5% equity to Finnmax, *Shark Tank*'s production company (a standard clause that was removed in late 2013). Pacque had to decide whether the exposure to the *Shark Tank* audience of 8 million people was worth the financial sacrifice.

What Would You Do?

Source: Colao, J. J. (2013, July 13). Is Shark Tank really worth 5% of your company? Business owners say, "Absolutely." *Forbes*. Retrieved from http://www.forbes.com/sites/jjcolao/2013/06/13/is-shark-tank-really-worth-5-of-your-company-business-owners-say-absolutely/#4485d1101b02

13.4 VENTURE CAPITALISTS (VCs)

>> **LO 13.4   Explain the role of venture capitalists (VCs) and how they finance entrepreneurs.**

Video
Venture Capitalists

Like angel investors, VCs are often former or current entrepreneurs, but unlike angels, they are mostly professional money managers. Like angel investors, VCs look for opportunities that are likely to return 10 times their investment in five years.[13]

Typically, these venture capital money managers form a venture capital limited partnership fund that earns money through ownership of equity in different companies. The fund usually goes through a 10-year cycle before it dissolves and the assets are distributed to each of the partners. In terms of investment in early-stage to late-stage ventures, VCs investment generally starts at $1M but there have been "megadeals" in excess of $100M.[14] Unlike angel investors, VCs are not really interested in smaller, seed-stage investments because it takes as much effort to monitor a small investment as it does a large one.[15]

The majority of VCs invest in businesses (mainly high-technology companies) that have proved there is a significant market for their product and service. It is extremely rare for VCs to invest in the seed stage of business. In fact, it is commonly believed that seed-stage entrepreneurs have a better chance of winning $1 million or more in the lottery than getting venture capital investment.[16] As Figure 13.3 illustrates, VCs invested in only 2% of seed-stage companies in 2014.[17]

However, when considering an investment in a business, many VCs actually look for entrepreneurial ventures that have received seed funding in the early stages because it legitimizes the entrepreneur, helps to validate the idea, and shows an ability to stimulate belief among the entrepreneur's personal network.[18] Investors attract other investors.

Even if VCs do invest in young companies, their investment often comes at a price; as they tend to take more equity, more control, and may even take over the running of the company. However, while it is rare for seed-stage entrepreneurs to receive venture capital, it is not impossible. For example, online mobile photo-sharing, video-sharing, and social networking service Instagram received $250,000 VC seed investment that returned $78 million to the VC fund. It is widely regarded to be one of the most successful seed investments in history.[19]

FIGURE 13.3

Venture Capital Investments by Stage

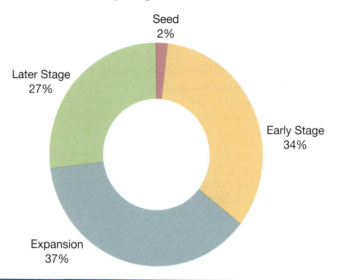

Credit: National Venture Capital Association Yearbook 2014 (March 2014). Thomson Reuters Figure 3.05 (on p 33) http://leeds-faculty. colorado.edu/bhagat/NVCA_Yearbook_2014.pdf

However, despite some success stories, the history of venture capital has been rocky to say the least. It is essential that entrepreneurs know about the highs and lows of venture capital before making a deal.

A Brief History of Venture Capital

One of the most useful ways for entrepreneurs and VCs to succeed in the future is to reflect on, and learn from, mistakes made in the past. Venture capital traces its roots back to the early 20th century. Wealthy families such as the Rockefellers, Bessemers, and Whitneys were looking for ways to earn profits by investing in promising young companies.

While venture capital was largely disorganized and somewhat informal at this stage, a more professional structure called American Research and Development (ARD) was created in 1946, by cofounder and Harvard Business School professor General George F. Doriot (considered the "father of venture capital"). Today, ARD is mostly recognized for its enormously successful investment in Digital Equipment Company (DEC) in 1957 when its initial investment of $70,000 was valued at over $355 million when DEC went public in 1968.

The introduction of the Small Business Investment Act of 1958 furthered the progress of the venture capital industry, as it officially allowed small business invest-ment companies (SBICs) to finance entrepreneurial ventures seeking startup capital. During the 1960s, the United States experienced a mild boom in the number of young companies that went public, but a recession in the early 1970s hit the SBICs, and many ended up in liquidation and sank into obscurity.

However, the venture capital industry began to experience a new high thanks to a 1979 rule that allowed pension funds to invest in venture capital for the first time. This opened the door to pension fund managers who rapidly invested huge amounts of money into new venture capital funds with the expectation of enor-mous returns. Huge successes of DEC, Apple, Genentech, and many more spurred more and more investment as each venture capital firm vied for the next success story. However, despite billions of investment in startups by multiple venture

RESEARCH AT WORK

Talk About the Losses[20]

Apple, Microsoft, Compaq, and Google are just a few well-known examples of companies to receive venture capital during their startup periods. The investment turned each of these companies into a household name. Yet, despite the number of success stories perpetuated by the media and the venture capitalist industry, the success of these venture-backed companies has proved to be the exception rather than the rule.

Recent research shows that venture-backed startups actually fail a lot more often than the industry cares to admit—as many as 3 out of 4. These findings are based on data from over 2,000 companies that received venture funding during the course of 6 years. So, why the silence?

Researchers discovered that VCs tend to "bury their dead very quietly." In other words, they prefer to talk about the wins and not the losses. It also depends on the definition of failure: for example, failure might be losing an entire investment in a company that is forced to liquidate its assets (which happens to 30% to 40% of US startups); or it could be failure to see any return, or merely to break even on their investments (which happens with 95% of startups). Whatever the definition of failure, VCs don't like talking about it.

According to David Cowan of Bessemer Venture Partners, there should be more talk about failures—not less: "People are embarrassed to talk about their failures, but the truth is that if you don't have a lot of failures, then you're just not doing it right, because that means that you're not investing in risky ventures."

CRITICAL THINKING QUESTIONS

1. **Why do you think VCs tend to "bury their dead quietly"?**

2. **Do you think it's important to learn about failures as well as successes? Why or why not?**

3. **What do you think you could learn from a VC about failed investments? Think of some questions you'd like to ask a VC on this topic ●**

capital firms during the 1980s, the returns declined. The firms had risked too much by overinvesting, and had failed to nurture or monitor the companies properly. Because of these problems, VCs became more cautious and limited investment in early-stage companies. As a result, growth in the venture capital industry slowed down from the late 1980s to the first half of the 1990s.

After this slow period, another boom was just around corner (known in retrospect as the dot.com bubble) as the Internet began to thrive and innovative Silicon Valley firms began to pop up. During the late 1990s, Amazon.com, America Online, eBay, Yahoo!, and Netscape were among the first tech firms that received venture capital funding. Blinded by the race to find the "next best thing," investors poured money into startup Internet companies without giving too much thought to how these companies would turn a profit, if ever.

The early dot.com businesses themselves made big mistakes. They had attracted venture capital because of the potential of the Internet—their whole theory relied on attracting huge numbers of people to their sites, without any clear strategies about how they could translate site visits into sales and sales into profits. These companies failed to plan properly, neglected research and development, and carried out limited promotion and advertising. As a result, hundreds folded.

When Internet stocks collapsed on the NASDAQ in 2000 (called the "dotcom crash"), so did the startups, leaving investors to deal with huge losses. Investors had overvalued the companies, and had based their investments only on ideas without proving they had market potential. As a result, VCs lost large portions of their investments.

FIGURE 13.4

Venture Capitalist Investment Over 20 Years

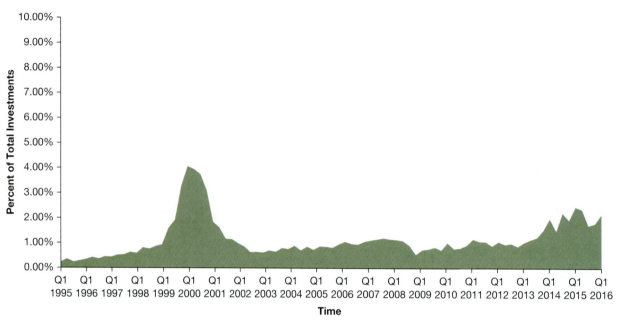

Source: Based on data from PricewaterhouseCoopers (2016) Historical Trend Data. Retrieved from https://www.pwcmoneytree.com/HistoricTrends/CustomQuery HistoricTrend

Following the crash, VCs have become a lot more cautious when investing in new ventures, and new ventures today have to do a lot more to prove themselves worthy of investment. The pattern of VC investments since 1995 is displayed graphically in Figure 13.4.

However, due to the gradual rise in venture capital investment in the years after recovery from the 2008 worldwide financial crisis, some experts predicted that another dot.com boom might be on the horizon. The rise of smartphones and tablets spawned the growth of a whole new generation of venture capitalist companies hoping to capitalize on this new market.[21] For example, messaging firm Snapchat received over $500 million in venture capital in its first five years. This has led to some questions over whether startups are expanding too rapidly, and causing them to overspend unnecessarily.[22] Both investors and entrepreneurs would be wise to learn from the mistakes made in the past in order to prevent history from repeating itself.

How Venture Capital Works

Video
How VCs Work

Today's VCs do not readily invest in seed-stage ventures as they once did, given the higher risk level. Yet there are many types of VCs out there, and the lines between informal and professional investors are blurring. It remains true, however, that professional VCs have the ability to catapult your venture from seed to high growth, so it's important to know how they operate.

Venture capital firms work within a specific investment portfolio, which means they have a defined list of the types of businesses in which they would like to invest. By narrowing these options, investors are often able to become experts in specific industries, which makes them better able to identify ventures that they think have the greatest potential.

VCs have very specific criteria for investing in an entrepreneurial venture, and these factors will very much influence the amount of investment made. Unlike banks, which seek return on capital through interest payments, VCs look for ventures that will earn them five to ten times their original investment. They place a high value on quality management teams with excellent business skills who can deliver on their commitments.

One of the most important criteria for assessment is you, the entrepreneur, and your management team.[23] The VC will base its decision on how well you work together, the complementary skills you have, and your shared commitment to growing the business. VCs take an interest in entrepreneurs who surround themselves with smart, talented, well-respected people who support their ideas.

In relation to the industry, your company will be assessed for industry–market fit, its anticipated growth rate, the value-added potential, and the age and stage of development of your enterprise. The VC will also ensure that your goals for growth, control, and harvest (the stage at which they will cash in their investment) are aligned with their goals and strategies. The decision regarding the amount of investment will be based on these criteria.

In short, investors look for three main things: great teams, big markets, and unique and innovative ideas. However, they do not give them equal weight: The team trumps everything else. Most investors would rather have an "A" Team with a "B" idea, than a "B" Team with an "A" idea.

Finding the right VC for your venture

We've discussed how VCs decide whether a given venture is right for their investment; now let's explore how you as an entrepreneur can find a VC that is right for you. First, recognize that venture capital is a long-term investment. Typically, a venture will not see an exit event until five to 10 years after launch.[24] All going well, additional funding will be provided by the VC every year or two as the company grows. Because you're going to be dealing with one another over a number of years, it is important to make the right match between the VC and the entrepreneur. If a good choice is made, you will have a mutually rewarding working relationship both financially and personally. It's also not uncommon to have more than one VC firm as an investor.

The process of choosing a suitable VC is going to involve in-depth research on your part, and the first step is to find ways to get in touch with them. VCs are an elusive bunch just as angels are; they prefer to be contacted through referrals from accountants, lawyers, bankers, and other professionals with experience of investment like business angels. The National Venture Capital Association is a useful resource for finding VCs. This site didn't work for me.

Once you have names and contact information, what information should you research and what kinds of questions should you ask? Table 13.5 lists some guidelines for this process.[25]

When you as an entrepreneur get the opportunity to meet with a VC, it is important to be prepared. You will be expected to explain clearly and concisely the market opportunity your business presents; the size and potential growth of your market; why customers will be attracted to your product/service; how your business makes money, or will make money in the future; how soon it is anticipated to reach profit; why you and your team are the right people for the job; and how your investor can exit the investment. By providing this information to the VC, you are displaying your confidence, knowledge, and commitment in your business, as well as reassuring the VC that you are in it for the long haul.

If the first meeting goes well, you will be invited for a second meeting that involves a formal presentation to several of the VC partners. This is the meeting that can either break or seal the deal, so it is crucial to allow yourself sufficient time to prepare. Following the second meeting, the VC partners will discuss whether they wish to invest in your company.

TABLE 13.5

Guidelines for Finding the Right VC for Your Startup

1. Find investors who can provide the amount of capital you need.
2. Check whether they are interested in investing in your company's current stage of growth.
3. Ensure they are experts in the industry you are working in and have a good track record of experience growing companies.
4. Look for VCs that can provide advice, contacts, moral support, and so on.
5. Make sure they have the time and commitment to support your venture.
6. Make sure they have a good reputation.
7. Check their history of building new companies.

Source: Jeffry Timmons & Stephen Spinelli, (2008) *New Venture Creation* 8th ed, McGraw-Hill Irwin: Boston, MA.

Why VCs might say no

VCs typically review over 100 plans and proposals a month, but usually thoroughly read and review one or two of these. On average, a partner in VC firms will do only one to three deals per year. This means a couple of things: Your venture really has to stand out from the crowd, and you should not take it personally if your firm is turned down. However, you can boost your chances of success by knowing why a VC may be likely to say no.

One of the most common reasons why VCs do not choose certain companies for investment is that the opportunity presented does not fit in with the fund's criteria. For example, the fund might invest only in companies within a specific geographic location, or industry sector, the deal might be considered too small/too big, or the business might not be quite mature enough for them to invest. As with angels and their criteria, some of these factors are beyond your control, but you can avoid wasting your time and the time of potential investors if you research their criteria ahead of time.

Another reason funds reject some applications is that they have a policy to review opportunities only via a referral. With such specific criteria, you as the entrepreneur need to carry out some careful research to find the most appropriate VC for your business, and go through the proper channels in order to reach VCs.

"Simpson, you promised you wouldn't tell anybody I turned down Bill Gates!"

Cartoon of investor who turned down Bill Gates
Credit: www.CartoonStock.com

VCs and entrepreneurs go through a process to build a trusting relationship that will last a long time. Decisions and deals are not made over night. If a VC shows

Find an Investor–Entrepreneur Pair

Investors and entrepreneurs usually have different perspectives. Sources of these differences include the size of the opportunity, the future growth potential of the business, appropriate business model, scalability, and company valuation, just to name a few. We often hear about the entrepreneur's side OR the investor's side, but a lot can be learned from comparing the two perspectives.

Your mindshift is to find an investor–entrepreneur pair. In other words, find an entrepreneur that had angel or venture capital financing and talk to the entrepreneur. Then talk to his/her investor. The order can be reversed; it doesn't matter whether you first talk to the investor or the entrepreneur.

Begin your conversation with a broad open-ended question such as: "Tell me about the process of receiving funding from investor X." Conversely, when talking to the investor, ask, "Tell me about the process of funding Company Y." Probe a lot, take notes, and then compare notes. What similarities and differences did you find?

CRITICAL THINKING QUESTIONS

1. **Was it easier than you expected to find an entrepreneur and investor to interview, or harder?**

2. **What obstacles or challenges did you encounter in your conversations?**

3. **Did you learn anything that surprised you or that ran counter to your expectations?** ●

---

interest in your venture, the next stage is an intensive due diligence process that the VC carries out to mitigate the risk of potentially investing in your company.

13.5 DUE DILIGENCE

>> LO 13.5 **Describe how investors carry out due diligence processes.**

Due diligence is a rigorous process carried out to evaluate an investment opportunity prior to a deal being finalized. When considering an investment opportunity, both angel investors and VCs conduct a due diligence process; but typically, angel investors and groups do not carry out as much due diligence as VCs due to time and resource constraints.

An angel or angel group generally conducts a proper analysis of the market opportunity to ensure it fits in with investment goals, and carries out background checks, legal checks, and financial analysis. Angels will also consider any personal conflicts that may get in the way of the deal; different ways in which they can add value; and ultimately whether they want to establish a long-term working relationship with the entrepreneur.[26] Table 13.6 lists the steps taken by angel investors when creating a due diligence plan.

Like angels, VCs are very careful when it comes to due diligence, particularly because of their history of making impulsive, wild investments in young companies. In general, investing in early-stage companies is risky, especially when millions of dollars are at stake, and VCs need to identify any potential red flags to ensure they are making a sound investment. During this process, entrepreneurs, their teams, and the company itself will undergo a vigorous appraisal, which generally lasts over a period of several weeks or even months. During this period, the backgrounds of

Due diligence: a rigorous process which involves evaluating an investment opportunity prior to the contract being signed.

Video
Due Diligence

TABLE 13.6

Due Diligence Process for Angels

Founders	Angels need to like and trust the entrepreneurial team before proceeding with the investment. Qualities such as leadership ability, honesty and integrity, intelligence, and good judgment tend to attract angel investment. They will check credentials to make sure the founders have the necessary skills to lead the venture, or at least have people in mind to provide those skills. To get to know the founders better, angels often meet entrepreneurs in a more relaxed environment and visit the company's premises in order to interact with the whole management team.
Legal	Angels will carry out a legal background check to ensure that there are no past or pending legal actions against the management team such as lawsuits, criminal convictions, and so on. Angels will also check to see if the founders own their intellectual property (IP) and have filed patents correctly—legal issues that we explore further in Chapter 15.
Market	Angels may conduct rigorous market analysis to establish the existence and size of the market for the product. This analysis includes identifying the customers and why they would want to buy the product/service; the competition—who they are/the size of their market share/ strengths and weaknesses; how the product is distributed; the pricing of the product; and how this new product differentiates itself from competitors.
Finance	Angels will check the financial risks involved before they proceed. This involves checking the accuracy of financial projections if they have been provided; cash flow and if the amount of money (together with the angel investment) is realistic enough to grow the business; the company's financial commitments and expenses—leases, salaries to employee and the entrepreneurs themselves, loans, debts, and so forth.
People	Angels may talk to a whole range of people before making a decision to invest. Some of these people include: existing customers of the entrepreneur's product/service; other angels (especially if the entrepreneur received angel investment in the past); other investors who may already be investing in the venture; and other competitors.
Exit Strategy	Angels will want to clarify exit strategies to better estimate when they will realize a return on their investment. There are several options for exiting.

the entrepreneurial team will be verified; references thoroughly checked; and corporate compliance, employment and labor, intellectual property rights, and legal issues reviewed.

During this time, it is important for the founding team to carry out its own due diligence on the VC. It is perfectly appropriate to ask VCs for the contact details of companies in their portfolio where they have achieved success, as well as those where the deals did not work out. Talking to others who have been involved with the VC is an invaluable way of garnering information that will help you decide whether or not you will be able to build a long-term successful relationship with them.

Exits/Harvesting

Video
A Firm's Exit

Part of the due diligence process involves the discussion of exit options. When VCs and business angels invest in a business, there is an expectation that they will receive a return on their investment when the firm exits the investment, within a certain time period, usually in around three to seven years. Typically, this money is repaid through one of three types of exit strategies: an IPO, mergers and acquisitions, or buyback.

An initial public offering (IPO) is a company's first opportunity to sell stocks on the stock market to be purchased by members of the general public. Smaller companies are often bought by larger companies through *acquisitions,* which are ways for bigger companies to increase their profitability and in some cases swallow the competition.

For example, Facebook purchased competitor WhatsApp in order to integrate it into Facebook and use its functionalities to enhance its own messaging services. A less common exit strategy is a *buyback,* which gives the entrepreneur an opportunity to buy back a venture capital firm's stock at cost plus a certain premium. However, buybacks are rare because the young company usually does not have the cash to buy out its investors, unless it has reached a highly profitable state.

Screenshot of WhatsApp
Credit:©iStockphoto.com/ hocus-focus

The due diligence process is complete when all the issues have been resolved to the satisfaction of both parties. Getting through the due diligence process is the final step before contracts are signed and you finally receive capital. It is also an essential part of building a foundation of trust and commitment with your investor—and remember how important that foundation is since you will be in the newly forged relationship for years to come.

13.6 THE ENTREPRENEUR'S DILEMMA

>> **LO 13.6** **Explain the money versus power trade-off and the funding life cycle.**

As we have described, there are many funding alternatives for would-be entrepreneurs. The type of financing an entrepreneur chooses often depends on her or his tolerance for varying types of risk. Quitting a corporate career risks the loss of a stable income and other corporate-related benefits. Investing personal finances comes with the risk of bankruptcy. Financing from family and friends risks ruining meaningful relationships. Accepting financing from investors runs the risk of eroding the entrepreneur's vision of creativity, company culture, and decision-making autonomy. Entrepreneurs, therefore, risk so much more than financial investments; they also risk personal relationships and the emotional well-being associated with the health of the business.

Yet being willing to take responsible, calculated risks is central to the entrepreneurial mindset. Instead of agonizing over what is given up in pursuit of an entrepreneurial opportunity, the key is to focus on what is to be gained.

Rich or King/Queen? The Trade-off Entrepreneurs Make

Very few entrepreneurs manage to make money and maintain full control of their businesses. Entrepreneurs who give up a bigger slice of equity to investors tend to build more valuable companies than those who give up less equity or none at all. Any investment comes with a price, and before you sign on the dotted line, you need to have a very clear idea of how you want to run your business, and what matters to you most.

Approaching Investors

A meeting between angel investors
Credit: ©iStockphoto.com/monkeybusinessimages

Acquiring capital from angel investors can be as elusive as acquiring it from a venture capitalist. As a serial entrepreneur and equity investor, Patrick Hull noted that relationship building and diligent preparation are keys to successful acquisition of capital from angel investors.

Angel investors mitigate risk by ensuring the entrepreneur is well prepared with a thorough and realistic financial plan, a good management team, and a detailed business plan. Additionally, as noted by Hull, angel investors are investing in both the company and the people within the company, making relationships crucial for funding decisions. Consequently, in addition to determining if your startup is compatible with the angel investor's funding preferences, it is equally important to discern if the investor's personality is compatible with your own.

An entrepreneur can gain insight from an investor's website on such details as typical investment amounts as well as funding preferences for an entrepreneurial organization's stage, size, geography, and industry. Gaining insight into the investor's personality, however, will require an investment of time and effort using networks of entrepreneurs. Gathering this data does not guarantee a meeting with an angel investor but it does increase the odds in the entrepreneur's favor.

Similarly, a meeting with an angel investor does not guarantee funding. Thorough preparation is critical, and it's an entrepreneur's responsibility to provide as much information as possible. The more answers the entrepreneur can provide, the more comfortable investors will be in establishing a partnership. The angel investor is responsible for filling in the risk-related gaps in the information provided and determining if there is compatibility between investor/entrepreneur personalities. Recognizing the substantial benefit that funding from an angel investor can have for a startup, it can be tempting for entrepreneurs to exaggerate aspects of the startup or provide dubious responses during meetings with potential investors.

Even if the angel investor does not provide funding, the meeting can lead to future funding or additional contacts for funding. Since an entrepreneur can't predict either the questions that will be posed or what value a potential investor may have, it is crucial to engage in every interaction ethically. Therefore, preestablished ground rules can provide guidance for ethical behavior in important, stressful, and unpredictable situations like meeting with potential investors.

CRITICAL THINKING QUESTIONS

1.   **You're in a meeting with an angel investor whose funding could jump-start your venture. How would you feel if you had to answer the investor's questions with, "I don't know" several times in a row?**

2.   **It's impossible to prepare thorough responses to all of the questions an angel investor may ask, particularly personality-related questions. What ground rules can you establish that will allow you to remain confident and ethical when not knowing the answers to an angel investor's questions?**

3.   **What would you do if you realized you had unintentionally provided critical but inaccurate information to an angel investor? ●**

Sources

Hull, P. (2013, April 26). 3 Tips to approach angel investors. *Forbes Entrepreneurs.* Retrieved from http://www.forbes.com/sites/patrickhull/2013/04/26/three-tips-to-approach-angel-investors/#24e34932330e

Santinelli, A. J. (*n.d.*). How to approach investors 101. *Babson College/Entrepreneurship Education.* Retrieved from http://www.babson.edu/executive-education/thought-leadership/education/Pages/how-to-approach-investors-101.aspx

Zwilling, M. (2013, November 17). How to make an ethical difference in your business. *Forbes Entrepreneurs.* Retrieved from http://www.forbes.com/sites/martinzwilling/2013/11/17/how-to-make-an-ethical-difference-in-your-business/#2a2982d5281f

By giving away equity, you will have less control over your decisions and may even be at risk of losing your position of CEO. Why? Because once you give up equity, directors will join the board and will take over much of the decision making, including the decision to either keep you as CEO or move you to a different position, or even push you out of the company altogether.

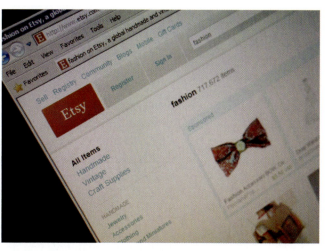

Online crafts marketplace Etsy originally founded by Rob Kalin
Credit: online crafts marketplace

For example, a study of 212 US startups from the late 1990s and early 2000s showed that 50% of the founders were no longer the CEO after three years. In fact, the same research shows that four out of five entrepreneurs are forced by investors to relinquish their CEO roles.[27] One of the most famous examples of an entrepreneur pushed out of his own company was the late Steve Jobs, who was fired by Apple's board of directors less than 10 years after he cofounded Apple Computers with Steve Wozniak. More recently, Rob Kalin, the founder of the online crafts marketplace Etsy, was fired as CEO, not once but twice. The first time he was replaced as CEO, yet returned to his post a year later. But not long after resuming his post, Kalin was replaced again, this time by Etsy's CEO.[28]

Being pushed out or moved to a "lesser" position can come as a real shock to entrepreneurs who have worked tirelessly on building their ventures from the ground up, as well as to employees who have worked alongside them. In fact, the way this leadership transition is handled by both the investor and the entrepreneur can make or break a company.

One of the most common mistakes founders make is believing they can grow the business through inspiration, passion, and perspiration. While these three key elements are helpful in getting a business off the ground, entrepreneurs need better

FIGURE 13.5

The Trade-Off Entrepreneurs Make

		FINANCIAL GAINS	
		WELL BELOW POTENTIAL	CLOSE TO POTENTIAL
CONTROL OVER COMPANY	LITTLE	Failure	Rich
	COMPLETE	King/Queen	Exception

Source: Wasserman, Noam. "The Founder's Dilemma." HBR, February 2008 issue. https://hbr.org/2008/02/the-founders-dilemma

resources to fully capitalize on future opportunities. As a company evolves, it needs different skills to grow into a more valuable business.

For example, a startup that has developed a product may not have the expertise or financial resources to market and sell it to customers, or the know-how to set up after-sales service. This means relying on people with different skills like financial executives, accountants, lawyers, and so on. More employees may need to be hired, and a new organizational structure put in place. All these elements can be overwhelming for a founder and team who lack these skills.

Of course, it is entirely possible to remain in full of control of your business by keeping as much equity as you can. You may have less financial investment to increase the value of your business, but if you have more interest in being in control (i.e., being the "King/Queen"), then this is a viable option for you.

Thinking about what matters most to you—to be rich or to be all-powerful—is a useful exercise in how you define success, and what it means to you. As Figure 13.5 illustrates, maximizing control over wealth and vice versa can negatively impact success. While the ideal would be to make tons of money and be completely in control, history shows that few entrepreneurs have managed to do both.

A View From the Top[29]

Let's use an example of a hypothetical startup to collate everything you have learned in this chapter so far. To begin, put yourself in the shoes of an entrepreneur who has an idea that has great potential. You are the only person working on this idea, and you own 100% of everything.

Finding a cofounder

As your idea starts to takes shape, you realize you need help. Developing a prototype is taking you a lot longer than you thought, and you could do with getting some advice. So you look for someone who is as enthusiastic about your idea as you are, and you begin to work together. Soon after, you ask your colleague to become your cofounder. You can't pay her in cash, so you agree to split the equity of the startup 50/50.

Finding early funding

You have your cofounder, but you have no funding to support you while you're working on the idea. You can't go to a VC just yet, as you have very little to show. Being a private company, you can take money from two main sources: accredited investors, or your family and friends. You decide to approach family and friends first, and you are fortunate enough to receive $15,000 from a wealthy uncle. In exchange, you give your uncle 5% equity in your business. You have six months to build your prototype and develop your business before the money runs out.

Registering the company

In order to give your uncle 5% equity, you register your company, which you can do through sites such as LegalZoom or through a lawyer (which is usually more expensive, unless you have a good friend who is a lawyer willing to give you a special deal). You set aside 20% of stock for future employees, a process known as an "option pool," which is a good way of attracting talent to your startup as it progresses. Early employees will be compensated with stock later on if they help the company go public.

Finding an angel

Even though your uncle's $15,000 will support your business for six months, you need to start looking for more funding right now, before you run out of cash. You start looking for an angel, but when you show her what you have, she estimates your business to be worth $1 million, and agrees to invest $200,000. You accept the offer and figure out how much equity you will give to the angel in return:

- ▶ $1,000,000 valuation + $200,000 investment = $1,200,000 post-money valuation.
- ▶ Then divide the investment by the post-money valuation $200,000/$1,200,000 = 1/6 = 16.7%.
- ▶ The angel gets 16.7% of the company, or 1/6.

Cutting the pie

Now you have the funding, but between giving equity to your cofounder, your uncle, and your angel, your control over your own company is shrinking. Yet, your pie is getting bigger with each investment.

Seeking venture capital

You are at the point where you have developed your prototype and gained traction with users. It's time to approach VCs. The VC values your company at $4 million and decides to invest $2 million. Using the same approach as the angel investor, that would mean that you would be giving away 33.3% of your company to the VC. Depending on how your company grows, you may get more rounds of funding to the point where a bigger company may want to buy your business, or you take the company public.

Going public

An IPO is an opportunity for you to sell stocks on the stock market to be purchased by members of the general public. Not only is this is a quicker way to generate cash, but it gives you the chance to return the cash invested by people like your uncle, your angel, and your VC. Your employees also get a chance to cash in on the stock options you kept aside for them in the early days. Investment bankers love IPOs because they get 7% of all the money earned from the IPO just by doing the paperwork and generating interest in your stock. For instance, say your startup generated $235,000,000 in an IPO. A total of $16.5 million of that would go to your investment banker.

The process of startup funding is summarized in Figure 13.6.●

FIGURE 13.6

How Startup Funding Works

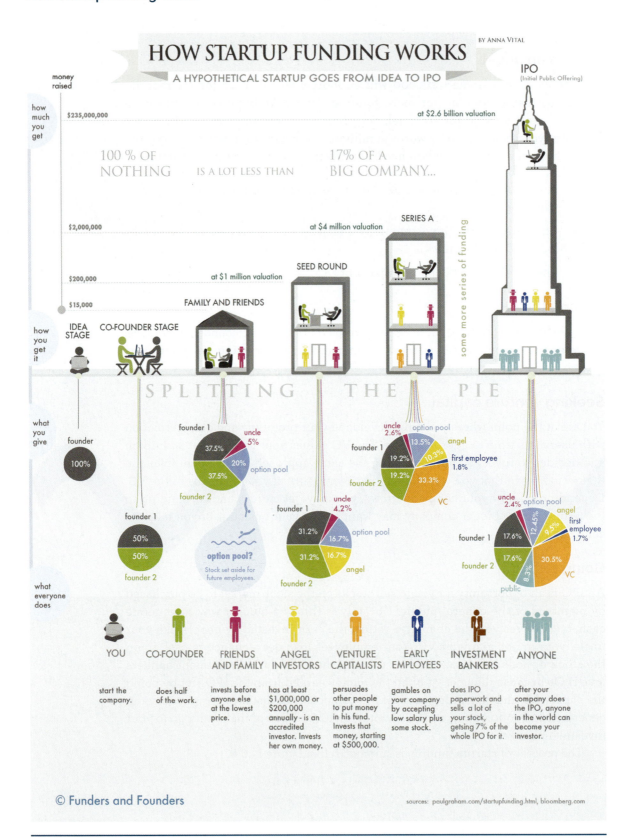

Credit: Anna Vital, "How funding works—Splitting the equity pie with investors." (May 9, 2013) http://fundersandfounders.com/how-funding-works-splitting-equity/ retrieved on May 4, 2015.

Get the edge on your studies at **edge.sagepub.com/neckentrepreneurship**

- ▸ Master the learning objectives using key study tools
- ▸ Watch, listen, and connect with online multimedia resources
- ▸ Access mobile-friendly quizzes and flashcards to check your understanding

13.1 Define equity financing for entrepreneurs and outline its main stages.

Equity financing is the sale of ownership stake within the company in exchange for funding. Seed-stage financing, startup financing and early-stage financing describe funds in support of different early-business objectives. As the organization grows, it may then seek out second- or later-stage financing through subsequent rounds of financing. Businesses may also choose to undergo an IPO, opening the firm to general market funding and offering an exit to early investors.

13.2 Illustrate the basics of enterprise valuation.

Investors use a variety of factors to come to valuation proposals, including market conditions, opportunities, competition, comparables and how much value a given venture can add to the mix.

13.3 Describe angel investors and how they finance entrepreneurs.

Angel investors are typically high-net-worth individuals who are accredited investors investing their own money in startup ventures. Other types of angels include corporate angels, professional angels, enthusiast angels, and micromanagement angels, each characterized by distinct goals and value-added capabilities.

13.4 Explain the role of venture capitalists (VCs) and how they finance entrepreneurs.

Venture capitalists differ from angels in the sense that they are professional money managers. Entrepreneurs should also exhibit at least as much caution as venture capitalists when seeking VC funding; the owners are likely to concede a significant ownership stake in the venture, and need to be certain of both why venture capital is absolutely necessary and which firm would provide the best guidance.

13.5 Describe how investors carry out due diligence processes.

To ascertain the prospects of any potential investment, angel investors and venture capitalists alike conduct due diligence processes of the firm under consideration. Essential to this process is identifying a method and timing for the investors to recoup their capital at exit, such as completing an IPO.

13.6 Explain the money versus power trade-off and the funding life cycle.

The typical "entrepreneur's dilemma" is choosing between retaining significant ownership and control versus securing substantial funding and losing majority ownership. The venture typically starts with finding partners and securing initial funding, followed by formal founding and registration of the business. As the business grows and additional financing is needed, angel and venture capital investments are sought out. Finally, the most successful of startups often accomplish an IPO.

KEY TERMS

Angel investor 332
Convertible debt 335
Due diligence 347

Early-stage financing 331
Equity financing 329
Seed-stage financing 331

Startup financing 331
Venture capitalist
   (VC) 333

CASE STUDY

Hyrum W. Smith, Cofounder of Franklin Covey Company

Hyrum W. Smith is the cofounder (along with Stephen R. Covey, author of *The 7 Habits of Highly Effective People*) of Franklin Covey Company and an originator of the Franklin Day Planning System, used by tens of millions of people throughout the world.

Born in 1943, Smith grew up in Honolulu, Hawaii, where his father was a professor in the Speech Department at The University of Hawaii. Smith learned early that he could sell things; an early success was his sales of newspaper subscriptions in the neighborhood. Over the years, he had jobs selling everything from soap and encyclopedias to microphones and insurance.

During his teenage years, Smith worked in Washington, DC, as an intern for Rep. Daniel Inouye (D-Hawaii), who went on to have a long and distinguished career in the U.S. Senate. Smith graduated from University High School in Honolulu in 1961. He attended Queens College of the City University of New York before accepting a call to serve a 2-year, full-time, voluntary mission for his church in Great Britain. During his time in England, Smith discovered he loved to teach and to speak publicly.

Upon his return to the United States in 1965, Smith intended to enroll at the University of Utah to study political science; however, instead he was drafted into the Army. He was accepted to Officer Candidate School (OCS), where he graduated with honors at the top of his class. As a newly minted Second Lieutenant, Smith was stationed in Germany, where he helped oversee a battery of Pershing missiles. Smith had married Gail Cooper four days after graduating from OCS; their first child was born during the couple's military assignment in Germany.

After completing his military tour of duty, Smith returned to Utah to study business at Brigham Young University (BYU), graduating with a bachelor's degree in 1970. During his time at BYU, he met future presidential candidate Mitt Romney, and at one time participated in a sales venture with Romney.

During his senior year at BYU, Smith was recruited by Connecticut Mutual Life Insurance, and accepted a sales job back in his home State of Hawaii. In 1972, he was offered a sales job with Automatic Data Processing (ADP) in Portland, Oregon. During his six years with ADP, he rose from entry-level salesman to International Vice President of Sales, a position that provided him with opportunities to oversee sales operations on three continents. During these years, his family continued to grow. Smith and his wife would eventually have five children and adopt one more.

In 1991 he considered a run for the U.S. House of Representatives representing a district in California. Ultimately, however, he decided to strike out on his own as an entrepreneurial motivational speaker.

However, Hyrum and his wife Gail were virtually broke financially. Working with a close friend, Richard Winwood, the two pooled $3,500 of their own money in 1983 to found HW Smith & Associates—a training company borne out Smith's passion for teaching. HW Smith created seminars for corporate companies, teaching employees how to be more productive at work. HW Smith & Associates was the forerunner of Franklin Institute, Franklin Quest, and then FranklinCovey.

By February 1984, they had attracted an investor who committed $200,000 to fund the first printing of the original Franklin Day Planners for a 20% stake in the company. Shortly before writing the check, the investor got cold feet and tried to pull out of his signed contract. Rather than becoming encumbered with legal action, Smith persuaded the investor to give them a 90-day, interest-free loan of $90,000 with the agreement that he would no longer have any stake in the company. The investor agreed to Smith's renegotiated terms. The first Day Planners rolled off the presses within days of receiving the $90,000.

The planner was not an instant success, but after seven months of very hard work by Smith and his associates, they were able to pay back the loan. From that point forward, all company growth and expansion was strictly revenue-based.

For the next decade and a half, the Franklin Institute enjoyed enormous growth. In the process, the Franklin Day Planner became a household name throughout North America and around the world as the market's top-notch personal planning tool. In 1992, Smith and his associates changed the name of the company to Franklin Quest and launched an Initial Public Offering (IPO) on the New York Stock Exchange (NYSE). Already a millionaire, Smith became a megamillionaire overnight. According to Smith, the investor who got cold feet back in 1984 would have added some $200 million to his portfolio had he maintained his original 20% stake in the company!

Also in 1992, Smith helped to found Smith & Henderson, a money management firm that has since evolved into Soltis Advisors. Today, Soltis is a highly successful firm with $2 billion under management.

By 1997, the Franklin Day Planning system was the most recognized and respected personal planning philosophy and system in the world, and had attracted the attention of Stephen R. Covey—author of the best seller *The 7 Habits of Highly Effective People*—and his associates at the Covey Leadership Center. Recognizing the similarities between the vision and mission of the two organizations, Franklin Quest acquired the Covey Leadership Center to form Franklin Covey, thereby adding the power of Covey's nomenclature to the company's brand.

Along the way, Smith authored several successful books and spoke publicly to live audiences all over the world. He was also awarded multiple honorary doctorates and other awards, including the Entrepreneur of the Year Award from the Brigham Young University's School of Business and the Silver Beaver Award from the Boy Scouts of America.

In 1999, Smith stepped down as chairman and CEO of Franklin Covey. He continued to serve as vice chairman of the board until his retirement in 2004. Always an entrepreneur, Smith did not let his "official" retirement signal an end to his professional activity, philanthropy, or investment activities. In 2002, he helped to found The Galileo Initiative, a seminar company that delivered soft-skills training based on Smith's own philosophical construct known as The Reality Model. Galileo went on to earn approximately $10 million in revenue.

Smith's philanthropic endeavors have been many and varied. From supporting young missionaries to helping needy college students and others, Smith and his wife have always been known for their generosity. Smith's grandest act of philanthropy included contributing $23 million to build, establish, and sustain Tuacahn Center for the Arts in St. George, Utah. Tuacahn is home to a charter high school with a focus on the performing arts. Thanks to Smith's generosity it also sports a 2,000-seat outdoor amphitheater where world-class theater and musical productions are held throughout the year.

While it might seem that Smith has found wealth and success at every turn, in fact he and his wife have also invested in various ventures that he describes as "financial disasters." Smith chalks it up to being part of the process. "As an investor, you are not going to succeed every time." His investment philosophy involves investing in people rather than products or services. "If the people are good, honest, smart, and competent, success is virtually assured. If the people are incompetent or dishonest, even the best product and service in the world is ultimately a poor gamble; so over the years, we have learned to invest in people."

In retirement, Smith decided, in his own words, to "reach for the brass ring one last time" by authoring yet another book and starting another training company. The name of his new book and company is: *The 3 Gaps*. The focus of the training is to "Close the Value Gap (whatever space exists between your values and behavior), the Productivity Gap (whatever space exists between your actions and your desired accomplishments), and the Belief Gap (whatever space exists between your beliefs and your actions on those beliefs). The book was published in 2016.

After a lifetime of meaningful service, contribution, philanthropy, and entrepreneurial success, Smith has two key pieces of advice for young entrepreneurs.

First, remember that lasting financial success is always the by-product of some other success that focuses on serving people. "If you start a company only to make money, you are likely to be extinct within three years." Smith points out that about two-thirds of the Fortune 500 Companies from 40 years ago are now gone. Why? Because, he says, they focused only on the bottom line. "Never allow the bottom line to govern your venture." Instead, he encourages you to focus on whatever authentic passion and belief you have deep down inside that what you are doing will make a positive and meaningful difference in people's lives. "Money honestly earned," he says, "is merely a byproduct of making a meaningful difference in the world."

Second, educate yourself in the art of language and communication. When Smith was a boy, his father had him memorize the following statement: "You cannot think any deeper than your vocabulary will allow you to." This concept deeply influenced Smith, and led him to study diligently to become a master of oral communication. He read widely, nurtured a love for the English language, and noticed that the highly successful people he knew had large vocabularies. While serving as a young missionary, he had the opportunity to hear a famous man with an unusually large vocabulary—Sir Winston Churchill—speak not long before he died. Churchill's oratory, his Mission President's abilities at the pulpit, and his own father's capacity for language, deeply influenced Smith and motivated him to work at and polish his skills as a public speaker. As a result, he is recognized as one of the finest speakers in America, commanding five-figure speaking fees.

Critical Thinking Questions

1. What was the financial cost to Smith and Winwood when their initial investor pulled out of his original contract? What was the benefit?

2. What non-monetary benefits might Smith and Winwood have obtained because their original investor got cold feet?

3. How are money benefits versus non-money benefits related to the "entrepreneur's dilemma?"

4. Hyrum Smith emphasizes the importance of following your own personal values. As an entrepreneur, which do you value more: to be "King or Queen" or to be "Rich" (viewed as a ratio using a scale of 0–100%)?

5. Whom do you presently know that you could potentially approach as an "Angel Investor" for your own entrepreneurial idea(s)? Whom could you approach for capital investment? For equity investment?

6. What due diligence would you need to do to make a compelling case to a potential angel investor? A capital investor? An equity investor?

Sources

Godfrey, R. L., Pulsipher, G. L., & Smith, H. W. (2011). *The 7 laws of learning: Why great leaders are also great teachers*. Springville, UT: Bonneville Books.

Godfrey, R. L. & Smith, H. W. (2009). *Home of the brave: Confronting and conquering challenging times*. New York, NY: Hachette.

Smith, H. W. (1994). *The 10 natural laws of successful time and life management*. New York, NY: Warner Books.

Smith, H. W. (2000). *What matters most: The power of living your values*. New York, NY: Fireside.

Smith, H. W. (2001). *The modern gladiator: Increasing productivity in the global age* [AudioBook]. FranklinCovey.

Smith, H. W. (2013). *The power of perception: 6 Steps to behavior change*. USA: Alexander's.

APPENDIX A
FINANCIAL STATEMENTS AND PROJECTIONS FOR STARTUPS

By Angelo Santinelli

Learning Objectives

A.1 Explain the purpose of financial projections for startups.

A.2 Describe financial statements as an essential part of financial projections.

A.3 Clarify the relationship between the three financial statements.

A.4 Describe the journey of cash through the cash conversion cycle.

A.5 Discuss how to build a pro forma financial statement.

A.6 Explain how to apply assumptions when building pro forma statements.

Outline

A.1 Financial Projections for Startups

A.2 Three Essential Financial Statements

A.3 Linkages Between the Three Financial Statements

A.4 The Journey of Cash: The Cash Conversion Cycle

A.5 Building Pro Forma Financial Statements

A.6 Building Assumptions: Operating Policies and Other Key Assumptions

A.1 FINANCIAL PROJECTIONS FOR STARTUPS

>> **LO A.1** **Explain the purpose of financial projections for startups.**

As we have explained in this textbook, developing an entrepreneurial mindset, testing and experimenting, building business models, and planning are all elements in The Practice of Entrepreneurship and now it's time to discuss another key element—financial projections. Through the iterative process discussed so far, entrepreneurs learn how to assess the problem–solution fit, product–market fit, competitive and industry fit, and now we will look at financial fit. Through action entrepreneurs develop assumptions, opinions, and a market perspective based on objective data and analysis. This primary data enables entrepreneurs to make a convincing case for financial projections, and prove that their startup is worth investment.

In Chapter 13, "Equity Financing for Entrepreneurs," we touched on the topic of financial projections. Potential investors (angels, VCs) sometimes decline to invest in a project because they feel the financial projections are exaggerated or not believable. This is because financial projections are often built on a foundation of untested assumptions and third party data sources that are interpreted to portray market size and growth that exaggerates or distorts the revenue projections.

In many cases, entrepreneurs first develop pitch decks or other similar planning tools before testing the feasibility of their ideas to confirm whether or not the idea is indeed an opportunity. As result, they lack the necessary data to support their financial projections, which means the exercise is nothing more than guesswork.

Presenting carefully thought-out financial projections to investors is an exercise in lowering perceived risk in both you as an entrepreneur and your idea. When you are able to frame the opportunity from the perspective of the target market(s), understand the resources required to capitalize on the opportunity, and know how to allocate those resources under varying market conditions, investors will be more inclined to have serious investment discussions. Similarly, the confidence and knowledge that you have developed from building realistic projections should make the process of convincing others, employees and investors alike, a little easier.

A.2 THREE ESSENTIAL FINANCIAL STATEMENTS

>> **LO A.2**   **Describe financial statements as an essential part of financial projections.**

Financial statements provide a window into the financial health and performance of a company. Every entrepreneur needs to understand the three essential financial statements: an income statement, a balance sheet, and a cash flow statement. The **income statement** (or profit and loss statement) is a financial report that measures the financial performance of your business on a monthly or annual basis. It shows sales and expense-related activities that result in profit or loss over a set period of time. The **balance sheet** is a financial report that shows what the company owes, and what it owns, including the shareholders' stake, at a particular point in time. The **cash flow statement** is a financial report that details the inflows and outflows of cash for a company over a set period of time. Each statement examines the company from a slightly different perspective, yet together they provide a holistic economic view of the company.

In the following sections, we will take a closer look at each of these three financial statements.

The Income Statement

The income statement measures the financial performance of your business on a monthly or annual basis. It subtracts the COGS (cost of goods sold) and expenses (administrative, marketing, research, and other operating expenses) from the total revenue to give you a net income figure, which will be either a profit or a loss. Using Table A.1 as a guide, let's explore the different line items of the income statement in further detail.

First, revenue is recorded on the income statement when the company makes a sale of a product or service and then delivers to the customer, thereby creating an obligation for the customer to issue payment to the company. It is important to note that there is a difference between a sale (revenue) and an order (bookings). An order may or may not become a sale. Orders become sales only when the product is shipped to and accepted by the customer. A sale is recorded on the income statement, while an order might only show up in a **backlog**—orders that have been received but not delivered to the customer. Also, the revenue number should be expressed net of any discounts offered. Table A.2 explains the distinctions between revenue, bookings, and backlogs.

COGS represents the total cost to manufacture a product. Costs are expenditures of raw materials, labor, and manufacturing overhead used to produce a product.

Income statement: a financial report that measures the financial performance of your business on a monthly or annual basis.

Balance sheet: a financial statement that shows what the company owes, what it owns, including the shareholder's stake, at a particular point in time.

Cash flow statement: a financial report that details the inflows and outflows of cash for a company over a set period of time.

Backlog: orders that have been received but not delivered to the customer.

TABLE A.1

Income Statement

Revenue	$$$$
(-) Cost of Goods Sold	$$
Gross Profit	$$
(-) Sales, General & Administrative	$
(-) Marketing	$
(-) Research & Development	$
(-) Depreciation & Amortization	$
Operating Profit	$$
(-) Interest Expense	$
(-) Taxes	$
Net Income	$$

Master the content
**edge.sagepub.com/
neckentrepreneurship**

For a service business, COGS may include the cost of service staff and associated overhead.

Subtracting COGS from revenue leaves you with three types of profit margins: gross margins, operating profit, and net income. A high gross margin percentage that remains consistently high over time can be an indicator of the company's long-term competitiveness.[1] It also shows that the company has sufficient funds for sales, marketing, product development, and other expenses.

Operating expenses are the expenditures that the company makes to generate income. These expenditures generally include sales, general, and administrative (SG&A); research and development (R&D); and marketing expenses. These expenses directly lower income.

Operating expenses: the expenditures that the company makes to generate income.

As we explored in Chapter 10, the income statement also reflects depreciation and amortization of your company's assets. Recall that depreciation really means the cost of wear and tear of your physical assets such as machinery, equipment, and the building in which you operate. Amortization works similarly to depreciation; the main difference is that amortization relates to intangible assets such as patents, trademarks, copyrights, and business methodologies. Amortization matches the useful life of an intangible asset with the revenue it generates.

If you have studied accounting in the past, you might hear depreciation referred to as a "noncash" expense that is usually ignored when calculating free cash flow or

TABLE A.2

Revenue, Bookings and Backlog

Revenue = Sale	Shown on the Income Statement net of any discounts when a customer receives and accepts an Order
Bookings = Order	An Order is a promise to purchase, which does not show up on the Income Statement until the customer receives and accepts the product or service
Backlog = Orders – Revenue	Orders that have been received but not delivered to the customer

EBITDA (Earnings Before Interest, Taxes, Depreciation, and Amortization). This is an accepted practice, but it avoids the obvious, which is that equipment and buildings eventually need to be replaced. From a short-term perspective, depreciation is a non-cash charge to earnings, but in the long term, someone has to write a check for replacement. It is best to ask your accountant about the various rules for depreciating assets.

The second most important profit margin to monitor is **operating profit,** which is the amount left over from revenue once all costs and expenses are subtracted.

Another component of EBITDA is **interest expense**, which shows the extent of the company's debt burden as well as representing any interest owed on borrowed money. Taxes are the last expense item before net income. This line item captures federal, state, and sometimes municipal taxes due for the period. Sales taxes are not recorded here.

The third profit margin item is **net income,** which indicates what is left after all costs, expenses, and taxes have been paid. It is important to note that there is a difference between income and cash; for instance, it is quite possible for a company to have positive net income, but have a negative cash flow, which causes it to struggle to pay its bills. We will explore this concept in more detail later.

The income statement alone does not reveal much about a company's long-term viability or financial health. It tells you little about how and when the company receives cash or how much it has on hand. For an accurate picture of financial health, the balance sheet and cash flow statements need to be analyzed.

The Balance Sheet

The balance sheet (see Table A.3) is a statement that shows a "snapshot" at a particular point in time of what the company has today (assets), how much it owes (liabilities), and what it is currently worth (shareholder equity).

As explained in Table A.4, the Balance Sheet gets its name from a basic equation, which must be equally balanced.[2]

Assets include cash, machines, inventory, buildings, and what you are owed and what you have the right to collect. **Current assets** include cash and other assets such as inventory, accounts receivable, and prepaid expenses that can be converted into cash within a year. Cash usually includes both cash and cash equivalents, or short-term, low-risk investments. Inventory represents what the company has to sell, as well as materials that are to be made into products. There are three basic types of inventory: raw materials, which include any goods or components used in the manufacturing process; work-in-process (WIP) or semi-finished products, which are partially assembled items awaiting completion; and finished goods, which are ready to be sold (see Figure A.1).

Accounts receivable refers to money owed to the company for goods or services provided and billed to a customer. When the company ships a good or provides a service to a customer on credit and sends a bill, the company has the right to collect this money. **Prepaid expenses** represent payments the company has already made for services not yet received. These are usually things like insurance, deposits, and prepayment of rent. Prepaid expenses are considered current assets because the company has already paid for these services and will not have to use cash to pay for them in the near future.

Fixed assets might also appear on the balance sheet as property, plant, and equipment (PP&E). These are productive assets that are not intended for sale and are used over time to produce goods, store them, ship them, and so on. This commonly includes land, buildings, equipment, machines, furniture, trucks, autos, and other goods that

Operating profit: the amount left over from revenue once all costs and expenses are subtracted.

Interest expense: the extent of the company's debt burden as well as representing any interest owed on borrowed money.

Net income: indicates what is left after all costs, expenses, and taxes have been paid.

Current assets: cash and other assets that can be converted into cash within a year.

Accounts receivable: money owed to the company for goods or services provided and billed to a customer.

Prepaid expenses: the payments the company has already made for services not yet received.

TABLE A.3

Balance Sheet

ASSETS (WHAT THE BUSINESS OWNS)		LIABILITIES (WHAT THE BUSINESS OWES)	
Current Assets		**Current Liabilities**	
Cash	$$	Accounts Payable	$$
Inventory	$$	Accrued Expenses	$$
Accounts Receivable	$$	Short-Term Debt	$$
Prepaid Expenses	$$	Other Current Liabilities	$$
Fixed Assets		**Long-Term Debt**	$$
Property, Plant, & Equipment	$$	**Shareholder Equity (What the Business Is Worth?)**	
Accumulated Depreciation	$$$	Retained Earnings	$$
		Capital Stock	$$
Total Assets	**$$$$**	**Total Liabilities and Shareholder Equity**	**$$$$**

have a useful life of 3 to 5 years, although the life of some assets, such as land and buildings, could be much longer. These assets are reported at cost less accumulated depreciation. Recall that depreciation is an accounting convention that appears on the income statement and represents the decline in value of the asset, due to age, wear, and the passage of time. Accumulated depreciation is the sum of all the depreciation charges taken since the asset was acquired.

Other types of assets

"Other assets" is a catchall category that includes items such as the value of patents, goodwill, and intangible assets. **Goodwill** represents the price paid for an asset in excess of its book value. You will see this on the balance sheet when the company has made one or more large acquisitions. **Intangible assets** represent the value of patents, software programs, copyrights, trademarks, franchises, brand names, or assets that cannot be physically touched. One important note is that only items that have been purchased can appear here. For instance, companies are not allowed to create a value for things like a brand name and place it on the balance sheet.

Another type of asset includes **long-term investments,** which refers to assets that are more than one year old and are carried on the balance sheet at cost or book value

Goodwill: the price paid for an asset in excess of its book value. You will see this on the balance sheet when the company has made one or more large acquisitions.

Intangible assets: the value of patents, software programs, copyrights, trademarks, franchises, brand names, or assets that cannot be physically touched.

TABLE A.4

The Balance Sheet Equation

What You Own	=	What You Owe + What You Are Worth
Assets	=	**Liabilities + Shareholder Equity**
Both sides of this equation must always be in balance.		

FIGURE A.1

Define Each Manufacturing Inventory

Long-term investments: assets that are more than one year old and are carried on the balance sheet at cost or book value with no appreciation.

Liabilities: economic obligations of the company, such as money owed to lenders, suppliers, and employees.

Current liabilities: bills that must be paid within one year of the date of the balance sheet.

Accounts payable: money owed by a business to its suppliers.

Accrued expenses: costs incurred by the company for which no payment has been made.

Short-term debt: the portion of long-term debt that must be paid within a year.

Other current liabilities: short-term liabilities that do not fall into a specific category, such as sales tax, income tax, and so forth.

Long-term debt: obligation for debt that is due to be repaid in more than 12 months.

Shareholder equity: the money that has been invested in the business plus the cumulative net profits and losses the company has generated.

Retained earnings: the cumulative amount of profit retained by the company and not paid out in the form of dividends to owners.

with no appreciation. Examples of long-term investments include cash, stock, bonds, and real estate. It is possible that the assets are worth much more, or much less, than the original cost, but the convention is to carry them at cost.

Liabilities and shareholder equity

Let's turn our attention to the other side of the balance sheet: liabilities and shareholder equity. **Liabilities** are economic obligations of the company, such as money it owes to lenders, suppliers, and employees.

Current liabilities are bills that must be paid within one year of the date of the balance sheet. They are organized based on who is owed the money. **Accounts payable** is money owed by a business to its suppliers. **Accrued expenses** are costs incurred by the company for which no payment has been made. For example, wages and taxes may be indicated on the balance sheet to be paid at a future date, but that payment hasn't occurred just yet. **Short-term debt** is the portion of long-term debt that must be paid within a year. A common example of short-term debt is money owed to lenders such as bank loans. **Other current liabilities** are short-term liabilities that do not fall into a specific category; these will include sales tax, income tax, and so forth.

Long-term debt is an obligation for debt that is due to be repaid in more than 12 months. Bank loans, finance and leasing obligations are all examples of long-term debt.

Shareholder equity represents the money that has been invested in the business plus the cumulative net profits and losses the company has generated (see Figure A.2). This is a liability that is not usually repaid over the normal course of business. Subtracting what the company owns (total assets) from what it owes (total liabilities) provides the percentage of its value to the owners, or its shareholders' equity.

There are two main components of shareholder equity. One component is **retained earnings**, the cumulative amount of profit retained by the company and not paid out in the form of dividends (a sum of money paid to shareholders from company profits) to owners. The other component is **capital stock**, which represents the original amount

FIGURE A.2

Total Shareholder Equity

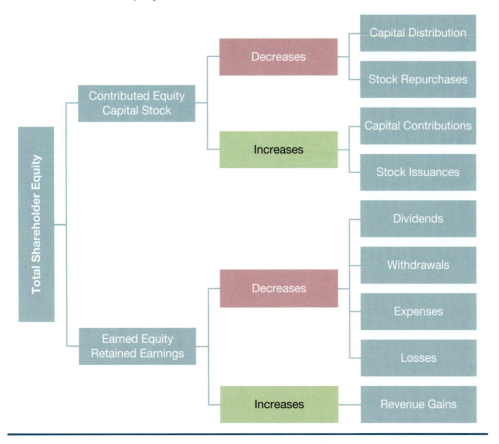

the owners paid into the company plus any additional paid-in capital to purchase stock in the company.

Shareholder equity increases when the company makes a profit (increase in retained earnings) or sells new stock to increase the capital stock. If the company has a loss, which lowers retained earnings, or pays a dividend, which also lowers retained earnings, these actions will result in a decrease in shareholder equity.

The Cash Flow Statement

The cash flow statement tracks the movement of cash into (cash inflows) and out of (cash outflows) the company over a period of time. Cash inflows include loans, sales, interest, and shares; while outflows include payment to suppliers, wages and salaries, and dividends to shareholders (see Table A.5).

The cash flow statement is like a cash register for the company. It shows the cash that is available at the beginning of the period—in other words, cash that is already in the register. It also shows cash received during the period such as cash from the sale of a product or service, or cash received from investments, borrowing, or the sale of assets and stock, less the cash paid out in the period. This is cash actually paid out to support operations necessary to make and sell a product or service, or cash used to pay down loans, taxes, or the purchase of assets. This then leaves you with cash at the end of the period. Only cash transactions affect cash flow and are considered on the cash flow statement.

Capital stock: the original amount the owners paid into the company plus any additional paid-in capital to purchase stock in the company.

TABLE A.5

Examples of Cash Inflows and Outflows

CASH INFLOWS	CASH OUTFLOWS
Loans	Payments to Suppliers
Sales	Wages & Salaries
Interest	Dividends to Shareholders
Shares	Taxes on Profits
Receipts from Debtors	Loan Payments

Cash flow statements are generally divided into two basic parts: cash generated from operations or profit-making activities, and cash generated from investment and financing activities. The first examines the profit-making inflows and expense outflows, while the second examines inflows and outflows of cash related to the purchase and sale of assets, and financing activities such as bank borrowing and stock sales. Together they form the full picture of cash moving through the company (Table A.6).

The first line of the cash flow statement is net income. The first thing to do when examining cash flow is to add back depreciation and amortization that appear on the income statement. As you may recall, these are considered "noncash" charges related to the declining value of tangible and intangible assets. So, even though a write-down, or charge, may appear on the income statement, no cash actually left the company. Since we want to determine only cash in this statement, we add back both depreciation and amortization expenses.

TABLE A.6

Cash Flow Statement

NET INCOME	$$$
(+) Depreciation & Amortization	$
(+) Sources: Decrease in Assets or Increase in Liabilities	$
(-) Uses: Increase in Assets or Decrease in Liabilities	$
Increase/(Decrease) Cash from Operations	**$$$**
(-) Net Property Plant & Equipment	$
Increase/(Decrease) Cash from Investments	**$$**
(+) Increase in Net Borrowing	$
(+) Sale of Stock	$
(-) Paying of Dividends	$
Increase/(Decrease) Cash from Financing	**$$**
Increase/(Decrease) in Cash *(Should be equal to cash on the Balance Sheet)*	**$$**

TABLE A.7

Inflows and Outflows of Cash

SOURCES (INFLOWS) OF CASH	USES (OUTFLOWS) OF CASH
• Decrease in Assets	• Increase in Assets
• Increase in Liability	• Decrease in Liability
• Increase in Shareholder Equity	• Decrease in Shareholder Equity
• Profit from Operations	• Loss from Operations

The next step is to examine the changes in the balances of current assets and current liabilities on the balance sheet. If a current asset balance increases, we are using cash. If a current asset balance decreases, we are adding cash. Conversely, an increase in a current liability balance adds cash, while a decrease in a current liability balance uses cash (Table A.7).

Initially, it is best to understand the inflows and outflows of cash related to the operating activities of the company by determining the sources (inflows) and uses (outflows) associated with current assets and current liabilities to arrive at the degree of cash flow from operations.

Next we shift our focus to cash changes stemming from investment and financing activities. One option might be to simply stockpile cash on the balance sheet, but this isn't the most productive use of cash. Another option might be to return cash to shareholders in the form of dividends, or to pay down any debt that the company may have amassed. And still another option might be to invest in productive assets such as machinery and equipment, or to acquire all or part of another business. This may show up as a separate line item in the cash flow as "Investments in Fixed Assets" or something similar.

Finally, you must examine cash inflows and outflows from financing activities such as selling stock, borrowing, or paying dividends. Borrowing money increases the amount of cash on hand. Conversely, paying down your debt lowers the amount of cash on hand, while the sale of stock by a company increases the amount of cash coming into the company.

Adding the cash flow from operations to the cash flow from investing and financing leaves us with either a cash increase or decrease for the period. If a company has either cash in the bank or access to additional cash, it can withstand negative cash flow for several periods. It is good business practice for entrepreneurial managers to strive to achieve profits and convert those profits into cash.

Net income versus cash flow

While net income (or profit) and cash flow are both crucial to the success of the business, there are important differences between the two.

Net income as it appears on the income statement is determined by accounting principles and includes accruals and noncash items such as depreciation and amortization. In other words, there are items on the income statement that determine net income for a period that do not represent actual cash coming in or going out of the company for that period. For instance, in respect of how revenue is recorded on the income statement, the credit sales are captured as an obligation to pay (asset) in the balance sheet as an account receivable. Even though no cash has changed hands, the revenue on the income statement still reflects the sale. This treatment also applies to expenses and capital expenditures on the income statement.

Cash flow, in contrast, deals only with actual cash transactions. A company's operating policies, production techniques, and inventory and credit-control systems will influence the timing of cash moving through the business; and this is what the entrepreneurial manager must master in order to convert profit into cash.

A.3 LINKAGES BETWEEN THE THREE FINANCIAL STATEMENTS

>> **LO A.3**   **Clarify the relationship between the three financial statements.**

The power of financial statements lie in the linkages. It is important to understand how the three financial statements are linked to one another and how decisions with regard to the operations of a company will impact its financial performance. A company's pricing and credit policies will have a direct impact on revenue, an income statement item; and accounts receivable, a balance sheet item. While each financial statement provides a different view of the company, each statement is also related to the other.

For instance, net income on the income statement is added to retained earnings on the balance sheet. The ending cash balance on the cash flow statement is equal to the cash on the balance sheet. Every entrepreneur needs to understand how cash and goods and services flow into and out of the company.

Figure A.3 shows what happens when a sale is made, the product or service is delivered, and the cash is collected. When a sale is made and the product or service is accepted by the customer, revenue on the income statement increases. Assuming that credit is extended for the sale, accounts receivable on the balance sheet also increases. Once the obligation to pay is met by the customer, accounts receivable decreases and the amount paid becomes a cash inflow on the cash flow statement. Additionally, when a sale is made, the value of the product is moved from inventory (a balance sheet item) to cost of goods (an income statement item).[3]

As with the *sales* cycle explained above, these types of connections between the various statements can be charted in similar fashion for the *expense* cycle, the purchase of fixed assets, and investments. When you understand how cash moves through the company, you begin to understand how policies related to credit, inventory, and payables can affect the time it takes for cash to be converted into products and returned back to the company at a profit.

A.4 THE JOURNEY OF CASH: THE CASH CONVERSION CYCLE

>> **LO A.4**   **Describe the journey of cash through the cash conversion cycle.**

Cash is used to purchase materials, which are then made into products. This creates obligations to make payments to certain suppliers of those materials, which is captured on the balance sheet in accounts payable. These products are stored, which appears on the balance sheet in inventory, and are eventually sold and delivered to customers. Then the company has the right to collect cash for the selling price of the products, which appears on the balance sheet in accounts receivable. Once collected, this cash

FIGURE A.3

Income Statement / Balance Sheet / Cash Flow Statement

Income Statement

Revenue	$$$$
(-) Cost of Goods	$$
Gross Profit	$$
(-) Sales, General & Administrative	$
(-) Marketing	$
(-) Research & Development	$
(-) Depreciation & Amortization	$
Operating Profit	$$
(-) Interest Expense	$
(-) Taxes	$
Net Income	$$

When a sale is made, Revenue increases on the Income Statement and an obligation to pay is incurred by the customer, which increases Accounts Receivable on the Balance Sheet.

When a sale is made, Revenue increases on the Income Statement and an obligation to pay is incurred by the customer, which increases Accounts Receivable on the Balance Sheet.

When a sale is made, Revenue increases on the Income Statement and an obligation to pay is incurred by the customer, which increases Accounts Receivable on the Balance Sheet.

Balance Sheet

Assets (What You Own)		Liabilities (What You Owe)	
Current Assets		Current Liabilities	
Cash	$$	Accounts Payable	$$
Inventory	$$	Accrued Expenses	$$
Accounts Receivable	$$	Short-Term Debt	$$
Prepaid Expenses	$$	Other Current Liabilities	$$
Fixed Assets		**Long-Term Debt**	$$
Property, Plant & Equipment	$$	**Shareholders' Equity (What You Are Worth)**	
Accumulated Depreciation	$$$	Retained Earnings	$$
		Capital Stock	$$
Total Assets	**$$$$**	**Total Liabilities and Shareholders' Equity**	**$$$$**

When Net Income on the Income Statement increases, Retained Earnings on the Balance Sheet increases. The opposite is also true. A decrease in Net Income will decrease Retained Earnings.

Cash Flow Statement

Net Income	$$$
(+) Depreciation & Amortization	$
(+) Sources: Decrease in Assets or Increase in Liabilities	$
(-) Uses: Increase in Assets or Decrease in Liabilities	$
Increase/(Decrease) Cash from Operations	$$$
(-) Net PP&E	$
Increase/(Decrease) Cash from Investments	$$
(+) Increase in Net Borrowing	$
(+) Sale of Stock	$
(-) Paying of Dividends	$
Increase/(Decrease) Cash from Financing	$$
Increase/(Decrease) in Cash	$$
(Should be equal to cash on the Balance Sheet)	

Cash Conversion Cycle (CCC): the number of days a company's cash is tied up in the production and sales process.

has now returned to the company. You hope that this journey produces more cash that is returned to the hands of the company. This journey is called the **cash conversion cycle (CCC)**, and it refers to the number of days a company's cash is tied up in the production and sales process. CCC can be calculated using the equation shown in Figure A.4.

Cash Conversion Cycle

Calculated in days, this equation shows how long the journey is for cash from the point of leaving the company to the point of return.

DSO is a measure of the number of days that it takes to collect on accounts receivable. Remember, if you do business in cash then your DSO is zero, but if you sell on credit, then this will be a positive number. DSO is calculated using the following equation:

DSO: a measure of the number of days that it takes to collect on accounts receivable.

> DSO = Average Accounts Receivable/Revenue per day
>
> Average Accounts Receivable = (Beginning Accounts Receivable + Ending Accounts Receivable)/2
>
> Revenue per day = Revenue/365

DOI is a measure of the average number of days it takes to sell the entire inventory of a company. DOI is calculated using the following equation:

DOI: a measure of the average number of days it takes to sell the entire inventory of a company.

> DOI = (Average Inventory)/COGS per day
>
> Average Inventory = (Beginning inventory + Ending inventory)/2
>
> COGS per day = COGS/365

DPO is a measure of the number of days it takes you to pay your bills. DPO is calculated using the following equation:

DPO: a measure of the number of days it takes you to pay your bills.

> DPO = Average Accounts Payable/COGS per day
>
> Average Accounts Payable = (Beginning Accounts Payable + Ending Accounts Payable)/2
>
> COGS per day = COGS/365

To calculate CCC, you need to include several items from the financial statements:

▸ Income statement

▸ revenue and COGS

▸ Balance sheet

- Beginning and ending inventory
- Beginning and ending accounts receivable
- Beginning and ending accounts payable

Note that for balance sheet items, because they capture a snapshot in time, you want to use an average over the period of time that you investigating. So if you are looking at one year, then you need to look at the ending period for the current year and the same ending period for the previous year.

Let's use an example to explore this equation in more detail. Suppose you are making men's shirts and selling them through a retail channel. The DOI is 80 days. You purchase enough cotton material to make a shirt. This purchase creates an obligation for the shirtmaker to pay (account payable) for this material in 30 days (DPO). The raw material arrives (inventory) and the manufacturing process begins.

At the end of 80 days, the completed shirt is sold to the retailer (DOI). The retailer now has an obligation to pay the shirtmaker (account receivable) and takes 40 days to pay for the completed shirt. This means that from the time cash left the shirtmaker 30 days after the purchase of raw material, it took 90 days for cash to make its way back to the shirtmaker. In this case the formula would be:

$$CCC = DSO + DOI - DPO$$

$$= 80 + 40 - 30$$

$$= 90$$

Figure A.5 illustrates this process.

Cash Conversion Cycle

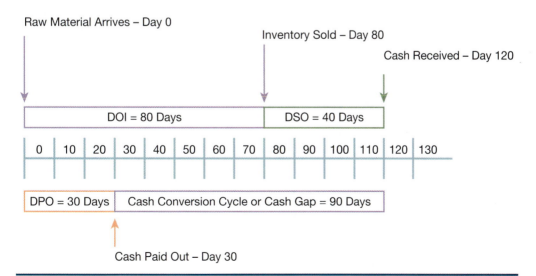

The cash conversion cycle, or days that it takes for cash to return to the business, must be funded. Any increase in sales usually results in an increase in working capital necessary to support this higher level of sales. Therefore, you must be able to fund the growth of the company.

As a stand-alone number the cash conversion cycle doesn't tell you much. Like many other metrics and ratios it must be compared over time and to other competitors in the industry. In general, a decreasing cash conversion cycle is a good thing, while a rising cash conversion cycle should motivate you to look a little more deeply into the management policies of the business to try and find the cash necessary to fund the company.

A.5 BUILDING PRO FORMA FINANCIAL STATEMENTS

>> **LO A.5**   **Discuss how to build a pro forma financial statement.**

Now that you have a better understanding of the three financial statements, it's time to turn our attention to developing projections or forecasted financial statements. When entrepreneurs are assessing the long-term viability of a business it's important to make projections and develop pro forma financial statements. Rather than looking at financial statements from what has happened, as we have been discussing we must now look at how to project what could happen. Pro forma financial statements give an idea of how the actual statement will look if the underlying assumptions hold true.[4]

The pro forma financial statement should include at least three scenarios of your financial forecast—each containing an income statement, the balance sheet, and the all-important cash flow statement. Each of these three scenarios should manipulate the various revenue and cost drivers in an attempt to determine where there is leverage in the business model to deal with what may go right and what may go wrong. All of your assumptions and estimates should be carefully documented and built into the model so that you can dynamically change them to conduct "what if" analyses in real time.

While there are many preexisting, dynamic, pro forma models on the Internet,[4] be mindful not merely to insert estimates randomly without corresponding backup for every assumption. Anyone who has been through this process knows that the numbers are estimates that will change over time. Nevertheless, you must be able to defend every assumption, and the components must logically support one another. In the end, the pro forma financial plans must be strategically compelling and operationally achievable, and they must convey both confidence and realism to investors.

Your goal is to determine how much absolute cash is required to get to cash flow break-even and how this cash might be logically staged so that you can achieve a step-up in valuation at each stage. It is worth noting that items will emerge that you have not considered and that items that you have considered will be magnified to either the positive or negative.

Creating pro forma statements can be a time-consuming process, but there are major benefits to doing so. First, it gives investors a degree of comfort that you understand how to build a business and execute the business model. Second, it shows that you have a good understanding of how the market may evolve and how to respond to these changes. Finally, it is a useful way of providing structure and discipline as operating decision points arise.

The Mechanics and Research

All too often entrepreneurs begin the process with an existing model or business planning software and, before long, find themselves tweaking elements of the model to "make the numbers work." Instead, it is best to set the spreadsheet models aside and

FIGURE A.6

The Mechanics

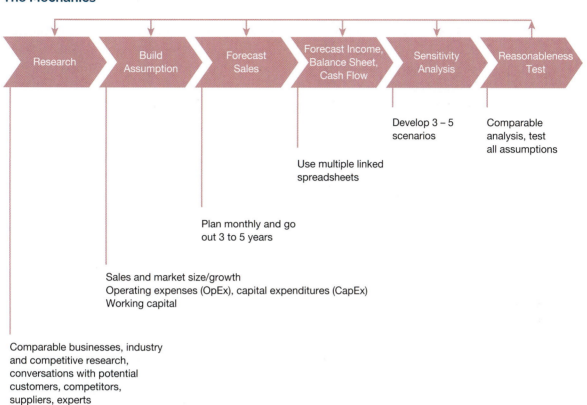

thoroughly research various business model elements that drive revenue and costs. This process requires both primary and secondary research. Figure A.6 outlines the overall process, or mechanics.

Research

Much of your research should focus on the customer and market size and growth potential. A common beginner mistake is to assume that an exceedingly large population is your market and all you will need to do is get 1% of that market to be successful.

While understanding the aggregate market size is useful, it is recommended that you segment your market in greater detail to better understand the various subgroupings and their respective buying habits and behaviors. Understand how they differ and how they are similar in terms of needs, expectations, price sensitivity, amount, and frequency of purchase, to name a few.

For the purpose of forecasting, it is also useful to understand how each subgroup is growing and changing over time. In general, the more you know about your primary and secondary target markets, the more reliable your forecasts will be.

Primary research refers to data gathered by yourself through sources such as focus groups, interviews, and surveys. **Secondary research** refers to data gathered from external sources: industry publications, company websites, government agencies, and the like. Secondary source articles and research reports can be useful as a means to get smart about an industry but, given the pace with which markets develop today, the data can get stale rather quickly. It is more beneficial to use primary data gathered in real time through observation, conversation, and rapid prototyping.

Primary research: refers to data gathered by yourself through sources such as focus groups, interviews, and surveys.

Secondary research: refers to data gathered from external sources such as industry publications, websites, government agencies, and so on.

One useful approach is to first determine the questions that need to be answered about your target market, channels of distribution, required resources, cost drivers, and revenue drivers. Next consider the data required to answer these questions. When you have gathered that data, then think about the primary and secondary sources of the data.

Remember to document the source of every assumption so that you can reference it if asked. Let's say that you want to start a pizzeria restaurant. Let's call it Town Pizza. Table A.8 lists some of the critical questions that you will want to answer before even opening a spreadsheet.

In addition to fundamental market research, it is also useful to find some yardsticks, or generally accepted rules of thumb for your industry. The best source of this information can usually be found by examining businesses that are comparable to yours in terms of industry and business model. There are numerous approaches to finding this information. Secondary sources are readily available on the Internet and include everything from historical data from public companies to industry associations and publications.[5] Similarly, primary data can be gathered through interviews with experts, business owners, potential customers, and observation. The comparable data will be extremely useful in both forming and validating your assumptions. In other words, everything covered in this text so far will help you build your assumptions.

TABLE A.8

Key Spreadsheet Questions

KEY QUESTIONS	DATA REQUIRED	SOURCES PRIMARY	SOURCES SECONDARY
Customer and Market • What is pizza consumption in the U.S.? Is it growing? • Who eats pizza, how much and when? • When is pizza consumed most? What days of the week? Time of year? • What is the population and composition of households in the area? What is the college population? What is the working population? • What percentage of these people will be likely diners? (lunch, dinner) • How can you estimate the traffic to the pizzeria and typical purchase order? **Revenue Drivers** • What else is sold at the typical pizzeria restaurant? (sandwiches, salads, pasta, beverages) • What is the consumption of these items relative to pizzas? • What is the average order? What are the average prices for each item? • What is the contribution margin? • What are breakeven points? **Cost Drivers** • What does it cost to make a pizza? A sandwich? A salad? etc.? • What is the average size of a pizzeria? • What does build out cost? • What are the typical operating expenses? (monthly, yearly) • What costs are fixed? Which are variable? • What fixed assets are needed? (equipment) What does it cost? Should you buy new or used? • What are the working capital requirements?	• U.S. pizza consumption data • Census data • Traffic patterns • Demographics • Typical pizza restaurant menu and pricing • Average pizzeria statistics • Ingredients cost • Real Estate data • Construction estimates • OpEx and CapEx for typical pizzeria	• Pizzeria owners, managers, and employees • Various customer segments of the pizzeria dining market • Associations • Consultants and experts • Accountants, Lawyers, Real Estate Agents • Suppliers • Contractors	• Industry research reports • Association research • Town Census • Periodicals • News articles • Websites/Blogs • New and Used Equipment sites • Annual Reports

Building Assumptions: Forecasting Sales

Forecasting sales can be a complex process. One useful way to estimate sales is the **Bottoms Up** or **Build Up Method**, a technique that involves first estimating revenue and costs from the smallest unit of sales and building up from there.

Let's apply this method to the Town Pizza example. As you can see from the revenue worksheet (Table A.9), Town Pizza sells pizza, sandwiches, salads, and drinks. By using the build up method you can present the assumptions gathered from your research to estimate revenue for a typical day, and then extrapolate what that revenue might be for a typical month and year.

As Table A.9 shows, the monthly revenue has been estimated at $26,280 or $315,360 per year before accounting for seasonal spikes. This foots pretty closely to the national average of $396,594, which does include seasonal spikes, so our bottoms up approach appears to be feasible.

Furthermore, you can examine the market data to see if there will be sufficient demand for our pizzeria by using a top down approach. As you can see in the assumptions, the town comprises 8,594 households, of which 62% are age 45 and younger. Just to be conservative, let's assume that your primary target market is people aged 45 and younger, and likely to be either college students or families. That would leave 16,517 people in town under the age of 45. Add to that the college students and workers who come into town each day and the figure becomes 23,541. So, if 94% of these people

Bottoms Up (or Build Up Method): Estimating revenues and costs from the smallest unit of sales, such as a day.

TABLE A.9

Revenue Worksheet

PRODUCT DESCRIPTION	SUGGESTED PRICE	EST. UNITS PER DAY	AVERAGE DAILY REVENUE
Pizza	$13.00	42	$546.00
Sandwich	$8.00	21	$168.00
Salad	$8.00	11	$88.00
Beverage	$2.00	37	$74.00
Total Average Daily Revenue			$876.00
Total Average Monthly Revenue @ 30 days/month			**$26,280.00**
* Does not account for seasonality spikes			

Assumptions:

US Pizza Market

- Average traffic—370 customers per month
- Average daily pizza sales = 42
- Sandwich sales are 50% of pizza sales
- Salad sales are 50% sandwich sales
- Beverages are 100% of pizza and sandwich sales
- Seasonal spikes – Super Bowl (Feb), Halloween (Oct), Thanksgiving (Nov), Christmas (Dec)
- Typical pizzeria average annual sales = $396,594.00
- 94% of Americans eat pizza; Average = 46 slices or 5.75 pizzas per year
- Pizza market is growing approximately 2% annually

Market Size / Growth

- Population = 27,982 (Households = 8,594), College Students = 5,974, Business employees = 1,050 (Total Pop 35,006)
- 62% of households < 45 years old (does not include college students and business employees)
- Growth 1% per year
- Currently 5 pizza restaurants in town

eat pizza and the average person eats 5.75 pizzas in a year, that means approximately 127,000 pizzas are eaten by this population yearly. If the average pizzeria serves 14,400 pizzas per year and there are currently only five pizzerias in town, then there should be room in the market for our Town Pizza.

The process of gathering the data and formulating the assumptions helps you better understand the business model and the levers that might be used to generate more revenue. For instance, will spending more on advertising and promotions bring more people to the store? This type of scenario or sensitivity analysis can be explored in more detail once you have completed building the integrated pro forma financial statements.

Now that you have this baseline to work with, you can plot out what the first two or three years of revenue might look like on a monthly, quarterly, and yearly basis. This would also allow you to make estimates for seasonal spikes or lows.

Building Assumptions: Cost of Goods and Operating Expenses

With a firm estimate on top line revenue, you can now turn your focus to estimating costs. The first cost item on the income statement is Cost of Goods Sold (COGS) (Table A.10). Recall that COGS includes the cost of raw materials and direct labor in the production of the product. Here you can once more use the buildup method to estimate the exact costs for each product, or as a first cut, you might want to use comparable data from a typical pizzeria.

Say you have found that the average raw materials and labor cost for a typical independent pizzeria is 30%. Given your estimated monthly revenue of $26,280, COGS would be $7,884, leaving you with a gross margin of $18,396 or 65%. Once again, our estimates are close to the average.

Businesses also incur operating expenses (see Table A.11), such as salaries, rent, advertising, marketing, and possibly research and development. These costs can also be estimated and validated through primary and secondary research. Reliable estimates can be accomplished through Internet research and validated through conversations with pizzeria owners, associations, accountants, lawyers, real estate brokers, and government officials, to name a few. It is worth sweating the details to get these

---

TABLE A.10

Cost of Goods Worksheet

PRODUCT DESCRIPTION	SUGGESTED PRICE	EST. COGS (%)	EST. UNITS PER DAY	COGS ($)
Pizza	$13.00	30%	42	$163.80
Sandwich	$8.00	31%	21	$52.08
Salad	$8.00	25%	11	$22.00
Beverage	$2.00	13%	37	$9.62
Total Daily COGS				$247.50
Total Monthly COGS				**$7,425.00**
Total Monthly Gross Margin				$18,855.00
(Total Monthly Revenue – Total Monthly COGS)				

TABLE A.11

Operating Expense Worksheet

OPERATING EXPENSE TYPE	ESTIMATED MONTHLY EXPENSE
Rent	$2,333.00
Labor	$7,925.00
Outside Services	$275.00
Credit Card Processing (1.9% of Sales)	$500.00
Utilities	$525.00
Advertising and Coupons	$100.00
Maintenance and Contingency	$500.00
Repair & Maintenance	$100.00
Insurance	$250.00
Office Supplies	$75.00
Equipment Rental	$250.00
Total Monthly Expenses	$12,833.00
Total Monthly Operating Profit **(Gross Margin – Operating Expense)**	**$6,022.00**

Assumptions:

Rent – 1000 sq. ft. at $28/year = $62,500.00

Labor – 1 Mgr, plus 3 hires

Fringe Rate = 15%

CC Processing – 1.9% of sales

estimates as close to the actual expenses as you possibly can. Once again, the buildup method is employed to round these numbers up to the monthly or yearly costs.

As you can see from the worksheet, the estimated operating profit is $6,022.00. This is not to be confused with net profit, which is profit after interest, depreciation, and taxes have been paid.

Labor Estimates

A more complex business that might involve research and development of a product and a greater number of employees would require a more detailed approach to structuring new hires. In many types of business people can account for 75% to 85% of operating costs. Therefore, the schedule of new hires must be carefully thought out and matched to product development and sales requirements and milestones.

Given the time and cost involved in screening, hiring, and onboarding new employees, a plan that takes these items into consideration should be constructed for each department. A common mistake is to hire people too quickly and terminate poor performers too slowly. However, regardless of the size or complexity of your business, it is good practice to build a simple table to estimate this expense separately (Table A.12).

TABLE A.12

Labor Estimates

POSITION	EST. ANNUAL / HOURLY WAGES	MARCH	APRIL	MAY	....
Manager	$31,200.00	$2,650.00	$2,650.00	$2,650.00	....
Hourly Employees					....
Kitchen Staff	1 @ $13 per hr. *	$2,297.00	$2,297.00	$2,297.00	....
Counter / Wait Staff	2 @ $11 per hr. *	$1,944.00	$1,944.00	$1,944.00	....
Benefits	15%	$1,033.00	$1,033.00	$1,033.00	....
Total Monthly Cost		$7,924.00	$7,924.00	$7,924.00	....

Assumptions:
- 1 Manager
- 1 Kitchen Staff
- 2 Counter Staff

With your top line revenue and operating expense worksheets completed, you can now turn your attention to expenditures necessary to build out and run the business (see Table A.13). These expenditures, or capital expenses, will not appear as a line item on your income statement. Since the expenditures will be used over a period of time, usually more than a year, they will appear on your balance sheet as an asset and on your cash flow statement as an outflow. What will appear on your income statement is depreciation, which reflects the annual decrease in value of these assets over their useful lives.

TABLE A.13

Capital Equipment and Other Expenditures Worksheet

EXPENDITURES	ESTIMATED COST
Pizza Ovens	$21,995.00
Walk-in Refrigerator	$10,500.00
Pizza Table / Work Tables	$13,000.00
Mixer	$3,500.00
Prep Sink / Dish Washer	$1,350.00
Pots & Pans	$500.00
Phone, POS, Coolers, CC Machine, Misc.	$1,000.00
Restaurant Build Out	$33,500.00
Signage	$1,250.00
Total Expenditures	**$95,595.00**

Assumptions:
- All prices assume new purchases; best efforts will be made to purchase used equipment in good repair.
- Build Out estimate provided by contractor for 1,000 sq. ft. including restroom. (Carpentry, electrical, plumbing labor included. Fixtures broken out separately.)

A.6 BUILDING ASSUMPTIONS: OPERATING POLICIES AND OTHER KEY ASSUMPTIONS

>> LO A.6   Explain how to apply assumptions when building pro forma statements.

As we saw earlier when describing the Cash Conversion Cycle (CCC), operating policies can greatly affect the speed at which cash makes its journey back to the company. In constructing pro forma financial statements, these policies need to be carefully considered and enforced by the company. Some of the more critical policies are as follows.[6]

▶ **Purchasing Policy** – The price and timing of raw materials, and other goods and services necessary to build, sell, and support products.

▶ **Pricing Policy** – How pricing will be determined for your products and services.

▶ **Compensation Policy** – The level of compensation and benefits for each type of position in the business.

▶ **Credit Policy** – The process and timing in which obligations to pay for products and services sold will be billed and collected.

▶ **Payables Policy** – The process and timing in which obligations to pay for goods and services received by the business will be paid.

▶ **Inventory Policy** – The level of various types of inventory (e.g., raw materials, work-in-process, finished goods) maintained and the speed with which inventory moves from the business to the customer.

Other critical assumptions can affect the timing of cash flows both into and out of the business. For instance, when do you expect to make the first sale, and how long will it take for the business to ramp up to full capacity? In our pizzeria example, it may take several months to obtain permits and complete a buildout of the restaurant before the grand opening. Then it may take several more months before advertising efforts begin to bring in the traffic that you anticipated would be necessary to achieve peak sales. This logic can also be extended to the productivity of new hires. Be sure to take into account the time and training it may take before new hires hit their stride and begin achieving the established sales quota.

Assumptions must also be considered for local, state, and federal taxes; interest; and inflation. Understand how your various expense-related items might increase over time as well. It is important to carefully document the source of every assumption made because it may be necessary to revisit it, or to defend it during due diligence.

Building Integrated Pro Forma Financial Statements

With your research and analysis completed and assumptions made, you are now ready to build integrated pro forma financial statements. The logical place to begin is with the income statement. Using the validated assumptions from the revenue worksheet, build out a monthly pro forma income statement, balance sheet, and cash flow statement for a minimum of two years, followed by years 3 through 5 on an annual basis. This time horizon will give you a good sense for the value-producing ability of the business.

Purchasing policy: The price and timing of raw materials and other goods and services necessary to build, sell, and support products.

Pricing policy: How pricing will be determined for your products and services.

Compensation policy: The level of compensation and benefits for each type of position in the business.

Credit policy: The process and timing in which obligations to pay for products and services sold will be billed and collected.

Payables policy: The process and timing in which obligations to pay for goods and services received by the business will be paid.

Inventory policy: The level of various types of inventory (e.g., raw materials, work-in-process, finished goods) maintained and the speed with which inventory moves from the business to the customer.

When building your pro forma statements, remember the linkages between the three financial statements described earlier. Also ensure you understand how changes on one statement can affect the other statements. Understanding these linkages and especially how cash makes its journey through the business can mean the difference between success and failure. It is essential that you understand how the growth in your business will be funded and the amount of funding you will need until your business is producing enough cash to survive without constant external funding.

The cash flow statement is used to determine when and how much funding is required to get the business off the ground and support growth in the earlier years. This can be achieved by leaving the third section, financing activities, blank to determine the cumulative amount of cash needed. View a set of sample financial statements on the companion site for this text.

Sensitivity Analysis

With the first full set of pro forma financial statements completed, you can now begin to address critical assumptions related to the revenue and cost drivers to test what your business might look like in different scenarios relating to customer traffic and seasonality, or cost of raw materials. For instance, if the restaurant were to open in the summer, might customer traffic be lighter due to vacationing college and high school students? If so, how might that affect revenue? Alternatively, what costs might need to be adjusted during peak selling months, and how might that affect cash flow and profitability?

During this analysis, a minimum of three scenarios is recommended: best case, worst case, and likely case. Thinking through the drivers and operating policies and understanding what can go right, what can go wrong, and what you would do to mitigate any controllable circumstances is probably the greatest benefit to building pro forma financial statements.

Reasonableness Test

Using comparable data that you gathered during your research, compare your statements to those of similar businesses. Unless you have an entirely new and disruptive business model, your numbers should not be too different from businesses of similar size and scope.

Specifically, take a look at your top line revenue and determine whether sales ramp too quickly or too slowly. Have you accounted for seasonal changes in demand? Does the rate of sales growth level off at some point in time? Do expenses continue to rise in lockstep with sales, or should you expect to achieve scale effects that allow COGS and other operating expenses to grow at a slower rate as sales increase? Are there other efficiencies to your business model that are reflected in your operating policies?

Consider all of the questions that a potential investor may have about your business model and its effects on your financial model, and be prepared to answer those using data from your research and comparable analysis. If certain numbers do not pass the reasonableness test, revisit your assumptions until you are comfortable and confident that you can defend the model. ●

Get the edge on your studies at **edge.sagepub.com/neckentrepreneurship**

▸ Master the learning objectives using key study tools
▸ Watch, listen, and connect with online multimedia resources
▸ Access mobile-friendly quizzes and flashcards to check your understanding

A.1   Explain the purpose of financial projections for startups.

Financial projections enable the entrepreneur to frame the opportunity from the perspective of the target market(s), understand the resources required to capitalize on the opportunity, and know how to allocate those resources under varying market conditions.

A.2   Describe financial statements as an essential part of financial projections.

The three essential financial statements are the income statement, the balance sheet, and the cash flow statement. The income statement measures performance on a monthly or annual basis. The balance sheet shows what the company owns and what it owes at a given point in time. The cash flow statement assesses the inflows and outflows of money over a period of time.

A.3   Clarify the relationship between the three financial statements.

While each financial statement provides a different view of the company, they are all needed to provide a complete picture. For example, a company's pricing and credit policies will have a direct impact on revenue, an income statement item; and on accounts receivable, a balance sheet item.

A.4   Describe the journey of cash through the cash conversion cycle.

The cash conversion cycle is the number of days a company's cash is tied up in the production and sales process. The number of days in the cycle is calculated by adding the Days Sales Outstanding (DSO) to Days Of Inventory (DOI) then subtracting Days Payable Outstanding (DPO).

A.5   Discuss how to build a pro forma financial statement.

The pro forma financial statement should include at least three scenarios of your financial forecast, each containing all three types of financial statements. Each scenario should manipulate revenue and cost drivers to show how the business can deal with what may go right and what may go wrong. It should show a best case, a worst case, and a likely case.

A.6   Explain how to apply assumptions when building pro forma statements.

Assumptions include operating policies, which determine the speed of the cash conversion cycle, as well as taxes, interest, inflation, and the time it will take to ramp up the business. When assumptions are applied, integrated financial statements can be created and sensitivity analysis and reasonableness test applied.

KEY TERMS

Accounts payable 364
Accounts receivable 362
Accrued expenses 364
Backlog 360
Balance sheet 360
Bottoms up/Build up method 375
Capital stock 364
Cash Conversion Cycle (CCC) 370
Cash flow statement 360
Compensation policy 379
Credit policy 379
Current assets 362

Current liabilities 364
DOI 370
DPO 370
DSO 370
Goodwill 363
Income statement 360
Intangible assets 363
Interest expense 362
Inventory policy 379
Liabilities 364
Long-term debt 364
Long-term investments 363
Net income 362

Operating expenses 361
Operating profit 362
Other current liabilities 364
Payables policy 379
Prepaid expenses 362
Pricing policy 379
Primary research 373
Purchasing policy 379
Retained earnings 364
Secondary research 373
Shareholder equity 364
Short-term debt 364

14 Developing Networks

"The most important action entrepreneurs and organization founders must take is to build a network of support for their new venture."

—Alex Steffen, author of *Worldchanging: A User's Guide for the 21st Century*

Learning Objectives

14.1 Explain the role of networks in building social capital.

14.2 Demonstrate the value of networks for entrepreneurs.

14.3 Describe different ways of building networks.

14.4 Illustrate the benefits of virtual networking.

14.5 Explain how networking can help to build the founding team.

Chapter Outline

14.1 The Power of Networks

14.2 The Value of Networks

14.3 Building Networks

14.4 Virtual Networking

14.5 Networking to Build the Founding Team

14.1 THE POWER OF NETWORKS

>> LO 14.1 Explain the role of networks in building social capital.

Over the course of this text, we have emphasized the fact that no entrepreneur is an island. Entrepreneurs need other people in order to succeed, and a strong network is key to this success. Studies show that by making connections with people who share our values, we are able to achieve more than if we had acted alone.[1]

The best networks can provide entrepreneurs with access to external sources of information, financing, emotional support, and expertise, and allow for mutual learning and information exchange. Network building is a dynamic process, which expands and evolves over time—continuously making purposeful and valuable connections is essential for business success.[2]

Through building networks, the most successful entrepreneurs develop **social capital,** which refers to our personal social networks populated with people who willingly cooperate, exchange information, and build trusting relationships with each other. Like physical capital (materials) and human capital (skills and knowledge), social capital is a productive asset. In other words, it's valuable.[3]

Social capital is less tangible than physical and even human capital because it "exists in the relationships among persons,"[4] and the value of these relationships can be difficult to assess and measure. However, in spite of its intangible nature, using social capital is a valuable way of getting work done, acquiring information, and finding resources of all types.

Social capital works through a wide range of channels. When you exchange ideas or information with someone at college, you are building social capital. Social capital can be found everywhere—in your local community, faith-based organizations, schools, clubs, online social media groups, and more.[5] Anywhere that provides the opportunity to interact socially will help you build social capital if you recognize the value in purposeful relationships.

Video
The Role of Networks

Social capital: personal social networks populated with people who willingly cooperate, exchange information, and build trusting relationships with each other.

John Hite and Franklin Yancey, Cofounders of College Comfort

Stadium seating at Ohio State, as designed by the cofounders of College Comfort.

Credit: Used with permission from John Hite and Franklin Yancey

John Hite's startup that made watching college sports games more comfortable, and more cool, made him a millionaire by his mid-twenties. His company was bought out by an earlier incarnation of IMG College—a collegiate sports marketing company—and he stayed on in leadership throughout that sale. Now, as a vice president at IMG, you might say Hite has the best of both worlds: the security and infrastructure afforded by an established company, and the personal satisfaction of staying on to lead his once-startup "baby" as it continues to grow and flourish.

It all started when Hite was an undergraduate majoring in business, hanging out at the legendary Lane Stadium at Virginia Tech. One fateful day in 1995, Hite watched as ROTC cadets collected the worn burlap seat cushions fans rented for a little extra comfort. John caught up with one of the young uniformed men and began asking questions. How much did the cushions cost to make? How much was the ROTC charging to rent them out? As the officer answered his questions, Hite was simultaneously wrapped up in his own internal dialogue: *What if the seats were plusher, more comfortable? What if they came in orange and maroon—Virginia Tech Hokie colors—and were emblazoned with the school logo? How much might the average Virginia Tech football fan pay for that—$4? $15? $20? More?*

Hite discussed his vision with fellow student Franklin Yancey, a longtime friend from childhood, and together they approached Virginia Tech administration with a pitch. Hite explains that the meeting didn't exactly go how the two had hoped. "'Get out of here! Go back to class!' was the general reaction," he says with a laugh, "because we were just students."

Undeterred, Hite and Yancey shopped their idea around and finally landed a contract with East Carolina University—which meant they had to learn seat cushion manufacturing, and fast. Through a contact of Yancey's father, they lined up an engineer who designed a device for bending steel, and they found a former Levi's plant nearby that had sewing and assembly capacity. Donning work gloves and blowtorches, the guys gave it a shot over Thanksgiving break, and their new company, College Comfort, was born.

"It was harder than we thought," Yancey told *Game Plan: People, Properties and Progress of IMG College.* (He, too, has remained with College Comfort through its subsequent sales, eventually landing as a vice president, along with Hite, at IMG College.) "We burned our hands. We could only make 50 a day. It was clear we couldn't do this on our own, so we reached out to a company in Wisconsin to bend the steel and ship the frames to Blackstone [where the old Levi's plant was located], where they cut and assembled a full seat."

In 1999, Virginia Tech finally came around, signing a contract, and in the ensuing years the duo networked tirelessly to sign colleges across the country. The early years were lean. They personally drove seats to games in their "company car" (a beat-up Jeep Cherokee). As the two crisscrossed the country networking and meeting with prospects, "lodging" for business meetings consisted of couches accommodated by their network of family and friends. "Each [set] of our parents cosigned loans for $30,000," explains Hite. "We used credit cards with balance transfers of 0%; I don't recommend doing that, but we did. We never ended up paying the 18% because we would transfer the balance once the 0% period was up."

The company, which began with 3,000 seat cushion rentals at its inaugural game, eventually grew to provide 80,000 seats in 40 schools across the nation before it was sold to ISP Sports in 2008. IMG Worldwide, a global leader in sports, fashion, and media, operating in more than 25 countries, acquired ISP Sports in 2010, again under the duo's leadership. In 2014 IMG was acquired by Hollywood-based WME, the world's leading entertainment and media agency. Hite and Yancey's division was valued at $75 million at the time of the sale. By the time the business was bought out, Hite and Yancey had managed to learn everything about running a business, thanks to their hard work, eagerness to learn, and extensive network.

Theirs is "a classic entrepreneurial success story, seeing something where nothing existed and then working incredibly hard to build on that vision," Ben C. Sutton, Jr., President of IMG College, told *Game Plan*. "John and Franklin were dogged and persistent in serving fans and their school partners, saw a path to even greater growth, and took advantage of our scale to build a market-leading business."

CRITICAL THINKING QUESTIONS

1. **How important were the networks of Hite and Yancey in achieving their goals?**

2. **Do you think Hite would have succeeded on his own? Why or why not?**

3. **What are some ways in which you can use your own network to attain your goals?** ●

Source: J. Hite, personal interview, January 4, 2015.

Social capital can be divided into three dimensions: the structural dimension, the relational dimension, and the cognitive dimension (see Figure 14.1). The structural dimension describes the components of your network, such as the type of social ties you may or may not have (i.e., the contacts in your network) and the degree to which these ties may be formal or informal.[6]

The relational side is what these contacts represent, such as a trusting relationship. When trust is present between two people, the relationship is stronger and an exchange of resources or overall support for your ideas or venture is greater.[7] You are more likely to enroll people into your idea when they trust you. It may also be helpful to think of your social capital as an "emotional bank account."[8] You can "make conscious efforts to make meaningful deposits in your relationships"[9] by actions you take with those in your network; making these deposits builds your "balance" so that when a "withdrawal" is needed, the relationship has the necessary social capital to cover it.

The cognitive dimension describes the degree of shared norms, visions, values, interpretations, and beliefs you may have with others. All of which provides a good foundation for working well together toward a common goal.[10]

Some observers argue that in the United States today, people are less likely to interact socially than they were in the past. Today, more time is spent at the workplace, commuting to work, and using devices like personal computers, smart phones, gaming

SAGE edge™

Master the content
edge.sagepub.com/
neckentrepreneurship

Video
Social Capital

FIGURE 14.1

Three Dimensions of Social Capital

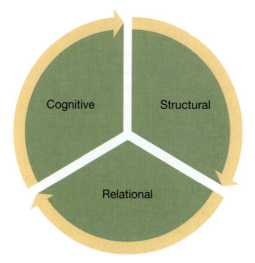

consoles, and television, leaving less time for volunteering, joining community groups, and socializing with friends, family, and neighbors. Even spending time participating in online social networks is not as "real" as the face-to-face social interaction of the past. The decline of community networks that used to be so prevalent in the past has led to a loss of social capital.[11] However, the good news is that anyone can build social capital if they make an effort to actively and purposefully form connections with others.

The Organisation for Economic Cooperation and Development (OECD), a global organization promoting economies throughout the world, identifies three main varieties of social capital:[12]

Bonds: the connections with family, friends, and others who have a similar cultural background or ethnicity.

Bridges: the links that go further than simply sharing a sense of identity; for example, making connections with distant friends or colleagues who may have different backgrounds, cultures, and so on.

Linkages: the connections to people or groups regardless of their position in an organization, society, or other community.

- ▸ **Bonds**: connections with people who are just like us, such as family, friends, and others who have a similar cultural background or ethnicity.

- ▸ **Bridges**: Links that go further than simply sharing a sense of identity; for example, making connections with classmates or colleagues who may have different backgrounds, cultures, or other characteristics.

- ▸ **Linkages**: Connections to people or groups regardless of their position in an organization, society, or other community.

There are many benefits to social capital. It creates a sense of shared value to the people who are connected in the network, especially when cooperation, trust, and mutual exchange are high. Our bonds with friends and family can be especially important when it comes to providing emotional, social, and economic support.

Famously, the most powerful contact in Bill Gates's network before Microsoft took off was his mother, Mary Gates. Mary Gates sat on the board of United Way with John Akers, a senior IBM executive. The relationship led to her son, Bill, pitching the Microsoft operating system to Akers, who awarded the contract to Gates. Microsoft would eventually surpass IBM as the most powerful computer company in the world.[13] Indeed, most networks begin by using our personal contacts for advice and support. For example, in the UK, more people are likely to secure jobs through personal contacts than through job advertisements.[14]

Take John Hite and Franklin Yancey, featured in *Entrepreneurship in Action*. Thanks to their network of family and friends providing accommodation, Hite and Yancey were able to travel across the country for business meetings with prospects, thus saving huge costs. Franklin Yancey also used his close personal network to find an engineer (a contact of his father's) who showed them how to make their first cushions. By the time Hite and Yancey' s business was sold, they had managed to learn everything there was to know about pitching, manufacturing, and engineering, thanks to social capital derived from their respective networks.

While personal bonds or "strong ties" to family and friends can be beneficial, they can also be restrictive. Forming connections with people who are too similar to ourselves can prevent us from seeing the bigger picture, as they are less likely to challenge our ideas, which may deprive us of valuable feedback and information.[15] In addition, when bonds are too strong, social capital can have a negative impact on society. As an extreme example, members of drug cartels are often bound together by personal loyalties, and their actions go against the interests of society and inhibit social and economic progress.[16]

That's why it is important to expand beyond our range of strong ties and capitalize on the external relationships or "weak ties" in our network, such as people we meet at trade shows and exhibitions, as well as potential investors and banks to capture a wider range of information. A combination of social bonds, bridges, and linkages is the best way of building a diverse and productive network. Let's explore the different ways we can build our network.

14.2 THE VALUE OF NETWORKS

>> **LO 14.2** **Demonstrate the value of networks for entrepreneurs.**

Video
The Power of Networks

Building relationships and social interaction are key to starting a business. An entrepreneur is required to interact with potential employees, resource providers, and other stakeholders.[17] Keep in mind that in a networking group of 20 to 40 people, the amount of possible referrals and leads that you could obtain from this group is almost incalculable.

Brian Pallas first realized the power of networks when he joined the Family Business Club at Columbia University, a club for students who came from high-net-worth families. However, with only 70 members, it was quite a limited network. By collating the clubs from Harvard, London School of Economics, and INSEAD, Pallas expanded the club globally, providing its members with the opportunity to network with trusted contacts all over the world.[18] This global club eventually became Opportunity Network—an organization that partners with top financial institutions to connect the "best banking clients" all over the world, giving them the opportunity to conduct very large, lucrative deals. The company aims to unite business leaders on a single platform to make it easier and more comfortable for a CEO in Manhattan to potentially partner with a senior manager in Africa.

Advantages to Networks

There are three main advantages to networks: private information, access to diverse skillsets, and power.[19] *Private information* is the type of information that is not available to the general public. Gathering unique information from network contacts, such as the release date of a new product, or what investors look for during a pitch, can give entrepreneurs the edge over the competition. The value of private information increases when trust is high in the network.

Secondly, networks provide *access to diverse skillsets*. A highly diverse network of contacts gives you a broader perspective of certain situations and allows you to trade information and skills with people who have different experiences and backgrounds from your own. By actively taking part in events and seeking out new contacts at meetings, you will be able to find people with complimentary skills and experience to help you grow your venture. As the late Nobel Prize winner Linus Pauling said, "The best way to have a good idea is to have a lot of ideas."[20]

Finally, networks can give you access to *power*—people in senior or executive positions who can provide expert advice and introduce you to other powerful people in their network. Additionally given the depth and breadth of your own network, you may actually have power.

Let's take a closer look at our personal networks and the different types of roles people play. First, people in your network can help you to progress by offering information and instruction, especially when trying to learn complex tasks. They can also refer you to others who might be able to assist in achieving difficult tasks.[21]

Second, people can help protect your venture by giving you advice when you are confronted with high-risk situations or are going through a rough patch. For example, when Mark Zuckerberg experienced confusion about the direction of Facebook in the early days, he sought advice from Steve Jobs, who urged Zuckerberg to take a trip to India to help him reconnect with Facebook's original mission. Zuckerberg took Jobs's advice and credits that trip for giving him clarity about the future of Facebook and his mission to provide Internet connectivity all over the world.[22]

TABLE 14.1

Types of Support

CAREER SUPPORT	PSYCHOSOCIAL SUPPORT	ROLE MODELING
• Sponsorship • Coaching • Exposure and visibility • Challenging assignments • Protections and preservation	• Encouragement and emotional support • Acceptance and confirmation • Counseling • Friendship • Personal feedback	• Behavior to emulate • Work ethic and values • Inspiration and motivation

Source: Murphy, W., & Kram, K. (2014). *Strategic relationships at work* (p. 23). New York, NY: McGraw-Hill.

Third, people can provide personal and emotional support by listening to your concerns, empathizing, and offering advice when required.

Finally, people become your role models. You can be inspired by their achievements, and in many cases, they represent what you would like to be when you progress as an entrepreneur.

In sum, networks can provide three types of support (Table 14.1): career support, psychosocial support, and role modeling.

Impression Management and Self-confidence

Despite the value of networking, other research has found that students in entrepreneurship classes often don't take advantage of networking opportunities provided to them in class. Students are given access to guest speakers, other entrepreneurs, and each other, yet often do not use these opportunities to build their networks. What stops students from networking effectively? Poor impression management and lack of confidence were the two biggest inhibiting factors identified during the study.[23]

Impression management: the concept of how people pay conscious attention to the way they are perceived and the steps they take to be perceived by others in a certain way.

Impression management is paying conscious attention to the way people perceive you and taking steps to be perceived in the way you want others to see you. When people interact with you, they form opinions. For example, the social cues that venture capitalists cue into are things like the following: How much does this person believe in this idea? How confident are they when speaking? How determined are they to make this work?[24] Research shows that entrepreneurs who display strong social competence are more likely to receive outside funding.[25]

You can manage the impressions others form of you by the way you dress, being aware of your body language, being polite and courteous, and being confident and open. Your attitude is also part of impression management: making an effort to interact with and learn from others goes a long way toward making a positive impression.

As one successful student entrepreneur, Jack, put it, "I want to meet some of these entrepreneurs and VCs that come [as guest speakers] to class—just meet these people, learn from their lives and experience what they've done—at least vicariously what they've done.... I really value trying to meet this person and getting to know them."[26] The outcome isn't defined beforehand, but "it just means doors aren't closed for you and you have more opportunities," Jack said.[27]

Lack of confidence also plays a part in students' reluctance to make connections with others. Fear of failure, of not asking the "right" questions, and insecurity about themselves and what they want to achieve are factors that may prevent students

RESEARCH AT WORK[28]

The "Dirtiness" of Professional Networking

Does professional networking make us feel "dirty"? A series of experiments shows that this very well might be the case. Inauthenticity and immorality were feelings found to be associated with professional networking, much more so than how we feel during our efforts to make new friends. In the first experiment, one group of participants was asked to write about a time when they deliberately set out to forge a professional relationship for personal gain; and another group was asked to write about a time where they had spontaneously made a professional contact. Each group was then presented with a number of word fragments, such as SH--ER, W--H, and S--P. Participants in the first group tended to fill in the blanks to make "cleansing" words, such as "shower," "wash," and "soap"; while those in the second group mostly filled in noncleansing words, such as "shaker," "with," and "ship."

In another experiment the groups were presented with one of two scenarios to read: attending a holiday party with the hope of making friends; or going to a company party with the intention of making business connections. Afterwards, they were asking to rate a list of consumer products (many of which included cleansing products) from 1 to 7. The group that had been presented with the professional networking scenario rated cleansing products higher than those who had read the fun, holiday party scenario.

However, in other experiments, researchers found that people with higher power (such as partners in a law firm) did not feel "dirty" about networking, and would not have been in the position to make partner without it. So what can "low power" people do? Harvard professor Francesca Gino says, "If you focus on what you can offer to the relationship, it might be an important mindset to have, and remove some of those feelings of inauthenticity." In other words, thinking about what you bring to the table, and the value you can contribute to a professional networking relationship, will help chase those uncomfortable, "dirty" feelings away.

CRITICAL THINKING QUESTIONS

1. **What do you think is easier—forging a professional relationship for personal gain or forming a spontaneous professional contact?**

2. **Would you consider deliberately forming a professional contact for professional gain "dirty"? Why or why not?**

3. **How would you go about forming your own professional relationships?** ●

from approaching guest speakers and asking questions. In some cases, networking is regarded negatively because some people may think of it as an insincere way of gaining a personal advantage.

While in college or even in this course you are taking, it may not seem important to network with your classmates. However, never underestimate the value of networking with your peers. As Jack was told by his professor, "You're sitting next to a potential CEO. You're sitting in class right now with someone that is going to go to Wall Street and could potentially get you a job next year, or could be your contact. And you're not talking to them. You're not meeting them."

The students you sit next to in class might become your cofounders, your partners, your advisors, your employers, your stakeholders, and even your mentors one day. Interact with them, learn from shared experiences, make connections, and use them to expand your network. Keep in mind that many of the most successful ventures are built on forging relationships at the university level. Dropbox founders Drew Houston and Arash Ferdowsi met at MIT; Instagram founders Kevin Systrom and Mike Krieger met at Stanford; and Stacey Bendet and Rebecca Matchet, founders of contemporary clothing company Alice and Oliva, met at the University of Pennsylvania.[29] Without being immediately conscious of it, these founders had become self-selected stakeholders before the venture had even existed. In the next section, we will explore the concept of self-selected stakeholders and their value to entrepreneurial ventures.

Self-Selected Stakeholders

Usually, entrepreneurs do not think about stakeholders such as employees, contractors, suppliers, customers, and the like until after the business has started. However, entrepreneurs need to understand the importance of a particular type of stakeholders called **self-selected stakeholders**.[30] These are the people who "self-select" into a venture in order to connect entrepreneurs with resources such as subject-matter expertise, funding, advice, introductions to others, new perspectives, feedback on concepts, acting as mentors, sharing war stories, and so on, in an effort to steer the venture in the right direction.

The first step to finding self-selected stakeholders is to think about the people you already know: your family and friends, people you have met at work, and people you encounter in school and social activities. These stakeholders may not even be part of the eventual founding team, but they are a valuable source of information and, potentially, investment.

A stakeholder self-selects into your venture to offer some type of short term or long-term commitment in an effort to steer your venture in the right direction. Unlike venture capitalists and other investors, your self-selected stakeholders do not need to be pitched to or sold to. They are helping you because they feel motivated to give you access to information and resources that you didn't otherwise have. When people self-select into your network without any hidden agenda or motive, there is a huge opportunity to collaborate with them to build a better business.

Indoor rock climbing business Gravity Vault, founded by Lucas Kovalcik and Tim Walsh

Self-selection also ties in with the concept of enrollment as discussed as part of The Practice of Entrepreneurship in Chapter 2. Key to building the network is the idea of enrolling people in your idea rather than selling them. You aren't asking for favors. You are sharing in hopes they want to be a part of your network. They have something to offer, and you have something of value to provide. Building your network is not a sales job. It's not about trying to convince someone to do something that he or she may not ordinarily do. Rather, people join your network because they want to. People enroll in your vision because they're moved by your enthusiasm or idea. They see something that they want to become part of.

Peter Senge, founding chairperson of the Society for Organizational Learning, offers the following three guidelines for enrollment.

1. Be enrolled yourself. If you're not buying the future vision, opportunity, or team, others won't, either.
2. Be truthful. Don't inflate the benefits beyond what they really are.
3. Let the other person choose. Don't try hard to "convince" them—that comes across as manipulative and ultimately hurts enrollment.[31]

One of the best ways to form a range of diverse connections with self-selected stakeholders is through shared activities.[32] Types of shared activities can include joining sports teams, clubs, community service ventures, and voluntary and charitable associations. These activities bring together all sorts of people from different experiences and backgrounds. Remember that new ventures require a variety of talents, from marketing to technology to finance; and confining yourself to a particular group whose experience mirrors yours is unlikely to expand your skillset. Your goal is to learn more about the talents of acquaintances to find areas of mutual interest.

Participating in a shared activity builds trust and passion, and allows for people to be themselves outside a formal environment in the attainment of a common goal. Team members can build a loyal bond that may transfer into a working relationship. For example, the franchised indoor rock climbing business, Gravity Vault, was founded by Lucas Kovalcik and Tim Walsh, who met through a mutual love of rock climbing.[33]

14.3 BUILDING NETWORKS

>> **LO 14.3** **Describe different ways of building networks.**

Forging connections goes beyond striking up conversations with friends and acquaintances; a really useful network expands to meeting other individuals in your geographic location. Check online for public calendars of local events, including public lectures at universities, Chambers of Commerce, and events announced in the local newspaper.

Video
Developing a Network

Many cities around the world have Meetup groups—local get-togethers of people who share a passion for interests ranging from hiking to sightseeing to biking to meditations to entrepreneurs. They provide a way to find people locally who share a common interest with you. Go to Meetup.com and enter your zip code to

TABLE 14.2

Top Organizations for Entrepreneurs

Entrepreneurs' Organization (EO)	The world's only peer-to-peer network solely for entrepreneurs. Connects entrepreneurs with over 10,000 peers and offers opportunities to attend global networking events.
Young Entrepreneur Council (YEC)	For entrepreneurs below the age of 40. Provides 24/7 peer-to-peer support, events, and a chance to take part in mentorship discussions.
Social Enterprise Alliance (SEA)	Provides members with subscriptions to a monthly newsletter, access to forums, the SEA Knowledge Center, consultation services, and networking opportunities at events.
Startup Grind	One of the largest organizations in the world and has connected over 215,000 founders in 185 cities internationally. It holds monthly events featuring successful local founders, innovators, and investors; and has provided entrepreneurs with connections to partners, funding, and mentors.[37]
Association of Private Enterprise Education (APEE)	An organization that provides entrepreneurship education and information and offers annual conferences as an opportunity to expand this knowledge.
United States Association Small Business and Entrepreneurship (USASBE)	Entrepreneurship community that focuses on entrepreneurship education, entrepreneurship research, entrepreneurship outreach, and public policy. Membership includes access to their online career center that offers networking opportunities with fellow entrepreneurs, educators, and policy makers.
Ashoka	For social entrepreneurs, Ashoka is the largest network for entrepreneurs who want to change the world. It provides startup financing and excellent networking opportunities.
The Entrepreneur's Club (TEC)	Holds 10 events a year and gives entrepreneurs a chance to network, swap ideas with peers, and listen to influential speakers like Steve Blank and Guy Kawasaki.

Source: Rampton, J. (2015, January 2). 12 Organizations entrepreneurs need to join. *Entrepreneur.* Retrieved from http://www.entrepreneur.com/article/241192

Analyzing My Network[34]

Have you ever stopped to think about the network you already belong to?

Think about the people in your current network. First, list these people in column format on a piece of paper. Try to list 15 to 20 people that you know. Next for each person, identify:

- with an (A) if they help you get work done,

- with a (B) if they help advance your career or entrepreneurial ideas,

- with a (C) if they provide personal support, and

- with a (D) if they are a role model.

Now, count how many As, Bs, Cs, and Ds you have. What type of people are most plentiful in your network? What type of people do you need more of and why? Keep in mind that entrepreneurs need all types in their network.

CRITICAL THINKING QUESTIONS

1. **How easy or difficult was it to think of 15 to 20 people in your current network? Could you think of more than 20 people?**

2. **Do you think the A, B, C, and D categories are a helpful way to categorize the members of your network? Would you use other categories instead or in addition?**

3. **How do you think others would categorize you as a member of their networks? What qualities do you possess that would be valuable to others in their networks?** ●

Source: Based on Murphy, W., & Kram, K. (2014). *Strategic relationships at work*. New York, NY: McGraw Hill.

see a wide variety of meetups near you. One group set up in Vancouver, Canada, is for the "Extremely Shy" and is the most active meetup group in Canada, as well as being one of the top 5 most active groups in the world.[35] Meetup is becoming so popular that the number of worldwide users has already reached 25 million.[36] Meetups typically run from one hour to all day, and they can feature formal presentations or simply be free-form networking events. Many Meetup groups focus on technology (such as the SaaS consortium) or skills (such as public speaking or podcasting).

There are more formal networking groups solely for the entrepreneur community. For example, Startup Colorado (startupcolorado.com) is a "regional initiative to increase the breadth and depth of the entrepreneurial ecosystem across Colorado's Front Range. Our mission is to multiply connections among entrepreneurs and mentors, improve access to entrepreneurial education, and build a more vibrant entrepreneurial community." Here Colorado-based entrepreneurs can find what local startup events are going on. There are many more organizations that entrepreneurs can join—see Table 14.2. Attending these events will expand your network and find self-selected stakeholders.

Learning How to Network

Networking is not just about collecting business cards. You may walk away from a networking event with a whole stack of business cards but with no meaningful relationships or connections forged. A business card isn't enough for someone to remember you by—you need to have meaningful conversations to maintain a relationship and provide value in a way that makes you memorable.

Networking is a two-way game. It's a targeted search, with a philosophy of contributing, giving value, sharing and exchanging information, and interacting with people.

Networking events

Before you attend a networking event, do your research. Think about who might be there, and decide whom you would like to meet. Think of what you are going to say before you arrive. Your list of topics does not have to be solely business related. You could talk about anything from business, to sports, to weekend plans, to industry events. Remember, relationships can be forged on mutual personal interests or hobbies, and not just business interests. However, it is always best to steer clear of potentially incendiary topics like politics, religion, and other issues that might elicit a strong emotional reaction.

Walking in to a room full of strangers can be daunting, but the good news is that like any other skill, the skill of networking can be learned. And in keeping with the theme of this book, it takes practice. One step in developing this skill is to make a habit of "reading" the room when you first walk in. How crowded or empty is it? Is there a focal point or an activity taking place that could be a conversation starter? If people are gathered in groups of various sizes, think about which groups you could approach and make a positive contribution. This involves looking at nonverbal cues such as body language and eye contact to identify whom to approach as a likely conversant, and whom to avoid. For example, a small, animated group may look appealing, but be aware that they might be in the middle of an intense discussion and may not be open to welcoming a newcomer at the moment.

Research shows that domineering people tend to take control of the conversation and avoid eye contact a lot of the time. People who are open to making new connections generally "adopt an open stance, shoulders apart and hands at their sides, turning slightly toward newcomers to welcome them," says networking expert Kelly Decker, of Decker Communications.[38] While influential people tend to lead conversations, good networkers will listen and show interest by nodding, leaning forward, raising their eyebrows, and mirroring the speaker's gestures; for example, tilting their heads in the same way.

When you start a conversation with someone or someone else approaches you for a conversation, commit fully to the discussion. Don't "look over the shoulder of the person you're talking to in case someone more interesting shows up."[39] Also be careful not to dominate the conversation; make sure you give some time and attention to letting the other person speak and offer thoughts and opinions. To disengage without leaving the person feeling they've been brushed off, look them in the eye, shake hands and say their name followed by "it's been good talking with you" or words to that effect.

If you are approaching a desired contact with a question, briefly introduce yourself, keep your question short, and explain why you are asking. This shows you have done your homework and have really thought about what you need to know. Then thank person for their help and follow up with a short note or email within 24 hours. After thanking the person via email or note, consider connecting on LinkedIn or other professional networking sites.

The give and take of networking

Bear in mind that networking is a two-way street. The *quid pro quo* (meaning something that is given or done in return for something) strategy is often used by networkers to initiate a business relationship.[40] The idea behind it is to first identify something your contact needs and then offer something of value. This could involve sharing some information, sending a link to an article about the subject in question, or offering your contact an introduction to someone who knows more about the subject.

Kare Anderson, author of *Mutuality Matters,* points out that when you do favors for somebody, they are more likely to repay them. Doing favors for others helps people with good ideas to find ways to capitalize on their opportunities. She provides a list of favors that may only take as little as 5 minutes, and are a great way of quickly building trusting relationships:

▶ Use a product and offer concise, vivid, and helpful feedback.

▶ Introduce two people with a well-written email, citing a mutual interest.

▶ Read a summary and offer crisp and concrete feedback.

▶ Serve as a relevant reference for a person, product, or service.

▶ Share, comment, or retweet something on Facebook, Twitter, LinkedIn, Tumblr, Google+, or other social places.

▶ Write a short, specific, and laudatory note to recognize or recommend someone on LinkedIn, Yelp, or other social place.[41]

Remember that many people who are new to networking events will be as nervous as you are. If you see someone standing alone, why not approach him or her? They are likely to be more welcoming because you have made an effort to strike up a conversation. More important, don't assume "anyone standing alone is a loser and should be avoided."[42] This person might end up being one of your most valuable contacts. In fact, never assume that anyone—regardless of who they are or what they do—can't be a worthwhile acquaintance (see Figure 14.2).

FIGURE 14.2

Variety Is the Spice of Networking

Credit: ©iStock.com/mattjeacock

Ivan Misner, founder of business networking organization BNI, tells the story of a financial advisor friend who received a huge portion of business referred to him by a gardener on Cape Cod in Massachusetts. The gardener worked in the gardens of the grandest homes on Cape Cod and had built up good professional relationships with wealthy families living there. When the gardener heard the financial advisor was trying to get referrals in the area, he mentioned his name to his contacts in the wealthy families, and that is how the financial advisor ended up getting a huge chunk of business.[43] So the moral of the story is, never underestimate the power of the "loner" or the person with a "low wage" job, or the person sitting next to you at an entrepreneurship event. Pursue all networking opportunities—you never know where they may lead. Networking is simply about human connection and connecting with all types of people.

Finally, make a real effort to remember names (this could involve mentally writing a person's name on or above their face) and use names during conversation to fully assimilate them. Write down information soon after you meet someone.[44]

Guy Kawasaki, author of *The Art of the Start,* provides some additional tips for networking:[45]

- Discover what you can do for someone else. Great networkers want to know what they can do for you, not what you can do for them.

- Ask good questions: the mark of a good conversationalist is to get others to talk a lot and then listen.

- Unveil your passions. Don't just talk about business—let the conversation expand into your hobbies as well.

- Read voraciously so that you have an array of information to draw on during conversations.

- Follow up with a short but personal note within 24 hours. Something like, "Nice to meet you. Hope your blog is doing well," is fine—but be sure to mention at least one personal item to show that you're not just sending a canned email.

- Prepare a self-introduction of seven to nine seconds (*not* a 30-second elevator speech). Tie it to why you're attending the event. This will help people figure out what to say to you.

Networking to Find Mentors

Mentors can be an invaluable resource for entrepreneurs as they offer advice based on years of experience, help you progress with your venture, and warn you of known pitfalls. Most well-known entrepreneurs credit their mentors for their success. Steve Jobs taught Mark Zuckerberg how to build a team; Bill Gates credits Warren Buffett for his ability to deal with complex problems; and Richard Branson references British airline entrepreneur Sir Freddie Laker for his advice and guidance when trying to get Virgin Atlantic off the ground.[46]

Web
Finding Mentors

Yet entrepreneurs may not just have one mentor; they may build up a network of mentors over time, which can be useful when you are seeking different perspectives or guidance during particular stages of your venture. Mentors can also play a very important role in larger companies. For example, instead of bosses at the multinational manufacturer W.L. Gore, new hires are assigned mentors—people who can guide them through Gore's famously unique nonhierarchical culture and address any questions, concerns, or issues the new hire may have.[47]

How do you go about finding your mentor? Look in your personal network—the ideal mentor might be right in front of you. Sometimes the person who knows you best can be the right fit for you. Following a long search through her external network, Brooke Stone, Founder and CEO of Brooke Stone Lifestyle Management, eventually realized that the best mentor for her was actually her father.[48]

Check out your college connections, too, as they can be a valuable resource for mentors. For example, Theranos founder and the world's youngest self-made billionaire, Elizabeth Holmes, discovered her mentor, Channing Robertson, Dean of Chemical Engineering, at Stanford. Roberston agreed to give Holmes the opportunity of working in Robertson's lab—a privilege not usually afforded to freshmen. That experience helped Holmes develop her relationship with her mentor and further her goal to provide needle-free blood testing. Anywhere you have the opportunity to form connections—networking events, Meetup groups, and so forth—may be the right step toward finding the right mentor for you.

However, for some entrepreneurs, asking someone to be your mentor can be daunting. Why would a successful business person or seasoned entrepreneur want to take the time to help you grow your fledgling new venture? The answer is that many mentors gain personal pleasure in sharing their experience to help others succeed. Now a mentor himself, Richard Branson is a champion of young entrepreneurial talent; he has said he gets "a real sense of pleasure from seeing talented people realize their ambitions and grow professionally and personally." Branson also believes that mentors can also learn a lot from their mentees, "As I've learned, in the process you can gain new insights and discover fresh approaches to doing business by simply discussing how things work."[50]

While face-to-face networking is essential for building valuable relationships, it is also possible to network from a remote location. In the next section, we will explore the benefits of virtual networking.

14.4 VIRTUAL NETWORKING

» LO 14.4   **Illustrate the benefits of virtual networking.**

Video
Virtual Networking

With the proliferation of online social networks, networking has definitely evolved! One of the speediest and simplest ways to connect with others is through social media. Twitter, LinkedIn, Facebook, Instagram, and YouTube all provide ways to connect with people who are experts in the field, potential stakeholders, or fellow entrepreneurs—anyone who can potentially help you develop, build, and grow your entrepreneurial venture. Some of these people may become self-selected stakeholders and eventually become part of your founding team. Let's explore how you can use these social media sites to build your network.

Twitter is one of the easiest ways to find people whom you don't know but who might become potential stakeholders (see Table 14.3). Signing on to Twitter is free (just choose a user name and a password) and easy (write a 160-character bio about yourself). You can upload a photo and you're ready to go.

To find others on Twitter who share your interests, you can do a search on Twitter (www.search.Twitter.com) by keyword and see everyone who is using that keyword at that very instant. You can also search for other people's bios through www.Twellow.com using keywords of your choice. If you want others to find you easily, then you can register with Twellow and write a longer biography. The longer length gives you a chance to use more keywords and to express yourself and your ideas in a bit more detail. You can also Tweet people directly and ask them questions or make comments on their Tweets, which allows you to establish contact more easily.

In addition to Twitter, you can interact with individuals or with the group as a whole through LinkedIn by asking questions or posting comments. LinkedIn also has a

TABLE 14.3

How to Network on Twitter

• Provide information and reply to questions ("@ replies").
• Provide a link to a useful article or study. For example, Aerospace Incubator promotes entrepreneurship & work force development in the space industry: http://ow.ly/jrF.
• Announce a new blog post if you have a blog.
• New blog post: Solving Scarce Resource Problems through Innovative IT: http://is.gd/O90y #innovation.
• Give a friend a toot: Congrats @bhc3 is #7 on Top 50 Geek Entrepreneur blogs: http://ow.ly/jPtA.
• Announce a new product or service you offer.
• Recommend a good book, video, expert, and so on.
• Disclose a bit about you: Woo hoo! Finished all 9 presentations for #AIIP conference!
• Show personality: Furl.net just got acquired by Diigo. This is a resource I cannot live without. And they did NOT consult with me beforehand. I'm shocked.
• Ask a question: Help! I need to record a one-hour webinar and am cheap. Which screencasting tool handles an hour-long call? Jing? Screentoaster? GoView?

section devoted specifically to Questions & Answers, which provides you with a view into the real-life challenges that business people face and the solutions that others offer. Anyone can post a question, and anyone can provide an answer. To reward helpful, quality answers, the question-asker can award the best answer with a "good answer" tag. As an entrepreneur looking to build your knowledge, you can use these tags to identify the best answers from which to learn. Posting answers is a good way to show your own expertise and to demonstrate your willingness to be of help to others. When you share information with others, they will feel more inclined to reciprocate. Table 14.4 lists a range of LinkedIn groups dedicated to entrepreneurs and small-business owners.

Entrepreneur John Neary credits his LinkedIn network for giving him the advice and encouragement needed to start his company Right Workplace—a new venture that focused on employee engagement and workplace culture improvement. Neary published detailed, informative posts about culture and leadership on LinkedIn, which won the admiration of his followers and attracted attention from potential clients. One of these clients ended up offering Neary a full-time CEO role, which he accepted.[51] This example illustrates the power of virtual networks when they are used productively.

Facebook has grown from a social platform to a business platform—most businesses have a presence on Facebook. It is also useful for posting articles on Facebook pages and connecting with others who share mutual interests. Facebook groups are also beneficial for connecting with others and starting dialogues around shared interests. There are also specific Facebook Groups for entrepreneurs (Table 14.5) that provide a forum for entrepreneurs to meet and exchange ideas. Don't be wary of connecting with your competitors—they are a valuable source of learning and inspiration.

Both Facebook and LinkedIn make it easy to find out which face-to-face conferences the people in your network are attending.

Unlike Twitter, LinkedIn, and Facebook, YouTube is less of a social networking and interaction site. However, you can use YouTube as a resource for identifying experts and getting video tutorials on a specific topic. When you find the expert on YouTube, you can use other social media like Twitter and LinkedIn to establish first contact.

TABLE 14.4

LinkedIn Groups Dedicated to Entrepreneurs

A Startup Specialists Group— Online Network for Entrepreneurs and Startups	With just under 200,000 members, this is one of the moderated LinkedIn communities for startups, founders, mentors, investors, and small business experts.
Band of Entrepreneurs	This group describes itself as "a nonprofit organization of, by and for entrepreneurs," and it provides support on topics like legal help, human resources, public relations, technology, and more. The group is open (meaning anyone can join) and has over 22,000 members.
Bright Ideas & Entrepreneurs	Founded in 2007 and now boasting over 17,000 members, this group aims to facilitate discussion and idea-sharing among entrepreneurs all over the world.
Entrepreneurs Meet Investors	Whether you're looking for funding to start a business or grow your existing company, this open group could help. It has a network of over 6,000 entrepreneurs and investors.
Entrepreneur's Network	Founded in 2008, this open group has over 24,000 members. It's dedicated to current and aspiring entrepreneurs looking to network and ask and answer questions.
On Startups—The Community for Entrepreneurs	This open group has over 500,000 members, making it the largest entrepreneurial startup group on LinkedIn. It is dedicated to discussing marketing, financing, operations, hiring, and all other things small business.
Social Entrepreneur Empowerment Network	Dedicated to social entrepreneurs; brings "together some of the world's most accomplished visionary leaders and conscious business experts," according to its profile. The open group aims to empower social entrepreneurs, and has over 16,000 members.
Women's Network of Entrepreneurs	Dedicated to female entrepreneurs and women in business who want to build their networks and share resources, this private group was founded in 2008 and has over 17,000 members.
Young Entrepreneur Connections	With almost 20,000 members, "designed to benefit all young entrepreneurs," according to its profile. The group is open and is a great opportunity for young professionals and entrepreneurs to network with small business owners, consultants, advisors, and more.

Source: Excerpted from Helmrich, B. (2016, March 23). 16 LinkedIn groups every entrepreneur should belong to. *Business News Daily.* Retrieved from http://www .businessnewsdaily.com/7185-entrepreneur-linkedin-groups.html

Instagram is also a useful networking tool. People can send short videos and photos to connect with others and showcase where they have been and what business activities they have been involved with. For example, Pete Cashmore, founder and CEO of leading news digital site Mashable, posts natural pictures that give his followers an insight into his professional life. Allowing people an insight into your professional life gives them the opportunity to get to know you and your business.

Social networking sites enable you to find and interact with people you might otherwise never meet who share your passion and could ultimately be a resource. For example, selective networking site FounderDating provides a global forum for entrepreneurs to connect with like-minded entrepreneurs, cofounders, and advisors. Applications from entrepreneurs to join FounderDating are first screened for skillsets (50% of the members are engineers), and if the applicants are accepted, they are given access to the network for a

Pete Cashmore, founder and CEO of Mashable.

Credit: Mireya Acierto/Getty Images Entertainment/Getty Images

$50 annual fee.[52] Teams that have connected through FounderDating have built new ventures together, including the team behind the 2011 startup Refresh.io—an app that to help build a robust profile of contacts on Facebook or LinkedIn that you may not follow too closely. Refresh.io was taken over and shut down by LinkedIn in 2015, with 12 of the original team of 15 joining LinkedIn to apply their technology into a range of LinkedIn products.[53]

Stakeholders can provide valuable resources to entrepreneurs as well, helping cocreate and bring the venture to life. Cocreation is a strategy that focuses on bringing people together to initiate a constant flow of new ideas that help to create ventures and transform businesses for the better in an uncertain and unpredictable world. For example, social entrepreneur John Louis Kiehl runs a charity for people in debt in France. Instead of fighting with the banks, Kiehl cocreates with financial institutions to identify the groups of customers who are most at-risk, in order to provide support and reduce the risk of excessive debt.[54]

In other countries around the world, online startup support networks are becoming more popular as a means of funding early-stage ventures. VC4Africa is Africa's largest online entrepreneurship network, which brings together venture capitalists, angels, and entrepreneurs to support Africa's rapidly growing startup scene. Through its 17,000 members, the network connects entrepreneurs with the knowledge, contacts, and financing necessary to build their businesses. To date, entrepreneurs have raised over $27 million in funding through VC4Africa.[55]

TABLE 14.5

Some Facebook Groups for Entrepreneurs

Entrepreneurs	A place for entrepreneurs to meet and share ideas and resources. The rules for marketing and selling on social networks are still being written in large part. This page is for entrepreneurs who recognize this sales and marketing opportunity and choose to be pioneers in the new medium.
Entrepreneur Magazine	The magazine for the small business community. Stay up to date with the latest business trends, opportunities, movers, and shakers through this Facebook page.
Ladies Who Launch	Inspires women to start businesses, grow existing companies, and tap into their creativity to develop essential services and products and enjoy the lifestyle of their dreams while doing it.
Social Media for Small Business	A series of "Social Media Guides" to help small and medium businesses effectively use these tools to grow and better serve customers.
Young Entrepreneurs	Focused on empowering individuals who have a vision of success. This group's purpose is to provide strategies for starting a successful business, and real live testimonials from actual entrepreneurs. It is also a marketing tool for those looking to network.
Urban Social Entrepreneurs	A nonprofit organization based on the ideas and principles of social entrepreneurism. It was created to make urban communities economically and socially stronger, through the development of a new generation of social entrepreneurs.
Social Media Today	From networking and community building to marketing and trend analysis, we help people understand what's going on in social media.

Source: Excerpted from The 25 Facebook groups for entrepreneurs. (2011, February 24). *Brandmaker News*. Retrieved from http://brandmakernews.com/business-brand/3561/the-25-facebook-groups-for-entrepreneurs.html

In the Philippines, incubators Ideaspace and Kickstart were set up to revive Manila's technology sector. The startup support groups have attracted interest from venture capitalists from Japan, Singapore, and the United States looking to invest in the growing tech scene. Philippine scientist Aisa Mijeno is one of the entrepreneurs funded by IdeaSpace for her revolutionary invention, the SALt Lamp (Sustainable Alternative Lighting), which does not require electricity but runs on salt and water, in response to the 16 million Filipinos living in remote places with no access to electricity.[56]

Maintaining Your Network

Once you've started to build your network, it's important to maintain it—something that's easier than ever to forget when your network is mainly virtual and you are not interacting face-to-face on a regular basis. Maintaining your network involves staying in touch through occasional interaction. Research shows we can really manage up to only 25 relationships, but we can maintain up to 150.[57]

This interaction can take the form of tweeting a useful piece of information, replying to a request for information, answering a question, or attending an event. For example, if you saw an interesting video on YouTube, send a link in seeing to people in your network who might be interested. If one of your stakeholders posts a question on LinkedIn to which you know the answer (or know someone who knows the answer), answer the question or recommend an expert. Figure 14.3 lists several skills important to maintaining relationships.

If you're a member of Meetup groups, then let your network know that you're attending an upcoming meeting. You can also Tweet your attendance or announce it on LinkedIn and Facebook. After the event, you can Tweet or email any people with whom you talked, by thanking them for the conversation. Another way to maintain your network is to provide value back to them by writing a blog. As an entrepreneur, you can use a blog as a way to showcase and share your thoughts and activities with your stakeholders.

Overall, the frequency of interactions you have with your stakeholders can vary over time. There will be times when you're actively seeking advice, which means you will have more interactions. Some stakeholders will want to be involved on a daily or weekly basis. Others are fine with less frequent interactions. Overall, maintaining relationships is a skill like any other, and it pays to learn it (see Figure 14.3).

FIGURE 14.3

Skills for Maintaining Relationships

Skills for Maintaining Relationships

- Curiosity
- Questioning
- Deep Listening

- Self-Management
- Accountability
- Intuition

Source: Adapted from Wendy Murphy & Kathy Kram. Strategic Relationships at Work. (New York: McGraw Hill. 2014).

ENTREPRENEURSHIP MEETS ETHICS

Ethics and Social Media in the Workplace

Consuming media, especially social media, has become more popular than ever

Credit: ©iStock.com/monkeybusinessimages

With over 2 billion of the world's population using social networks, social media is more popular than ever. But what does this mean for social media in the workplace? According to CareerBuilder, 28% of employers have fired employees for conducting non-work-related activities during the working day, including shopping online, or checking Facebook; while 18% of employers have discharged employees because of unprofessional posts on social media. Because of incidents like these, many companies, big and small, have established policies related to social networking in the workplace. Yet, when it comes to social networking, are these policies enough to establish acceptable behavior in the workplace?

In 2012, a study was carried out by the Ethics Resource Centre (ERC) to explore the possible relationship between ethical behavior and social media. The ERC produced a survey called the National Business Ethics Survey (NBES) to relay how social media has influenced employees' perspectives of ethics at work.

The survey studied the differences in behaviors between active social networkers (people who spend over 30% of their working day on social media) in comparison with other US workers who are less active on social media. It found that active social networkers were more likely than the other workers to add a client/customer on a social network, blog or tweet negative messages about their organization or colleagues, upload vacation pictures to the company network to share them with colleagues, and retain copies of confidential work documents to bring to another job if necessary.

While the report concludes that "active social networkers show a higher tolerance for activities that could be considered unethical," Dr. Patricia J. Harned, president of the ERC, states that the findings do not necessarily call the character of the social networkers into question. Harned says, "It appears that they are more willing to consider things that are 'gray areas'—issues that are not always clear in company policies as wrong: and that's an area for further study."

CRITICAL THINKING QUESTIONS

1. **Do you think ethics should be addressed in social media policies? Why or why not?**

2. **What would you regard as "acceptable behavior" when it comes to using social media in the workplace?**

3. **As the founder of a startup with several employees, how would you address the issue of ethics in relation to social media usage?** ●

Sources

Lauby, S. (2012, March 17). Ethics and social media: Where should you draw the line?" *Mashable*. Retrieved from http://mashable.com/2012/03/17/social-media-ethics/#ILPOfjM.gqq9

Rapacon, S. (2016, February 5). How using social media can get you fired. *CNBC*. Retrieved from http://www.cnbc.com/2016/02/05/how-using-social-media-can-get-you-fired.html

statista: The Statistics Portal (*n.d.*). Retrieved from http://www.statista.com/topics/1164/social networks/

By participating in social networking sites, you build credibility, transparency, and trust. If people get an insight into your professional life, see the connections you have made, and what thoughts and information you share, they will get to know you and want to build a relationship with you. Whether you're networking in person or online, it is important to look for potential candidates for your founding team. The next section focuses on how you can network to build a founding team.

14.5 NETWORKING TO BUILD THE FOUNDING TEAM

>> LO 14.5   **Explain how networking can help to build the founding team.**

Founding team: a group of people with complementary skills and a shared sense of commitment coming together in founding an enterprise to build and grow the company.

A **founding team** is a group of people with complementary skills and a shared sense of commitment coming together in founding an enterprise to build and grow the company. The founding team usually consists of the founder and a few other cofounders who possess complementary skills. While there is no "right size" for the number of people on a founding team, two to four seems to be the typical number.

The goal of the founding team is to build and grow the company and provide economic and social returns for themselves, employees, other owners, and potential investors. Research shows that more and more, new fast-growth ventures have been founded by entrepreneurial teams rather than sole entrepreneurs. In fact, overall, studies have shown that ventures started by teams typically perform better than those started by solo founders.[58] When researchers asked venture capitalists the most important factors to new venture success, their response was, "the lead entrepreneur and the quality of the team."[59]

When considering potential founding team members, it is helpful to ask yourself two questions: "Can I build the company without them?" and "Can I find someone else just like them?" If the answer to both questions is no, then you have most likely discovered a cofounder. However, if the answer to both questions is yes, then you can still keep them in your network, maintain the relationship, and potentially hire them at a later date as employees.[60]

Researchers have cited the most likely outlets where entrepreneurs find their founding teams: colleagues in organizations where they were previously employed; organizations similar to the founding firm; prior working relationships across organizations (e.g., buyers, suppliers, consultants); family members and friends; and deliberate search by the lead entrepreneur.[61]

Usually team members are found in the network of the lead entrepreneur. This means most founding teams have a lead entrepreneur (usually, but not always, the team CEO) who creates the vision; has full belief in the venture; and has the motivation and passion to persevere, inspire team members, and make judgements and decisions during difficult times.[62] The late Steve Jobs is a good example of a lead entrepreneur and visionary who worked with cofounder Steve Wozniak to bring his invention of the first PC model to life. But remember, most startups are executed by a team. Bill Gates and Paul Allen founded Microsoft and started the company with nine founding team members.

Characteristics of a Great Founding Team

Video
Building a Team

Finding the right cofounders to build and scale your venture can make all the difference between your business succeeding or failing. The most successful teams are composed of members who possess the experience, skills, and abilities to manage complex problems, cope with pressure, and overcome obstacles to achieve rapid growth.

Positive social relations within the team are also key when it comes to providing social and emotional support.[63] Bernd Schoner, cofounder of RFID tech startup ThingMagic, started with friends from MIT he had worked with before. They thought they knew each other well enough to start a company, but they found that "outside pressure causes people to act differently," which caused "extreme turmoil." Schoner has learned from this experience and believes that founding teams must have the right balance of personalities and characteristics in order to achieve success.[64]

Jenn Houser, a serial entrepreneur and cofounder of Upstart Bootcamp, has outlined the following useful characteristics to look for when you are evaluating potential cofounders.[65]

Possess the right skills

Houser recommends identifying the top three to five business operations you need to carry out well over the next three years; then ask yourself who has the skills and expertise to accomplish these operations. She points out the importance of examining the track record of each candidate. Whether or not the person is a friend, she or he should be considered only if they've demonstrated the ability to do the job.

Take a hands-on approach

During the startup stage, you and your cofounders will be doing everything—from answering the phone to ordering office supplies. Make sure your chosen cofounders are not only willing but happy to do whatever it takes to achieve goals.

For example, Alan Jones, a member of the leadership team with Blue Chilli, a startup based in Sydney, Australia, often takes on the role of receptionist for the company. Although Jones has 20 years of startup experience, including roles with Yahoo, HomeScreen Entertainment, and Macworld, he doesn't mind getting his hands dirty for the good of the business. Jones says:

The Microsoft founding team

Credit: Courtesy Microsoft/ ZUMApress/Newscom

If 20 years in startups has taught me anything, it's that 90% of building a success-
ful early-stage startup is just getting sh*t done, whatever needs doing, whenever
it needs doing, and not being precious about it. A lot of that is what we call 'con-

cierging,' but a bunch of it is just taking out the trash and restocking the toilet rolls when that needs doing. Like some other startup accelerators, BlueChilli is growing fast and kicking goals, but like most accelerators (and most startups) we need to run tight on overheads, be smart on what we spend money on, and when.[66]

Use positive problem solving

You want to choose entrepreneurial team members who are curious and driven—people who see problems not as obstacles but as challenges that must be overcome in a creative and innovative way. An entrepreneurial mindset is required for all team members.

Leave ego at the door

Team success depends on collaboration and a collective willingness to work for the good of the enterprise. Cofounders with a big ego or a personal agenda are less likely to work well with others. One way to find out if potential cofounders have big egos is to ask them about a time when they achieved team success, and listen carefully to the number of times they say "I" or "we" in their response.

David Balter, founder of word-of-mouth media and marketing company BzzAgent, warns of the dangers of a large ego, blaming his own tendency to believe his own hype for the struggles his agency faced during the 2009 recession. He says, "My attitude prevented us from seeing changes coming until they were choking our business. Innovative clients who wanted to try new concepts didn't get it. In the world according to Balter, there was only Balter's view."[67] Having learned the hard way, Balter now believes that humility is an essential trait for entrepreneurs, as it helps to make smarter decisions and ensure the longevity of startups.

Share similar attitudes toward values, goals, and risk

Jenn Houser advises that cofounders need to be aligned with the goals to be achieved, the values they share, and the risks they may need to take to get there. The best relationships are based on trust, and your team should feel comfortable about discussing potential ethical dilemmas and how they will be resolved. Before you commit, she recommends investing several days with your cofounders in hashing out every detail of the business and how the partnership arrangement will work.

Care deeply

While cofounders need to have the intelligence, skills, and experience to achieve goals, they also need to be care deeply about the enterprise. Someone who doesn't care deeply about the success of the startup may be likely to become unavailable when things get tough, or even to jump ship at a crucial moment. Plenty of passion combined with a high degree of smarts can even compensate for limitations in the area of experience. Finding a cofounder who has complementary skills and equal enthusiasm for your ideas can help minimize risk and increase the odds of startup success.[68]

Many startups fail because the cofounders came together too quickly rather than spending time together first. Spending time with your potential cofounders on a startup weekend or working together in a previous job allows for more bonding and building a relationship of trust and respect. The bottom line is connecting with your cofounders is like entering into a marriage on both an emotional and financial basis. Get to know each other first, before you commit, and make sure the others feel the same way about you as you do about them. Atish Davda, founder of liquidity manager EquityZen, has created a list of attributes to look for in founding team members (Figure 14.4).

FIGURE 14.4

Key Attributes of Founding Team Members

Source: Adapted from Atish Davda, "How You Can Build an Incredible Founding Team" Creator (December 12, 2014) https://creator.
wework.com/knowledge/can-build-incredible-founding-team/ retrieved on November 24, 2015.

The Value of Team Diversity

Diversity comes in many forms. We often think of diversity as referring to demographic characteristics such as age, gender, race, and ethnicity; but diversity is also found in people's career paths and goals, viewpoints, educational backgrounds, and life experiences. Let's examine how diversity relates to networking to build your founding team (see Figure 14.5).

Homogeneous and heterogeneous teams

Which do you think is more important: **homogenous teams**, whose members possess the same or similar characteristics such as age, gender, ethnicity, experience, and educational background; or **heterogeneous teams,** meaning a group of people with a mix of knowledge, skills, and experience? While there is no proven conclusive research to suggest that homogenous is better than heterogeneous or vice versa, the results of studies argue the benefits and disadvantages of both.

In homogeneous teams, members are likely to feel included because of their shared backgrounds, cultures, languages, and experiences. This helps the team to communicate more effectively and avoid misunderstandings as well as prejudices. However, sharing similarities does not mean that personality conflicts do not exist—any team, whether homogeneous or heterogeneous, is liable to have conflicts at times. Further, studies have shown that lack of diversity in homogeneous teams can stifle creativity and information processing. Indeed, it is difficult to form a homogeneous team without others feeling excluded because they do not share the same characteristics as the team members.[69]

In a heterogeneous team, there is a greater mix of experiences, skills, ethnicities, and backgrounds. A diverse set of collective characteristics can aid decision making and expand a "group's set of possible solutions and allows the group to conceptualize

Audio
The Importance of Diversity

Homogenous team:
a group of people with the same or similar characteristics such as age, gender, ethnicity, experience, and educational background.

Heterogeneous team: a group of people with a mix of knowledge, skills, and experience.

FIGURE 14.5

Dimensions of Diversity

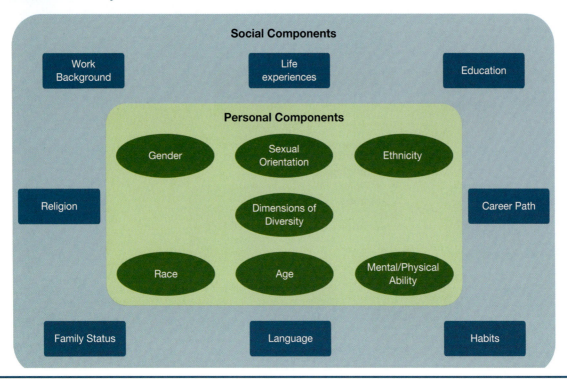

Sources: Gardenswartz, Lee, and Rowe, Anita (2003). Diverse Teams at Work: Capitalizing on the Power of Diversity.
Mor Barak, Michael, E.; Cherin, David; Berkman, Sherry. 1998. Organizational and personal dimensions in diversity climate: Ethnic and gender differences in employee perceptions. *Journal of Applied Behavioral Science*, 34(1): 82–104.

problems in new ways."[70] Studies have found that this type of team tends to have a higher degree of creativity and innovativeness than homogeneous teams.[71]

Researchers have argued, however, that team diversity alone will not necessarily result in better performance. What matters more than demographic diversity (age, gender, race, etc.) is team commitment and **cognitive comprehensiveness**, a process in which team members examine critical issues with a wide lens and formulate strategies by considering diverse approaches, decision criteria, and courses of action. Team-level cognitive comprehensiveness is positively related to entrepreneurial team effectiveness. Effective teams also tend to have a high level of member commitment, encourage each other to use different approaches, offer different perspectives on problems, and use a range of potential solutions to solve problems.[72]

Finally, there are certain drawbacks to heterogeneous teams. Groups that have a greater mix can find it more difficult to communicate and understand each other, especially if they have to navigate across different languages and cultural backgrounds. This may lead to some members feeling misunderstood or isolated, which may produce conflicts and emotions among members of the entrepreneurial team, resulting in poor performance.[73]

Groupthink and healthy conflict

A healthy team could be considered as one whose members are from diverse backgrounds, hold complementary skills and experiences, and have commitment to the venture. And even though conflict arising from personality difference can

Cognitive comprehensiveness: a process in which team members examine critical issues with a wide lens and formulate strategies by considering diverse approaches, decision criteria, and courses of action.

be destructive, there is such a thing as healthy conflict. Testing and challenging assumptions is a state that gets the team out of **groupthink**—a phenomenon where people share too similar a mindset, which inhibits their ability to spot gaps or errors. Patrick Lencioni, author of *The Five Dysfunctions of a Team*, states that "productive debate over issues is good for a team." Disagreeing on issues makes things uncomfortable, but it builds clarity. "If you don't have conflict on a team, you don't get commitment," Lencioni said. "If people don't weigh in, they won't buy in."[74] Healthy conflict builds clarity; for example, if team members point out flaws in an idea, then they can work together to build it into a more robust idea.

The challenge is to ensure that constructive conflict over issues does not degenerate into dysfunctional interpersonal conflict.[75] In other words, team members need to be able to argue without taking it personally or impairing their ability to work together. In her study of teams, Stanford University Professor Kathleen Eisenhardt found teams that engaged in healthy conflict shared six traits:

▸ developed multiple alternatives to enrich the level of debate;

▸ shared commonly agreed-upon goals;

▸ work with more information rather than less;

▸ injected humor into the decision process;

▸ maintained a balanced power structure; and

▸ resolved issues without forcing consensus.[76]

Overall, the teams worked with more, rather than less, information and debated on the basis of facts, not emotions. When teams stay with the topic of the debate and argue their points productively, there is less chance of personal attack.

Another way to ensure that the conflict remains healthy is through the most widely used team assessment tool in the world, Myers-Briggs Type Indicator. Myers-Briggs assesses personality types through a self-report questionnaire that gives team members insights into their own communication styles and the styles of others. Knowing each other's personality style helps avoid personal conflict. For example, if you know one of your teammates has a very direct communication style, then you're less likely to take personal offense during a debate.

Alfred P. Sloan, legendary CEO of General Motors, was a great advocate of healthy debate: "Gentlemen, I take it we are all in complete agreement on the decision here," Sloan said. After everyone around the table nodded affirmatively, Sloan continued: "Then I propose we postpone further discussion of this matter until our next meeting to give ourselves time to develop disagreement and perhaps gain some understanding of what the decision is all about."[77] Sloan's strategy is related to the problem of groupthink.

One way of preventing groupthink and promoting healthy conflict is the use of a devil's advocate to challenge assumptions and encourage different perspectives. For example, Ori Hadomi, CEO of Israel-based medical technology startup Mazor Robotics, appoints one of the team's executive members to play devil's advocate to prevent the team from being "too positive" about their assumptions. By asking the right questions and challenging assumptions, the devil's advocate helps the team assess risk,

Groupthink: a phenomenon where people share too similar a mindset, which inhibits their ability to spot gaps or errors.

"Emphasize our unique differences, pass it down."

This cartoon describes the concept of groupthink.
Credit: Cartoon Resource / Alamy Stock Vector

Video
Working With a Team

manage expectations, and ensure the rest of the team is thinking realistically about goal achievement.[78]

However, not all teams welcome the presence of a devil's advocate. In a classic study in decision making carried out in the early 1960s, several groups of managers were formed to solve a complex problem. The groups were identical in size and composition, except that half the groups included a devil's advocate, whose role was to challenge the group's conclusions, and force the others to critically assess their assumptions and the logic of their arguments. The groups with the devil's advocate performed significantly better than the other groups by generating better quality solutions to problems.

After a short break, the groups were told to eliminate one person from their group. In each group, it was the devil's advocate whom the group chose to ask to leave. Despite the fact that the devil's advocate was the reason for the team's high performance and competitive advantage, the members chose to eliminate that member because he or she made them feel uncomfortable. "I know it has positive outcomes for the performance of the organization as a whole, but I don't like how it makes me feel personally."[79] However, as we have learned, while we may think engaging in conflict is awkward and uncomfortable, it can be valuable and constructive if it is carried out in the right way.

In sum, healthy and constructive conflict is good, provided team members are clear on the organization's goals and free of hidden agendas. Steve Jobs said it best when he stated, "It's okay to spend a lot of time arguing about which route to take to San Francisco when everyone wants to end up there, but a lot of time gets wasted in such arguments if one person wants to go to San Francisco and another secretly wants to go to San Diego."[80] ●

SUMMARY

14.1 Explain the role of networks in building social capital.

Networks provide social capital such as access to sources of financing, information, expertise, and support; and networks can be excellent sources for loyalty. They allow for learning and information exchange; and social capital enables access to a range of resources, including venture capitalists, angel investors, advisors, banks and trade shows.

14.2 Demonstrate the value of networks for entrepreneurs.

Relationships are key to business success, and entrepreneurs in particular will need to skillfully interact with a vast array of stakeholders. Networks provide entrepreneurs with access to private information, diverse skillsets, and power. Networks can also be relied on for personal and emotional support.

14.3 Describe different ways of building networks.

Building a network extends beyond socializing with friends and acquaintances, and it often involves active participation in organized networking events. In a new relationship, it is better to give value to get value; value is a two-way game.

14.4 Illustrate the benefits of virtual networking.

Social media sites and other forms of virtual networking provide additional channels to meet or interact with stakeholders from the world over. Entrepreneurs have a number of different virtual communities in which they can participate, with many communities offering access to a specific subset of interests in entrepreneurship. Common social media platforms like Facebook also contain groups that are similar in fashion to online entrepreneurship communities.

14.5 Explain how networking can help to build the founding team.

One of the most valuable things an entrepreneur can do is connect with individuals who serve as great complements on a founding team. Research even suggests that team-started ventures are more successful than solo-founded ventures. Networking skills can often be relied on as the means to that end.

KEY TERMS

Bonds 386
Bridges 386
Cognitive
   comprehensiveness 406
Founding team 402

Groupthink 407
Heterogeneous team 405
Homogenous team 405
Impression
   management 388

Linkages 386
Self-selected
   stakeholders 390
Social capital 383

CASE STUDY

Jason Miner, Director of IT; Cardon Health Care

Entrepreneurs are good at building relationships and networking with others to accomplish worthy objectives. Jason Miner is an outstanding example of an effective entrepreneur inside a large organization. who built and cultivated a wide network within an organization to accomplish his professional goals.

Entrepreneurs don't only start and build their own companies. Sometimes they apply principles of entrepreneurship to bring about positive changes within organizations that are faltering or failing. They build their own opportunities within the companies they already work for, and they accomplish them through effective networking and other social interactions that are backed up by good ideas, self-discipline, and due diligence.

Miner graduated from high school in Utah in 1996, and earned a vocational scholarship to a local campus of the state college, which he attended for two semesters. His mantra in college was, "Just get smarter, and work hard in my classes." After proactively seeking out employment opportunities, he landed a job at Cardon Health Care. He had zero experience in health care, but they liked the fact that he could speak Spanish, and they were willing to train.

Cardon specializes in providing financial counseling to uninsured hospital patients. As a Cardon representative, Miner would interview people who had recently been in the emergency room, talk to them about their options, and communicate further with them over the phone. He worked part-time at Cardon for 25 to 30 hours a week while he attended school. In time, he earned a bachelor's degree in political science with a minor in Spanish.

Things had not been going well for Cardon at one of the hospitals, and Miner was given an opportunity to represent the company at the hospital with the goal of turning things around. He recalls being "really excited" about the chance to right the ship. Going to work in the hospital was challenging, but satisfying. Since patients had no way of getting treatments they needed without Cardon's help, the work was meaningful to Miner. During his time there, he helped people get heart transplants, liver transplants, and walk again after serious accidents. There were times when he felt instrumental in saving people's lives.

Because of his excellent people skills, Cardon began to build a network of doctors and other important hospital employees. This provided him with many opportunities to establish a noteworthy reputation through positive, professional, social interactions combined with doing excellent work. Miner enjoyed his work, and ended up supervising Cardon's work at the hospital for about three years. In the process, he was successful in turning things around.

By working hard and diligently applying his entrepreneurial mind, Miner became an industry expert. His expertise and track record of success opened up another opportunity, this time in management. A few years later, he was promoted again, providing him with another leadership opportunity: he was now running an entire office, managing 30 to 40 people in the process. He now had an entire leadership team of supervisors reporting to him that he was responsible to train, delegate, and so on.

Miner had always been a hobbyist when it came to computers. As an office manager, he had his team work on about 60 different computers. The problem was that the IT Department was in Texas, and Miner's office was in Utah. As a result, he ended up getting increasingly involved in the IT side of the business because he could work with and fix computers. If his office got a new shipment of computers, he would be the guy to set it all up. If something broke, he would fix it. When network and Wi-Fi issues cropped up, he would address them. As a result, he ended up getting some extra pay from all the IT work he was doing outside of normal business hours. And as word got around that he could fix things, members of his team started coming to him with their computer issues.

Things really got interesting when Miner started programming, which he got involved in to solve specific problems that cropped up. Twice a month, he had to complete a pay review, which was important, but tedious, time-consuming work that was well below his pay grade. Eventually, it dawned on him that he could write a program that could do the pay review for him. He figured if he succeeded, he could get his weekends back.

He succeeded. The result was cutting 8 to 12 hours of work down to 30 minutes, 25 of which he could be doing other things while the computer completed the pay review. The increased efficiency of this and other programming efforts were staggering. Amazingly, he had found a way to solve real business problems by pursuing his hobby!

When people around the office learned what Miner was doing, the demand for his skills increased. Others had similar problems they were dealing with, and they were excited to learn that Miner could write a program that would solve their problem, too. He ended up spending all the time he personally had saved writing code for other people. In the process, his office and company became far more efficient.

About this same time, Cardon had determined their old computing system was outdated, and it was time to replace it with a new one. When Miner heard the news, he became vocal in his desire to be involved because he knew there was a better way, and he knew what to do. It was challenging to get his entrepreneurial voice heard at first because he wasn't officially part of the IT Department. But he had built a good network and over time; the IT director got to know him and learned about all the things he had done to increase office efficiency. Word then spread to the CEO, who informed the head of IT that Miner needed to be involved.

Next came a call from IT headquarters in Texas. They had created a new position for Miner. If he was willing to move to Texas, Cardon would make him the project manager of the entire system conversion. He would work with computer programmers and developers to make sure the system was built right and properly tested. Miner accepted the promotion, which came with yet another raise.

Over the past several years, Miner has gone from managing five or six people and outsourcing much of the work to managing a team of 30 that does all programming in-house. This promotion led to another pay raise, and he's had several more in the intervening time. As the director of IT for Cardon, Miner has hired almost everyone who currently works in his department. He has also overseen the acquisition of two smaller companies, and retained several people from those company's IT departments.

Through networking and cultivating key relationships, Jason Miner built the exact opportunity he wanted within a company, and he refused to give up until he succeeded. At this point in his career, through his networking skills, he has been able to gain not only the IT leadership skills but enough technical skills that he could get a technical job and write code all day for just about any other company, if needed. He is set for long-term success in his career, come what may—although for the time being, he is happy right where he is. This case study demonstrates the entrepreneurial power of networking, personal vision, and effective social interactions—backed up by hard work.

Critical Thinking Questions

1.   What are you currently *not* doing (in person) that you could be doing to build better relationships and effectively network both inside *and* outside of your school or organization?

2.   What are you currently *not* doing (virtually) that you could inside and outside of your school or organization?

3.   Think of an activity (video games, social media, TV, Internet surfing) that you could cut back on to pursue personal growth, seek out professional opportunities, and build relationships (network). Set a goal to cut back on the time spent in this activity, and determine what activity (reading, research, conversation, etc.) will take its place.

Sources
This story is reprinted, with minor changes, with permission of Dr. Jordan R. Jensen, the copyright holder, from the following book:
Jensen, J. R. (2015). *Self-action leadership: The key to personal and professional freedom*. Bloomington, IN: authorHouse.

15 Navigating Legal and IP Issues

With contributions from
Richard Mandel, JD

UNITED STATES PATENT   SHEET 1 *of*

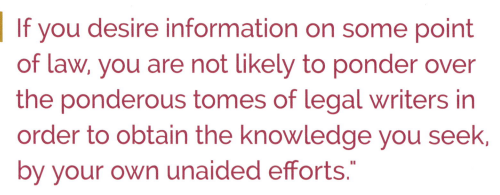

"If you desire information on some point of law, you are not likely to ponder over the ponderous tomes of legal writers in order to obtain the knowledge you seek, by your own unaided efforts."

—Felix Adler, Professor of Political and Social Ethics

Learning Objectives

15.1 Discuss how legal considerations can add value to entrepreneurial ventures.

15.2 Explain the most common types of legal structures available to startups.

15.3 Outline the most common legal errors made by startups.

15.4 Define IP and how it affects entrepreneurs.

15.5 Assess the global impact of IP theft.

15.6 Describe the common IP traps experienced by entrepreneurs.

15.7 Explain the legal requirements of hiring employees.

Chapter Outline

15.1 LEGAL CONSIDERATIONS

>> **LO 15.1** Discuss how legal considerations can add value to entrepreneurial ventures.

Just as there are laws regulating who can drive a car or open a bank account, there are laws related to starting a business. Entrepreneurs are usually much more interested in their firm than in doing legal research, but dealing with the law is part of the process. When it comes to legal considerations, seeking expert advice is essential. Most entrepreneurs either lack the skills to understand the legalities of setting up a business or neglect the legal side altogether. Facebook cofounder Mark Zuckerberg made several big legal mistakes in the early startup stage, including setting up Facebook as the wrong business structure. While Zuckerberg may excel at anticipating user needs, he was certainly no expert in legal matters.[1]

As described in *Entrepreneurship in Action*, FlexGround's Corey Hague spent lots of time researching the law in order to benefit his employees and enhance the way FlexGround would operate. Yet he still sought out advice and consulted with an attorney.

Before you meet with a legal expert, it is important to be prepared by knowing a certain amount of information in order to ask the right questions and make the best decisions for your new venture. Legal experts are in a great position to add value to your business if they are the right fit. And that "if" is important: While some lawyers may be great at drawing up contracts and preparing documentation, not all can work with startups and small businesses. Because startup companies face a variety of unique legal issues and funding challenges that are simply not experienced by more established companies, one of the most important things to look for in a lawyer is familiarity and comfort in working with startups. You will also want to look for one who understands the industry you are in.

Video
The Value of Legal Considerations

Corey Hague, FlexGround

Corey Hague, founder of Flexground

Credit: Used with permission from Corey Hague

Corey Hague is the founder of FlexGround, a multimillion-dollar regional leader in alternative surfacing that has seen astronomical growth since its official founding in 2010, netting over $8 million in revenue in 2014 alone.

By its fifth year in operation, the company was employing over 40 people and had opened operations in Nevada and Northern California. It has received many accolades, including being honored by *Inc.* magazine in 2014 as #11 in its list of top construction companies, and its spongy, colorful, poured-in-place, rubber safety surfacing was named one of *Inc.*'s "500 Coolest Products."

Hague attributes FlexGround's success to its seasoned four-member leadership team and to "treating customers like absolute gold." Corey's father, Greg, "is a very direct, hardcore businessperson," according to his son. "He wants to make money and he knows how to do it." Corey's brother, Bill Sr., has special strengths in managing employees, says Corey. "One of the best lessons dad ever told me, he asked 'what is a problem?' The answer: 'A problem is just a set of facts compounded by emotion. . . . It's just a set of facts that require tweaking.'"

Corey's father, Greg, is also an attorney, and his advice is simple: "Know the law better than any of your competitors." Corey spent a great deal of time researching tax laws in the various states FlexGround operates in: Arizona, California, and Nevada. "I've been able to take advantage of labor laws [to benefit my company and its employees]." With the assistance of a labor attorney, Corey crafted a bonus policy, which is "in essence a fee for showing up early. It's good because I can pay my guys more where my competitors don't. It helps me attract good labor and be fair to my guys," while staying in compliance with labor laws.

Laws differ from state to state, which means FlexGround's various entities must operate differently. The company is made up of four different companies: three LLCs (FlexGround LLC and FlexGround Products LLC in Arizona and FlexGround Nevada LLC in Nevada) and one corporation (FlexGround Surfaces Inc. in California). "Every time I open a new center, I set it up as its own company," says Hague. "So if something bad happens in one, it doesn't affect the others."

Today, 60% of FlexGround's business comes by way of government contracts; the remaining 40% is private, and of that 40%, a very large portion is a nationwide daycare chain.

"We are highly innovative," says Hague, "and we found a few ideas that could separate us, make us a little more impenetrable [to the competition]." One is a repair system for FlexGround's rubber surfacing that allows clients to easily and cheaply make their own repairs. The second is an in-ground, randomized water sprayer called the Splashground, which is offered to commercial customers purchasing safety surfacing.

"We figured out a way [to do it] without burying it in the cement with a big water pump," Hague says, comparing the FlexGround innovation to those at malls, rec centers, and water parks, which typically cost upwards of $50,000. Patents take forever, explains Corey—his oldest took 3.5 years for approval, though FlexGround's inventions are temporarily protected with provisional patent applications—but they're necessary. "We were small, and we knew it," says Hague. Without patent protection, "the big guys could have heard of our work, copied it, and taken me out of business with their money."

"I think everyone would say, unless they're being dishonest, you start a business to make money," says Hague, when reflecting on his definition of success. But there's more to it than that. "The culture we have created in and among our offices, we have very happy employees, they love coming to work, and we've never had anyone quit. That's certainly success for me—their happiness. Also, in general, I think we have changed the marketplace [with our focus on customer service]. . . . Happy employees, happy customers, a nice, healthy bottom line—that's success." To aspiring entrepreneurs, Hague advises: "Be prepared to give everything short of your life, if necessary. . . . Be prepared for the onslaught of stress, emotion, highs and lows. . . . If you're really not dedicated to it, don't even attempt it. That's why 85% of companies fail in the first year, and then many more fail in years 2 or 3. . . . The level of dedication needed is unfathomable."

FlexGround is one of the fastest growing companies in the United States this decade, and it's unlikely the company will slow down any time soon.

CRITICAL THINKING QUESTIONS

1.   **How does the Hague family take legal considerations into account to benefit FlexGround?**

2.   **Laws differ from state to state. How would you go about ensuring your startup was legally set up?**

3.   **What steps would you take to protect your product/service from being copied by competitors?** ●

Source: C. Hague, personal interview, February 2, 2015.

Master the content
edge.sagepub.com/
neckentrepreneurship

For example, if you are in the fashion industry, you will need a lawyer who has some experience in the many areas that are likely to affect your business, including textile production, international trade, manufacturing law, and e-commerce.

How much does it cost to hire a lawyer? Startup legal costs vary widely, depending on the type of business you are setting up. A simple home-based cupcake-baking business may cost only a few hundred dollars in legal fees, whereas a larger, more complex enterprise is likely to cost a good deal more. In general, a business attorney will charge upwards of $200 per hour, but a simple startup may only need one or two hours of work to draw up the required documents. Some legal practices provide a free one-hour consultation for new clients and/or payment plans for startups. Before you decide on a lawyer, do some research and compile a list of four or five possible candidates, their qualifications, and their rates. Like anything else worthwhile that you need to buy for your business, it pays to shop around.

Of course, there are a wide range of free resources regarding legal issues and documents available through the Internet to entrepreneurs looking for advice. However, be careful using these resources as they may not be strictly accurate or relevant to the type of business you are trying to set up. Using certain sites online (See Table 15.1) is a good way to gather research and identify the type of legal counsel you might need. While legal advice can be expensive, the expense far outweighs the risks of attempting to do it all yourself with the help of free, potentially risky information online.

Entrepreneurs can also receive legal support from clinics operated at law schools all over the United States that provide legal assistance to entrepreneurs. For example, second- and third-year law students at the law clinic in Santa Clara University in California provide affordable legal services to entrepreneurs looking to set up a business or for advice on the legal issues that may arise from running a business.[2] Apart from clinics, law school websites can also be useful for legal information, as they may provide certain forms or documentation for no charge. Washburn University of Law, in particular, provides a wide range of forms and information, which can be accessed for free.[3]

The United States government also provides resources for entrepreneurs. One such resource is the Unites States Patent and Trademark Office (USPTO), which provides a pro bono legal program to support entrepreneurs. The Small Business Administration also sponsors the SCORE association, a network of volunteer business counselors throughout the United States and its territories, who are trained to serve as counselors, advisors, and mentors to aspiring entrepreneurs and business

TABLE 15.1

Useful Online Legal Resources

Business.gov	Includes information on a broad range of business and business law topics, small business guides, governmental forms and FAQs, and links to state regulations and local governments across the United States. http://business.usa.gov/
IRS.gov/Businesses	Provides information for various types and sizes of businesses, including information on small business and self-employed persons, industry-specific information, and links to all 50 states in such categories as: Doing Business in the State; Taxation; Employer Links; and other General information of interest to businesses. http://www.irs.gov/businesses/index.html
D.O.L. Office of Small and Disadvantaged Business site	Includes links to a wealth of information and resources regarding federal and state employment and labor relations laws: http://www.dol.gov/oasam/programs/osdbu/
Securities Laws and Regulations	Provides information on federal securities laws and regulations, research guides and tools, special information for small business. http://www.sec.gov/
Business Entity Formation	Common steps in starting a business. http://business.usa.gov/top-programs-and-services-recommended-starting-your-business
NOLO Press	Offers low-cost DIY kits for setting up business entities. http://www.nolo.com/legal-encyclopedia/llc-corporations-partnerships
General Information	Legal Issues and Forms from the entrepreneurship law editorial team of Entrepreneurship.org. http://entrepreneurship.org/entrepreneurship-law/general-information-legal-issues-and-forms.aspx

owners. These resources can be incredibly useful in finding out the different legal requirements for your venture. Armed with this information, you will have a better chance of finding the right legal help when the time comes.

The best lawyers not only will be able to provide legal counsel but will also add value, not just in the startup phase but potentially for many years as your business grows.[4] They will have experience with early-stage startups, know the industry, and be up front with their fee structure. They may also have an impressive list of contacts, which can be very useful in connecting you with investors and advising you on fundraising. What's more, a good lawyer will be a person you can actually relate to. The best way to hire legal experts is the same way you would hire an employee. When the time comes, ask yourself, "Is this the right person to advise and represent my company?"

15.2 TYPES OF LEGAL STRUCTURES

Video
Common Legal Structures

>> LO 15.2   **Explain the most common types of legal structures available to startups.**

One of the most important choices entrepreneurs make when starting a business is choosing the right type of legal structure for their company. The type of structure affects the authorities you need to notify regarding your business, tax and other contributions you may have to pay, the records and documentation you will need to maintain, and how decisions are made about the business.

As legal structures vary from state to state (and country to country), it is essential that entrepreneurs do as much research as possible before deciding on a particular form of organization. Depending on your situation, there are several structures to choose from, and it is important to understand the differences among them. If, after researching the question, you are still not sure which one best suits your business, then paying a few hundred dollars for a legal consultation can be a worthwhile investment. Let's examine some of the most common legal structures used in the United States.

Sole Proprietorship

A **sole proprietorship** refers to a person who owns a business but has not formed a separate entity to run it. This is the simplest and most inexpensive form of legal structure for startups, but it is rarely the correct choice. It means the business is completely managed and controlled by you, the owner, and that you are entitled to all the profits your business makes. However, it also means you are personally exposed to all the risks and legal responsibilities or liabilities of the business. The main reason why sole proprietorship is the most common choice of business structures is simply that many entrepreneurs are not well versed in the legalities. But many large organizations began as sole proprietorships; for example, eBay was a sole proprietorship owned by founder Pierre Omidyar for three years before he joined with other partners.[5]

> **Sole proprietorship:** a person who owns a business and has full exposure to its liabilities.

Forming a sole proprietorship is quite simple. In many jurisdictions and industries, there is no legal filing at all to set yourself up as a business owner.[6] If your business is in an industry and/or a location where licenses or permits are necessary, you may just need to pay a nominal fee to obtain the right license or permit. For example, for a painting business you might need a home improvement contractor license; for any retail business you will likely need a sales tax permit. Because you and your business are treated as one entity, you have to file only one personal tax return outlining your income and expenses. (You do, however, have to use a separate form, Schedule C, to report your business income.)[7] The business's income is added to whatever other income you (and your spouse) may have and is taxed at your personal income tax rate.

However, as previously mentioned, you are also held personally liable for any problems the business incurs (see Figure 15.1). There can be quite a lot of pressure to running a sole proprietorship, especially when it comes to fulfilling all your financial obligations. For example, say you have borrowed money to run your business, but you lose a major customer, which leaves you unable to repay the loan. Or say an employee of yours is involved in an automobile accident while on the job and injures another driver; you as sole proprietor are fully responsible for dealing with the injured person's claims. Either of these scenarios could potentially mean having to sell personal assets such as your car, your investments or even your house to raise the money. You could even be driven to personal bankruptcy. The other business structures we will discuss all provide at least a minimal level of protection against such personal losses.

General Partnership

A **general partnership** involves two or more people who have made a decision to manage and share in the profits and losses of a business. Like a sole proprietorship, setting up a general partnership is relatively low-cost and straightforward. As each partner reports profits and losses on individual tax returns rather than the corporate level, a process called pass-through taxation, taxes are also paid at your personal income tax rates.

> **General partnership:** two or more people who have made a decision to co-manage and share in the profits and losses of a business.

For example, say you and your business partner decide to open a café. To qualify for general partnership legal status, you and your partner must be involved in the

FIGURE 15.1

The Sole Proprietor

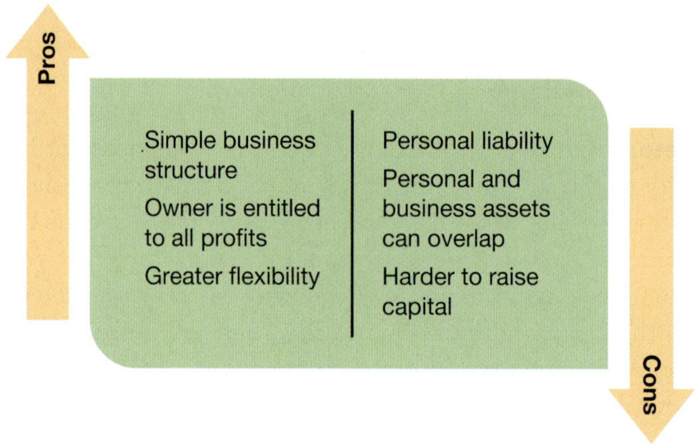

Pros	Cons
Simple business structure	Personal liability
Owner is entitled to all profits	Personal and business assets can overlap
Greater flexibility	Harder to raise capital

business, and contribute toward setting up and paying the costs of running the café. You and your partner will split the profits and losses between you.

While partnership arrangements can be quite flexible, it is wise to have a formal partnership agreement drafted by a legal expert to lay out the terms of the partnership. Typically, this agreement will cover the percentage of shares you are each entitled to, your individual rights and duties, and the consequences of one of you leaving the business for any reason.

Sharing the burden of running the business with someone else can be a great asset to a startup. However, like the sole proprietorship legal structure, in a general partnership each partner is still personally liable for the company's financial obligations. In a worst-case scenario, this means that if one partner is responsible for running the company into the ground, the other partner will still be liable. And if the offending partner cannot pay, the other partner would be liable for the full amount. Therefore, before entering into a general partnership it is essential that the partners know each other well and establish a high degree of trust.

C Corporation

C corporation: (sometimes known as a "C-corp") a separate legal and taxable entity created by the state government and owned by an unlimited number of shareholders.

A **C corporation** (sometimes known as a "C-corp") is a separate legal entity created by the state government and owned by an unlimited number of shareholders. This means that the corporation, not the shareholders, is legally liable for its actions. The most money that shareholders can lose is their personal investment—the value of their stock.

Another advantage to the C corporation is transferable ownership, which means it can issue shares of stock to investors in exchange for capital. In addition, because the corporation is a separate entity, it benefits from continuous existence, which means that it will still survive after the demise of its owners. This allows the corporation to plan for the future.

Many people believe that corporations are so complex that they are usually reserved for larger, more established businesses with numerous employees. In reality, however, corporations normally are not very time-consuming or expensive to set up. Many corporations are owned by only one or a few stockholders who elect themselves as directors and officers.

An alleged disadvantage is double taxation: The corporate profit is taxed twice— first on the profit it makes; and secondly, the shareholders are taxed on the dividends. However, in a startup, corporate profits are often paid out to the owners as additional compensation (which means that corporate tax is eliminated on nonexistent corporate profits). Otherwise these profits are often retained to fund the growth of the startup, thus eliminating any current tax on dividends (the sum of money paid to shareholders from company profits) and leaving only the corporate tax at a rate calculated without adding the additional income of stockholders and their spouses.

S Corporation

An **S corporation** (sometimes known as an "S-Corp") is a corporation whose stockholders elect special treatment for income tax purposes. For all other purposes, it is identical to a C corporation. In order to qualify as an S-Corp, the corporation must be a US domestic corporation. In addition, it must have no more than 100 shareholders, who in most cases must be individual US citizens or legal immigrants (not corporations, partnerships or trusts) and all of whom must own only one class of common stock (ordinary shares).

Unlike the C-corp, the S-corp does not have to deal with double taxation, as there is only one level of tax to pay. Similar to a partnership, the income and losses are passed through to the company's shareholders' tax returns and taxed at the individual rates. This is especially attractive for corporations expecting to lose money in the short term, as such losses will offset other income earned by shareholders, acting as a so-called "tax shelter." S-Corps often consider a later switch to C-Corp status because their growth may be limited by the restricted number and types of shareholders permitted. Another reason for switching to C-Corp status is the fact that an S-Corp's future retained earnings would be taxed to stockholders as so-called "phantom income"—earnings are taxed but not received by the individual.

> **S corporation:** (sometimes known as an "S-Corp") - a certain type of corporation which is eligible for, and elects special taxation status.

Limited Liability Company (LLC)

A **limited liability company (LLC)** is a business structure that combines the pass-through taxation aspects of a partnership with the limited liability benefits of a corporation without being subject to the eligibility requirements of an S corporation.

This means that profits and losses are reported on individual tax returns; therefore double taxation does not apply, and there is potential tax sheltering from losses while personal assets are protected. Modern limited liability company statutes allow LLCs to have continuous existence similar to corporations. And just as with partnerships and corporations, it is advisable for the LLC's owners (called "members") to enter into ownership agreements, often contained within an operating agreement that serves the combined purposes of bylaws and stockholder agreements in corporations. LLCs are rapidly replacing S corporations as the entity of choice for many startup businesses. FlexGround, featured in *Entrepreneurship in Action,* is made up of four different companies, three of which are LLCs (FlexGround LLC and FlexGround Products LLC in Arizona and FlexGround Nevada LLC in Nevada).

> **Limited liability company (LLC):** a form of business structure that combines the taxation advantages of a partnership with the limited liability benefits of corporation without being subject to the eligibility requirements of an S corp.

Limited Partnership and Limited Liability Partnership (LP and LLP)

There are a variety of other forms of business entity that may be used in certain circumstances. One example is the limited partnership, a pass-through tax entity made up of two kinds of partners: general partners, who manage the business but have personal exposure for its liabilities; and limited partners, who are essentially silent investors but are protected from liabilities.

Recently, however, the limited partnership has been largely replaced by the limited liability company. It acts as a pass-through entity, grants limited liability to *all* members, and does not prohibit any member from getting involved in management.

Another example is the limited liability partnership. This is essentially a general partnership that, in exchange for registering with the state and paying an annual fee, gets a form of limited liability for its partners. However, the partners are still not protected from the consequences of wrongful acts committed by themselves and in some cases by their employees. This form is popular generally only among firms of licensed professionals, such as lawyers and accountants, who want to avoid classifying their partners as employees of the business. This means that these employers do not have to comply with employment laws and regulations (such as mandatory or enforced retirement).

The principal types of legal structures we have described are summarized in Table 15.2.

TABLE 15.2

Types of Legal Structures

BUSINESS ENTITY	STRUCTURE	LIABILITY	TAXATION	NOTES
Sole Proprietorship	One owner	Unlimited	Pass-through	
General Partnership	Two or more partners	Unlimited Joint & Several	Pass-through	
C Corporation	Stockholders, directors, officers	Limited	Taxable entity	Potential double tax on dividends
S Corporation	Stockholders, directors, officers	Limited	Pass-through	Subject to eligibility requirements
Limited Liability Company (LLC)	Members, optional board of managers	Limited	Pass-through	May elect to be taxable entity
Limited Partnership	General partners, limited partners	General partners: Unlimited Limited partners: Limited	Pass-through to all partners	Limited partners largely prohibited from management
Limited Liability Partnership (LLP)	Two or more partners	Limited with some restrictions	Pass-through	Generally used only for professional practices
Benefit Corporation (under corporate law)	Stockholders, directors, officers	Limited	May be either C corp or S corp, if eligible	Charter sets forth social purpose(s)

Source: Richard Mandel has provided the above table.

Benefit Corporation

In Chapter 1, we mentioned a **benefit corporation** (or B-corp) as a form of organization certified by the nonprofit B Lab, which ensures that strict standards of social and environmental performance, accountability, and transparency are met. B Lab certification ensures that the for-profit company fulfills its social mission. It is available to businesses operating as any one of the business entities mentioned above (not just corporations).

Video
A Benefit Corporation

In addition to the B Lab certification, many states have enacted statutes creating a new form of business entity also called a B or Benefit corporation that is not subject to the fiduciary obligations of other business corporations. A B corporation must justify all its actions as contributing ultimately to increased shareholder wealth.[8]

On the contrary, a statutory B corporation declares in its charter one or more social benefit goals. This protects it and its managers from lawsuits from shareholders claiming that the company is spending more time or resources on social issues than on maximizing profit.

A statutory B corporation is similar to a corporation as it also has shareholders and employees. However, the main difference lies in the fact that managers in a statutory B corporation are held responsible for ensuring the right balance is met between pure profit and its declared social benefit goals.

Not-for-Profit Entities

Not-for-profits are not technically a different form of business entity. **Not for profit** is a tax status available to corporations, LLCs, trusts, and other structures that meet specific criteria set out in the Internal Revenue Code.

All not-for-profits are exempt from income tax on their profits (so-called "surplus"), and some are also eligible to receive donations that are tax deductible to their donors. Only those companies described in Section 501(c) of the tax code are eligible; these include not only charitable organizations, but also such organizations as business leagues, civic leagues, labor organizations, chambers of commerce, social clubs, fraternal organizations, cemetery companies, and the like.

Those also eligible to receive tax deductible contributions are the smaller list of organizations in Section 501(c)(3), including religious, educational, scientific, and charitable institutions. One important condition applicable to all, however, is that none of the organization's earnings are permitted to benefit the individuals. In other words, although not-for-profits can pay reasonable compensation to employees, they cannot have shareholders; all profit must be reinvested in the business and used for the organization's exempt purpose.

Not for profit: a tax status granted to companies performing functions deemed by Congress to be socially desirable that exempts them from income tax and, in some cases, allows them to receive tax deductible donations.

15.3 LEGAL MISTAKES MADE BY STARTUPS[9]

>> **LO 15.3**   **Outline the most common legal errors made by startups.**

It is very common for entrepreneurs to make mistakes at the very beginning of their ventures. Even the most successful entrepreneurs have fallen into legal traps in the early stages of setting up. As we mentioned, one of the best ways to avoid costly mistakes is by hiring the right legal counsel. Some entrepreneurs rely on friends and family who offer free advice or steep discounts. Although it is always useful to get input from people you know or through contacts, never let that be a substitute for seeking professional guidance from a lawyer experienced in startups and expert in the legal areas that are most relevant to your business.

As mentioned in the previous section, it is vital to choose the right business structure for your company. Choosing the wrong entity could incur higher taxes than necessary or expose you to significant personal liabilities. It is also important to be aware that business structures differ from state to state; setting up the wrong structure puts you at risk for financial penalties. In California and Nevada, for example, licensed professionals such as doctors, lawyers, architects, and accountants are legally permitted to form an LLP, but are not allowed to operate as an LLC.

Keep in mind that experienced investors generally invest only in C corporations, so if you want to seek immediate external funding, you might be better off forming a C corporation rather than an LLC or an S-corp. However, if you don't plan to seek external financing until some time down the road, be aware that it is normally relatively easy and inexpensive to convert to a C corporation from any of the pass-through entities.

Video
Legal Errors

Vesting: the concept of imposing equity forfeitures on cofounders over a certain period of time on a piecemeal basis should they not stay with the company.

It is essential that you enter into a written agreement with your cofounders early on that formalizes the terms of the business (see Table 15.3). This is necessary regardless of the form of entity you have chosen. It may be a partnership agreement in a general or limited partnership, a stockholder agreement in an S or C corporation, or an operating agreement in an LLC; but the purpose of the agreement is the same. Failing to enter into this agreement is almost certain to cause problems later on.

One of the most high-profile instances of this is the dispute between the twin brothers Cameron and Tyler Winklevoss and Facebook's cofounder, Mark Zuckerberg.[10] The twins alleged that they had a verbal agreement with Zuckerberg to create programming for a new site called Harvard Connections. A few months later, Zuckerberg built Facebook—a rival site. The lack of any formal agreement in place has resulted in a lengthy court battle with the twins accusing Zuckerberg of stealing their idea.

Make sure you have the right processes in place when issuing shares to friends and family; otherwise you risk noncompliance with securities laws. For example, issuing shares to people who are not accredited investors or using the services of someone who is not a registered broker to sell stock can result in severe consequences, including refunding the investment, penalties, fines, and even criminal prosecution.

It is also important to ensure you have the right vesting schedule in place to protect the other cofounders. **Vesting** is the concept of imposing equity forfeitures on cofounders over a certain period of time on a piecemeal basis should they not stay with the company. Without a formal vesting schedule in place, it is possible for a cofounder to walk away from the company at any time with a chunk of the equity, leaving the

Cameron Winklevoss and Tyler Winklevoss, who sued Mark Zuckerberg over the Facebook idea

Credit: Cyrus Moghtader/Splash News/Newscom

remaining cofounders working to increase the wealth of a noncontributing owner. A similar concern arises when including equity in a compensation package for an employee. Vesting is discussed in more depth later in this chapter.

TABLE 15.3

Points to Be Addressed in a Founder Agreement

- Decide who gets what percentage of the company's equity.
- For pass-through entities, decide who gets what percentage of the company's taxable and distributable profits (they may not be the same).
- For pass-through entities, decide who gets what percentage of the company's losses (for tax purposes).
    - The above three do not have to be the same (e.g., you might want to direct losses to the person with the most outside taxable income), but there are serious tax compliance issues that must be dealt with if they are not.
- Outline the roles and responsibilities of the founders.
- In the event of one founder leaving, decide whether the company and/or other founders can buy back that founder's shares, and if so, how will the price be determined.
    - The answer and price may be different for different circumstances; for example, leaving as a result of death versus leaving to take another job. Rather than a given amount, price can be expressed as a financial formula or determined by some form of arbitration by a third party.
- Decide how much time each founder is expected to commit to the business.
- Define salaries (if any) and how they might change as time goes on.
- Outline how the daily and key decisions are to be made.
    - One such key decision would involve deciding whether to issue additional equity to later investors, employees, and so on.
- Decide who will serve initially as officers, board members, managing partners or managers.
- Agree on the circumstances that might result in a founder being removed from the business and whether this would trigger a repurchase of his/her equity.
- Set out the restrictions on founders' ability to resell their equity to third parties.
- State the assets or cash each founder invests in the business along with any obligation to make additional contributions under any circumstances.
- Decide how the sale of the business will be decided.
- Outline what will happen in the event of one founder not complying with the terms of the agreement.
- Decide whether the founders will be subject to confidentiality, invention assignment, or noncompetition agreements.
- Determine if the equity will be subject to a vesting schedule (see discussion later in this chapter).
- Agree on the overall goals and vision for the business.

Source: Adapted from Richard Harroch, "10 Big Legal Mistakes Made by Startups," *Forbes* (October 3, 2013) http://www.forbes.com/sites/allbusiness/2013/10/03/big-legal-mistakes-made-by-startups/ retrieved on August 4, 2015. (http://www.forbes.com/sites/allbusiness/2013/10/03/big-legal-mistakes-made-by-start-ups/#503948ee488f)

In the next section we explore the issue of IP (intellectual property) ownership, which can also cause complex legal complications if not handled correctly from the outset.

15.4 INTELLECTUAL PROPERTY (IP)

>> LO 15.4 Define IP and how it affects entrepreneurs.

Intellectual property (IP) describes intangible personal property created by human intelligence, such as ideas, inventions, slogans, logos, and processes. Intellectual property law includes the copyright, trademark, and patent protections

Intellectual property (IP): intangible personal property created by human intelligence, such as ideas, inventions, slogans, logos, and processes.

Video
Intellectual Property

for physical and nonphysical property that is the product of original thought and that can, in some sense, be owned. Intellectual property is a valuable asset for which entrepreneurs need to create an IP strategy that supports and evolves with the business. Intellectual property rights (IPR) legally protect inventions.[11] IP is the backbone of innovation all over the world because it plays a significant role in economic growth and development—both inside the United States and internationally.

Many startups are dependent on IP protection, regardless of industry or line of business—from manufacturing to tech enterprises to restaurants, IP is essential to the survival of small businesses. Without it, powerful companies like Amazon, Google, eBay, or Staples would never have gotten off the ground.[12]

Companies that depend on intellectual property
Credit: ©iStockphoto.com/AnatoliiBabii

Entrepreneurs and small businesses are becoming increasingly dependent on protecting their IP in order to bring their products and services to market. In fact, protecting IP has become more important to entrepreneurs than ever before.[13] The late Steve Jobs realized the importance of protecting IP early on: "From the earliest days at Apple, I realized that we thrived when we created intellectual property. If people copied or stole our software, we'd be out of business."[14]

IP is one of the most valuable assets for startups when it comes to transforming ideas and innovations into real market value. It is also one of the major things that investors look for in a startup. A 2013 article in *Forbes* magazine asserted that out of the 65 questions investors ask startups, four of them will relate to IP.[15] If the IP is usable and owned by the startup, not only will investors be more comfortable in investing, but it can also increase the valuation of the new venture. Protecting your IP also prevents competitors from trying to copy your products and services.

However, IP can also be complex, confusing, and entirely misunderstood. In the flurry of setting up new ventures, many entrepreneurs neglect the issue of IP and fail to seek advice from experts. Yet, if the IP isn't in place, then the whole venture can collapse.

Determining IP ownership is not straightforward. For instance, say you start working to create IP for a venture while still employed at another company, or when you have just left a job. In many employment contracts and under the law of most jurisdictions, the rights to inventions that substantially relate to the employee's old job description belong to the company.[16] This means that your former employer owns the IP on your inventions—not you. It is fundamental in the early stage of a startup that you seek legal advice from an IP attorney and review employee contracts and applicable law to determine if there is anything that might prevent you from attaining IP ownership.

Furthermore, a startup may use an independent contractor or a third party to help develop an innovation or trademark. Without a formal agreement in place, that third party has a right to a portion of any IP that results from her contribution, even though she may have been paid to create it. Table 15.4 outlines some more resources for IP information.

TABLE 15.4

Resources for IP Information

U.S. Patent and Trademark Office	The site offers a wealth of information about patents, trademarks and IP law and policy.
U.S. Copyright Office	The authoritative source for information about copyright.
InventNow	Tied to nonprofit innovation site Invent.org, this youth-oriented microsite puts the complexities of managing an IP portfolio into simple steps.
Google Patents	Google Patents delivers information on more than 7 million existing patents.
Pat2PDF	A web-based tool that finds patents and downloads them as PDFs.
Inventors Digest	An online hub loaded with inventor and IP developer news, as well as IP trends and tips.
PatentWizard	Designed by a patent attorney, the site helps you take the critical first steps toward filing an early provisional patent.
Patent Pro	This full-featured (and incredibly complex) PC-based patent filing software takes work to learn, but can help entrepreneurs create a working patent.

Source: Adapted from Jonathan Blum, "How to Protect Your Intellectual Property Rights" *Entrepreneur* (July 26, 2011) http://www.entrepreneur.com/article/220039 retrieved on August 2, 2015.

Finally, be aware of the relationship between IP and hackathons—events where software and hardware developers intensively collaborate to generate new ideas and inventions. A number of popular innovations, such as the ideas for Twitter and GroupMe, arose from hackathons.

When organizations hold internal hackathons whose participants are their own employees, they automatically retain the IP of whatever creative innovations arise. However, taking part in an external hackathon is not so clear-cut, especially if you are already an employee at a tech organization. Developing a proof-of-concept prototype product at a hackathon and then disclosing it could destroy any chance of patenting it in the future. Even worse, with so many people involved, it is not clear who can claim IP ownership of the innovation.[17] Similar issues can arise in the context of group projects in college classwork. In summary, it behooves you as an entrepreneur to educate yourself about IP and to seek legal guidance whenever appropriate.

Many types of innovations have arisen from hackathons

Credit: epa european pressphoto agency b.v. / Alamy Stock Photo

The Four Types of Intellectual Property[18]

IP is an essential asset to a company as it provides opportunities for others to invest or collaborate, and allows the founders to license, exchange or even franchise out their IP. In order to protect their IP, entrepreneurs need to be very knowledgeable about the different types during the early days of their business. There are four types of IP that fall under the protection of US law: copyright, trademark, trade secrets, and patent.

Copyright

Copyright: a form of protection provided to the creators of original works in the areas of literature, drama, art, music, film and other intellectual areas.

Copyright is a form of protection provided to the creators of original works in the areas of literature, music, drama, choreography, art, motion pictures, sound recordings, and architecture. It is important for tech entrepreneurs to be aware that computer code is classified as a literary work for purposes of copyright protection.[19] Another crucial thing to remember is that copyright does not protect ideas; it protects the tangible expression of the idea, such as in written materials or recordings. Generally, US copyright lasts for the duration of the author's life plus 70 years.

Copyright infringement cases can prove costly. For example, in a recent lawsuit, a US jury came to the conclusion that "Blurred Lines," a song created by Pharrell Williams and Robin Thicke, was too similar to the late Marvin Gaye's "Got to Give It Up." Williams and Thicke were instructed to pay $7.4 million in compensation to the Gaye family for loss of profits.[20]

Some limited uses of copyrighted material are allowed without the permission of the copyright owner; this is called "fair use." Generally, it must be shown that the work is of a type meant to be copied, the use is for a noncommercial purpose, it constitutes only a small portion of the work, and won't have a negative effect on the market for the work. Fair use is a "gray area" in US law; there are no absolute rules or boundaries around what is and is not fair use.

Trademark (and service mark)

Trademark: Any word, name, symbol, or device used in business to identify and promote a product. Its counterpart for service industries is the service mark.

Any word, name, symbol, or device used in business to identify and promote a product is a **trademark**; its counterpart for service industries is the service mark. Although the law affords some limited protection to trademarks without registration, a federally registered trademark generally lasts 10 years and, if still in use, can be renewed every 10 years thereafter.

In 2009, Gucci filed a lawsuit against Guess in New York and Milan, citing trademark infringement, due to the similar "G" stamp that appeared on a line of Guess shoes. Four years later, the New York courts found in favor of Gucci, but the Milan courts ruled in favor of Guess. Gucci has challenged the Milan ruling.[21] Trade and Service Marks are the legal basis of most branding campaigns.

Trade secret

Trade secret: confidential information that provides companies with a competitive edge and is not in the public domain, such as formulas, patterns, compilations, programs, devices, methods, techniques, or processes.

A **trade secret** is any confidential information that provides companies with a competitive edge and is not publicly known or accessible, such as formulas, patterns, customer lists, compilations, programs, devices, methods, techniques, or processes. Trade secrets last for as long as they remain secret; they are protected from theft under federal and state law. Companies can protect their trade secrets by having their employees and contractors sign nondisclosure, work-for-hire, and noncompete agreements or clauses. Famous examples of trade secrets allegedly include the recipe for Coca-Cola's beverages, KFC's ingredients, and the formula for WD-40.[22]

Patent

Patent: a grant of exclusive property rights on inventions through the U.S. and other governments.

A **patent** is a grant of property rights on inventions through the U.S. government. It excludes others from making, using, selling, or importing the invention without the

MINDSHIFT

Patent Search

What is the coolest product that you own or would like to own? This can be anything from the stylus you may use on a tablet computer to a Frisbee you would play with in a park.

Your Mindshift task is to find the patent for this item. Use Google Patents (google.com/patents) or the "quick search" function from the United States Patent and Trademark Office (http://patft.uspto.gov/). While you are searching, pay attention to the sections and content you see in patents: the abstract, the description, the patent's claim, and so on.

Once you have a good idea of what a patent looks like, try to find a patent that pertains to one of your own original ideas.

CRITICAL THINKING QUESTIONS

1. **How easy or difficult was it to think of a cool product for your patent search? What factors came into play?**

2. **Did you find many other patents for products related to the one you were searching for?**

3. **What did you learn that surprised you or went against your expectations?** ●

---

patent owner's consent. In order to be granted a patent, the product or process must present a new or novel way of doing something, be nonobvious, or provide some sort of solution to a problem.

In the United States, the invention must not have been made public in any way before one year prior to the filing application date (the one-year grace period does not exist in most other countries. Laws of nature, physical phenomena, mathematical equations, scientific theories, the human body or human genes, and abstract ideas cannot be patented. However, it is possible for a mobile app to be patented if it meets the criteria of the U.S. Patent and Trademark Office (PTO).

The duration of a patent is generally 20 years from the filing date of application, and it can be costly to file a patent. The Beer Brella (Patent No. 6,637,447) is an example of a novel and arguably useful invention, which provides shade for bottle of beer on a hot day.[23] It may not be a scientific breakthrough, but it qualifies for patenting.

It is important to note that while copyright protects artistic expression and trademark protects brand, there is no way of protecting or patenting an idea. Of course, the whole innovation must begin with an idea, but an idea must be turned into an invention before it can qualify for patenting.[24] This does not necessarily mean creating a prototype, but you must be able to meaningfully describe the invention, how it is made, and how others could use it. For example, the "beer brella" would have started out as an idea, but the inventors would have needed to flesh out the concept and create a sketch of it in order to explain its intended use.

In summary, IP rights are the basis for every single business; without them, entrepreneurs would be less likely to risk bringing new innovations to the marketplace; investors would not invest; and customers would end up with less choice. Fewer businesses means more unemployment and less economic growth.[25] The importance of IP cannot be overestimated—this is why it can be so devastating to businesses of any size when IP is compromised.

Audio
The Power of Patents

15.5 GLOBAL IP THEFT

>> **LO 15.5**   Assess the global impact of IP theft.

Video
The Global Impact of IP Theft

Any business that has a trademark, trade secret, patent, or copyright is dependent on IP protections. Millions of people all over the world violate IP laws every day. Ignoring copyright by downloading your favorite song from a peer-to-peer website without paying for it is exactly the same as going into a music store and stealing a CD, yet people who would otherwise characterize themselves as law-abiding do it all the time. IP theft costs the United States almost $300 billion every year, and it has a huge negative impact on legitimate businesses.[26]

Consider this scenario. You have just launched your T-shirt business with a trademarked brand, and sales are really taking off. A few months later, you come across another website set up in a different country that is selling counterfeit versions of your T-shirts for a fraction of the price. You start losing sales, your brand becomes tainted, investors think twice about investing in your company, and your reputation becomes damaged—and all because someone has stolen your unique trademark and copied it for financial gain.

A study from MarkMonitor shows that global online piracy is rife in the area of digital content such as movies, music, software, games, and e-books; whereas counterfeiting is prolific across most items, including clothing, footwear, electronics, sports goods, and pharmaceuticals.[27]

Why does IP protection sometimes fail? IP rights are territorial, which means that while your rights may be protected in the United States, they are not necessarily protected in a different country. Developed countries such as the United States impose strict IP laws, but countries like China and India take a less stringent approach and have a rich history of IP rights violations, with China being the top country for online piracy, counterfeiting, and theft of trade secrets.[28]

A counterfeit Louis Vuitton bag

Credit: AP Photo/Greg Baker

There is a strong market in the United States for counterfeit goods made in China. In one example, U.S. Customs and Border Protection in the Port of Miami seized over $10 million of counterfeit Burberry and Louis Vuitton clothing and jewelry in a shipment that had arrived from China bound for sale in the United States.[30] Indeed, clothing giant Burberry was awarded $100 million in a lawsuit for trademark infringement by a range of Chinese websites.[31]

Major corporations can afford to wage massive legal battles and get compensation for IP theft, but how can a startup or a small business protect its IP in different territories? Entrepreneurs who are seeking to sell their innovations abroad must first conduct a search to ensure their company's name and brand can be used in the foreign country. Then, they must register for local IP ownership within that country or extend US registrations to foreign countries at the beginning of the process. Also, it would be wise for them to seek proper IP counsel to protect their IP rights abroad.

RESEARCH AT WORK

Patent Trolls[29]

US patents have encouraged innovation, but they have also become subject to patent trolls—individuals or firms who own patents but have never actually produced useful products of their own. Patent trolls issue legal complaints against alleged patent infringers in an effort to extract a licensing fee for the duration of the life of the patent. AT&T, Google, Verizon, Apple, and Blackberry are only a few of the thousands of companies being sued every year by patent trolls.

The endless patent litigation has led to significant damage to innovation. Research findings have shown that it reduces VC investment in startups; it also decreases research and development, as the more research firms carry out, the more likely they are to be sued for patent infringement. The biggest impact of patent trolls is on small startups. One survey of software startups reported that because of this issue, 41% were forced to either exit the business or change strategy. U.S. congressional leaders and the White House have called for reforms to address the negative effects of lengthy patent litigation.

CRITICAL THINKING QUESTIONS

1. **How would you protect your startup against patent trolls?**

2. **Do you think individuals or firms have the right to hold patents without producing any useful products of their own? Why or why not?**

3. **What are the effects of patent trolls on startups? ●**

In addition, ensure your systems are watertight. For example, in 2012, when Skyhigh Networks, a cybersecurity startup, received $6.5 million in funding, its founders noticed high activity in outsiders trying to hack into its network in order to steal its IP. Fortunately, the company had prepared for this eventuality and was not affected.[32]

Finally, don't depend wholly on your patent for your business strategy. Building customer relationships, promoting your trademarked brand, providing quality products and services, and implementing rapid innovation will also help you defend your business against the effects of IP theft.

In addition, one significant development taking place in China might help to curb the level of IP theft. In recent years more and more people in China are applying for patents to protect their own innovations from competitors and as an effort to improve its negative history of IPR. In 2012, China announced its new goal of producing innovations that are "designed in China" rather than "made in China."[33] This indicates that China is more invested in its own homegrown ideas, which may result in less IP theft in the future.

YOU BE THE ENTREPRENEUR

Security is vital for any company. Customers and clients count on a company to keep their information safe, and the company counts on its system to not harm its image. Entrepreneurs constantly worry about breaches in security and the possible ramifications of a hack.

Steve Ells, CEO and Founder of Chipotle, had to deal with a situation involving possible legal issues and had to make the right decision to save his company's image. Ells started

Chipotle with the idea of serving food that came from naturally grown ingredients, including naturally raised meat—a new twist on the restaurant industry. He bases his business on honesty and transparency. This came into question when Chipotle's Twitter account was hacked by someone who tweeted vulgar language and symbols. One of the tweets spoke about President Obama and changed Chipotle's logo to a swastika. Many people became outraged by the insulting words, and Chipotle had to find a way to respond.

Then, in 2015, Chipotle faced more controversy following an E. coli outbreak across nine states that left over 50 people ill. Steve Ells has been fighting to save the restaurant's reputation and win back customers.

What Would You Do?

Sources
Shandrow, Kim. (2015, February 9). *Hackers hijack Chipotle's Twitter account, tweet f-bomb and n-word insults. Entrepreneur,* 12. U.S. Food and Drug Administration. Retrieved from http://www.fda.gov/Food/RecallsOutbreaksEmergencies/Outbreaks/ucm470410.htm

15.6 COMMON IP TRAPS[34]

>> **LO 15.6**   **Describe the common IP traps experienced by entrepreneurs.**

Web
IP Traps

IP can be a minefield, and many inventors fall into some common traps that hamper the potential of exciting innovations. Patenting can cost thousands of dollars, and some inventors find that they earn less than the cost of the patent. For example, Robert Kearns, the inventor of the intermittent windshield wiper, sued car manufacturers Chrysler and Ford for copying the technology he had patented. Following a court battle that spanned decades, Kearns was finally granted a total of $40 million in compensation, which may sound like a lot, but it is nothing in comparison to what Kearns would have made if he had been credited with his invention from the beginning. Let's explore the common IP pitfalls and how entrepreneurs can avoid them.

Publicly Disclosing Your Innovation

You might be bursting to tell the world about your discoveries—but don't. Disclosing your new product or service in public before you have filed a patent application means that in most countries you will not be permitted to patent it at all. (We've mentioned the one-year grace period in the United States.) For example, a professor at Imperial College London, Robert Perneczky, discovered a protein that had the potential to significantly improve the chances of spotting the onset of Alzheimer's disease. However, Perneczky failed to qualify for a patent because of a detailed article he had written about his discovery that had been published in an academic paper. Because Perneczky's idea had been disclosed to the public, he was prevented from patenting it.

While it is impractical to avoid disclosing anything at all about your discoveries, try to refrain from revealing every single step. One way of protecting your IP that works in the United States is to file a provisional patent application before you take your idea public. This secures your rights as the inventor and gives you 12 months to complete the research and develop your idea into a working prototype. However, you will have to file a full patent application as soon as the 12 months is up; otherwise the knowledge it holds will become publicly available. Also, your invention cannot have changed substantially from the date of the initial filing. Bear in mind that the

United States has changed from being a "first to invent" to a "first to file" country, which means that if an inventor waits too long to file a patent application, he or she may lose out to someone else who is working on a similar innovation.

Failure to Protect Product and Processes

As Robert Kearns learned, it is easy for innovations to be copied by others. This is why it is important for entrepreneurs to ensure their products and processes are fully protected. Some inventors and other scientists protect their products by building unique markers into them; for example, a unique chemical "thumbprint" can reveal through a simple test if someone else has copied their product. Another option some entrepreneurs use is to license their innovation to a larger organization that has all the tools already in place to protect and commercialize the invention. The inventor then profits through a stream of royalties.

The intermittent windshield wiper, invented by Robert Kearns, who sued Chrysler and Ford for copying the idea.

Credit: ©iStockphoto.com/ deepblue4you

Inability to Determine Originality

Entrepreneurs often build on existing products, tools, and techniques to create their innovations. However, the outcome must be considered both novel and useful if it is to qualify for IP protection. This means ensuring that products and services contain enough features to significantly improve the way they are used by others with the intention of solving a problem. For example, when Jeffrey Percival and his research team developed the Star Tracker 5000—a low-cost device that determines the space rocket's altitude and tracks stars—the concern was it was not original enough, as it was mostly formed of standard components. To make his product more original, Percival added an algorithm that rapidly transmits digitized images. By enhancing the features of the product, Percival was able to license it to NASA for its space missions.

Failure to Assign Ownership

In the early stages of a startup, a number of people may be formally involved in contributing to the innovation process. But as Mark Zuckerberg learned through the Winklevoss twins' lawsuit, it is best to make formal agreements regarding IP ownership prior to any further development in order to decide who owns and controls the innovation, and who doesn't. Ownership can even vest in people you haven't paid, people you have paid but who haven't signed a formal assignment of ownership, or people who have otherwise made a valuable contribution to the innovation.

For example, InBae Yoon invented a medical device used to withdraw fluid from a body cavity called the trocar, which he subsequently licensed to a larger organization. However, Yoon had originally collaborated with electronic technician Young Jae Choi to create the product. Yoon failed to pay Choi for his work or obtain an assignment of his rights. Some years later, a rival competitor discovered the technician's involvement, amended the patent to assign him partial ownership, and won a court case to secure a separate licensing agreement with Choi to allow them to use the product. The same kinds of problems can arise with people who may have coauthored copyrighted material or helped to design a logo for a company's trademark.

Failure to Protect IP in Global Markets

As we mentioned earlier, IP rights are territorial, which means that while your rights may be protected in the United States, they are not necessarily protected in a different country. For example, in China, Apple Inc. lost a court battle with Chinese technology firm Proview International Holdings, which claimed it owned the iPad trademark in the Chinese market.[35] The case seriously threatened Apple's ability to sell the iPad in China. Apple finally agreed to pay $60 million in 2012 to settle the two-year dispute.

Entrepreneurs hoping to sell in different territories need to get the right legal advice and carry out due diligence before even starting their business, in order to understand how to navigate any obstacles up front. Otherwise, they risk running into some major difficulties along the way.

15.7 HIRING EMPLOYEES[36]

>> **LO 15.7**   **Explain the legal requirements of hiring employees.**

Video
Legal Requirements for Hiring

There may come a time when you need to hire some help when your business takes off. Yet there's more to the hiring process than interviewing and selecting the best person for the job. As an employer, you need to understand federal and state labor laws in order to protect both your business and your employees. In this section we describe some of the regulatory steps you need to consider when hiring your first employee.

Equal Employment Opportunity

Employers in the United States need to be aware that federal laws prohibit discriminating against employees on the basis of race, sex, creed, religion, color, national origin, or age. Workers with disabilities are also protected, though employers can refuse to hire on the basis of a disability if it prevents the worker from fulfilling job tasks. Some states forbid discrimination on the basis of sexual orientation.

Globally, the rules are not the same. For example, the global rights index provided by the International Trade Union Confederation (ITUC) shows that while countries such as Austria, Finland, Netherlands, Norway, and Uruguay score the highest for equality at work, the level of inequality in other countries is rising. The report showed that countries such as China, Belarus, Egypt, Colombia, and Saudi Arabia are among the worst in the world for equal opportunities and workers' rights.[37]

Employer Identification Number (EIN)

Before you hire your first employee, make sure you get an employer identification number (EIN). You will need to use this on documents and tax returns for the IRS. It is also necessary when reporting employee information to state agencies. There is also a regulatory requirement to register your newly hired employee with your state directory within 20 days of the hire date. You can apply for the EIN online.

Navigating Legal and Intellectual Property Issues

Entrepreneurs need to be careful not to disclose inventions before a patent is filed.

Credit: ©iStockphoto.com/SebastianGauert

Protection of IP encourages innovators to risk investing time and money by ensuring they will be the primary beneficiaries of profit when the invention is introduced into the market. When evaluating ethics related to IP, there are sometimes clear-cut courses of action, but more often there are multiple possible solutions, each of which is more or less ethically acceptable.

The first step is to know the law and understand how it applies to the business activity at hand. IP laws are complex, so the guidance of a qualified IP attorney is often well worth the investment. Once you know the legalities, there are still questions of right and wrong to be answered.

As an example, entrepreneurs may experience IP issues when inventions are disclosed before a patent is filed and without a nondisclosure agreement. Under these circumstances, the person to whom the IP has been disclosed is legally able to recreate the invention and take it to market without compensating the original innovator. Doing so is legal, but is it ethical?

CRITICAL THINKING QUESTIONS

1. **Why is it important to protect intellectual property?**

2. **Whose responsibility is it to protect intellectual property?**

3. **When is the best time to apply for intellectual property protection?** ●

Sources

Bagley, C. (2003, March 3). *Top ten legal mistakes made by entrepreneurs.* Retrieved from Harvard Business School: http://hbswk.hbs.edu/item/top-ten-legal-mistakes-made-by-entrepreneurs

BRAINMASS. (n.d.). *Ethical issues in intellectual property.* Retrieved from BRAINMASS.com: https://brainmass.com/business/business-culture-in-china/ethical-issues-intellectual-property-556131

Telford, E. (2013, October 15). *Why intellectual property allows you to be an entrepreneur.* Retrieved from Entrepreneur.com: http://www.entrepreneur.com/article/229407

webGURU. (n.d.). *Ethics case studies.* Retrieved from webGURU: Guide for Undergraduate Research: http://www.webguru.neu.edu/professionalism/research-integrity/ethics-case-studies

Unemployment and Workers' Compensation

Register with your state's labor department to pay state unemployment compensation taxes, which provide temporary relief to employees who lose their jobs. Depending on the size of your business, most states will require you to register for workers' compensation insurance to protect against any work-related injuries. (Some states make exceptions for very small businesses.)

Withholding Taxes

To comply with IRS regulations, you will need to withhold part of your employee's income and keep records of employment taxes for at least the most recent four years. You will need to report these wages and taxes every year. There may also be a requirement to withhold state income taxes, depending on the state in which your employees are located.

Employee Forms

Make sure you set up personnel files containing important documents for each employee that you hire. Each employee must fill out a W-4 form that lets you, as the employer, know how much money to withhold from their paychecks for federal tax purposes. You can ask employees to fill out this form every year if they wish to change the withholding amount. This form does not have to be filed with the IRS. The Form 1-9 is another form you need to complete within three days of hiring your new employee; this requires employers to verify the new employee's eligibility to work in the United States. In addition, you must file IRS Form 940 every year to report federal unemployment tax, which provides payment of unemployment compensation to employees who have lost their jobs.

Benefits

As an employer, you will need to decide what sorts of benefits you plan to provide your employees. The law requires you to pay and withhold Social Security taxes and an additional rate for Medicare and to pay for unemployment insurance. For businesses with over 50 employees, you must also provide family and medical leave and health insurance. In a few states, employers must provide a certain number of paid sick days. You are not required by law to provide life insurance, retirement plans, or regular vacation leave; but by offering a competitive benefits program, you will have a better chance of attracting high-caliber employees. If you choose to provide these optional benefits, be aware that they are subject to many regulations; consultation with an accountant experienced in such benefits is a worthwhile investment.

FIGURE 15.2

Example of a required workplace poster

Credit: FRANCIS DEAN/DEAN PICTURES/Newscom

Workplace Posters

As an employer, you will be required to post specific federal and state notices in the workplace that inform employees of their rights under labor laws. The Department of Labor and Small Business administration websites are useful resources for finding out which types of posters you need to display in your workplace (see Figure 15.2).

Safety Measures

All employers have a responsibility to their employees to maintain a safe and healthy workplace environment. This means training employees to do their jobs safely, ensuring the workplace is free from hazards, maintaining safety records, and reporting any serious accidents at work to government administrators. You should also have provisions in place such as medical treatment and rehabilitation services to support employees who are injured on the job.

The Employee Handbook

Although you are not legally required to have an employee handbook, it is a great way of communicating your policies and guidelines, as well as setting the tone for the kind of behavior you might expect from your new employees. It needs to be a true reflection of the way you want your business to operate. For example, you might prefer your employees not to blog about the company, text during working hours, or dress in a certain way. However, be aware that the law limits what an employer can require of employees in these respects.

In addition to outlining company benefits, compensation, pay, and promotions, the manual might also include details of the company's attendance policy, lunch breaks, any bans on smoking, policies around employee harassment and discrimination, leave policies, and so on. To give your new employee more of an idea of what your business is about, it is also useful to include a bit about the company background, its mission statement, position in the market, and who its customers are. However, it is not advisable to include language that could be interpreted as promises of future employment or benefits. In some cases, these statements have been held to be contracts enforceable by employees claiming to have relied on them.

The key to complying with legal requirements is being organized. Maintaining payroll records, filing tax returns on time, keeping your employees informed, and ensuring you are up to speed with federal reporting requirements go a long way toward running an efficient business. Some essential resources for hiring employees are summarized in Table 15.5.

Many companies include a dress code in the employee handbook

Credit: Anthony Redpath/Getty Images

TABLE 15.5

Resources for Hiring Employees

EIN	Form SS-4 from the IRS website: www.irs.gov
Workers compensation	state unemployment tax agencies at http://workforcesecurity.doleta.gov/map.asp
Withholding taxes	information and forms at www.irs.gov
Employee benefits	information at https://www.sba.gov/content/required-employee-benefits
Workplace poster	legal requirements at http://www.dol.gov/whd/resources/posters.htm
Safety measures	safety rules at www.osha.gov
Employee handbook	see www.nolo.com

Source: US Small Business Administration. "Hire Your First Employee" https://www.sba.gov/content/hire-your-first-employee retrieved on August 4, 2015

Hiring a Contractor or an Employee?[38]

When hiring people, it is important to distinguish between contractors and employees. Many startups and small businesses use independent contractors because of the advantages they bring. For example, it generally saves money to hire contractors because they don't require contributions toward health care, compensation insurance, or any other benefits. In addition, there can be cost-saving benefits when it comes to office space and equipment, as contractors will usually provide their own.

Furthermore, working with independent contractors gives employers greater flexibility in hiring and letting go of workers. For example, you could hire contractors for a specific project, and then let them go when the job is finished. Equally, if you do not like their work, you never have to see them again. There can also be valuable cost savings in hiring contractors who are experts in their field and are ready to hit the ground running, which means saving time and money on training.

Legally, independent contractors are not protected by the same laws as employees, which means there is less chance of dealing with the same legal claims that could be brought by employees. However, there are some disadvantages to hiring independent contractors. Because contractors have autonomy in what, when, and how they perform their job duties, you may feel you have less control over them. Also, independent contractors may be present for only a short period of time before leaving again, which might be disruptive to the other employees.

Finally, it is important to be aware that the classification of workers as independent contractors or employees is not your choice. The classification is dictated by the facts of the relationship. State and federal agencies are very strict on workers who are classified as contractors versus employees, and you may risk facing government audits as a result.

Misclassifying independent contractors and employees could have costly legal consequences. For example, if the individual you thought you were hiring as an independent contractor actually meets the legal definition of an employee, you may need to pay back wages, taxes, benefits, and anything else an employee would receive in your company—health insurance, retirement, and so on. Table 15.6 outlines some of the main differences between employees and contractors.

TABLE 15. 6

Differences Between Employees and Contractors

EMPLOYEE	CONTRACTOR
Duties are dictated or controlled by others.	Decides what, when, and how duties are performed.
Works solely for employer.	Provides services to other clients.
Uses tools or materials provided by employer.	Supplies own tools or materials.
Working hours set by employer.	Sets own working hours.
Tax, benefits, and pension paid by employer.	Pays own tax, benefits, and pension.
Expenses paid for by employer.	Pays own expenses.
Tasks must be performed by the employee.	Can subcontract work to others.
Employer provides annual and personal leave.	Not provided with annual and personal leave.
Paid regularly (weekly, monthly, etc.) as per employee contract.	Provides an invoice when work is performed and the task is completed.
Provided with training.	Does not receive training.

Source: "Hire a Contractor or an Employee," US Small Business Association https://www.sba.gov/content/hire-contractor-or-employee retrieved on August 2, 2015.

The FedEx Ground division of FedEx operated using the independent contractor model for decades: workers had to pay not only for their own uniforms, scanners and other tools, but they also had to buy their own trucks and the fuel, insurance, and maintenance for those trucks. They did not receive overtime pay or any other benefits. However, a California court ruling stated that FedEx had misclassified over 2,000 drivers as independent contractors, largely because of the extent to which FedEx controlled the drivers. FedEx eventually settled the long-running dispute for $228 million in 2015.[39]

Whether the person you hire is a contractor or an employee depends on all of the factors listed above, but the most significant factor is the amount of control the employer has over the work being carried out.[40] For example, if you expect the person to show up at the same time every day and work a set period of hours, and you expect to closely oversee her duties, then you will have hired an employee rather than retained a contractor.

Compensating Employees

It is often the case that a startup's need for additional employees outstrips the company's ability to pay in cash. When faced with this resource constraint, entrepreneurs often come up with alternative ways to compensate employees such as giving them flexible hours, additional days off, and small perks such as gift cards or a lunch paid for by the company.

Compensation in the form of equity

Entrepreneurs often attempt to obtain services from employees and contractors in exchange for a share of the business. This raises two legal issues.

First, as mentioned earlier in the context of issuing shares to friends and family, issuance of shares to employees and contractors risks noncompliance with securities laws. Although the workers are not investing cash in the business, their time and labor is considered an investment under the law, triggering the protection of securities regulation. Therefore, just as much care must be paid to having the right processes in place when issuing shares to employees and contractors as when issuing shares to traditional investors.

Second, it is important to note that income tax is triggered any time an individual receives any form of property in exchange for performing services, not just when he or she is paid in cash. Therefore, the receipt of shares as compensation for work can result in an unexpected tax bill. This may not seem much of a problem in the early days of a startup when the shares may not be worth very much, but could become an issue later on.

However, if the shares are subject to a vesting schedule, the problem becomes magnified as the tax may not apply until the shares have vested (when, it is hoped, they will have greatly increased in value). This same problem exists when founders' stock is made subject to a vesting schedule, since by doing so, you are tying the retention of stock to the performance of services. There are tax techniques available to mitigate, and in some cases eliminate, this unwelcome tax issue, so be sure to consult competent tax professionals before agreeing to pay compensation in the form of equity.

Unpaid internships

The thought of receiving the services of enthusiastic young interns looking for work experience rather than financial compensation can be very attractive to the resource-constrained startup. However, bear in mind that such arrangements are generally illegal. The Fair Labor Standards Act provides a minimum wage, overtime pay, and other protections to most workers. Putting an intern to work in your business normally requires compliance with these requirements. The Department of Labor has directly addressed the issue of unpaid interns and published a 6-part test to determine its legality.[41]

In summary, the internship must be solely for the benefit of the intern's education, the services provided must be of a kind that does not displace other employees, and the employer must not benefit from the arrangement. Many companies demand that the intern receive academic credit from an educational institution as a way of complying with regulations, but even in that case, the intern's services must not benefit the company or replace duties that could be provided by paid employees. ●

Get the edge on your studies at **edge.sagepub.com/neckentrepreneurship**

‣   Master the learning objectives using key study tools
‣   Watch, listen, and connect with online multimedia resources
‣   Access mobile-friendly quizzes and flashcards to check your understanding

SUMMARY

15.1 Discuss how legal considerations can add value to entrepreneurial venture.

Understanding the legal considerations applicable to the business is as important as understanding user needs. Taking legal considerations into account may add value to the firm. Whether it is a lawyer, free website content, or some form of legal expert, obtaining competent legal advice will certainly help improve the performance of the venture.

15.2 Explain the most common types of legal structures available to startups.

The most common types of legal structures include: Sole Proprietorship, General Partnership, C corporation, S corporation, Limited Liability Company (LLC), Limited Partnership, Limited Liability Partnership (LLP), and Benefit Corporation. In addition, most of these business structures can be run as a not-for-profit provided the company complies with IRS section 501(c).

15.3 Outline the most common legal errors made by startups.

Startups may make some common mistakes that could be expensive. The most common mistakes they make are in choosing the legal structure of the venture, not having a written agreement defining the many parameters of their relationship, not paying close enough attention to forming the right vesting schedules, and issuing shares to people who are not accredited investors.

15.4 Define IP and how it affects entrepreneurs.

IP is intangible personal property created by human intelligence, as a result of creativity such as inventions, trade secrets, slogans, logos, and processes. The four main types of IP are copyright, trademark/service mark, trade secret, and patent. It behooves entrepreneurs to understand IP because startups are by definition innovative and likely to involve the creation of IP.

15.5 Assess the global impact of IP theft.

Millions of people all over the world violate IP laws every day by ignoring copyright. IP theft costs the United States almost $300 billion every year.

15.6 Describe the common IP traps experienced by entrepreneurs.

Entrepreneurs often make mistakes in the following areas:

- Public disclosure of an invention or innovation;
- Failure to protect products, processes, brands, and so on;
- Inability to determine originality;
- Failure to allocate ownership; and
- Failure to protect IP in global markets.

15.7 Explain the legal requirements of hiring employees.

Legal requirements related to hiring employees include registering employees with the state labor department, keeping records of employee tax history, preparing the appropriate legal documentation, and complying with safety regulations.

KEY TERMS

C corporation 418
Copyright 426
General partnership 417
Intellectual property (IP) 423
Limited liability company (LLC) 419
Not for profit 421
Patent 426
S corporation 419
Sole proprietorship 417
Trade secret 426
Trademark 426
Vesting 422

CASE STUDY

Robert Donat, Founder & CEO of GPS Insight

In ten years, Robert Donat, founder and CEO of GPS Insight, built his technology software company from nothing into a corporation with 105 employees, with growing revenues for 2014 of $25 million per year. How did he do it? By meeting a growing need in service and trucking industries—a huge market that includes 20 million trucks. GPS Insight uses its proprietary global positioning system (GPS) software to track 100,000 trucks in the United States, Canada, UK, and Australia.

GPS Insight does far more than just "track" the location of each truck it serves. Through unmatched software technological systems, GPS Insight offers a host of unique "insights" that provide their customers with an unprecedented amount of data, empowering fleet managers and executives with the knowledge of just about everything there is to know about each truck in their fleet—including where the driver of that truck is and what he or she has been doing.

GPS Insight then organizes the data it collects to produce a variety of reports that provide customers with invaluable information that leads to heightened efficiency and cost savings. From a truck's whereabouts, speed, and ignition status, to messaging, driver identification, and diagnostics, GPS Insight helps its customers see where their vehicles are, run reports on where their trucks have been, how many stops they have made, miles traveled, landmark visits to customers, acceleration statistics, who is driving which vehicle, and so forth.

This data is then used to schedule reports, keep up with state mileage taxing, find out which customers are not being serviced, recover stolen vehicles, and discover which drivers are cheating on their hours or otherwise not doing their job.

Generating, organizing, and reporting this extremely valuable data has benefited GPS Insight customers to the tune of a stellar 5-1 return on their investment (ROI). No wonder GPS Insight has been growing at the extraordinary rate of 30% in recent years, not to mention garnering an impressive array of industry awards, including CEO Robert Donat's being recently named the Innovator of the Year by the Industry Leaders of Arizona (see http://www.gpsinsight.com/about/newsroom/awards-achievements for a full list of GPS Insight awards). And with 12 million trucks not utilizing GPS that could potentially be served, it appears that GPS Insight's future growth potential is almost limitless.

Robert Donat attributes GPS Insight's success in part to good timing. While the industry space in which GPS Insight plays has existed for many years, Donat says that the early 21st century was really the "sweet spot" in which to enter the playing field. But jumping in at the right time was only one variable in Donat's remarkable success. Donat was also an extremely hard worker with a courageous willingness to take risks for entrepreneurial growth.

Robert Donat was born and raised in suburban Chicago. The Donats didn't have much money, and Robert learned early on that if he wanted more than his 50-cent per-week allowance, he was going to have to earn it on his own. As a young boy, he delivered newspapers and mowed lawns. By the time he was in 7th grade, he had earned enough money to buy his own computer—and then taught himself how to program it.

When Robert graduated from college in 1991 (he started in 1987, the year of "Black Monday"), the job landscape in the financial industry was unfortunately bleak. Unable to find desirable employment, Robert joined the Army, where he was eventually commissioned as an artillery officer. He later earned two master's degrees at DePaul University in computer science and finance. Despite Donat's forays into the academic realms of finance, his life ambition was ultimately to be, in his words, a "technology geek."

He was eventually able to combine his financial training and tech ambitions while working for Citadel Investment Group in Chicago, and then by serving as a technology consultant for hedge funds and trading funds. He also gained additional experience as a "geek" by learning the science and art of database architecture.

While working for Citadel, Donat—always the entrepreneur—picked up side work with a dotcom startup called eCrush, which he describes as a teenage version of the online dating service Match.com. Like so many other technology companies of its era, eCrush took a huge blow when the dotcom bubble burst in the early 2000s. Working on a virtually nonexistent budget, Donat and others banded together to save the company and make it successful. In 2006, the reinvigorated company was sold to Hearst Magazines Digital Media (a leading publisher of monthly magazines including *Seventeen*, *Marie Claire*, and *Good Housekeeping*).

The $400,000 he made from its 2006 sale to Hearst, in concert with his experience building a business with extremely meager resources, prepared Donat to eventually build GPS Insight into a "lean and mean" organization. This developed capacity as a nimble innovator enabled him to accomplish tasks and build processes at GPS Insight for literally tens of millions of dollars cheaper than many of his larger competitors.

In 2004, two years before he sold eCrush, Donat and his family moved from Chicago to Scottsdale, Arizona, where his wife had grown up. Seeking a new start in the financial industry, Donat was disappointed to discover that the specific financial market niche he sought was severely lacking in his new locale. As a midcareer professional uninterested in commuting to financial hubs to work, Donat began to reinvent himself when he learned that a friend needed help tracking a fleet of 300 trucks. An industry-leading GPS tracking company encouraged him to start a consulting business around their existing product, and told him if he did, they would send Robert all the business he could handle.

Quickly discovering that the existing products on the market were not very good, and that existing vendors were not providing quality service to their customers, Donat identified an ideal space with a potentially perfect storm of opportunity to combine his education, experience, tech savvy, and entrepreneurial vision into a successful business. Thus GPS Insight was born.

With a clear vision of his potential, Donat acquired every penny he could possibly "beg, borrow, or leverage" to start GPS Insight. He even went so far as to liquidate the equity on his home and cash out his 401k, stock, and other holdings. This, plus the $400,000 he had earned from the sale of eCrush and a $200,000 infusion from an investor for a 5.5% stake in the new company, provided Donat with the nearly $2 million he needed to get GPS Insight off the ground.

The first few years were extremely challenging and stressful. When the Great Recession hit in 2008, several GPS Insight customers went bankrupt, leaving many invoices forever unpaid. But Donat and his company remained determined to meet each challenge and rise above it. It took $40 million in revenue for GPS Insight to earn its first dollar of profit, but through continual customer-centric innovation and careful frugality, it has since made an additional $60 million in revenue in the past four years alone, including a substantial amount of well-earned profit.

Looking back, Donat attributes his success in large part to effectively listening to customers and being innovative in adapting products to their needs. Customer service lies at the heart of GPS Insight's mission. For example, they process 100 million database queries per day, 15 million pieces of vehicle data per day, and 1 million customer queries per day. They have also sent over 73 million alerts to customers, providing them with invaluable "insight" empowering them to proactively address issues related to fleet efficiency and results. The result has been a $500 million customer ROI since the company's inception.

As the founder and CEO of a successful software technology company, Donat also understands the potential legal and IP challenges that come with being a successful entrepreneur in an industry awash with patents. To date, GPS Insight has been hit with half a million dollars' worth of patent lawsuits. The challenges posed by these "patent trolls"—as Donat not-so-affectionately refers to corporate technology "ambulance chasers" who seek to suck money out of technology companies over the pettiest of matters, based on the complicated particulars of legal fine print— have caused Donat plenty of angst and stress over the years.

Despite the difficulties of dealing with these legal and IP issues, Donat has managed to stay above the fray to lead his company to become the most successful and profitable organization of its size in the industry. GPS Insight remains the only high-quality, independently owned, US-based GPS fleet tracking company.

According to Donat, the business model of a "patent troll" essentially involves buying patents from individuals who develop patents on obscure, semi-obvious elements of a technological process and then proactively seek out anyone who might be infringing on the patent in any conceivable way. The trolls then require businesses to license their patent or they will file legal suit. Donat explains that while some of these patents are easily invalidated, or invalid to begin with, lawyers have a lot of leverage to sue people over just about anything; and, as a result, some of the trolls are genuine "shake-down artists."

According to Donat, "patent trolls" suck billions of dollars of productivity out of the economy, and over time, even the courts have become less sympathetic with their extortionist designs. Donat also credits the Obama administration for making progress in limiting the power of trolls. The 44th president has indeed made progress in this area. According to one article, "The history books will remember [Obama] for setting off a chain of reforms that made predatory patent lawsuits a virtual memory. Obama is the patent troll slayer" (Kravets, 2014). Senator Patrick Leahy (D-Vermont) has also been a champion of inhibiting the power and influence of patent trolls, and has said: "The United States patent system is vital for our economic growth, job creation, and technological advancement. Unfortunately, misuse of low-quality patents through patent trolling has tarnished the system's image."

In the meantime, corporate heads like Robert Donat of GPS Insight will continue to expect the periodic lawsuit from patent trolls. According to Donat, any technology company making revenue north of $10 million per year can expect to become a target of patent trolls.

However, Donat points out that patent trolls are not all bad. Some, he explains, effectively play the role of "Robin Hood," to help smaller companies from being driven out of business by larger corporations.

In battling patent trolls in court, Donat explains that fighting to win in court usually isn't financially viable. In his words, "You might fight it out tooth and nail in court and eventually win, but if it costs you a million dollars in legal fees, and you help your competition avoid that troll in the meantime, it just isn't worth it." As a result, Donat says the most financially responsible course of action involves moving through the legal process as slowly as possible, paying them off as little as possible, and chalking it up to a pseudo "tax" you simply have to put up with if you are going to be in business in the technological industry. While GPS Insight's patent wars have been minimal enough to not require a set-aside legal budget for future battles, such legal budgeting is not uncommon among large corporations, especially technology-based corporations.

Despite the angst, stress, and cost of patent trolls, Robert Donat is sitting in the "catbird seat" these days as he continues to watch the company he built become increasingly successful by providing valuable service to clients. Through visionary customer service, courageous entrepreneurial risk-taking, and an endless supply of discipline, diligence, and hard work, GPS Insight has made an impressive mark on their industry, and has a bright future.

Critical Thinking Questions

1. Robert Donat is an effective example of leveraging the financial damage that patent trolls can incur in a business. How might you apply what you learned from Robert's experience to the development, design, and patenting of your own products and services in the future?

2. What kinds of preventive actions can you take to avoid legal mistakes and other common IP traps that typically ensnare startups?

3. In what ways do your entrepreneurial ideas involve the development of intellectual property and/or patents? What legal considerations will you need to take into account in the pursuit of your business-building objectives?

Sources

2014 EY Finalist. *Short interview with Robert Donat.* Retrieved from https://www.youtube.com/watch?v=aO_wOAwiBTk

GPS Insight website: Retrieved from www.gpsinsight.com

GPSInsight.com. *Short interview with Robert Donat.* Retrieved from http://www.gpsinsight.com/fleet-tracking/the-gps-insight-difference

Kravets, D. (2014, March 20). *History will remember Obama as the great slayer of patent trolls.* Wired.com. Retrieved from http://www.wired.com/2014/03/obama-legacy-patent-trolls/

Moore, P. (2014, June 27). Robert Donat has GPS Insight going in the right direction. *Denver Business Journal.* Retrieved from http://www.bizjournals.com/denver/print-edition/2014/06/27/robert-donat-has-gps-insight-going-in-the-right.html?page=all

Robert Donat: The Road to Success for a Growing Technology Company. Interview with Robert Donat. Golden Bridge Awards. Retrieved from http://www.goldenbridgeawards.com/people/Robert-Donat.html

Wyatt, E. (2013, June 5). Obama orders regulators to root out "patent trolls." *The New York Times.* Retrieved from http://www.nytimes.com/2013/06/05/business/president-moves-to-curb-patent-suits.html?_r=0

7

—10

12

16

Marketing and Pitching Your Idea

The purpose of a pitch is to stimulate interest, not to close a deal."

—Guy Kawasaki, author and entrepreneur

Learning Objectives

Chapter Outline

16.1 THE ROLE OF MARKETING AND PITCHING IN ENTREPRENEURSHIP

>> **LO 16.1** Discuss the role of marketing and pitching in entrepreneurship.

Throughout this book we have shown how to find new ideas and opportunities, test and experiment, build sound business models, find the best way to plan for your venture, source investors, build networks, and think about different ways to fund your business. By now you are likely to have one or more ideas for a product or service that is needed by particular customer segments. Now it's time to think about your pitch to customers, to investors, to employees, and other stakeholders who can play a role in the development and growth of your idea or business. All the knowledge and experience you have gained up to this point leads to one thing: the pitch.

Typically, a **pitch** is the act of clearly presenting and describing a product or service to others. The purpose of the pitch is not to make your audience immediately fall in love with your idea, but to present something so captivating that it starts a discussion that grows toward a favorable outcome. In Chapter 9 we described the different types of plans used by entrepreneurs, which included a pitch deck—a brief slide presentation highlighting many of the essential elements found in a feasibility study and a business plan. In this chapter, we focus more on *how* to pitch than *what* to pitch (see Appendix B: The Pitch Deck).

Andrew Loos credits his network for his success in pitching his marketing agency Attack! to other marketing agencies and brands. Entrepreneurs might also pitch to prospective investors for funding, or to people they want to hire or partner with.

However, it is important to keep in mind that the pitch is a package, not simply a presentation. Your pitch package determines how the world sees you, your team, your idea, and your company. In order to be "pitch ready" you need to spend time crafting the pitch based on all the knowledge you have gained so far, as well as designing the impression you want to make on others.

Video
Basics of the Pitch

Pitch: the act of clearly presenting and describing a product or service to others.

Andrew Loos, Managing Partner and Cofounder, Attack! Marketing

Andrew Loos, cofounder of Attack! Marketing
Credit: Used with permission from Andrew Loos

Andrew Loos cofounded Attack! Marketing in 2001. Attack! is a marketing agency that provides experiential strategy and activation to lifestyle brands. It has locations in New York, Los Angeles, and San Francisco, and employs between 40 and 60 people in-house, with a contractor network of over 80,000 across the United States and Canada.

Before cofounding Attack!, Loos took on a number of freelance roles with marketing agencies all over the country to run regional promotional marketing campaigns to support himself until he could fulfil his dreams in the film industry. However, during his experience as a freelance marketer, he noticed something that would send him down a very different career path:

> [A]gencies and brands were spending millions of dollars on the concept of the campaign—the giveaways, the data collection, the logistics, etcetera, yet neglecting to engage the consumer in a proper way. It was my observation, at the time, that if a customer was encouraged by the right brand ambassadors to try something new—taste, touch, smell—then they would be on the right path to falling in love with the brand, and remaining loyal to it. Yet these campaigns were being led by people that the consumer was unable to relate to. They were missing the human element.

Having witnessed fitness promotions led by visibly unfit people, and teen modeling promotions spearheaded by people in their late 30s or early 40s, Loos decided it was time to act. With a good business partner, Loos cofounded Attack! with the vision of revolutionizing the consumer experience during live marketing events. He began to pitch to contacts he had made at the agencies, and this is what he told them: "Each campaign needs to be represented by somebody they can relate to; someone who can draw in consumers. These are people who look like your brand, who use your brand, and who already love your brand. They are the ones that will appeal to your targetmarket in the field."

Loos was also able to show that by neglecting the human element, agencies were suffering financially because of low trial rates and low conversion numbers. In other words, they weren't getting enough customers to justify the marketing dollars spent. They were losing money! With his approach, the agencies saw a significant increase in the number of people who tried out their products and services, and more conversions. Loos created a new approach in consumer marketing—his own unique human approach.

Loos did not write a formal business plan to sell his concept to agencies. His ideas were based on his observations while he was working in the marketing field. Furthermore, he had a good enough relationship with agency people to pitch certain concepts to them, experiment with ideas, and test out new technology that helped connect ambassadors to campaigns involving brands they already loved and consumed.

Eventually, Attack! started to take on services that the agencies no longer wanted to do in-house such as staffing, scheduling, logistics, and a huge range of reporting. In addition to being a provider of staffing and logistics for agencies, Attack! has also evolved into a strategic partner to brands, using creative concepts and consumer analysis to better understand the brand and its target market.

Loos says he owes a lot of his success to the relationships he has built up over the years and believes that the "network is key," especially when it is based on trust and honesty. He also confesses that he had a few hiccups in the early days of starting a business. "We never wanted to say 'no' to a client in case they never came back to us again, so we would say 'yes' to duties that we could not fulfil. We fell flat on our face a couple of times until we learned that saying 'no' is better than faking it and letting the client down. We needed to stick to what we were good at and that's what we did."

And his advice for aspiring entrepreneurs who are just starting out? "Test the marketplace. Don't just create a service or product that your family or friends think is special. Assess your competition, the viability of the idea, and the cost. The key is experimentation—stay in the lab a little longer. [And] don't do it all by yourself. Find business partners that can inspire you, motivate you, and support you while you're building a business."

2. **If you are just starting out, how can you create a network of contacts to pitch to?**

3. **Do you agree with Loos that it's better to say "no" than to "fake it 'til you make it"? Why or why not?** ●

Source: Personal Interview, A. Loos, September 15, 2014.

CRITICAL THINKING QUESTIONS

1. **How did Andrew Loos get buy-in from his agency contacts? What made his pitch attractive to them?**

However well you think you know your product or service, you will not be in a position to pitch it properly until you have explored it from a strategic marketing perspective. The success of a new venture ultimately depends on how well it competes in the marketplace, so marketing is a significant part of launching any new venture.

Marketing is a method of putting the right product in the right place, at the right price, at the right time. Marketing for entrepreneurs involves showing how a product meets customer needs, pricing the products in a way that accurately represents the value perceived by the customer, promoting products in innovative ways to reach customers, implementing delivery of the products, and maintaining the relationship with the customer even after the sale is made.[1]

Getting all these elements to balance is tricky. It requires a lot of research and commitment to ensure your product is line with your marketing vision. This is why it helps to use an established marketing framework to help develop your marketing strategy.

16.2 THE BASIC PRINCIPLES OF MARKETING[2]

>> **LO 16.2** **Explain the principles of marketing and how they apply to new ventures.**

In traditional marketing, companies develop the **marketing mix**—a framework that helps define the brand and differentiate it from the competition. This framework helps companies with crystallizing their offering and how they intend to take it to market.

Traditionally, the marketing mix is made up of four main elements, known as the 4 Ps: product, price, promotion, and place (see Figure 16.1). It is important to be familiar with the 4 Ps, as they are still relevant to entrepreneurs with limited resources. Each of the 4 Ps needs to be considered in relation to each other, in order to build the best overall marketing strategy of your offering.

The **product** describes anything tangible or intangible (such as a service) offered by the company. This includes the features, the brand, how it meets customer needs, how and where it will be used, and how it stands out from competitors.

$SAGE edge™

Master the content
edge.sagepub.com/
neckentrepreneurship

Marketing: a method of putting the right product in the right place, at the right price, at the right time.

Marketing mix: a tool that helps to define the brand and how it differentiates from the competition.

Product: anything tangible or intangible (such as a service) offered by the company that includes the features, the brand, how it meets customer needs, how and where it will be used, and how it stands out from competitors.

FIGURE 16.1

Elements of the Marketing Mix

A good way of assessing your product is to try and look at it objectively—as if you were someone seeing it for the first time. Then ask yourself some critical questions, such as, "Is this product or service suitable for my target market?" and "Is this something today's customers will want or need?" or "How can I market this product better than my competitors?" By repeatedly asking these questions, you will have a better understanding of your product or service and how it fits into the marketplace.

The **price** covers the amount that the customer is expected to pay for the product, its perceived value, and the degree to which the price can be raised or lowered depending on market demand and how competitors price rival products. Again, get into the habit of continually examining the pricing structure of your products and services to ensure it is appropriate for your target market. Depending on changes in the market, you may need to raise or lower your price. Make a point of frequently examining competitors pricing in order to price your products accordingly.

The third element of the marketing mix is **promotion:** all the ways in which companies tell their customers about their offering. This may involve advertising online, through social networking, direct mail, in the press, or even on TV if you have the budget. It also includes public relations such as being featured in blogs, newspapers, magazines—all free aspects of promotion. Both large and small companies need to continually experiment with finding ways to promote their products and services in order to find out what works and what doesn't. Whatever promotional tactic might work one day, may not work the next, so continuous development of new strategies is essential to retaining and increasing your target customer base.

Finally, **place** describes the location where the product is actually distributed to your target market: trade fairs, retail stores, catalogs, mail order, online, and so forth. You can always revisit where you sell your product. For example, if you're selling retail products, you might start off selling online and then also decide to rent a retail space in order to make your company more visible to your target market. Ask yourself where else you could sell your products, and what changes you need to make in order to reach your target market. Wherever you choose to sell, it is essential that

Price: the amount that the customer is expected to pay for the product, its perceived value, and the degree to which the price can be raised or lowered depending on market demand and how competitors price rival products.

Promotion: the activities that involve all the ways in which companies tell their customers about their offering.

Place: the location where the product is actually distributed to your target market; for example, trade fairs, retail stores, catalogs, mail order, online, and so forth.

your customers receive the best buying information on your product or service to help them make a buying decision.

Any pitch requires a discussion of who the customer is and how you are going to reach them; therefore, it is a good idea to use the 4 Ps framework to evaluate the strength and completeness of your marketing approach. Important questions can be answered using the 4 Ps framework:

Video
Marketing Principles

- What are the benefits and features of my product? (Product)
- What is the value of my offering, and what are customers willing to pay? (Price)
- How will they know my business exists? (Promotion)
- How will the customers be reached? Where will they buy my product or service? (Place)

The marketing mix is constantly changing; you don't simply develop it and move on. By continually reviewing and tweaking your marketing mix, you will be better able to adjust to an ever-changing competitive environment.

While the 4 Ps model is arguably the most recognized, newer marketing models have been developed to enhance the traditional model. Some of them extend the 4 Ps to 7 Ps, including **people,** which refers to the people responsible for every aspect of sales and marketing; **packaging,** which is a process that explores every single visual element of the external appearance of an offering through the eyes of your customer; and **positioning,** which is a marketing strategy that focuses on how customers think or talk about product and a company relative to competitors.[3]

People are an important part of the marketing mix and the marketing strategy. They are responsible for enforcing every aspect of your sales and marketing activities. Hiring the right people with the right skills and abilities to market your products effectively is at the core of any marketing strategy. Often in the early days of a startup the entrepreneur is wearing many hats and is playing the role of chief marketing officer and salesperson.

It is also important to objectively assess the visual element of the packaging of your product or service. Remember, your packaging represents you and your company, and first impressions count. Always be prepared to adjust elements of your packaging to encourage potential buyers to buy your product. Packaging is also an important part of branding, which we will discuss in the next section.

Positioning is something that should be at the forefront of every entrepreneur's mind. What are people saying about you, your company, and your product when you're not present? What are the words that people use about you to describe you and your offerings to other people? Knowing what other people think of you and your product determines the extent to which they will buy from you, and how much they are willing to pay. Be vigilant in monitoring what other people think about you, especially on social media, and be sure to make the changes you need to enhance interaction with your target customer because positioning is at the heart of branding.

Branding

Branding is the process of creating a name, term, design, symbol, or any other feature that identifies a product or service and differentiates it from others. Your brand is a promise to your customers, letting them know what they can expect from your offering and how it differentiates you among your competitors. The face of your brand is your logo, which should also be integrated into your website, packaging, and promotional materials to communicate your brand message.

People: the people who are responsible for every aspect of sales and marketing.

Packaging: a process that explores every single visual element of the external appearance of an offering through the eyes of your customer.

Positioning: a marketing strategy that focuses on how your customers think or talk about product and a company relative to competitors.

Branding: the process of creating a name, term, design, symbol, or any other feature that identifies a product or service and differentiates it from others.

A **brand strategy** is a long-term plan to develop a successful brand. It involves how you plan to communicate your brand messages to your target customers. This brand message can be channeled through your advertising, distribution, and packaging.

Two of the most classic and powerful brands include Coca-Cola, which has managed to differentiate itself from other sodas through its consistent strategic branding; and Nike, which involves famous athletes as part of its branding strategy, encouraging people to buy its products through the transfer of the emotional attachment they may feel for these star athletes. Over the years, both of these brands have evolved their branding strategies to appeal to generations of customers. See Figure 16.2 for the world's ten most powerful brands.

While there isn't one "right" way to guarantee brand success, you can start by defining the brand you would like for your company by answering the following questions:

> ▸ What is the primary goal of your company?
>
> ▸ What are the best features and benefits of your products or services?
>
> ▸ What are your customers and prospective clients already saying about you and your company?
>
> ▸ What sorts of qualities do you want them to associate with your company?

Your responses will help you to create a brand name that resonates with your target customers.

Alexandra Watkins, founder of San Francisco-based Eat my Words, a company that specializes in creating catchy brand names, believes that brand names should

Brand strategy: a long-term plan to develop a successful brand; it involves how you plan to communicate your brand messages to your target customers.

FIGURE 16.2

Top 10 Most Powerful Brands in the World

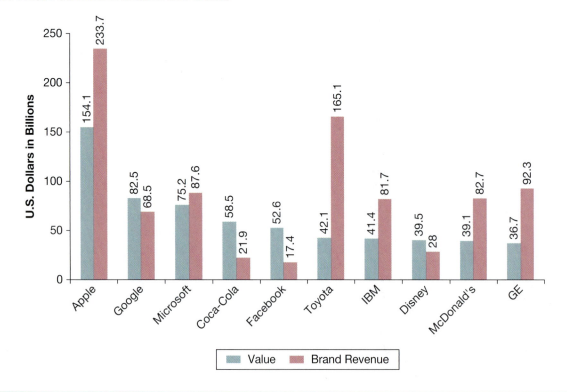

Source: Forbes. (2016). The World's Most Valuable Brands. Retrieved September 19, 2016, from http://www.forbes.com/powerful-brands/list/#tab:rank

make people smile rather than scratch their heads. On this basis, she devised the Eat My Words® SMILE and SCRATCH Test™ (see Table 16.1)—a fun way to test your company or product name to see if you should keep it or scratch it off the list. Some of the names Watkins claims have passed the Test include SPOON ME for a chain of frozen yogurt stores; BLOOM, a natural energy drink for women; and NEATO for a home-cleaning robot.

A successful brand all starts with a name. It could be a family name, which can add credibility to the business, or an obscure name that has nothing to do with the actual product. For example, the Starbucks logo has incredible brand recognition around the world but it has no relationship to coffee whatsoever, yet its name is unique and memorable. Or you could go with an edgy name like Go Daddy—a domain registration and website hosting company—which, through its unusual name and unique logo of a man in sunglasses, has managed to capture over 50% of the US market of new domain names. Bob Parsons, Go Daddy's founder and CEO, believes that Go Daddy's edgy branding strategy is key to brand recognition and success, especially when enhanced with its provocative advertising featuring "Go Daddy Girls" dressed in tight white tank tops. Parsons says, "The edgier the brand is, the better it works. The point is to keep it fun." Whatever name you choose, make sure it passes the Smile test first.[4]

Some experts believe that a strong brand can be created by just using one word—a concept first introduced by marketing professional and author, Al Ries, who believed it made the brand easier for consumers to remember. Many top companies such as Google, Salesforce, Uber, and Hubspot have adopted this approach.[5] The key to defining your brand is knowing what your customers think of you and acting on that knowledge to build a successful brand. Following are some steps to building a brand in a systematic way.[6]

Design a logo. Your logo is the gateway to your overall brand image. It triggers people's emotions and perception of the brand and answers questions such as: Who are you? What do you do? and What's in it for me? When designing a logo, make sure it shows up well in different types of media, its design and message are clear, and it is

TABLE 16.1

Eat My Words® SMILE and SCRATCH Test™

SMILE, the qualities of a powerful name:
Simple—one, easy-to-understand concept **M**eaningful—your customers instantly "get it" **I**magery—visually evocative, creates a mental picture **L**egs—carries the brand, lends itself to wordplay **E**motional—empowers, entertains, engages, enlightens
SCRATCH it off the list if it has any of these deal-breakers:
Spelling-challenged—you have to tell people how to spell it **C**opycat—similar to competitor's names **R**andom—disconnected from the brand **A**nnoying—hidden meaning, forced **T**ame—flat, uninspired, boring, nonemotional **C**urse of Knowledge—only insiders get it **H**ard-to-pronounce—not obvious, relies on punctuation

Domain registration and web hosting company GoDaddy uses edgy branding to make the company more memorable.

Credit: NetPhotos/Alamy Stock Photos

instantly recognizable. Put your logo everywhere you can—on your company website, social media, packaging, email signature, and all written communication.

Spread the word. Get your brand out into the world. Social media is a great way for cash-strapped entrepreneurs to spread the word about their brand. Keep track of your online followers, and listen to what they have to say about your brand. Engage with your followers, be responsive to their needs, and reward them for following your brand.

Know your customer. Knowing what your customer wants is key to building a successful brand. In order to achieve brand success, you need to know how your brand is perceived—who loves it, who hates it, and who would recommend it—what would make it stronger, how customers feel about competitor brands, and the extent to which customers will emotionally connect with your brand. You can find out this information through surveys and by keeping an eye on your followers and observing how they behave over a certain time period.

Become your brand. Incorporate your brand into every aspect of your business. In an office environment, this includes how you greet people over the phone and what you and your employees wear. For example, if your aim is to promote sophistication through your brand, then you may want your employees to choose a polite yet formal manner over the phone, and to dress smartly.

Write a tagline. While can be difficult to capture the essence of brand in one succinct statement, a tagline is important for communicating your brand message. Keep your tagline short, simple, clear, and memorable. (See Figure 16.3 for the world's catchiest taglines.)

Always deliver on your brand promise. Customers are more likely to buy into your brand if it consistently meets and exceeds their expectations.

Be consistent with your brand. While it is possible to tweak a logo or a tagline, make sure you always retain the brand voice and deliver on your brand promise.

FIGURE 16.3

The World's Catchiest Taglines

Nike	Just Do It
Apple	Think Different
McDonald's	I'm Loving It
Verizon	Can You Hear Me Now? Good.
L'Oréal	Because You're Worth It
California Milk Processor Board	Got Milk?
M&Ms	Melts in Your Mouth, Not in Your Hand
Lay's	Betcha Can't Eat Just One
Meow Mix	Tastes So Good, Cats Ask For It By Name
The New York Times	All the News That's Fit to Print

Reframing the 4 Ps[7]

A five-year study conducted by Harvard Business School, involving 500 managers and customers across numerous countries, presented the argument that because of the new relationships businesses have with customers, the traditional 4 Ps model is narrow and outdated and is not strictly relevant in a modern business environment.

According to this research, the 4 Ps model over emphasizes product technology and quality, understates the necessity of explaining the value of the product and why customers need it, and distracts businesses from promoting themselves as important sources of information and problem solving. Researchers believe that a solutions-focused approach is needed when it comes to marketing products. Today's customers have far more input into the business–customer relationship, which necessitates a new framework that better reflects what the customer wants and cares about.

The study inspired the S.A.V.E framework—Solution, Access, Value, Education—which reinterprets the 4 Ps model by transferring the emphasis from *products* to solutions, *place* to access, *price* to value, and *promotion* to education (see Figure 16.4). Let's examine these factors one-by-one.

Solution rather than product: researchers argue that businesses tend to get caught up in the features and functions of their product, when all customers really want to know is how the product solves their problems. S.A.V.E. advocates marketing a product based on how it meets customer needs, rather than emphasizing its features.

Access rather than place: here, the focus is on how accessible your company is to your target customer. The exact location where someone can purchase your product is not so important. This approach considers the customer's journey from where they first hear of your company to actually making the purchase. Customers want to see that businesses care about customer feedback, and are available if they need advice and support.

Value over price: customers are drawn to value more than to price. This means that entrepreneurs need to build a strong case for showing customers why their product offers superior value to the competition, rather than focusing on the actual price tag.

Web
Products as Solutions

FIGURE 16.4

The S.A.V.E. Framework

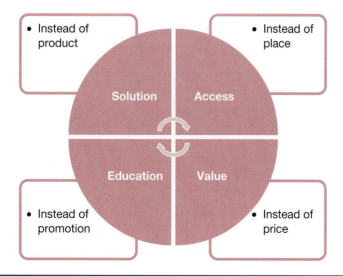

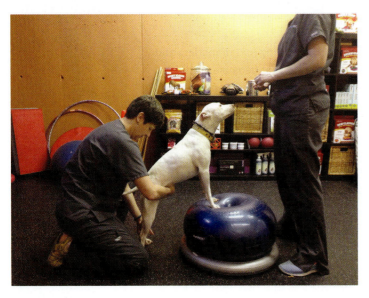

FlowDog - physical therapy for dogs.

Credit: Used with permission from FlowDog

Education rather than promotion: today's businesses are in a good position to educate customers by providing information that they want to read that is up to date and relevant. This helps to build a relationship of familiarity and trust before a purchase is even made.

Figure 16.5 compares how the message of FlowDog, a Boston-based physical therapy facility for dogs, is influenced according to the 4 Ps on one hand, and the S.A.V.E. model on the other.

Regardless of how many marketing models there are out there, the lesson is to take a broad approach to encompass all the elements that are relevant to your business. Then, test them, tweak them, and adjust them where needed.

In this section, we have described the traditional marketing approaches used predominantly by larger companies. However, new ventures have to think a bit more creatively to get noticed.

FIGURE 16.5

FlowDog: The 4 Ps versus S.A.V.E.

4 Ps	S.A.V.E.
Product FlowDog provides the following: • Physical therapy for orthopedic and neurological conditions • Hydrotherapy for therapeutic swimming in a pool heated 84-89 degrees Fahrenheit. • Fitness swimming for weight loss, weight management and cross training • Massage to increase blood flow and relieve muscle tension • Reiki for stress reduction • Acupuncture for pain and tension relief • Physical therapy products to supplement service (e.g., special harnesses, toys to improve cognition)	**Solution** FlowDog brings peace of mind to the dog owner by providing an array of therapeutic services for a complete solution that increases the quality of life of postsurgical, injured, and aging dogs. By providing hands-on treatment, owner education, and products to use at home, FlowDog gives dogs every opportunity to fully recover, prevent injury, and even prolong life.
Place FlowDog is located in Waltham, MA. The facility is located in an office park area and is zoned for a dog-related business. There is ample parking.	**Access** FlowDog is conveniently located to dog owners in both Boston and the surround for suburbs. With strong relationships with Boston-area vets, customers are often referred to FlowDog by their primary veterin or specialty/surgical hospital.
Price An initial evaluation for physical therapy is $185/hour and follow-up appointments are $110. Other treatments (massage, reiki, acupuncture) range in price from $40 to $80. FlowDog rates are competitive with other facilities in the Boston area.	**Value** Physical therapy reduces recovery time after surgery and reduces prolonged medication usage. It is often used as an alternative to surgery or as a way of preventing surgery. On average, dog owners can expect to pay $2,500 to $3,500 for a common knee surgery such as an ACL tear. Overall, FlowDog's focus is on prolonging the dog's life.
Promotion FlowDog advertises in local dog newsletters, vet offices, and online. The company uses Facebook to communicate with customers about upcoming events.	**Education** The FlowDog website offers case studies of dogs who have recovered from or better managed various medical conditions such as arthritis, cruciate tears, and spinal injuries. Because each dog is unique, a special treatment plan is created after the initial evaluation that meets the needs of both dog and owner.

16.3 ENTREPRENEURIAL MARKETING

>> **LO 16.3**   **Compare entrepreneurial marketing with traditional marketing.**

Because entrepreneurship is more accessible than ever—meaning it's easier than ever to start but not necessarily run a business—the need for a more entrepreneurial approach to marketing is paramount. Sometimes traditional marketing just isn't enough (or even too much) for the startup. Keep in mind that even though it's easy to start a business, it's still very hard to keep it going. Paying extra attention to the marketing side of your business will help you increase the odds of success.

The main challenge facing a young company is the ability to compete against bigger, better known, more established companies that have not only the marketing resources to promote their offering on a much grander scale, but also the name recognition. How can a startup with a skeleton staff, no history, hardly any resources, zero brand awareness, no graphic design team or advertising consultants, and very little budget hope to compete against these bigger companies?

The good news is that today's entrepreneurs don't need millions of dollars to make an impact. Many new ventures have stormed the marketplace on a shoestring marketing budget. Facebook, Twitter, Instagram, Uber, Craigslist, and Zipcar are only a few relatively recent companies to have gained millions of customers in a short period of time, with very little marketing budget.[8] None of these companies went down the traditional advertising route: they had no billboards, no TV or radio advertising campaigns, no big budget for advertising in newspapers and magazines.

Video
Why Entrepreneurial
Marketing

Traditional Marketing Versus Entrepreneurial Marketing

The new ventures we have just mentioned used **entrepreneurial marketing,** which is a set of processes adopted by entrepreneurs based on new and unconventional marketing practices in order to gain traction and attention in competitive markets.[9]

Unlike traditional marketing, which is mostly centered on the product and how it can make money, in entrepreneurial marketing entrepreneurs adopt an interactive marketing approach with their customers. They set up a dialogue and build long-term relationships with them, adapting the business to meet customer needs. These personal interactions are further enhanced by word of mouth and recommendations. Table 16.2 explains the differences between traditional marketing and entrepreneurial marketing.

Entrepreneurial marketing: a set of processes adopted by entrepreneurs based on new and unconventional marketing practices in order to gain traction in competitive markets.

Features of Entrepreneurial Marketing

Innovation, risk taking, resourcefulness, value creation, and proactivity are some of the main features of entrepreneurial marketing. It focuses on building trust, finding out customer preferences, and creating long-term competitive advantage. It also provides the entrepreneur with the opportunity to highlight the company's strengths while showcasing the different ways the product adds value.

Entrepreneurial marketing involves the creative use of affordable, innovative, and easy-to-use marketing tools such as viral videos, social media (Twitter, Facebook, etc.) and mass emailing to grab the attention of the customer. Just as we talked about bootstrapping in Chapter 12, entrepreneurial marketing is also part of an entrepreneur's bootstrap strategy. These tools can be a very effective way of

TABLE 16.2

Traditional Marketing Versus Entrepreneurial Marketing

TRADITIONAL MARKETING	ENTREPRENEURIAL MARKETING
• Big cash investment • Main focus is on the product • Goal is to maximize profit • Short-term relationship with customer • Delivers marketing message as a monologue	• Investment of time, energy, creativity, commitment. • Main focus is on the customer. • Goal is to meet and satisfy customer needs. • Long-term interactive relationship with customer • Delivers marketing message as a dialogue

showing how your business stands out from the crowd. For example, Zappos was one of the first companies to use social media as its main marketing strategy. Zappos was able to attract a large customer base very quickly by emphasizing free, easy returns on shoe purchases and excellent customer service.[10]

Entrepreneurial marketing tools are not just reserved for entrepreneurs; more and more large, established companies are using the same tools in different ways to draw attention to their products. While these industry giants may have a bigger budget and enormous resources, that should not stop new entrepreneurs from waging their own successful campaigns. Entrepreneurial marketing tools level the playing field: with a bit of knowledge, imagination, and ingenuity entrepreneurs can make their products and services be heard and seen in very noisy marketplaces. Let's take a look at how some companies their products and services be heard and seen in very noisy marketplaces.

Guerrilla Marketing

Guerilla marketing:
a low-budget strategy that focuses on personally interacting with a target group by promoting their products and services be heard and seen in very noisy marketplaces.

One form of entrepreneurial marketing is **guerrilla marketing,** which is a low-budget strategy that focuses on personally interacting with a target group by promoting products and services through surprise or other unconventional means. A successful guerrilla marketing campaign enhances the customer's perception of value, inspires word of mouth, and increases sales.

Guerrilla marketing strategies are almost limitless: email, interactive poster campaigns, advertisements on cars, T-shirts, street branding (writing marketing messages with paint or chalk on pavements or walls), characters in costume, flashmobs (where a large group of people seemingly come out of nowhere to perform an act in a public place), projecting images/videos/messages in public areas through laser or beamer, and even YouTube videos that can go viral in minutes.

When guerilla campaigns go viral, they can reach a huge audience. For example, to heighten awareness of its company, Ontario-based Alphabet Photography posted a flashmob video on YouTube called "Christmas Food Court Flash Mob, Hallelujah Chorus." It shows a group of talented performers bursting into song, and lots of surprised reactions from unsuspecting onlookers. Since being posted in 2010, the video has received over 45 million views, which made it the most watched flashmob video on YouTube.

Example of an interactive ad campaign for King Solomon's Casino.
Credit: mark peterson/Corbis Historical/Getty Images

There is even a guerilla marketing technique called snow branding, which involves making imprints of the product's name and brand during the night on snow-covered pavements, walls, cars and the like.[11] When people emerge the next morning, they are surprised by these novel images that are aimed to create a good feeling, a sense of awareness, and a positive memory of the company's brand.

Guerilla marketing strategies are also used by major companies. In an effort to boost its digital platform, Coca-Cola famously filmed what happened when they put "the happiness machine" on a college campus—a vending machine that gives out seemingly endless cans of Coca-Cola, plus a few more surprise gifts such as bunches of flowers, balloon animals, pizzas, and giant sandwiches. Coca-Cola successfully managed to create a connection with the audience—not through giving away free stuff, but by giving them a "dose of happiness" that they would share with their friends.[12]

While guerrilla marketing can be a creative and affordable way to reach your desired target market, it has its limitations. In order to conduct a successful Guerrilla campaign, you need to have a good understanding of your target market and where the high traffic exists; for example, subway, mall, university campus, and so on. You also need to get the timing right: should you conduct the campaign during business hours, at weekends, or morning, or night?

Guerrilla marketing can also be difficult to measure: how do you know the good feeling or memory you're giving your customer is going to translate into sales? Monitoring the media (newspapers, radio) for mentions of your campaign, and taking the time to scout blogs, forums, and social networks to see who is talking about your company and your product is a good start in measuring the campaign's impact on sales.

Finally, you need to have a good sense of the community and any legal, social, or moral restrictions that may cause a negative reaction to a campaign. Rich Tu, founder of the event management app Pozzle, found this out the hard way. After plastering New York City with hundreds of stickers bearing his company's logo, Tu was arrested, jailed for 24 hours, and sentenced to perform 21 hours of community service.[13]

Planning a guerrilla marketing campaign requires commitment, creativity, consistency, patience, and a true understanding of your target market. Getting it right could have big payoffs. What's more, many Guerrilla efforts can be done quite inexpensively, so what do you have to lose? Take action, test, and see what works with your customer base.

Video
Guerilla Marketing

Example of street branding
Credit: Ethan Miller/Getty Images News/Getty Images

16.4 MARKETING THROUGH SOCIAL MEDIA

>> LO 16.4   **Assess the value of social media for marketing opportunities.**

Video
Social Media for Marketing

Social media has become an essential business tool for entrepreneurs to market their products and services and themselves. When used properly, social media can launch businesses into new levels of success. For example, Rachel Mielke, owner of Canadian-based jewelry company Hillberg & Berk, saw a 2,000% increase in sales over the course of four years, thanks to marketing her business on Facebook and Twitter.[14]

Robert Herjavec, Shark Tank investor and founder of BRAK Systems

Credit: Monica Schipper/Getty Images Entertainment/Getty Images

Social media is also a valuable way of following market trends, finding new employees, and building and maintaining relationships with customers. It is the most powerful way of spreading word of mouth about your products and services. This is why it is so important for entrepreneurs to create their own social media strategy. Table 16.3 lists some of the most popular forms of social media.

Social media is also a useful way to find potential stakeholders. Social media sites like Twitter, LinkedIn, Facebook, Instagram, and YouTube all provide ways to connect with people who are experts in the field, or fellow entrepreneurs—anyone who can potentially help you develop, build, and grow your venture. Some of these people may become self-selected stakeholders or may even become part of your founding team.

Robert Herjavec, a Shark Tank investor and the founder of Toronto-based Internet security firm BRAK Systems, believes that social media is essential for attracting customers to products and services. As an example, Herjavec points to one of the startups he invests in called The Natural Grip, maker of gloves for people who do gymnastics and weightlifting. By finding out where these athletes like to "hang out" on Facebook, the company was able to engage with them and gain a mass of new customers.[18]

Getting the Most From Social Media

Anyone can engage in social media, but it takes a smart, dedicated entrepreneur to use social media wisely and productively. The most successful social media strategies start with solid research. Take a look at how your competitors use social media. What kind of content do they share with their customers and followers? What sort of language do they use to engage their followers? It also helps to read blogs and join discussions about subjects that are relevant to your business. Contributing to conversations helps you learn more about what is important to your customers, and helps to boost your profile and showcase your knowledge about a particular area.

After conducting your research, think about the goals you would like to achieve. Do you want your social media presence to attract customers, increase recognition of your brand, or both? Many companies use social media to provide efficient customer service; for example, online food ordering company Seamless provides round-the-clock customer service on Twitter, and low-cost airline JetBlue tweets if there are airline delays and responds quickly to tweets from frustrated passengers.

Next, think about ways in which you can measure your online presence. For example, you can catalog the number of visits to your site, the number of followers, the types of comments people make about your business, and who they share them with. It also helps to design your strategy around your target audience—how do you engage them? What media platforms do they use the most? Choose one or two social media sites to begin with that fit in with your industry and your target market.

Once you have launched your social media campaign, make sure you post regular updates. Followers will expect to see quick messages on Twitter several times a day, and longer blog posts or articles on Facebook at least a couple of times a

TABLE 16. 3

Popular Forms of Social Media

Facebook
• Over 1 billion active users.
• Easier to create and maintain than a website.
• Tools that support interaction with customers.
• Helps foster a loyal following.
• Provides access to a huge audience when messages spread through networks.
Instagram (owned by Facebook)
• Over 400 million active users.
• Photo, videosharing, and social network site.
• Visual marketing tool that engages followers through high quality, innovative images and video footage.[15]
Twitter
• Over 320 million active users.[16]
• Third most popular search engine after Google and YouTube.
• Allows users to share information and build relationships.
• Supports instant interaction with potential customers.
YouTube
• Over 1 billion active users.[17]
• Most popular site after Google and Facebook.
• Easy and inexpensive way to engage customers.
• Showcases the human side of business and builds trust.
LinkedIn
• 100 million members.
• The biggest professional network in the world.
• Geared to professional rather than social networking.
• Tools that help to create a network of business contacts.
• Access to discussion groups that help boost profile and showcase your expertise.
Blogs
• The oldest form of social media.
• Companies with blogs get 55% more web traffic and 126% higher sales lead growth than those that don't.

Source: Business Development Bank of Canada. *Social media: A guide for entrepreneurs* (p. 4). (2012, October). Retrieved from http://trenval.on.ca/wp-content/uploads/2015/03/SMeBook_2012_EN.pdf

week. Be vigilant about monitoring your social media—every day, check for new followers, any feedback, questions, or complaints. Then make sure you address them all. In addition, check out who your new followers are and how many of them have retweeted your posts. Who has viewed your LinkedIn profile? How many people have viewed or subscribed to your YouTube channel? Also, keep a close watch on your competitor's sites—what are people saying about them? Is your business mentioned in customer reviews on their site?

Posting interesting content online on a regular basis is one of the best ways of getting feedback from your followers and growing your online community. If you are a confident public speaker, then videos are also a powerful way of building trust with potential customers by letting them get to know you before they buy from you. For example, Pierre Martell of Martell Home Builders posted a video on YouTube consisting of short interviews with contractors offering advice and renovation tips, and displayed his company banner in the background. He also promoted his business on Twitter and Facebook, which drove traffic to his business website. Thanks to his social media marketing efforts, Martell has seen a vast increase in sales and a reduced sales conversion time.[19]

Creating Content That Drives Sales

Whether you are using up-to-the-minute social media or traditional media such as magazines, newsletters, and other print collateral, the content matters. Let's take a closer look at how you can create interesting, engaging content online that ultimately translates into sales.

For many of us, the word *sales* evoke images of the pushy salesman using hard-sell tactics to pressure us into buying stuff we don't need. So, it's time to let go of that outdated image and realize that today, most of us spend 40% of our time at work "selling" in one way or another: persuading, influencing, and convincing others in ways that don't necessarily translate into an immediate purchase.[20] In this sense, we are all salespeople, whether we realize it or not.

Take enterprise software company Atlassian, for instance. Rather than sending out salespeople to knock on doors and convince other companies to buy from them, Atlassian provides a trial version of one of its products to be downloaded on its website. Some people who test the product then call the support team at Atlassian, who are there to answer questions and to provide more information. There are no traditional salespeople at Atlassian to pressure inquiring customers into long-term commitments; in fact, Atlassian does not have a sales team at all. Instead, inquiries turn into sales as a result of the support team helping to understand customer needs, showing them how to use the product, and providing them with helpful information.

Sales has evolved from using hard core sales techniques to a soft sell through content such as that provided by Atlassian: It is genuine and creative, adds value, and builds relationships. Social media is not about advertising your business or self-promotion. Instead, it aims to educate, inspire, and entertain people enough that they will grow to trust you and your brand. It is a way for your customers to get to know the human side of your business.

The key to good content is quality. If you can create content that is meaningful to your audience, they will share it through their own social networks—think tweets, retweets, likes, comments, reviews. It also helps to get in touch with people in a similar market who already have a large number of followers, and build a relationship with them. For example, if you have a product designed for mothers of young children, then you could get a list of the top mommy bloggers, send them the product and get them talking about it. All going well, the product will be picked up by a company that will have heard

A cyclist using GoPro to video the ride.

Credit: ©iStockphoto.com/ Paolo Cipriani

of it through your more high-profile mommy bloggers. Over time, they may even share some of your content with their audiences, which gives your business an even larger platform to promote itself. In return, you can share some of their content in order to develop a mutually beneficial relationship.

It is important to be available to your online community. Publishing content regularly through blogs, infographics, videos, tweets, and taking part in conversations is essential if you want to maintain a loyal following. Getting your users involved is an even better way of spreading the word about your company.

Take entrepreneur Nick Woodman, founder of high-definition action camera company GoPro. Woodman adopts user-generated visual content, which regularly goes viral, by inviting his customers to shoot videos of themselves skydiving, climbing, surfing, diving, skiing, and snowboarding. These videos allow viewers a glimpse into extreme sports that they may never have entered themselves. This type of content is a powerful and affordable way of spreading the word about GoPro, with the added value of providing visual stimulation and building customer loyalty to the brand.[21]

Your Website

However you choose to market your content, it is always important to build a decent platform that showcases you, your company, and your content. This is where a good quality website can make a real difference in attracting customers.

When you are marketing through social media, your website needs to stand out from the competition. Websites with crisp, clean designs with a clear description of your product or service, together with simple, uncluttered pages that flow well in relation to each other, tend to be the most successful. It is particularly important that your website be quick and easy to navigate on both a large computer screen and a mobile device. Recent studies show that smartphones are the most popular way to browse the Internet in the UK.[22]

Site builder tools like Squarespace and Webflow and content management systems like WordPress have made it easier for entrepreneurs on a tight budget to build their own sites. There is also the option of using professional web designers to build custom solutions if your startup is very much Internet-based, but

Example of a well-designed startup website (Evernote)

Credit: Mark Richardson / Alamy Stock Photo

this will be more expensive. Whatever method you choose, do seek guidance to ensure you are using the best possible search engine optimization. This is what enables people to find you online via Google or other search engines, so it is worth the investment. Because Google search results also take into account the amount of times websites are shared in social media, it is also important that your site includes links to your social media pages and vice versa, in order to boost Google search rankings.

Remember that the act of building a website will not encourage visitors to flock immediately to your site. Attracting an audience takes time and patience. It won't be perfect from the very start, but will evolve over time in line with industry fluctuations and the response you get from your audience. Table 16.4 illustrates ten tips to help you avoid mistakes in building your first website.

TABLE 16.4

Top 10 Tips for Building Your First Website

Inaccessibility	Make sure your website is available to everyone, including those with a disability. Can the size of the text be easily changed to cater to the visually impaired? Does your color scheme provide the right contrast between text and background design so the content can be easily viewed?
Difficult-to-find contact information	Some sites bury their contact information, which can be frustrating for people trying to get in touch. Easy-to-find contact information including a phone number and address is essential to new businesses, as it gives your site visitor the confidence that they are dealing with a genuine business, rather than a fraudulent one.
Overusing the "wow" factor	Flash can add pizzazz to your site but don't overdo it—not everyone has flash or even has enough bandwidth to support it. The same goes for graphics—use them sparingly as too many will slow down the functionality of your site. Similarly, don't go to town on audio and never let it play automatically—always let your visitors choose if they want to hear it or not.
Slow load times	We are an impatient bunch. A recent study by Akamai Technologies showed that on average, online shoppers will wait only 4 seconds for a website to load before doing their shopping elsewhere.[23] If your website is not loading within 4 seconds, then identify the elements that are slowing it down (Flash, large images, etc.) and remove them.
Not getting picked up by search engines	If you want to achieve higher rankings, you need to do at least the basics. These include a site map, concise and relevant content, use of standard mark-up tags that are recognized by search engines as well as meta tags such as keywords. Seek professional advice on this if you have the budget.
Long sections of text	A wall of text is difficult and frustrating to read online. Visitors want to see text in digestible chunks that they can scan quickly. To break up the text and to make it more user friendly, include subheads, bulleted lists, highlighted keywords, and short paragraphs—all written in jargon-free simple language.
Poor navigation	There is nothing more off-putting for online visitors than a disorganized, poorly structured site. The user experience should be as smooth as possible and populated by links and menus, all of which should work and should be frequently tested. Ask yourself how many clicks a visitor will need to access a piece of information on your site. Make their journey as easy and speedy you can.
Not monitoring your site	There is no excuse for not keeping an eye on your site. There are many free tools available. They provide valuable insights into the type of visitors that your site attracts, including factors such as where they come from, what content they read the most, and what links are the most popular.
Not updating your content	Don't be one of those people whose site displays outdated information, or creates blogs once in a blue moon. Frequently published fresh, new content is a way of building credibility with your audience.
Failing to link to social platforms	Your business will most likely have its own Facebook page, a Twitter and LinkedIn account, and maybe a Pinterest board. Visitors to your website should be able to move from your site to your social media presence as smoothly as possible, and vice versa. Connecting your social media to your website is essential to drive traffic to your site.

Source: Scocco, D. (n.d.). 43 Web design mistakes you should avoid. Retrieved from www.dailyblogtips.com

16.5 MARKETING YOURSELF

>> **LO 16.5**   **Practice how to make a good impression during your pitch.**

So far, we have focused on the role of marketing in entrepreneurship and the different ways of marketing new ventures through social media. In this section, we will explore one of the most fundamental parts of marketing your business—marketing you, the entrepreneur.

At the early stages of a new venture, you are marketing yourself just as much you are marketing a product, service, or company. Most investors will invest in you first and foremost, and not just in your idea. Investors will want to see that they can build a long-term relationship with you over a period of years and that you are capable of collaborating to build the business. This is why it is worth spending time figuring out how you're going to market yourself, and not just your company, before you pitch anything.

Research shows that people will unconsciously decide whether they like you or not within one tenth of a second. People decide in less than 90 seconds if they want to hear more about an idea or not, and it takes between 7 and 20 seconds to create a first impression.[24] So we have less than 20 seconds to make a good first impression and less than 90 seconds to engage our audience in our ideas. How you deliver your pitch really counts. How you even walk into the room matters!

Research shows that we have less than 20 seconds to make a good first impression.
Credit: ©iStockphoto.com/laflor

Researchers conducted an experiment that compared first impressions with assessments built over a period of months. They compared the ratings given to college professors by students at the end of the semester with ratings of the same professors given by another group of students based on three ten-second video clips, which they were shown before the lectures. The results showed that both groups of students had pretty much the same opinions of the professors. This experiment indicates that a ten-second first impression gleaned from the second group of students was almost as powerful as the impressions the other students had derived while interacting with professors over the course of an entire semester. Such is the power of first impressions.[25]

While we can train ourselves on what to say, we are often ill-prepared on how to say it. Given that 93% of our communication is nonverbal, it is essential that you focus on other factors that could get in the way of conveying a positive first impression. For example, slouching while standing or sitting, avoiding eye contact, frowning, relying on technical jargon, reading slides, speaking too fast or too slowly, untidy physical appearance, and gesturing too much are all actions that can put off your audience. Research has shown that 93% of our communication is nonverbal:

- 55% of the message is conveyed through facial expression
- 35% of the message is conveyed through expression voice tone
- 7% of the message is conveyed through words.[26]

Another factor in nonverbal communication is the nonvisual dimension. We all see the world differently, so it pays to be aware of the different sensory learning styles of your audience in order to build a rapport. Numerous studies have shown that people learn information in different ways. For example, some are visual learners, while others are auditory or kinesthetic learners.[27] In preparing your pitch, you can use these learning preferences to your advantage by using various kinds of media. For example, you might present a slide show with images. Ensuring that you describe your ideas and concepts clearly and confidently will appeal to auditory learners. If available, bring a prototype of your product along to give your audience something to touch and feel.

How to Make a Good First Impression

Preparation is key when it comes to making a good first impression. Table 16.5 illustrates some tips that will help you achieve a positive impression of yourself and your business.

Video
Making a Good Impression

TABLE 16.5

Tips for Making a Good First Impression

- Be aware of your body language: analyze a video of yourself pitching and study your pose, gestures, and facial expressions.

- Learn from others: don't just practice your own body language, learn from other speakers and analyze their posture, expressions, and the gestures they make while they are presenting.

- Be open and confident: people who are expressive, animated, and easy to read are more likeable than ones who are more guarded.

- Discover areas in common: we are more likely to get along with people with whom we share common interests. Find out what common interests you may have with your audience and connect on this level.

- Learn to listen: listening to others shows that we care enough about them to listen to what they are saying. Don't interrupt or try to complete someone else's sentences.

- Manage your image: analyze your grooming and how you dress. Does what you wear reflect you and your business? Does your general grooming correspond to how you want your audience to perceive you?

- Get that handshake right: studies have found that a firm handshake makes a better impression than a weak one (which implies passivity).

- Be polite and courteous: good manners go a long way toward making a good first impression.

Source: Adapted from Gregoire, C. (2014, May 30). "How to make the perfect first impression. *Huffington Post*. Retrieved from http://www.huffingtonpost.com/2014/05/30/the-science-and-art-of-fi_n_5399004.html

While meeting people in person is one of the best ways to market yourself, marketing yourself and your company through social media can also help make a positive impression, boost your business, and enhance customer engagement.

16.6 THE ART OF PITCHING

>> **LO 16.6**   Describe the pitch process and different types of pitches.

Video
Pitching the Venture

The pitch is fundamental to marketing you as well as your venture, and the power of the pitch and how much time it takes to develop a good one cannot be underestimated. Imagine that you have been invited to pitch to an investor. Prior to the pitch, you must carry out a number of actions to prepare to ensure that you are "pitch-ready." This involves doing some due diligence to really understand your audience and their needs and expectations, so you can tailor your pitch accordingly.

There are two main parts to the "perfect pitch"—the content, which includes your value proposition, the problem and the solution, and the resources required; and the communication.

When pitching to potential investors, employees, customers, and colleagues, you will need to prepare a "pitch deck," previously introduced in Chapter 9 and further detailed in Appendix B that follows this chapter. It is a brief presentation, usually in the form of approximately 10–12 slides, that provides your audience with a synopsis of your idea or venture.

While there are different types of pitching, every pitch must end with a "call to action"—the action you would like your audience to take after you have finished your presentation. Never leave a presentation without some kind of request. This could come in the form of money, advice, a sale, a contact, or a second meeting. While you will usually use your pitch deck during face-to-face meetings, a powerful video pitch is also an effective way to present to an audience.

RESEARCH AT WORK[28]

Pitching Trustworthiness

What is the relationship between trust and early-stage investors' interest in investment during a pitch? Is trust really a factor when it comes to investing, or do investors focus primarily on seeking economic gains?

These are the questions Lakshmi Balachandra, a professor at Babson College, sought to find out. Balachandra carried out an experiment by studying 101 videos of entrepreneurs pitching to a network of angel investors from the Tech Coast Angels (TCA) in California—the largest angel group in the country. The results showed that trustworthiness displayed by entrepreneurs during the pitch had a direct impact on whether the angels would invest or not. In fact, angels who perceived trustworthiness were 10% more likely to invest. Angels were also more likely to rate "coachability" three times more important than competence during the trustworthiness assessments. For instance, investors will have more confidence that they can help "coach" or make up any skills that are lacking if the entrepreneur comes across as being trustworthy.

Other factors that led to an assessment of trust included the number of meaningful social network connections; the ability for entrepreneurs to accept suggestions, critique, and feedback; and shared commonalities between the angels and the entrepreneurs, such as background and expertise. It is clear from this research that entrepreneurs need to demonstrate trustworthiness while pitching.

CRITICAL THINKING QUESTIONS

1. **Give some reasons why trustworthiness is so important to potential investors.**

2. **Explain the relationship between trustworthiness and coachability. How can an entrepreneur demonstrate coachability during the pitch?**

3. **What are some ways you can demonstrate trustworthiness during a pitch? ●**

The key to presenting a sure-fire pitch is to be prepared. If you are presenting live, then make sure you get to the venue early to set up. Technology can be known to malfunction, so in case the projector doesn't work, or your laptop fails, make sure you have spare copies of your presentation backed up, as well as printed versions. It also helps to check how much time you have to present at the beginning of the meeting; this shows you are respectful of everyone's time, as well as ensuring that they will commit their time to you.

Audio
Making a Pitch

If you are presenting with your team, decide in advance who is going to do the talking. Usually, the CEO will do most of the talking, with the rest of the team presenting one or two slides that relate specifically to their areas of expertise. Make sure that one of you is taking notes during the presentation. Not only does it show that you are listening to your audience and are willing to learn, but you will find those notes valuable afterward.

When the presentation is over, make sure you summarize what has been said to make sure you have noted down the right information. If your audience has made requests for more information or asked questions to which you didn't have the answers at the time, then be conscientious and send them everything within the day. Above all, never try to cover up mistakes you may have made. People like honesty, and it is important to show your audience how you have learned from your failures.

Finally, delivering a successful pitch is all about practice. Take videos of yourself presenting, and improve the parts you don't like.

Pitch Approaches

For the past few decades, the "elevator pitch" was the standard way to pitch an idea. This meant that if you happened to find yourself in an elevator with someone important,

YOU BE THE ENTREPRENEUR

The pitch or "elevator 15-second commercial" is a crucial part of an entrepreneur's journey. To gain support, funding, and connections, entrepreneurs need to be able to pitch their ideas at a moment's notice. In business, it's all how you present an idea, first and foremost. Then you have to have the numbers to back it up. This process can be seen clearly on the television show *Shark Tank*, where Michael Tseng, founder of Plate Topper, had firsthand experience.

Michael Tseng is a very well-educated businessman and had developed a product he thought was the next big thing. Tseng went on *Shark Tank* and gave his pitch for the Plate Topper, a microwave-safe food cover. He asked for $90,000 for a 5% stake in his company. He made a great pitch to the investors, and received substantial offers in the beginning; but when he didn't accept any of the offers it rubbed the investors the wrong way. The "sharks" started to pull their offers off the table.

What Would You Do?

Source: Liew, J. (2012, November 5). *Shark Tank's lessons in the art of negotiation. Entrepreneur*, 1–3.

you would be able to pitch your idea from the point of the doors closing, to when they opened again. The idea was to use this short amount of time (less than one minute) to explain why your business is exciting and unique. Today, thanks to a more democratic working structure that allows us easier access to influential people, and new technology that provides us with a whole set of tools to get in touch others, the "elevator pitch" has evolved into several different forms. Though the speed and brevity of the elevator pitch is still important, the actual elevator is not!

Let's explore some pitch approaches that have been found to be successful.

The storytelling approach

Regardless of to whom you are presenting, it is essential that you articulate your idea clearly and tell a compelling story. Indeed, storytelling is part of our nature, and it is a powerful way of engaging and connecting with people.[29] Many of us make decisions based on stories that move or inspire us. Opening a pitch with "I have a story to tell" immediately alerts the audience that you have something interesting to say.

All stories are based on a three-part narrative arc, which can be traced back to ancient Greece and the stories of the philosopher Aristotle. Aristotle's arc still applies to storytelling today: an introduction that presents the characters and ideas; the climax that outlines the problem at its height and how your solution can overcome the most complex of issues; and the resolution that explains how you expect things to work out.[30]

A story will be successful only if it is authentic and is told with genuine enthusiasm and energy. Starbucks founder Howard Schultz is known as an excellent storyteller who has used examples drawn from his personal life to ignite passion in others. According to Schultz, the philosophy behind Starbucks was based on his father's failure to find any meaning or fulfilment in his work. When his father ended up with a work injury and no compensation or health insurance, Schultz vowed that he would create the type of company that he could feel passionate about—one that both inspires and takes care of its staff.[31]

One way of using the storytelling approach is to use the Pixar Pitch.[32] Every movie made by Disney Pixar follows a narrative structure that can be summed up in six chronological sentences:

1. Once upon a time, . . .
2. Every day, . . .
3. One day, . . .
4. Because of that, . . .
5. Because of that, . . .
6. Until finally, . . .

Let's apply the Pixar Pitch to Attack! Marketing, as described in this chapter's *Entrepreneurship in Action* feature (see p. 446).

Starbuck's founder Howard Schultz relays stories from his personal life to inspire others.
Credit: David Becker/ZUMA Press/Newscom

▸ <u>Once upon a time</u>, advertising agencies and brands in the United States were focusing solely on the concept of the campaign.

▸ <u>Every day</u>, millions of dollars would be spent on data collection, giveaways, and logistics, which neglected to engage the customer in a meaningful way, resulting in low trial rates and conversion numbers.

▸ <u>One day</u>, we developed a business called Attack! that revolutionized the consumer experience by introducing the human element, allowing consumers to taste, touch, and smell the products during live marketing events.

▸ <u>Because of that</u>, more consumers fell in love with the brand.

▸ <u>Because of that</u>, agencies saw a significant increase in the number of people who tried out the products and services, and more conversions as a result.

▸ <u>Until finally</u>, the Attack! philosophy became so widely accepted that more and more advertising and marketing agencies began to adopt it.

The key to telling a good story is to tell the right story to the right audience. This involves understanding what type of people they are. Do your research. Who are they? What are their wants and needs? What is the best way of moving them? Don't be afraid to make your story interactive by asking your audience for input—this makes them feel part of the story, and it will encourage them to become more engaged with your idea.[33]

In fact, successful pitches all have to do with drawing people into your story. A recent study of the Hollywood pitch process showed that when pitchers invited studio executives to collaborate on an idea, there was a better chance of the project being green-lighted. However, pitches were unsuccessful when the pitcher doesn't listen properly or is unwilling to accept feedback or constructive criticism. Bringing people into your story and allowing them to participate is a powerful way of getting the buy-in you need.

Social Media and Marketing

Social media websites rely heavily on the number of website hits they receive every day.

Credit: ©iStockphoto.com/franckreporter

Although social media increases the permeability of communication to consumers directly without print or TV intermediaries, its accessibility also means consumers can no longer rely on marketing messages having been vetted through journalistic standards. Consumers must, therefore, acquire information on the trustworthiness of companies from word-of-mouth reviews by friends and strangers. Trust then becomes the prized currency of social media business marketing.

Trust is, unfortunately, declining. Edelman's 2010 Trust Barometer study indicated that people who view their social media friends as credible sources of brand information fell from 45% in 2008 to 25% in 2010.

There are several potential reasons for the decline of trust in social media. One is the trade-off of quantity of Facebook "likes" and retweets over quality of meaningful engagement among companies and customers. In a similar vein, paying people to post positive social media messages about a new product without disclosing their financial incentives is an ethical oversight, even if it is perfectly legal.

Historically, ethical failures in the general business environment have harmed innocent people and sometimes resulted in only minor consequences—or none at all—for the offending company. Conversely, ethical failures in social media tend to primarily harm the offending organization. Ironically, when unethical practices are discovered in social media, the offending company is punished by the very people the organizations are trying to woo as customers.

In this quickly evolving social media environment, there are few or no historical precedents to use as a guide to solving the ethical dilemmas. Customers and their data are easier for startups to access, creating a potential for companies to grow their customer base quickly. Social media can, however, be a double-edged sword as customers use social media to rapidly and widely disseminate their perceptions of a company's ethical lapses. These lapses, however unintentional, can be deadly, particularly for a startup.

CRITICAL THINKING QUESTIONS

1. **How can you draw attention to your company and educate your customers in the overcrowded marketplace on social media without resorting to practices that are borderline unethical?**

2. **Suppose someone fraudulently posts unflattering material about your company on social media. How can you best respond and clear your good name?**

3. **What can you do to remedy a customer's negative perceptions before it goes viral?** ●

Sources

Edelman Trust Barometer. (2010). *2010 annual global opinion leaders study.* Retrieved from Edelman Trust Barometer: http://www.edelman.com/insights/intellectual-property/edelman-trust-barometer-archive/

Lievertz, M. (2010, December 3). Ethical frameworks in business and their application to social media marketing. *Academia.edu,* 1-16. Retrieved from http://www.academia.edu/1400018/Ethical_Frameworks_in_Business_and_Their_Application_to_Social_Media_Marketing

Moore, J. (2010, June 17). *3 steps to ethical social media marketing.* Retrieved from Social Media Examiner: http://www.socialmediaexaminer.com/3-steps-to-ethical-social-media-marketing/

Ray, A. (2013, Apriil 23). *Ethics in social media marketing: Responding to the Boston tragedy.* Retrieved from Social Media Today: http://www.socialmediatoday.com/content/ethics-social-media-marketing-responding-boston-tragedy

Vinjamuri, D. (2011, November 3). *Ethics and the five deadly sins of social media.* Retrieved from Forbes/CMO : http://www.forbes.com/sites/davidvinjamuri/2011/11/03/ethics-and-the-5-deadly-sins-of-social-media/#29bfaaab37ad

MINDSHIFT

Pitch Practice

Because entrepreneurs are so close to their ideas, they can easily fall into the trap of thinking they are pitching their idea clearly when in fact they are not being very clear in their communication. What is clear in your head may not be clear in the minds of the people you are pitching to. Give this experiment a try.

- First, create a 30–60 second pitch. No need to go into great detail. Just talk about what the idea is, the problem it solves, and how it will work.

- Second, identify a person to pitch to and deliver your 30- to 60-second pitch.

- Third, once you have finished pitching, ask the person to tell you in his or her own words what your idea is.

Repeat this process five times with different types of listeners.

CRITICAL THINKING QUESTIONS

1. **Were your listeners able to articulate your idea in their own words more accurately than you expected, or less so?**

2. **Over the course of your five pitches, did you notice any pattern in areas of your message that your listeners misinterpreted or didn't catch?**

3. **In what ways would you improve your pitch in the future for greater clarity and effectiveness?** ●

The question approach

Asking questions as part of your pitch, rather than making statements, is a powerful way to encourage others to respond, or at least think more deeply about the answer. One of history's most successful question pitches was launched by Ronald Reagan during his presidential campaign in 1980, when he was trying to unseat the incumbent president, Jimmy Carter. Reagan asked the question, "Are you better off now than you were four years ago?" The question prompted voters to really think about their own personal circumstances, which moved them to take action and vote.

The Twitter approach

This type of pitch challenges you to capture the essence of your idea within the 140 character limit. Steve Jobs managed to easily manage this for every Apple product he pitched—iPod: "1,000 songs in your pocket"; Macbook Air, "The World's thinnest notebook." While investors may not invite you to pitch via Twitter, the actual concept helps to succinctly summarize your idea to engage your audience.

Finally, delivering a successful pitch is all about practice. Practice it at least ten times in front of friends, family, or other entrepreneurs who have already been through the process. Refine your pitch based on their feedback and advice. While the content of a pitch is important to get right, how you market yourself and communicate the message is vital when it comes to engaging your audience.

In this chapter, we have explored the different elements of the pitch package and the importance of marketing your idea, company, and yourself in person and through social media.

In Chapter 1 we started the textbook with an open letter. In that letter, we talked about the journey that you are on—a journey we call entrepreneurship. Because we started the book with a letter, we think it's only appropriate to end with a letter! ●

Dear Student,

We suspect you are reading this now because you are at the end of your course. This part of the journey is over, but it's really just the beginning. You may have an idea that you love and want to take forward. Or you may realize that your idea is not that strong, but you still have a desire to search for that right idea, at the right time, for the right reason . . . for you! You may have even realized that entrepreneurship is a lot of hard work, and you are just not quite ready to commit to starting and running your own business at this time. Maybe it's something you will do later in life. Who knows? Don't try to predict the future. Remember, entrepreneurs create the future.

Regardless of where you are, we hope you realize the most important outcome of going through this textbook. You are thinking and acting more entrepreneurially than ever before. This goes beyond the ability to start a business. You have developed a life skill that will reward you no matter what you choose to do next. You have the courage to take action under conditions of uncertainty. You know how to use what you have to start something new. You know how to identify what people need. You know how to create and identify new ideas that meet those needs and test them with real people to get real results. You can quickly vet whether the idea is a viable business opportunity. And you know how to think about marketing yourself and your ideas, as well as building a network of people to help you get things done. These skills will take you far.

Congratulations for becoming entrepreneurial. Keep up The Practice.

Action trumps everything.

The Authors

Get the edge on your studies at **edge.sagepub.com/neckentrepreneurship**

▸   Master the learning objectives using key study tools
▸   Watch, listen, and connect with online multimedia resources
▸   Access mobile-friendly quizzes and flashcards to check your understanding

SUMMARY

16.1   Discuss the role of marketing and pitching in entrepreneurship.

The pitch is the entire act of presenting a product concept. It is meant to be brief and enticing, and well developed to take the interests of the intended audience into account. Marketing is a method of putting the right product in the right place, at the right price, at the right time.

16.2   Explain the principles of marketing and how they apply to new ventures.

The right product, in the right place, at the right price, at the right time. For entrepreneurs, this extends to identifying needs, serving those needs, communicating the value proposition, supplying the product or service, and supporting the customer relationship from then on.

16.3   Compare entrepreneurial marketing with traditional marketing.

Entrepreneurial marketing represents more interactive marketing focused on customers (instead of the product) and rapid adaptation to changing consumer needs. Hallmarks of entrepreneurial marketing are innovation, risk-taking, resourcefulness, value creation, and proactivity—attributes supported by smaller, more agile startup companies.

16.4   Highlight the value of social media for marketing opportunities.

Social media is ubiquitous, and in many cases entirely free for the entrepreneur to use. It allows direct access to individual customers and general access to billions of potential customers. Furthermore, the structuring of the content is often a guided process; and users tend to be well-versed in the presentation of content, regardless of the social media venue.

Social media strategies help to attract customers, increase recognition of your brand, and provide efficient customer service. Creating interesting content as part of a social media strategy can also help to drive sales.

16.5   Practice how to make a good impression during your pitch.

Many investors, when asked, might confess that when choosing investment opportunities, they're more interested in the people behind the product than the product itself. First impressions are created extremely quickly, and they tend to endure. Presenters need to be cognizant of their body language, confident, well-groomed, and good listeners.

16.6   Describe the pitch process and different types of pitches.

Preparing a pitch involves thorough understanding of the audience, deliberate framing of the problem and solution, the resources required (the "ask"), and the method by which all of this will be communicated. Some popular pitches include the elevator pitch, the rocket pitch, the storytelling pitch, the Pixar pitch, the question pitch, and the Twitter pitch.

KEY TERMS

Brand strategy 450
Branding 449
Entrepreneurial
   marketing 455
Guerrilla marketing 456

Marketing 447
Marketing mix 447
Packaging 449
People 449
Pitch 445

Place 448
Positioning 449
Price 448
Product 447
Promotion 448

Steve Jobs, Cofounder of Apple Computer

What is the difference between a good idea and a good idea that is realized and actually makes it to market? While there are many answers to this question, two fundamental elements stand out above all others. First, a good idea must be translated into a quality product or service that actually works. Second, an effective sales pitch must be made to investors and customers.

This case study chronicles the professional journey of Apple's visionary and chief executive Steve Jobs, a man widely regarded as one of the most innovative and successful entrepreneurs of the last half-century. Jobs had great ideas. But great ideas alone were not what created Apple's; Computer a capable team, willing investors, and interested customers were the variables that ultimately catapulted Apple to the top of its industry.

Among all the companies that make tablet computers, mp3 players, smartphones, and other devices, how is it that Apple came to be so completely dominant in the portable self-computing and communication industry? The short answer is the company's founder and former CEO: Steve Jobs, also known as the "father of the digital revolution." Few entrepreneurs in history have had as great an impact, not only on their industry, but on the entire world. How could your impact be anything other than legendary when your name is synonymous with the iPod, the iPad, and the iPhone?

What is it that made Apple so wildly successful in selling these three specific products? Many, when answering this question, are apt to respond, "It's because they have great marketing." It is true that Apple spends large sums of money on carefully strategized marketing campaigns that are cutting-edge, catchy, and attractive. But would a company enjoy the kind of perennial success Apple has experienced so lavishly in the past decade if its product didn't meet and exceed expectations? Brilliant marketing campaigns can buy you quarterly, or even annual successes, but perennial success that lasts a decade or more can come only from consistently producing high-quality products that customers *want* to buy.

Distilled to its essence, entrepreneurial success is a direct by-product of giving customers the products or services they want more than any other option on the market. Yes, Jobs was legendary in his attention to detail and cosmetic beauty, and yes, he had a compelling vision of entrepreneurial leadership. But in the end, Jobs—and Apple's—earned its success because customers wanted what they had to offer more than they wanted whatever anybody else was offering. Jobs's understanding of what the customer really wanted surpassed that of any of his competitors.

Traditionally speaking, such knowledge is derived through market research. Jobs, who was not a big fan of market research, once told *Business Week*: "A lot of times, people don't know what they want until you show it to them." This assertion, which may come across as typical Jobs hubris, nevertheless captures the penetrating nature of his commitment to his own inspired vision. Arrogant? Perhaps; but he was proved to be right, not as a matter of individual opinion, but by the cash votes of hundreds of millions of satisfied customers. Perhaps no one in the past generation has exhibited a more creative, compelling, and at times tyrannical brand of entrepreneurial leadership than Steve Jobs. One can only imagine what Jobs might have yet accomplished in his storied career had cancer not cut short his life in 2011.

Steve Jobs was born and raised in the San Francisco Bay area, not far from the area that later became known as Silicon Valley—where he would someday serve as CEO of Apple not once, but twice. His intellect was evident at a young age, leading him to skip a grade of school. He did not, however, thrive in formal school environments and was known for being mischievous and habitually uninterested in typical classroom instruction.

As a teenager, Jobs became increasingly fascinated with electronic devices. One of his high school friends was Steve Wozniak, who would eventually cofound Apple with Jobs. While Jobs gets most of the credit for building Apple as a company, Wozniak was, in fact, the engineering genius behind the construction of the actual computer hardware. Wozniak was the wizard wonk while Jobs was the sales, marketing, and visionary genius.

After high school, Jobs enrolled at Reed College in Portland, Oregon, but quickly became disenchanted with life as a college student. He also felt he was wasting his working-class parents' hard-earned money on the private school's expensive tuition. He dropped out after only six months and spent the following year and a half randomly auditing various courses that interested him. One such course on calligraphy proved hugely influential in Apple's later development—and subsequent worldwide proliferation—of a wide variety of computer fonts. Jobs then embarked on a seven-month journey of personal discovery in India. There he studied, and began practicing, elements of Zen Buddhism, a spiritual philosophy that would continue to influence him the rest of his life.

After his return from India, Jobs worked with Wozniak at an early video game company called Atari. Riding the coattails of Wozniak's legendary genius working with computer hardware, Jobs found success making improvements to a circuit board game called *Breakout*.

In 1976, Jobs and Wozniak founded the Apple Computer Company, where Wozniak built the first Apple Macintosh computer. Jobs's vision at Apple was audaciously ambitious. He did not see himself as just another businessman with a genius computer geek at his side (Wozniak). He saw himself as a visionary leader—an inspired entrepreneur who was destined to change the world of human computing.

Apple did not become successful overnight. Like all entrepreneurs who build a company from the ground up, Jobs, Wozniak, and a growing number of colleagues and employees worked extremely hard and faced many challenges in Apple's early years. Eventually, their efforts paid off handsomely. Within a decade of starting their company in the garage of Jobs's parents' home in Los Altos, California, Apple had become a $2 billion dollar company with 4,000 employees. Their little startup had grown to become a household name, and the Los Altos-Santa Clara Valley region was becoming famous as Silicon Valley. In 1984, Apple purchased its first Super Bowl television advertisement.

A year earlier, Jobs had convinced Pepsi CEO John Sculley to join Apple's executive team. In making the pitch, Jobs famously asked Sculley: "Do you want to spend the rest of your life selling sugared water, or do you want a chance to change the world?" Sculley was intrigued enough by Jobs's offer to join Apple as its new CEO. Ironically, Sculley and the rest of Apple's Board of Directors ended up tangling with Jobs; and by the end of 1985, Jobs was forced out of his own company, a move he later described as "devastating."

As he suffered through the fallout of his epic freeze-out from the company he himself had founded, Jobs considered leaving Silicon Valley for good. But he decided instead to stay and start over because he loved his work too much to turn his back on it. Reflecting, years later, on this painful experience, Jobs commented, "Sometimes life hits you in the head with a brick. Don't lose faith. I'm convinced that the only thing that kept me going was that I loved what I did."

Continuing the work he felt so passionate about, Jobs completely reinvented himself over the next half-decade. He started by building another computer company from the ground up. The company was called NeXT. He was also instrumental in building and then leading the animated motion picture studio Pixar, which was eventually bought by Disney for over 7 billion dollars. In his personal life, he fell in love with and married the woman who would be his wife for the rest of his life.

The irony of Jobs's 1985 firing from Apple was extended in the 1990s, but this time, in reverse. Desperately seeking a technological edge that would make their new operating system successful, Apple turned to Jobs and NeXT. The move proved genius, and in 1997 Jobs once again became CEO of Apple.

Jobs's strong leadership not only saved Apple from bankruptcy but transformed the company into the most valuable publicly traded corporation on the planet. The fuel behind Apple's extraordinary prosperity came partly in the form of desktop and laptop computers but was mostly derived from the unprecedented sales of Apple's unique versions of mp3 players, tablet computers, and smartphones. Today, it is not an exaggeration to say that the iPod, iPad, and iPhone changed the world.

In 2003, Jobs was diagnosed with pancreatic cancer, from which he eventually died of in 2011. In intervening years, Jobs experienced varying degrees of productive vitality and declining health. He remained CEO of Apple up until six weeks before his death.

The influence of Steve Jobs's life and career are incalculable. By translating his extraordinary vision and ideas into the right sales pitch at the right time to the right person or organization, he was able to achieve unprecedented results in his industry. He left behind a legacy that will continue to touch the lives of entrepreneurs and others for all time. Some of the most memorable insights Jobs has offered to aspiring entrepreneurs came in a commencement address at Stanford University in 2005. In his speech, which has over 30 million hits on YouTube, Jobs talked about looking back on one's life versus looking forward, and emphasized the importance of trusting your inner voice.

> You can't connect the dots looking forward; you can only connect them looking backwards. So you have to trust that the dots will somehow connect in your future. You have to trust in something—your gut, destiny, life, karma, whatever. This approach has never let me down, and it has made all the difference in my life.

Critical Thinking Questions

1. What were some of the successful pitches that Steve Jobs made during his illustrious career with Apple and NeXT? Why were they successful?

2. What was Jobs's unorthodox marketing philosophy, and why do you think he was so successful at "showing" the customers what they "wanted?"

3. What role do you think the principle of "marketing yourself" played in helping Jobs overcome his initial failure with Apple to eventually regain the top spot at his old company?

4. Had social media been around in the 1980s and 90s, how do you think Jobs might have utilized it to further market his ideas and products? How might you utilize social media to market your own ideas in today's world?

Sources

Blumenthal, K. (2012). *Steve Jobs: The man who thought different*. New York, NY: Feiwel and Friends.

Gallo, C. (2009). *The presentation secrets of Steve Jobs: How to be insanely great in front of any audience*. New York, NY: McGraw Hill; Isaacson, W. (2011). *Steve Jobs*. New York, NY: Simon & Schuster.

Jobs, S. (2005). *Steve Jobs 2005 Stanford Commencement Address* (video). Delivered June 12, 2005. Retrieved from https://www.youtube.com/watch?v=UF8uR6Z6KLc

Jobs, S. (2005). "You've got to find what you love," Jobs says. The 2005 Stanford Commencement Address of Steve Jobs (transcript). *Stanford News*. Delivered
June 12, 2005. Retrieved from http://news.stanford.edu/news/2005/june15/jobs-061505.html

Mui, C. (2011, October 17). Five dangerous lessons to learn from Steve Jobs. *Forbes*. Retrieved from http://www.forbes.com/sites/chunkamui/2011/10/17/five-dangerous-lessons-to-learn-from-steve-jobs/

Reinhardt, A. (interviewer) (1998, May 12). Steve Jobs on Apple's resurgence: "Not a one-man show." *Business Week*. Retrieved from http://www.businessweek.com/bwdaily/dnflash/may1998/nf80512d.htm

Steve Jobs: Father of the digital revolution. (2011, October 14). Retrieved from http://people.bukiki.com/2011/10/14/steve-jobs-father-of-the-digital-revolution/#axzz1rOXXhAMP

APPENDIX B
THE PITCH DECK

Learning Objectives

B.1 Describe the pitch deck and its importance to potential investors.

B.2 Explain the content of pitch deck slides.

B.3 Anticipate and prepare for the types of questions that may be asked during the question and answer period.

Outline

B.1 Overview of the Pitch Deck

B.2 Pitch Deck Slides

B.3 The Question and Answer Period

B.1 OVERVIEW OF THE PITCH DECK

>> **LO B.1** Describe the pitch deck and its importance to potential investors.

The pitch deck is a brief presentation that highlights the essential elements of the TRIM framework (Team, Resources, Idea, and Market) as discussed in Chapter 9. The pitch deck should articulate the purpose of the venture (the idea), who is served by the venture (market), how the venture will be successful (resources), and who will execute the venture (team). It's a story that is told to convince the listener that your idea is compelling enough to warrant further investigation.

As highlighted in Chapter 9, there are many types of plans. The business plan has historically been the most popular, but in the past decade the pitch deck has become one of the most valuable tools an entrepreneur can have when trying to raise startup capital or find other types of resources. A pitch deck is a good way to describe your business to a potential investor; it can also be used for meetings with potential partners, advisors, employees or even a reporter who might be doing a story on your startup! Any stakeholder who has a vested interest in your business could be an audience for your pitch.

Chapter 9 introduced Guy Kawasaki's 10 essential slides, but there are no strict rules for pitch deck length or style. For example, some people suggest that the pitch deck should have only 5 slides while others recommend 6, 10, 11, 12, 15, or even 30 slides.[1] Regardless of the slide count or style, all pitch decks need to answer the same fundamental questions. These include the following:

- What is the problem/need?
- How will you solve the problem or meet the need in a unique way?
- Who is the customer, and are there enough customers to build a viable venture?
- What is the size/extent of the market for this product/service idea now and in the future?
- How will you reach, acquire, and keep the customer?
- Whom will you compete with, and how are you different?

- ▶ What is the revenue/expense model?
- ▶ What capabilities does your team have to execute the venture?
- ▶ What is your call to action?

Typically, an initial meeting with a possible investor will be 30 minutes to one hour, but you should not use all of this time to present. Generally your pitch should not exceed 20 minutes, but different situations call for different pitch lengths. For this reason, we suggest being prepared to give a 1-, 3-, 10-, 15-, and 20-minute version. Whatever time is allotted for your pitch, it's important to leave room for questions. One of the biggest mistakes entrepreneurs make during a pitch is failing to leave time for questions at the end of the pitch.[2] If you can anticipate the questions in advance, it is also smart to create some backup slides with the answers to show that you have done your homework.

B.2 PITCH DECK SLIDES

>> LO B.2 Explain the content of pitch deck slides.

While there is no one "right" pitch deck format, we have provided you with a basic template to follow that will help answer the essential questions. We use the company, India in a Box, that was introduced in Chapter 9 as a pitch deck example. If you recall, India in a Box, uses a subscription model to deliver authentic Indian meals that can be prepared by customers in minutes.

Slide #1: Title

The title slide should include the name of the company, logo, your name, and contact information. This is the first slide your audience will see and will likely be on-screen the longest while they wait for you to present. Don't be boring here. Pay attention to

---

FIGURE B.1

Example Title Slide

Source: Shyam Devnani (Contact information has been removed for publication.)

slide design. In addition, consider putting your name and company on every slide so your audience will remember you and your company.

Slide #2: Company Purpose/Description

The purpose or vision slide is a quick overview of your company. Why does your company exist? Develop one sentence that describes what your company does. For example, it is a useful exercise to fill in the following blanks:

{Company} is _____ for _____ that _____.

For example: FlowDog **is** an aquatic and rehabilitation center **for** dogs **that** suffer from physical injuries.

{Company} sells _____ to _____ in order to _____.

For example: VentureBlocks **sells** computer-based simulations **to** educators **in order to** help teach core topics related to entrepreneurship.

You could also include a type of comparison with a widely known brand, which will help the listener to immediately grasp the concept. For example, "we are the Uber for pets" or "we are the Netflix for video games."[3]

FIGURE B.2

Example Company Purpose/Description Slide

Source: Shyam Devnani

Slide #3: The Problem/Need

Describe the problem that your company is solving or how you are addressing a customer need. Additionally, you should describe how the problem is currently being solved by other companies, and point out any inefficiencies in how it is being solved,

FIGURE B.3

Example Problem/Need Slide

Source: Shyam Devnani

or why the existing solutions are insufficient. Keep in mind that you need to prove to your audience that the problem is a big one. As venture capitalist Skylar Fernandes says, you need to solve the customer's #1 problem—not the #10 problem![4]

Slide #4: The Solution

The solution is really your value proposition, because if you can solve the customer's problem or fulfill their need in a unique way, then you are already creating value. Don't just type the solution on a slide. If possible offer a live demonstration. If the product or service is not yet fully developed, show a prototype or a picture of a prototype. If the solution is web-based, a mockup landing page is a must.

    Another option is to show a **use case**[5]—a methodology used in the software industry to illustrate how a user will interact with a specific piece of software.[6] Figure B.4 illustrates a use case to show how easy it is to prepare a meal from India in a Box. For entrepreneurs, use cases are also a good way of showing an audience how customers will interact with their products or services and how their lives are made easier through the interaction.

Use Case: a methodology used in the software industry to illustrate how a user will interact with a specific piece of software.

Slide #5: Why Now?

There is a window of opportunity for many new ventures. You need to convince your audience that the time is now for your new product or service. This means pointing out trends or changes that prove that your company is timely. For example, a new ride-sharing service called Chariot for Women was introduced in Boston after news stories surfaced about allegations and complaints against other ride-sharing services

FIGURE B.4

Use case highlighting cooking instructions

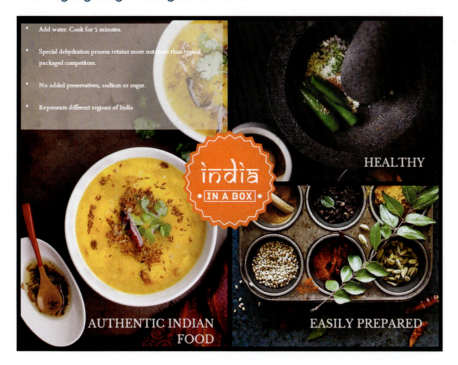

Source: Shyam Devnani

FIGURE B.5

Example Solution Slides

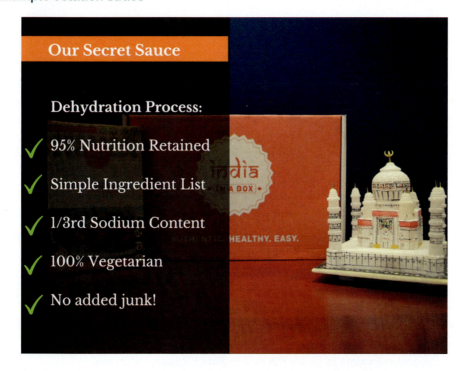

Source: Shyam Devnani

FIGURE B.6

Example Why Now? Slide

Source: Shyam Devnani

involving rape and sexual assault. Chariot for Women is similar to Uber and Lyft, but just for women. Both the customers and drivers are women, and the service also transports children under the age of 13. The time is now for Chariot for Women because it meets the needs of customers who have been put off by the perceived dangers of other ride-sharing services, as well as their perceived lack of thoroughness in carrying out background checks on their drivers.[7]

Slide #6: Market Opportunity

The solution is powerful only if there is a market of customers willing to pay for the product or service. When it comes to creating your market opportunity slide, it is important to think through three important acronyms that represent different subgroups of the market: TAM, SAM, and SOM.[8]

> **TAM,** or Total Available Market, refers to the total market demand for a product or service.

> **SAM,** or Serviceable Available Market, is the section of the TAM that your product or service intends to target.

> **SOM,** or Share of Market, is the portion of SAM that your company is realistically likely to reach.

To explain these acronyms in further detail, let's take the example of an entrepreneur pitching a gourmet donut café concept Let's call it The Gourmet Donut Co. The café will serve high-end coffee and tea, and unique-flavored, gourmet donuts such as maple bacon or ham and cheese, in addition to the traditional glazed and chocolate. The entrepreneur wants to locate the café in Baton Rouge, Louisiana.

TAM: (Total Available Market)—the total market demand for a product or service.

SAM: (Serviceable Available Market)—the section of the TAM that your product or service intends to target.

SOM: (Share of market)—the portion of SAM that your company is realistically likely to reach.

The TAM market covers all the possible customers who visit donut shops or cafés in the United States. If you were to open coffee shops all over the US, then you could potentially generate revenues from TAM. While your intention is not to run your business to this scale, you could always produce this statistic to your audience as overall evidence of the popularity of donut shops and cafes.

The SAM is a little more specific than TAM as it describes the demand for your types of products within your reach; in this case, the café or donut market in the Baton Rouge area. In other words, if you had no competition in the Baton Rouge area, then you could potentially generate revenues from SAM. Keep in mind, however, that you always have competition.

The SOM describes the share of the market you can realistically reach with your café in Baton Rouge. This involves working out the percentage of SAM that you could potentially service. For example, in this case SOM may be a particular geographic radius within the city of Baton Rouge. You would need to figure out how much market share you could capture, given the degree of competition, and the geographic radius. To better visualize TAM, SAM, and SOM for your audience, you could use a graphic like Figure B.7 in your presentation.

It is important for investors to see that you have thought through TAM, SAM, and SOM, so they have a better idea of the fraction of the market you intend to target. If you cannot prove that you have a good chance of penetrating the local market, then they will be unable to see the growth potential of your business.

FIGURE B.7

TAM, SAM, SOM

FIGURE B.8

Example Market Opportunity Slide

THE MARKET

Over 5 million Indians and 130,000 Indian students in the US.

Indians are the largest international nationality for students represented in the US.

Source: Shyam Devnani

Slide #7: Getting Customers

After depicting the market size and showing the target market, it is essential that you demonstrate an understanding of your customers—who they are and how you will reach them. This is where you talk about your interactions with customers and what you have learned about them during the planning process.

Using the café and donut example above, it's not enough to simply describe that your target market consists of 125,000 people living in a particular geographic area within the city of Baton Rouge. You also need to show that you have done your homework to better understand what kinds of people are likely to go to a café that serves high-end coffee and funky, gourmet donuts!

Additionally, you need to articulate how you will reach those customers, what they are willing to pay, and how you intend to keep them coming back. Here you can begin to really build a market size number in terms of dollars using a simple calculation. For example:

number of customers x price x frequency of purchase = market size $

You can do this calculation for a day, week, month or year, and it should connect to your overall financials. Let's think about this for a single day. On an average day you may anticipate that 300 customers will enter the café and the average receipt based on 1 coffee and 1 donut is $7.50. Three hundred customers x $7.50 x 1 purchase = $2,250 total receipts for an average day. If there are 30 days in a month, then total monthly receipts could be $67,500. As a result the annual revenue could be $810,000.

Slide #8: Competitor Analysis & Differentiation

The competitor analysis shows how your company differentiates itself from others providing similar solutions, or how it has carved out a unique space that fulfills unmet

FIGURE B. 9

Example Getting Customers Slide

Source: Shyam Devnani

needs. Competition is a good thing because it shows that there is a market for products and services. The key is to show how you are doing something better, different, and more compelling. A strong analysis will show the audience your competitive advantage—the source of why or how you will outperform others.

The competitive grid analysis compares your company to your most significant competitors and details their strengths and weaknesses relative to your own business. Figure B.10 illustrates an example of a competitive grid analysis for a new business called "Best Cuts," comparing it to two different competing hair salons in terms of pricing, capacity, location and other attributes.

Another way to compare your company with the competition is to use a positioning matrix illustrating how you intend to position your business relative to the competition. Figure B.11 illustrates this concept with the Gourmet Donut Co. example.

The competitive matrix positions your company relative to the competition on selected variables. In Figure B.11, we look at the competition for the Gourmet Donut Co. based on price and flavors. Other possible variables could be price and quality or flavors and healthfulness of ingredients such as processed versus all-natural. But in the example here, we will stick with price and flavors. After analyzing the competition in the Baton Rouge market, you can see that there are five donut shops that offer basic flavors of donuts at a low price such as Dunkin' Donuts and Krispy Kreme. Their coffee is priced low as well. Starbucks and CC's offer expensive donuts, though basic flavors, and high-end coffee. You can see from the matrix that The Gourmet Donut Co. is positioning itself very differently with its gourmet flavors.

Showing that you have done your homework on the competition is essential. One of the worst mistakes entrepreneurs can make in a pitch is claiming they have no

FIGURE B.10

Example of Competitive Grid Analysis

Competitive Grid

Competitor	Bobo Salon and Styling	Johnny's Hair	BEST CUTS
Offerings	Men's/women's cut/styles/color perms	Men's cuts only	Men's/ women's cut/ style/ color/ perms
Service Prices	Starts at $38	Starts at $50	Starts at $30
Retail Prices	100% markup	100% markup	75% markup
Location	High traffic, highly visible	Moderate traffic, highly visible	High traffic, not visible
Expertise	20+years, up-to-date trends	15+ years, young hairstylists	13+ years, up-to-date trends
Service	Set hours, little schedule flexibility	Manager never there	Custom hours to suit clients needs
Turnover	Low	High	Sole stylist
Capacity	11 active chairs	8 active chairs	1 active chair
Client Base	Over 4000	?	Over 300

Source: http://www.slideshare.net/smarty23b/sample-business-plan-presentation2)

FIGURE B.11

Gourmet Donut Co. Competitive Positioning

competition. You will always have competition, and how you define that competition is important. Remember when you acquire a customer you are taking them away from someone or something else. Who is that someone or something else? For example, before there was iTunes, there were music stores. Though iTunes was a great innovation, it still had competition.

Example Competitor Analysis & Differentiation Slide

Source: Shyam Devnani

Slide #9: Traction

Traction describes all the work you've done to date to build your venture. Your audience, especially investors, want to see the actions you have taken to construct your venture and the milestones you have achieved. Examples of traction include the following:

▸ Early customer adoption and showing you have revenue

▸ Completion of customer research

▸ Working website

▸ Working prototype or minimum viable product

▸ Submission of patent application

▸ Formation of team

▸ Product testing

▸ Contracting of suppliers

▸ Creation of first batch of product

▸ Successful crowdfunding campaign (where relevant)

▸ Securing of space (in the case of retail)

▸ Securing of investment or loans

Other evidence of traction includes recognition and press. For example, if you have won pitch competitions or been mentioned in blogs, magazines, TV shows, or other media, then you can talk about it here.

You could also include your future milestones or planned next steps. These could include expansion into new locations or overseas; the number of customers you intend to reach (for example, one million customers); or hiring more staff and employees.

FIGURE B.13

Example Traction Slide

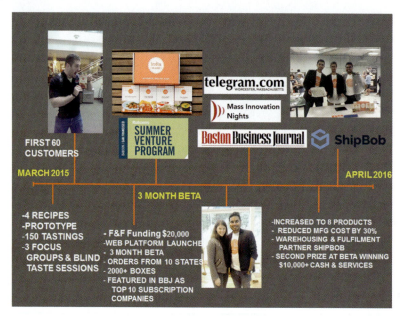

Source: Shyam Devnani

Slide #10: Financials

Your financials need to demonstrate that you have a clear understanding of potential profit and loss. It's important to highlight the key drivers of revenue and expenses, but keep it at the highest levels for now. In other words, you should not present a detailed income statement, cash-flow statement, and balance sheet (see Financial Appendix at p. 359 for further explanation); but you do need to show at least three years of revenue projections. Be realistic with these projections, and explain the assumptions underlying the projections. Have back up slides of detailed financials if asked about them during the question and answer period.

In Figure B.14 Shyam shows 3-year profit potential for India in a Box. You may also want to consider showing three different scenarios such as best case, worst case, and likely case. This shows investors and others that you are trying to be as realistic as possible with your projections.

Slide #11: Team

Showing you have a strong team with the right skillsets is more important than you might think. Your audience may not be convinced that the opportunity is there, but if the team is strong, then it's more likely that the team will be able to pivot as necessary

FIGURE B.14

Example Financials Slide

FINANCIALS

	YEAR 1	YEAR 2	YEAR 3
REVENUE	$261,000	$ 820,000	$ 2,540,000
EXPENSES	$ 132,000	$ 343,000	$ 980,000
GROSS PROFIT	$ 129,000	$ 477,000	$ 1,560,000
SG&A	$ 84,000	$ 225,000	$ 530,000
NET PROFIT	$45,000	$252,000	$1,030,000

61% GROSS PROFIT MARGIN | **$1 Million** PROFIT YEAR 3

Source: Shyam Devnani

to give the business the best possible chance for success.[9] The team slide should include a list of all team members, providing photos, their experience, and education. If you have a board of advisors, then include those names as well. Talent attracts other talent. So if you have an amazing team, you might even consider moving this slide to the beginning of your presentation.

FIGURE B.15

Example Team Slide

TEAM

SHYAM DEVNANI
CEO AND FOUNDER

SUCHETA GEHANI
HEAD OF NUTRITION

GURMEET KOCCHAR
OPERATIONS

6+ years in Food-tech, Business and Nutrition

Source: Shyam Devnani

Slide #12: Call to Action

The call to action is often the most forgotten slide! It doesn't matter if you are pitching to a venture capitalist, an angel investor, an audience in a pitch competition, your professor, a friend, your class, or your grandmother, you must always have a call to action. By this point in the presentation, you've likely spent about 15 minutes presenting your idea. So now it's time to ask for something.

What you ask for depends on your audience. If you are presenting to an investor, you are probably asking for money. If this is the case, then you need to say how you plan to use the money. For example: "I'm asking for $200,000 for 20% of the company. The money invested will primarily be used for . . . (e.g., building out the sales channel, customer acquisition through marketing, packaging, redesign, hiring)." If you are pitching to your classmates, you might be asking for feedback on the idea. If you are pitching to your professor, you might be asking him or her to act as an advisor. If so, then tell your professor what you are looking for in an advisor. If you need team members, ask for them, but be specific in the skillsets you are looking for. The bottom line is, don't ever pitch without asking for something at the end, because you could be missing a major opportunity.

FIGURE B.16

Example Call to Action Slides

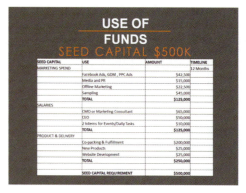

Source: Shyam Devnani

B.3 THE QUESTION AND ANSWER PERIOD

>> **LO B.3**   **Anticipate and prepare for the types of questions that may be asked during the question and answer period.**

During the question and answer period (Q&A) at the end of your presentation, the title slide should be showing. As we mentioned earlier, it is also useful to have a series of backup slides that can help you answer the most anticipated questions. In addition, you will likely pitch to more than one audience, so remember to incorporate answers to new questions that may have arisen in previous meetings.

For pitches in front of investors, or application to incubators, or pitch competitions, you can be sure that some of the following questions will be asked.[10]

Team Questions

▸ Why is the team capable of executing what you have proposed today?

▸ How do you divide up responsibilities among the team members?

- What is the equity split among team members?
- How are decisions made among the team members?
- Who is the boss?
- Who came up with the original idea?
- Who else do you need to add to your team in the short term?
- What obstacles have you faced, and how did you overcome them?
- Are you open to changing your idea?

Product/Customer Questions

- What makes customers try your product/service?
- What is the technology behind your product?
- How does your product work in more detail?
- What are the risks?
- What is the next step in your product evolution?
- Where do most of your customers come from today?
- How many customers do you have today?
- Who is going to be your first paying customer?
- How are you understanding customer needs?
- How do you really know people want this?

Competition Questions

- What competitor do you fear the most?
- Are the barriers to entry high or low? In other words, is it easy for competitors to enter the same market?
- How much money have your competitors made?
- Why do you think you are unique among your competitors?
- Can the competition do what you are doing if they want to?
- Why hasn't this already been done?

Financial Questions

- How did you calculate your market size?
- What are the assumptions behind your revenue projections?
- Are your numbers comparable to those of your competitors?
- What happens if you don't achieve your projected revenue?
- If I invest, what exactly are you going to do with the cash and what impact will it have on your business?
- What is the typical cycle between making initial customer contact and closing the sale?
- How much does it cost to acquire one customer?

Growth Questions

▶ If your startup succeeds, what additional areas might you be able to expand into?

▶ Are there other applications for your product/service/technology?

▶ How are you defining success?

▶ How big do you want to grow?

▶ What is a likely exit strategy for this business?

▶ What competition do you fear most?

▶ Where do your growth projections come from?

Regardless of how prepared you are, there may be some questions that still take you by surprise. Two-time technology entrepreneur Caroline Cummings, who raised $1 million for her startup, wrote a blog post on the 10 most unexpected questions she was asked during her pitch to a venture capitalist (see Table B.1). These questions show that investors are interested in who you are as a person and how you think just as much as they are interested in the opportunity you present to them!

The pitch deck process is essential to engaging an audience in order to generate interest, and to secure commitment and, where appropriate, investment. The key to a good presentation is preparation. By creating the number of slides that succinctly outline the nature of your company, presenting with passion and knowledge, and taking the time to prepare the responses to the questions you might be asked, you will have a better chance of engaging the right people to join you on your journey to entrepreneurial success.

TABLE B. 1

10 Most Unexpected Questions

Who believes in you, and how can I get in touch with them?
What entrepreneurs do you admire and why?
How do you track trends in your market?
Can you tell me a story about a customer using your product?
How do you know how much money you need, and could you scale your business with less?
How can I connect with five customers who have used your product?
What will your market look like in five years as a result of using your product or service?
What mistakes have you made thus far in this business, and what have you learned?
What if three to five years down the road we think you are not the right person to continue running this company—how will you address that?
Have you ever been fired from a job? Tell us about it.

Source: Cummings, C. (2013, February 22). The 10 questions I didn't expect to be asked by investors: Bplans Blog. Retrieved from http://articles.bplans.com/the-10-questions-i-didnt-expect-to-be-asked-by-investors/

Get the edge on your studies at **edge.sagepub.com/neckentrepreneurship**

▸ Master the learning objectives using key study tools
▸ Watch, listen, and connect with online multimedia resources
▸ Access mobile-friendly quizzes and flashcards to check your understanding

SUMMARY

B.1 Describe the pitch deck and its importance to potential investors.

The pitch deck is a brief presentation that highlights the essential elements of the TRIM framework discussed in Chapter 9. It is one of the most valuable tools an entrepreneur can have when trying to raise startup capital or find other types of resources.

B.2 Explain the content of pitch deck slides.

While there are no strict rules for length or style, your slides should include the following information: title, company purpose/description, the problem/need, the solution, why now?, market opportunity, getting customers, competitor advantages and differences, traction, financials, team, and call to action.

B.3 Anticipate and prepare for the types of questions that may be asked during the question and answer period.

When it comes to the question and answer period, expect the unexpected. In this regard, it is useful to prepare a series of backup slides that can help you answer the most anticipated questions.

KEY TERMS

SAM 480
SOM 480

TAM 480
Use Case 478

GLOSSARY

Accounts payable: money owed by a business to its suppliers.

Accounts receivable: money owed to the company for goods or services provided and billed to a customer.

Accrued expenses: costs incurred by the company for which no payment has been made.

Active search: method used by entrepreneurs in attempting to discover existing opportunities.

Advertising Revenue Model: the amount of revenue gained through advertising products and services

AEIOU framework: acronym for *Activities, Environments, Interactions, Objects,* and *Users*—a framework commonly used to categorize observations during fieldwork.

Alertness: the ability some people have to identify opportunities.

All-benefits: a type of value proposition that involves identifying and promoting all the benefits of a product or service to target customers, with little regard to the competition or any real insight into what the customer really wants or needs.

Analytical strategies: actions that involve taking time to think carefully about a problem by breaking it up into parts, or looking at it in a more general way in order to generate ideas about how certain products or services can be improved or made more innovative.

Angel investor: a type of investor who uses his or her own money to provide funds to young startup private businesses run by entrepreneurs who are neither friends nor family.

Backlog: orders that have been received but not delivered to the customer.

Balance sheet: a financial statement that shows what the company owes, what it owns, including the shareholder's stake, at a particular point in time.

Behavior focused strategies: methods to increase self-awareness and manage behaviors particularly when dealing with necessary but unpleasant tasks. These strategies include: self-observation, self-goal setting, self-reward, self-punishment, and self-cueing.

Benefit corporation (or B-Corp): a form of organization certified by the nonprofit BLab that ensures strict standards of social and environmental performance, accountability, and transparency are met.

Bonds: the connections with family, friends, and others who have a similar cultural background or ethnicity.

Bootstrapping: the process of building or starting a business with very little funding or capital or virtually nothing at all.

Bottoms Up (or Build Up Method): Estimating revenues and costs from the smallest unit of sales, such as a day.

Brand strategy: a long-term plan to develop a successful brand; it involves how you plan to communicate your brand messages to your target customers.

Branding: the process of creating a name, term, design, symbol, or any other feature that identifies a product or service and differentiates it from others.

Bridges: the links that go further than simply sharing a sense of identity; for example, making connections with distant friends or colleagues who may have different backgrounds, cultures, and so on.

Brokers: the people who organize transactions between buyers and sellers.

Building approach: a concept that assumes that opportunities do not exist independent of entrepreneurs, but are instead a product of the mind.

Bundled pricing: a type of pricing strategy whereby companies package a set of goods or services together and then sell them for a lower price than if they were to be sold separately

Business model canvas (BMC): a type of visual plan that depicts the business on one page by filling in nine blocks of a business model.

Business model: a conceptual framework that describes how a company creates, delivers, and extracts value.

Business plan: a formal document that provides background and financial information about the company, outlines your goals for the business, and describes how you intend to reach them.

C corporation: (sometimes known as a "C-corp") a separate legal and taxable entity created by the state government and owned by an unlimited number of shareholders.

Capital stock: the original amount the owners paid into the company plus any additional paid-in capital to purchase stock in the company.

Cash Conversion Cycle (CCC): the number of days a company's cash is tied up in the production and sales process.

Cash flow statement: a financial report that details the inflows and outflows of cash for a company over a set period of time.

Challenging: the process of building on past failures by braving new encounters.

Cognitive comprehensiveness: a process in which team members examine critical issues with a wide lens and formulate strategies by considering diverse approaches, decision criteria, and courses of action.

Compensation policy: The level of compensation and benefits for each type of position in the business.

Competition-led pricing: a type of pricing strategy when prices are guided by other businesses selling the same or very similar products and services.

Constructive thought patterns: models to help us to form positive and productive ways of thinking that can benefit our performance.

Convergent thinking: a thought process that allows us to narrow down the number of ideas generated through divergent thinking in an effort to identify which ones have the most potential.

Convertible debt: (also known as convertible bond or a convertible note)—a short-term loan that can be turned into equity when future financing is issued.

Copyright: a form of protection provided to the creators of original works in the areas of literature, drama, art, music, film and other intellectual areas.

Corporate entrepreneurship (or intrapreneurship): a process of creating new products, ventures, processes, or renewal within large organizations.

Corporate social responsibility (CSR): describes the efforts taken by corporations to address the company's effects on environmental and social well-being in order to promote positive change.

Cost of goods sold (COGS): the value of goods sold when a sale takes place.

Cost-led pricing: a type of pricing strategy that involves calculating all the costs involved in manufacturing or delivering the product or service, plus all other expenses, and adding an expected profit or margin by predicting your sales volume to get the approximate price.

Creation logic: a form of thinking that is used when the future is unpredictable.

Creativity: the capacity to produce new ideas, insights, inventions, products, or artistic objects that are considered to be unique, useful, and of value to others.

Credit policy: The process and timing in which obligations to pay for products and services sold will be billed and collected.

Crowdfunding: the process of raising funding for a new venture from a large audience (the "crowd"), typically through the Internet.

Crowdsourcing: the process of using the Internet to attract, aggregate, and manage ostensibly inexpensive or even free labor from enthusiastic customers and like-minded people.

Current assets: cash and other assets that can be converted into cash within a year.

Current liabilities: bills that must be paid within one year of the date of the balance sheet.

Customer value proposition (CVP): a statement that describes exactly what products or services your business offers and sells to customers.

Customer-led pricing: a type of pricing strategy when you ask customers how much they are willing to pay, and then offer it at that price.

Customers: people who populate the segments of a market served by the offering.

Data Revenue Model: a type of revenue model whereby companies generate revenue by selling high-quality, exclusive, valuable information to other parties.

Decision makers: the type of customers (similar to economic buyers) who have even more authority to make purchasing decisions as they are positioned higher up in the hierarchy.

Deliberate practice: a method of carrying out carefully focused efforts to improve current performance.

Design thinking: a thinking process most commonly used by designers to solve complex problems and navigate uncertain environments.

Development strategies: actions that involve enhancing and modifying existing ideas in order to create better alternatives and new possibilities.

Deviance: a situation where an entrepreneur defies legal and ethical boundaries leading to mismanagement of the venture.

Direct cross-subsidies: pricing a product or service above its market value to pay for the loss of giving away a product or service for free or below its market value.

Divergent thinking: a thought process that allows us to expand our view of the world to generate as many ideas as possible without being trapped by traditional problem-solving methods or predetermined constraints.

Diversified market: a variety of services that for two customer segments with different needs and problems, and which bear no relationship to each other.

DOI: a measure of the average number of days it takes to sell the entire inventory of a company.

DPO: a measure of the number of days it takes you to pay your bills.

DSO: a measure of the number of days that it takes to collect on accounts receivable.

Due diligence: a rigorous process which involves evaluating an investment opportunity prior to the contract being signed.

Early-stage financing: a stage of financing which involves larger funds provided for companies that have a team in place and a product or service tested or piloted, but has little or no revenue.

Earned-income activities: the sale of products or services that are used as a source of revenue generation.

Economic buyers: the type of customers who have the ability to approve purchases, such as office managers, corporate VPs, or even teens with their own allowances.

Effectuation: the idea that the future is unpredictable yet controllable.

End users: the type of customers who will use your product. Their feedback will help you refine and tweak the product.

Enterprising nonprofits: a form of social entrepreneurship where both the venture mission and the market impact are for social purposes.

Entrepreneur: an individual or a group who creates something new—a new idea, a new item or product, a new institution, a new market, a new set of possibilities.

Entrepreneurial marketing: a set of processes adopted by entrepreneurs based on new and unconventional marketing practices in order to gain traction in competitive markets.

Entrepreneurial mindset: the ability to quickly sense, take action, and get organized under uncertain conditions.

Entrepreneurial self-efficacy (ESE): the belief that entrepreneurs have in their own ability to begin new ventures.

Entrepreneurs inside: the types of entrepreneurs who think and act entrepreneurially within organizations.

Entrepreneurship: a discipline that seeks to understand how opportunities are discovered, created, and exploited, by whom, and with what consequences.

Equity crowdfunding: a form of crowdfunding that gives investors the opportunity to become shareholders in a company.

Equity financing: the sale of shares of stock in exchange for cash.

Established business owners: the people who are still active in business for over three and a half years.

Expanding: the broadening or the acquisition of new skills that enable people to generate ideas and share knowledge.

Experiment: a method used to prove or disprove the validity of an idea or hypothesis.

Exploratory experimentation: a method whereby market tests are conducted to get early feedback and acquire important learning and information.

Exposing: the skills required to open ourselves to diverse and fluctuating circumstances and events.

Fair pricing: the degree to which both businesses and customers believe that the pricing is reasonable.

Family enterprise: a business that is owned and managed by multiple family members, typically for more than one generation.

Feasibility study: a planning tool that allows entrepreneurs to test the possibilities of an initial idea to see if it is worth pursuing.

Financial viability: defines the revenue and cost structures a business needs to meet its operating expenses and financial obligations.

Finding approach: a concept that assumes that opportunities exist independent of entrepreneurs and are waiting to be found.

Fixed mindset: the assumption held by people who perceive their talents and abilities as set traits.

Founding team: a group of people with complementary skills and a shared sense of commitment coming together in founding an enterprise to build and grow the company.

Franchise: a type of license purchased by a franchisee from an existing business, to allow them to trade under the name of that business.

Franchising Revenue Model: a type of revenue model whereby franchises are sold by an existing business to allow another party to trade under the name of that business.

Freemium Revenue Model: a type of revenue model whereby free (mainly web-based) basic services are mixed with premium or upgraded services.

General partnership: two or more people who have made a decision to co-manage and share in the profits and losses of a business.

Goodwill: the price paid for an asset in excess of its book value. You will see this on the balance sheet when the company has made one or more large acquisitions.

Grit: the quality that enables people to work hard and sustain interest in their long-term goals.

Groupthink: a phenomenon where people share too similar a mindset, which inhibits their ability to spot gaps or errors.

Growth mindset: the assumption held by people who believe that their abilities can be developed through dedication, effort, and hard work.

Guerilla marketing: a low-budget strategy that focuses on personally interacting with a target group by promoting their products and services be heard and seen in very noisy marketplaces.

Habit: a sometimes unconscious pattern of behavior that is carried out often and regularly.

Habit-breaking strategies: actions that involve techniques that help to break our minds out of mental fixedness in order to bring about creative insights.

Heterogeneous team: a group of people with a mix of knowledge, skills, and experience.

Homogenous team: a group of people with the same or similar characteristics such as age, gender, ethnicity, experience, and educational background.

Hybrid model of social entrepreneurship: an organization with a purpose that equally emphasizes both economic and social goals.

Hypothesis: an assumption that is tested through research and experimentation.

Ideation: a creative process that involves generating and developing new ideas based on observations gained during the inspiration process to address latent needs.

Imagination-based strategies: actions that involve suspending disbelief and dropping constraints in order to create unrealistic states, or fantasies.

Implementation: a process involving the testing of assumptions of new ideas to continuously shape them into viable opportunities

Impression management: the concept of how people pay conscious attention to the way they are perceived and the steps they take to be perceived by others in a certain way.

Improvisation: the art of spontaneously creating something without preparation

Inattention: a condition whereby an entrepreneur becomes sidetracked from the core business.

Income statement (or profit and loss statement): a financial report that measures the financial performance of your business on a monthly or annual basis.

Income statement: a financial report that measures the financial performance of your business on a monthly or annual basis.

Influencers (or opinion leaders): the type of customers with a large following who have the power to influence our purchase decisions.

Infrastructure: the resources (people, technology, products, suppliers, partners, facilities, cash, etc.) that an entrepreneur must have in order to deliver the CVP.

Insight: an interpretation of an observation or a sudden realization that provides us with a new understanding of a human behavior or attitude that results in some sort of action.

Inspiration: the problem or opportunity that stimulates the quest for a solution.

Intangible assets: the value of patents, software programs, copyrights, trademarks, franchises, brand names, or assets that cannot be physically touched.

Intellectual property (IP): intangible personal property created by human intelligence, such as ideas, inventions, slogans, logos, and processes.

Intelligent failures: a way of describing failures that provide valuable new knowledge that can help a startup innovate and stride ahead of its competition.

Interest expense: the extent of the company's debt burden as well as representing any interest owed on borrowed money.

Intermediation Revenue Model: the different methods by which third parties such as brokers (or "middlemen") can generate money.

Interpersonal strategies: actions that involve group members stimulating each other to come up with new or improved ideas.

Introductory offer: a pricing method to encourage people to try a new product by offering it for free or at a heavily discounted price.

Inventory policy: The level of various types of inventory (e.g., raw materials, work-in-process, finished goods) maintained and the speed with which inventory moves from the business to the customer.

Investor model: a context for crowdfunding that gives backers an equity stake in the business in return for their funding.

Lack of ability: the lack of skillset to get the job done.

Latent needs: needs we don't know we have.

Lending model: a context for crowdfunding where funds are offered as loans with the expectation that the money will be repaid.

Liabilities: economic obligations of the company, such as money owed to lenders, suppliers, and employees.

Licensing Revenue Model: a way of earning revenue by giving permission to other parties to use protected intellectual property (patents, copyrights, trademarks) in exchange for fees.

Limited liability company (LLC): a form of business structure that combines the taxation advantages of a partnership with the limited liability benefits of corporation without being subject to the eligibility requirements of an S corp.

Linkages: the connections to people or groups regardless of their position in an organization, society, or other community.

Long-term debt: obligation for debt that is due to be repaid in more than 12 months.

Long-term investments: assets that are more than one year old and are carried on the balance sheet at cost or book value with no appreciation.

Loss leader: a pricing method whereby a business offers a product or service at a lower price in an attempt to attract more customers

Marketing mix: a tool that helps to define the brand and how it differentiates from the competition.

Marketing: a method of putting the right product in the right place, at the right price, at the right time.

Mass market: a large group of customers with very similar needs and problems.

Microloan: a very small, short-term loan often associated with entrepreneurs in developing countries.

Multiparty business: a type of free model that involves giving one party product or service free, but charging the other party(s).

Multisided markets: platforms that serve two or more customer segments that are mutually independent of each other.

Nascent entrepreneurs: individuals who have set up a business they will own or co-own that is less than three months old and has not yet generated wages or salaries for the owners.

Natural reward strategies: types of compensation designed to make aspects of a task or activity more enjoyable by building in certain features, or by reshaping perceptions to focus on the most positive aspects of the task and the value it holds.

Necessity-based entrepreneurs: individuals who are pushed into starting a business because of circumstance such as redundancy, threat of job loss, and unemployment.

Needs: human emotions or desires that are uncovered through the design process.

Net income: indicates what is left after all costs, expenses, and taxes have been paid.

New business owners: individuals who are former nascent entrepreneurs and have been actively involved in a business for over three months but less than three and a half years.

Niche market: a small market segment comprising customers with specific needs and requirements.

Not for profit: a tax status granted to companies performing functions deemed by Congress to be socially desirable that exempts them from income tax and, in some cases, allows them to receive tax deductible donations.

Observation: the action of closely monitoring the behavior and activities of users/potential customers in their own environment.

Offering: what you are offering to a particular customer segment, the value generated for those customers, and how you will reach and communicate with them.

Operating Expenses: the costs of running your business, including your rent, utilities, administration, marketing/advertising, employee salaries, and so on.

Operating expenses: the expenditures that the company makes to generate income.

Operating profit: the amount left over from revenue once all costs and expenses are subtracted

Opportunity: an apparent way of generating profit through unique, novel, or desirable products or services that have not been previously exploited.

Opportunity-based entrepreneurs: individuals who make a decision to start their own businesses based on their ability to create or exploit an opportunity, and whose main driver for getting involved in the venture is being independent or increasing their income, rather than merely maintaining their income.

Other current liabilities: short-term liabilities that do not fall into a specific category, such as sales tax, income tax, and so forth.

Packaging: a process that explores every single visual element of the external appearance of an offering through the eyes of your customer.

Passion: an intense positive emotion, which is usually related to entrepreneurs who are engaged in meaningful ventures, or tasks and activities, and which has the eff ect of motivating and stimulating entrepreneurs to overcome obstacles and remain focused on their goals.

Patent: a grant of exclusive property rights on inventions through the U.S. and other governments.

Patronage model: a context for crowdfunding that describes the fi nancial support given by backers without any expectation of a direct return for their donations.

Pattern recognition: the process of identifying links or connections between apparently unrelated things or events.

Payables policy: The process and timing in which obligations to pay for goods and services received by the business will be paid.

People: the people who are responsible for every aspect of sales and marketing.

Pitch: the act of clearly presenting and describing a product or service to others.

Pivot: a quick reaction and sometimes a change in direction.

Place: the location where the product is actually distributed to your target market; for example, trade fairs, retail stores, catalogs, mail order, online, and so forth.

Plan: a written description of the future you envision for your business, including what you plan to do and how you plan to do it.

Planning: a description of the future one envisions for a business, including what one plans to do and how one plans to do it.

Points-of-difference: a type of approach that focuses on the product or service relative to the competition and how the offering is different from others on the market.

Positioning: a marketing strategy that focuses on how your customers think or talk about product and a company relative to competitors.

Potential entrepreneurs: individuals who believe they have the capacity and know-how to start a business without being burdened by the fear of failure.

Predictive logic: a form of thinking that sees entrepreneurship as a linear process in which steps are followed and outcomes are—ideally—predictable.

Prepaid expenses: the payments the company has already made for services not yet received.

Price: the amount that the customer is expected to pay for the product, its perceived value, and the degree to which the price can be raised or lowered depending on market demand and how competitors price rival products.

Pricing policy: How pricing will be determined for your products and services.

Primary research: refers to data gathered by yourself through sources such as focus groups, interviews, and surveys

Prior knowledge: the preexisting information gained from a combination of life and work experience.

Process Inadequacy: The wrong (or lack of) processes set up in the organization causing communication breakdown.

Product: anything tangible or intangible (such as a service) offered by the company that includes the features, the brand, how it meets customer needs, how and where it will be used, and how it stands out from competitors.

Product-market fit: an offering that meets the needs of customers.

Professional Revenue Model: professional services on a time and materials contract.

Promotion: the activities that involve all the ways in which companies tell their customers about their offering.

Psychological pricing: a pricing method intended to encourage customers to buy on the basis of their belief that the product or service is cheaper than it really is.

Purchasing policy: The price and timing of raw materials and other goods and services necessary to build, sell, and support products.

Recommenders: The type of customers who have the power to make or break a sale.

Relationship-seeking strategies: plans of action that involve consciously making links between concepts or ideas that are not normally associated with each other.

Resonating-focus: a type of CVP that describes why people will really like your product and focuses on the customers and what they really need and value.

Retained earnings: the cumulative amount of profit retained by the company and not paid out in the form of dividends to owners.

Revenue Model: a key component of the business model and identifies how the company will earn income and make profits.

Revenue: the income gained from sales of goods or services.

Reward-based crowdfunding: a context for crowdfunding which involves rewarding backers for supporting a project.

Royalties: a share of the proceeds of a business from one party to another.

S corporation: (sometimes known as an "S-Corp") - a certain type of corporation which is eligible for, and elects special taxation status.

Saboteurs: the type of customers who can veto or slow down a purchasing decision.

SAM: (Serviceable Available Market)—the section of the TAM that your product or service intends to target.

Search strategies: actions that involve using memory to retrieve information to make links or connections based on past experience that are relevant to the current problem using stimuli.

Secondary research: refers to data gathered from external sources such as industry publications, websites, government agencies, and so on.

Securing: the capacity to focus on and sustain new ideas.

Seed-stage financing: a stage of financing in which small or modest amounts of capital are provided to entrepreneurs to prove a concept.

Segmented market: a marketing strategy that involves breaking customer segments into groups according to their different needs and problems.

Self-cueing: the process of prompting that acts as a reminder of desired goals, and keeps your attention on what you are trying to achieve.

Self-goal setting: the process of setting individual goals for ourselves.

Self-leadership: a process whereby people can influence and control their own behavior, actions, and thinking to achieve the self-direction and self-motivation necessary to build their entrepreneurial business ventures.

Self-observation: a process that raises our awareness of how, when, and why we behave the way we do in certain circumstances.

Self-punishment (or self-correcting feedback): a process that allows us to examine our own behaviors in a constructive way in order to reshape these behaviors.

Self-reward: a process that involves compensating ourselves when we achieve our goals. These rewards can be tangible or intangible.

Self-selected stakeholders: the people who "self-select" into a venture in order to connect entrepreneurs with resources in an effort to steer the venture in the right direction

Serial Entrepreneurs (or habitual entrepreneurs): the type of entrepreneurs who start several businesses, whether simultaneously or one after the other.

Serial Entrepreneurs (or habitual entrepreneurs): the type of entrepreneurs who start several businesses, whether simultaneously or one after the other.

Shareholder equity: the money that has been invested in the business plus the cumulative net profits and losses the company has generated.

Short-term debt: the portion of long-term debt that must be paid within a year.

Skill of creativity: requires a general openness to the world and relates to unleashing our creative ability to create and find opportunities and solve problems.

Skill of empathy: developing the ability to understand the emotion, circumstances, intentions, thoughts, and needs of others.

Skill of experimentation: best described as acting in order to learn—trying something, learning from the attempt and building that learning into the next iteration.

Skill of play: frees the imagination, opens up our minds to a wealth of opportunities and possibilities, and helps us to be more innovative as entrepreneurs.

Skill of reflection: helps make sense of all of the other actions required of play, empathy, creativity and experimentation.

Skimming: a form of high pricing method, generally used for new products or service that face very little, or even no competition.

Social capital: personal social networks populated with people who willingly cooperate, exchange information, and build trusting relationships with each other.

Social consequence entrepreneurship: a for-profit venture whose primary market impact is social.

Social entrepreneurship: the process of sourcing innovative solutions.

Social purpose ventures: businesses created by social entrepreneurs to resolve a social problem and make a profit.

Sole proprietorship: a person who owns a business and has full exposure to its liabilities.

SOM: (Share of market)—the portion of SAM that your company is realistically likely to reach.

Stakeholders: the people or groups affected by or involved with the achievements of the social enterprise's objectives.

Startup financing: a stage of financing in which the money is provided to entrepreneurs to enable them to implement the idea by funding product research and development.

Startup: a temporary organization in search of a scalable business model.

Storyboarding: an easy form of prototyping that provides a high-level view of thoughts and ideas arranged in sequence in the form of drawings, sketches, or illustrations.

Subscription Revenue Model: a type of model that involves charging customers to gain continuous access to a product or service.

Sweat equity: the increase in value or ownership interest created as a result of hard work.

TAM: (Total Available Market)—the total market demand for a product or service.

Target-return pricing: a pricing method whereby the price is based on the amount of investment you have put into your business.

Theory of Effectuation: the idea that the future is unpredictable yet controllable and entrepreneurs can "effect" the future.

Total Entrepreneurial Activity (TEA): the percentage of the population of each country between the ages of 18 and 64, who are either a nascent entrepreneur or owner-manager of a new business.

Trade secret: confidential information that provides companies with a competitive edge and is not in the public domain, such as formulas, patterns, compilations, programs, devices, methods, techniques, or processes

Trademark: Any word, name, symbol, or device used in business to identify and promote a product. Its counterpart for service industries is the service mark.

TRIM (Team, Resources, Idea, Market) framework: a planning tool that identifies the types of people needed for the team, the resources available and needed, the details of the idea, and the potential market for the product or service.

Uncertainty: the lack of clarity about future events that can cause entrepreneurs to take unreasonable actions.

Unit Sales Revenue Model: the amount of revenue generated by the number of items (units) sold by a company.

Use Case: a methodology used in the software industry to illustrate how a user will interact with a specific piece of software.

Utility and Usage Revenue Model: a pay-as-you-go model that charges customers fees on the basis of how often goods or services are used.

Value-based pricing: a pricing method that involves pricing a product based on how it benefits the customer.

Venture capitalist (VC): a type of professional investor who generally invests in early-stage and emerging companies because of perceived long-term growth potential.

Venture philanthropy funding: a combination of financial assistance such as grants with a high level of engagement by the funder.

Vesting: the concept of imposing equity forfeitures on cofounders over a certain period of time on a piecemeal basis should they not stay with the company.

Wicked problems: large, complex social problems where there is no clear solution, where there is limited, confusing, or contradictory information available, and where a whole range of people with conflicting values engage in debate.

Work integration social enterprise (WISE): a social enterprise whose mission is to integrate people who have been socially excluded into work and society through productive activity.

NOTES

CHAPTER 1

1. PBS News Hour interview transcript. Retrieved from http://www. skaggsisland. org/sustainable/muhammadyunus.htm

2. Yunus, M., & Jolis, A. (2007). *Banker to the poor: Micro-lending and the battle against world poverty.* New York: Public Affairs.

3. Rindova, V., Barry, D., & Ketchen, D. J. (2009). Entrepreneuring as emancipation. *Academy of Management Review, 34,* 477–491.

4. Gladwell, M. (2008). *Outliers: The story of success.* New York: Little, Brown.

5. Feloni, R. (September 24, 2014). How Uber CEO Travis Kalanick went from a startup failure to one of the hottest names in Silicon Valley. *Business Insider.* Retrieved from http://www.businessinsider.com/ uber-ceo-travis-kalanicks-success-story-2014-9?IR=T

6. Blank, S., & Dorf, B. (2012). *The startup owner's manual: The step-by-step guide for building a great company.* K&S Ranch.

7. Neck, H. M., Greene, P. G., & Brush, C. B. (2014). *Teaching entrepreneurship: A practice-based approach.* Northampton, MA: Edward Elgar.

8. Sarasvathy, S. D. (2008). *Effectuation: Elements of entrepreneurial expertise.* Northampton, MA: Edward Elgar.

9. Morris, M. H. (1998). *Entrepreneurial intensity: Sustainable advantages for individuals, organizations, and societies.* Westport, CT: Quorum.

10. Neck, H. M., & Greene, P. G. (2011). Entrepreneurship education: Known worlds and new frontiers. *Journal of Small Business Management, 49,* 55–70.

11. Brown, P. (November 6, 2013). Entrepreneurs are "calculated" risk takers—The word that can be the difference between failure and success. *Forbes.* Retrieved from www.forbes.com/sites/ actiontrumpseverything/2013/11/06/ entrepreneurs-are-not-risk-takers-they-are-calculated-risk-takers-that-one-additional-word-can-be-the-difference-between-failure-and-success/

12. Schlesinger, L., Kiefer, C., & Brown, P. (2012). *Just start: Take action, embrace uncertainty, create the future.* Cambridge, MA: Harvard Business School Press.

13. Costello, C., Neck, H., & Williams, R. (2011). *Elements of the entrepreneur experience.* Babson Park, MA: Babson Entrepreneur Experience Lab. Retrieved from http:// elab.businessinnovationfactory.com/ sites/default/files/pdf/BabsonBIF-eLab-NVE-V1-2012rev.pdf

14. Gralla, P. (October 31, 2011). Bill Gates—I helped Steve Jobs create the Mac. *Computerworld.* Retrieved from www. computerworld.com/article/2471512/ microsoft-windows/bill-gates—i-helped-steve-jobs-create-the-mac.html

15. Young Entrepreneurs Council. (March 23, 2014). 10 Ways it pays to work with your competitors. *Huffington Post.* Retrieved from http://www.huffingtonpost.com/ young-entrepreneur-council/10-ways-it-pays-to-work-w_b_4637818.html

16. Spors, K. K. (January 9, 2007). Do start-ups really need formal business plans? Studies find often time wasted gathering data with no link to success. *Wall Street Journal.* Retrieved from http://www.wsj .com/articles/SB116830373855570835

17. Costello, C., Neck H., & Williams, R. (2011). *Elements of the entrepreneur experience.* Babson Park, MA: Babson Entrepreneur Experience Lab. Retrieved from http:// elab.businessinnovationfactory.com/ sites/default/files/pdf/BabsonBIF-eLab-NVE-V1-2012rev.pdf

18. The Babson Entrepreneur Experience Lab in partnership with the Business Innovation Factory. Retrieved from www.businessinnovationfactory. com/interactive/era-analysis/era-analysis.html

19. Landstrom, H. (1999). The roots of entrepreneurship research, *New England Journal of Entrepreneurship, 2*(2), 9–20.

20. Hebert, R. & Link, A. (1989). In search of the meaning of entrepreneurship. *Small Business Economics. 1,* 39–49.

21. Drucker, P. (1985). *Innovation and entrepreneurship: Practice and principles* (p. 21). New York: Harper & Row, 1985. See also http://www.economist.com/ node/13565718

22. Schumpeter, J. A. (1934). *The theory of economic development* (p. 66). Cambridge, MA: Harvard University Press.

23. Kirzner, I. 1973. *Competition and entrepreneurship.* Chicago: University of Chicago Press.

24. Schumpeter, J. A. (1976). *Capitalism, socialism and democracy.* New York, NY: Harper & Row.

25. Venkataraman, S. (1997). The distinctive domain of entrepreneurship research. *Advances in Entrepreneurship, Firm Emergence and Growth, 3,* 119–138.

26. Pritzker, P. (March 28, 2014).The new "economic census" will help unleash the economic magic of U.S. government data. *Forbes.* Retrieved from http://www.forbes. com/sites/realspin/2014/03/28/the-new-economic-census-will-help-unleash-the-economic-magic-of-u-s-government-data/#16957e856e1a

27. Covin, J. G., & Miles, M. (1999). Corporate entrepreneurship and the pursuit of competitive advantage. *Entrepreneurship: Theory and Practice, 23*(3), 47–63.

28. Brush, C. (January 28, 22014). Are you a corporate entrepreneur? *Forbes.* Retrieved from www.forbes.com/ sites/babson/2014/01/28/are-you-a-corporate-entrepreneur/

29. Costello, C., Neck, H., & Dziobek, K. (2012). *Entrepreneurs of all kinds: Elements of the entrepreneurs inside experience.* Babson Park, MA: Babson Entrepreneur Experience Lab. Retrieved from http:// elab.businessinnovationfactory.com/ sites/default/files/pdf/babsonBIF-elab-EI-V2-2012rev.pdf

30. *Intermarche: Inglorious fruits and vegetables.* (n.d.). Retrieved from http:// adsoftheworld.com/media/ambient/ intermarche_inglorious_fruits_and_ vegetables

31. Judd, R. J., & Justis, R. T. (2007). *Franchising: An entrepreneur's guide* (4th ed.). Stamford, CT: Cengage Learning.

32. Franchise Direct website. Retrieved from www.franchisedirect.com/blog/10-random-and-interesting-franchise-facts/

33. Frannet website. Retrieved from www .frannet.com/index.php/franchising-basics/franchise-facts

34. Small Business Association website. Retrieved from www.sba.gov/content/ buying-existing-business

35. Interview with Chris Cranston, FlowDog.

36. Neck, H. M. (2010). Social entrepreneurship. In B. Bygrave & A. Zacharakis (Eds.), *The portable MBA in entrepreneurship* (pp. 411–436). Hoboken, NJ: Wiley.

37. Neck, H. M., Brush, C., & Allen, E. (2009). The landscape of social entrepreneurship. *Business Horizons, 52,* 13–19; Mair, J., & Marti, I. (2006). Social entrepreneurship research: A source of explanation, prediction and delight. *Journal of World Business, 41,* 36–44.

38. Roominate™ raises over $1 million for the debut of its new line of connected building kits. (2015, September 15). *Business Wire.* Retrieved from http://www.businesswire.com/ news/home/20150915005580/en/ Roominate%E2%84%A2-Raises-1-Million-Debut-Line-Connected.

39. Schwab Foundation for Social Entrepreneurship website. Retrieved from www.schwabfound.org/content/ lo-chay and https://www.youtube .com/watch?hl=fr&v=8bykbVECV rE&gl=FR

40. B Corporation website. Retrieved from https://www.bcorporation.net/what-are-b-corps

41. Clifford, C. (2012, June 11). B corps: The next generation of company. *Entrepreneur.* Retrieved from www.entrepreneur.com/ blog/223762

42. Warby Parker website. Retrieved from www.warbyparker.com/buy-a-pair-give-a-pair

43. Habbershon, T. G., Williams, M., & MacMillan, I. C. 2003. A unified systems perspective of family firm performance. *Journal of Business Venturing, 18.* 451–465.

44. Aileron. (2013, July 31). The facts of family business. *Forbes.* Retrieved from www.forbes.com/sites/aileron/2013/07/31/the-facts-of-family-business/

45. The University of Vermont College of Business website. Retrieved from www.uvm.edu/business/vfbi/?Page=facts.html

46. https://www.virgin.com/richard-branson/opportunity-missed

47. Family Enterprise USA (FEUSA). (2013). *2013 Survey of family firms.* Retrieved from http://c.ymcdn.com/sites/www.familyenterpriseusa.org/resource/resmgr/annual_survey/2013_feusa_annual_survey_res.pdf

48. Ethical entrepreneurs win first Yunus Social Business Awards, Greater Manchester Chamber of Commerce website. Retrieved from http://www.gmchamber.co.uk/stories/member-news-ethical-entrepreneurs-win-first-yunus-social-business-awards

49. Geromel, R. (2012, April 27). Israeli Nobel Prize Winner: Entrepreneurship is the only way to maintain peace. *Forbes.* Retrieved from www.forbes.com/sites/ricardogeromel/2012/04/27/israeli-nobel-prize-winner-entrepreneurship-is-the-only-way-to-maintain-peace/

50. President Obama on National Small Business Award Winners. (2009, May 19). Retrieved from https://www.whitehouse.gov/video/President-Obama-on-National-Small-Business-Award-Winners#transcript

51. Unreasonableatsea website. Retrieved from http://unreasonableatsea.com/overview/

52. Braun, A. (2014). *The promise of a pencil: How an ordinary person can create extraordinary change.* New York: Scribner.

53. The Global Entrepreneurship Monitor (GEM) website. Retrieved from http://www.gemconsortium.org/

54. Kelley, D., Singer, S., & Herrington, M. (2015). *Global entrepreneurship monitor 2015 global report.* Global Entrepreneurship Research Association. Retrieved from http://www.gemconsortium.org/docs/download/3106

55. Kelley, D., Singer, S., & Herrington, M. (2015). *Global entrepreneurship monitor 2015 global report.* Global Entrepreneurship Research Association. Retrieved from http://www.gemconsortium.org/docs/download/3106

56. Kelley, D., Singer, S., & Herrington, M. (2015). *Global Entrepreneurship Monitor 2015 Global Report.* Global Entrepreneurship Research Association. Retrieved from http://www.gemconsortium.org/docs/download/3106

CHAPTER 2

1. Schlesinger, L., Kiefer, C., & Brown, P. (2012). *Just start: Take action, embrace uncertainty, create the future.* Cambridge, MA: Harvard Business School Press.

2. Noyes, E. and Brush, C. 2012. Teaching Entrepreneurial Action: Application of the Creative Logic. In A. C. Corbett and, J. A. Katz (eds.), *Advances in Entrepreneurship, Firm Emergence and Growth,* Vol 14: 253–280.

3. Greenberg, D., McKone-Sweet, K., & Wilson, H. J. (Eds.). (2011). *The new entrepreneurial leader: Developing leaders who will shape social and economic opportunities.* San Francisco, CA: Berrett-Koehler.

4. Blank, S., & Dorf, B. (2012). *The startup owner's manual: The step-by-step guide for building a great company.* K&S Ranch.

5. Here we are building on the work of Sarasvathy. Rather than use the terms "effectual" and "causal," we are using "prediction" and "creation," respectively. Effectuation theory assumes that causal is not needed; however, we promote the use of both types of thinking. In the startup world, creation comes before prediction. Use of the terminology "creation" and "prediction" rather than "effectual" and "causal" can be found in Schlesinger, L., Kiefer, C., & Brown, P. (2012). *Just start: Take action, embrace uncertainty, create the future.* Cambridge, MA: Harvard Business School Press; Greenberg, D., McKone-Sweet, K., & Wilson, H. J. (Eds.). (2011). *The new entrepreneurial leader: Developing leaders who will shape social and economic opportunities.* San Francisco, CA: Berrett-Koehler; Noyes, E., & Brush, C. (2012). Teaching entrepreneurial action: Application of creative logic. In A. C. Corbett & J. A. Katz (Eds.), *Entrepreneurial action: Advances in entrepreneurship and firm emergence and growth* (pp. 253–280); Neck, H. M., Greene, P. G., & Brush, C. B. (2014). *Teaching entrepreneurship: A practice-based approach.* Northampton, MA: Edward Elgar.

6. Read, S., Sarasvathy, S., Dew, N., & Wiltbank, R. (2011). *Effectual entrepreneurship.* New York, NY: Routledge.

7. Sarasvathy, S. D. (2008). *Effectuation: Elements of entrepreneurial expertise.* Northampton, MA: Edward Elgar.

8. Dew, N., Read, S., Sarasvathy, S. D., & Wiltbank, R. (2009). Effectual versus predictive logics in entrepreneurial decision-making: Differences between experts and novices. *Journal of Business Venturing, 24,* 287–309.

9. Neck, H. M., Greene, P. G., & Brush, C. B. (2014/2015). Practice-based entrepreneurship education using actionable theory. In M. Morris (Ed.), *Annals of Entrepreneurship Education and Pedagogy* (pp. 3–20). Northampton, MA: Edward Elgar.

10. Neck, H. (September 9, 2014). Entrepreneurship requires practice: Part 1—The five practices. *Forbes.* Retrieved from www.forbes.com/sites/babson/2014/09/09/entrepreneurship-requires-practice-part-1-the-five-practices/

11. Ries, E. (2011). *The lean startup: How today's entrepreneurs use continuous innovation to create radically successful businesses.* New York, NY: Crown Business.

12. Neck, H. (September 9, 2014). Entrepreneurship requires practice: Part 1—The five practices. *Forbes.* Retrieved from www.forbes.com/sites/babson/2014/09/09/entrepreneurship-requires-practice-part-1-the-five-practices/

13. Neck, H. (September 9, 2014). Entrepreneurship requires practice: Part 1—The five practices. *Forbes.* Retrieved from www.forbes.com/sites/babson/2014/09/09/entrepreneurship-requires-practice-part-1-the-five-practices/

14. Hamidi, D. Y., Wennberg, K., & Berglund, H. (2008). Creativity in entrepreneurship education. *Journal of Small Business and Enterprise Development, 15,* 304–320.

15. Brockbank, A., & McGill, I. (2007). *Facilitating reflective learning in higher education* (2nd ed.). New York, NY: Open University Press.

16. Neck, H. M., Greene, P. G. & Brush, C. (2014). *Teaching entrepreneurship: A practice-based approach.* Northampton, MA: Edward Elgar Publishing; Brockbank, A., & McGill, I. (2007). *Facilitating reflective learning in higher education* (2nd ed.). New York, NY: Open University Press.

17. Hedburg, C., & Luecke, R. (2005, July 25). Jim Poss. Babson Case Study #130-C04 A-U.

18. Bigbelly website. Retrieved from http://www.bigbelly.com/

19. Blank, S., & Dorf, B. (2012). *The startup owner's manual: The step-by-step guide for building a great company.* K&S Ranch.

20. Wagner, E. T. (September 12, 2013). Five reasons 8 out of 10 businesses fail. *Forbes.* Retrieved from www.forbes.com/sites/ericwagner/2013/09/12/five-reasons-8-out-of-10-businesses-fail/

21. Campbell, A. (July 7, 2005). Business failure rates highest in first two years. *Small Business Trends.* Retrieved from http://smallbiztrends.com/2005/07/business-failure-rates-highest-in.html

22. Neck, H. M., & Greene, P. G. (2011). Entrepreneurship education: Known worlds and new frontiers. *Journal of Small Business Management, 49,* 55–70.

23. Neck, H. M., Greene, P. G., & Brush, C. B. (2014/2015). Practice-based entrepreneurship education using actionable theory. In M. Morris (Ed.), *Annals of entrepreneurship education and pedagogy* (pp. 3–20). Northampton, MA: Edward Elgar.

24. Mask, C. (November 4, 2014). The 4 reasons why people start their own businesses. *The Business Journals.* Retrieved from http://www.bizjournals.com/bizjournals/how-to/growth-strategies/2014/11/4-reasons-why-people-start-their-own-businesses.html?page=all ; and Wells, C.

(2015, May 26). Why some entrepreneurs feel fulfilled—But others don't: Money is only part of the equation; The latest research offers surprising insights into the path to satisfaction. *Wall Street Journal* [Eastern edition, New York, N.Y.], p. R.1.

25. Sarasvathy, S. D. (2008). *Effectuation: Elements of entrepreneurial expertise*. Northampton, MA: Edward Elgar.

26. Concept of affordable loss is based on the previously cited words of Saras Sarasvathy.

27. Santinelli, A., & Luecke, R. (June 11, 2010). Vera Bradley (A). Babson Case Study #656-C-10.

28. Vera Bradley website. Retrieved from www.verabradley.com

29. Santinelli, A., & Luecke, R. (June 11, 2010). Vera Bradley (A). Babson Case Study #656-C-10.

30. Baron, R. A., & Henry, R. A. (2010). How entrepreneurs acquire the capacity to excel: Insights from research on expert performance. *Strategic Entrepreneurship Journal, 4*, 49–65.

31. Baron, R. A., & Henry, R. A. (2010). How entrepreneurs acquire the capacity to excel: Insights from research on expert performance. *Strategic Entrepreneurship Journal, 4*, 49–65.

32. Duvivier, R. J., van Dalen, J., Muijtjens, A. M., Moulaert, V., van der Vleuten, C., & Scherpbier, A. (2011). The role of deliberate practice in the acquisition of clinical skills. *BMC Medical Education, 11*, 101–108.

33. Wasserman, N. (2014, August 25). How an entrepreneur's passion can destroy a startup. *Wall Street Journal*. Retrieved from http://online.wsj.com/articles/how-an-entrepreneur-s-passion-can-destroy-a-startup-1408912044

34. Schwartz, M. A. (2008). The importance of stupidity in scientific research. *Journal of Cell Science, 121*(11), 1771.

CHAPTER 3

1. McKean, E. (2005). *New Oxford American dictionary* (2nd ed.). New York, NY: Oxford University Press.

2. Dweck, C. (2006). *Mindset: The new psychology of success*. New York, NY: Random House.

3. Wiseman, R. (2003). *The luck factor: The four essential principles*. New York, NY: Hyperion.

4. Bronson, P. (2007, August 3). How not to talk to your kids. *New York Magazine*. Retrieved from http://nymag.com/news/features/27840/

5. Dweck, C. Information obtained from Carol Dweck's website. Retrieved from http://mindsetonline.com/changeyourmindset/firststeps/

6. Ireland, R. D., Hitt, M. A., & Sirmon, D. G. (2003). A model of strategic entrepreneurship: The construct and its dimensions. *Journal of Management, 29*, 963–990.

7. Cardon, M. S., Wincent, J., Singh, J., & Drnovsek, M. (2009). The nature and experience of entrepreneurial passion. *Academy of Management Review, 34*, 511–532.

8. Warren, R. (2013, September 7). 101 Best inspirational quotes for entrepreneurs. *Business Insider*. Retrieved from http://www.businessinsider.com/101-best-inspirational-quotes-for-entrepreneurs-2013-9

9. Cardon, M. S., Wincent, J., Singh, J., & Drnovsek, M. (2009). The nature and experience of entrepreneurial passion. *Academy of Management Review, 34*, 511–532.

10. Brännback, M., Carsrud, A., Elfying, J., & Krueger, N. (2006). *Sex, [drugs], and entrepreneurial passion? An exploratory study*. Paper presented at the Babson College Entrepreneurship Research Conference, Bloomington, IN.

11. Baron, R. A. (2008). The role of affect in the entrepreneurial process. *Academy of Management Review, 33*, 328–340.

12. Cardon, M. S., Wincent, J., Singh, J., & Drnovsek, M. (2009). The nature and experience of entrepreneurial passion. *Academy of Management Review, 34*, 511–532.

13. Duhigg, C. (2012, February 27). How you can harness the power of habit. *NPR*.

Retrieved from http://www.npr.org/2012/02/27/147296743/how-you-can-harness-the-power-of-habit

14. Information in this section taken from D'Intino, R. S., Goldsby, M. G., Houghton, J. D., & Neck, C. P. (2007). Self-leadership: A process for entrepreneurial success. *Journal of Leadership & Organizational Studies, 13*(4), 105–120.

15. Manz, C., & Neck, C. (2004). *Mastering self-leadership: Empowering yourself for personal excellence* (3rd ed.). Saddle River, NJ: Pearson Prentice Hall).

16. Neck, H. M. (2010). Idea generation. In B. Bygrave & A. Zacharakis (Eds.), *Portable MBA in entrepreneurship* (pp. 27–52). Hoboken, NJ: Wiley.

17. List of awards retrieved from http://blitab.com/

18. Hamidi, D. Y., Wennberg, K., & Berglund, H. (DATE). Creativity in entrepreneurship education. *Journal of Small Business and Enterprise Development, 15*, 301–320.

19. Neck, H. M. (2010). Idea generation (at pp. 34–35). In B. Bygrave & A. Zacharakis (Eds.), *Portable MBA in entrepreneurship* (pp. 27–52). Hoboken, NJ: Wiley.

20. Adams, J. (2001). *Conceptual blockbusting* (4th ed.). Cambridge, MA: Perseus.

21. Pink, D. H. (2005). *A whole new mind: Why right-brainers will rule the future*. New York, NY: Riverhead Books.

22. Nielsen, J. A., Zielinski, B. A., Ferguson, M. A., Lainhart, J. E, & Anderson, J. S. (2013). An evaluation of the left-brain vs. right-brain hypothesis with resting state functional connectivity magnetic resonance imaging. *PLoS ONE, 8*(8), e71275. doi:10.1371/journal.pone.0071275

23. Right brain, left brain, debunked. (2013, August 8). *Huffington Post*. Retrieved from http://www.huffingtonpost.com/2013/08/19/right-brain-left-brain-debunked_n_3762322.html

24. Csikszentmihalyi, M. (1996). *Creativity: Flow and the psychology of discovery and invention*. New York, NY: Harper Collins.

25. Hmieleski, K., & Corbett, A. (2008). The contrasting interaction effects of improvisational behavior with entrepreneurial self-efficacy on new venture performance and entrepreneur work satisfaction. *Journal of Business Venturing, 23*, 482–496.

26. Retrieved from http://iangotts.files.wordpress.com/2012/02/using-improv-in-business-e2-v1.pdf

27. Tutton, M. (2010, February 18). Why using improvisation to teach business skills is no joke. *CNN*. Retrieved from http://edition.cnn.com/2010/BUSINESS/02/18/improvisation.business.skills/

28. Zagorski, N. (2008, Fall). The science of improv. *Peabody Magazine*. Retrieved from http://www.peabody.jhu.edu/past_issues/fall08/the_science_of_improv.html

29. Schwartz, K. (2014, April 11). Creativity and the brain: What we can learn from jazz musicians. *Mindshift*. Retrieved from http://blogs.kqed.org/mindshift/2014/04/the-link-between-jazz-improvisation-and-student-creativity/

30. McGee, J. E., Peterson, M., Mueller, S., & Sequeira, J. (2009). Entrepreneurial self-efficacy: Refining the measure. *Entrepreneurship Theory & Practice, 33*, 965–988.

31. Godwin, J. L., Neck, C. P., & D'Intino, R. S. (2016). Self-leadership, spirituality and entrepreneurial performance: A conceptual model. *Journal of Management, Spirituality, and Religion, 13*(1), 64–78.

32. Caprino, K. (May 23, 2012). 10 Lessons I learned from Sara Blakely that you won't hear in business school. *Forbes*. Retrieved from http://www.forbes.com/sites/kathycaprino/2012/05/23/10-lessons-i-learned-from-sara-blakely-that-you-wont-hear-in-business-school/#78efd58d7442

33. Schwarzer, R., & Jerusalem, M. (1995). Generalized Self-Efficacy Scale. In J. Weinman, S. Wright, & M. Johnston (Eds.). *Measures in health psychology: A user's portfolio. Causal and control beliefs* (pp. 35–37). Windsor, England: NFER-NELSON. Scale retrieved from http://userpage.fu-berlin.de/~health/engscal.htm

34. Conflict minerals are natural resources extracted in conditions of conflict and human rights abuses. These minerals are used by rebels and armies, in the DRC (Democratic Republic of Congo) in particular, to help finance the conflict.

CHAPTER 4

1. Sharir, M., & Lerner, M. (2006). Gauging the success of social ventures initiated by individual social entrepreneurs. *Journal of World Business, 41,* 6–20, at p. 7.

2. Retrieved from http://www.un.org/waterforlifedecade/scarcity.shtml

3. Cheriakova, A. (2013, October 28). The emerging social enterprise: Framing the concept of social entrepreneurship. *The Broker.* Retrieved from http://thebrokeronline.eu/Articles/The-emerging-social-enterprise

4. Mair, J., & Marti, I. (2006). Social entrepreneurship research: A source of explanation, prediction, and delight. *Journal of World Business, 41,* 36–44.

5. Churchman, C. W. (1967). Wicked problems. *Management Science, 14*(4), B-141 & B-142; Conklin, J. (2006). *Dialogue mapping: Building shared understanding of wicked problems.* Chichester, England: Wiley. See also http://www.cognexus.org/id17.htm

6. Retrieved from http://www.kickstart.org/success-stories/kenya/samuel-ndungu-mburu/

7. Brown, T. (2008, June). Design thinking. *Harvard Business Review,* 84–92).

8. Rosenberg, T. (2013, January 16). A hospital network with a vision. *International New York Times Opinionator.* Retrieved from http://opinionator.blogs.nytimes.com/2013/01/16/in-india-leading-a-hospital-franchise-with-vision/?_r=0

9. Gaynor, T. (2015, December 18). 2015 likely to break records for forced displacementStudy. *UNHCR: The UN Refugee Agency.* Retrieved from http://www.unhcr.org/5672c2576.html

10. Chanoff, S. (2015, March 11). Entrepreneurship: A new front in the refugee crisis. *Huffpost.* Retrieved from http://www.huffingtonpost.com/sasha-chanoff/a-new-front-in-the-refuge_b_6832244.html

11. Neck, H. M., Brush, C., & Allen, E. (2009). The landscape of social entrepreneurship. *Business Horizons, 52,* 13–19.

12. PACT apparel introduces new organic cotton, fair trade certified line. (2014, March 7). *Fair Trade USA.* Retrieved from http://fairtradeusa.org/press-room/press-release/pact-apparel-introduces-new-organic-cotton-fair-trade-certified-line#

13. O'Neill, M. (2013, January 22). Help Whole Kids Foundation, PACT crowdsource 100 urban gardens across America," *AdWeek Blog Network: Social Times.* Retrieved from http://www.adweek.com/socialtimes/urban-gardens-across-america/117841

14. Reyes, M. (2015, May 18). West Point-born sisters add glam to military goods. *New York Post.* Retrieved from http://nypost.com/2015/05/18/west-point-born-sisters-add-glam-to-military-goods/

15. Marshall, A. (2014, September 30). Let's talk about zoo poop. *The Atlantic: Citylab.* Retrieved from http://www.citylab.com/cityfixer/2014/09/lets-talk-about-zoo-poop/380947/

16. Food Corps website. Retrieved from https://foodcorps.org/about

17. Lelon, E. (2014, July 10). The baby saving revolution: Obama and Beyonce embrace founder, Jane Chen (you will too). *Huff Post Business Blog.* Retrieved from http://www.huffingtonpost.com/elise-lelon/the-baby-saving-revolution-nonprofit_b_5570683.html

18. Building Impact website. Retrieved from http://buildingimpact.org/news/press/

19. Blanding, M. (2013, August 12). Entrepreneurs and the "hybrid" organization. *Forbes Blog.* Retrieved from http://www.forbes.com/sites/hbsworkingknowledge/2013/08/12/entrepreneurs-and-the-hybrid-organization/

20. BCorporation Blog Post. Sustainable Harvest. (2013, January 1). Retrieved from http://www.bcorporation.net/blog/sustainable-harvest

21. Sistare, H. (2013, February 28). Better World Books continue to innovate. *Triple Pundit.* Retrieved from http://www.triplepundit.com/2013/02/better-world-books-continues-to-innovate/

22. Better World Books website. Retrieved from http://www.betterworldbooks.com/info.aspx?f=our_impact

23. Lipin, A. (2015, April 30). Interview with Jennifer McFadden, Associate Director of Entrepreneurship at SOM. *Yale Entrepreneur.* Retrieved from http://yaleentrepreneur.com/2015/04/30/34758/

24. Cohen, R., & Bannick, M. (2014, September 20). Is social impact investing the next venture capital?" *Forbes.* Retrieved from http://www.forbes.com/sites/realspin/2014/09/20/is-social-impact-investing-the-next-venture-capital/

25. Examples of impact investment funds, *Impactbase* Retrieved from http://www.impactbase.org/info/examples-impact-investment-funds

26. VPP website. Retrieved from http://www.vppartners.org/about-us

27. SJF Ventures website. Retrieved from http://www.sjfventures.com/case-studies

28. SJF Ventures website. Retrieved from http://www.sjfventures.com/

29. Achates Power wins $14 million military engine project. (2015, March 31). *PR Newswire.* Retrieved from http://www.prnewswire.com/news-releases/achates-power-wins-14-million-military-engine-project-300057973.html

30. Mulupi, D. (2015, February 18). How this company built a business by charging phones in rural Tanzania. *How We Made It in Africa.* Retrieved from http://www.howwemadeitinafrica.com/how-this-company-built-a-business-by-charging-phones-in-rural-tanzania/47016/

31. Miller, T. (2014, June 16). Haiti rising: Record loan backed by Muhammad Yunus will create 300 quality jobs. *Kiva Blog.* Retrieved from http://blog.kiva.org/kivablog/2014/06/16/haiti-rising-record-loan-backed-by-muhammad-yunus-will-create-300-quality-jobs

32. Lidksy, D. (2015, February 9). 13. Inventure: Most Innovative Companies 2015. *Fast Company.* Retrieved from http://www.fastcompany.com/3039583/most-innovative-companies-2015/inventure

33. Mitchell, R., Agle, B., & Wood, D. (1997). Toward a theory of stakeholder identification and salience: Defining the principle of who and what really counts. *Academy of Management Review, 22,* 853–866.

34. Suchman, M. C. (1995). Managing legitimacy: Strategic and institutional approaches. *Academy of Management Review, 20,* 571–610.

35. Retrieved from http://www.c-e-o.org/about-us

36. Rao, S. (2010, April 14). Moving from a "me" to an "other-centered" universe. *Huffpost Healthy Living.* Retrieved from http://www.huffingtonpost.com/srikumar-s-rao/how-to-be-happy-moving-fr_b_570730.html

37. The halo effect. (2015, June 27). *The Economist.* Retrieved from http://www.economist.com/news/business/21656218-do-gooding-policies-help-firms-when-they-get-prosecuted-halo-effect

38. The halo effect. (2015, June 27). *The Economist.* Retrieved from http://www.economist.com/news/business/21656218-do-gooding-policies-help-firms-when-they-get-prosecuted-halo-effect retrieved on October 30, 2015.

39. Adams, S. (2015, September 17). The companies with the best CSR reputations in the world. *Forbes.* Retrieved from http://www.forbes.com/sites/susanadams/2015/09/17/the-companies-with-the-best-csr-reputations-in-the-world/

40. Cook, G. (2012, November 29). The autism advantage. *The New York Times Magazine.* Retrieved from http://www.nytimes.com/2012/12/02/magazine/the-autism-advantage.html?_r=0

41. Specialist People Foundation website. Retrieved from http://specialistpeople.com/

42. Specialist People Foundation website. Retrieved from http://specialistpeople.com/

43. Cheriakova, A. (2013, October 28). The emerging social enterprise: Framing the concept of social entrepreneurship. *The Broker.* Retrieved from http://thebrokeronline.eu/Articles/The-emerging-social-enterprise

44. Leung, P. (2014, December 4). Guys with criminal records get a new start in Kendall Square. *Boston Globe.* Retrieved from https://www.bostonglobe.com/magazine/2014/12/04/guys-with-criminal-records-get-new-start-kendall-square/KuLo6Nr7i5RUUl0d1aFYqL/story.html

45. From Ashoka website. Retrieved from https://www.ashoka.org/fellow/saskia-ni%C3%B1o-de-rivera

46. Ycenter website. Retrieved from http://y-center.org/story/#story1

47. Kashyap, S. (2015, July 20). From Philadelphia to Mozambique: An Indian's journey to create a socially-impactful programme. *Your Story*. Retrieved from http://yourstory.com/2015/07/dhairya-pujara/

48. Field, A. (2014, June 11). Incubating impact: Why a New York City program's pairing MBAs and social enterprise," *Forbes*. Retrieved from http://www.forbes.com/sites/annefield/2014/06/11/a-new-10-week-program-matches-mbas-with-social-enterprises/

CHAPTER 5

1. Mitton, D. G. (1989). The complete entrepreneur. *Entrepreneurship: Theory and Practice, 13*, 919.

1. Baron, R. A. (2006). Opportunity recognition as pattern recognition: How entrepreneurs "connect the dots" to identify new business opportunities. *Academy of Management Perspectives, 20*, 104–119.

2. Bellis, M. (*n.d.*).Liquid paper—Bette Nesmith Graham (1922–1980). *About Money*. Retrieved from http://inventors.about.com/od/lstartinventions/a/liquid_paper.htm

3. Helmer, J. (2013, August). How a squinting dog inspired a $3 million company. *Entrepreneur Magazine*. Retrieved from http://www.entrepreneur.com/article/227–358

4. Maheshwari, S. (2013, June 25). The house that Snuggie built. *BuzzFeed* Retrieved from http://www.buzzfeed.com/sapna/the-house-that-snuggie-built

5. Business Management Degrees. (2016). Bizarre inventions that made serious bucks. Retrieved from http://www.business-management-degree.net/bizarre-inventions-that-made-serious-bucks/

6. Thompson, D. (2012, June 15). Forget Edison: This is how history's greatest inventions really happened. *The Atlantic*. Retrieved from http://www.theatlantic.com/business/archive/2012/06/forget-edison-this-is-how-historys-greatest-inventions-really-happened/258–525/

7. Thompson, D. (2012, June 15). Forget Edison: This is how history's greatest inventions really happened. *The Atlantic*. Retrieved from http://www.theatlantic.com/business/archive/2012/06/forget-edison-this-is-how-historys-greatest-inventions-really-happened/258525/

8. Fallows, J. (2013, November). The 50 greatest breakthroughs since the wheel. *The Atlantic*, Retrieved from http://www.theatlantic.com/magazine/archive/2013/11/innovations-list/309536/

9. See, for example, https://www.whitehouse.gov/omb/intellectualproperty

10. Smith, G. F. (1998). *Quality problem solving* (Chapter 6, pp. 133–135). Milwaukee, WI: ASQ Quality Press.

11. This section is heavily sourced from three primary works: Alvarez, S. A. & Barney, J. B. (2007). Discover and creation: Alternative theories of entrepreneurial action. *Strategic Entrepreneurship Journal, 1*, 11–26. DeTienne, D. R., & Chandler, G. N. (2004). Opportunity identification and its role in the entrepreneurial classroom: A pedagogical approach and empirical test. *Academy of Management Learning and Education, 3*, 242–257. Baron, R. A. (2006). Opportunity recognition as pattern recognition: How entrepreneurs "connect the dots" to identify new business opportunities. *Academy of Management Perspectives, 20*, 104–119.

12. Climbing Mount Everest is work for supermen. (1923, March 18). *The New York Times*. Retrieved from http://graphics8.nytimes.com/packages/pdf/arts/mallory1923.pdf

13. Alvarez & Barney (2007) used the term discovery, but finding is analogous.

14. Sarasvathy, S. D. (2008). *Effectuation: Elements of entrepreneurial expertise*. Northampton, MA: Edward Elgar. Alvarez, S. A., & Barney, J. B. (2007). Discover and creation: Alternative theories of entrepreneurial action. *Strategic Entrepreneurship Journal, 1*, 11–26.

15. Baron, R. A. (2006). Opportunity recognition as pattern recognition: How entrepreneurs "connect the dots" to identify new business opportunities. *Academy of Management Perspectives, 20*, 104–119.

16. Baron, R. A. (2006). Opportunity recognition as pattern recognition: How entrepreneurs "connect the dots" to identify new business opportunities. *Academy of Management Perspectives, 20*, 104–119 at p. 105.

17. Fiet, J. O. (2000). The theoretical side of teaching entrepreneurship. *Journal of Business Venturing, 16*, 1–24. Fiet, J. O. (2002). *The systematic search for entrepreneurial discoveries*. Westport, CT: Quorum Books.

18. Kirzner, I. M. (1973). *Competition and entrepreneurship*. University of Chicago Press: Chicago, IL. Kirzner, I. M. (1997). Entrepreneurial discovery and the competitive market process: An Austrian approach. *Journal of Economic Literature, 35*, 60–85.

19. The invention of footballThe story behind the ball we all know. (*n.d.*). *The Inventions Handbook*. Retrieved from http://www.inventions-handbook.com/invention-of-football.html

20. Epstein, R. (1996). *Cognition, creativity, and behavior*. Westport, CT: Praeger.

21. Baron, R. A. (2006). Opportunity recognition as pattern recognition: How entrepreneurs "connect the dots" to identify new business opportunities. *Academy of Management Perspectives, 20*, 104–119.

22. Shane, S. (2000). Prior knowledge and the discovery of entrepreneurial opportunities. *Organization Science, 11*, 448–469.

23. McKelvie, A. & Wiklund, J. (2004). How knowledge affects opportunity discovery and exploitation among new ventures in dynamic markets. In J. E. Butler (Ed.), *Opportunity identification and entrepreneurial behavior* (pp. 219–239). Greenwich, CT: Information Age.

24. Tabaka, M. (2015, September 9). 5 Entrepreneurs with surprising educational backgrounds. *Inc*. Retrieved from http://www.inc.com/marla-tabaka/5-entrepreneurs-with-surprising-educational-backgrounds.html

25. Baron, R. A. (2006). Opportunity recognition as pattern recognition: How entrepreneurs "connect the dots" to identify new business opportunities. *Academy of Management Perspectives, 20*, 104–119. The concept of pattern recognition comes from a rich research stream in cognition. See, for example, Matlin, M. W. (2002). *Cognition* (5th ed.). Fort Worth, TX: Harcourt College.

26. Baron, R. A. (2006). Opportunity recognition as pattern recognition: How entrepreneurs "connect the dots" to identify new business opportunities. *Academy of Management Perspectives, 20*, 104–119.

27. Baron, R. A. (2006). Opportunity recognition as pattern recognition: How entrepreneurs "connect the dots" to identify new business opportunities. *Academy of Management Perspectives, 20*, 104–119.

28. Baron & Shane textbook chapter 3, page 69, figure 3.2.

29. DeTienne, D. R., & Chandler, G. N. (2004). Opportunity identification and its role in the entrepreneurial classroom: A pedagogical approach and empirical test. *Academy of Management Learning and Education, 3*, 242–257.

30. Entrepreneur Staff. (2011, July 25). Food trucks 101: How to start a mobile food business. *Entrepreneur*. Retrieved from https://www.entrepreneur.com/article/220060

31. Tozzi, J. (2012, April 17). Driver's ed for would-be food truck entrepreneurs. *Bloomberg*. Retrieved from http://www.bloomberg.com/news/articles/2012-04-17/drivers-ed-for-would-be-food-truck-entrepreneurs

32. Reddy, S. (2011, June 14). Every bride expects a lovely food truck. *The Wall Street Journal*. Retrieved from http://online.wsj.com/news/articles/SB10001424052702303714704576383682135167132

CHAPTER 6

1. Clark, K. & Smith, R. (2008). Unleashing the Power of Design Thinking. *dmi Review, 19*(3), 815.

2. Malone, L. (2013, November 15). The bike helmet that's invisible, *Sydney Morning Herald.* Retrieved from http://www .smh.com.au/executive-style/fitness/ the-bike-helmet-thats-invisible-20131115- 2xkvd.html

3. Austin, H., & Kosinski, M. (2013, November 15). Invisible bicycle helmet—An airbag for the head. *NBC News.* Retrieved from http://www.nbcnews.com/tech/ innovation/invisible-bicycle-helmet- airbag-head-f2D11599972

4. Austin, H., & Kosinski, M. (2013, November 15). Invisible bicycle helmet—An airbag for the head. *NBC News.* Retrieved from http://www.nbcnews.com/tech/ innovation/invisible-bicycle-helmet- airbag-head-f2D11599972

5. Liedtka, J., & Ogilvie, T. (2011). *Designing for growth: A design thinking toolkit for managers.* New York, NY: Columbia University Press. [location 168 of 3511, Kindle.]

6. Brown, T., & Katz, B. (2009). *Change by design: How design thinking transforms organizations and inspires innovation* (p. 17). New York, NY: Harper Collins.

7. Neck, H. (2012, March 8). What is design thinking and why do entrepreneurs need to care? *BostInno.* Retrieved from http:// bostinno.streetwise.co/2012/03/08/ what-is-design-thinking-and-why-do- entrepreneurs-need-to-care/

8. Berger, W. (2012, September 17). The secret phrase top innovators use. *Harvard Business Review.* Retrieved from https://hbr.org/2012/09/the-secret- phrase-top-innovato/

9. Image is from human centered design: An introduction, p. 14. *IDEO.* Retrieved from http://d1r3w4d5z5a88i. cloudfront.net/assets/guide/ Field%20Guide%20to%20Human- Centered%20Design_IDEOorg_English- ee47a1ed4b91f3252115b831528 28d7e.pdf

10. Brown, T., & Katz, B. (2009). *Change by design: How design thinking transforms organizations and inspires innovation* (p. 18/19). New York, NY: Harper Collins.

11. Helping you find your inner adult. (*n.d.*). *IDEO case study.* Retrieved from http:// www.ideo.com/work/helping-you-find- your-inner-adult

12. Brown, T., & Katz, B. (2009). *Change by design: How design thinking transforms organizations and inspires innovation* (pp. 18/19, 172–174). New York, NY: Harper Collins.

13. Brown, T., & Katz, B. (2009). *Change by design: How design thinking transforms organizations and inspires innovation* (pp. 18/19, 51–52). New York, NY: Harper Collins.

14. Keith, S. (2012, November 18). How Dan Houser helped turn Grand Theft Auto into a cultural phenomenon. *The Guardian*, pp. 1–5.

15. Hasso Plattner Institute of Design at Stanford. *An introduction to design thinking: Process guide.* Retrieved from https://dschool.stanford.edu/ sandbox/groups/designresources/ wiki/36873/attachments/74b3d/ ModeGuideBOOTCAMP2010L. pdf?sessionID=68deabe9f22d5b 79bde83798d28a09327886ea4b

16. Hasso Plattner Institute of Design at Stanford. *An introduction to design thinking: Process guide.* Retrieved from https://dschool.stanford.edu/ sandbox/groups/designresources/ wiki/36873/attachments/74b3d/ ModeGuideBOOTCAMP2010L. pdf?sessionID=68deabe9f22 d5b79bde83798d28a093278 86ea4b

17. Brown, T., & Wyatt, J. (2010, July). Design thinking for social innovation: IDEO. *Development Outreach: World Bank Institute.* Retrieved from https://open knowledge.worldbank.org/ handle/10986/6068

18. Gelles, D. (2016, February 13). The commute of the future? Ford is working on it. *New York Times.* Retrieved from http:// www.nytimes.com/2016/02/14/business/ the-commute-of-the-future-ford-is- working-on-it.html?smprod=nytcore- ipad&smid=nytcore-ipad-share&_r=2

19. MIT Age Lab website. Retrieved from http://agelab.mit.edu/agnes-age-gain- now-empathy-system

20. Chion, J. (*n.d.*). What it's like to work at Ideo. Retrieved from https://medium. com/@jimmmy/what-its-like-to-work- at-ideo-6ca2c961aae4

21. The ladder example is borrowed from Dev Patnaik, cofounder of Jump Associates.

22. Wheeler, R. (*n.d.*). Alex F. Osborn: The Father of Brainstorming. Retrieved from http://russellawheeler.com/resources/ learning_zone/alex_f_osborn/

23. Brown, T., & Katz, B. (2009). *Change by design: How design thinking transforms organizations and inspires innovation* (pp. 89–90). New York, NY: Harper Collins.

24. Brown, T. (2008, June). Design thinking. *Harvard Business Review*, 84–92.

25. Overholt, Z. (2010, March 26). Shimano officially abandons coasting group. *Bike Rumor.* Retrieved from http://www .bikerumor.com/2010/03/26/shimano- officially-abandons-coasting-group/

26. Gray, S. (2010, May 4). Insights—What are they really? *Quirk.* Retrieved from http:// www.quirk.biz/resources/article/4878/ insights

27. Gray, S. (2010, May 4). Insights—What are they really? *Quirk.* Retrieved from http:// www.quirk.biz/resources/article/4878/ insights

28. Williams, L. (2011, April 11). The key to design insights: See the world differently. *The Atlantic.* Retrieved from http://www.theatlantic.com/ business/archive/2011/04/the-key- to-design-insights-see-the-world- differently/237117/

29. AEIOU framework. (*n.d.*). Retrieved from http://help.ethnohub.com/guide/aeiou- framework

30. Tool, K. (2011, March 28). Design thinking and three ways to improve our observation skills. *Design Due.* Retrieved from https://designdue.wordpress. com/2011/03/28/design-thinking- and-three-ways-to-improve-our- observation-skills/

31. Brown, T. (2012, November 27). One design thinking tip you can use right now. *Design Thinking.* Retrieved from http:// designthinking.ideo.com/?p=784

32. Material in this section is adapted from: Brush, C., & Santinelli, A. (2013, July). Tips for effective in-depth market research interviews. Babson College, MA; Giff. (2012, December 6). 12 tips for early customer development interviews, revision 3. Retrieved from http:// giffconstable.com/2012/12/12-tips- for-early-customer-development- interviews-revision-3/

33. Slideshare. (*n.d.*). Retrieved from http:// www.slideshare.net/stockerpartnership/ innovation-tools-empathy- mapping?related=1

34. Stanford Design School. (*n.d.*). Empathy map. Retrieved from http://dschool. stanford.edu/wp-content/themes/ dschool/method-cards/empathy- map.pdf

35. Liedtka, J., & Ogilvie, T. (2011). *Designing for growth: A design thinking toolkit for managers.* New York, NY: Columbia University Press. [location 168 of 3511, Kindle.]

36. Liedtka, J., & Ogilvie, T. (2011). *Designing for growth: A design thinking toolkit for managers.* New York, NY: Columbia University Press. [location 168 of 3511, Kindle.]

CHAPTER 7

1. Ries, E. (2011). *The lean startup* (p. 56). New York, NY: Crown Business.

2. Dyer, J., Gregersen, H., & Christensen, C. (2011). *The innovator's DNA: Mastering the five skills of disruptive innovators* (p. 143/ ibook). Boston, MA: Harvard Business Review Press.

3. Retrieved from http://steveblank. com/2014/06/23/keep-calm-and-test-the- hypothesis-2-minutes-to-see-why/

4. Dyer, J., Gregersen, H., & Christensen, C. (2011). *The innovator's DNA: Mastering the five skills of disruptive innovators* (p. 143/ ibook). Boston, MA: Harvard Business Review Press.

5. Thomke, S., & Manzi, J. (2014, December). The discipline of business experimentation. *Harvard Business Review*, 70–79, at 72.

6. Steps of the scientific method. (2014, December 27). Retrieved from http://www.sciencebuddies.org/science-fair-projects/project_scientific_method.shtml

7. Story of Amazon and Jeff Bezos is from Dyer, J. Gregersen, H., & Christensen, C. (2011). *The innovator's DNA: Mastering the five skills of disruptive innovators* (p. 144–145/ibook). Boston, MA: Harvard Business Review Press.

8. Davenport, T. H. (2009, February). How to design smart business experiments. *Harvard Business Review*, 68–76.

9. Blank, S. & Dorf, B. (2012). *The startup owner's manual* (pp. 87–88). California: K&S Ranch.

10. Ries, E. (2011). *The lean startup* (pp. 57–58). New York: Crown Business.

11. Baribeau, S. (2013, September 4, 2013). How Tony Hsieh pivoted Zappos into a $1.2 billion Amazon acquisition. *Fast Company*. Retrieved from http://www.fastcompany.com/3000591/how-tony-hsieh-pivoted-zappos-12-billion-amazon-acquisition

12. Anderson, E. T. & Simester, D. (2011, March). The step-by-step guide to smart business experiments. *Harvard Business Review*, 98–105.

13. Anderson, E. T., & Simester, D. (2011, March). The step-by-step guide to smart business experiments. *Harvard Business Review*, 98–105.

14. Anderson, E. T., & Simester, D. (2011, March). The step-by-step guide to smart business experiments. *Harvard Business Review*, 98–105.

15. Thomke, S., & Manzi, J. (2014, December). The discipline of business experimentation. *Harvard Business Review*, 70–79, at 71.

Tuttle, B. (2013, April 9). The 5 big mistakes that led to Ron Johnson's ouster at JC Penney. *Time*. Retrieved from http://business.time.com/2013/04/09/the-5-big-mistakes-that-led-to-ron-johnsons-ouster-at-jc-penney/

16. Thomke, S., & Manzi, J. (2014, December). The discipline of business experimentation. *Harvard Business Review*, 70–79, at 79.

17. Ariely, D. (2009, May). Why businesses don't experiment. *Harvard Business Review*, 34.

18. Ries, E. (2011). *The lean startup* (p. 56). New York: Crown Business.

19. Reid, A. (2013, December 9). *Business Vancouver*. Retrieved from https://www.biv.com/article/2013/12/andrew-reid/

20. Dholakia, U., & Durham, E. (2010, March). One café chain's Facebook experiment. *Harvard Business Review*, p. 26.

21. This whole section is based on material from Dyer, J. Gregersen, H., & Christensen, C. (2011). *The innovator's DNA: Mastering the five skills of disruptive innovators*. Boston, MA: Harvard Business Review Press.

22. Dyer, J., Gregersen, H., & Christensen, C. (2011). *The innovator's DNA: Mastering the five skills of disruptive innovators* (p. 149/ibook). Boston, MA: Harvard Business Review Press.

23. Dyer, J., Gregersen, H., & Christensen, C. (2011). *The innovator's DNA: Mastering the five skills of disruptive innovators* (p. 141 Kindle ed.). Boston, MA: Harvard Business Review Press.

24. Dyer, J., Gregersen, H., & Christensen, C. (2011). *The innovator's DNA: Mastering the five skills of disruptive innovators* (p. 141 Kindle ed.). Boston, MA: Harvard Business Review Press.

25. McKean, E. (2014, September 16). Five entrepreneurial lessons from my life as a dressmaker. *Biz Journals.com*. Retrieved from http://www.bizjournals.com/bizjournals/how-to/growth-strategies/2014/09/5-entrepreneurial-lessons-of-dressmaker.html?page=all

26. Buchenau, M., & Suri, J. F. Experience prototyping. *DIS '00: Proceedings of the 3rd Conference on Designing Interactive Systems: Processes, Practices, Methods, and Techniques*, (pp. 424–433). Retrieved from http://dl.acm.org/citation.cfm?id=347642

27. Dyer, J., Gregersen, H., & Christensen, C. (2011). *The innovator's DNA: Mastering the five skills of disruptive innovators* (pp. 159–160/ibook). Boston, MA: Harvard Business Review Press.

28. Retrieved from https://www.renttherunway.com/pages/about#about-definition

29. Storyboarding. (2014, December 27). Retrieved from http://www.instructionaldesign.org/storyboarding.html

30. Bourque, A. (2012, November 17). 4 powerful reasons to storyboard your business. Retrieved from http://www.socialmediatoday.com/content/4-powerful-reasons-storyboard-your-business-ideas

31. Thorn, K. (2011, August). The art of storyboarding. Retrieved from http://elearnmag.acm.org/featured.cfm?aid=2024072

32. Bourque, A. (2012, November 17). 4 powerful reasons to storyboard your business. Retrieved from http://www.socialmediatoday.com/content/4-powerful-reasons-storyboard-your-business-ideas

33. The Common Craft Blog. (2014, December 27). Retrieved from https://www.commoncraft.com/explainer-tip-creating-simple-storyboards

34. Foundation of Management & Entrepreneurship at Babson College. Retrieved from http://www.babson.edu/Academics/undergraduate/academic-programs/fme/Pages/default.aspx

CHAPTER 8

1. Skarzynski, P., & Gibson, R. (2008). *Innovation to the core: A blueprint for transforming the way your company innovates* (p. 112). Boston, MA: Harvard Business School Press.

2. Blank, S., & Dorf, B. (2012). The startup owner's manual: Step-by-step guide for building a great company (pp. 87–88). California: K&S Ranch.

3. Amit, R. (2014, November 18). The latest innovation: Redesigning the business model. Knowledge@Wharton. Retrieved from http://knowledge.wharton.upenn.edu/article/redesigning-business-model/

4. Hopkins, R. (2010, February 17) Stuck? Take a look at your business model. *Bloomberg*. Retrieved from http://www.bloomberg.com/news/articles/2010-02-17/stuck-take-a-look-at-your-business-model

5. Johnson, M., Christensen, C., & Kagerman, H. (2008, December). Reinventing your business model. *Harvard Business Review*, 1–11.

Osterwalder, A., & Pigneur, Y. (2010). *Business model generation: A handbook for visionaries, game changers, and challengers*. Hoboken, NJ: Wiley.

6. Scott, M. (2014, February 27). Copycat business model generates genuine global success for start-up incubator. Retrieved from http://www.nytimes.com/2014/02/28/technology/copycat-business-model-generates-genuine-global-success-for-start-up-incubator.html?_r=0

7. Winter, C. (2012, February 29). How three Germans are cloning the web. *Bloomberg Business Week Online*. Retrieved from http://www.businessweek.com/articles/2012-02-29/the-germany-website-copy-machine

8. Rocket Internet. (*n.d.*). About: Global infrastructure. Retrieved from https://www.rocket-internet.com/about

9. Winter, C. (2012, February 29). How three Germans are cloning the web. *Bloomberg Business Week Online*. Retrieved from http://www.businessweek.com/articles/2012-02-29/the-germany-website-copy-machine

10. Amit, R. (2014, November 18). The latest innovation: Redesigning the business model. Knowledge@Wharton. Retrieved from http://knowledge.wharton.upenn.edu/article/redesigning-business-model/

11. Anderson, J., Narus, J., & van Rossum, W. (2006, March). Customer value propositions in business markets. *Harvard Business Review*, 91–99.

12. Amit, R. (2014, November 18). The latest innovation: Redesigning the business model. Knowledge@Wharton. Retrieved from http://knowledge.wharton.upenn.edu/article/redesigning-business-model/

13. Johnson, M., Christensen, C., & Kagerman, H. (2008, December). Reinventing your business model. *Harvard Business Review*, 1–11, at 3.

14. Johnson, M. W. (2010, February 3). A new framework for business models strategy and innovation. Retrieved from http://www.innosight.com/innovation-resources/a-new-framework-for-business-models.cfm

15. Johnson, M., Christensen, C., & Kagerman, H. (2008, December). Reinventing your business model. *Harvard Business Review*, 1–11.

16. Osterwalder, A., & Pigneur, Y. (2010). Business model generation: A handbook for visionaries, game changers, and challengers (p. 129). Hoboken, NJ: Wiley.

17. Sundelin, A. (2009, December 10). Tata Motors—Inexpensive cars for modular distribution. *The Business Model Database*. Retrieved from http://tbmdb.blogspot.com/2009/12/business-model-example-tata-motors.html

18. Sundelin, A. (2009, December 10). Tata Motors—Inexpensive cars for modular distribution. *The Business Model Database*. Retrieved from http://tbmdb.blogspot.com/2009/12/business-model-example-tata-motors.html; Fogarty, J. (2009, April 7). Tata's Nano: How'd they do it? *Seeking Alpha*. Retrieved from http://seekingalpha.com/article/129832-tatas-nano-howd-they-do-it

19. Johnson, M., Christensen, C., & Kagerman, H. (2008, December).

Reinventing your business model. *Harvard Business Review*, 1–11.

20. Avey, L. (May 5–6, 2009), Cofounder of 23andMe, presented at the World Innovation Forum, New York City.

21. Mooney, C. (2015, July 7). Many Americans still lack access to solar energy. Here's how Obama plans to change that. *Washington Post*. Retrieved from https://www.washingtonpost.com/news/energy-environment/wp/2015/07/07/many-americans-lack-access-to-solar-energy-heres-how-obama-plans-to-change-that/

22. Anderson, J., Narus, J., & van Rossum, W. (2006, March). Customer value propositions in business markets. *Harvard Business Review*, 91–99.

23. Blank, S., & Dorf, B. (2012). The startup owner's manual: The step-by-step guide for building a great company (pp. 87–88). California: K&S Ranch.

24. Business model canvas customer segments. (2014, May 31. Retrieved from https://www.youtube.com/watch?v=VJdaCvviktk

25. Blank, S. (2013, May 28). Startup: Class no. 002 Business Model Canvas Customer Segments. Retrieved from https://www.youtube.com/watch?v=mweYqciVLxE

26. Forman, L. (2014, August). Illustrating customer segments and value propositions

with ridiculous toys.. Retrieved from http://www.slideshare.net/leslieforman/customer-segments-value-proposition-based-on-business-model-canvas-framework-presented-to-chile-startup-school-on-october-12-2011-leslie-forman

27. Diet Coke vs. Coke Zero: What's the difference. (2012, September 5). *Huffington Post*. Retrieved from http://www.huffingtonpost.com/2012/01/11/diet-coke-vs-coca-cola-zero_n_1199008.html

28. Coke Zero Ads Aim Clearly at the Lads. (2006, July 8). *The Grocer*. Retrieved from http://www.thegrocer.co.uk/fmcg/-coke-zero-ads-aim-clearly-at-the-lads/111665.article

29. Osterwalder, A., & Pigneur, Y. (2010). *Business model generation: A handbook for visionaries, game changers, and challengers* (p. 21). Hoboken, NJ: Wiley.

30. Osterwalder, A., & Pigneur, Y. (2010). *Business model generation: A handbook for visionaries, game changers, and challengers* (p. 21). Hoboken, NJ: Wiley.

31. This section borrows heavily from Osterwalder, A., & Pigneur, Y. (2010). *Business model generation: A handbook for visionaries, game changers, and challengers.* Hoboken, NJ: Wiley.

32. Retrieved from http://airwaysnews.com/blog/2014/04/04/day-in-life-southwest-737/

CHAPTER 9

1. The top 10 dare *devil* entrepreneurs who embrace risk. #9 Elon Musk. *Addicted to Success*. Retrieved from http://addicted2success.com/entrepreneur-profile/the-top-10-daredevil-entrepreneurs-who-embrace-risk/, An introduction to business Plans. *Entrepreneur*. Retrieved from http://www.entrepreneur.com/article/38290 retrieved on June 6, 2015.

2. Roam, D. (2008). *The back of the napkin: Solving problems and selling ideas with pictures*. New York, NY: Penguin Books.

3. Pior-Ohngren, K. (2011, July 11). Five businesses born at a bar. *Entrepreneur*. Retrieved from http://www.entrepreneur.com/article/219834

4. Herold, C. (2011). *Double double: How to double your revenue and profit in three years*. Austin, TX: Greenleaf Book Group Press.

5. Blank, S. (2013, May). Why the lean start-up changes everything. *Harvard Business Review*, 65–72.

6. Innovative alternatives to the traditional business plan. (2015, March 17). *Investintech.com* Retrieved from http://www.investintech.com/resources/blog/archives/5503-alternatives-business-plan.html

7. Berry, T. (2012, August 9). Should you create your business plan on Pinterest? *Entrepreneur*. Retrieved from http://www.entrepreneur.com/article/224157

8. Blank, S. (2013, May). Why the lean start-up changes everything. *Harvard Business Review*, 65–72.

9. An introduction to business plans. *Entrepreneur*. Retrieved from http://www.entrepreneur.com/article/38290

10. Weinberger, J., & Hughes, L. (2014, March 2). Stay-at-home mom makes millions from pretzels (p. 1). *CNBC*.

11. Young Entrepreneur Council. (2013, January 13). The 10 reasons why you should write a business plan. *Small Business Trends*. Retrieved from http://smallbiztrends.com/2013/01/10-reasons-write-business-plan.html

12. Timmons, J., Zacharakis, A., & Spinelli, S. (2004). *Business plans that work: A guide for small business*. New York, NY: McGraw-Hill.

13. Zwilling, M. (2013, November 6). The 10 reasons not to write a business plan. *Entrepreneur*. Retrieved from http://www.entrepreneur.com/article/229804

14. Neck, H. (2013, May 21). What comes before the business plan? Everything. *Forbes*. Retrieved from http://www.forbes.com/sites/babson/2012/05/21/what-comes-before-the-business-plan-everything/

15. Neck, H. (2013, May 21). What comes before the business plan? Everything. *Forbes*. Retrieved from http://www.forbes.com/sites/babson/2012/05/21/what-comes-before-the-business-plan-everything/

16. Gross, B. (2015). Bill Gross: The single biggest reason why start-ups succeed. TED 2015, 6:40, filmed March 2015. Retrieved from http://www.ted.com/talks/bill_gross_the_single_biggest_reason_why_startups_succeed?utm_campaign=ios-share&utm_medium=social&source=email&utm_source=email

17. Henricks, M. Do you really need a business plan?" *Entrepreneur*. Retrieved from http://www.entrepreneur.com/article/198618

18. Hull, P. (2013, February 28). 5 Tips for a great business plan. *Forbes*. Retrieved from http://www.forbes.com/sites/patrickhull/2013/02/28/5-tips-for-a-great-business-plan/

CHAPTER 10

1. This section is adapted from *Revenue models: A quick guide*. Retrieved from http://www.bmnow.com/revenue-models-quick-guide/

2. Frizell, S. (2014, July 7). *Here's what Facebook can do with your personal data in the name of science*. Retrieved from http://time.com/2949565/heres-what-facebook-can-do-with-

your-personal-data-in-the-name-of-science/

3. Dawson, A. (2014, September 26). Ello review—Is this new ad-free social

network any good? *Mirror*. Retrieved from http://www.mirror.co.uk/news/technology-science/technology/ello-review—new-ad-free-4327663

4. Reinink, A. (2009, September 14). Don't cut out the middleman—Become one. *Entrepreneur*. Retrieved from http://www.entrepreneur.com/article/203310

5. Loeb, S. (2013, December 21). How does Pandora make money? *vatortv*. Retrieved from http://vator.tv/news/2013-12-21-how-does-pandora-make-money

6. Daley, J. (2015, January 10). 6 Wacky franchises you won't believe actually exist. *Entrepreneur*. Retrieved from http://www.entrepreneur.com/article/240715

7. *Revenue models: A quick guide*. Retrieved from http://www.bmnow.com/revenue-models-quick-guide/

8. *Revenue models: A quick guide*. Retrieved from http://www.bmnow.com/revenue-models-quick-guide/

9. The concept was popularized by Chris Anderson's 2009 book, *Free: The future of a radical price*. New York, NY, Hyperion.

10. Greenslade, R. (2011, January 26). Profitable *Metro* can't stop making money, but we still need "proper" newspapers." *The Guardian*. Retrieved from http://www.theguardian.com/media/greenslade/2011/jan/26/metro-national-newspapers

11. Osterwalder, A., & Pigneur, Y. (2010). *Business model generation: A handbook for visionaries, game changers, and challengers*, p. 104. Hoboken, NJ: Wiley.

12. Weiss, G. (2014, September 17). With $28 million in new funding, Porch is the 1-year-old startup looking to remodel the home improvement market. *Entrepreneur*. 1–5.

13. The information in this section is heavily drawn from Andrew Zacharakis and Angelo Santinelli (working paper from Babson College).

14. London's quirkiest cafes: in pictures (2014, November 6). *The Telegraph*. Retrieved from http://www.telegraph.co.uk/travel/destinations/europe/united-kingdom/england/london/galleries/Londons-quirkiest-cafes/ziferblatcafe/

15. Section on revenue drivers is derived from Carter, D. P. (2011, June 7). *The four fundamental drivers of revenue*. Retrieved from http://www.davidpaulcarter.com/2011/06/07/the-four-fundamental-drivers-of-revenue/

16. Kumar, V. (2014, May). Making freemium work. *Harvard Business Review*. Retrieved from https://hbr.org/2014/05/making-freemium-work/ar/1

17. Seave, A. (2014, August 27). New research helps find the perfect strategy for "freemium" business models. *Forbes*. Retrieved from http://www.forbes.com/sites/avaseave/2014/08/27/choosing-the-perfect-strategy-for-freemiums/#7e90921e4bcd

18. This section on pricing is sourced from Clark, D. (2014, October 6). How to determine what you should charge customers. *Entrepreneur*. Retrieved from http://www.entrepreneur.com/article/238086

19. YouTube. (2010, January 29). 9 pricing rules for entrepreneurs. *StartUpMe*. Retrieved from https://www.youtube.com/watch?v=redLOAIkEvI

20. This section is based on Team YS. (2010, July 27). *10 Pricing strategies for entrepreneurs*. Retrieved from http://yourstory.com/2010/07/10-pricing-strategies-for-entrepreneurs-2

21. O' Reilly, T. (2013, April 13). Loss leaders—How companies profit by losing money. *CBC Radio*. http://www.cbc.ca/radio/undertheinfluence/loss-leaders-br-how-companies-profit-by-losing-money-1.2801812

22. Symester, C. (2015, August 28). FREE Uber taxi ride worth £10 for new customers with voucher code. *Mirror*. Retrieved from http://www.mirror.co.uk/money/free-uber-taxi-ride-worth-5863754

23. Riley, J. (2012, September 23). *Pricing—Pricing strategies*. Tutor2u. Retrieved from http://www.tutor2u.net/business/gcse/marketing_pricing_strategies.htm

24. Riley, J. (2012, September 23). *Pricing—Pricing strategies*. Tutor2u. Retrieved from http://www.tutor2u.net/business/gcse/marketing_pricing_strategies.htm

CHAPTER 11

1. Wagner, E. (2013, October 22). 9 Lessons from a 10-time startup failure. *Forbes*. Retrieved from http://www.forbes.com/sites/ericwagner/2013/10/22/9-lessons-from-a-10-time-startup-failure/

2. Hough, K. (2012, April 25). 10 Greatest startup failures of all time. *Techli*. Retrieved from http://techli.com/2012/04/10-greatest-startup-failures/#

3. Edmondson, A. C. (2011, April). Learning from failure. *Harvard Business Review*. Retrieved from https://hbr.org/2011/04/strategies-for-learning-from-failure

4. Hahn, J. D. (2013, July 30). 10 Startups that failed but should have succeeded. *Complex*. Retrieved from http://uk.complex.com/pop-culture/2013/07/10-startups-that-failed-but-should-have-succeeded/napster

5. Honigman, B. (2014, June 27). 33 Entrepreneurs share their biggest lessons learned from failure. *The Huffington Post*. Retrieved from http://www.huffingtonpost.com/brian-honigman/35-tech-entrepreneurs-failure_b_5529254.html

6. Cancialosi, C. (2015, April). 5 Signs your organization has outgrown you. *Forbes*. Retrieved from http://www.forbes.com/sites/chriscancialosi/2015/04/27/5-signs-your-organization-has-outgrown-you/#1faa91d6b917

7. Del Castillo, M. (2013, April 29). Awkward. How to take the power back and still be friends. *Upstart Bizjournal*. Retrieved from http://upstart.bizjournals.com/entrepreneurs/hot-shots/2013/04/29/nick-tippmann-takes-over-nibletz.html

8. Lentz, H. (2014, November 24). Ayloo founders shed Light on why their startup failed. *Creating Genius Magazine*. Retrieved from http://cgeniuslife.com/ayloo-founders-shed-light-vegastech-startup-failed/?cbg_tz=0

9. Giang, V. (2014, July 31). How 4 successful entrepreneurs came back after startup failure. *Fast Company*. Retrieved from http://www.fastcompany.com/3033745/hit-the-ground-running/how-4-successful-entrepreneurs-came-back-after-startup-failure

10. Honigman, B. (2014, June 27). 33 Entrepreneurs share their biggest lessons learned from failure. *The Huffington Post*. Retrieved from http://www.huffingtonpost.com/brian-honigman/35-tech-entrepreneurs-failure_b_5529254.html

11. Sastray, A., & Penn, K. (2014). *Fail better: Design smart mistakes and succeed sooner* [p. 1 Kindle]. Cambridge, MA: Harvard Business Review Press.

12. Shepherd, D. A. (2003). Learning from business failure: Propositions of grief recovery for the self-employed. *Academy of Management Review, 28*, 318–328; McGrath, R. (1999). Falling forward: Real options reasoning and entrepreneurial failure. *Academy of Management Review, 24*, 13–30.

13. Svane, M. (2014, December 17). Failure sucks. *Recode*. Retrieved from http://recode.net/2014/12/17/failure-sucks/

14. Shepherd, D. A. (2003). Learning from business failure: Propositions of grief recovery for the self-employed. *Academy of Management Review, 28*, 318–328.

15. Never too big to fail. (2012, September). Indiana University Research Blog. Retrieved from http://research.indiana.edu/2012/09/never-too-big-to-fail/

16. Singer, S., Amoros, J. E., & Moska, D. (2014). *Global Entrepreneurship Monitor 2014 Global Report*. Retrieved from http://www.gemconsortium.org/report

17. McGregor, H. A., & Elliot, A. J. (2005). The shame of failure: Examining the link between fear of failure and shame. *Personality and Social Psychology Bulletin, 31*, 218–231, at 219.

18. McGregor, H. A., & Elliot, A. J. (2005). The shame of failure: Examining the link between fear of failure and shame. *Personality and Social Psychology Bulletin, 31*, 218–231, at 229.

19. Strategies for managing fear of failure are from Loder, V. (2014, October 30). How to conquer the fear of failure—5 Proven strategies. *Forbes*. Retrieved from http://www.forbes.com/sites/vanessaloder/2014/10/30/how-to-move-beyond-the-fear-of-failure-5-proven-strategies/

20. Vinnedge, M. (2010), September 19). Arianna Huffington: Pushing the limits.

21. Heber, A. (2015, July 13). Chart: The fear of failure rates for entrepreneurs around the world. *Business Insider Australia*. Retrieved from http://www.businesinsider.com.au/chart-the-fear-of-failure-rates-for-entrepenuers-around-the-world-2015-7

22. Griffith, E. (2014, December 2). Amazon CEO Jeff Bezos: "I've made billions of dollars of failures." *Fortune*. Retrieved from http://fortune.com/2014/12/02/amazon-ceo-jeff-bezos-failure/

23. Edmondson, A. C. (2011, April). Strategy for learning from failure. *Harvard Business Review*, 48–55.

24. Pharrell Williams: Happy and grateful. (2014, April 13). *CBS News*. Retrieved from http://www.cbsnews.com/news/pharrell-williams-happy-and-grateful/

25. Cooper, B. B. (2013, May 9). The 13 biggest failures from successful entrepreneurs and what they've learned from them. *Buffer Social*. Retrieved from https://blog.bufferapp.com/failure-entrepreneur-12-successful-entrepreneurs-tell-us-the-biggest-lessons-theyve-learned

26. Porter, M. E., Lorsch, J. W., & Nohria, N. (2004, October). Seven surprises for new CEOs. *Harvard Business Review*, 62–72.

27. Danner, J. (2015, May 11). How to make the other 'F' word work for you (not against you). *Fortune*. Retrieved from http://fortune.com/2015/05/11/how-to-make-the-other-f-word-work-for-you-innovation/

28. Seelig, T. (2009, July 28). Fail in order to succeed. *CreativyRulz*. Retrieved from http://creativityrulz.blogspot.com/2009/07/fail-in-order-to-suceed.html

29. Perkins-Gough, D. (2013, September). The significance of grit: A conversation with Angela Lee Duckworth. *Educational Leadership*, 71(1). Retrieved from http://www.ascd.org/publications/educational-leadership/sept13/vol71/num01/The-Significance-of-Grit@-A-Conversation-with-Angela-Lee-Duckworth.aspx

30. Del Giudice, M. (2014, October 14). Grit trumps talent and IQ: A story every parent (and educator) should read. *National Geographic*. Retrieved from http://news.nationalgeographic.com/news/2014/10/141015-angela-duckworth-success-grit-psychology-self-control-science-nginnovators/

31. Perkins-Gough, D. (2013, September). The significance of grit: A conversation with Angela Lee Duckworth. *Educational Leadership*, 71(1). Retrieved from http://www.ascd.org/publications/educational-leadership/sept13/vol71/num01/The-Significance-of-Grit@-A-Conversation-with-Angela-Lee-Duckworth.aspx

32. Del Giudice, M. (2014, October 14). Grit trumps talent and IQ: A story every parent (and educator) should read. *National Geographic*. Retrieved from http://news.nationalgeographic.com/news/2014/10/141015-angela-duckworth-success-grit-psychology-self-control-science-nginnovators/

33. Giang, V. (2014, July 28). 8 Women entrepreneurs share how they conquered their biggest roadblocks. *Fast Company*. Retrieved from http://www.fastcompany.com/3033532/hit-the-ground-running/8-women-entrepreneurs-share-how-they-conquered-their-biggest-roadbloc

34. Siskar, K. (2015, July 14). What makes a successful entrepreneur? Circumstance, genetics, and perseverance. *The Huffington Post*. Retrieved from http://www.huffingtonpost.com/kevin-siskar-/what-makes-a-successful-e_b_7793914.html

35. Perlis, M. (2013, October 29). 5 Characteristics of grit—How many do you have?" *Forbes*. Retrieved from http://www.forbes.com/sites/margaretperlis/2013/10/29/5-characteristics-of-grit-what-it-is-why-you-need-it-and-do-you-have-it/

36. Ungerleider, N. (2011, December 15). How FAILFaire turns epic fails into successes. *Fast Company*. Retrieved from http://www.fastcoexist.com/1679000/how-failfaire-turns-epic-fails-into-successes

37. Kanter, B. (2013, April 17). Go ahead, take a failure bow. *Harvard Business Review*. Retrieved from https://hbr.org/2013/04/go-ahead-take-a-failure-bow&cm_sp=Article-_-Links-_-End%20of%20Page%20Recirculation

38. Kanter, B. (2013, April 17). Go ahead, take a failure bow. *Harvard Business Review*. Retrieved from https://hbr.org/2013/04/go-ahead-take-a-failure-bow&cm_sp=Article-_-Links-_-End%20of%20Page%20Recirculation

CHAPTER 12

1. Sharp, G. (2014). *The ultimate guide to bootstrapping* [Kindle ed., LOC 166]. Real. Cool. Media.

2. National Venture Capital Association Yearbook 2016, p.3.

3. Inc Staff. (2001, November 15). Brief profiles of 2001 Inc 500 companies. *Inc.* Retrieved from http://www.inc.com/magazine/20011115/23533.html

4. Sharp, G. (2014). *The ultimate guide to bootstrapping* [Kindle ed., LOC 173]. Real. Cool. Media.

5. Retrieved from http://newsandinsights.businessgrowthfund.co.uk/qa-with-ralph-kugler-chairman-of-afg-media

6. Sharp, G. (2014). *The ultimate guide to bootstrapping* [Kindle ed., LOC 155]. Real. Cool. Media.

7. Sharp, G. (2014). *The ultimate guide to bootstrapping* [Kindle ed., LOC 182]. Real. Cool. Media.

8. Retrieved from http://www.seattlepi.com/business/article/Birth-of-a-Startup-Step-1-Find-your-dream-1077256.php

9. Sharp, G. (2014). *The ultimate guide to bootstrapping* [Kindle ed., LOC 147]. Real. Cool. Media.

10. Garson, J. (2010). *How to build a business and sell it for millions*. New York, NY: St. Martin's Press.

11. This section is based on Sharp, G. (2014). *The ultimate guide to bootstrapping* [Kindle ed.]. Real. Cool. Media.

12. Steinberg, S. (2008). *The crowdfunding bible* [Kindle ed., LOC 78]. read.me Press.

13. Mollick, E. (2014). The dynamics of crowdfunding: An exploratory study. *Journal of Business Venturing, 29*, 1–16, at 2.

14. Anderson, C. (2010, February). Atoms are the new bits. *Wired*, 59–67.

15. Owen, J. (2014, September 12). 3d-printed wikihouse 4.0. *The Independent*. Retrieved from http://www.independent.co.uk/incoming/3dprinted-wikihouse-40-the-50000-house-you-can-download-from-the-internet-9727424.html

16. Mollick, E. (2014). The dynamics of crowdfunding: An exploratory study. *Journal of Business Venturing, 29*, 1–16, at 3.

17. Zipkin, N. (2015, December 28). The 10 most funded Kickstarter campaigns ever. *Entrepreneur*. Retrieved from http://www.entrepreneur.com/article/235313

18. Fundable. (n.d.). *Crowdfunding statistics*. Retrieved from https://www.fundable.com/crowdfunding101/crowdfunding-statistics

19. Kickstarter. (*n.d.*). *Kickstarter basics*. Retrieved from https://www.kickstarter.com/help/faq/kickstarter+basics?ref=footer

20. Kuppuswamy, V., & Bayus, B. (2014, January 29). *Crowdfunding creative ideas: The dynamics of project backers in Kickstarter*. (UNC Kenan-Flagler Research Paper No. 2013-15).

21. Kickstarter statistics listed on https://www.kickstarter.com/help/stats?ref=foote These statistics change daily.

22. Kickstarter. (*n.d.*). *Our rules*. Retrieved from https://www.kickstarter.com/rules?ref=footer

23. Buck, S. (2012, May 13). 9 Essential steps for a killer Kickstarter campaign. *Mashable*. Retrieved from http://mashable.com/2012/05/13/kickstarter-tips/

24. Kuppuswamy, V., & Bayus, B. (2014, January 29). *Crowdfunding creative ideas: The dynamics of project backers in Kickstarter*. (UNC Kenan-Flagler Research Paper No. 2013-15, p. 22).

25. Belleflamme, P., Lambert, T., & Schwienbacher, A. (2014). Crowdfunding: Tapping the right crowd. *Journal of Business Venturing, 29*, 585–609, at 589.

26. Statt, N. (2015, November 18). The Coolest Cooler is turning into one of

Kickstarter's biggest disasters. *The Verge.* Retrieved from http://www.theverge.com/2015/11/18/9758214/coolest-cooler-amazon-kickstater-shipping-production-delay

27. Campbell, P. (2015, June 18). Babies, degrees, cosmetic surgery: How to crowdfund your life. *The Telegraph.* Retrieved from http://www.telegraph.co.uk/lifestyle/11683562/Babies-degrees-cosmetic-surgery-how-to-crowdfund-your-life.html

28. Mollick, E. (2014). The dynamics of crowdfunding: An exploratory study. *Journal of Business Venturing, 29,* 1–16, at 2.

29. Ambani, P. (2014, May 30). Top 15 Crowdfunding platforms in Europe. *Crowdsourcing Week.* Retrieved from http://crowdsourcingweek.com/top-15-crowdfunding-platforms-in-europe/

30. Mollick, E. (2014). The dynamics of crowdfunding: An exploratory study. *Journal of Business Venturing, 29,* 1–16.

31. O'Grady, C. (2014, August 1). Reinventing the patron. *The Skinny.* Retrieved from http://www.theskinny.co.uk/tech/features/reinventing-the-patron

32. Steinberg, S. (2008). *The crowdfunding bible* [Kindle ed.]. read.me Press.

33. Belleflamme, P., Lambert, T., & Schwienbacher, A. (2014). Crowdfunding: Tapping the right crowd. *Journal of Business Venturing, 29,* 585–609.

34. Diallo, A. (2014, January 24). Crowdfunding secrets: 7 Tips for Kickstarter success. *Forbes.* Retrieved from http://www.forbes.com/sites/amadoudiallo/2014/01/24/crowdfunding-secrets-7-tips-for-kickstarter-success/

35. Dewey, C. (2014, August 28). Ryan Grepper, inventor of the 'Coolest' Cooler, failed many times before raising $13 million on Kickstarter. *Washington Post.* Retrieved from http://www.washingtonpost.com/news/

the-intersect/wp/2014/08/28/ryan-grepper-inventor-of-the-coolest-cooler-failed-many-times-before-raising-11-million-on-kickstarter/

36. Pofeldt, E. (2014, May 26). Secrets to crowdfunding success. *Forbes.* Retrieved from http://www.forbes.com/sites/elainepofeldt/2014/05/26/secrets-to-crowdfunding-success/

37. Kuppuswamy, V., & Bayus, B. (2014, January 29). *Crowdfunding creative ideas: The dynamics of project backers in Kickstarter.* (UNC Kenan-Flagler Research Paper No. 2013-15).

38. Mollick, E. (2014). The dynamics of crowdfunding: An exploratory study. *Journal of Business Venturing, 29,* 1–16, at 8.

39. Mollick, E. (2014). The dynamics of crowdfunding: An exploratory study. *Journal of Business Venturing, 29,* 1–16, at 2.

CHAPTER 13

1. Mathisen, T. (2014, April 29). The List: CNBC First 25. *CNBC.* Retrieved from http://www.cnbc.com/2014/04/29/25-google-team--sergey-brin-larry-page-eric-schmidt.html

2. Venture capital. (*n.d.*). *Small Business Notes.* Retrieved from http://www.smallbusinessnotes.com/business-finances/venture-capital.html

3. Shane, S. (2008, September). *The importance of angel investing in financing the growth of entrepreneurial ventures* (a working paper for the Small Business Association). Retrieved from http://www.angelcapitalassociation.org/data/Documents/Resources/AngelGroupResearch/1d%20-%20Resources%20-%20Research/19%20Angel_Investing_in_Financing_the_Growth_of_Entrepreneurial_Ventures.pdf

4. Asheesh, A. (2006, May 15). Raising money using convertible debt. *Entrepreneur.* Retrieved from http://www.entrepreneur.com/article/159520

5. Prive, T. (2013, March 12). Angel investors: How the rich invest. *Forbes.* Retrieved from http://www.forbes.com/sites/tanyaprive/2013/03/12/angels-investors-how-the-rich-invest/

6. Adams, P. (2014, January 12). How do angel investors differ from venture capitalists? [Rockies Venture Club blog.] Retrieved from http://www.rockiesventureclub.org/colorado-capital-conference/how-do-angel-investors-differ-from-venture-capitalists/

7. Hayden, B. (2015, March 20). Entrepreneurs can pay it forward through angel investing. *Entrepreneur.* Retrieved from http://www.entrepreneur.com/article/243759

8. Bygrave, W. (2010). Equity financing: Informal investment, venture capital, and harvesting. In B. Bygrave & A. Zacharakis (Eds.), *Portable MBA in entrepreneurship* (pp. 161–195). New York, NY: Wiley.

9. This section is sourced from: Finding an angel. (*n.d.*). *Small Business Notes.* Retrieved from http://www.smallbusinessnotes.com/business-finances/finding-an-angel.html

10. Stengel, G. (2014, May 28). Entrepreneurship and angel investing are breaking barriers for women. *Forbes.* Retrieved from http://www.forbes.com/sites/geristengel/2014/05/28/entrepreneurship-and-angel-investing-are-breaking-barriers-for-women/

11. Stengel, G. (2013, May 22). How women angels and entrepreneurs are beating investment odds. *Forbes.* Retrieved from http://www.forbes.com/sites/geristengel/2013/05/22/how-women-angels-and-entrepreneurs-are-beating-investment-odds/

12. Robehmed, N. (2013, October 16). There are few minority entrepreneurs, and they rarely get funding. *Forbes.* Retrieved from http://www.forbes.com/sites/natalierobehmed/2013/10/16/there-are-few-minority-entrepreneurs-and-they-rarely-get-funding/

13. Timmons, J., & Spinelli, S. (2008). *New venture creation* (8th ed., p. 457). Boston, MA: McGraw-Hill Irwin.

14. Retrieved from http://nvca.org/pressreleases/58-8-billion-in-venture-capital-invested-across-u-s-in-2015-according-to-the-moneytree-report-2/

15. Hadzima, J., Jr. All financing sources are not equal. *Boston Business Journal* reprint. Retrieved from http://web.mit.edu/e-club/hadzima/all-financing-sources-are-not-equal.html

16. Frazier, D., Franklin, B., & Taylor, J. (2014). *National Venture Capital Association Yearbook* (p. 13). New York, NY: Thomson Reuters.

17. Bygrave, W. (2010). Equity financing: Informal investment, venture capital, and

harvesting. In B. Bygrave & A. Zacharakis (Eds.), *Portable MBA in entrepreneurship* (pp. 161–195, at p. 176). New York, NY: Wiley.

18. Reich, D. (2014, January 4). Raising money from friends and family. *Forbes.com.* Retrieved from http://www.forbes.com/sites/danreich/2013/01/04/raising-money-from-friends-and-family/

19. Singerman, B. (2012, July 29). The paradox of VC seed investing. Retrieved from http://techcrunch.com/2012/07/29/the-paradox-of-vc-seed-investing/

20. Gage, D. (2012, September 20). The venture capital secret: 3 out of 4 start-ups fail. *The Wall Street Journal.* Retrieved from http://www.wsj.com/articles/SB10000872396390443720204578004980476429190

21. Colombo, J. (*n.d.*). The Dot-com bubble. *The Bubble Bubble.* Retrieved from http://www.thebubblebubble.com/dotcom-bubble/

22. Austin, S. (2015, January 2). Snapchat cracks top 10 largest U.S. venture-capital deals. *The Wall Street Journal.* Retrieved from http://blogs.wsj.com/digits/2015/01/02/snapchat-cracks-top-10-largest-u-s-venture-capital-deals/

23. Timmons, J., & Spinelli, S. (2008). *New venture creation* (8th ed., p. 456). Boston, MA: McGraw-Hill Irwin.

24. Retrieved from http://www.angelblog.net/Venture_Capital_Exit_Times.html

25. Timmons, J., & Spinelli, S. (2008). *New venture creation* (8th ed., p. 458). Boston, MA: McGraw-Hill Irwin.

26. Prithivi, S. (2011, August 24). Angel investing series part II: Due diligence, sealing the deal and post-investment relationship. *Tech.co.* Retrieved from http://tech.co/angel-investing-series-part-ii-2011-08

27. Wasserman, N. (2008, February). The founder's dilemma. *Harvard Business Review*. Retrieved from https://hbr.org/2008/02/the-founders-dilemma

28. Inc. staff. (2016, June). A brief history of the fired founder: 6 Founders who were fired from their companies. *Inc.* Retrieved from http://www.inc.com/magazine/201606/inc-staff/ss/fired-founders.html

29. Vital, A. (2013, May 9). *How funding works—Splitting the equity pie with investors.* Retrieved from http://fundersandfounders.com/how-funding-works-splitting-equity/

APPENDIX A

1. Buffet, M., & Clark, D. (2008). *Warren Buffet and the interpretation of financial statements* (p. 33). New York, NY: Scribner.

2. Ittelson, T. R. (2009). *Financial statements: A step-by-step guide to understanding and creating financial reports* (pp. 15–17). Pompton Plains, NJ: Career Press.

3. Ittelson, T. R. (2009). *Financial statements: A step-by-step guide to understanding and creating financial reports* (pp. 79–82). Pompton Plains, NJ: Career Press.

4. http://www.businessdictionary.com/definition/pro-forma.html

5. EZ Numbers website, http://www.eznumbers.com; Lonee Corporation website, http://marketing.lonee.com

6. Bizminer website, http://www.bizminer.com; IBISWorld website, http://www.ibisworld.com; Statista website, http://www.statista.com

7. Smith, R. L., & Smith, J. K. (2004). *Entrepreneurial finance* (pp. 144–146, 2nd ed.). Hoboken, NJ: Wiley.

CHAPTER 14

1. Cope, J., Jack, S., & Rose, M. (2007). Social capital and entrepreneurship: An introduction. *International Small Business Journal, 25*, 213–219, at 213.

2. Cope, J., Jack, S., & Rose, M. (2007). Social capital and entrepreneurship: An introduction. *International Small Business Journal, 25*, 213–219, at 216.

3. Tsai, W., & Ghoshal, S. (1998). Social capital and value creation. The role of intrafirm networks. *Academy of Management Journal, 41*, 464–476.

4. Coleman, J. S. (1988). Social capital in the creation of human capital. *American Journal of Sociology: Supplement, Organizations and Institutions: Sociological and Economic Approaches to the Analysis of Social Structure, 94*, 95–120.

5. Bettertogether website. (n.d.). Retrieved from http://www.bettertogether.org/socialcapital.htm

6. A/L Muniady, R., Al Mamun, A., Mohamad, M. R., Permarupan, P. Y., Zainol, N. R. B. (2015). The effect of cognitive and relational social capital on structural social capital and micro-enterprise performance. *Sage Open.* Retrieved from http://sgo.sagepub.com/content/5/4/2158244015611187

7. Uzzi, B. (1996). The sources and consequences of embeddedness for the economic performance of organizations: The network effect. *American Sociological Review, 61*, 674–698.

8. Stephen R. Covey Blog. (2009, May 8). Posts tagged "emotional bank account." Retrieved from http://www.stephencovey.com/blog/?tag=emotional-bank-account Withdrawing too much without depositing will not create any value or trust within your network.

9. Covey, S. (2004). *The seven habits of highly successful people.* New York, NY: Simon & Schuster.

10. A/L Muniady, R., Al Mamun, A., Mohamad, M. R., Permarupan, P. Y., & Zainol, N. R. B. (2015). The effect of cognitive and relational social capital on structural social capital and micro-enterprise performance. *Sage Open.* Retrieved from http://sgo.sagepub.com/content/5/4/2158244015611187

11. OECD Insights: Human Capital. (n.d.). Retrieved from http://www.oecd.org/insights/37966934.pdf

12. OECD Insights: Human Capital. (n.d.). Retrieved from http://www.oecd.org/insights/37966934.pdf

13. Uzzi, B., & Dunlap, S. (2005, December). How to build your network. *Harvard Business Review*, 52–60, at 53.

14. OECD Insights: Human Capital. (n.d.). Retrieved from http://www.oecd.org/insights/37966934.pdf

15. Cope, J., Jack, S., & Rose, M. (2007). Social capital and entrepreneurship: An introduction. *International Small Business Journal, 25*, 213–219, at 2–14.

16. Casson, M., & Della Giusta, M. (2007). Entrepreneurship and social capital: Analyzing the impact of social networks on entrepreneurial activity from a rational action perspective. *International Small Business Journal, 25*, 220–44, at p. 221.

17. Hoehn-Weiss, M., Brush, C., & Baron, R. (2004). Putting your best foot forward? Assessments of entrepreneurial social competence from two perspectives. *Journal of Private Equity, 7*(4), 17–26.

18. Guttman, A. (2015, October 29). How a business school student used his personal network to build a startup valued at $100 Million. *Forbes.* Retrieved from http://www.forbes.com/sites/amyguttman/2015/10/29/how-a-business-school-student-used-his-personal-network-to-build-a-100-million-dollar-business/

19. Uzzi, B., & Dunlap, S. (2005, December). How to build your network. *Harvard Business Review*, 52–60.

20. Science quotes by Linus Pauling. (n.d.). *Today in Science History.* Retrieved from http://todayinsci.com/P/Pauling_Linus/PaulingLinus-Quotations.html

21. Murphy, W., & Kram, K. (2014). *Strategic relationships at work.* New York, NY: McGraw Hill.

22. D'Onfro, J. (2015, September 27). Mark Zuckerberg says that visiting an Indian temple at the urging of Steve Jobs helped him stick to Facebook's mission. *TECH Insider.* Retrieved from http://www.techinsider.io/mark-zuckerberg-visited-india-thanks-to-steve-jobs-2015-9

23. Neck, H. An ethnographic study of entrepreneurship education: Trajectories connecting the classroom to the real world. Unpublished working paper.

24. Pentland, A., & Heibeck, T. (2009, October 31). Great ideas vs. confidence: Which counts more? *Psychology Today.* Retrieved from http://www.psychologytoday.com/blog/reality-mining/200910/great-ideas-vs-confidence-which-counts-more-0]

25. Hoehn-Weiss, M., Brush, C., & Baron, R. (2004). Putting your best foot forward? Assessments of entrepreneurial social competence from two perspectives. *Journal of Private Equity, 7*(4), 17–26.

26. Neck, H. An ethnographic study of entrepreneurship education: Trajectories connecting the classroom to the real world. Unpublished working paper.

27. Neck, H. An ethnographic study of entrepreneurship education: Trajectories connecting the classroom to the real world. Unpublished working paper.

28. Nobel, C. (2015, February 9). Professional networking makes people feel dirty. *Harvard Business School Working Knowledge.* Retrieved from http://hbswk.hbs.edu/item/professional-networking-makes-people-feel-dirty

29. Which leading entrepreneurs met their business partners at school? (2013, May 14). *Nerdwallet.* Retrieved from http://www.nerdwallet.com/blog/loans/student-loans/entrepreneurs-college-alumni-networks/

30. Sarasvathy, S. D. (2008). *Effectuation: Elements of entrepreneurial expertise.* Northampton, MA: Edward Elgar.

31. Senge, P. M. (1990). *The fifth discipline: The art and practice of the learning organization.* New York, NY: Doubleday/Currency.

32. Uzzi, B., & Dunlap, S. (2005, December). How to build your network. *Harvard Business Review*, 52–60, at 58.

33. Murphy, B. (2014, March 31). 50 Ways to find co-founders. *Inc.* http://www.inc.com/bill-murphy-jr/50-ways-to-find-co-founders.html

34. Based on Murphy, W., & Kram, K. (2014). *Strategic relationships at work.* New York, NY: McGraw Hill.

35. Meetup blog. (*n.d.*). Extremely shy—Looking for friends. Retrieved from http://www.meetup.com/extremely-shy-looking-for-friends/

36. Loten, A. (2015, March 13). Meetup aims to get people off the Internet. *Wall Street Journal.* Retrieved from http://www.wsj.com/articles/meetup-com-aims-to-get-people-off-the-internet-1431538570

37. Information obtained from the Startup Grind website. Retrieved from https://www.startupgrind.com/about-us/

38. Murphy, B. (2015, October 19). 9 Smart habits of highly effective networkers. *Inc.* Retrieved from http://www.inc.com/bill-murphy-jr/9-smart-habits-of-highly-effective-networkers.html

39. Murphy, B. (2015, October 19). 9 Smart habits of highly effective networkers. *Inc.* Retrieved from http://www.inc.com/bill-murphy-jr/9-smart-habits-of-highly-effective-networkers.html

40. Spencer, S. (2011, December 14). Business networking that works . . . It's called quid pro quo. *Forbes.* Retrieved from http://news.yahoo.com/business-networking-works-called-quid-pro-quo-190953397

41. Anderson, K. (2013, July 17). Pay it forward with the five-minute favor. *Forbes.* Retrieved from http://www.forbes.com/sites/kareanderson/2013/07/17/pay-it-forward-with-the-five-minute-favor/

42. Murphy, B. (2015, October 19). 9 Smart habits of highly effective networkers. *Inc.* Retrieved from http://www.inc.com/bill-murphy-jr/9-smart-habits-of-highly-effective-networkers.html

43. Misner, I. (2009, January 14). You never know whom they know. *Entrepreneur.* Retrieved from http://www.entrepreneur.com/article/199542

44. Rollag, K. (2015). *What to do when you're new.* New York, NY: Amacom.

45. Based on material in Kawasaki, G. (2015). *The art of the start* (p. 199). New York, NY: Penguin.

46. Three famous billionaire entrepreneurs and their mentors. (2015, February 12). *Small Business BC.* Retrieved from http://smallbusinessbc.ca/article/three-famous-billionaire-entrepreneurs-and-their-mentors/

47. Deutschman, A. (2004, December 1). The fabric of creativity. *Fast Company.* Retrieved from http://www.fastcompany.com/51733/fabric-creativity

48. Renton, D. (2014, July 18). Finding the perfect mentor: Stories from 4 successful entrepreneurs. *Grasshopper Blog.* Retrieved from http://grasshopper.com/blog/finding-the-perfect-mentor-stories-from-4-successful-entrepreneurs/

49. Elizabeth Holmes Interview from The Academy of Achievement. (2014). Retrieved from http://www.achievement.org/autodoc/page/holoint-6

50. Branson, R. (2012, July 24). Network early, network often. *Daily Monitor.* Retrieved from http://www.monitor.co.ug/Business/Prosper/Network-early--network-often/-/688616/1461204/-/1028mhh/-/index.html

51. Neary, J. (2014, August 26). From executive to entrepreneur and back with the help of my LinkedIn network. *LinkedIn Official Blog.* Retrieved from http://blog.linkedin.com/2014/08/26/from-executive-to-entrepreneur-and-back-with-the-help-of-my-linkedin-network/

52. FounderDating. (*n.d.*). Retrieved from http://founderdating.com/about/

53. Cutler, K.-M. (2015, April 2). LinkedIn buys Refresh.io to add more predictive insights to its products. *TechCrunch.* Retrieved from http://techcrunch.com/2015/04/02/linkedin-buys-refresh-io-to-add-more-predictive-insights-to-its-products/

54. Ashoka. (2014, February 4). Why co-creation is the future for all of us. *Forbes.* Retrieved from http://www.forbes.com/sites/ashoka/2014/02/04/why-co-creation-is-the-future-for-all-of-us/

55. Nsehe, M. (2015, March 1). Angel investors invest $27 million in African startups listed on VC4Africa. *Forbes.* Retrieved from http://www.forbes.com/sites/mfonobongnsehe/2015/03/01/angel-investors-invest-27-million-in-african-startups-through-vc4africa/

56. Balea, J. (2014, November 13). This Philippine startup wants to light up poor homes with lamp powered by salt and water. *TechInAsia.* Retrieved from https://www.techinasia.com/salt-light-poor-homes-philippines/

57. Uzzi, B., & Dunlap, S. (2005, December). How to build your network. *Harvard Business Review, 83* (12), 52–60.

58. Aldrich, H. E., & Kim, P. H. (2007). Small worlds, infinite possibilities? How social networks affect entrepreneurial team formation and search. *Strategic Entrepreneurship Journal, 1*, 147–165, at 149.

59. Timmons, J. A. (1994). *New venture creation: Entrepreneurship for the 21st century* (p. 19, 4th ed.). Burr Ridge, IL: Irwin; Cooper, A. C., & Daily, C. M. (1997). Entrepreneurial teams. In D. L. Sexton & R. W. Smilor (Eds.), *Entrepreneurship 2000* (pp. 127–150). Chicago, IL: Upstart. [Cooper & Daily proclaimed, "Entrepreneurial teams are at the center of the crucial activities of the firm" (p. 144)].

60. Blank, S. (2013, July 29). Building great founding teams. Retrieved from http://steveblank.com/2013/07/29/building-great-founding-teams/

61. Cooper, A. C., & Daily, C. M. (1997). Entrepreneurial teams. In D. L. Sexton & R. W. Smilor (Eds.). *Entrepreneurship 2000* (pp. 127–150). Chicago, IL: Upstart.

62. Cooney, T. M. (2005). Editorial: What is an entrepreneurial team? *International Small Business Journal, 23*, 226–235, at 228.

63. Aldrich, H. E., & Kim, P. H. (2007). Small worlds, infinite possibilities? How social networks affect entrepreneurial team formation and search. *Strategic Entrepreneurship Journal, 1*, 147–165, at 149.

64. Vozza, S. (2014, July 2). The only 6 people you need on your founding startup team. *Fast Company.* Retrieved from http://www.fastcompany.com/3032548/hit-the-ground-running/the-only-6-people-you-need-on-your-founding-startup-team

65. Houser, J. (2011, June 21). How to build an insanely great founding team. *Inc.* Retrieved from http://www.inc.com/articles/201106/how-to-build-an-insanely-great-team.html

66. Jones, A. (2015, February 3). Don't like menial tasks? Don't be a startup founder. *BlueChilli.* Retrieved from https://www.bluechilli.com/blog/dont-like-menial-tasks-dont-be-a-startup-founder/

67. Balter, D. (2011, June 23). The humility imperative: CEOs, keep your arrogance in check. *Inc.* Retrieved from http://www.inc.com/articles/201106/the-humility-imperative-ceos-keep-your-arrogance-in-check.html

68. Spors, K. (2009, February 23). So, you want to be an entrepreneur. *Wall Street Journal/Small Business Reports.* Retrieved from http://www.wsj.com/articles/SB123498006564714189

69. Sommers, S. R., Warp, L. S. & Mahoney, C. (2008). Cognitive effects of racial diversity: White individuals' information processing in heterogeneous groups. *Journal of Experimental Social Psychology, 44*, 1129–1136.

70. Surowiecki, J. (2005). *The wisdom of crowds* (p. 36). New York, NY: Anchor Books.

71. Schwenk, C. R., & Cosier, R. A. (1980). Effects of the expert, devil's advocate, and dialectical inquiry methods on prediction performance. *Organizational Behavior and Human Performance, 26*, 409–424.

72. Chowdhury S., (2005). Demographic diversity for building an effective entrepreneurial team: Is it important? *Journal of Business Venturing, 20*, 727–746.

73. Chowdhury S., (2005). Demographic diversity for building an effective entrepreneurial team: Is it important? *Journal of Business Venturing, 20*, 727–746.

74. Patrick Lencioni presentation at the World Business Forum, Oct. 6, 2009. For summary, see http://www.vault.com/blog/pink-slipped-make-your-layoff-pay-off/world-business-forum-building-winning-teams-with-patrick-

lencioni/; see Lencioni, P. (2002). *The five dysfunctions of a team.* San Francisco, CA: Jossey-Bass.

75. Eisenhardt, K., Kahwajy, J., & Bourgeois, L. J., III. (1997, July-August). How management teams can have a good fight. *Harvard Business Review, 75,* 77–85.

76. Eisenhardt, K., Kahwajy, J., & Bourgeois, L. J., III. (1997, July-August). How management teams can have a good

fight. *Harvard Business Review, 75,* 77–85.

77. Guru Alfred Sloan. (2009, January 30). *The Economist.* Retrieved from http://www.economist.com/node/13047099

78. Bryant, A. (2011, December 24). Every team should have a devil's advocate. *The New York Times.* Retrieved from http://www.nytimes.com/2011/12/25/business/ori-hadomi-of-mazor-

robotics-on-choosing-devils-advocates.html?_r=0

79. Boulding, K. (1964). Further reflections on conflict management. In R. Kahn, & E. Boulding, (Eds.), *Power and conflict in organizations.* New York, NY: Basic Books.

80. Eisenhardt, K., Kahwajy, J., & Bourgeois, L. J., III. (1997, July-August). How management teams can have a good fight. *Harvard Business Review, 75,* 77–85.

CHAPTER 15

1. Abramowitz, Z. (2015, March 23). How lawyers can add value for startups. *Above the Law.* Retrieved from http://abovethelaw.com/2015/03/how-lawyers-can-add-value-for-startups/

2. *The Entrepreneurs' Law Clinic. (n.d.).* Santa Clara University. Retrieved from http://law.scu.edu/elc/

3. Source for legal research on the web. Retrieved from http://www.washlaw.edu/

4. Abramowitz, Z. (2015, March 23). How lawyers can add value for startups. *Above the Law.* Retrieved from http://abovethelaw.com/2015/03/how-lawyers-can-add-value-for-startups/

5. Successful entrepreneurs who started out as sole proprietors. (n.d.). *Gaebler.com* Retrieved from http://www.gaebler.com/Successful-Entrepreneurs-Who-Started-Out-As-Sole-Proprietors.htm

6. http://www.inc.com/guides/2010/10/how-to-start-a-sole-proprietorship.html

7. http://www.moneyedup.com/2010/08/how-sole-proprietorship-works/

8. See, e.g., California Corporations Code Sections 2500, et seq., and Massachusetts General Laws Ch. 156E.

9. This section is heavily based on http://www.forbes.com/sites/allbusiness/2013/10/03/big-legal-mistakes-made-by-startups/

10. Adetunji, J. (2010, December 10). They sued Mark Zuckerberg for $65m. But it was not enough. *The Independent.* Retrieved from http://www.independent.co.uk/life-style/gadgets-and-tech/news/they-sued-mark-zuckerberg-for-65m-but-it-was-not-enough-2155946.html

11. Intellectual property rights for innovative entrepreneurship. The Innovation Policy Forum. Retrieved from https://www.innovationpolicyplatform.org/content/intellectual-property-rights-innovative-entrepreneurship.

12. Keating, R. J. (2013). *Unleashing small business through IP: Protecting intellectual property, driving entrepreneurship* (p. 36). Vienna, VA: Small Business & Entrepreneurship Council. Retrieved from http://www.sbecouncil.org/wp-content/uploads/2013/06/IP+and+Entrepreneurship+FINAL.pdf

13. Keating, R. J. (2013). *Unleashing small business through IP: Protecting intellectual property, driving entrepreneurship* (p. 36). Vienna, VA: Small Business &

Entrepreneurship Council. Retrieved from http://www.sbecouncil.org/wp-content/uploads/2013/06/IP+and+Entrepreneurship+FINAL.pdf

14. Isaacson, W. (2011). *Steve Jobs* (p. 396). New York, NY: Simon & Schuster.

15. Harroch, R. (2013, June 10). 65 Questions venture capitalists will ask startups. *Forbes.* Retrieved from http://www.forbes.com/sites/allbusiness/2013/06/10/65-questions-venture-capitalists-will-ask-startups/

16. McKenna, C. (2015, April 3). Do you really own all your intellectual property? *The National Law Review.* Retrieved from http://www.natlawreview.com/article/do-you-really-own-all-your-intellectual-property

17. Steele, A. (2013, June 11). Who owns Hackathon inventions? *Harvard Business Review.* Retrieved from https://hbr.org/2013/06/who-owns-hackathon-inventions

18. Purvis, S. (n.d.). The fundamentals of intellectual property for the entrepreneur. Presentation, U.S. Patent and Trademark Office, Department of Commerce. Retrieved from http://www.uspto.gov/sites/default/files/about/offices/ous/121115.pdf

19. Retrieved from www.copyright.gov/circs/circ61.pdf

20. Slind-Flor, V. (2015, March 12). Blurred Lines, Aero, White Oak: Intellectual Property. *Bloomberg Business.* Retrieved from http://www.bloomberg.com/news/articles/2015-03-12/-blurred-lines-aereo-white-oak-tenax-intellectual-property

21. Karmali, S. (2013, May 7). Gucci loses legal battle against Guess. *Vogue.* Retrieved from http://www.vogue.co.uk/news/2013/05/07/gucci-loses-guess-lawsuit—logo-copyright-case

22. Halligan, R. M., & Haas, D. (2010, February 19). The secret of trade secret success. *Forbes.* Retrieved from http://www.forbes.com/2010/02/19/protecting-trade-secrets-leadership-managing-halligan-haas.html

23. Quinn, G. (2008, April 20). Obscure patent: The Beerbrella. *IPWatchDog.* Retrieved from http://www.ipwatchdog.com/2008/04/10/obscure-patent-the-beerbrella/id=146/

24. Quinn, G. (2014, February 15). Protecting ideas: Can ideas be protected or

patented? *IPWatchDog.* Retrieved from http://www.ipwatchdog.com/2014/02/15/protecting-ideas-can-ideas-be-protected-or-patented/id=48009/

25. Keating, R. J. (2013). *Unleashing small business through IP: Protecting intellectual property, driving entrepreneurship* (p. 36). Vienna, VA: Small Business & Entrepreneurship Council. Retrieved from http://www.sbecouncil.org/wp-content/uploads/2013/06/IP+and+Entrepreneurship+FINAL.pdf

26. Woollacott, E. (2013, May 23). US should get tough on Chinese IP theft, committee warns. *Forbes.* Retrieved from http://www.forbes.com/sites/emmawoollacott/2013/05/23/us-should-get-tough-on-chinese-ip-theft-committee-warns/

27. Keating, R. J. (2013). *Unleashing small business through IP: Protecting intellectual property, driving entrepreneurship* (p. 36). Vienna, VA: Small Business & Entrepreneurship Council. Retrieved from http://www.sbecouncil.org/wp-content/uploads/2013/06/IP+and+Entrepreneurship+FINAL.pdf

28. Kadkol, A. (2015, May 3). Thirteen countries on U.S. priority watch list. *News Everyday.* Retrieved from http://www.newseveryday.com/articles/15378/20150503/thirteen-countries-u-s-priority-watch-list.htm

29. Bessen, J. (2014, November). The evidence is in: Patent trolls do hurt innovation. *Harvard Business Review.* Retrieved from https://hbr.org/2014/07/the-evidence-is-in-patent-trolls-do-hurt-innovation

30. $10.9 million in counterfeit clothing, jewelry seized at Port of Miami. (2012, June 14). *Channel 6 South Florida News.* Retrieved from http://www.nbcmiami.com/news/109-Million-in-Counterfeit-Clothing-Jewelry-Seized-at-Port-of-Miami-159078005.html

31. Burberry earns $100 million in counterfeiting lawsuit. (2012, May 18). *Huffington Post.* Retrieved from http://www.huffingtonpost.com/2012/05/18/burberry-100-million-lawsuit-counterfeiting_n_1526790.html

32. Retrieved from http://blogs.wsj.com/cio/2013/11/06/early-stage-startups-vulnerable-to-ip-theft/

33. Perkowski, J. (2012, April 18). Protecting intellectual property rights in China. *Forbes*. Retrieved from http://www.forbes.com/sites/jackperkowski/2012/04/18/protecting-intellectual-property-rights-in-china/2/

34. Most of this section is based on: Kotha, R., Kim, P. H., & Alexy, O. (2014, November). Turn your science into a business. *Harvard Business Review*, 92(11), 106–114.

35. Lococo, E. (2012, July 2). Apple pays Proview $60m to resolve iPad trademark dispute. *Bloomberg Business*. Retrieved from http://www.bloomberg.com/news/articles/2012-07-02/

apple-pays-60-million-to-end-china-ipad-dispute-with-proview

36. Hire your first employee. Retrieved from https://www.sba.gov/content/hire-your-first-employee

37. Burrow, S. (2015, June 10). Top ten worst countries for workers' rights: The ranking no country should want. *Huffington Post*. Retrieved from http://www.huffingtonpost.com/sharan-burrow/top-ten-worst-countries-f_b_7553364.html

38. Hire a contractor or an employee. (*n.d.*). *U.S. Small Business Administration*. Retrieved from https://www.sba.gov/content/hire-contractor-or-employee

39. Wood, R. (2014, August 27). FedEx misclassified drivers as independent contractors, rules Ninth Circuit. *Forbes*. Retrieved from http://www.forbes.com/sites/robertwood/2014/08/27/fedex-misclassified-drivers-as-independent-contractors-rules-ninth-circuit/

40. See, e.g., Internal Revenue Service Publication 15-A, Employer's Supplemental Tax Guide 2016.

41. U.S. Department of Labor, Wage, and Hour Division Fact Sheet #71: Internship Programs Under the Fair Labor Standards Act.

CHAPTER 16

1. Crane, F. G. (2012, September 12). *Marketingfor entrepreneurs: Concepts and applications for new ventures*, p. 3. Thousand Oaks, CA: SAGE. [Kindle ed.]

2. Much of this section is based on Manktelow, J. (*n.d.*). The marketing mix and the 4Ps of marketing. *MindTools*. Retrieved from http://www.mindtools.com/pages/article/newSTR_94.htm

3. Retrieved from http://www.entrepreneur.com/article/70824

4. Retrieved from https://www.entrepreneur.com/article/219314

5. Pono, M. (2016, May 3). How industry leaders create strong brands. *Medium*. Retrieved from https://www.linkedin.com/pulse/how-industry-leaders-create-strong-brands-myk-pono

6. Williams, J. (*n.d.*). The basics of branding. *Entrepreneur*. Retrieved from https://www.entrepreneur.com/article/77408

7. Ciotti, G. (2013, July 23). The new 4Ps of marketing. *Help Scout*. Retrieved from http://www.helpscout.net/blog/new-4ps-of-marketing/

8. The Kauffman Foundation. (*n.d.*). Founder School video. Retrieved from http://www.entrepreneurship.org/Founders-School/Transcripts/Entrepreneurial-Marketing/Transcript-Quad-Marketing-Approach.aspx

9. *Entrepreneurial marketing*. (*n.d.*). Retrieved from http://www.marketing-schools.org/types-of-marketing/entrepreneurial-marketing.html

10. *Entrepreneurial marketing*. (*n.d.*). Retrieved from http://www.marketing-schools.org/types-of-marketing/entrepreneurial-marketing.html

11. *Guerilla marketing von Luoupus—Snow branding in Leipzig*. (2010, January 17). YouTube video. Retrieved from https://www.youtube.com/watch?v=_JcuDxT88_Y

12. Edelstein, M. (2010, July 21). How Coca-Cola created its "Happiness Machine." *Mashable*. Retrieved from http://mashable.com/2010/07/21/coke-happiness-machine/

13. Brooks, C. (2012, March 12). 5 Crazy marketing gimmicks gone horribly wrong. *Business News Daily*. Retrieved from http://www.businessnewsdaily.com/2174-guerilla-marketing-wrong.html

14. Business Development Bank of Canada. (2012, October 12). *Social media: A guide for entrepreneurs*, p. 4. Retrieved from http://trenval.on.ca/wp-content/uploads/2015/03/SMeBook_2012_EN.pdf

15. Statista. (*n.d.*). Retrieved from http://www.statista.com/statistics/272014/global-social-networks-ranked-by-number-of-users/

16. Statista. (*n.d.*). Retrieved from http://www.statista.com/statistics/272014/global-social-networks-ranked-by-number-of-users/

17. Retrieved from https://www.youtube.com/yt/press/en-GB/statistics.html

18. Shandrow, K. L. (2016, March 28). "Shark Tank" star Robert Herjavec's top 5 small-business marketing tips. *Entrepreneur*. Retrieved from https://www.youtube.com/watch?v=_JcuDxT88_Y

19. Business Development Bank of Canada. (2012, October 12). *Social media: A guide for entrepreneurs*, p. 4. Retrieved from http://trenval.on.ca/wp-content/uploads/2015/03/SMeBook_2012_EN.pdf

20. Pink, D. (2012.) *To sell is human*, p. 21. New York, NY: Penguin.

21. Bobowski, K. (2014, July 1). How GoPro is transforming advertising as we know it. *Fast Company*. Retrieved from http://www.fastcompany.com/3032509/the-future-of-work/how-gopro-is-transforming-advertising-as-we-know-it

22. Hern, A. (2015, August 5). Smartphone now most popular way to browse internet—Ofcom Report. *The Guardian*. Retrieved from http://www.theguardian.com/technology/2015/aug/06/smartphones-most-popular-way-to-browse-internet-ofcom

23. Mintzer, R. (2014, May 27). The 10 most deadly mistakes in website design. *Entrepreneur*. Retrieved from http://www.entrepreneur.com/article/234129

24. Gregoire, C. (2014, June 12). How to make the perfect first impression. *Huffington Post*. Retrieved from http://www.huffingtonpost.com/2014/05/30/the-science-and-art-of-fi_n_5399004.html

25. Mackay, J. (*n.d.*). The weird science behind first impressions. *Crew*. Retrieved from http://blog.crew.co/weird-science-first-impressions/

26. *Body language for entrepreneurs*. (*n.d.*). Retrieved from Udemy.com Course.

27. *Body language for entrepreneurs*. (*n.d.*). Retrieved from Udemy.com Course.

28. Balachandra, L. (2011, August 2). *Pitching trustworthiness: Cues for trust in early-state investment decision-making*. Submitted to the Carroll School of Management in partial fulfillment of the requirements for the degree of Doctor of Philosophy (working paper).

29. Monarth, H. (2014, March 11). The irresistible power of storytelling as strategic business tool. *Harvard Business Review*. Retrieved from https://hbr.org/2014/03/the-irresistible-power-of-storytelling-as-a-strategic-business-tool/

30. Neck, H. (2015, July 14). The entrepreneurial skillset of storytelling. *Forbes*. Retrieved from http://www.forbes.com/sites/babson/2015/07/14/the-entrepreneurial-skillset-of-storytelling/ retrieved on September 20, 2015.

31. Gallo, C. (2013, December 19). What Starbucks CEO Howard Schultz taught me about communication and success. *Forbes*. Retrieved from http://www.forbes.com/sites/carminegallo/2013/12/19/what-starbucks-ceo-howard-schultz-taught-me-about-communication-and-success/ retrieved on September 20, 2015.

32. Pink, D. (2012.) *To sell is human*, p. 171. New York, NY: Penguin.

33. Zwilling, M. (2013, January 25). Entrepreneurs who master storytelling win more. *Forbes*. Retrieved from http://www.forbes.com/sites/martinzwilling/2013/01/25/entrepreneurs-who-master-storytelling-win-more/

APPENDIX B

1. 5 slides: http://techcrunch.com/2010/11/02/365-days-10-million-3-rounds-2-companies-all-with-5-magic-slides/

    6 slides: http://avc.com/2010/06/six-slides/10 slides: http://guykawasaki.com/the-only-10-slides-you-need-in-your-pitch/

    11 slides: http://articles.bplans.com/what-to-include-in-your-pitch-deck/

    12 slides: http://www.forbes.com/sites/chancebarnett/2014/05/09/investor-pitch-deck-to-raise-money-for-startups/#5dcf25b84863

    15 slides: https://www.entrepreneur.com/article/240065

    30 slides: http://www.slideshare.net/Sky7777/the-best-startup-pitch-deck-how-to-present-to-angels-v-cs

2. http://techcrunch.com/2010/11/02/365-days-10-million-3-rounds-2-companies-all-with-5-magic-slides/

3. http://articles.bplans.com/what-to-include-in-your-pitch-deck/

4. http://www.slideshare.net/Sky7777/the-best-startup-pitch-deck-how-to-present-to-angels-v-cs

5. http://www.slideshare.net/PitchDeckCoach/sequoia-capital-pitchdecktemplate

6. http://www.bridging-the-gap.com/what-is-a-use-case/

7. http://techcrunch.com/2016/04/08/chariot-for-women-is-a-new-ride-sharing-service-for-women-only/

8. Discussion of TAM, SAM, and SOM is based on the following: https://www.caycon.com/blog/2013/10/understanding-market-size-or-demystifying-tam-sam-and-som/; http://leanplan.com/tam-sam-som-potential-market/; http://www.slideshare.net/PersianGuru/market-sizing-20130129

9. Sampson, M. (2011, March 23). Invest in people, not ideas. Retrieved from https://michaelsampson.net/2011/03/23/invest-people/

10. Question list was compiled from author experience, but some questions may be found at http://techcrunch.com/2012/04/27/be-concise-the-top-questions-asked-at-a-y-combinator-interview/; http://www.forbes.com/sites/allbusiness/2013/06/10/65-questions-venture-capitalists-will-ask-startups/#50987df18202

NAME INDEX

SUBJECT INDEX